P. Vanderbilt Spader

Weather Record for New Brunswick, New Jersey

From 1847 to 1890

P. Vanderbilt Spader

Weather Record for New Brunswick, New Jersey
From 1847 to 1890

ISBN/EAN: 9783337341695

Printed in Europe, USA, Canada, Australia, Japan

Cover: Foto ©Suzi / pixelio.de

More available books at **www.hansebooks.com**

WEATHER RECORD

FOR

NEW BRUNSWICK, NEW JERSEY,

1847-1890.

By P. VANDERBILT SPADER,

Northwest Corner of George and Church Streets.

PRINTED FOR PRIVATE CIRCULATION ONLY.

Somerville, N. J.:
Press of the Unionist-Gazette.
1890.

INTRODUCTION.

These records have grown from a small beginning. If I had known, when I commenced them, what a tax it would have become, I am afraid that I would never have undertaken them.

Among my earliest recollections was that of seeing my father looking at the thermometer. He never recorded his observations. Neither did I until June, 1847, when I began keeping a daily journal. In this I used to record only the extremes of heat and cold, and remarkable changes in the weather. I continued this until December, 1851, when my father commenced recording and which he continued more fully than I had done until March, 1855. I then continued, only recording the extremes as before, until January, 1857, when I purchased a little volume, 32 mo., published by Mason Brothers, called the "New York Almanac and Weather Book." The meteorological records in this book were supplied by Mr. E. Meriam, of Brooklyn. The calendar was interleaved with ruled pages to keep a record for the current year. Here I commenced keeping a daily record on January 8th, 1857.

During all this time the observations had been made from a London thermometer of the ordinary kind, but on February 1, 1857, I bought two of G. Tagliabue's self-registering thermometers of Rutherford's invention. After two years of publication this handy little volume of Mason's (price 25 cents,) failed for want of support. I then kept my records on sheets of note paper and pasted them in the American Almanac, 12 mo. In 1861 this publication failed for want of support. I then had a book made of large quarto size, and on April 1, 1862, commenced a fuller record which I have kept up until this date, including observations of the rain-fall.

In May, 1862, I broke my maximum thermometer, and I then

bought two of James Green's self-registering thermometers, and I have used his instruments ever since.

My rain-gauge is five inches in diameter, and is the one recommended by the Smithsonian Institute. It is placed four feet from the ground with no obstruction near it. Light falls of snow I always melted and recorded in the column of "Rain and Melted Snow," and I only recorded the depth of snow by actual measurement, whenever it overflowed the gauge, and I always measured it with the ordinary rule. In the yearly amount of rain and snow I estimate 1.00 inch of snow to 0.10 of an inch of rain. Any fall of rain or snow less than 0.01 is not recorded.

My thermometers are placed in the alley on the west side of my house, and are five feet from the ground and protected from the sun and all reflection and from the rain and snow, and detached from the building.

I do not offer this volume to the public for criticism. I simply call it a Weather Record. I have kept the record merely for pleasure and personal satisfaction, and it has finally grown into this volume, and, thinking it might interest my townsmen, and lead some one to improve on it, I have printed it at my own expense to be given to my friends and such of my acquaintances as may wish to preserve it. I say this to disarm any criticism on what some might consider egotistical in the above remarks, and to stop any fault-finding that I had not made a complete meteorological record. To have done this would have required too much labor and too much time. Let anyone undertake it and he will see for himself.

I did not sit up o' nights as a general thing, but went to bed at 11 P.M. and got up 7 A.M., and my "remarks" generally cover the hours from 7 A.M. to 11 P.M., but if I was awakened by a shower in the night I would note the time.

The only originality about this book is that after I used Mr. Meriam's blanks for the first two years, every form since used is my own and although not scientific is still satisfactory to the ordinary observer.

JANUARY 1st, 1873.

P. S.—From the above date it will be seen that I contemplated printing my records at the end of the year 1872, but for some reason or other it was not done, and my daily observations of the temperature now extend from January, 1857, to April 30, 1890, —33¼ years; and the rain-fall from January, 1854, to March, 1862, —8 years, from the records of Prof. George H. Cook, Rutgers College; and my own records from April, 1862, to December, 1889, 28 years: making altogether 36 years.

For easy reference, tables of maximum and minimum temperatures for every month, and the rain-fall for every month will be found at the end of the volume.

The average rain-fall for 33 years, 1854-1886, was 45.95 inches; but the great rains of 1887, 1888 and 1889 have increased the average of 36 years to 46.82 inches.

The rain-fall for 1887 was 51.84 inches; for 1888, 59.00 inches, and for 1889, was 61.30 inches.

I would finally say that my thermometers and rain-gauge are in the same location they were placed when I commenced my observations.

The brick part of my house where this record was kept, on the northwest corner of George and Church streets, was built by my father, P. Spader, in 1816, and I was born in it on December 1st, 1829.

In my last monthly report (for April) in the "Fredonian," I made the following remarks, viz: "I am compelled to stop these reports by failing sight, but they will be continued by younger hands."

I have given my instruments to my young friend, Charles V. Meyers of Bayard street, who takes great interest in the matter, is thoroughly competent for the work and will continue the monthly reports.

He has a much better exposure for the instruments than I had, and, therefore, the maximum record will be somewhat higher, and the minimum will be somewhat lower than my record has been.

P. VANDERBILT SPADER.

May 1, 1890.

WEATHER RECORD

FOR

NEW BRUNSWICK, NEW JERSEY,

FOR THE YEARS

1847-1896.

Weather Record for New Brunswick, N. J.

1847-1852.

Thermometer.

Year	Month	Day	7 A. M.	12 M.	3 P. M.	REMARKS.
1847	June	24			82	
	"	25			88	
	"	26			95	
	"	28			94	
	September	2–5			86	
	November	29	20			
	"	30	14			
	December	14			70	
1848	April	19				Snow 9 A. M. to 12 M.
	May	5			76	
	June	3			90	
	"	16			100	
	"	17			100	
1849	January	3	10			
	"	10	0			
	"	11	−4			
	June	23			96	
1850	April	6				Snow 6 in., com. on 5th, 7 P. M.
	May	28			85	6 P. M. 80°; 6:30 P. M. 45°.
	June	20			90	
	"	21			93	
	December	30	17			
	"	31	17			Snow 12 to 4 P. M., 2 in.
1851	January	1	17			
	April	20				Snow for half an hour.
	May	28			88	
	July				94	First week in July.
	September	11			96	
	"	12			97	
	"	13			96	
	"	14	60			
	December	16	13		15	
	"	17	8		13	
	"	18	8		18	
	"	19	14		22	
	"	24	7		18	
	"	26	10		15	Snow storm.
	"	27	−11		15	Coldest for many years.
	"	28			34	Raining.
	"	29			44	55° change since 27th.
1852	January	13	12			
	"	14	17			
	"	18	12			Snow all day. Mercury stationary
	"	19	10		12	
	"	20	−2	3	5	
	"	21	2		16	
	"	22	8			
	"	23	8			

1852-1853.

Year	Month	Day	Thermometer 7 A.M.	12 M.	3 P.M.	REMARKS.
1852	January	24	6			
	"	25			40	
	February	19				Northern lights (brilliant). Whole month cold, mercury frequently below 10°.
	"	20	-8			
	March	14			68	
	"	17				One foot of snow.
	April	5 & 6				Snow on both days.
	May	6			76	
	"	7			80	
	"	8			80	
	"	10			80	
	"	25			86	
	June	15			90	June 10th, gas first lighted in stores and dwellings and a few street lamps.
	"	16			95	June 11th, all street lamps lighted.
	"	17			90	
	July	7				For the last week 86° to 88°.
	"	8			90	
	"	9-12			86-89	
	"	21			92	
	"	22			95	
	August	15			87	Aug. 10th, gas first in street lamps at city expense.
	"	16			87	
	October	7			80	
	"	8			80	
1853	January	16	16	12	10	
	"	17	12			
	"	18	16			
	"	26	20		16	
	"	27	12			
	"	28	14			
	February	15	16			
	"	20	18			
	"	21	26			
	March	15	17			
	April	24				Showered 2 or 3 hours.
	May	16			80	
	"	17			84	
	"	18			84	Near sundown east wind set in and shower in the night.
	"	19			70	
	"	20			48	

WEATHER RECORD FOR NEW BRUNSWICK, N. J.

1853-1854.

Year	Month	Day	Thermometer 7 A.M.	Thermometer 12 M.	Thermometer 3 P.M.	REMARKS
1853	May	29			82	
	June	15			84	
	"	16			85	
	"	17			87	
	"	18			82	
	"	19			88	
	"	20			92	
	"	21			95	
	"	22		84	95	
	"	23			91	
	"	24			81	
	"	25			70	
	"	26			56	
	"	30			89	From this date to July 8th 80° to 87°
	July	9			90	
	"	31			88	
	August	10			92	
	"	11			91	
	"	12			94	
	"	13			93	
	"	14			93	
	September	5			87	
	"	6			90	
	"	7		82	88	
	"	17			76	
	"	18			80	
	"	19			82	
	December	20	20			
	"	21	18			
	"	22	24			
	"	23	24			
	"	28	20		17	
	"	29	13			
1854	January	3	2			
	"	22	13			
	"	23	19			
	"	24	16			
	"	25	13			
	"	28	18			
	"	29	10			
	"	30	21			
	February	2			60	
	"	3	18			Snow—a difference of 42°
	"	4	17			
	"	5	14		30	
	"	6	20			
	"	7	14			

1854.

Thermometer.

Year	Month	Day	7 P.M.	12 M.	3 P.M.	REMARKS.
1854	February	20				Severe snow storm.
	"	21				Snow drifted very much.
	"	22	20			
	"	23	20			
	"	24	19			
	March	17			76	1st to 17th pleasant, 18th gets colder and a difference of 54° between 17th and 19th.
	"	19	22			
	April	14–17				Over 2 ft. of snow. Commenced 5 P.M. on Apr. 14th and continued till 8 A.M. on 15th—the rest of 15th and 16th it rained and snowed alternately, and on 16th at 1 P.M. commenced snowing and continued uninterruptedly till 8 A.M. on 17th, Friday to Monday. The "oldest inhabitants" do not recollect a storm like this at this season of the year.
	June	27			90	
	"	28			90	
	"	29			90½	
	"	30			84	
	July	1			83	
	"	2			84	
	"	3			92	
	"	4			96	
	"	5			96	
	"	6			85	
	"	7			86	
	"	8			88	
	"	9			86	
	"	10			76	
	"	11–17			80	and above every day.
	"	18			91	
	"	20			98	
	"	21			97	
	"	22			93	
	"	23			90	
	"	24			85	
	"	25			86	
	"	26			87	
	"	27			93	
	"	28			84	
	"	29			85	
	"	30			90	

Weather Record for New Brunswick, N. J.

1854-1856.

Year	Month	Day	Thermometer 7 A.M.	12 M.	3 P.M.	Remarks
1854	July	31			83	
	August	1			92	
	"	2	84		92	Hottest morning this summer.
	"	3			88	
	"	13			92	
	"	13-21			84-87	No rain in 3 weeks.
	"	22			99	
	"	24	70		84	Difference of 29°.
	"	25			95	Fine showers.
	"	26			90	
	September	3			90	
	"	4			85	
	"	5			88	
	"	6			92	
	"	7			87	
	"	8			88	
	"	9			92	
	"	10			60	
	December	5	21			
	"	6	24			
	"	7	32			
	"	8	13			
	"	9	14			
	"	20	15			
	"	21	5	11	18	
	"	22	19			
	"	23	9	17		
	"	30	13			
1855	January	14	17		20	
	"	24	15			
	February	6	3	1	2	Never has been so low all day in my recollection.
	"	7	-5	-3	5	Snowed all day after 11 A. M.
	"	8	16		26	Snowed till 5 P. M.
1856	January	9	-5	-1		January remarkable for cold and quantity of snow. Dec. 28th 5 inches fell, partly washed away by rain Jan. 2nd and 3rd. On the 5th snow fell about 20 inches on a level. On the 12th 4 inches partly washed away by rain. On 27th and 28th 7 inches more, and more yet at the end of the month—6 weeks of the finest sleighing. According to "Newark Daily Advertiser," it snowed in 8 days 33 inches falling. Average temperature 21¼°.
	"	10	-2			
	February	3	5		10	
	"	4	3			
	"	5	8			
	"	6	6			
	"	11	3		10	
	"	12	2			
	March	9	10		15	
	"	10	4		14	
	July	18			103	
	"	27			101	
	December	18	9			
	"	19	7			

January, 1857.

Year	Month	Day	Thermometer 7 A. M.	Thermometer 12 M.	Thermometer 3 P. M.	REMARKS.
1857	January	1				
"		2				
"		3				
"		S 4				
"		5				
"		6				
"		7				
"		8	4	12	16	
"		9	8			
"		10	20			Snow.
"		S 11	25			Snow.
"		12	10			
"		13	13			
"		14	16			
"		15	24			
"		16	5	15	17	
"		17	20			
"		S 18	0	-1	-1	(1 P. M. 0) snow from noon 18th, until noon 19th drifted several feet in depth.
"		19	8		12	
"		20	14		21	
"		21	24		34	
"		22	12	12	10	
"		23	-3		8	
"		24	-10	4	11	6 P. M. 13°, wind southwest.
"		S 25	2			
"		26	-8		18	
"		27	28		37	Rain.
"		28	31		35	Snow.
"		29	31		35	Snow.
"		30	17			
"		31	30		35	Snow and rain.

February, 1857.

Date	Thermometer Lowest	Thermometer Highest	Weather Morning	Weather Afternoon	REMARKS
S 1	33½	40½	Clear	Clear	On Feb. 1, 1857, I commenced using G. Tagliabue's self-registering thermometer.
2	17	22	"	"	
3	10½	24	"	"	
4	17½	38½	Cloudy	Cloudy	
5	35½	39½	"	"	
6	34	46	Clear	Clear	
7	36½	48½	Cloudy	Cloudy	
S 8	45½	60	Rainy	Rainy	
9	25	30½	Clear	Clear	
10	20½	34½	"	"	
11	8	21½	"	"	
12	13½	28	"	"	
13	27	40	Rain	Rain	
14	33	45½	Clear	Clear	
S 15	35	52½	Rainy	"	
16	37½	63½	Foggy	"	
17	48	59½	"	"	
18	45	60½	"	"	
19	44½	65½	Clear	Rainy	
20	34	37	Rainy	"	
21	34	49	Clear	Clear	
S 22	32	48	"	"	
23	34	54	"	"	
24	39	65	"	"	
25	52½	65½	Cloudy	"	
26	37	40½	Clear	"	
27	26	36	Cloudy	Snow	
28	28½	41	Clear	Clear	

Weather Record for New Brunswick, N. J.

March, 1857.

Date.	Thermometer.		Weather.		REMARKS.
	Lowest.	Highest.	Morning.	Afternoon.	
S 1	32½	43	Cloudy	Cloudy	Commenced snowing 8 P. M.
2	17½	20	Snow	"	Continued snowing till 2 P. M.
3	10½	27	Clear	Clear	
4	19	37½	"	"	
5	25½	44	"	Rain	
6	37½	41	"	Clear	
7	26	29	"	"	
S 8	18	32½	"	"	
9	21	36½	Cloudy	Snow	Commenced snowing 11 A. M.
10	19½	29	Clear	Clear	
11	15	38	Cloudy	Cloudy	Snow 6 to 9 P. M.
12	24	31	Clear	Clear	
13	16	32½	"	Cloudy	
14	27½	40	Snow	Clear	
S 15	32	46	Clear	"	
16	35½	49½	Cloudy	"	
17	37	52	Clear	"	
18	39½	61½	Cloudy	"	
19	50½	55	Rain	Rain	
20	34	48½	Clear	Clear	
21	36½	55½	"	"	
S 22	39½	55	"	"	
23	38½	45½	Cloudy	Cloudy	
24	39	53	"	"	
25	44	50	"	"	
26	32½	43½	Clear	Clear	
27	33½	49	"	"	
28	36½	45½	"	Cloudy	
S 29	37½	51	"	"	
30	40	53	"	"	
31	40½	58	"	Clear	

April, 1857.

Date.	Thermometer.		Weather.		REMARKS.
	Lowest.	Highest.	Morning.	Afternoon.	
1	45	50½	Cloudy	Rain	
2	17	32	Clear	Clear	
3	23	42	"	"	
4	30	57	"	"	
S 5	43½	65½	Cloudy	Cloudy	
6	55	62	Rain	Rain & Snow	
7	27	39	Clear	Clear	
8	32	50	"	"	
9	37	52	"	"	
10	40	53	Cloudy	Rain	
11	42	58	Clear	"	
S 12	47	51	Rain	"	
13	38½	49	Cloudy	"	
14	39	48	Rain	Cloudy	
15	39	50½	Clear	Clear	
16	34	47	"	Rain	
17	33½	45	"	Clear	
18	35	51½	"	"	
S 19	37½	45	Cloudy	Rain	
20	37	45	Rain	"	
21	38	42	"	"	
22	36½	50	Clear	Clear	
23	37½	55	"	"	
24	43½	54	"	"	
25	41	59	"	"	
S 26	38½	57½	Clear	Cloudy	
27	47	60½	Rain	Clear	
28	45	60	Clear	"	
29	43	57	"	"	
30	39½	58½	"	"	

Weather Record for New Brunswick, N. J.

May, 1857.

Date.	Thermometer. Lowest.	Thermometer. Highest.	Weather. Morning.	Weather. Afternoon.	Remarks.
1	39½	56	Clear	Clear	
2	47	60	Rain	Rain	
S 3	55½	65½	Clear	Cloudy	
4	50½	61½	Rain	"	
5	55½	70	"	Clear	
6	53½	61½	Clear	"	
7	49	65	"	"	
8	49	68	"	"	
9	48	72½	"	"	
S 10	49	77½	"	"	
11	42½	55½	"	"	
12	43½	59	"	"	
13	43	66	"	"	
14	52	55	Rain	Rain	
15	50½	56	"	"	
16	50	62	Cloudy	Clear	
S 17	48	60	Clear	"	
18	42½	54	Cloudy	Cloudy	
19	44½	48	Rain	Rain	
20	42	50	"	"	
21	46½	57	Rain	Cloudy	
22	49	72½	Clear	Clear	
23	56	74	"	"	
S 24	55	75	"	"	
25	57½	79½	"	"	
26	59½	82	"	"	
27	64	77½	"	"	Shower.
28	63	77	"	"	Shower.
29	63	73½	"	"	
30	58	72	"	"	
S 31	59½	76	"	"	

June, 1857.

Date	Thermometer Lowest	Thermometer Highest	Weather Morning	Weather Afternoon	Remarks
1	66½	73	Rain	Shower	
2	67	72	Clear	Clear	
3	58	76	"	"	
4	63	71½	"	Cloudy	
5	55	67	"	Clear	
6	52	69	"	"	
S 7	57	65	Cloudy	Showers	
8	56	66½	"	Cloudy	
9	56½	66	Rain	Rain	
10	55	61	"	Cloudy	
11	57	70	"	Showers	
12	56½	74	Clear	Clear	
13	66	78	"	"	
S 14	68	80	"	"	
15	62½	74	"	"	
16	64½	70	Cloudy	Cloudy	
17	56	62½	"	"	
18	58	64	"	"	
19	59	70	Rain	Rain	
20	66	78	Clear	Clear	
S 21	68½	78	"	"	
22	65	75	"	Showers	
23	57½	71	"	Clear	
24	57½	75	"	"	
25	61½	79	"	"	
26	64½	85½	"	"	
27	65	84½	"	"	
S 28	66	78	Cloudy	"	
29	64	71½	Rain	Cloudy	
30	60½	63	"	Rain	

WEATHER RECORD FOR NEW BRUNSWICK, N. J.

July, 1857.

Date.	Thermometer.		Weather.		REMARKS.
	Lowest.	Highest.	Morning.	Afternoon.	
1	57	63	Rain	Rain	
2	54½	59	"	"	
3	52½	59½	Cloudy	Cloudy	
4	57	67½	"	"	
S 5	58½	73	Clear	Clear	
6	63½	79	Rain	"	
7	65½	79½	Clear	"	
8	66½	81	"	"	
9	63	79	"	"	
10	67	77	"	"	
11	66	81	"	"	
S 12	69	85	"	"	
13	72	85	"	"	
14	70	82	Cloudy	"	
15	72½	84	Clear	Showers	
16	70½	80	"	Clear	
17	68½	81½	"	"	
18	71½	82	"	"	
S 19	73	83	"	"	
20	71½	85	"	"	
21	72	85	"	Showers	
22	68	80	"	Clear	
23	71	75½	Showers	Showers	
24	65	77	Clear	"	
25	70	80	"	Clear	
S 26	71½	83	Cloudy	"	
27	73	84½	Clear	"	
28	73	85	"	Showers	
29	71½	80	"	Clear	
30	67½	70	Rain	Rain	
31	64	71	Cloudy	Cloudy	

August, 1857.

Date.	Thermometer.		Weather.		REMARKs.
	Lowest.	Highest.	Morning.	Afternoon.	
1	64½	78	Clear	Clear	
S 2	65	80	"	"	
3	64	80½	"	"	
4	65½	82	"	Rain	
5	69	74	Rain	"	
6	68½	76	Cloudy	Shower	
7	65½	77½	Clear	Clear	
8	63½	79	"	"	
S 9	69	80½	"	"	
10	69	78	Cloudy	Rain	
11	66½	79	Clear	Clear	
12	65	78	"	"	
13	70	86	"	"	
14	75	89	"	"	
15	77½	84	"	"	
S 16	67½	77	"	"	
17	69	79	Cloudy	"	
18	66	71	Shower	Cloudy	
19	65	73	Clear	Shower	
20	63	75	"	Clear	
21	59½	74	"	"	
22	60½	73	"	Cloudy	
S 23	63	75	"	"	
24	60½	72	"	"	
25	54½	74	"	"	
26	57½	76	"	"	
27	63	77½	"	"	
28	67½	80	Rain	Clear	
29	65	77	Clear	"	
S 30	59½	72	"	"	
31	57½	75	"	"	

September, 1857.

Date.	Thermometer.		Weather.		REMARKS.
	Lowest.	Highest.	Morning.	Afternoon.	
1	62	77	Clear	Clear	
2	64½	77	"	"	
3	61	77	"	"	
4	62	77	"	"	
5	67½	80	"	"	
S 6	69	75	"	"	
7	54	67	"	"	
8	50	68	"	"	
9	52½	72	"	"	
10	57½	71½	"	"	
11	63	79	"	"	
12	63	74	"	"	
S 13	63	68	"	Rain	
14	67	75	Rain	Cloudy	
15	67	76	Clear	Clear	
16	57½	71	"	"	
17	61½	78	Rain	"	
18	69	76	Clear	"	
19	53	57	Rain	Rain	
S 20	51½	64	Cloudy	Cloudy	
21	53	61	"	"	
22	56½	62	Rain	Rain	
23	56	61	Clear	Clear	
24	46	66	"	"	
25	49½	66	"	"	
26	51	77	"	"	
S 27	58	76½	"	"	
28	60	74	"	"	
29	53½				Absent from home.
30					

Weather Record for New Brunswick, N. J.

October, 1857.

Date.	Thermometer. Lowest.	Thermometer. Highest.	Weather. Morning.	Weather. Afternoon.	Remarks.
1	------	------	------	------	42° lowest while absent.
2	------	------	------	------	70° highest while absent.
3	------	------	------	------	
S 4	50	63	Clear	Clear	
5	50½	63	"	"	
6	47½	65	"	"	
7	49	66	"	"	
8	48	68	"	"	
9	48	68	"	"	
10	50	62	"	"	
S 11	48	62	"	"	
12	48	66	"	"	
13	55	69	Rain	Cloudy	
14	61	68	Cloudy	Rain	
15	61	65	Rain	"	
16	56	63	Clear	"	
17	48	59	"	Clear	
S 18	46½	51	"	"	
19	46½	63	Cloudy	Cloudy	
20	46½	48	Clear	Clear	
21	36½	45	"	"	
22	35	51	"	"	
23	39½	51	Cloudy	Cloudy	
24	45	54	Rain	Rain	
S 25	52½	57	"	"	
26	50	57	"	"	
27	49	51	Cloudy	"	
28	41	48	"	Cloudy	
29	44	49	"	"	
30	45	52	"	"	
31	45	51	Rain	"	

Weather Record for New Brunswick, N. J.

November, 1857.

Date	Thermometer Lowest	Thermometer Highest	Weather Morning	Weather Afternoon	Remarks
S 1	38	52	Clear	Clear	
2	42	59	"	"	
3	42	52	"	"	
4	35	50	"	"	
5	37	63	"	Rain	
6	57	65	"	"	
7	58	65	"	Clear	
S 8	55	65	Cloudy	Cloudy	
9	60	74	Clear	Clear	
10	55	57	Cloudy	"	
11	36½	51	Clear	"	
12	36½	54	"	"	
13	44	56	Cloudy	"	
14	40	45	Clear	"	
S 15	27	40	"	"	
16	30	43	Cloudy	Rain	
17	40½	50	Clear	Cloudy	
18	35	50	Cloudy	"	
19	45	60	Clear	Rain & snow	
20	29	31	"	Clear	
21	22	34	"	"	
S 22	30	45	Snow	"	
23	35	59	Clear	Rain	
24	29	33½	"	Clear	
25	20	24	"	"	
26	18	31	"	"	
27	22½	43	"	"	
28	27	48	"	"	
S 29	28	50	"	"	
30	39	55	Cloudy	Cloudy	

Weather Record for New Brunswick, N. J.

December, 1857.

	Date.	Thermometer.		Weather.		REMARKS.
		Lowest.	Highest.	Morning.	Afternoon.	
	1	46½	55	Rain	Clear	
	2	35	47	Clear	"	
	3	37½	47	"	"	
	4	36½	41	"	"	
	5	33	39	Snow	Cloudy	
S	6	32	48	Rain	Rain	
	7	42	55	Clear	Clear	
	8	37	54	Cloudy	"	
	9	45	58	Rain	Rain	
	10	47	50	Cloudy	Clear	
	11	33	39	"	Cloudy	
	12	24	35	Clear	Clear	
S	13	23½	40	"	"	
	14	30	50	"	"	
	15	37	48	"	"	
	16	38	48	Cloudy	Cloudy	
	17	37	55	"	"	
	18	50	58½	Rain	Clear	
	19	42	46	Clear	"	
S	20	31	39	"	"	
	21	28	47	"	Rain	
	22	44	51	Cloudy	Cloudy	
	23	34	42	Clear	Clear	
	24	38	47	"	"	
	25	26½	28	Cloudy	Cloudy	
	26	22	26	"	"	Snow 8 A. M. to 5 P. M.
S	27	14	25	Clear	Clear	
	28	22½	38	Cloudy	Cloudy	
	29	34	37	Rain	Rain	
	30	33	42	"	"	
	31	35	46	Cloudy	Clear	

January, 1858.

Date.	Thermometer. Lowest.	Thermometer. Highest.	Weather. Morning.	Weather. Afternoon.	REMARKS.
1	35	50	Clear	Clear	
2	36½	45	"	"	
S 3	35	43½	"	"	
4	37	52	"	"	
5	38	49	"	Cloudy	
6	34	36	Snow	"	
7	32	40	Clear	Clear	
8	21½	30	"	"	
9	24	38	Snow	Cloudy	
S 10	33	40	Clear	Clear	
11	34	61	Rain	Rain	
12	43½	50	Clear	Clear	
13	34	48½	"	"	
14	38½	45	"	"	
15	32	46½	Cloudy	Rain	
16	41	55	Rain	Cloudy	
S 17	37	40	Clear	Clear	
18	28½	39	Cloudy	"	
19	35	41	Clear	Cloudy	
20	29½	40	"	Clear	
21	30	45	"	"	
22	34	37	"	"	
23	18	32	"	"	
S 24	37	46	"	Cloudy	
25	40	55	Cloudy	Clear	
26	42½	58	Rain	Cloudy	
27	44	50	Clear	Clear	
28	36	41	"	Cloudy	
29	32	38	Cloudy	"	
30	23½	33½	Clear	Clear	
S 31	19½	32½	"	"	

February, 1858.

Date.	Thermometer. Lowest.	Thermometer. Highest.	Weather. Morning.	Weather. Afternoon.	REMARKS.
1	19½	32	Clear	Rain	
2	29½	41½	Cloudy	Cloudy	
3	37½	44	Clear	Clear	
4	34½	40	Cloudy	Cloudy	
5	29	33½	Clear	Clear	
6	22	33	"	"	
S 7	27½	45	"	"	
8	32½	37½	Cloudy	"	
9	28	49	Clear	"	
10	41½	43½	"	"	
11	12½	21½	"	"	
12	15	28½	Cloudy	"	
13	20	24½	"	Snow	
S 14	17	27	Snow	Cloudy	
15	22	30	Cloudy	Clear	
16	19½	33	"	Cloudy	
17	9	22	Clear	Clear	
18	10	26½	"	"	
19	12	16	Snow	Snow	Coldest 10 A. M.
20	20	29	"	"	Snowed till 2 P. M.
S 21	20	32	Clear	Clear	
22	21	27½	"	Cloudy	
23	10	25	"	Clear	
24	– 1	28	"	"	
25	10	35	"	"	
26	26	35	"	"	
27	14	41	"	"	
S 28	26½	45½	Cloudy	Cloudy	

Weather Record for New Brunswick, N. J.

March, 1858.

Date	Thermometer		Weather		Remarks
	Lowest	Highest	Morning	Afternoon	
1	37	41	Cloudy	Snow	8 p. m.
2	23	26	Clear	Clear	
3	15	25½	"	"	
4	11½	23	"	"	
5	7½	14½	"	"	
6	7	26	"	"	
S 7	15	31	"	"	
8	18	25	Snow	Snow	11 a. m.
9	16½	28	Clear	Cloudy	
10	24½	40	"	Clear	
11	20	49½	"	"	
12	29½	42	"	"	
13	32	44	"	"	
S 14	32½	44½	Cloudy	Rain	
15	39½	51½	"	Cloudy	
16	40	57½	Clear	Clear	
17	39	62	"	"	
18	52½	65½	"	"	
19	44	57	"	"	
20	35	53½	Clear	"	
S 21	39½	59	Rain	"	
22	39½	50	Clear	"	
23	35½	44	Cloudy	"	
24	31	51½	Clear	"	
25	36½	60½	"	"	
26	39½	50½	"	"	
27	33½	48	"	Cloudy	
S 28	40½	45½	Cloudy	"	
29	37	55½	Clear	Clear	
30	39½	57	"	"	
31	37	58	"	"	

Weather Record for New Brunswick, N. J.

April, 1858.

Date	Thermometer Lowest	Thermometer Highest	Weather Morning	Weather Afternoon	Remarks
1	37	59	Clear	Clear	
2	40	57	"	"	
3	48½	67	"	"	
S 4	48½	59	"	"	
5	39½	60½	"	Rain	10 P. M.
6	46	53	"	Cloudy	
7	32	52½	"	Clear	
8	30	51½	"	Light rain	
9	43	65	Shower	Clear	Thunder shower, 3 A. M.
10	45	68	Clear	"	
S 11	42	46	Rainy	Rainy	
12	41½	45	Rain	Rain	
13	38	48½	"	"	
14	43	57	Cloudy	Rain	10 P. M.
15	47	58	Clear	Clear	
16	47	56	Rainy	"	
17	42	63	Clear	"	
S 18	43	59	"	"	
19	45½	51	Rainy	Cloudy	
20	44	46	Rain	Rain	
21	41½	58½	"	Clear	
22	42½	65	Clear	"	
23	51½	68½	Cloudy	Rain	
24	41	51	Clear	Clear	Frost.
S 25	36	46	Cloudy	Cloudy	Frost.
26	34	49	Clear	Clear	Frost.
27	36½	43	Cloudy	Cloudy	
28	37½	57	Clear	Clear	
29	38	64	"	"	
30	53	77	Shower	"	

May, 1858.

Date.	Thermometer.		Weather.		REMARKS.
	Lowest.	Highest.	Morning.	Afternoon.	
1	60	66	Cloudy	Cloudy	
S 2	48	59	"	Clear	
3	43½	58	Clear	"	
4	47	58½	Cloudy	Cloudy	
5	49	60½	Rain	Rain	
6	55	67	Cloudy	Clear	
7	57	64	Rainy	Rainy	
8	54½	65	Clear	Clear	
S 9	50	64	Cloudy	"	
10	53½	61	Rainy	Rainy	
11	52½	64	Rain	Rain	
12	54	60	Clear	Clear	
13	48½	72	"	"	
14	51	56½	Rain	Cloudy	
15	50	71	"	Showers	
S 16	50½	62	Cloudy	Clear	
17	47½	60	"	Cloudy	
18	51	53½	Rain	"	
19	49	57	Cloudy	"	
20	50	59	"	Rain	
21	46½	61	Clear	Clear	
22	45	62	"	"	
S 23	45	69½	"	Cloudy	
24	54	76	"	Sh'r & cloudy	
25	57	63½	Cloudy	Rain	
26	51	54	Rain	"	
27	47½	52	"	"	
28	48	60½	Clear	Clear	
29	44½	56	Cloudy	"	
S 30	47½	61	Clear	"	
31	48	68	"	"	

WEATHER RECORD FOR NEW BRUNSWICK, N. J.

June, 1858.

Date	Thermometer. Lowest.	Highest.	Weather. Morning.	Afternoon.	REMARKS.
1	54	65	Cloudy	Clear	
2	54	75	Clear	"	
3	56½	75	"	"	
4	62	75	Cloudy	Cloudy	
5	64½	81	Clear	Clear	
S 6	69	85	"	"	
7	66	81	"	"	
8	70½	83	"	"	
9	64½	82	"	"	
10	70½	85½	"	"	
11	74½	86	"	Shower	
12	61	63½	Rain	Rain	55° at 3 P. M.
S 13	51½	62½	Cloudy	Cloudy	
14	57	63	"	"	
15	55½	62½	"	"	
16	58	69½	"	Clear	
17	56	71	Foggy	"	
18	58½	81	Clear	"	
19	63½	83½	"	"	
S 20	68½	85	"	"	
21	69	85	"	"	
22	68	76	"	"	
23	62	78	"	"	
24	64½	82½	"	"	
25	72½	89	"	"	
26	76	91	"	"	
S 27	75	89½	"	"	
28	74½	91	"	"	
29	76	89	"	"	
30	73	89½	"	"	

Weather Record for New Brunswick, N. J.

July, 1858.

Date	Thermometer Lowest	Thermometer Highest	Weather Morning	Weather Afternoon	REMARKS
1	67	79	Clear	Clear	
2	64½	79½	"	"	
3	71¼	83	"	Shower	Shower A. M.
S 4	74	88	"	Clear	
5	69½	81	"	"	
6	63½	79	"	"	
7	63	82	"	"	
8	63	84	"	"	
9	70	84	Shower	"	
10	73½	88½	Clear	"	
S 11	77	90½	"	"	
12	76	88½	"	"	
13	75	82½	Showers	Showers	
14	69½	74½	Cloudy	Clear	
15	64½	79	Clear	"	
16	66	79	"	"	
17	65½	83	"	"	
S 18	70½	77	Cloudy	Shower	
19	62½	78	Clear	Clear	
20	61	77½	"	Cloudy	Shower P. M.
21	65½	77½	Shower	Clear	
22	68	83	Clear	"	
23	62	79	"	"	
24	62	75	"	"	
S 25	58½	72	"	"	
26	58½	75½	"	"	
27	64½	84½	"	"	
28	70	83	"	"	
29	67½	83	"	"	
30	74	85½	"	Showers	
31	67½	79	"	Clear	

August, 1858.

Date	Thermometer Lowest	Thermometer Highest	Weather Morning	Weather Afternoon	Remarks
S 1	65	77½	Clear	Cloudy	
2	68½	72	Rain	Rain	
3	62½	71	"	"	
4	65	75	"	Cloudy	
5	68	75	Clear	Clear	
6	69	85	"	"	
7	68	80	"	"	
S 8	65	79½	"	"	
9	62½	78	"	"	
10	64½	81	"	"	
11	67	79	"	"	Shower P. M.
12	70	78½	"	Shower	Shower A. M.
13	68½	76	"	Clear	
14	65	74	Cloudy	Cloudy	
S 15	65½	77½	"	Clear	
16	66½	83	Clear	"	
17	68½	84	"	Cl'dy & sh'ry	
18	68½	85	"	Clear	
19	67½	71	"	"	
20	52½	72	"	"	
21	66	80	"	"	
S 22	67½	77	"	"	
23	55½	69	"	"	
24	49½	72	"	"	N. Y.
25	55	75	"	"	
26	56½	75	"	"	
27	64½	78½	Cloudy	Cloudy	
28	70½	75	Shower	Shower	
S 29	66	75½	Clear	Clear	
30	59½	72	"	"	
31	63½	76	"	"	

September, 1858.

Date.	Thermometer. Lowest.	Thermometer. Highest.	Weather. Morning.	Weather. Afternoon.	REMARKS.
1	60	77½	Clear	Clear	
2	66	77	"	"	
3	64½	82½	"	Slight show'r	
4	72	78	"	Showers	
S 5	61	78	"	Clear	
6	61½	78	"	"	
7	58½	80	"	"	4:30 P. M.
8	61	80	"	"	
9	62½	82	"	"	
10	66	84	"	"	
11	68	75½	Cloudy	Rain	
S 12	61½	73	Clear	Clear	
13	52	70	"	"	
14	52½	70	"	"	
15	53	69½	Cloudy	Rain	
16	62¼	72	Rain	"	
17	56	65	Clear	Clear	
18	52	67½	"	"	
S 19	52½	71	"	"	
20	55	74½	"	"	
21	60¼	79½	"	"	
22	57	62½	"	"	
23	40	58¼	"	"	
24	47	57	Rain	Rain	
25	47	59	Clear	Clear	
S 26	41	62	"	"	
27	43½	64	"	"	
28	45½	63½	"	"	
29	43¼	69	"	"	
30	55½	76	"	"	

October, 1858.

Date.	Thermometer.		Weather.		REMARKS.
	Lowest.	Highest.	Morning.	Afternoon.	
1	62	74½	Clear	Clear	
2	49	65	"	"	
S 3	49	75	"	"	
4	64½	85	"	"	
5	60	69	"	"	
6	50½	66	"	"	
7	54	66	Rain	Cloudy	
8	47	56	Clear	Clear	
9	43	58	"	"	
S 10	44	63	"	"	
11	46	60	Cloudy	Cloudy	
12	50	61	"	"	
13	56	61½	Rain	Rain	
14	58	62	Clear	Clear	
15	48	61	"	"	
16	42	64	"	"	
S 17	48½	69	"	"	
18	50½	67	"	"	
19	53½	68½	"	"	
20	48½	70	"	"	
21	49	60½	"	"	
22	51½	60	Rain	Rain	
23	56	66	Cloudy	Clear	
S 24	48	60	Clear	Rain	
25	42	53	"	Clear	
26	36	51	"	"	
27	33½	59	"	"	
28	36½	60	"	"	
29	45	62	Cloudy	Rain	
30	49	64	Rain	"	
S 31	54	66	Clear	Clear	

November, 1858.

Date.	Thermometer Lowest	Thermometer Highest	Weather Morning.	Weather Afternoon.	REMARKS.
1	49½	62¼	Clear	Clear	
2	48	53	Cloudy	Cloudy	
3	43½	51	Rain	Rain	
4	45½	51	"	"	
5	44½	52	Cloudy	Cloudy	
6	47	51	Rain	Rain	
S 7	41	52	Clear	Clear	
8	39½	55	"	"	
9	40½	50	"	Cloudy	
10	43	50	"	Clear	
11	36½	47	"	"	
12	31¼	42	"	"	
13	31	48	Cloudy	Cl'dy & rain	
S 14	28	38	Clear	Clear	
15	28	37	Cl'dy & snow	Snow	
16	23½	36	Clear	Clear	
17	33	43	"	"	
18	34	43	"	"	
19	35	43½	"	"	
20	27	42	"	"	
S 21	35	38½	Rain & snow	Rain & snow	
22	33½	43	Clear	Cl'dy & rain	
23	37	42½	Cloudy	Cloudy	
24	39	43	"	"	
25	35	40½	Clear	Clear	
26	33½	39	"	"	
27	33	39	"	"	
S 28	32	36	Snow	Rain & snow	
29	30½	36	Cloudy	Clear	
30	25	41	Clear	"	

WEATHER RECORD FOR NEW BRUNSWICK, N. J.

December, 1858.

Date.	Thermometer. Lowest.	Thermometer. Highest.	Weather. Morning.	Weather. Afternoon.	REMARKS.
1	25	32½	Clear	Clear	
2	23½	38	Cloudy	Rain	
3	30½	45	Clear	Cloudy	
4	38½	43½	Cloudy	"	
S 5	34	43	Rain	Rain	
6	37½	48½	Clear	Clear	
7	33	43	Cloudy	Rain	
8	36	43	Rain	"	
9	25	29	Clear	Clear	
10	19	31	"	"	
11	25½	39	"	"	
S 12	29½	39	"	Cloudy	
13	33½	45	Rain	Rain	
14	40	65	"	"	
15	54	57½	"	"	
16	39	45	Clear	Clear	
17	32	45	"	"	
18	23½	30	"	"	
S 19	13½	37	Cloudy	Cloudy	
20	35	42	Snow	"	
21	37	42	Rain	Rain	
22	37½	43	Clear	Clear	
23	32	47	"	Rain	
24	36	38	"	Clear	
25	19½	34	"	"	
S 26	19½	39	"	Cloudy	Rain 10 P. M.
27	34½	46	"	Clear	
28	34½	42	"	Cloudy	
29	30	33½	Cloudy	Snow	3 P. M.
30	23	26	Snow	Cloudy	
31	35	40	Rain	Rain	

January, 1859.

Date	Thermometer Lowest	Thermometer Highest	Weather Morning	Weather Afternoon	REMARKS
1	36½	41	Rain	Cloudy	
S 2	29	39	Clear	Clear	
3	27	32½	Cloudy	Snow	
4	26	35	Snow	Cloudy	10 inches.
5	27	37	Clear	Clear	St. Augustine.
6	30	43½	"	"	
7	35	40½	Rain	Rain	
8	26½	28	Clear	Clear	3 P. M. 20°.
S 9	11	21	"	"	
10	−5½	2	"	"	Coldest 10 A. M.
11	5½	10	Cloudy	Cloudy	Snow squalls P. M.
12	4½	28	"	"	
13	21¼	35	"	"	
14	31	44	"	Clear	
15	31	43	Clear	"	
S 16	35	41	"	"	
17	34	45	"	"	
18	24	33	"	"	
19	22½	45½	"	"	
20	27	56	"	"	
21	29	61½	Cloudy	Rain	
22	37½	42	"	Clear	
S 23	14	24½	Clear	"	
24	16½	32	"	"	
25	21¼	39	"	"	
26	31	45	"	"	
27	29	38	Cloudy	Rain	Got warm in the night.
28	50	54	Foggy	Foggy	
29	37	44	"	Cloudy	
S 30	34	39	Clear	Clear	
31	27	35	"	"	

February 1859.

Date	Thermometer Lowest	Thermometer Highest	Weather Morning	Weather Afternoon	REMARKS.
1	26	43	Clear	Clear	
2	31	42	"	Rain	Rain 5 P. M.
3	31	35	Rainy	Rainy	Snow squall 9 P. M.
4	30	39	Clear	Cloudy	
5	24	33	"	Clear	
S 6	27	36	Cloudy	Snow	6 inches.
7	26	32	"	Clear	Cleared 10 A. M.
8	12	33½	"	Rain	Clear 10 to 12 A. M.
9	37½	41	Rainy	Rainy	
10	26	31	Clear	Clear	
11	15½	27	Cloudy	Cloudy	
12	22	30½	"	"	Snowed a little all day.
S 13	23	31	Clear	Clear	
14	24	35	"	"	
15	30½	43	Cloudy	Rain	
16	36	49	Rain	Clear	
17	33½	46	Clear	Cloudy	
18	37	42	Rain	"	
19	32	46	Clear	Rain	Commenced raining 6 P. M.
S 20	40	57	Foggy & rain	Clear	Cleared 5 P. M.
21	34	39	Clear	"	
22	30	48	Rain	"	
23	36	57	Clear	"	
24	41	49½	Cloudy	"	
25	26	32	"	Snow	Commenced snowing 10:30 A. M.
26	23½	37	Snow	Snow & rain	Cleared 5:30 P. M.
S 27	25	47	Clear	Clear	
28	36½	48	"	"	

Weather Record for New Brunswick, N. J.

March, 1859.

Date	Thermometer Highest	Thermometer Lowest	Weather Morning	Weather Afternoon	REMARKS.
1	32	36	Clear	Clear	
2	19	35	"	"	
3	25	34	Cloudy	Snow & rain	Snow 12 M. to 6 P. M. and then rain.
4	33	50	Clear 8 A. M.	Clear	Rain 6 to 10 P. M.
5	39½	47	"	"	
S 6	38½	51	"	"	
7	34½	50	"	Rain	Commenced raining 3 P. M.
8	40½	45	Cloudy	"	
9	35½	51	Clear	Clear	
10	33	50	"	"	
11	35	50	Cloudy	Rainy	
12	49½	63	Rainy	Clear	
S 13	43	63	Clear	"	
14	41	50	"	Cl'dy & rain	Commenced raining 7 P. M.
15	45	60	Rain	Cloudy	Clear 4 to 8 P. M.
16	40	54	Cloudy	Clear	
17	36	61	Clear	"	Clouded over 5 P. M.
18	49	62	Rain	Cloudy	Clear 8 P. M.
19	44	48	Cloudy	"	
S 20	36	52	Clear	Clear	
21	33½	53½	"	"	
22	43½	62	"	Cloudy	Rain 8 P. M.
23	46½	61	"	Clear	
24	41	58	Cloudy	Rain	
25	45	55	Rain	Clear	Cleared 3 P. M.
26	41	46	Cloudy	Cloudy	Cleared 7 P. M.
S 27	34½	56	"	Clear	
28	42	56	Clear	"	Clouded over 5 P. M.
29	44	58	Rain	"	Cleared 4 P. M.
30	44½	54	Cloudy	"	Cleared 9 A. M.
31	39	54½	Clear	"	

Weather Record for New Brunswick, N. J.

April, 1859.

Date.	Thermometer. Lowest.	Highest.	Weather. Morning.	Afternoon.	REMARKS.
1	37½	58	Clear	Clear	
2	38	58	"	Cloudy	Rain 7 P. M.
S 3	45	55	Rain	"	
4	44	50	Clear	Clear	
5	34	44	"	"	
6	31½	48	"	"	
7	35	53	"	"	Cloudy 12 to 3 P. M.
8	41	47	"	Cloudy	10 A. M. to 5 P. M.
9	31½	49	"	Clear	
S 10	36½	46	Cloudy	Cloudy	
11	41½	45	Rain	"	
12	39	55	Cloudy	Clear	Clear from 1 to 8 P. M.
13	47	61	"	"	3 to 5 P. M.
14	45	47	Rain	Rain	
15	38	57	Clear	Clear	
16	41	46	"	"	
S 17	37	55	"	Cloudy	
18	42½	52½	Cloudy	Clear	
19	38	58	Clear	"	
20	43	60	"	"	
21	45	63½	"	Cloudy	10:30 P. M. rain.
22	50	54	Rain	Rain	21st pears and cherries flowered.
23	43	57	"	"	
S 24	40	57	Clear	Clear	
25	46½	61	Cloudy		Cloudy nearly all day.
26	49	69½	"		Cloudy and showery all day.
27	54	56	Rain	Rain	
28	43	56	Cloudy	Cloudy	
29	42½	62	Clear	Clear	
30	45	73½	"	"	

May, 1859.

Date.	Thermometer. Lowest.	Thermometer. Highest.	Weather. Morning.	Weather. Afternoon.	REMARKS.
S 1	50	64	Clear	Clear	
2	44½	71½	"	"	
3	51½	63	"	"	
4	44	66	"	"	
5	43	69	"	"	
6	49	72½	"	"	
7	57½	80	"	"	
S 8	60½	81½	"	"	
9	62	81	"	"	
10	51	55	Cloudy	Rain	Easterly storm.
11	46	50	Rain	"	
12	46	61¼	Cloudy	Cloudy	Cleared 8 P. M.
13	52½	70	Clear	Clear	
14	59	70¼	Cloudy	"	
S 15	53¼	65¼	Clear	"	
16	47½	61	"	"	
17	48	58	Rainy	Cloudy	
18	54	65	Cloudy	Rainy	
19	55½	65	Rainy	Cloudy	
20	59	68	Cloudy	Rain	
21	57	66	Rain	"	
S 22	59	68	Cloudy	"	Cleared 4 P. M.
23	52	69	Clear	Clear	
24	51	73	"	"	
25	53	74	"	"	
26	54½	77	"	"	
27	58½	81	"	"	Rain 9 P. M.
28	54	67	"	"	
S 29	51½	75	"	"	
30	62	72	"	"	
31	58	67	Cloudy	Cloudy	

June, 1859.

Date	Thermometer Lowest	Highest	Weather Morning	Afternoon	REMARKS
1	59	68	Rain	Cloudy	
2	63½	81	Clear	Clear	Rain in the night.
3	65	76	Shower		Shower all day.
4	57	60	Cloudy	Cloudy	
S 5	43	63	Clear	Clear	
6	48	66	"	"	
7	51	71	"	"	
8	56	75	"	"	
9	53	70	"	"	
10	54½	76½	"	"	Rain 4 P. M.
11	44	62	"	"	
S 12	45	67	"	"	
13	51½	72½	Cloudy	Shower	
14	67	80½	Clear		Light shower in the afternoon.
15	67½	85	"	Clear	
16	73½	81½	"	"	Shower 4 and 11 P. M.
17	62½	65	Rain	Rain	Northeast storm.
18	59½	72	Clear	Clear	
S 19	54½	73	"	"	
20	59½	66	Rain	Rain	
21	63½	76	Cloudy	Clear	Clear part P. M.
22	64½	73	"	"	Clear part P. M.
23	63	73	"	"	
24	63	68	"	Cloudy	
25	65	77	Clear	Clear	
S 26	62	77	"	"	
27	62	80	"	"	
28	64	81½	"	"	
29	73	89	"	"	Shower 9 P. M.
30	67½	74	"	"	

Weather Record for New Brunswick, N. J.

July, 1859.

Date	Thermometer Lowest	Thermometer Highest	Weather Morning	Weather Afternoon	REMARKS
1	55	76	Clear	Clear	
2	63	85	Cloudy	"	Shower 10:30 P. M.
S 3	70	79	Shower	Shower	Very hard 3 P. M.
4	54	69	Clear	Clear	
5	53½	69	"	"	
6	53½	71½	"	"	
7	56½	75	"	"	
8	64½	77½	"	"	
9	64½	80	"	"	
S 10	64½	81	"	"	
11	66	86½	"	"	
12	71	90	"	"	
13	76	90	"	"	Hard shower 5:30 P. M.
14	70½	82½	"	"	
15	70½	77	"	Cloudy	
16	68	71	Rain	Rain	Easterly storm.
S 17	65	81	Clear	Clear	Clear 8 A. M.
18	70	83	"	"	
19	71	77	Showery	Cloudy	
20	69	84	Clear	Shower 3 P.M.	Cleared 9 A. M.
21	62½	74	"	Clear	Clouded over 4 P. M.
22	66	77	" 8 A. M.	"	Shower 10 P. M.
23	65	74	Clear	"	
S 24	57½	76	"	"	
25	64	77	"	"	
26	68	78	Cloudy	Cloudy	Cleared 4 P. M.
27	60	77	Clear	Clear	
28	59½	76	"	"	
29	60	77½	"	"	
30	62	77	"	"	
S 31	64	73	Cloudy	"	

August, 1859.

Date.	Thermometer.		Weather.		REMARKS.
	Lowest.	Highest.	Morning.	Afternoon.	
1	58½	79	Clear	Clear	
2	67	80	"	"	
3	68	86	"	"	
4	72	89	"		Hard shower afternoon & evening
5	73	80			Shower all day.
6	66½	77½	Clear	Clear	
S 7	62	80	"	"	
8	66	79	"	"	
9	63½	79½	"	"	
10	63½	79	"	"	
11	62	77	"	"	
12	68	78½	"	"	Rain 8 P. M.
13	71	80			Cloudy and showery all day.
S 14	68½	81	Clear	Clear	
15	69	78	"	"	
16	61	72	"	"	
17	56	72	"	"	
18	56	75	"	"	
19	59	77	"	"	
20	60	74	"	"	
S 21	57½	75	"	"	
22	57½	75	"	"	
23	60	75	"	"	
24	67	77	Rain	Rain	
25	67	79	"	Clear	
26	65	78½	Clear	"	Shower 9 P. M.
27	65	78	"	"	
S 28	63½	70	Cloudy	"	
29	51½	69	Clear	"	
30	50	70	"	"	
31	55	75½	"	"	Shower 8 P. M.

Weather Record for New Brunswick, N. J.

September, 1859.

Date	Thermometer Lowest	Thermometer Highest	Weather Morning	Weather Afternoon	REMARKS.
1	55½	72½	Clear	Clear	
2	61	70	"	"	
3	50	73	"	"	Clouded over 5 P. M.
S 4	66	77			Cloudy most of the day.
5	56	64	Cloudy	Rainy	
6	57	69	Clear	Clear	
7	49½	68	"	"	
8	53½	70	"	"	
9	53	72	"	"	
10	56	73	"	Cloudy	
S 11	64	76	Rainy	Rainy	Shower all day.
12	62	75	Clear	Clear	
13	58	75	"	"	Shower 4 P. M.
14	50	65	"	"	
15	46½	60	"	"	
16	50	60	Rain	Rain	Easterly storm.
17	55	61	"	"	Easterly storm.
S 18	54	70	Clear	Clear	
19	52	71½	"	"	
20	62	72	"	Rain	
21	65	68	Rain	"	Easterly storm.
22	54½	63	"	"	Easterly storm.
23	57	67	"	"	Easterly storm.
24	61	68	Cloudy	Cloudy & rain	Easterly storm.
S 25	60	68	"	Clear	Part of afternoon.
26	57½	72	Clear	"	
27	58	72	"	"	
28	64½	75½	"	"	
29	56½	66½	"	Cloudy	
30	57½	65	"	Clear	

October, 1859.

Date.	Thermometer.		Weather.		REMARKS.
	Lowest.	Highest.	Morning.	Afternoon.	
1	49	68½	Clear	Clear	Rain 8 p. m.
S 2	59½	67	Cloudy	"	Part of afternoon.
3	49	65	Clear	"	
4	50	73	"	"	
5	53	72½	"	"	
6	51	60	"	"	
7	43	62	"	"	
8	52	68	Cloudy	Rain	Thunder shower 3:30 p. m.
S 9	48	55	"	Cloudy	
10	42	54	Rain	Clear	Easterly storm.
11	41	61	Clear	"	
12	46	60	"	"	
13	47	66	"	"	
14	58	71	"	Rain	
15	49	57	"	Clear	
S 16	40	54	"	"	
17	41	60	Cloudy	Cloudy	
18	57½	65	Rain	Clear	
19	42	51	Clear	"	
20	41	45	Cloudy	"	
21	32½	43	Clear	"	
22	32	44	"	Cloudy	
S 23	39	52	Cloudy	Clear	
24	35	53½	Clear	"	
25	45½	59	"	"	
26	33	41	"	Snow 5 p. m.	1 inches snow.
27	30	40	Cloudy	Clear	
28	33	46	Clear	"	
29	36	45	Cloudy	Cloudy	
S 30	39	45	"	"	
31	39	46	"	"	

November, 1859.

Date.	Thermometer.		Weather.		REMARKS.
	Lowest.	Highest.	Morning.	Afternoon.	
1	35½	49	Clear	Clear	
2	32½	51	"	"	
3	36½	51	"	"	
4	37½	60	"	"	
5	45	66	"	"	
S 6	43	55	"	"	
7	38	53	"	"	
8	42	58	"	"	
9	45	59	Cloudy	"	
10	53	62	Foggy	Cloudy	
11	50	52½	Clear	Clear	
12	36	63½	Cloudy	Cloudy	
S 13	38	66½	"	"	Rain 11 A. M. to 2 P. M.
14	30	38	Clear	Clear	
15	31	44	"	"	Cloudy part P. M.
16	31	54	"	"	
17	37½	60	Foggy	"	
18	49	58	Rain	Rain	
19	55	66	"	Cloudy	Clear part P. M.
S 20	43	50	Clear	Clear	
21	34	50	"	Cloudy	Rain 6 P. M.
22	42	51	Rain	Clear	
23	44	50	Clear	"	
24	33	38	"	"	
25	30	38	"	Cloudy	Warm at night.
26	45	59	"	Clear	
S 27	41	46	Cloudy most all day		
28	38	47	Clear	Clear	
29	34	46	"	"	
30	34	53	Cloudy most all day		

42 WEATHER RECORD FOR NEW BRUNSWICK, N. J.

December, 1859.

Date.	Thermometer.		Weather.		REMARKS.
	Lowest.	Highest.	Morning.	Afternoon.	
1	43	63	Clear	Clear	
2	54½	67	"	"	
3	32	36	Cloudy	Snow, hail & rain.	
S 4	26	36	Raining and freez' all day		
5	34	39	Drizzly all day........		
6	36	47	" "	"	
7	45	64	" "	"	
8	21½	26	Clear	Clear	
9	17½	31	"	Cloudy	
10	26	28	"	Clear	
S 11	16½	32	Cloudy middle of day		
12	29	40	" "	"	
13	18½	31	Clear	Cloudy	
14	26	33	Snow flurries all day		
15	27	32	Clear	Clear	
16	19½	37	"	"	
17	19½	42	Cloudy	Rain 4 P. M.	
S 18	29	44	Clear	Clear	
19	37	45	"	"	
20	35	42	Rain	Rain	
21	32	34	Cloudy	Clear	
22	22½	29½	Clear	Cloudy	
23	21	30	"	Clear	
24	18½	23½	"	"	
S 25	17	35	"	"	
26	29	47	Cloudy	"	
27	32½	35	Clear	"	
28	8½	16	Cloudy	Cloudy	Snow 1 to 3 P. M.
29	6	30	"	"	Snow 7 P. M. 6 in.
30	25	30	"	Clear	
31	19½	24	Clear	Cloudy	

Weather Record for New Brunswick, N. J.

January, 1860.

Date.	Thermometer. Lowest.	Thermometer. Highest.	Weather. Morning.	Weather. Afternoon.	REMARKS.
S 1	3	15	Cloudy	Cloudy	Clear in the evening.
2	2	14½	Clear	Clear	
3	5	25	"	Cloudy	
4	20½	28	Cloudy	Snow	11 A. M. to 5 P. M.—3 inches.
5	9	21	Clear	Clear	
6	2½	22	"	"	
7	10	40	Cloudy	Rain	5 P. M.
S 8	34	41	Foggy	Clear	
9	29½	43½	Clear	"	
10	34	40	Cloudy	Cloudy	
11	34	45	"	"	
12	31	35	Snow	Clear	5 P. M.—2 inches snow.
13	22	34	Clear	Cloudy	
14	26	36	Snow till 10	and then rain	3 inches snow.
S 15	33	41	Cloudy	Clear	
16	32	46	Clear	"	
17	31	40	Cloudy	Rain	Clear 3 P. M.
18	28	38	Clear	Cloudy	
19	30½	36	"	Clear	
20	28	42	"	"	
21	34	50	"	"	
S 22	35	49	"	"	
23	36	44	"	"	
24	31½	48	"		Clouded over 3 P. M.
25	43	55	Cloudy	Clear	
26	31½	36	"	Cloudy	Snow 7 P. M.—2 inches.
27	22½	31	Clear	Clear	
28	20	36	Cloudy	Cloudy	Clear 9 P. M.
S 29	20	35	Clear	Clear	
30	29	48½	"	"	
31	35½	50	"	Cloudy	Snow 7 P. M. till 11 A. M. Feb. 1st —5 inches.

Weather Record for New Brunswick, N. J.

February, 1860.

Date.	Thermometer.		Weather.		REMARKS.
	Lowest.	Highest.	Morning.	Afternoon.	
1	6	12	Snow	Clear	
2	-½	14	Clear	Cloudy till 7 P.M.	
3	-1	23	"	Clouded over 3 P. M.	
4	18½	30	Cloudy	Clear	
S 5	15	37	"	Cloudy	
6	35	47	Foggy & driz-zly all day		
7	37½	45	Clear	Clear	
8	28½	40	"	"	
9	27	47	"	"	
10	19½	23½	Clear & blus-tering all day		
11	14	27	Clear	Cloudy	Snow 6 P. M.
S 12	19	29½	"	Clear	
13	21	43	"	Cloudy	Rain 10 P. M.
14	39	44	"	"	
15	27	31	Cloudy	Snow	Snow 11 A. M.—9 in.
16	25½	34	"	Clear	
17	10	20	Clear	"	
18	11	28	Snow	Snow, rain & hail—6 in.	
S 19	18	26	Clear	Clear	
20	13	34	"	"	
21	20	43	"	"	
22	34	56	Cloudy	Rain	
23	44	65	Clear	Clear	Shower 3 P. M.
24	41	48½	"	Cloudy	Rain 5 P. M. and then snow and rain.
25	27	37	"	Clear	Snow-flurries—P. M.
S 26	28½	41	"	"	
27	32	53	"	"	
28	40	57	Clear but lit-tle hazy		
29	38	53	Cloudy	Cloudy	

Weather Record for New Brunswick, N. J.

March, 1860.

Date.	Thermometer.		Weather.		REMARKS.
	Lowest.	Highest.	Morning.	Afternoon.	
1	40	60	Rain.	Cloudy	Clear in evening.
2	46	64	Clear	Clear	
3	40	55	"	Rainy	
S 4	46	54	"	Clear	High wind.
5	36	61	"	"	High wind.
6	48	59	"	Cloudy	
7	41	46	Rain.	"	
8	38	48	Cloudy	Rainy	
9	32	45	Snow	Clear	
10	28½	32	Clear.	Cloudy	
S 11	27	42½	Cloudy	Clear.	Cloudy again 10 P. M.
12	34½	50	Rainy	Rainy	
13	30	38	Cloudy	Cloudy.	
14	27½	46	Clear	Clear.	
15	31½	51½	"	"	
16	32½	54	"	"	
17	36	54	Cloudy	"	Foggy 9 P. M.
S 18	38	55	Foggy	"	
19	41	53	Cloudy	Cloudy.	Rain 7 to 8 A. M.
20	42½	55	"	Clear.	
21	31½	39	Clear 10 A. M. to 5 P. M.		Highest point 7 A. M.
22	27	36	Cloudy.	Cloudy	Snow flurries.
23	24	46	Clear	Clear.	Clouded 7 P. M.
24	34	45	"	"	Snow flurries.
S 25	29½	40	"	"	
26	32	43	"	Cloudy.	
27	28½	47	"	Clear	
28	32½	53	"	"	Clouded 5 to 10 P. M.
29	35½	58½	"	"	
30	39	67½	"	"	
31	43	69	"	"	

Weather Record for New Brunswick, N. J.

April, 1860.

Date	Thermometer Lowest	Thermometer Highest	Weather Morning	Weather Afternoon	Remarks
S 1	51	68	Clear	Cloudy	Rain 8 p. m.
2	31	40½	"	Clear	
3	28½	52	Cloudy	Cleared	3 p. m.
4	43½	61	Clear	Showers	
5	47	64	"	Clear	Clouded 5 p. m.
6	43	55½	"	"	Rained last night.
7	37	54	"	"	
S 8	41	55	Rain	Cloudy	Easterly storm.
9	51	62	"	Rainy	Easterly storm.
10	45½	50	"	"	Easterly storm.
11	41½	51	"	"	Cleared 9 p. m.
12	38½	58	Clear	Clear	
13	44	55	"	"	
14	40½	49	"	"	Philadelphia.
S 15	28½	53½	"	"	Philadelphia.
16	34	45½	"	Cloudy	Drizzly.
17	38	73	Cloudy	Clear	
18	39	57	Clear	"	
19	38	62	"	"	
20	49	60	Cloudy	Cloudy	
21	55½	77	Clear	"	St. Joseph.
S 22	42½	47	Rain	"	Pears and cherries flowered.
23	43½	57	Cloudy	"	
24	42	54	"	Clear	
25	36	50	Clear	Rain & snow from 4 to 5 p. m.	
26	33	53	"	Clear	Frost.
27	34	58	"	"	Frost.
28	38½	60	"	Cloudy	
S 29	45	58	"	Clear	
30	41½	61	"	"	

WEATHER RECORD FOR NEW BRUNSWICK, N. J.

May, 1860.

Date	Thermometer Lowest	Thermometer Highest	Weather Morning	Weather Afternoon	REMARKS
1	41½	52½	Cloudy	Rain	Easterly storm.
2	47½	58	Rain	Cloudy	Easterly storm.
3	50	60	Cloudy	"	Easterly storm.
4	45	69	Clear	Clear	
5	51	72	"	"	
S 6	53	77	"	"	
7	62	81	"	"	Clouded 6 P. M.
8	56	59	Cloudy	Cloudy	East wind.
9	53½	60	"	"	East wind.
10	55	60	Rain	"	East wind.
11	55	60	"	"	East wind.
12	54	70	Cloudy	"	East wind.
S 13	59	71	"	Clear	East wind.
14	58	68	Showers	Showers	East wind.
15	52	65	Clear	Clear	East wind.
16	50	70	"	Cloudy	East wind.
17	51	56	Cloudy	"	East wind.
18	53	66	"	"	East wind.
19	58½	70½	Showers 7 A. M. & 6 P. M.		Rest of day clear.
S 20	56	69	Clear	Clear	
21	50¼	57½	Cloudy	Cloudy	East wind.
22	46¼	66	"	Clear	Thunder shower last night.
23	53	70	Clear	"	East wind.
24	52	72	"	"	
25	54	76	"	"	East wind.
26	64½	72	Cloudy	Hard shower	East wind.
S 27	57	60	Drizzly	Rainy	East wind.
28	53	62	Rainy	Cloudy	East wind.
29	52	68	Clear	Clear	East wind.
30	51	68	Cloudy	Cloudy	East wind.
31	58	75	Rain	Clear	Shower 6 P. M.

June, 1860.

	Thermometer.		Weather.		
Date.	Lowest.	Highest.	Morning.	Afternoon.	REMARKS.
1	58	71	Clear	Clear	The seventeen-year locusts have appeared.
2	58	77	"	"	
S 3	57	78	"	Cloudy	
4	60	74	"	"	Rain 7 P. M.
5	61	69	Showery	"	Wind east.
6	61½	73	Cloudy	Clear	Cleared 10 A. M.
7	61½	76	Clear	"	
8	60	75	"	"	Shower 5 to 7 P. M.
9	56	70	"	"	
S 10	55	68	"	"	
11	53	74½	"	"	Philadelphia.
12	53	75	"	"	Philadelphia.
13	53½	76½	"	"	Philadelphia.
14	58	77	"	"	Philadelphia.
15	59½	79	"	"	
16	62½	76	"	Cloudy	Shower 1:30 to 3:30 P. M.
S 17	63	75	"	Clear	East wind.
18	59½	76	"	"	
19	61	72	Heavy show'r morning and evening.		
20	60½	76	Clear	Cloudy	Shower 11 A M.
21	57	66	Cloudy	"	East wind.
22	56	72	Clear	Clear	East wind.
23	55½	75	"	"	East wind.
S 24	60	72	"	"	East wind.
25	55	76	"	"	East wind.
26	61½	85½	"	"	First warm night.
27	70	80	Cloudy	"	
28	66	83	Clear	"	
29	71	91	"	"	
30	72	89	"	"	

July, 1860.

Date.	Thermometer. Lowest.	Highest.	Weather. Morning.	Afternoon.	REMARKS.
S 1	67½	75	Light shower	Clear	Cleared 4 P. M.
2	60½	80	Clear	"	
3	65	76	Cloudy nearly all day		
4	70	82	Clear	Clear	Shower 3:30 P. M.
5	69	76	Rainy	Rainy	Easterly storm.
6	57½	68	Cloudy	Clear	East wind.
7	56½	70	Clear	"	East wind.
S 8	60½	74	Cloudy	Cloudy	East wind.
9	66	86	Clear	Clear	
10	68½	85	"	"	
11	68	79	"	"	
12	58	75	"	"	
13	57½	75	"	"	East wind.
14	59½	79	"	"	East wind.
S 15	61	83	"	"	
16	69½	90	"	"	Shower 5 P. M.
17	67	81	"	"	
18	61½	83	"	"	
19	71	88	Cloudy	Cleared 5 P.M.	
20	74	91	Clear	Clear	Great meteor 9:50 P. M.
21	74	86	Cloudy	Cloudy	Clear 9 P. M.
S 22	64½	80	Clear	Clear	
23	69	84	Rain	"	
24	58½	76	Clear	"	
25	59	82	"	"	
26	63½	85	"	"	Shower 2:30 to 3 P. M.
27	68	80	Cloudy	"	Heavy showers 12 to 3 A. M.
28	59	74	Clear	"	
S 29	63	75	Cloudy	Cloudy	Rain 9 P. M.
30	70	85	Clear	Clear	On S. S. Great Eastern to Cape May.
31	71	82	"	"	At Cape May.

Weather Record for New Brunswick, N. J.

August, 1860.

Date.	Thermometer.		Weather.		REMARKS.
	Lowest.	Highest.	Morning.	Afternoon.	
1	59	76½	Clear	Clear	At Cape May.
2	56½	80	"	"	At Cape May.
3	60	80	"	"	At Philadelphia.
4	67	84	"	"	Shower 9 A. M. and 9 P. M.
S 5	71	84	"	"	
6	66½	82½	"	"	
7	66½	88	"	"	
8	73½	87½	"	"	Shower 9 P. M.
9	74½	86½	"	"	
10	71½	87½	"	"	
11	70	74	Cloudy	Cloudy	
S 12	63½	78	Clear	"	
13	71	83	Showers	Heavy rain	After 4 P. M.
14	62	67	Rain	Rainy	Clear 9 P. M.
15	55½	71½	Clear	Clear	
16	56½	72½	"	"	
17	57½	76	"	"	
18	62½	81	"	"	Shower 6 P. M.
S 19	67	79½	"	"	
20	72½	79½	"	"	
21	71½	80	Cloudy	Rain	
22	68½	78	Rain	Shower 2 P.M.	Clear 9 A. M. to 2 P. M.
23	70	77½	Heavy rain	Clear	
24	71	77	Cloudy	Cloudy	Rain in the night.
25	69	80	Clear	Clear	
S 26	64½	76½	"	"	
27	63	78	"	"	
28	63	71	"	Rainy	
29	56	73	"	Clear	
30	56½	75	"	"	
31	62	77	Cloudy	"	

WEATHER RECORD FOR NEW BRUNSWICK, N. J.

September, 1860.

Date	Thermometer Lowest	Thermometer Highest	Weather Morning	Weather Afternoon	REMARKS.
1	58½	75	Clear	Clear	
S 2	56	69	"	"	
3	57	71	"	"	
4	54½	74	"	"	
5	63	78	"	"	
6	68	78	Rainy	"	
7	66½	81	Clear	"	
8	71	84	"	Cloudy	Shower 6:30 P. M.
S 9	57	63½	Cloudy	Clear	Rain before daybreak.
10	49	65	Clear	"	
11	56	64	Cloudy	Cloudy	
12	53	57	"	Clear	Rain before daybreak.
13	48	65	Clear	"	
14	48	69	"	"	
15	51½	72	"	"	
S 16	55	74	"	"	Fog A. M.
17	62½	71	Cloudy	Cloudy	
18	63	73	Clear	Clear	
19	65	77	Cloudy	"	Rain before daybreak.
20	67	76	Rain	Rain	Clear 9 A. M. to 2 P. M.
21	57	64	Cloudy	Clear	Cleared 9 A. M.
22	48	66	Clear	"	
S 23	54½	71½	"	"	
24	57	76	"	"	
25	63	73	"	"	Shower 10 A. M. and shower and hail 3 P. M.
26	54	64	"	"	
27	49½	56	Cloudy	Cloudy	
28	50	63	Clear	Clear	
29	41	53	"	"	Clouded over 6 P. M.
S 30	44	53	Cloudy	Cloudy	Cleared 9 P. M.

Weather Record for New Brunswick, N. J.

October, 1860.

Date.	Thermometer. Lowest.	Thermometer. Highest.	Weather. Morning.	Weather. Afternoon.	Remarks.
1	42	57	Rainy	Rainy	Easterly storm.
2	55	72	Cloudy	Clear	Cleared 10 A. M.
3	53½	64	Clear	"	
4	49½	63	"	Cloudy	
5	58	68½	"	Clear	Philadelphia.
6	50	55½	"	"	Philadelphia.
S 7	39	58	"	"	Philadelphia.
8	49	70	Cloudy	"	Rain before daybreak.
9	44	56	Clear	"	
10	46	64	"	"	
11	53	67	"	"	
12	48	57	"	"	
13	39½	55	"	"	Cloudy 6 P. M.
S 14	44½	51	Cloudy	Rain	Snow 10 P. M.
15	34½	50	Clear	Clear	
16	36	55	"	"	
17	41	60	"	Cloudy	
18	51	58	"	Clear	Cloudy 9 A. M. to 3 P. M.
19	45	59	Cloudy	Cloudy	Rain 8 P. M.
20	50	56½	Rain	Rain	
S 21	52	58	"	"	
22	53½	58	Foggy	Cloudy	
23	54	62	Cloudy	Clear	
24	53	63	Clear	"	
25	46	64	"	"	
26	50	67	"	"	Foggy A. M.
27	41	58	"	"	
S 28	44	57	Cloudy	Cloudy	
29	53½	68	"	"	
30	58	65	Foggy	"	
31	61	74	Cloudy	Clear	Cloudy again 8 P. M.

November, 1860.

Date	Lowest	Highest	Morning	Afternoon	Remarks
1	61½	74½	Clear	Clear	
2	61	67	Cloudy	Cloudy	Clear 9 A. M. to 5 P. M.
3	61	63	Rain	Rain	
S 4	53	55	Clear	Clear	Cleared 9 A. M.
5	40	61	"	"	Clouded 5 P. M.
6	48	52½	Cloudy	"	Cleared 9 A. M.
7	37	50	Clear	"	
8	36	52	"	"	
9	38	50	"	Cloudy	Rain 7 P. M.
10	45	56	Rain	Rain	
S 11	43½	49	Cloudy	Rainy	
12	43	55	"	Clear	Cloudy 8 P. M.
13	44½	55	Clear	"	
14	39	58	"	"	
15	40	55	"	"	
16	41	53	"	"	
17	40	55	"	Cloudy	
S 18	46	54	Rain	"	
19	42	55	Cloudy	"	
20	40	48	Clear	Clear	
21	33	41	"	Cloudy	
22	30½	42	"	Clear	
23	34	59	Rain	Rain	
24	24	38	Clear	Clear	Warmest 8 A. M., coldest 12 M.
S 25	15	36	"	"	River frozen over.
26	21	39	"	Cloudy	Warm during night.
27	50	54	Rain	Rain	
28	38	42	Cloudy	Clear	
29	29½	43	Clear	"	
30	34½	46	Cloudy	Rain	

December, 1860.

Date.	Thermometer. Lowest.	Thermometer. Highest.	Weather. Morning.	Weather. Afternoon.	REMARKS.
1	35	38	Clear	Cloudy	Snow squall in night.
S 2	26	36	Cloudy	Clear	Clear 1 to 6 P. M.
3	30½	40	Clear	"	Cloudy 7 P. M.
4	33	39	Snow 8 A. M.	Snow	5 inches.
5	23	35	Clear	Clear	
6	24	35	"	Cloudy	
7	28	38	"	Clear	
8	27	37	Snow	Cloudy	4 inches; clear 8 P. M.
S 9	17½	35	Clear	Clear	
10	24	40	Cloudy	Rain	Rain 10 A. M.
11	35	38	"	Clear	
12	24	38	"	"	
13	31	38	Clear	"	
14	14½	20½	"	"	
15	10	19	Cloudy	Cloudy	Cleared 6 P. M.
S 16	12	30	Clear	Clear	
17	21½	37	"	"	
18	23½	34	"	"	
19	23	52	Cloudy	Rain	Snow flurry 6 A. M.
20	42	47	"	Cloudy	
21	37	44	Clear	Clear	Cloudy 9 P. M.
22	37	45	Rain	"	Cleared 2 P. M.
S 23	24½	31	Clear	"	
24	20	30	"	"	
25	23	33	"	"	Cloudy 1 to 4 P. M.
26	25¼	36	Cloudy	"	Cleared 10 A. M.
27	27	35	Clear	"	Cloudy 5 P. M.
28	25	35	Cloudy	"	
29	23½	37	"	Cloudy	
S 30	32	43	"	Rain	
31	28	36	"	Clear 4 P. M.	Snow squall before day.

Weather Record for New Brunswick, N. J.

January, 1861.

Date	Thermometer Lowest.	Thermometer Highest.	Weather Morning.	Weather Afternoon.	REMARKS.
1	18½	34	Clear	Clear	
2	23	40	"	"	
3	33	36	Rain	Cloudy	
4	27	33	Cloudy	"	Snow 10 A. M. to 12 M.; clear 12 to 4 P. M.
5	27	35	Clear	Clear	
S 6	27	40	"	"	Cloudy 6 P. M.
7	35	47	Cloudy	Cloudy	Clear 6 P. M.
8	36	41	"	"	Clear part A. M.
9	33	41	"	Snow	Very wet snow—3 inches.
10	28	35	"	Cloudy	Clear 12 to 5 P. M.
11	12	24	Clear	"	Snow 4 P. M.—2 inches.
12	17	27	Cloudy	"	Cleared 6 P. M.
S 13	- 1	13	Clear	Clear	Wind southwest A. M.
14	2	35	Cloudy	Snow	10 A. M. to 6 P. M. and then rain.
15	30	37	"	Cloudy	
16	34	39	Rain	"	
17	35½	44	Clear	"	Clouded over 3 P. M.
18	33	38	Cloudy	Snow	1 to 2:30 P. M. and then rain.
19	34	44	Clear	Clear	
S 20	34	38	Cloudy	"	Clear part A. M.
21	25	33½	Clear	"	
22	20½	30	"	"	
23	17	31	"	"	Clouded 6 P. M.
24	24	39	Snow		3 A. M. to 12 noon—4 inches and then rain.
25	35	38	Cloudy	Cloudy	
26	28	34	"	Snow	2 to 9 P. M.—3 inches.
S 27	24½	32	"	Clear	Cleared 9:30 A. M.
28	16	33	"	"	Snow squall before day; cleared 10 A. M.
29	23	40	"	Cleared	3 P. M.
30	26	32	Clear	Clear	Warmest 7:30 A. M.
31	16	27	"	"	

Weather Record for New Brunswick, N. J.

February, 1861.

Date.	Thermometer.		Weather.		REMARKS.
	Lowest.	Highest.	Morning.	Afternoon.	
1	14½	38	Clear	Cloudy 1 P.M.	Rain to 6 P. M.—warmest in the night.
2	46	51	R'ny & foggy all day.		
S 3	33	36	Cloudy	Cloudy	Clear 9 to 12 A. M.
4	26	36	"	Clear	
5	26	40	Clear	Cloudy	
6	33½	43	Cloudy	Clear	
7	36	48	"	Clear & cl'dy Alternately.	
8	- 6	13	Clear	Clear	Cloudy 8 P. M.
9	9¼	32	Cloudy	Cloudy	Clear 3 to 7 P. M.
S 10	33	44	"	"	Clear 2 to 9 P. M.
11	36	60	Clear	"	
12	50	59	Rain	Clear	
13	41½	52	Clear	"	
14	35	55	"	Cloudy	3 P. M.
15	34	43	Rainy	Rainy	
16	37	52	Clear	Cloudy	4 P. M. and rain 8 P. M.
S 17	36½	42	"	"	4 P. M.
18	28	36½	"	"	
19	29	36	"	"	3 P. M.
20	35	43	Snow till 10 Clear.		
21	30½	36	Clear	Cloudy	Part P. M. Heavy snow squall 11 A. M.
22	27	40	"	Clear	Cloudy 6 P. M.
23	34	56	Cloudy	Cloudy	Rainy 5 P. M.
S 24	37	45	"	Clear	15° 8 A. M., 37° at noon—falling all day.
25	20½	40	Clear	"	
26	30½	52	"	"	Cloudy 9 A. M. to 2 P. M.
27	34	59	"	"	
28	39½	63	"	"	

Weather Record for New Brunswick, N. J.

March, 1861.

Date.	Thermometer.		Weather.		REMARKS.
	Highest.	Lowest.	Morning.	Afternoon.	
1	49	67	Clear	Clear	Cloudy 8 P. M., and light rain in the night.
2	47	62	"	"	
S 3	45½	74	"	"	
4	45	55	Cloudy	"	Clear 10 A. M.
5	34	40	Clear	"	
6	24	40	"	"	
7	14	25	"	"	
8	17	39	"	"	Cloudy 5 P. M.
9	50½	54	Rain 7½ A. M. to 4 P. M.	Clear 7 P. M.	
S 10	34	42	Cloudy	Cloudy	
11	24½	37	Clear	Clear	
12	30	51	"	Cloudy	
13	40	53	Cloudy	Rainy	
14	29	33	Snow	Snow	3 inches.
15	27	35	Cloudy	Cloudy	1 inch snow in night.
16	28	47	Clear	Clear	
S 17	41	46	"	"	
18	14	28	"	Cloudy 2 P. M.	Snow 9 P. M.
19	14	27½	Snow 2 inches	Clear	Cleared 2 P. M.
20	14	36	Clear	"	Snow 9 P. M.
21	31	35	Rain till 6:30 A. M. & then	Snow all day. 6 inches.	
22	26	42	Cloudy	Clear	Cleared 9 A. M.
23	30	50	Clear	"	Cloudy 6 P. M.
S 24	39½	46	"	"	
25	30	50	"	"	Cloudy 6 P. M.
26	40	66	Cloudy nearly all day.		
27	57	61	Cloudy. Rain 3 A. M. to 6 P. M., and then clear.		
28	39	52	Clear	Clear	Cloudy 3 to 6 P. M.
29	38	60	"	"	
30	46	64	"	"	
S 31	35	50	"	"	

WEATHER RECORD FOR NEW BRUNSWICK, N. J.

April, 1861.

Date	Thermometer Lowest	Thermometer Highest	Weather Morning	Weather Afternoon	REMARKS
1	33½	42	Cloudy	3 P. M. snow, hail and rain.—East wind.	
2	32½	43	Cloudy most all day	East wind.	
3	34½	44	" "	"	East wind.
4	32½	52	Clear.	Clear	East wind.
5	35	57	"	"	East wind.
6	41½	56	"	"	East wind.
S 7	38½	54	"	"	East wind.
8	37½	52	"	Cloudy	East wind.
9	30½	48	Cloudy most all day	East wind.	
10	36	54	Clear.	Clear.	East wind.
11	35	64	"	"	East wind.
12	38	60	"	"	Cloudy 6 P. M.—East wind.
13	53	62	Rain all day except from 3 to 9 P. M.—East wind.		
S 14	50½	64	Clear.	Clear.	
15	45	55	"	Cloudy.	Rain 4 P. M.
16	42	45	Rain.	Rain.	East wind.
17	37	43	Rainy	Cloudy	
18	34½	51	Clear	Cloudy nearly all afternoon.	
19	45	53	"	" "	" "
20	36	55	"	Clear	
S 21	44	65	Cloudy	"	Cleared 9 A. M.
22	48½	72½	Clear.	"	
23	58	83	"	"	Pears and cherries flowered.
24	50	66	"	"	
25	51	66	"	"	
26	49	67	"	"	
27	47	75	"	"	
S 28	50½	70	Cl'dy & show'y all day		
29	48	73	Clear	Clear	
30	53	75	"	"	2 to 5 P. M. Cloudy.

Weather Record for New Brunswick, N. J.

May, 1861.

Date	Thermometer Lowest	Thermometer Highest	Weather Morning	Weather Afternoon	Remarks
1	45½	56	Clear	Clear	Rain 7 to 9 A. M. and cloudy again 8 P. M.
2	35	50	"	"	
3	35½	47	"	Little snow	and then rain. Frost last three mornings.
4	36½	49	Rain	Rain	Heavy snow 7 to 9 A. M.; cleared 4 P. M.
S 5	35	59	Clear	Clear	Frost this A. M.
6	43	64	Rain	Rain	
7	51	66½	Clear	Clear	
8	54	65	"	Cloudy	Nearly all P. M.
9	46	65	"	Clear	
10	43	60	"	Cloudy	Rain 4 P. M.
11	47	68	"	Clear	
S 12	50	69	"	"	Cloudy 6 P. M. Rain 11 P. M., with thunder, etc.
13	57½	65	Cloudy	Cloudy	
14	55	75	Rain	Clear	Rain till 8 A. M. and cloudy rest of A. M.
15	55	69	Clear	"	
16	53½	66	"	"	
17	47½	59	"	"	
18	44	61	"	"	
S 19	42½	61	Cloudy 8 to 12 A. M. and again 6 P. M.; rain 9:30 P. M.		
20	50½	55	Rain till 5 P. M. and cloudy afternoon.		
21	48	65	Clear	Clear	
22	46	65	"	"	
23	48½	68	"	"	
24	48	69	"	"	
25	50½	74	Rain	"	
S 26	57	75	Clear	"	Cloudy early part P. M.
27	61	74	Showery	"	
28	51½	70	Clear	"	
29	52	62	"	"	Rain 6 to 8 A. M.
30	45	67	"	"	Frost.
31	49½	72	"	"	

Weather Record for New Brunswick, N. J.

June, 1861.

Date	Thermometer Lowest	Thermometer Highest	Morning	Afternoon	REMARKS
1	53	75	Clear	Clear	
S 2	59	74½	"	Cloudy	Shower 2:30 P. M.
3	64	79	Rain	Clear 2¼ P. M.	Shower 10 P. M.
4	65½	71	Rainy	Rainy	
5	58½	64	Cloudy	Cloudy	
6	51½	60	Rain till 3 P. M. and cloudy afterwards.		
7	58	67½	Cloudy	Clear 3 to 7 P. M. and then rain.	
8	60	72½	Clear	Heavy show'r	
S 9	59	73	"	Clear	
10	58	81	"	"	Cloudy 6 P. M.
11	65	75	Showery	all day	Clear 6 P. M.
12	61½	82	Clear	Clear	
13	62½	75	"	"	
14	55½	74	"	"	
15	62¼	83½	"	"	Shower 11 P. M.
S 16	71½	80	"	"	Cloudy 7 P. M.
17	63½	73	"	"	
18	56	71	"	"	
19	55	77	"	"	Shower in night.
20	63½	79	"	"	
21	59½	71	"	Cl'y & show'y	
22	64	81	"	Clear	
S 23	62	85	"	"	Shower 7 P. M.
24	59½	75	"	"	
25	54½	78	"	"	
26	64	78	"	Cloudy most P. M.—shower 7 P. M.	
27	66	79	"	Clear	
28	67	81	"	Cloudy most P. M.	
29	67	78	"	Clear	
S 30	62	72½	"	Cloudy	

July, 1861.

Date	Thermometer Lowest	Thermometer Highest	Weather Morning	Weather Afternoon	REMARKS
1	63	74	Cloudy most all day		Shower 10 P. M.
2	60½	67	Clear	but blustering	Comet first seen.
3	55	79½	Clear	Clear	
4	60½	82	"	"	
5	62	82½	"	"	
6	62½	81	"	Cloudy	
S 7	69½	86½	Cloudy	Clear	
8	71½	91	Clear	"	
9	75	89½	"	"	Rainy after 6 P. M.
10	73½	87½	"	"	Shower 9 P. M.
11	69½	82	"	"	
12	63½	78	"	"	
13	59	76½	"	Cloudy	Rainy 6 to 9 P. M.
S 14	62	65	Cloudy	Rainy	
15	60	75	Clear	Clear	9 A. M. to 8 P. M. and then cloudy.
16	62½	80	"	"	Shower 6 P. M. and cloudy.
17	67	82	"	"	
18	67	84	"	"	Comet last seen.
19	68½	80	Rainy	"	
20	67½	85	Showers	"	
S 21	63½	78	Clear	"	
22	65	73½	"	Cloudy	Most P. M.
23	63½	75	"	"	Most P. M.
24	59	75	"	"	Most P. M.
25	59½	76	"	Clear	
26	60½	79	"	"	
27	64	81	"	"	
S 28	66½	82	"	"	Cloudy 8 P. M.
29	71	83	Cloudy	"	Shower 9:30 P. M.
30	70	86	Clear	"	
31	69½	87½	"	"	

August, 1861.

Date	Thermometer Lowest	Thermometer Highest	Weather Morning	Weather Afternoon	REMARKS
1	73½	85	Clear	Clear	
2	72½	86	Cloudy	"	Clear about 10 A. M.
3	72	88	"	"	Clear about 10 A. M.
S 4	72½	90	"	"	Clear about 10 A. M.
5	74½	90	Clear	"	
6	73½	89	"	"	
7	72	80½	"	"	Cloudy 6 P. M.
8	67½	72	Cloudy	Cloudy	Rain 4 to 5 A. M.
9	64	72	"	"	Rain 8 to 8:30 A. M.
10	68½	87	"	Clear	Clear 10 A. M.
S 11	70¼	84	Clear	"	Cloudy 7 P. M.
12	70½	73	Cloudy	East'rly st'rm at 3 P. M.	
13	61¼	64	Rainy	Rainy	
14	54	67	Cloudy	Clear	
15	55	71	Clear	"	
16	54	71	"	Cloudy	3 P. M.
17	62½	69	Rainy	"	Clear 4 to 7 P. M.
S 18	63	77	Clear	"	most P. M.
19	69	76	Cloudy most all day.		
20	66	73	Clear	Clear	
21	58	73	"	"	
22	61½	78	Cloudy most all day.		Heavy rain after 6:30 P. M.
23	62	73	Clear	Clear	
24	57	76	"	"	
S 25	61½	77	"	"	
26	60	75	"	"	Cloudy in evening.
27	62	77	"	"	Cloudy evening.
28	66	75	Cloudy most all day.		
29	68½	75	Clear	Cloudy till 6 P. M., and then clear.	
30	64¼	78	"	Clear	
31	58	73	"	"	

Weather Record for New Brunswick, N. J.

September, 1861.

Date.	Thermometer.		Weather.		REMARKS.
	Lowest.	Highest.	Morning.	Afternoon.	
S 1	54½	72	Clear	Clear	
2	55	76½	"	"	
3	62	82	Cloudy most all day		Shower 3:30 P.M. & rain after 7 P.M.
4	67	75	Cloudy	Clear	Clear 9 A. M.
5	58	70	Cloudy most all day		
6	64	75	Clear	Clear	
7	65	78	"	"	
S 8	61½	72	"	"	Cloudy in evening.
9	62¼	78	Cloudy most all day		Rain 8 to 9 P. M.
10	59½	68	"	" " "	
11	64	72½	Rainy	Rainy	
12	63	73	Clear	Clear	
13	59	75	"	"	
14	59	77	"	"	Foggy A. M.
S 15	63½	80	"	"	
16	66	75	"	"	
17	64	71	Cloudy	Rain	Easterly storm.
18	60	65½	"	Cloudy	Easterly storm.
19	62	72½	Clear 9 A. M.	Clear	Philadelphia 5:30 P. M.
20	62½	79	Clear	"	Philadelphia.
21	65	80	Cloudy most all day		
S 22	55	61½	Cloudy	Clear 6 P. M.	Rain before day.
23	48½	71	Clear	Clear	
24	50	70	"	"	
25	50	69	"	"	
26	52¼	72½	"	"	
27	57½	76	Cloudy	Rainy	
28	59½	65	Clear	Clear	
S 29	47½	63	"	"	
30	46½	65	"	"	

Weather Record for New Brunswick, N. J.

October, 1861.

Date.	Thermometer.		Weather.		REMARKS.
	Lowest	Highest	Morning.	Afternoon.	
1	47½	65½	Clear	Clear	
2	50	67	Cloudy most all day		
3	60½	77	Clear	Clear	
4	56½	72½	"	"	
5	61½	81	"	"	
S 6	69	85	"	"	
7	71	76	"	Cloudy	Rain after 5 P. M.
8	58	65	Rain	Clear	Clear 5 P. M.
9	49	63	Clear	"	
10	52½	61	Cloudy	Cloudy	Rain after 5 P. M.
11	57	68	"	Clear	Cloudy again 9 P. M.
12	56	61	"	"	Rain before day; cleared 10 A. M.
S 13	49½	59	"	"	Clear 8 A. M.
14	45	60	Clear	"	
15	48	68	"	"	
16	52	65	Cloudy	Cloudy	
17	59	69	"	"	
18	64½	73	Rain	Clear	
19	63½	74	Foggy	Rainy	
S 20	56	63½	Clear	Clear	Cloudy 6 P. M.
21	45	57	"	Cloudy	
22	48	59	"	"	Rain 9 P. M.
23	54	61	Cloudy	"	Clear 5 P. M.
24	42	52½	Clear	Clear	
25	34	54	"	"	First frost on morning of the 25th.
26	45	57	Cloudy	Cloudy	Rain 8 P. M.
S 27	49	56	Clear	Clear	
28	35	52½	"	"	
29	38½	60	"	"	
30	40½	61	"	"	Cloudy morning and evening.
31	40½	56	"	"	

November, 1861.

Date.	Thermometer. Lowest.	Thermometer. Highest.	Weather. Morning.	Weather. Afternoon.	REMARKS.
1	40	56	Clear	Cloudy	
2	48	64	Rain	Rain	Violent storm.
S 3	53	59	Clear	Clear	
4	43	52	"	"	Cloudy part P. M.
5	38	56	"	Cloudy	Rain 6 to 8 P. M.; cleared 10 P. M.
6	43	56	Cloudy	Rain	
7	46	52	Clear	Clear	
8	37½	51	"	Cloudy	
9	43	50	Rain	Rain	
S 10	39	49	Clear	Clear	
11	39	57	Cloudy	Cleared 4 P. M	
12	40	52	Clear	Clear	
13	37	48	Cloudy most all day		Clear sunrise.
14	43	49	Clear	Cloudy	Most P. M.
15	36	42	Cloudy	"	Light rain before day.
16	33	39	Clear 9 A. M.	Clear with heavy flying clouds.	
S 17	34	45	"	Clear	
18	33	45	"	"	
19	31	46	"	"	
20	30	45	"	"	
21	31	47½	"	"	
22	31	44	"	"	Cloudy 5 P. M.
23	37½	50	Rain till 4 A. M., and cloudy afterwards.		
S 24	34	45	Clear	Clear	Cloudy 4 P. M.
25	30	38½	"	Cloudy 2 to 6 P. M.; light snow before day.	
26	31	41	"	Clear	
27	31	44	"	Cloudy	Raining after 5 P. M.
28	36	45	Clear sunrise but cloudy most of day.		
29	40	50	Foggy & misty all day	Rainy after 8 P. M.	
30	35	44	Rain till 8 A. M.	Cleared about noon.	

WEATHER RECORD FOR NEW BRUNSWICK, N. J.

December, 1861.

Date	Thermometer Lowest	Thermometer Highest	Weather Morning	Weather Afternoon	REMARKS
S 1	32	48	Cloudy most all day		
2	34	38	Clear	Cloudy	
3	23	32	"	Clear	
4	19	34	"	"	
5	28	46½	"	"	
6	35	48	Cloudy	Cloudy	Clear 3 to 8 P. M.
7	39	50	Foggy	Clear	5:30 P. M., Philadelphia.
S 8	33½	57	"	"	
9	38	61	"	"	
10	43	54	"	Cloudy most P. M.	
11	47½	53½	Rainy	Clear	
12	25	37	Clear	"	
13	25½	32	"	"	
14	41	48½	"	"	
S 15	37	43	"	"	
16	29	48	"	"	
17	38	47	"	"	
18	34½	47	Cloudy	Cloudy	Cleared 5 P. M.
19	30½	51½	Clear	Clear	Cloudy 6 P. M.
20	38	48	Cloudy	Cleared	2 P. M.
21	21	29	Clear	Clear	
S 22	22	34	"	Cloudy	Clouded over 10 A. M.
23	31	43	Rain till 4 P. M. and snow rest of day.		
24	25	29	Clear	Clear	
25	18	20	"	"	Cloudy part A. M.
26	17½	35	"	Cloudy	
27	30	38½	Rain	Clear	Cleared 8 A. M.
28	19½	28½	Clear	"	
S 29	22	35½	Cloudy	Cloudy	
30	28½	38	Clear	Clear	Cloudy part A. M.
31	24½	41½	Cloudy most all day		

Weather Record for New Brunswick, N. J.

January, 1862.

Date	Thermometer Lowest	Thermometer Highest	Weather Morning	Weather Afternoon	Remarks
1	35	53	Clear	Clear	
2	25	31	"	"	
3	17	26	"	"	Cloudy 6 P. M.
4	16½	25½	Cloudy	"	
S 5	10	26½	Clear	"	
6	15	24	Snow	Snow flurries	6½ inches.
7	19	33	Clear	Clear	Cloudy part P. M.
8	7	29½	"	"	Cloudy 5 P. M.
9	23½	40¼	Rain	"	Foggy night.
10	31½	42	Foggy & misty all day		
11	29¼	35	Clear	Cloudy	Hail and snow 9 P. M.
S 12	30¼	45½	Dense fog all day		Rain 9 P. M.
13	32	36	Cl'r part A.M.	Cloudy	36° at 7:30 A. M.; 32° at 8 A. M., and growing colder all day.
14	18	24	Cloudy	Clear	Cloudy again 9 P.M.
15	17½	39	Rain	Rain	Snow before day between 12 and 1 o'clock A.M.; large fire in Commerce Square. Dayton and others burnt out.
16	30	34	Clear	Clear	
17	24½	36½	Cloudy	Cloudy	
18	30½	39	"	Foggy & misty	Rain 8 to 12 A. M.
S 19	33½	39	Rain	Rain	
20	34	38½	"	"	
21	32	35	Cloudy	Cloudy	
22	29	37	"	"	
23	25½	37	"	"	Foggy early A. M.
24	30½	35	"	"	Snow and hail 8 P. M.
25	30	39	Rain	Rain	3 inches of slush.
S 26	29	35	Clear	Clear	
27	26	34	"	"	Cloudy part A. M.
28	23	31	Cloudy 9 A.M. Snow 1 to 7 P. M. and then rain—3 inches.		
29	26½	37½	Foggy & misty all day		
30	34	40	Rain	Misty	
31	26½	37	Clear	Clear	

NOTE.—There has been but one clear day between the 5th and 26th, and nearly the whole time the wind has been from the East.

Weather Record for New Brunswick, N. J.

February, 1862.

Date.	Thermometer.		Weather.		REMARKS.
	Lowest.	Highest.	Morning.	Afternoon.	
1	28	37	Snow	Snow	3 inches.
S 2	28	33	Clear	Clear	Cleared 7 A. M.
3	17	31	Cloudy	Snow	5 inches.
4	22½	32	Cloudy most all day.		
5	18½	33	Clear	Clear	
6	17	40	Cloudy	Rain	
7	35	41	Clear	Clear	
8	22½	36½	"	Cloudy	Snow squalls P. M.
S 9	22	34	Cloudy	Clear	Cleared 9 A. M.
10	13	29½	Clear	"	
11	18	34	"	Cloudy	Snow 7 P. M.; 1 inch.
12	31½	43	"	Clear	Cleared 7 A. M.
13	28½	43	Cloudy	"	Cleared 10 A. M.
14	33	41½	"	Clear part of P. M.	
15	22	32	"	Snow 12 to 5 P. M.; 2 inches.	
S 16	16	32	Clear	Clear	Cloudy part of evening.
17	21	34½	Cloudy	Rain, hail and snow.	
18	30	39	"	Clear	Foggy 9 P. M.
19	28	39	"	Snow 2:30 to 4	and then heavy rain, and had showers during the night accompanied with lightning.
20	34	41	Clear	Clear	
21	23	35	"	Cloudy	
22	29½	40	Cloudy	"	
S 23	34	43½	"	"	
24	37	45	Foggy & rainy	Cleared	5 P. M., with violent gale; foggy and misty until the afternoon; rained very hard from 2 to 3 P. M.; about 4 P. M. wind changed to N. W. and blew a terrific gale the whole night, unroofed houses, etc.
25	16	29	Clear	Clear	
26	21	36	"	Cloudy	Cloudy 8 A. M.
27	29½	37	Snow	Cloudy till 4 P. M., and then clear; 4 inches.	
28	18	26	Clear	Cloudy most of P. M.	

Weather Record for New Brunswick, N. J.

March, 1862.

Date.	Thermometer.		Weather.		REMARKS.
	Lowest.	Highest.	Morning.	Afternoon.	
1	20½	35	Clear	Clear	
S 2	23	37	"	"	Cloudy part P. M.
3	26½	43½	Cloudy	Rain	Rain 8 A.M.; lightning in evening.
4	30	34	Cloudy most all day and very blustery.		
5	31	40	Cloudy	Snow all P.M. but melts.	
6	28	35½	"	Clear	
7	19	38½	Clear	"	
8	30½	44	"	"	
S 9	35	46	"	"	
10	34	53	Cloudy and damp all day		
11	37	45½	Clear	Clear	
12	36	51	Cloudy	"	
13	35	42½	Cloudy most all day and rainy evening.		
14	35½	43	Cloudy and damp all day		
15	36½	41	Rain	Rain	
S 16	32½	43	Cloudy	Cloudy	
17	30	40	Cloudy most all day		Snow before day.
18	29	39½	Clear	Clear	
19	28½	44	"	"	Cloudy evening.
20	36	42	Cloudy	Cloudy	Rain 9 P. M.
21	34	44	Rain	"	Snow before day.
22	36½	44	Cloudy	Clear partly	Heavy snow 9 A. M. to 1 P. M., but melted as it fell.
S 23	38	47	"	Clear partly.	
24	36	49	Clear most all day		
25	35	40	Cloudy most all day		
26	29	45	Clear	Clear.	First dusty day.
27	32	51	"	"	
28	35	49½	"	"	
29	28	46	"	Cloudy	Clear again 8 P. M.
S 30	30	48	"	"	
31	38½	49	Cloudy	"	Most all P. M.

Weather Record for New Brunswick, N. J.

April, 1862.

Date.	Thermometer. Lowest.	Thermometer. Highest.	Weather. Morning.	Weather. Afternoon.	Prevailing Wind.	Rain and Melted Snow in inches.	Snow in inches.	Remarks.
1	40	50	Cloudy	most all day.	E.			Clear at sunrise, but clouded over soon after. Clear part of evening.
2	35	48	"	Cloudy	E.			
3	42	65	Clear	Clear	N. W.	0.07		Light rain before daybreak.
4	42	58	"	"	W.			Clouded at 6 P. M. and continued so most of the evening.
5	42½	45½	Cloudy	Cloudy	E.	0.34		Rain from 10:30 A. M. to 3 P. M. Cleared 9 P. M.
S 6	36	56	Clear	Clear	W.			Clouded over 3 P. M.
7	34	47	"	Cloudy	W.			
8	33	38½	Cloudy	Snow	N. E.		5.	Snow very hard from 11 A. M., but drifted. Melted first few hours.
9	30½	42	"	Cloudy	N. E.			Continued snowing until 5 A. M. Commenced again 8 P. M.
10	31	47½	Clear	Clear	N. E.		8.	Cleared 7 A. M.
11	32½	54	"	"	W., N., E.			
12	36	56	"	"	E., S. W.			
S 13	37	56½	"	"	N.W., E., S.			
14	40½	61½	"	"	S. W.			Cloudy part of morning and evening.
15	44	63½	Cloudy	Cloudy	N. E., S.			Clear part of morning.
16	51½	71	Clear	Clear	S. E., S. W.			Cloudy part of morning.
17	54	75½	Cloudy	"	S. W.			Cleared at 8 A. M.
18	58	78	Clear	"	S. W.	0.15		Clouded over 7 P. M., and shower 8 to 9 P. M.
19	62	70	"	"	N.W., N.E.			Cloudy evening.
S 20	46	54	Rain	Cloudy	E.	0.16		Rained all the morning, gently. Clear part afternoon.
21	44	50	"	Rain	E.	1.47		Rained 7 A. M. to 5 P. M. gently, and after that high winds.
22	45½	60	Clear	Clear	S.			Sun rose clear, but greater part of day was cloudy.
23	45	57	"	"	N. W.			Cloudy part of afternoon.
24	36½	56	"	"	W.			Clear but hazy.
25	40½	51	Cloudy	"	N. E., S.			Clear 3 P. M.
26	39½	57	Clear	"	E.			
S 27	38½	59	"	"	E.			
28	41	55½	Cloudy	Cloudy	E.	0.03		Misty rain 9 P. M.
29	47½	56	"	Rain	S. W.	0.37		Gentle rain 9:30 A. M. to 3 P. M. Cleared 5 P. M. Shower 11 P. M.
30	47½	61	Clear	Clear	E.	0.04		Pears and cherries flowered.
						2.63	13.	

Weather Record for New Brunswick, N. J.

May, 1862.

Date.	Thermometer. Lowest.	Thermometer. Highest.	Weather. Morning.	Weather. Afternoon.	Prevailing Wind.	Rain and Melted Snow in inches.	Snow in inches.	REMARKS.
1	48	52	Rain	Rain	E.			Rained quite hard all day, with some intermission.
2	50	59	"	Cloudy	E.	1.32		Rained hard all the morning, cloudy afterward and foggy night.
3	53	67	Cloudy	Clear	E., S. W.			Cleared 9 A. M.
S 4	48	64	Clear	"	W.			
5	50	65	"	Cloudy	W.	0.04		Light shower 4 P. M., and steady rain from 7 P. M.
6	46½	58	"	Clear	N. W.	0.15		Very blustery with heavy flying clouds.
7	48½	63½	"	"	N. W.			Very blustery with heavy flying clouds.
8	41½	62½	"	"	N. W.			Very blustery.
9	48	76	"	"	S. W.			Very blustery.
10	59	79	"	"	W.			Very blustery; air so filled with dust as to obscure the sun during the afternoon.
S 11	48	64	"	"	N. E.			
12	47	67	"	"	S. W.			
13	51½	76	"	"	S. W.	0.04		Clouded over 4 P. M., with two or three light showers in the evening.
14	56½	63	Cloudy	"	E.			Cleared 3 P. M.*
15	46½	67	Clear	"	E.			Clouded over 7 P. M.
16	55½	72	Cloudy	"	E.			
17	54	75	Clear	"	S. W.			
S 18	55	74	"	"	E.			
19	61	72	Cloudy	"	W.			Cloudy part of afternoon.
20	51	67	Clear	Cloudy	E.			
21	56½	60½	Cloudy	"	E.			Misty night with flashes of lightning.
22	58	80	"	Clear	W.			Cleared 10 A. M.
23	59	81½	Clear	"	S. W.			Showers all around the country, but only 5 minutes sprinkle here.
24	53½	64½	Cloudy	Cloudy	E.			Clear from 9 A. M. to 1 P.M. and in the evening after 8 P. M.
S 25	44	66½	Clear	Clear	E.			
26	46	70	"	"	E.			Cloudy 8 P. M.
27	54½	62	Rain	Cloudy	N. E.	0.63		Rained gently from midnight till 4 P. M.
28	58½	66	Cloudy	"	N. W.	0.03		Light sprinkle between 1 and 3 P.M.; cleared off 4:15 P.M.
29	45	69½	Clear	Clear	W.			
30	54½	66½	"	Rainy	E.			Clouded over 11 A. M., with light sprinkle now and then all day and night.
31	56	67½	Cloudy	Clear	E.	0.12		Cleared 10 A. M.
						2.33		

*On May 13 I commenced using James Green's self-registering thermometer.

June, 1862.

Date.	Thermometer. Lowest.	Highest.	Weather. Morning.	Afternoon.	Prevailing Wind.	Rain and Melted Snow in inches.	Snow in inches.	REMARKS.
S 1	55½	60½	Rainy	Cloudy	E.	0.08	----	Gentle rain nearly whole morning after 7 A.M.; afternoon and evening misty.
2	60	72	Cloudy	"	E.	0.02	----	Rain 8 to 9 A. M.—clear from 3:30 to 5:30 P. M.
3	63½	77	Cloudy most all day.		E.	----	----	
4	64	65	Rain	Rain	E.	3.33	----	Thermometer falling all day rained gently 6 A. M. to 12, but afternoon and night very hard.
5	56½	65½	Cloudy	Cloudy	E.	----	----	
6	58½	68½	Clear	Clear	E.	----	----	Cloudy part of evening.
7	55½	74½	"	"	E.	1.12	----	Hard shower 7:15 and rain all evening.
S 8	56	61½	Cloudy	Cloudy	E.	0.03	----	Rained quite hard for 15 minutes at 7:20 A. M.—clear part of evening.
9	48	65	Clear	Clear	E.	----	----	Cloudy part of morning.
10	51½	65¼	"	Rainy	E.	0.26	----	Clouded over 8 A. M.—light rain between 2 and 3 P. M. and steady rain after 7 P.M.
11	56½	67½	Cloudy	Clear	S. W.	0.02	----	Clear part of morning—flying clouds afternoon with shower 6 P. M.
12	57	80	Clear	"	S. W.	----	----	
13	64½	83	"	"	N. W.	0.24	----	Heavy shower 6½ to 7½ P. M.
14	66½	78½	"	Cloudy	N. W.	----	----	Clouded over 3:30 P. M. and several showers after 7 P.M.
S 15	56	68½	Rain*	Clear	N. E.	0.76	----	Rained until 8 A. M.—cleared 1 P. M.
16	47	64½	Clear	"	N. E.	----	----	
17	48½	69	"	"	S. W.	----	----	
18	58	77	Cloudy	"	S. W.	0.46	----	Cleared 8 P.M.; clouded over again 3 P. M.; hard shower 8:30 to 10:30 P. M.
19	60	76½	Clear	"	S. W.	----	----	
20	57	70	"	"	N. W.	----	----	Cloudy from 10 A.M. to 2 P.M.
21	54½	75	"	"	S. W.	----	----	Cloudy part of evening.
S 22	63	75½	"	"	N. W.	----	----	
23	56	74	"	Rain	E.	----	----	Clouded over 2 P. M. and rain all evening after 5:30 P. M.
24	59½	64	Rain	Misty	E.	0.29	----	Did not rain much after 8 A. M., but misty all day and night.
25	59	69	Cloudy	Shower	E.	0.10	----	Clear part of morning and part of afternoon.
26	62	75½	"	Clear	E	0.11	----	Clear part of morning—little shower 12 M.—cloudy part of evening.
27	62½	82½	Clear	"	W.	----	----	
28	64	81	"	"	S. W.	----	----	
S 29	68	82	"	"	S.	----	----	Clouded over 6 P. M.
30	68½	77½	Cloudy	"	E.	0.28	----	Rain before daybreak and from 10 to 12 M.—light shower 2 P. M.
						7.10		

Weather Record for New Brunswick, N. J.

July, 1862.

Date	Thermometer Lowest	Thermometer Highest	Weather Morning	Weather Afternoon	Prevailing Wind	Rain and Melted Snow in inches	Snow in inches	REMARKS.
1	60	73	Clear	Clear	N. W.			
2	56½	66½	Cloudy	Rain	E.			
3	55½	65	"	Cloudy	N. E.	1.77		Cleared off 6 p. m.; rained gently afternoon but violently evening and night of 2nd.
4	55	76	Clear	Clear	S. W.			
5	60	82½	"	"	S. W.			Cloudy part of afternoon.
S 6	69	89	"	"	S. W.			
7	76	88½	"	"	N. W.	0.80		Clouded over 5 p. m. Violent gale with thunder shower 7:30 to 8 p. m.
8	68	84	Cloudy	"	W.			
9	71	84	Clear	"	S. W.			Cloudy parts of morning and afternoon.
10	70	74½	Cloudy	Cloudy	N. W.			
11	60	73	Clear	Clear	E.			
12	56	78	"	"	W.			Clouded over 6 p. m.
S 13	62	83	"	"	S. W.			
14	67	84½	"	"	S. W.			
15	71	86	"	"	S. W.	0.11		Clouded over 4 p. m.; shower 5:30 to 6:30 p. m.; clear evening.
16	70½	86	"	"	S. W.	0.20		Clouded over 6 p. m.; showery evening after 7:30 p. m.
17	67½	78	"	"	N. W.			
18	65	74½	Cloudy	"	E.			Cleared 8 a. m.
19	58	71½	Clear	"	E.			
S 20	61	77½	Cloudy	Cloudy	S. W.	0.07		Shower 4 p. m. and 6:30 p. m.; clear part of evening
21	67½	70	"	"	E.			Misty part of day.
22	63½	71½	Clear	Clear	E.			Cloudy evening.
23	62½	68½	Cloudy	Cloudy	E.			Clear part of morning; rainy evening and night after 7 p. m.
24	63	69½	Cloudy & misty all day.		E.	0.30		
25	64	78½	Cloudy	Clear	N.		0.12	Cleared 8 a. m.
26	64	80	Clear	Cloudy	S. W.	2.35		Clouded over 4 p. m.; hard shower from 5:30 to 9:30 p. m.
S 27	64	77	Cloudy	"	W.			Cleared 8 a. m.
28	61½	81½	Clear	"	S. W.			
29	67½	84	"	"	S. W.			
30	68	83	"	"	S. W.	0.08		Shower before daybreak.
31	68	79½	"	"	N.			Cloudy part of afternoon.
						5.80		

Weather Record for New Brunswick, N. J.

August, 1862.

Date	Thermometer Lowest	Thermometer Highest	Weather Morning	Weather Afternoon	Prevailing Wind	Rain and Melted Snow in inches	Snow in inches	REMARKS.
1	67¼	81	Clear	Clear	N. E.			
2	67	83	"	"	N.			
S 3	68	84	"	"	S. E.			
4	73½	82½	Cloudy	"	S. E.	0.02		Light rain 5:30 A. M.; cleared 8 A. M.; northern lights 9 P. M.
5	73	87	"	"	S. W.	0.21		Cleared 11 A. M.; showery evening after 7:15.
6	70½	82	Clear	"	N.			
7	66	77½	"	"	E.			Cloudy part of afternoon.
8	68	91½	"	"	S. W.			Warmest day since I have kept a daily record—6 years.
9	76	91½	"	"	S. W.	0.26		Shower from 6 to 7 P. M.; cloudy afterwards; cleared 10:30 P. M.
S 10	73	82	"	"	N.			
11	64½	82½	"	"	E.			
12	73	88½	Cloudy	Cloudy	S. W.	0.23		Clear 8:30 A. M. to 1:30 P. M.; showery 1:45 to 2:45 P. M.; cleared 9 P. M.
13	64	76½	Clear	Clear	E.			
14	57½	79½	"	"	S. W.			Clouded over 6 P. M.
15	68½	79½	Cloudy	"	N. W.	0.04		Showery before daybreak; clear part of the morning.
16	58	72	Clear	"	N.			
S 17	54	71	"	"	N. E.			
18	52½	71½	"	"	N. E.			
19	57	76	"	"	S. W.			
20	57½	81	"	"	S. W.			
21	61½	80	"	"	S. W.			
22	67	82½	Cloudy	"	S. W.	0.07		Shower 2:30 P. M.; cloudy evening.
23	69½	78½	"	"	S. W.	0.13		Shower before daybreak and sprinkle during morning; clear part of morning.
S 24	60½	68	Clear	"	E.			Cloudy part of afternoon.
25	51	72½	"	"	E.			
26	56½	80	"	"	S. W.			
27	66	84	"	"	S. W.			
28	71½	82	Cloudy	"	S. W.	0.23		Cloudy most of morning, with 2 or 3 sprinkles; shower 4:45 P. M.
29	64	80	Clear	"	N. W.			
30	56	69½	"	"	E.			
S 31	52	75	"	Cloudy	S. W.	0.10		Shower 10 to 12 P. M.

1.29

September, 1862.

Date	Thermometer Lowest	Thermometer Highest	Weather Morning	Weather Afternoon	Prevailing Wind	Rain and Melted Snow in inches	Snow in inches	REMARKS.
1	66½	82½	Cloudy most all day.		S. W.	0.60		Clear part of morning and afternoon; high winds and rain 7 to 10 P. M.
2	58½	63	Clear	Clear	N. W.			
3	45½	66	"	"	N. W.			Frost.
4	50	73½	"	"	S. W.			
5	55½	78½	"	"	S. W.			
6	60½	82	"	"	S. W.			
S 7	63	84	"	"	S. W.			Cloudy part of morning.
8	65	84	"	"	S. W.			Cloudy part of morning.
9	68	78	"	"	N. E.			
10	57	76	"	"	N. E.			Cloudy part of evening.
11	66½	77½	Cloudy most all day.		N. E.			Clear part of morning and afternoon; rainy night.
12	69	72½	Rain	Rain	S. E.	2.15		Rained hard all morning and from 3:30 to 7 afternoon; clear part of evening.
13	59	71	Clear	Clear	N. E.			
S 14	55	65	"	Cloudy	N. E.			Clouded over 9 A. M.; clear parts of afternoon and evening.
15	58½	69	Cloudy	"	S. W.			Clear part of evening.
16	62	68	"	"	E.	0.30		Rain before day; clear part of morning.
17	64	69½	"	Misty	S.	0.05		Light rain from 1 to 2 P. M.
18	65½	76½	"	Clear	S. E.			Cleared 9 A.M.; cloudy evening.
19	64	78	Clear	"	N. W.			
20	60	70	Cloudy most all day.		S. W.			
S 21	60	73½	Clear	Clear	E.			
22	56	72½	"	"	E.			
23	53	72	"	"	S. W.			
24	54½	72½	Cloudy	Cloudy	W.			Clear part of morning; cleared 7 P. M.
25	48	63½	Clear	Clear	N. E.			
26	46	67	"	"	N. E.			
27	46½	70	"	"	S. E.			Cloudy part of evening.
S 28	60	68½	Cloudy	Cloudy	N. E.			
29	61½	77	"	Clear	N. W.			Cleared 8 A. M.
30	60	72½	Clear	Cloudy	E.			Clear part of afternoon.

3.10

Weather Record for New Brunswick, N. J.

October, 1862.

Date	Thermometer. Lowest	Thermometer. Highest	Weather. Morning	Weather. Afternoon	Prevailing Wind.	Rain and Melted Snow in inches.	Snow in inches.	REMARKS.
1	58½	62½	Rain	Rain	E.			Rained hard all morning, but with intermissions afternoon and night.
2	58½	64	"	Cloudy	N. E.	2.65		Rained until 9 A. M.; misty evening.
3	61	74	Cloudy	Clear	E.	0.04		Misty part of morning; cleared 2 P. M.
4	64	80½	"	"	S. W.	0.03		Cleared 9 A. M.; cloudy most of evening with little rain.
S 5	57½	65	Clear	"	N.			
6	44	60½	"	"	All points			
7	57	77	"	"	S. W.			
8	63½	82	"	"	S. W.			
9	62	78½	"	"	S. W.			
10	60½	69	Cloudy	Rain	E.			Rain 10:30 A. M. to 3 P. M., and misty afternoon and evening.
11	60	62	Rain	Cloudy	N.	0.95		Stopped raining 7:30 A. M; clear part of morning.
S 12	50	56	Cloudy	"	N. E.			
13	48	56	Rain	"	N. E.	0.20		
14	51	61½	Cloudy	Clear	All points			Clouded over 6 P. M.
15	51	62	Clear	"	N. E.			Clouded over 5 P. M.
16	48½	59	Cloudy	Cloudy	N. E.			
17	53½	63	Clear	Clear	N. W.	0.03		Light sprinkle before day.
18	43½	60	"	"	All points			
S 19	43	64½	"	"	S. W.	0.04		Clouded over 5 P. M. and rained at intervals from 6:30 to 9 P. M.
20	44	52	"	"	N. W.			
21	36	62	"	"	S. W.			
22	50	55	"	"	N. W.			
23	41	51½	"	"	N. W.			
24	33	60	"	"	N. W.			
25	45	59½	"	"	S. W.			Foggy morning—hazy all day; clouded over 5 P.M.
S 26	45½	51½	Cloudy	Rain	N. E.			Rained gently all afternoon and hard in the evening and night.
27	45	47	Rain	Cloudy	N. E.	1.27		Cleared 5 P. M.
28	34	52	Clear	Clear	All points			Hazy night.
29	37	57½	"	"	All points			
30	40	56	"	"	W.			
31	45	65	"	"	S. W.			

5.21

November, 1862.

	Date.	Thermometer. Lowest.	Thermometer. Highest.	Weather. Morning.	Weather. Afternoon.	Prevailing Wind.	Rain and Melted Snow in inches.	Snow in inches.	REMARKS.
	1	48	69	Clear	Clear	S. W.			Cloudy evening.
S	2	51¼	69	"	"	S. W.			Cloudy part of evening.
	3	48½	55	"	"	W.			
	4	37	49	"	"	E.			Cloudy part of evening.
	5	37	58	"	Cloudy	S. W.			Clouded over 5 P. M.
	6	43½	44	Cloudy	"	N.	0.36		Rain before day; clear part of morning.
	7	28	34	Snow	Snow	N. E.		5.00	Snow 7:15 A. M. to 4 P. M. violently, and moderate rest of day; ther. lowest 3 P. M., highest 8 A. M.
	8	27½	39	Cloudy	Cloudy	N. E.			Snow squall 11:30 A. M.; com. again 9 P.M. & snowed violently until 2 P. M. of 9th; 10 in. on ground
S	9	33	36½	Snow	"	N. W.		8.00	besides what melted on
	10	33	44	Clear	Clear	W.			Saturday; cleared 8 P. M.
	11	27	46	"	"	S. W.			Clear part of the afternoon and evening.
	12	37	49	Cloudy	Cloudy	S. W.	0.16		Clear part of morning; rain after 4 P. M. at intervals.
	13	41	51	Clear	Clear	W.			Foggy morning.
	14	32	54½	"	"	W.			Cloudy part of afternoon.
	15	38	49½	"	"	N. E.			
S	16	28	42	Cloudy	Cloudy	N. E.			Sun rose clear.
	17	37	48	"	Rain	N. E.	0.70		Rain parts of morning and afternoon till 6 P. M.; cleared 10 P. M.
	18	42½	51½	"	Cloudy	N. E.			Sun rose clear.
	19	44½	54	Misty	Misty	S. E.			Rain part of morning and afternoon.
	20	53	65½	Cloudy	Rain	S. W.	0.38		Rain before day and after
	21	46	54	Rain	Misty	N. E.	2.30		4 P. M.
	22	38½	45	Cloudy	Cloudy	N. W.			Sun shone a little at noon; clear part of the evening.
S	23	34	39	Clear	Clear	N. W.			Cloudy part of the afternoon.
	24	30	41½	"	"	W.			
	25	29½	50	"	Cloudy	S. W.			Clouded over 3 P. M.; light rain after 5 P. M.
	26	41	47	Rain	"	W.	0.35		Rain till 9 A. M.; clear part of afternoon.
	27	34	42	Clear	Clear	W.			Hazy evening.
	28	33	44	Cloudy	"	W.			Cloudy part of afternoon.
	29	34½	49	"	Rain	N. E.	0.06		Sun rose clear; rained lightly parts of afternoon.
S	30	34	46	Clear	Clear	S. W.			Clouded over 6 P. M.
							4.31	13.00	

WEATHER RECORD FOR NEW BRUNSWICK, N. J.

December, 1862.

Date.	Thermometer. Lowest.	Highest.	Weather. Morning.	Afternoon.	Prevailing Wind.	Rain and Melted Snow in inches	Snow in inches	REMARKS.
1	41	50½	Rain	Cloudy	S. W.	0.13		
2	35	41	Clear	Clear	N. W.			
3	30	37	Cloudy	Cloudy	N. E.			Cleared off 7 P. M.
4	26	37½	Clear	Clear	S. W.			
5	27	41½	"	Snow	S. W.		4.00	Clouded over 9 A. M.; snow 4 P. M., at first with little rain.
6	26½	30	"	Clear	N. W.			Heavy snow squall 10:30 to
S 7	13½	19½	"	"	N. W.			10:45 A. M.
8	12½	25	"	"	S. W.			Clouded over 6 P. M.
9	22½	32	"	"	N. E.			
10	16	36½	"	"	S. W.			
11	30	44½	"	"	S. W.			
12	30½	49½	"	"	S. W.			
13	32½	49	Cloudy	Cloudy	E.			Clear part of morning.
S 14	38	51	"	Clear	S. W.			Cleared 2 P. M.; foggy evening.
15	37	63	"	"	S. W.			Cleared 10 A. M.
16	43	53	Rain	"	N. W.	0.22		
17	32	39	Clear	"	N. W.			Heavy flying clouds all day.
18	20½	29½	"	"	N. W.			
19	24	40	"	"	N. W.			Cloudy part of afternoon.
20	10½	15	"	"	N.			
S 21	7½	20½	"	"	S. W.			Clouded over 6 P. M.
22	19	32	Cloudy	Cloudy	S. W.			Clear part of afternoon and evening.
23	27½	47	Clear	Clear	N.			Cloudy part of morning and part of afternoon.
24	27½	37	"	Cloudy	E.			
25	34	42	Cloudy	"	S. W.			Cloudy part of evening.
26	38	54	Clear	"	S. W.	0.07		Rain 9 P. M.
27	44½	52½	Cloudy	most all day.	W.			
S 28	35½	45	"	Clear	N.			Cleared 8 A. M.
29	33	51	Clear	"	S. W.			
30	36	45	Cloudy	Cloudy	N. E.			Rain 5:30 P. M.; snow afterwards.
31	30	36	Rain } Snow }	"	N. W.	0.40		Cleared 10 P. M.
						0.82	4.00	

Rain and melted snow, 9 months, 35.59 inches.

January, 1863.

Date	Thermometer Lowest	Thermometer Highest	Weather Morning	Weather Afternoon	Prevailing Wind	Rain and Melted Snow in inches	Snow in inches	REMARKS
1	22¼	35	Clear	Clear	N. W.			
2	20½	38½	"	"	N. W.			
3	22	44	"	"	N. W.			
S 4	25	48	"	"	E.			Cloudy part of evening.
5	37¼	51	"	"	S. W.			Rain 5 p. m.
6	33	42	Cloudy	Cloudy	W.	0.12		Cloudy part of morning.
7	30	32	Clear	Clear	N. W.			Cloudy part of morning;
8	21	31	Cloudy	Cloudy	S. W.			light snow in the evening.
9	26	34	"	"	N. E.			
10	32	50	"	Rain	E.			Commenced rain 4 p. m.
S 11	36½	43	"	Clear	W.	1.10		Cleared 8 a. m.
12	33½	41	Clear	"	N. W.			Cloudy part of morning and afternoon.
13	30½	39½	"	Cloudy	E.			
14	37½	54	Cloudy	"	S. W.			Shower after 9 p. m.
15	44	55	"	"	N. E.	0.14		Rain before day.
16	44	61½	Rain	Rain	S. W.	0.85		
17	22½	25½	Clear	Clear	N. W.			
S 18	13	25½	"	"	N. E.			
19	17½	32	"	"	E.			
20	22	33½	"	Cloudy	E.			Clouded over 8 a. m.
21	32	37	Cloudy	Rain	N. E.			Commenced raining 8:30 a. m., with little snow, and very violent wind all day.
22	34	39	"	Cloudy	N. E.	0.83		
23	34½	46	"	Clear	N. W.			
24	37	44	Clear	Cloudy	E.			Cloudy part of morning.
S 25	39	48	Cloudy	Clear	W.			
26	36½	48	"	Cloudy	S. W.			
27	41	51½	"	Misty	All points.			
28	33½	37	Snow	Snow	N. E.			Commenced snow before day and snowed very hard all day; all melted as it fell until noon.
29	31¼	36	Clear	Clear	N.		8.00	Snow till 11 a.m.; cleared 12 m; cloudy part of afternoon.
30	25¼	40	"	Cloudy	S. W.			Cloudy part of morning; snow squall 3 p. m.; clear evening.
31	28½	39	"	Clear	S. W.			Cloudy part of morning.
						3.04	8.00	

February, 1863.

Date.	Thermometer. Lowest.	Highest.	Weather. Morning.	Afternoon.	Prevailing Wind.	Rain and Melted Snow in Inches.	Snow in Inches.	REMARKS.
S 1	25	44½	Clear	Cloudy	N. E.			Clouded over 9 A. M.
2	33	34	"	Clear	N. W.			
3	22½	24½	Cloudy	"	N. E.			Cloudy part of afternoon.
4	4	10½	Clear	"	N.			
5	1	35	Cloudy	Snow	N. E.			Snow 8 A. M. to 12 M.; commenced again 4 P. M., but turned to rain 7 P.M. with wind S. E.; rainy night.
6	48	49	Rain	Cloudy	S. W.	1.60		
7	32½	38½	Clear	Clear	N. W.			
S 8	30	44	"	Cloudy	W.			Clouded over 3 P. M.
9	37	46	Cloudy	"	E.			Clear part of afternoon.
10	37	52	Clear	Clear	W.			
11	32	40	Cloudy	Cloudy	All points.			Clear part of morning; snow 7:30 P. M.
12	33½	39½	Rain	Rain	E.			Rained with intermissions all day and night.
13	28	33½	Clear	Clear	N. W.	0.35		
14	19½	33½	"	"	E.			
S 15	29	44	Rain	Cloudy	S. W.	0.15		Cleared 6 P. M.
16	33½	40½	Clear	Clear	N. W.			
17	30	31½	Cloudy	Snow	N. E.			Snowed moderately from 10:30 A. M. to 5 P. M.; clear part of evening.
18	25	39	Clear	Cloudy	N. E.			Rain 10 P. M.
19	35½	46½	Rain	Rain	N. E.			
20	42	50	"	Clear	W.	0.85		Rained till 9 A. M.; heavy flying clouds during afternoon.
21	26	29½	Clear	"	N.			
S 22	17	20	Cloudy	Snow	N. E.			Snow 8:30 A. M. violently all day and drifted very much.
23	14½	28	Clear	Clear	N. E.		8.00	
24	8	29	Cloudy	Cloudy	All points.			Clouded over 7 A. M.
25	23	39	Clear	Clear	W.			
26	33	41	Rain	Rain	E.			Rain commenced 8 A. M.; foggy evening.
27	37	50½	Cloudy	Clear	W.	0.80		Rain before day. Dr. Anthony Bournomille died A. M.
28	35	43½	"	Cloudy	E.			
						3.45	8.00	

WEATHER RECORD FOR NEW BRUNSWICK, N. J.

March, 1863.

Date	Thermometer Lowest	Thermometer Highest	Weather Morning	Weather Afternoon	Prevailing Wind	Rain and Melted Snow in inches	Snow in inches	REMARKS
S 1	37	44	Rain	Rain	E.	0.62		Cleared off 5 P. M.
2	37½	49	Clear	Clear	S. W.			
3	35	55	Rain / Snow	"	S. W.	0.10		Cleared 11 A. M.; cloudy part of afternoon.
4	25	30½	Clear	"	N. W.			Cloudy parts of morning and afternoon.
5	15½	29½	"	"	N. W.			
6	23½	38½	Cloudy	Cloudy	S. W.		1.00	Snow 6:30 A. M. to 9 A. M.
7	34½	38	Snow	Rain	N. E.	0.83		Rain mixed with snow from 8 A. M. to 9 P. M.
S 8	30½	35½	Snow / Rain	Cloudy	N. E.	0.63		Snow and rain again 10 P.M.
9	32	44	Cloudy	Clear	W.			Cleared 8 A. M.
10	31	37	"	Cloudy	All points			Commenced snowing 8 P. M.
11	29	40	Snow	Clear	W.		4.00	Snowed till 9 A. M.; cleared 11 A. M.; snow flurry 10 P. M.
12	23½	30½	Clear	"	N. W.			
13	16	25½	"	"	N. W.			Cloudy part of afternoon.
14	19½	34	"	"	W.			Cloudy part of afternoon.
S 15	15½	27	"	"	N. E.			Clouded over 5 P. M.
16	21	28	Cloudy	Cloudy	N. E.			Snowed a little all morning.
17	18	41	Clear	Clear	S. W.			Cloudy part of evening.
18	35	43	Cloudy	"	N. E.	0.10		Rain before day.
19	22	34½	Clear	"	N. E.			
20	21½	31	"	"	N. E.			
21	20	27	Cloudy	Cloudy	S. E.			Rain 9 P. M.
S 22	36	52	Clear	Clear	N.	0.30		Rain before day; cloudy part of evening.
23	35½	51½	"	Cloudy	E.			
24	38	45	Cloudy	"	E.			Rain 9 P. M.
25	42	61½	Rain	"	S.	0.53		Showery morning; cleared 8:30 P. M.
26	40½	50½	Clear	"	N. W.			Clear evening.
27	33½	44	"	Clear	N. W.			Cloudy part of morning.
28	31½	45	Cloudy	Rain	S. E.			Clouded over 7 A. M.
S 29	34½	39	Rain	Clear	N. W.	0.56		Stopped raining 7 A. M. and cleared 9 A. M.
30	31½	46	Clear	"	N.			Cloudy 9 A. M.
31	35½	38½	Snow / Rain	Rain	N. E.	1.18		Rain till 6 P. M.; cleared 9:30 P. M.
						4.85	5.00	

No ice crop gathered here this winter.

April, 1863.

Date.	Thermometer. Lowest.	Thermometer. Highest.	Weather. Morning.	Weather. Afternoon.	Prevailing Wind.	Rain and Melted Snow in inches.	Snow in inches.	REMARKS.
1	31	38	Clear	Clear	N. W.			
2	31½	50½	Cloudy	Cloudy	S. W.	0.04		Rain part of evening.
3	36	47½	Clear	Clear	N.			
4	29½	35	Cloudy	Snow Rain	N. E.			Snow commenced 2:30 P. M. and soon turned into rain and hail.
S 5	32	41½	Rain	Cloudy	N. E.	0.92		
6	34½	52½	Clear	"	S. W.	0.02		Light rain after 7 P. M.
7	41	45½	Cloudy	"	N.			Rain 5:30 P. M. and 10 P. M. snow.
8	31½	41½	"	"	N. W.	0.18		Ground covered with snow this morning.
9	32	52½	Clear	Clear	N. W.			
10	33	59½	"	"	S. W.			
11	43½	66½	"	"	S. W.			First dusty day.
S 12	46½	69½	"	Cloudy	S. W.	0.19		Clouded over 3 P. M.; rain 6 to 7 P. M.; cleared 9 P. M.
13	41½	49½	Cloudy	"	N. E.			Sun rose clear; clouded over between 6 and 7 A. M. cleared 6 P. M.
14	35½	58	Clear	Clear	E.			
15	39½	51½	Cloudy	Cloudy	E.			Clear part of morning; rain 4 to 6 P. M. and commenced again 10 P. M.
16	44½	50	Rain	Misty	N. E.	2.88		
17	46	55½	Cloudy	Cloudy	S. W.	0.02		Light rain 10 P. M.
18	47	59	"	"	N. E.			Clear part of afternoon.
S 19	50½	65	Clear	Clear	All points.			Cloudy part of afternoon.
20	50	61	"	Cloudy	E.			Clouded over 11 A. M.
21	41	53½	Cloudy	Clear	E.	0.20		Rain before day, cleared 8 A. M.
22	34	60½	Clear	"	E.			
23	37½	60½	"	Cloudy	E.			Clouded over 1 P. M.; rain 6:20 P. M.
24	48	54½	Rain	"	N. E.	1.60		Commenced raining again 7:45 P. M.
25	46½	54	Clear	Clear	N.	0.35		Heavy flying clouds parts of morning and afternoon.
S 26	37½	58	"	"	N.			
27	41	68½	"	"	S. W.			
28	45½	69	"	Cloudy	S. W.			
29	54	60	Rain	"	N. E.	0.13		
30	52½	64	Cloudy	"	E.	0.07		Clear parts of morning and afternoon; rain 5:30 to 6 P. M.
						6.60		

May, 1863.

Date.	Thermometer. Lowest.	Thermometer. Highest.	Weather. Morning.	Weather. Afternoon.	Prevailing Wind.	Rain and Melted Snow in inches.	Snow in inches.	REMARKS.
1	46	67	Clear	Clear	N. E.			
2	47½	72½	"	"	S. W.			Cloudy part of morning; pears and cherries flowered.
S 3	52	62	"	"	E.			Clouded over 8 P. M.
4	51	69	Cloudy	Cloudy	S. W.	0.01		Clear part of afternoon; light rain 5:30 P. M.
5	53½	55	"	"	N. E.	0.07		Light rain till 8 A. M.; rain again 10 A. M.
6	42	48	Rain	Rain	N. E.			
7	41	48½	"	Cloudy	N. E.	2.22		Rain till 7 A. M.; misty rest of morning.
8	42	53	Cloudy	"	N. E.			
9	41	67	Clear	Clear	W.			
S 10	49½	76	"	"	S. W.			
11	60	82½	"	"	S. W.			
12	59	85	"	"	S. W.	0.08		Clouded over 9 P. M.; shower 10:30 P. M.
13	56½	72	Cloudy	Cloudy	N. E.	0.37		Clear from 9 A. M. to 3 P. M.; rain from 5 to 6 P. M.
14	56	61	"	"	N. E.	0.11		Rain before day; rain again 7 to 8 P. M.
15	50	65	Clear	Clear	N. W.			
16	48½	70½	"	"	S. W.			
S 17	55	65	Cloudy	Rain	S. E.	0.42		Shower afternoon & evening.
18	47½	65	Clear	Clear	N. W.			
19	46	69½	"	"	N. W.			
20	50	76	"	"	S. W.			
21		80¼	"	"	S. W.			Cloudy part of morning.
22	60	87	"	"	N. W.			
23	62	84	"	"	S. W.			Thermometer highest at noon; wind shifted to the east about 1 P. M.
S 24	57½	68	Cloudy	Cloudy	E.			Clear part of the morning.
25	49	58½	"	"	E.	0.04		Rain before day.
26	50	63½	"	Clear	S. W.			Cleared 3 P. M.
27	50	72½	Clear	"	N. E.			
28	52½	79	"	"	S. W.			
29	57	77	"	"	S. W.			
30	64½	79	Cloudy	"	S. W.	0.05		Clear part of morning; shower 12:30 P. M.
S 31	68	80	"	"	S. W.	0.40		Heavy black clouds passing all day; shower 3:45 P. M.
						3.77		

WEATHER RECORD FOR NEW BRUNSWICK, N. J.

June, 1863.

Date.	Thermometer.		Weather.		Prevailing Wind.	Rain and Melted Snow in inches.	Snow in inches.	REMARKS.
	Lowest.	Highest.	Morning.	Afternoon.				
1	63½	78	Clear	Clear	S. W.			
2	55½	72½	"	"	W.			
3	59½	67	Cloudy	"	N. E.			Cleared 5 P. M.
4	51	68	Clear	"	N. W.			
5	53½	72	"	"	S. W.			
6	58	69	C'y m'st all day	All points.	0.04			Rain before day.
S 7	55½	66	Clear	Clear	N.	0.02		Rain before day; cloudy part of afternoon.
8	50	67	"	"	N. W.			Heavy flying clouds all day.
9	55½	76½	Cloudy	"	N. W.	0.03		Clear part of morning and cloudy part of afternoon; rain 6 A. M.
10	55½	82	Clear	Cloudy	S. W.			
11	61	75½	Cloudy	"	S. W.	0.20		Rainy evening after 5 P. M.
12	65	74½	"	"	E.	0.92		Light rain 8 A. M.; heavy rain 5:30 to 7:30 P. M.; clear part of afternoon.
13	61½	64½	Misty	"	E.	0.06		Light rain part of morning, and misty rest of morning.
S 14	57½	72½	Clear	Clear	S. W.			
15	61½	88	"	"	S. W.			
16	60½	74½	"	"	N. W.			
17	53	79	"	Cloudy	S. W.	0.22		Showers 9:30 A. M and 5 P. M. the latter hard; cloudy part of the morning and clear part of afternoon.
18	62	78	C'dy Hazy	all day	All points			Cloudy morning and evening; hazy in middle of day.
19	65	67½	Rain	Cloudy	E.	0.17		Rain till 9 A. M.
20	57½	63½	Cloudy	"	E.			
S 21	56	62	"	"	S. E.	0.38		Misty part of day; heavy shower 9:40 P. M.
22	57	69½	"	"	S. W.			Clear part of afternoon and evening.
23	56½	70½	Clear	Clear	N. W.			Heavy flying clouds part of day; sprinkle 3:15 P. M.
24	58	73	"	"	N. W.			Heavy flying clouds part of day.
25	56½	76½	"	"	W.			
26	62½	68½	Cloudy	Rain	E.	0.42		Clear part of morning; rain 9 A. M. to 8 P. M.; partly clear evening.
27	58	73	Clear	Clear	E.			
S 28	55	73½	Foggy	"	S. E.			Cleared 8 A.M.; clouded over 10 P M.
29	60½	72	Cloudy	"	S. E.			Cleared 4 P. M.
30	63	79½	Clear	"	S.			
						2.46		

WEATHER RECORD FOR NEW BRUNSWICK, N. J.

July, 1863.

Date.	Thermometer.		Weather.		Prevailing Wind.	Rain and Melted Snow in inches.	Snow in inches.	REMARKS.
	Lowest.	Highest.	Morning.	Afternoon.				
1	62	76½	Clear	Cloudy	S. W.			Clouded over 9 A.M.; clear a short time about 7:30 P.M.
2	68	80	Cloudy	"	S. W.			Cleared 9 P. M.
3	68	83	Cloudy most all day.		S. W.			
4	69	78	"	Cloudy	S. E.	0.36		Shower about 1 A. M.
S 5	67	71½	"	"	S. E.	0.06		Several light sprinkles during the day.
6	69	72½	"	"	S. E.	0.05		Light rain between 10 and 12 A.M.; cleared 8 P.M.
7	67½	79	"	Clear	S. E.			Cloudy part of afternoon.
8	70	78	"	Rain	S. E.	2.32		Partly clear part of morning, commenced raining 1 P.M.
9	67½	78½	"	Cloudy	N. E.	0.15		Clear 9 A.M. to 4 P.M.; shower 5 P.M.; com. rain' 9:45 P.M.
10	68½	72	Rainy most all day.		N. E.	0.84		Cleared 8:30 P. M.
11	67	80	Cloudy	Clear	S. W.			Clear from 10 A.M. to 8 P.M.
S 12	69	79	"	Cloudy	S. W.	0.07		Shower 7:30 to 9 P. M.
13	69	76	"	"	E.			Com. raining 9 P. M.
14	67	76	Rain	"	N. E.	0.25		Rained till 8 A. M.; partly clear part of evening.
15	70	81	Cloudy	Hazy	S. W.	0.38		Shower 3 A.M. and 7 A.M.; sun shines most of afternoon.
16	67½	82	Hazy	Rain	S. W.	3.80		Rain from 4:15 to 10 P.M.; in 2 hrs. 3.70 inches fell.
17	63	72	Cloudy	"	N. E.	1.03		Rain from 4 to 10 P. M.
18	64	74	"	Cloudy	E.	0.01		Partly clear part of afternoon; light sprinkle 7 P.M.
S 19	67	78	"	Clear	N. E.			Cleared 10 A. M.
20	67	79	"	"	S. E.			Cleared 9 A.M.; hazy evening.
21	69½	79	"	"	N. W.	0.03		Shower 8:10 A. M.; violent wind in southwest in A.M.
22	61	76	Clear	"	N. E.			First clear day this month.
23	61½	77½	"	"	All points.			
24	65	78½	Cloudy	"	S.			Cloudy part of afternoon.
25	68½	82	"	Cloudy	S.	0.27		Shower 2 P.M.; clear part of afternoon.
S 26	71	84	"	Clear	S. W.	0.39		Shower 1 A.M., cleared 8 A.M.
27	73	82	Clear	Cloudy	S. W.	0.02		Clouded over 10 A M.; light rain 2:30 to 6 P.M.; clear part of evening
28	68½	81½	Cloudy	Hazy	S. W.			Clear 8 A. M. to 3 P. M.
29	71½	77½	"	Cloudy	S. W.	0.33		Shower before day; sun shines part of afternoon.
30	69½	82½	"	"	S. W.	0.17		Shower 12:30 P. M.; clear part of evening.
31	71	82	"	Clear	S. W.	0.06		Shower 12:15 P. M.; cloudy part of afternoon.
						10.59		

August, 1863.

Date	Thermometer Lowest	Thermometer Highest	Weather Morning	Weather Afternoon	Prevailing Wind	Rain and Melted Snow in inches	Snow in inches	REMARKS
1	71½	82	Cloudy	Cloudy	S. W.			Cleared 7 P. M.
S 2	75	88	Clear	Clear	S. W.			
3	75½	90	"	"	S. W.			
4	74½	83	"	"	E.			Cloudy part of morning.
5	73½	85	"	"	S. W.			
6	70	85	"	"	S. W.			Cloudy part of afternoon; sprinkle 2:30 P. M.
7	67½	82½	"	"	S. E.			
8	72½	85½	Cloudy	"	S. W.	0.12		Shower 6 A.M.; heavy clouds afternoon and evening; sprinkle 8:10 P. M.
S 9	73	89	Clear	"	S. W.			Cloudy part of evening and looks showery.
10	73	89	"	"	S. W.			Cloudy part of evening and looks showery.
11	74½	90½	"	"	S. W.	0.07		Cloudy part of afternoon; shower 2:45 P. M.; the highest 12 M.
12	73½	83½	"	"	N.	0.02		Shower before day; partly cloudy part of afternoon.
13	68½	80½	"	"	N. E.			
14	70	83½	Cloudy	"	S. W.			Partly clear part of morning.
15	73	85½	Clear	"	N. W.			
S 16	71	82	"	Cloudy	S. E.	1.21		Cloudy part of morning; showery 1 P. M., and from 5:40 to 7:40 P. M.
17	67	84	Cloudy	Clear	N. E.			Sunshine part of morning; cleared 4 P. M.
18	56	71½	Clear	"	N. E.			
19	58	78½	"	"	S. W.			
20	65	83	"	"	S. W.			
21	65½	84	"	"	S. W.			Cloudy part of evening.
22	71	85	Cloudy	"	W.			Cleared 10 A. M.
S 23	72½	88	Clear	"	S. W.			
24	73½	87	"	"	S. W.			
25	74	84½	"	Show'ry	S. W.			Light shower in the afternoon and heavy ones in the evening.
26	60	71	Cloudy	Clear	N.	1.37		Shower before day.
27	56½	71	Clear	"	N. E.			Cloudy part of afternoon.
28	55	66	Cloudy	Cloudy	N. E.			Misty parts of day.
29	63	80	"	Clear	S. W.	1.29		Light shower before day, and heavy ones from 4 to 5 P. M., and 7:30 to 8:30 P. M.
S 30	52½	65	Clear	"	N. W.			
31	53½	67	"	"	N. E.			
						4.08		

September, 1863.

Date	Thermometer Lowest	Thermometer Highest	Weather Morning	Weather Afternoon	Prevailing Wind	Rain and Melted Snow in inches	Snow in inches	REMARKS
1	56½	67½	Cloudy	Cloudy	N. E.			Partly clear part of afternoon and evening.
2	53	70½	Clear	Clear	E.			
3	53	70½	"	"	E.			
4	58½	68	Cloudy	"	N. E.			
5	52	70	Clear	"	N. E.			
S 6	55	76½	"	"	S. W.			
7	65	77	Cloudy	Cloudy	S. W.			Clear 8 to 12 A. M.; light sprinkle in the afternoon; cleared 8 P. M.
8	62	76	Clear	Clear	S. W.			Cloudy parts of morning and evening.
9	67	73¾	Cloudy most all day.		N. E.			
10	56	68	Clear	Clear	N. E.			
11	50	68	"	Cloudy	E.			Clear part of afternoon.
12	57	73¾	Cloudy most all day.		S. W.	0.02		Rain 10:30 P. M.
S 13	64	70	"	Cloudy	N. E.	0.14		Clear part of morning; rainy evening.
14	63	69	"	"	E.			Cleared 9 P. M.
15	59	74½	"	Clear	S. W.			
16	63½	77¼	"	"	S. W.			
17	68½	80½	"	"	S. W.			Clear part morning; shower 3:30 P. M.
18	70	77	Sh'w'ry	Cloudy	S. E.	0.69		No rain after 2:30 P. M.
19	54½	57	Cloudy	Rain	N.	0.19		Clear part of the morning; rain 11 A. M. to 6 P. M.
S 20	50	56¼	"	Cloudy	N.			Cleared 9 P. M.
21	43½	65	Clear	Clear	W.			Clouded over 8 P. M.
22	48	56½	"	"	N.			
23	40½	58½	"	"	N. E.			
24	40½	64½	"	"	S. W.			
25	50½	60	Cloudy	Cloudy	N. W.	0.09		Clouded over 7 A. M.; rain 1:30 to 3:30 P. M.
26	44½	57½	Clear	Clear	N.			
S 27	41	63	"	"	N.			
28	42½	64½	"	"	All points.			
29	42½	65½	"	"	E.			Foggy morning.
30	46½	67½	"	"	S. W.			
						1.13		

WEATHER RECORD FOR NEW BRUNSWICK, N. J.

October, 1863.

Date.	Thermometer. Lowest.	Highest.	Weather. Morning.	Afternoon.	Prevailing Wind.	Rain and Melted Snow in inches.	Snow in inches.	REMARKS.
1	46	70½	Clear	Clear	S. W.			
2	50	69	Cloudy	Cloudy	S. E.	0.40		Rainy after 6:30 P. M.
3	61½	69	"	"	W.			Clear part of morning.
S 4	56½	68½	"	Clear	All points			Cloudy part of afternoon.
5	49	58½	Clear	"	N. W.			
6	43½	59	"	"	N. W.			Cloudy 2 to 5 P. M.
7	41	62½	"	Cloudy	N. E.	0.02		Misty evening after 7 P. M.
8	54	63	Cloudy	Rain	E.	0.21		Rain at intervals, 2:30 to 5:30 P. M. Cleared 6 P.M
9	45½	61	Clear	Clear	W.			
10	47½	60½	Cloudy	most all day.	N. E.			Rainy evening after 9 P. M.
S 11	46½	57½	Clear	Clear	N. E.	0.22		
12	40	54½	"	"	N. W.			
13	37	55	"	"	N. E.			
14	41	62½	"	Cloudy	S. W.			Cloudy 3 to 7:30 P. M. and clouded over again 9:30 P. M.
15	49	69	"	Clear	S. W.			Foggy morning; cloudy part of afternoon.
16	58½	65	Cloudy	Rain	S. E.	1.54		Light rain before day; commenced again 10 A. M.
17	58	69½	Clear	Clear	S. W.			
S 18	53	75½	"	"	S.			
19	58½	67	Cloudy	"	N. W.			Cleared 2:45 P. M.
20	45½	62	Clear	"	"			
21	44½	69	"	"	W.			
22	44½	58	"	"	N. W.			
23	41	61½	"	Cloudy	S. E.			Clear part of evening.
24	49	52	Rain	Rain	N. E.	0.55		
S 25	40½	47	Cloudy	Cloudy	N. E.			Cleared 8 P. M.
26	33½	45½	Clear	Clear	N. E.			
27	33	46	"	"	N. E.			Clouded over 7 P. M.
28	33	48½	"	"	N. E.			
29	29½	52½	"	"	N. E.			Cloudy part of evening.
30	42½	56½	Cloudy	Rain	N. E.	0.08		Clear part of morning; misty and rainy after 3 P. M.
31	52½	63	"	Clear	S. W.	0.24		Rain 10:15 A.M. to 1:30 P.M. Cleared 3:30 P. M.
						3.26		

November, 1863.

Date.	Thermometer. Lowest	Thermometer. Highest.	Weather. Morning.	Weather. Afternoon.	Prevailing Wind.	Rain and Melted Snow in inches.	Snow in inches.	REMARKS.
S 1	40	53	Clear	Clear	N. W.	----	-----	
2	35	53	"	"	N. E.	----	-----	
3	40½	59	Cloudy	"	S. W.	----	-----	Light sprinkle during morning; cleared 2 P. M.
4	39	54½	Clear	"	N. W.	----	-----	
5	41	66	Cloudy	most all day.	S. W.	----	-----	
6	50	58½	Clear	Clear	N. W.	----	-----	Very windy, with heavy flying clouds part of afternoon, with rain squalls.
7	36	57	Cloudy	most all day.	S. W.	----	-----	
S 8	39½	53½	Clear	Cloudy	N. W.	----	-----	Clear part of the afternoon.
9	32½	42½	"	"	N. E.	----	-----	Cloudy part of morning.
10	31½	40½	Cloudy	Clear	N. W.	----	-----	Clear part of morning.
11	29½	46	Clear	"	S. W.	----	-----	Cloudy part of evening.
12	37	59½	"	"	S. W.	----	-----	
13	38	62½	"	Hazy	S. W.	----	-----	
14	42½	56	Cloudy	Cloudy	E.	----	-----	Misty, rain at intervals after 5 P. M.
S 15	52½	62½	Rain	"	E.	0.21	-----	Cleared 3 to 5 P. M.; cleared finally 7 P. M.
16	38	51	Cloudy	Rain	S. W.	----	-----	Rain 2 to 6 P. M.
17	45	51½	Rain	"	N. W.	0.13	-----	Did not rain from 8 to 11:30 A. M.; partly clear part of evening.
18	41	48	"	Cloudy	S. W.	0.27	-----	Cleared 6 P. M.
19	38½	58	Clear	Clear	S. W.	----	-----	
20	40	62½	"	Cloudy	S. W.	----	-----	Clear part of afternoon.
21	46½	52	Rain	Rain	N. E.	1.00	-----	Rained steady from 7 A. M. to 9:30 P. M.
S 22	42	50½	Clear	Clear	N. W.	----	-----	
23	34	50½	"	"	N. E.	----	-----	Clouded over 8 P. M., and rained before 12 P. M.
24	38	51	Rain	Misty	N. E.	0.54	-----	
25	46½	49½	Clear	Clear	N. W.	----	-----	Clouded over 6 P. M.
26	34	47	"	"	N. W.	----	-----	
27	30½	48	"	"	S. W.	----	-----	
28	36	48½	Misty & rainy		All points.	----	-----	
S 29	40	42½	Cloudy	Cloudy	N.	0.27	-----	Rained before day; clear part of afternoon.
30	28½	39½	"	Clear	N. W.	----	-----	Snow squalls 9:30 to 11:30 A. M.; cloudy part of afternoon.
						2.42		

December, 1863.

Date.	Thermometer. Lowest.	Thermometer. Highest.	Weather. Morning.	Weather. Afternoon.	Prevailing Wind.	Rain and Melted Snow in inches.	Snow in inches.	REMARKS.
1	22	35	Clear	Clear	S. W.	----	----	
2	31	48	"	"	S. W.	----	----	Cloudy part of afternoon.
3	29½	41½	"	"	All points.	----	----	Cloudy part of afternoon.
4	31	50½	Cloudy	"	S. W.	----	----	Foggy morning; cloudy part of afternoon.
5	38	51	Clear	"	W.	----	----	Cloudy part of afternoon.
S 6	24	38	"	"	N. E.	----	----	
7	17½	32	"	"	N.	----	----	
8	19½	41	"	"	S. W.	----	----	
9	25	47	"	"	N. W.	----	----	Cloudy parts of morning and afternoon.
10	15½	26½	"	"	N. W.	----	----	
11	13½	27	Cloudy	Snow	N. E.	----	----	Clear part of morning; com. snowing 3:15 P. M., and hail and rain 8 P. M.
12	25½	40	"	Misty	N. E.	0.30	----	
S 13	38½	59	Rain	Clear	S.	0.43	----	Rain till 2 P.M.; cleared 4:30 P. M.
14	42½	60	"	"	S. W.	0.23	----	Cloudy parts of afternoon and evening.
15	36½	40	Clear	"	W.	----	----	
16	28½	36½	"	"	N. W.	----	----	Cloudy parts of afternoon and evening.
17	30½	39	Rain	Rain	N. E.	----	----	Rain 7 A. M.
18	35½	46	"	Clear	N. W.	1.70	----	Rain till 9 A. M.
19	30	33	Clear	"	W.	----	----	
S 20	22	28½	"	Cloudy	N. W.	----	----	Cloudy 8 A.M. to 2 P.M., and clouded over again 5 P.M.
21	25	31½	Cloudy	most all day.	N. W.	----	----	
22	21½	33	"	Clear	N. E.	----	----	Cleared 10 A. M.; partly cloudy after 7 P. M.
23	10½	24	Clear	"	N.	----	----	
24	15	24	"	"	N.	----	----	
25	15½	30	"	"	N. E.	----	----	
26	18½	35½	"	"	All points.	----	----	
S 27	26	36½	Rain	Cloudy	S. W.	----	----	Rain again 7 P. M.
28	33½	41	"	Rain	N. E.	1.75	----	
29	35	41	Cloudy	Clear	S. W.	0.34	----	Clear part of morning.
30	31½	47	Clear	"	S. W.	----	----	
31	33½	38½	Cloudy	Snow / Rain	E.	----	----	Snow at intervals 1 to 6 P.M. and then a warm rain set in.
						4.75	----	

Rain and melted snow for 1863; 52.50 inches.

Weather Record for New Brunswick, N. J.

January, 1864.

Date	Thermometer Lowest	Thermometer Highest	Weather Morning	Weather Afternoon	Prevailing Wind	Rain and Melted Snow in inches	Snow in inches	REMARKS
1	52	53	Rain	Clear	S. W., N. W.	0.66		Rain till 10 A. M.; cloudy part of afternoon; ther. 5 P.M. 28°; 9 P. M. 17°.
2	7	13½	Clear	"	W.			Very high wind; 46° change in less than 24 hours.
S 3	11	26½	Cloudy	"	S. W.			
4	23	30½	"	Snow	S.W.,N.,N.E.			Snow 3 P. M. to 9 P. M.
5	23	31	Snow	Clear	N.E.,S.,N.W.		2.00	Snow 8:30 A. M. to 11 A. M.; cleared 3 P. M.; first snow without rain.
6	14½	24	Clear	"	S. W.			
7	7½	30	"	Cloudy	N. E., N. W.			Snow 8 P. M.
8	12½	19½	Snow	Clear	N. E., N. W.		4.50	Snowed till 11 A. M.
9	12½	16½	Clear	"	W.			
S 10	8½	25½	"	"	S. W.			
11	10½	27	"	"	S. W.			
12	12½	31½	"	"	S. W.			
13	13½	31½	Cloudy	Cloudy	S. W.			A few stars visible overhead in the evening.
14	20	38½	C'y m'st all day		S. W., S. E.			
15	27½	40	Misty	Cloudy	N.E.,S.,S.W.			Cleared off 5 P. M.; heavy clouds passing over 9 P.M.
16	25	31½	Clear	Clear	N. W.			
S 17	16½	34	"	"	All points			Clouded over 9 A.M. to 3 P.M.
18	26	41	Rain	Rain	N. E.			Rain 9 A. M.
19	38	46	"	Cloudy	N.E., S., S.W.	1.38		Clear parts of P.M. and evening; rain again 5 to 6 P.M.
20	29	35	Cloudy	Clear	W.			Cleared 10 A. M.
21	26	34	"	Cloudy	E.			Clear 3 P. M. to 7 P. M.
22	31	45½	C'y m'st all day		N.E., S., S.W.			Cleared finally 8:30 P. M.
23	30½	45½	Clear	Clear	S. W.			
S 24	30½	51	"	Cloudy	S. W.			Clouded over 10 A. M.; clear 4:30 to 8 P. M.
25	41	53½	"	Clear	W.			Clouded over 7:30 P. M.
26	37	54½	"	"	S. W., N.			
27	34	56½	"	"	S. W.			
28	34½	56½	"	"	N. E.			
29	36	58	"	"	W., N. E.			
30	36½	45	Cloudy	Misty	N. E.	0.04		Light rain 6:30 A. M.
S 31	34½	43	"	Cloudy	N. E.			
						2.08	6.50	

February, 1864.

Date.	Thermometer. Lowest.	Thermometer. Highest.	Wind. Morning.	Wind. Afternoon.	Prevailing Wind.	Rain and Melted Snow in inches.	Snow in inches.	REMARKS.
1	33½	44	Rain	Rain	S. E.	0.59		No rain after 5 P. M.
2	33	45	Cloudy	Cloudy	S. W.			Foggy morning; partly clear part of morning.
3	32	40	Clear	"	N. W.			Clouded over 10 A. M.
4	29	38½	"	Clear	S. W.			Cloudy parts of morning and afternoon.
5	31	49½	"	"	S. W.			
6	36	48	Cloudy	Cloudy	N. E.			
S 7	35½	47½	Clear	"	N. W.			Clouded over 9 A. M.; cleared off 7 P. M.
8	32½	45½	"	Clear	S. W.			
9	29	36	"	"	S. W., N. W.			
10	20	26½	"	"	N. W.			
11	10	29	"	"	N. W., S. W.			
12	27	43½	Cloudy	"	S. W., N. W.			Cleared off 3 P. M.
13	29	40½	Clear	"	S. W.			
S 14	35½	51½	Cloudy	"	S. W., N. W.			Violent wind all afternoon.
15	23	35	Clear	Cloudy	N., S. W.			
16	30½	35½	Cloudy	Clear	S. W., N. W.			Snowed 11 A. M. to 1:30 P. M.; cleared 2:30 P. M.; cloudy part of evening with snow squall; violent wind.
17	6½	9½	Clear	Cloudy	N. W.			Cloudy 11 A. M. to 8 P. M.; violent wind all day.
18	3	18	"	Clear	N. W., S. W.			
19	4	18	"	"	N. W.			
20	11½	33½	"	Cloudy	S. W.			Clear part of afternoon.
S 21	23	45	"	"	N. E., S. E.			
22	33½	52	Cloudy	most all day.	N. E.			
23	34	56	Clear	Clear	S. W.			Clouded over 6 P. M. John Bayard Kirkpatrick died 1 P. M.
24	43½	54	Cloudy	"	S. W.	0.05		Light rain before day; cleared 9 A. M.
25	34½	51	Clear	Cloudy	S. W.	0.07		Light rain part of evening after 5 o'clock.
26	38	40½	Cloudy	Clear	S. W., N. W.			Snow 11:45 A. M. to 1:30 P. M.; cleared 3 P. M.
27	26	43½	Clear	Cloudy	S. W.			Clouded over 3 P. M.
S 28	36	51½	Cloudy	"	S. W.			
29	41½	43½	"	"	N. W.	0.13		Rain part of morning.

0.84

Weather Record for New Brunswick, N. J.

March, 1864.

Date.	Thermometer. Lowest.	Thermometer. Highest.	Weather. Morning.	Weather. Afternoon.	Prevailing Wind.	Rain and Melted Snow in inches.	Snow in inches.	REMARKS.
1	31½	34½	Cloudy	Snow	N. E.			Com. snowing 8:15 A. M. and continued all day, first few hours; melts as it falls.
2	26	37½	Clear	Clear	N. W.		5.50	Cloudy part of evening.
3	21	35½	"	"	W., S. W.			
4	24½	45	"	Cloudy	S. W.			
5	36	54½	Cloudy	Rainy	All points.	0.56		Rained at intervals during afternoon and evening; cleared 10 P. M.
S 6	33½	50	Clear	Clear	N. W.			Cloudy part of afternoon.
7	33	49	"	"	N. W.			Cloudy part of morning.
8	31½	50½	"	Cloudy	E.			Cleared 9 P. M.
9	35	52½	"	Clear	N. W.			
10	32½	45½	Cloudy	Rain	E.			Clouded over 7 A. M.; commenced raining 5 P. M.
11	38	47	Rain	Cloudy	N. E.	0.31		Rain till 7 A. M.; rain again part of evening.
12	39	53	Clear	Clear	S. W.			
S 13	37	57½	"	"	All points.	0.03		Cloudy part of afternoon; shower 3:30 P. M.
14	35	45½	"	"	N. W.			Cloudy part of morning.
15	31½	46	"	"	S. W., N. W.			Cloudy part of afternoon and part of evening with heavy snow squalls 4 to 5 P. M.
16	28½	34½	"	Cloudy	N. W.			Cloudy part of morning; cleared 5 P. M.
17	27½	39½	"	Clear	N. W., S. W.			Cloudy part of morning and part of afternoon.
18	31	52½	"	"	S. W.			Cloudy part of morning.
19	33	43½	Cloudy	"	N. W.			Cleared 7 A. M. and clouded over again 6 P. M.
S 20	30½	42	Clear	Cloudy	S. W., N. W.			Clouded over 4 P. M.
21	20	32	"	Clear	N. W.			
22	19½	35½	"	Cloudy	N. E.			
23	20	35	Snow	"	N.		1.00	Snowed till 11 A.M., but very fine and drifted much.
24	27	50½	Clear	Clear	N. W.			
25	30½	53½	"	Cloudy	S. E.			Clouded over 8 A. M.
26	39	41	Rain	Rain	N. E.	1.62		
S 27	35	53	Clear	Clear	N.			
28	36½	54	"	"	N. E.			
29	38	45½	Cloudy	Cloudy	E.			Partly clear part of afternoon.
30	36½	41½	Snow } Rain {	Rain	N. E.			
31	36½	41½	Cloudy	Cloudy	N. E.	1.02		Cleared 7 P. M.
						3.54	6.50	

April, 1864.

Date	Thermometer Lowest	Thermometer Highest	Weather Morning	Weather Afternoon	Prevailing Wind	Rain and Melted Snow in inches	Snow in inches	REMARKS
1	37	49	Clear	Cloudy	N. E., S. E.			
2	39	43	Misty	Rain	N. E.			
S 3	37	49	Rain	Cloudy	N. E.	0.85		Rain till 10 A. M.; sunshine part of morning; cleared 8 P. M.
4	35½	46½	Clear	"	N. E.			Clouded over 4 P. M.
5	34	42½	Snow	Misty } Rain }	N. E.	0.13		Snow 6:30 to 10 A. M., with high wind.
6	38	54	Clear	Cloudy	N. E.			Clouded over 4 P. M.; partly
7	39	60½	"	Clear	N. E.			clear part of evening.
8	37	63½	"	"	N. E.			Cloudy part of evening.
9	45	55½	Cloudy	Cloudy	N. E., S. E.			Clear part of afternoon; rain 11 P. M.
S 10	40	46½	Rain	Rain	S. E., N. E.	2.27		Rained hard with violent S. E. wind until 2 P.M.; misty evening; wind N. E.
11	38	43½	Cloudy	Cloudy	N. E.	0.02		Light sprinkle 1:30 to 3 P. M.; clear part of evening.
12	38½	55	"	Clear	E.			Wind from W. part of A. M.
13	38	46½	"	Rain } Snow }	N. E.	0.24		Rain part of morning; rain and snow till 6 P.M.; showered 3 hours. The wind has been E. for 20 consecutive days and all the rain during that time has been accompanied with violent gales.
14	36	52	C'y m'st all day		S. W.	0.01		Light sprinkle during day.
15	37	53	Clear	Cloudy	N. W.			Clear part of P.M. and ev'ng.
16	39	55½	"	"	N. E., S. W.			Clear part of P.M. and ev'ng.
S 17	37½	56½	"	Clear	N. W.			Cloudy evening.
18	39½	57	"	Cloudy	N. W.			Clouded over 5 P. M.
19	39	53½	"	"	N. E.			Clear part of evening.
20	41	50	"	"	N. E.			
21	40	55½	"	Clear	N. W.			Cloudy part of afternoon.
22	39	63	"	"	S. W.			Cloudy evening.
23	49½	74	Cloudy	"	S. W.			
S 24	57½	71	Clear	Cloudy	W., E.			Clouded over 4 P. M.; commenced raining 9:30 P. M.
25	54½	63	Rain	"	S. E.	0.25		Rain part of afternoon.
26	53	61½	C'y m'st all day		S. W.	0.17		Showers 8 A. M. and 5 P. M.
27	51	64½	C'y m'st all day		N. W.	0.04		Showers 6 P. M.; pears and cherries flowered.
28	36	52½	Clear	Cloudy	N.			Cloudy part of morning.
29	37	61	"	Clear	N. W.			
30	41	62½	"	"	N. E., S.	0.26		Clouded over 5 P. M.; rain 9 P. M.
						4.24		

Weather Record for New Brunswick, N. J.

May, 1864.

Date.	Thermometer. Lowest.	Thermometer. Highest.	Wind. Morning.	Wind. Afternoon.	Prevailing Wind.	Rain and Melted Snow in inches.	Snow in inches.	REMARKS.
S 1	48	60½	Cloudy	Clear	N. W.	----	----	Cleared off 3 P. M.
2	40	66	Clear	"	S.	----	----	Clouded over 9 P. M. and rained 11 P. M.
3	38½	54½	Cloudy	most all day.	S. W.	0.66	----	Rain till 3 A. M; light sprinkle from 6:30 to 7:30 P. M.
4	42	59½	Clear	Clear	N. W.	----	----	Cloudy part of afternoon.
5	44	70½	"	"	S. W.	----	----	
6	48½	78½	"	"	S. W.	----	----	Pears and cherries did not get into full bloom till to-day.
7	57	80	"	"	S. W.	0.05	----	Cloudy 5 to 9 P. M.; shower 6 P. M.
S 8	53½	82	"	"	N. E., S. W.	----	----	
9	59	81½	"	"	S. W.	----	----	Cloudy 5 to 9 P. M.; shower all around; but few drops here.
10	60½	84	"	"	S. W.	----	----	Cloudy evening.
11	59	69	Cloudy	most all day.	N. E.	----	----	
12	54	63	"	Cloudy	N. E.	----	----	
13	56½	68	"	"	E.	----	----	Sunshine part of the morning; shower 9 P. M.
14	60	67	Rain	Rain	S. E.	----	----	Showers all day and evening.
S 15	57½	64½	Misty	"	N. E.	1.62	----	
16	56½	65½	Rain	Cloudy	N. E.	0.10	----	
17	59	71	Cloudy	Clear	S. E.	----	----	
18	58	72½	Clear	Cloudy	N. E.	0.35	----	Clouded over 2:30 P. M., and rained 3 to 4 P. M.
19	60½	69½	Cloudy	Clear	N. E., S. E.	0.04	----	Rain before day and sprinkle 1 P. M.; clear part of morning and cloudy part of afternoon.
20	57	73½	Clear	"	S. W.	----	----	
21	61	80	"	"	S. W.	----	----	Clouded over 6 P. M., with showers all around.
S 22	65½	74	"	"	All points.	0.04	----	Rain before day and showers 6:30 P. M.; cloudy part of evening.
23	51	71½	Cloudy	"	S. W.	----	----	Cleared 9 A. M.
24	61½	72	"	Cloudy	S. E.	----	----	
25	56½	63	"	"	E.	0.30	----	Rain 12:30 A. M.
26	57	63	Rain	Rain	N. E.	----	----	Commenced raining 6 A. M.
27	58½	73	Cloudy	Clear	S. W.	2.92	----	Rained till 6 A. M., light showers 3 and 5:30 P. M.
28	60	72	Clear	Cloudy	N. W.	----	----	Clear part of afternoon.
S 29	49½	64½	"	Clear	N. W.	----	----	Cloudy part of evening.
30	54½	74	"	"	S. W.	----	----	Hazy morning.
31	60	81½	"	"	S. W.	----	----	

6.08

June, 1864.

Date.	Thermometer Lowest.	Thermometer Highest.	Weather. Morning.	Weather. Afternoon.	Prevailing Wind.	Rain and Melted Snow in inches.	Snow in inches.	REMARKS.
1	64	82½	Clear	Clear	S., W.			Shower 10:15 P. M.
2	56	64	Rain	"	N. E.	0.18		Commenced raining 7 A. M. cloudy part of afternoon.;
3	52½	70½	Clear	"	N., S.			
4	53½	73½	"	"	All points.			
S 5	56½	65½	Cloudy	Cloudy	N. E.	0.20		Rain part of morning.
6	63½	80½	Clear	"	S. W.	0.69		Clouded over 4 P.M.; shower 5 to 7 P. M.
7	52	67½	"	Clear	N. W.			
8	51½	72½	"	Cloudy	S. W.			Clouded over 4 P. M.
9	61	80	Cloudy most all day.		S. W.	0.65		Rain before day and showers 4 and 8 P. M.
10	53	61	Clear	Clear	N.			
11	46½	62	Cloudy	"	N. W., S. W.			Clear part of morning and cloudy evening.
S 12	51	64½	Clear	"	N. E.			
13	48½	67½	"	"	N. W.			
14	50½	72½	"	"	All points.			
15	60	73½	Cloudy	"	S. W.			
16	59½	80	Clear	"	N. W.			
17	62½	79	"	"	N. E.			
18	56½	73½	"	"	S. E.			
S 19	53	76½	"	"	S. W., S.			
20	56½	81	"	"	S. W.			
21	64	73	"	"	N. E., S. E.			
22	54½	76	"	"	S. W.			
23	63½	87½	"	"	N. W.			
24	64½	84½	"	"	S. W.			
25	71	94	"	"	W.			Warmest day in eight years.
S 26	75½	95	"	"	W.			4 P.M. showers all around with high winds, but few drops here.
27	74½	84	"	"	N. W., N. E.			
28	53½	75	"	"	N.			
29	54	78	"	"	S. W.			
30	58½	75	"	Cloudy	S. W.	0.40		Light showers 3:30 and 7:30 P.M. and heavy shower 11:30 P. M.
						2.12		

WEATHER RECORD FOR NEW BRUNSWICK, N. J.

July, 1864.

Date	Thermometer Lowest	Thermometer Highest	Weather Morning	Weather Afternoon	Prevailing Wind	Rain and Melted Snow in inches	Snow in inches	REMARKS
1	62½	76	Cloudy	Cloudy	All points			
2	68½	72	"	"	E.	0.05		Light showers 9:30 A. M. and 3:30 P. M.
S 3	66	82	Clear	Clear	N. W.			
4	61	78½	"	"	N. W.			
5	60	80½	"	"	N. W.			
6	62	82½	"	"	S. W.			Cloudy part of morning; cloudy again 10 P. M.
7	69	79½	C'y m'st all day		S. W.			Light sprinkle in evening.
8	70	75½	Cloudy	Clear	N. E.	0.10		Rain before day and 10 A. M.; cleared 4 P. M.
9	62	82½	Clear	"	S. W.			
S 10	63	83½	"	"	S. W.			Cloudy part of evening.
11	70	89	"	"	S. W.			Cloudy part of morning.
12	73	87½	"	"	N.			Cloudy part of afternoon.
13	69	85	"	"	N. E.			
14	66½	81½	"	"	E.			
15	63	78½	"	"	N. E.			
16	60	79½	"	"	N. E.			
S 17	60	85	"	"	N. E., S. E.			From 17th to 25th there has been a haze of more or less density overspreading the sky, day and night.
18	64	80	"	"	E.			
19	65	83	"	"	All points			
20	66	87	"	"	S. W.			
21	72½	77¼	"	"	N. W.			
22	58	72	"	"	N. W.			
23	54½	77½	"	"	N. W.			
S 24	57	81½	"	"	S. W.			
25	65	76½	Rain	Cloudy	N. E., S., S.W.	1.50		Rain 4 to 10 A. M.; cleared 6 P. M.
26	63½	79½	Clear	Clear	S. W.			Cloudy part of afternoon.
27	66½	84	"	"	S. W.			Cloudy evening.
28	69¼	87	"	"	S. W.			
29	69	89	"	"	S. W., N.			Cloudy part of afternoon.
30	66	86	"	"	N. W., S. W.			
S 31	70½	90½	"	"	N. W.			
						1.65		

August, 1864.

Date	Thermometer Lowest	Thermometer Highest	Weather Morning	Weather Afternoon	Prevailing Wind	Rain and Melted Snow in inches	Snow in inches	REMARKS
1	73	91½	Clear	Clear	S. W.			
2	76	89½	"	Cloudy	S. W.	0.05		Light shower 4:30 to 6:30 P. M.
3	73½	84	C'y m'st all day.		S.W., S., N.E.	0.58		Shower 1 to 2:30 P. M. and sprinkle in evening.
4	67	77	Cloudy most all day.		N. W.	0.08		Shower 3 and 8:30 P. M.
5	68½	76	"	" "	"	N. W.		
6	70½	79	"	Clear	E.			
S 7	72	88	Clear	"	W.			
8	66½	85½	"	"	W.			Hazy all day and night.
9	69	86	"	"	W.			Hazy all day and night.
10	70	90½	"	"	S. W.			Hazy all day and night.
11	74	92½	"	"	N. W.			Hazy all day and night.
12	75	83	"	"	S. E.			Hazy all day and night.
13	71½	89½	Cloudy	"	S. E.	0.14		Cleared 9 A. M.; shower 10 P. M.
S 14	74	88½	Clear	"	N.			
15	70	83½	"	"	S. E.			
16	68½	81½	"	"	S. E.			
17	74	85½	Cloudy most all day.		S. W.	1.16		Rain 7:45 to 11 A. M. and 4 to 7 P. M.
18	69	79½	"	" "	N. E.			
19	65	76½	Clear	Cloudy	N. E.			
20	67½	75	"	Clear	N. E.			Cloudy parts of day.
S 21	65	71	M'sty } Rain }	most all day.	N. E.	0.14		
22	68½	79	Cloudy	Shower	S. W.	0.95		Heavy shower 8 P.M.; sunshine part of day.
23	68	77½	"	Clear	W.			Clear part of morning.
24	65	80½	"	"	S. W.			Cleared 8 A. M.
25	69	83	Clear	"	S. W.			Cloudy part of afternoon.
26	71	81½	"	Cloudy	N. W.			Clear part of afternoon.
27	66½	77½	Cloudy	Clear	S. W., N. W.	0.27		Rain before day and sprinkle 9:30 A. M.
S 28	64½	75½	Clear	"	N. W.			Cloudy part of afternoon.
29	58	75	"	"	S. W.			Cloudy part of afternoon.
30	58	73½	"	"	N. W.			
31	57½	71	"	"	N. W., N. E.			Cloudy part of evening.
						3.37		

Weather Record for New Brunswick, N. J.

September, 1864.

Date.	Thermometer. Lowest.	Highest.	Weather. Morning.	Afternoon.	Prevailing Wind.	Rain and Melted Snow in inches.	Snow in inches.	REMARKS.
1	57½	71	Clear	Clear	N. E.			
2	55½	75	"	"	N. E.			
3	62½	74½	Cloudy	most all day.	S. E.			
S 4	63	65½	Rainy	" "	" S. E.	0.21		Rained at intervals all day but set in steady 6:30 P.M.
5	59½	62	Rain	Rain	N. E.	1.90		Rained till noon; commenced again 3 P. M.
6	54	60	"	Cloudy	N. E.	1.09		Rain till 10 A. M.; sprinkle during afternoon.
7	53	67	Clear	Clear	N. E.			
8	51	62½	"	"	N. E.			Cloudy parts of morning and afternoon.
9	55	68	Cloudy	most all day.	W.	0.02		Rain before day.
10	60	76	"	Clear	N. W.			Cleared 7 A. M.
S 11	60	63½	Rain	Cloudy	N. E.	0.51		Clear part of afternoon.
12	55½	61½	Cloudy	"	N. E.			Clear part of evening.
13	52½	59	"	"	N.			
14	53	65	Clear	"	S. W.	0.04		Cloudy part of morning; light showers 4:30 and 6:30 P. M.
15	58	72½	Cloudy	Clear	S. W.			Cleared 8 A. M.
16	54½	67	Clear	"	N. W.			
17	49	69	"	"	S. W.			
S 18	55½	74½	"	Cloudy	S. W.	0.15		Clear part of afternoon; shower 10 P. M.
19	62	68	"	Clear	N. W.			
20	50	68½	"	"	S. W.			
21	54	71	Cloudy	most all day.	S. W.			
22	63	69½	"	" "	" E.			
23	60½	72	"	" "	" S. E.	0.04		Rain part of morning.
24	66	77½	"	" "	"	0.27		Rain before day and showers 4:30 and 5:30 P. M.
S 25	53	60½	Clear	Clear	N. W.			
26	46	64½	"	"	N. W.			Cloudy part of morning.
27	55	75½	"	"	S. W.			
28	60	72½	"	Cloudy	S. W.			Shower 6:10 P. M.
29	64	77½	Cloudy	Clear	S.	0.38		Rain before day; showers 8 to 10 A. M.
30	67½	71	"	Cloudy	N.	0.06		Cleared 8 P. M.
						4.07		

October, 1854.

Date	Thermometer Lowest	Thermometer Highest	Weather Morning	Weather Afternoon	Prevailing Wind	Rain and Melted Snow in inches	Snow in inches	REMARKS
1	48½	60¼	Cloudy	Rain	N. E.			Commenced raining 5 P. M.
S 2	51½	60½	Rain	Cloudy	N. E.	0.46		Rained at intervals during evening after 5 P. M.
3	54	60	Cloudy	"	N. E.			
4	56	66	"	"	S. W.			Clear part of evening.
5	62½	72	"	"	N. E.			
6	61	72	"	"	S.			Partly clear part of evening.
7	64	69	Clear	Clear	N. W., S. W.			
8	54	59½	"	"	W.			
S 9	40½	47	Cloudy most all day.		N. W.			
10	34½	56	Clear	Clear	S. W.			Frost.
11	41½	58	"	"	N. W.			
12	38	57	Cloudy	Rain	E.	0.72		Clear part of morning; rain 2:30 P. M.
13	43	52	Clear	Clear	N. W.			Cloudy part of morning and part of evening.
14	39½	53	"	"	N. W.			
15	40	59½	"	"	W.			
S 16	44	61	Cloudy	"	W.			
17	40	58	Clear	"	N. W.			
18	36	62	"	"	S. W.			
19	39	53	"	Cloudy	N. W.			Clear part of afternoon.
20	45	56	"	Clear	W.			Clouded over 7:30 P. M.
21	43	57½	"	"	N. W.			
22	42	55	Cloudy	Cloudy	N. E.	0.01		Light rain 9 A. M.
S 23	43	54	Clear	Clear	N. W.			Cloudy part of afternoon.
24	41	57	Cloudy	"	All points.			Clear part of morning.
25	44	58	Clear	"	N. E.			
26	41	58	"	"	N. W.			
27	44	60	Cloudy	Cloudy	S. W.			Commenced raining 7:45 P.M.
28	54	61	Clear	"	S. W.	0.52		Rained till 6.30 A. M.; cleared off 7 A. M.; violent gale all day.
29	48½	56	Cloudy most all day.		N. W.			
S 30	42½	57	Clear	Clear	W.			
31	44	56	"	"	W.			Cloudy part of afternoon.

1.71

WEATHER RECORD FOR NEW BRUNSWICK, N. J.

November, 1864.

Date	Thermometer Lowest	Thermometer Highest	Weather Morning	Weather Afternoon	Prevailing Wind	Rain and Melted Snow in inches	Snow in inches	REMARKS.
1	40	47	Clear	Clear	N. W.			
2	32	46½	"	"	W.			Cloudy parts of afternoon and evening.
3	37¼	50	"	Cloudy	N. E.			Misty after 8 P. M.
4	45¾	63	Rain	Clear	S. W.	2.07		Rained till 10 A. M.; clear part of morning and cloudy part of afternoon.
5	40¼	47	Cloudy most all day.		N. W.			
S 6	31½	51	Clear	Cloudy	S. W.			Clouded over 3:30 P. M.
7	43	57	Rain	Rain	S. W.	0.98		Rained till 4:30 P. M.
8	53	61	Cloudy	Cloudy	E.			Foggy morning; rained parts of day.
9	58	68	Rain	"	S. W.	0.18		Rain part of morning.
10	63½	67	"	Clear	S. W.	0.42		
11	41	49½	Clear	"	S. W.			Cloudy parts of morning and evening.
12	38	54	Cloudy most all day.		S. W.	0.01		Light rain during evening.
S 13	35	39½	Clear	Clear	N. W.			Cloudy parts of day.
14	31½	39	"	"	N. W.			
15	26	37	"	Snow Hail	S. W.			Clouded over 8 A. M.; snow 10:40 A. M. to 3 P. M.; cleared off 6 P. M.
16	29	43½	"	Clear	N. W.			
17	30	43	Cloudy	Cloudy	N. E.			Clear part of morning; misty and rainy evening.
18	40	51¼	"	Rain	S., W., N.	0.28		Rain before day and parts of afternoon.
19	40½	44½	"	Clear	N.			Theophilus M. Holcombe died.
S 20	33½	44½	"	Rain	N. E.			Rain at 10:30 A. M., and rained at intervals during afternoon and evening.
21	42¼	49½	"	"	N. E.	0.28		
22	37½	42	Clear	Cloudy	N. W.	0.80		Partly clear part of afternoon.
23	27	32	"	Clear	N. W.			Robert Minturn died.
24	23	35	"	"	S. W.			
25	28	43½	"	"	S. W.			
26	30	43½	"	Cloudy	All points			
S 27	37	50	"	Clear	W.	0.02		Rain before day.
28	32	48	"	Cloudy	N. E., S. E.			Clouded over 10:30 A. M.
29	46	60¼	"	"	S. W.			Clear part of afternoon.
30	49	67½	"	Clear	W.			
						5.04		

December, 1864.

	Date.	Thermometer. Lowest.	Thermometer. Highest.	Weather. Morning.	Weather. Afternoon.	Prevailing Wind.	Rain and Melted Snow in inches	Snow in inches.	REMARKS.
	1	41	55½	Clear	Cloudy	W.	----	----	Clouded over 3 P. M.
	2	43	53	Cloudy	"	N. E.	----	----	Rain 8 P. M.
	3	46	53	Foggy	"	S. W.	0.26	----	Cleared off 9 P. M.
S	4	40½	45½	Clear	Clear	W.	----	----	
	5	31	44½	"	Cloudy	All points.	----	----	Clouded over 3 P. M.; partly clear during evening.
	6	34	44	Cloudy	"	N. E.	0.02	----	Light rain about noon; foggy evening.
	7	38½	59	Foggy	"	S.	0.09	----	Rain at intervals during day.
	8	31½	36½	Clear	Clear	N. W.	----	----	Coldest 3 P.M.; ther. 36½° 8 A.M.; clouded 6 P.M.
	9	15½	29½	"	"	N. W., N. E.	----	----	Clouded over 5 P. M.
	10	25½	36½	Snow	Cloudy	N. E.	----	6.00	Snowed till 9 A. M.
S	11	33½	38	Rain	Rain	N. E.	0.25	----	Rain at intervals till 5 P.M.
	12	8	28	Clear	Clear	S. W.	----	----	
	13	15½	28½	Cloudy	Cloudy	S.	----	----	Ther. highest 10 P. M.
	14	27½	40½	Snow / Rain	Clear	S. W.	0.22	----	Snow before day, and then rain till 10 A. M.
	15	18½	27	Clear	Cloudy	N., S. E.	----	----	Com. snowing 6:30 P.M.
	16	22	36	Cloudy	"	N. E.	----	3.00	Stopped snowing before daybreak; com. raining 6 P.M.
	17	30½	40½	F'g'y / Cl'dy	Clear	N. E., N. W.	0.22	----	Cleared 4 P. M.; George P. Kinnan died at Minneapolis on 16th.
S	18	31	40	Clear	Cloudy	N. W., N. E.	----	----	Clouded over 3 P. M.
	19	33½	41½	Rain	Rain	S. W.	0.19	----	Rain at intervals all day.
	20	26	30	Clear	Clear	N. W.	----	----	
	21	20½	39	Snow	Cloudy	N. E.	0.33	3.00	Snow 8 A.M. to 12:30 P.M. and then turned to rain.
	22	26	26	Clear	Clear	N. W.	----	----	Ther. 8 A. M. at 26° and grows colder all day;
	23	9	21½	"	"	S. W.	----	----	cloudy part of morning.
	24	18	32	Cloudy	Cloudy	S. W.	----	----	Clear part of morning.
S	25	22	37	Clear	Clear	S. W.	----	----	
	26	29½	39½	Rain	Rain	N. E.	----	----	Rained steady all morning and part of afternoon and then misty.
	27	37½	41½	Misty	all day.	N. E.	0.70	----	
	28	37½	43½	Rain	Cloudy	N. E., W.	0.30	----	Clear part of afternoon.
	29	36½	36½	Cloudy	Clear	N. W.	0.12	----	Rain before day; cleared 10 A.M.; ther. 36½° at 8 A.M., and grows colder all day.
	30	26	37	"	most all day.	S. W.	----	----	
	31	34	41	Snow	Snow	N. E.	----	3.00	Snow till 6 P.M.; snow heavy and packed close.
							2.70	15.00	

Rain and melted snow for 1864—40.84 inches.

January, 1865.

Date	Thermometer. Lowest.	Thermometer. Highest.	Weather. Morning.	Weather. Afternoon.	Prevailing Wind.	Rain and Melted Snow in inches.	Snow in inches.	REMARKS.
S 1	16½	24	Clear	Clear	N. W.			
2	16¼	27	"	"	S. W.			Cloudy part of morning and afternoon.
3	8½	30	"	Cloudy	N. W.		2.00	Clear part of afternoon; snow 8 P. M.
4	26	31	Cloudy	Clear	N. W.			Cleared 10 A. M.
5	9	24	Clear	Cloudy	S. W.			Clear part of afternoon.
6	19	44	Cloudy	Rain	S. W., N. E.			Rain at intervals during afternoon, till 5 P. M. and then steady.
7	35	38½	Rain	Cloudy	N. E.	1.05	0.50	Rain till 10 A. M.; snow squalls afternoon; cleared 7:30 P. M.
S 8	9	20	Clear	Clear	N. E.			
9	16	33½	Cloudy	most all day.	S. W.			
10	31	50	Rain	Cloudy	N. E.	1.05		Rain at intervals during afternoon till 8 P. M.
11	24	28	Clear	Clear	N. W.			
12	21½	33	"	"	S. W.			
13	28½	41	"	"	S. W.			Clouded over 8 P. M.
14	33½	39	Snow	"	S. W., N. W.	0.11		Snow 7 to 12 A. M., but all melts; cleared 2 P. M., but cloudy part of evening.
S 15	22½	28	Clear	"	N. W.			Clouded over 8:30 P. M.
16	24	26½	"	"	N. W.		0.50	Snow squalls before day, and 8:45 A. M.
17	17½	24	Cloudy	Snow	N. E.		2.50	Snow 9:30 A. M. to 4:30 P. M.
18	8	18	Clear	Clear	N. W.			
19	3½	19	"	Cloudy	S. W.			Snow 8 P. M.
20	7½	23½	"	Clear	N. W.		2.00	Stopped snowing before day.
21	8	25½	Cloudy	Cloudy	N. E.			
S 22	23½	34	"	"	N. E.			Rain 9 P. M.
23	32	36½	Rain	Rain	N. E.	0.58		Foggy morning; no rain after 6 P. M.
24	27½	29½	Clear	Clear	N. W.			Cloudy part of morning and clouded over 8 P. M.
25	16½	20	"	"	N. W.			
26	12	18	Cloudy	most all day.	W.			
27	9	14½	Clear	Clear	W.			Cloudy part of morning.
28	6	16½	"	Cloudy	N. W.			Clear part of afternoon.
S 29	10½	31	"	"	N. W.			Cloudy part of morning.
30	19½	32	"	Clear	N. W.			
31	20½	37½	"	Cloudy	S. W.			
						2.79	7.50	

February, 1865.

Date	Thermometer Lowest	Thermometer Highest	Weather Morning	Weather Afternoon	Prevailing Wind	Rain and Melted Snow in inches	Snow in inches	REMARKS
1	33	35½	Cloudy	Cloudy	N. W.			Clear part of evening.
2	23	32½	Clear	Clear	N.			
3	17	32½	"	Cloudy	N. E.			Light snow 7 to 10:30 P. M.
4	20½	42½	Cloudy	Clear	S. W.			Sprinkle 11 A. M.; cleared 1:30 P. M., but cloudy again part of afternoon.
S 5	36	38	Clear	"	N. W.			Snow squall 11:20 A. M.; ther. falls to 31°, grows colder all day; violent wind and clouds.
6	19	28½	"	"	N. W.			
7	19½	34	Cloudy	Snow } Rain	N. E.			Snow 12:20 to 7:30 P. M., and then rain; ther. 34° 10 P. M.
8	35½	35½	"	Cloudy	S. W.	1.14		Rain till 6 A. M.; ther. 35° 7:30 A. M.; grows colder all day.
9	21½	26	Clear	Clear	N. W.			
10	15½	28	"	Cloudy	S. W.			Clouded over 9 A. M.
11	23½	29	"	Clear	N. W.			
S 12	15	18½	Snow	Snow	N. E.		3.00	Snow till 5 P. M.; cleared 10 P. M.; snow drifted very much.
13	2	20	Clear	Clear	N. W.			
14	10	28½	"	"	S. W.			
15	16	34½	"	Snow } Rain	N. E.			Clouded over 11 A. M.; snow 11:45 A.M. to 4 P.M.; snow and rain till 6 P.M. and then steady rain; ther. 34° 11 P. M.
16	33½	40½	Cloudy	Clear	S. W.	1.48		Cleared 10 A.M.; cloudy part of afternoon. J. G. McDowell died.
17	32	43	Clear	Cloudy	S. W.			Clouded over 3 P.M.; clear part of evening.
18	31½	42	"	Clear	N. W.			
S 19	30½	36	"	"	N. W.			Cloudy part of morning.
20	29	37½	"	"	N. W.			
21	24	39	"	"	N. E.			
22	24	42	"	"	S. W.			Clouded over 5 P. M.; light sprinkle 9 P. M.
23	36	43	Cloudy	Cloudy	S. W.	0.04		Light sprinkle during morning.
24	31	36½	Clear	Clear	N.			
25	25½	42½	"	Cloudy	E.			Clouded over 2 P. M.; commenced raining 5 P. M.
S 26	34	50	Rain	Clear	S. W.	1.77		Rain till 7 A. M.; cleared 2 P. M.
27	33½	43½	Clear	"	N. W.			
28	31	36½	Cloudy	Cloudy	N. E.			Snow flurries during A. M.
						1.43	3.00	

March, 1865.

Date.	Thermometer. Lowest.	Thermometer. Highest.	Weather. Morning.	Weather. Afternoon.	Prevailing Wind.	Rain and Melted Snow in inches.	Snow in inches.	REMARKS.
1	30½	41½	Clear --	Cloudy	N. E.	----	----	
2	34	37	Cloudy	Rain --	E.	----	----	Snow flurry 8 A.M.; snow 1 P.M., but soon turn to rained.
3	35	42½	Rain --	Cloudy	N. E., N. W.	0.83	----	
4	38	57	" --	Clear --	E., S., W.	0.75	----	Rain till noon; cleared 3 P.M.
S 5	28½	39½	Clear --	" --	N. E.	----	----	
6	22½	40½	" --	" --	N. W.	----	----	
7	28½	48½	" --	" --	S. W.	----	----	
8	35	54½	C'y m'st all day.		All points.	----	----	Foggy morning; clear 10 A.M. to 2 P.M., rain 5 P.M.
9	42	53½	Rain --	Cloudy	N. E.	1.15	----	
10	45	45	Cloudy	Clear --	N. W.	0.10	----	Rain before day and misty part of morning; ther. 45° 7:30 A.M. and falling all day; cleared 3 P.M.
11	21	35	Clear --	" --	S. W.	----	----	Cloudy part of afternoon.
S 12	26	33½	" --	" --	N. W.	----	----	
13	30½	58	Cloudy	" --	S. W.	----	----	
14	37½	54½	Clear --	" --	S. E.	----	----	
15	52	64	Cloudy	Cloudy	S. W.	0.12	----	Clear part of morning; rain 5 P.M.
16	57	71½	"	Clear --	S. W.	----	----	Clear 10 A.M. to 9 P.M.; violent gale at midnight.
17	39	53½	"	" --	S. W.	0.34	----	Rain before day; cleared 8 A.M.; cloudy part of evening.
18	48½	57½	Clear --	" --	N. W.	----	----	
S 19	34	55	" --	" --	S. W.	----	----	Clouded over 9 P.M.
20	44½	69	" --	" --	S. W.	----	----	Cloudy part of morning; light sprinkle 8 A.M.
21	46	73	" --	" --	S. W.	0.09	----	Clouded over 5 P.M. and rain at intervals after 7 P.M.
22	57	59	Cloudy	most all day.	W.	----	----	8 A.M. 59°; ther. com. falling and at 3 P.M. was 43½° lowest; light rain 4:30 P.M.
23	41	54½	Clear --	Clear --	W.	0.04	----	Cloudy part of afternoon; shower 3:30 P.M.
24	36	43½	" --	Cloudy	W.	----	----	Clear part of afternoon; light flurries of rain and snow.
25	34½	45½	" --	"	N. W.	----	----	Clear part of evening; violent wind all the week.
S 26	35	48½	Cloudy	Clear --	N. W.	----	----	
27	31½	54	Clear --	" --	W.	----	----	
28	39	51	" --	" --	S. E.	----	----	
29	37	59	" --	Hazy --	S. E.	----	----	Clouded over 5 P.M.
30	46½	55½	Rain --	Rain --	N. E.	----	----	
31	49	54	" --	" --	N. E.	0.84	----	
						4.26	----	

April, 1865.

Date.	Thermometer. Lowest.	Thermometer. Highest.	Weather. Morning.	Weather. Afternoon.	Prevailing Wind.	Rain and Melted Snow in inches.	Snow in inches.	REMARKS.
1	40	55½	Clear	Clear	N. W.	0.75		Stopped raining before day; cloudy part of afternoon.
S 2	39¼	56½	"	"	N. W.			
3	36	58	"	"	S. E.			Cloudy part of afternoon and evening.
4	44	52	Cloudy	Cloudy	S. E.			Cleared off 8 P. M.
5	42	67	"	most all day.	S. W.			
6	55½	62½	"	Cloudy	S. W.	0.03		Light sprinkle 10 A. M. to 1 P. M.; clear part of evening.
7	57½	65	"	"	S. W.	0.10		Showers during afternoon.
8	42½	53¾	Clear	Clear	N. W.			
S 9	38	52½	Cloudy	Cloudy	E.			Clear part of morning.
10	41	51	Rain	Rain	N. E.	0.52		No rain after 7 P. M.
11	44	52½	Cloudy	Cloudy	S. E.			Commenced raining 10 P. M.
12	46	60	"	"	S. W.	0.40		Rain before day.
13	51	58	"	Clear	N. W.	0.04		Rain before day; cloudy part of evening. Pears and cherries flowered.
14	42	61	"	"	S. W.			
15	45½	63	Clear	Rain	S.	0.15		Rain 3 to 9 P. M.
S 16	50½	61	Cloudy	Cloudy	N. W.	0.07		Showery afternoon; clear part of afternoon and evening.
17	39	56	Clear	Clear	N. E., S. W.			
18	40	67½	Cloudy	"	S. W.			Sprinkle 3 P. M.; cleared off 4 P. M.
19	48	69	Clear	"	N. W.			
20	48½	56	"	Rain	S. E.			Clouded over 9 A. M.; commenced raining 4 P. M.
21	43	51	Cloudy	Misty	N. E.	0.93		
22	46	66	Foggy	Cloudy	N. W.			Clear part of afternoon.
S 23	44	50½	Clear	Clear	N. W.			Cloudy part of afternoon.
24	37	58½	"	"	N. W.			
25	41	63	"	"	E.			
26	44	73	"	"	S. W.			
27	55	76	"	"	S. W.			
28	56	75	"	"	S. W.			
29	60	72	Cloudy	Rain	S. W.	1.00		Clouded over 7 A. M.; rain 5:15 to 10 P. M
S 30	46	61	Clear	Clear	N.			Clouded over 6 P. M.

3.99

May, 1865.

Date.	Thermometer. Lowest.	Thermometer. Highest.	Weather. Morning.	Weather. Afternoon.	Prevailing Wind.	Rain and Melted Snow in inches.	Snow in inches.	REMARKS.
1	50	56½	Rain	Cloudy	N. E.	0.19		Cleared off 9 P. M.
2	41½	57	Clear	"	N. E.			
3	50	64	"	Clear	N.			
4	43	62	"	Cloudy	S. W.			
5	52	66½	"	Clear	S. E.			Cloudy parts of morning and afternoon.
6	53	55	Rain	Cloudy	S. E.	0.48		Rain 7:10 to noon; clear 8 to 10 P. M.
S 7	50	65½	Clear	Clear	N. W.			
8	52	71	"	Cloudy	S. W.			Cloudy part of morning; com. raining 6 P. M.
9	63½	65	Rain	Rain	N. E.	1.34		Rained till 4:30 P. M.
10	50½	60½	Cloudy	Cloudy	S. E.			Clear part of morning.
11	53	73	"	"	S. W.	0.08		Rain 6 to 8 A. M.; violent shower 6:30 P.M. and rain rest of night.
12	44½	58½	Rain	Clear	N. E.	1.20		Rained till 9 A. M.; cloudy part of afternoon.
13	45	61½	Clear	"	N. E., S.W.			
S 14	48½	70	"	Cloudy	S. W.			Clouded over 4 P. M.
15	55	74	"	Clear	S. W.			
16	54½	75½	"	"	S. W.			
17	57	82	"	"	S. W.			
18	65	66	Cloudy	Cloudy	E.			Rain 10:15 to 11:30 P. M.
19	51	61	"	"	N. E.	0.41		Rain before day.
20	50½	77½	"	most all day.	S. W.	0.30		Rain 6 to 7 A. M.
S 21	63½	70½	Show'rs all day.		S. W.	0.76		Heavy showers before 7 A. M. and light sprinkle rest of day; clear parts of day.
22	64½	71½	Rain	Clody	S.	0.75		Rain till 9 A. M.; shower 11 P. M.
23	60	70½	Cloudy	Clear	N.			Cleared 10 A. M.
24	49½	68	Clear	"	N. E., S.W.			
25	55	72	"		N. W.			
26	52	68½	"	Cloudy	All points.			
27	53½	60	Rain	Rain	N. E.			
S 28	51	57½	Cloudy	Cloudy	N. E.	0.73		Rain before day.
29	54	68	"	most all day.	S. W.			
30	57½	75	Clear	Clear	W.			
31	54½	76	"	"	S. W.			

6.24

Weather Record for New Brunswick, N. J.

June, 1865.

Date	Lowest	Highest	Weather Morning	Weather Afternoon	Prevailing Wind	Rain and Melted Snow in inches	Snow in inches	REMARKS
1	61	80½	Clear	Clear	S. W., S. E.			
2	65	73½	"	"	S. E.			Cloudy part of evening.
3	59	74	"	"	S. E.			
S 4	64	85	"	"	S. W.			
5	70	83½	"	Cloudy	S. W., E.	0.38		Showers 3 and 8 P. M.
6	62½	66	Cloudy	"	N. E.			
7	61	70	"	"	S. W.			Cleared 9 P. M.
8	66	82½	Clear	Clear	S. W.	0.02		Shower 9 P. M.
9	70	85	"	"	S. W.			Commenced raining 9 P. M.
10	68	79	Cloudy	Cloudy	S. W.	1.05		Rain before day; shower 10 A. M. and rain 2:30 to 6 P.M.
S 11	64	74	"	Clear	N. E., S. E.			Cleared 9 A. M.
12	57½	76½	Clear	"	S. W.			
13	64	81	Cloudy	"	S. W.			Cleared 7:30 A. M.; cloudy part of evening.
14	66	74	"	"	N. E.			Cleared 7:30 A. M.; cloudy part of evening.
15	61	66½	"	Cloudy	E.			Partly clear part of afternoon.
16	62½	74	"	"	E.			Clear part of evening.
17	68	82	"	Clear	S. W.			
S 18	68½	85½	Clear	"	S. W.			
19	69½	75	Cloudy	"	N. E.			Cloudy part of evening.
20	69	78	"	most all day.	S.	0.06		Rain 6:30 to 8 P. M.
21	70	81	"	Clear	S. W.			Cleared 10 A. M.; cloudy evening.
22	67½	83	Clear	"	S. W.	0.08		Shower 3:30 P. M.
23	65	78½	"	"	S. W.			
24	62	82½	"	"	S. W.			
S 25	68	84½	Cloudy	"	S. W.			Cleared 8 A.M.; cloudy part of afternoon.
26	67½	75	Rain	Rain	S.	0.49		Rain at intervals 7:30 A. M. to 7 P.M.; cloudy part of evening.
27	64	76½	Clear	Clear	N. W.			
28	59	78½	"	"	W.			
29	67	85	"	"	S. W.			
30	73	83½	"	"	S. W.			Clouded over 7 P. M. and showers after 8 P. M.
						2.31		

Weather Record for New Brunswick, N. J.

July, 1865.

Date.	Lowest.	Highest.	Weather Morning.	Afternoon.	Prevailing Wind.	Rain and Melted Snow in inches.	Snow in inches.	REMARKS.
1	71½	80½	Cloudy	Clear	S. W.			Light sprinkle 7 A. M.; cleared 4 P. M.; shower after 8 P. M.
S 2	71	81	"	"	W.	0.34		
3	63	79½	Clear	"	N. W.			
4	66	85	"	"	W.	0.88		Clouded over 7 P. M., and rain with heavy thunder 10:30 to 11:30 P. M.
5	70½	80	Cloudy	"	N.			
6	59	75	Clear	"	N. E., S. W.			Cloudy parts of morning and afternoon.
7	66½	90	"	"	S. W.	0.04		
8	72	81	"	"	N. W.			
S 9	69½	81	"	"	N.	0.17		Shower before day.
10	60	71½	Cloudy	Cloudy	N. E.			
11	63½	70	Rain	"	N. E.	0.36		Rain at intervals till 11 A. M.
12	65½	70	Cloudy	"	S. E.	0.03		Light shower at 3 P. M.
13	67	79½	"	Clear	N. W.			Cleared 8 A. M.
14	55	72½	Clear	"	N. W.			
15	55½	74½	"	"	S.			Cloudy parts of afternoon and evening.
S 16	65½	79	Cloudy most all day.		S. E.			Com. raining 5 P. M., with heavy showers during the night.
17	66	73	Rain	Clear	N.	1.85		No rain after 9 A. M.; cleared 11 A. M. Greatest freshet since 1810.
18	58	76	Clear	"	N. W., S. W.			
19	61	80	"	Cloudy	S. W.			Com. raining 7:15 P. M.
20	71	80½	"	Clear	N. W.	0.60		
21	67	84	Cloudy	"	W.			Cleared 8 A. M.
22	66½	69½	Rain	Cloudy	N. E.	3.30		Heavy thunder showers 2:30 to 7 A. M.; cleared 7:30 P. M.
S 23	61	77½	Clear	Clear	N.			
24	65	78½	"	"	N. W.			Cloudy parts of morning and evening.
25	69	86	Cloudy most all day.		S. W.	0.03		Shower 6 to 7 P. M.
26	71	81	Clear	Clear	W.			
27	69	81½	"	"	W.			
28	69½	86	"	"	S.			Cloudy part of evening.
29	75½	83½	"	"	N. W.			Cloudy part of evening.
S 30	70½	78	"	"	N. E.			Cloudy parts of morning and evening.
31	64	78	"	"	N. E., S. E.			

7.10

August, 1865.

Date	Thermometer Lowest	Thermometer Highest	Weather Morning	Weather Afternoon	Prevailing Wind	Rain and Melted Snow in inches	Snow in inches	REMARKS
1	65	77½	Clear	Clear	S. E.			Cloudy 7 A. M. to 2 P. M.
2	65½	81	"	"	S. E.			Cloudy parts of day.
3	70	85½	"	"	S. W.	0.15		Shower 5:15 P. M.; cloudy part of evening.
4	70½	86½	"	"	S. W.			
5	72	84½	Cloudy most all day.		S. W.			Light shower 3:15 to 6:30 P. M.
S 6	71½	80	"	Rain	S. W.	1.87		Light shower 6 A. M.; clear part of morning; heavy shower afternoon and evening till 11 P. M.
7	70½	79½	"	most all day.	S. W.	0.04		Shower 3:30 P. M.
8	61½	76½	Clear	Clear	N. W.			
9	64	77½	"	"	All points.			
10	63	78½	"	Cloudy	S. W.			Clear part of evening.
11	67	77½	"	Clear	N. W.			
12	63½	76	Cloudy	"	N.			Clear part of morning.
S 13	57½	75½	Clear	"	N., S. W.			
14	57½	76½	"	"	S. W.			Cloudy part of afternoon.
15	59½	77½	"	"	W., E.			
16	61	78½	"	"	S. E.			
17	66	73½	Cloudy	Cloudy	N. E.			Cleared off 6 P. M.
18	65	72½	"	Clear	N. E.			Cleared off 4:30 P. M.
19	63	76½	"	"	N. E., S. W.			Cleared off 9 A. M.
S 20	63½	82½	Clear	"	S. W.			
21	68½	84½	Cloudy	"	S. W.			Cleared off 8 A. M.
22	68	74½	"	Rain	N. E.	0.41		Heavy shower 12:15 A. M.; clear part of afternoon; easterly rain set in 4:30 P. M.
23	54½	67	Clear	Clear	N. W.	0.74		Rain till 2 A. M.
24	49½	65½	"	"	N. W.			
25	52½	71	"	"	N. W., S. W.			
26	54½	75½	"	"	S. W.			
S 27	62	79	"	"	W., N.			Cloudy part of morning.
28	54½	71½	"	"	N. W.			Cloudy evening.
29	63	75	C'y m'st all day.		All points			
30	60½	79	Clear	Clear	S. W.			
31	62½	79	Cloudy	"	S. W.			Cleared off 10 A. M. Water pipes have been placed in all the principal streets during the last two months.
						3.21		

WEATHER RECORD FOR NEW BRUNSWICK, N. J. 111

September, 1865.

	Date.	Lowest.	Highest.	Morning.	Afternoon.	Prevailing Wind.	Rain and Melted Snow in inches.	Snow in inches.	REMARKS.
	1	67½	84	Clear	Clear	S. W.			
	2	72	79	Rain	Cloudy	S. W.	1.28		Rain till 9 A.M.; clear part of afternoon; rain 8:30 to 11 P. M.
S	3	72	79½	Cloudy	"	N.			Cleared off 8 P. M.
	4	71½	78½	"	"	S. W., S. E.			Partly clear part of morning.
	5	71	78½	"	Clear	S. W.			Cleared 3 P. M.
	6	72½	86	"	"	S. W., N. W.	0.02		Cleared 10 A.M.; cloudy part of afternoon with shower 3:30 P. M.
	7	66	81	Clear	"	N. W., S. W.			
	8	67½	73	Cloudy	Rain	N. E.	0.87		Rain 1:15 to 11 P. M.
	9	64	69	"	Cloudy	N. E.			
S	10	65	73	"	"	E.	0.04		Light shower before day; clear 3 to 8 P. M.; misty evening.
	11	69	79	"	Clear	N. E., S. W.			Cleared 10:30 A. M. Lyman A. Chandler died.
	12	71	82	"	"	S. W., S. E.			Cleared 10 A. M.
	13	73	80½	Clear	"	S. E.			
	14	73	83	Cloudy	"	S. W.			Cleared 8 A. M.
	15	73	83½	"	"	N. W.			Cleared 8 A. M.; cloudy part of afternoon.
	16	60½	76	Clear	"	N. E.			
S	17	56½	77½	"	"	S. W.			
	18	64	69½	Cloudy	Cloudy	N. E.	0.48		Rain 5:30 to 9 P. M.
	19	46	63	Clear	Clear	N. E.			
	20	48	69	"	"	S. W.			
	21	56½	74	"	"	S. W.			Cloudy part of morning.
	22	60½	76½	"	"	N. E.			
	23	61½	65½	Cloudy	Cloudy	N. E.			
S	24	63	72½	"	Clear	S. W.			Clear part of morning.
	25	65½	73½	"	most all day.	S. W.	0.03		Light sprinkle during morning and 2:15 P. M.; clear evening.
	26	57½	68	Clear	Clear	N. E.			
	27	50½	67	"	"	N. E., S. E.			
	28	48	70	"	"	N. W.			
	29	51	73	"	"	S. W.			
	30	52	77	"	"	S. W.			
							2.72		

October, 1865.

Date	Thermometer. Lowest	Thermometer. Highest	Weather. Morning	Weather. Afternoon	Prevailing Wind.	Rain and Melted Snow in inches.	Snow in inches.	REMARKS.
S 1	59½	69½	Clear	Clear	N. W.			
2	50½	66½	"	"	S. W., N. W.			
3	45	58½	"	"	N. W.			
4	46	53	Cloudy most all day.		N. W.	0.03		Light rain 7 A. M.
5	41½	54½	Clear	Clear	N. W.			Cloudy part of afternoon.
6	43	59½	"	"	N. W.			
7	43	65½	"	"	W., S. W.			
S 8	53	73	"	"	S.W., N. W.			
9	52	70	"	"	N. W.			
10	56	80	"	"	W.			Hottest day for the time since I have kept record (10 years,) and the dustiest.
11	57½	67	"	"	N. E., S. W.			Cloudy part of morning.
12	58½	63	"	"	N. W.			Ther. 63° 8 A. M., and then commenced falling with violent wind from the N. W.
13	38½	55	"	"	N. W., S. W.			
14	35½	56½	"	Cloudy	E.			Commenced raining 7:45 P. M. It has been so dry that there has been no killing frost till morning of 14th.
S 15	49	57½	Rain	"	N. W.	1.00		Rain till 10 A. M.; partly clear part of A. M.; sprinkle during P. M.; cleared 8 P. M.
16	45½	52½	Clear	Clear	N. W.			
17	38½	55	"	"	N. W.			
18	47	63	Cloudy	Rain	S. E.			Commenced raining 3 P. M.
19	58	62½	"	most all day.	S. W.	1.58		During eclipse (10 A. M.) ther. fell to 52°; light sprinkle P. M.
20	49	56½	Clear	Clear	N. W.			
21	43½	54	"	"	N. W.			
S 22	38	53	"	"	N.W., S. W.			
23	42½	56	Cloudy	"	S. W., N. W.			Clear part of morning.
24	37½	53½	Clear	"	N. E.			Cloudy part of morning.
25	36	50½	"	"	N. E., S. E.			
26	33½	54	"	"	All points.			
27	45	58	Cloudy	Cloudy	S. E.			Commenced raining 8 P. M.
28	53½	67	Rain	Clear	S. W.	1.18		Rain till 5 P. M.; cleared 9 A. M.; shower 3 P. M.
S 29	42	49	Clear	"	N. W.			
30	35½	50	"	"	All points.			Cloudy part of morning
31	40	54	Cloudy	Rain	N. E.	0.83		Light sprinkle during A. M.; rain 12 to 5:30 P. M.; cleared 6 P. M.
						4.62		

Weather Record for New Brunswick, N. J.

November, 1865.

Date	Thermometer Lowest	Thermometer Highest	Weather Morning	Weather Afternoon	Prevailing Wind	Rain and Melted Snow in inches	Snow in inches	REMARKS
1	37½	54½	Clear	Clear	All points.			
2	39	57½	Cloudy	Rain	S.	0.12		Rain 12 to 5 P. M.
3	47	55	"	Cloudy	N. E.			
4	47½	54	Rain	Rain	N. E.	1.22		Rain 5:30 A. M. to 9 P. M.; cleared 11 P. M.
S 5	42	47½	Clear	Clear	N. W.			Cloudy part of morning and part of evening.
6	32½	46	"	"	S. W.			Cloudy part of evening.
7	37	41	"	"	N. W.			
8	26½	40	"	"	N. E., S. W.			
9	32	54	"	"	S. W., N. W.			
10	35	45½	"	"	N.			Cloudy part of evening.
11	26	42	"	"	N. E.			
S 12	26	43½	"	"	N. W., S. W.			
13	33	59	"	"	S. W.			
14	40½	61½	"	"	S. W.			
15	36	63½	"	"	S. W.			
16	41	68	"	"	S. W.			
17	51½	68½	Cloudy	"	S. W.			Foggy morning.
18	48	57½	"	"	N. W.			Cleared 9 A. M.; cloudy evening.
S 19	46	53	"	Cloudy	N. E.			
20	43	50	"	"	N. E.			Commenced 9 P. M.
21	42	44	Rain	Misty	N. E.	1.83		Cleared 9 P. M.
22	38½	43½	"	Cloudy	S. W.	0.23		Rain till 9 A. M., and rain again part of evening.
23	38½	47½	"	"	S. W., N. E.	0.17		Light rain till 10 A.M.; rain 4 to 5 P. M. with snow; cleared 8 P. M.
24	36½	51	Clear	Clear	N.			
25	37	48	"	"	N.			Cloudy part of morning.
S 26	35	48	"	"	N. W.			
27	31½	46	"	"	N. W.			Cloudy part of afternoon.
28	32	38½	"	"	N. W.			Clouded over 6 P. M.
29	30	37¾	Cloudy	Cloudy	N. E.			
30	34	47	"	Clear	N. E., W.			Cleared 8 A. M.; clouded over again 6 P. M.
						2.57		

December, 1865.

Date.	Thermometer. Lowest.	Thermometer. Highest.	Weather. Morning.	Weather. Afternoon.	Prevailing Wind.	Rain and Melted Snow in inches.	Snow in inches.	REMARKS.
1	40	44	Cloudy	Clear	W.	0.05		Rain before day; clear 11 A.M.
2	30½	55½	Clear	"	S. W.			
S 3	43	57	Cloudy	most all day.	S. W.			
4	46½	55	Foggy	Cloudy	N. E., S. W.			Partly clear after 9 P. M.
5	44	46	Cloudy	Clear	N. W.			Cleared 9 A.M.; cloudy part of afternoon.
6	27	39½	Clear	"	N. W.			
7	34	41	Rain	Rain	All points.	1.15		Rain till 4 P.M.; cleared 5 P. M.; cloudy part of evening.
8	26	32½	Clear	Clear	N. W.			
9	25½	40	"	Cloudy	S. W.	0.28		Snow 4 to 8 P. M. and then rain.
S 10	32	42½	Cloudy	Clear	S. W., N. W.			Cleared 10 A.M.; cloudy part of afternoon.
11	30	46	Clear	"	E.			Clouded over 9 P. M.
12	37	54	Rain	Rain	S. E.			
13	45	49	Clear	Cloudy	N. W.	1.18		Clouded over 3 P. M.; light sprinkle of rain with hail after 6 P. M.
14	33	37½	Cloudy	Clear	N. W.			Cleared 8:30 A. M.
15	16½	24	Clear	"	N. W.			
16	14	33½	"	"	N. W.			Clouded over 9 P. M.
S 17	22½	30	Cloudy	Cloudy	N. E.			Clear part of evening.
18	27	39½	"	most all day.	N. E.			
19	33	48	"	Cloudy	S. W.	0.10		Rain before day and light sprinkle in evening.
20	37	39	"	"	N. W.			Snow 6 to 11 P.M., and then rain.
21	32½	39	Clear	Clear	N. W.	0.78		Cleared 7½ A.M; snow squall 9 A. M.; cloudy part of afternoon.
22	18½	24½	"	"	W.			Cloudy part of morning.
23	15	25	"	"	S. W.			
S 24	17	46	Snow } Rain }	Rain	S. W.	1.38	2.50	Snow till 8:30 A.M. and then rain till 6 P. M.
25	34	42	Clear	Clear	S. W.			Foggy evening.
26	30	38	Foggy	Foggy	N. E.			Misty evening.
27	36	63	Rain	Cloudy	S W.	0.18		Clear part of evening.
28	40	48	Cloudy	"	N. E.	0.04		Rain part of afternoon; cleared 7 P. M.
29	35	42	Clear	Clear	N. W.			
30	29½	35½	Cloudy	Snow	N. E.		5.50	Snow 8 A. M. to 7 P. M.
S 31	24	34½	"	Cloudy	N. E.			Clear part of morning.
						5.14	8.00	

Rain and melted snow for 1865—51.23 inches.

January, 1866.

	Date.	Thermometer. Lowest.	Thermometer. Highest.	Wind. Morning.	Wind. Afternoon.	Prevailing Wind.	Rain and Melted Snow in inches.	Snow in inches.	REMARKS.
	1	32	40½	Rain	Cloudy	W.	0.26	----	Rained till 11 A. M., and sprinkle 4 P. M.
	2	33	36	Cloudy	"	N. E.	---	----	Commenced snowing 9 P. M.
	3	28	35½	"	"	N., S. W.	----	1.50	Clear part of evening.
	4	25½	34	"	Clear	N. W.	----	----	Cleared 11 A. M.; cloudy
	5	8	18½	Clear	"	N. W.	----	----	part of evening.
	6	15	27	"	"	S. W.	----	----	Clouded over 7 P. M.
S	7	14½	18	Cloudy	"	N. E.	----	----	Snow squall 9 A. M. Ther. 7:30, 18°; 9, 14°; 11, 18°; 4 P. M., 12°; 10 P. M., 3°; bar. 10 P. M., 30.87.
	8	-11½	8	Clear	"	N.	----	--	Coldest morning I have ever known; noon ther. -1°; bar. 30.89 10 A. M.; very high wind on the
	9	1½	26	"	"	N.	----	----	7th and 8th.
	10	16	37½	"	"	N. W.	----	----	Cloudy evening.
	11	29½	38	Cloudy	"	N. W.	----	----	Cleared 7:30 A. M.
	12	26	41	"	Cloudy	W., S. E.	0.03	----	Light snow 7 A. M., and light rain 8 P. M.
	13	34	47	"	Clear	S. W.	0.04	----	Clear part of A. M.; cloudy part of P. M.; shower with hail 4:45 P. M.
S	14	36	36	Clear	"	N. W.	----	----	Ther. 36° 7:30 A. M., falling all day; cloudy part A. M.
	15	5½	21½	"	Cloudy	N.	----	----	Com. snowing 8:30 P. M.
	16	16½	35	Snow	Clear	N. E., N. W.	0.05	6.00	Snowed till 3 A. M., & drizzly 5 to 8 A. M.; cleared 1 P. M, and cloudy part of evening.
	17	22	34	Clear	"	S. W.	----	----	Cloudy part of morning.
	18	28½	41½	Cloudy	"	S. W.	----	----	Cleared 10 A. M.
	19	26½	43½	"	"	N. E., S. W.	----	----	Cleared 10 A.M.; m'ly eveni'g
	20	36	46	Foggy	Cloudy	S. W.	0.05	----	Light rain during afternoon,
S	21	14½	21	Clear	Clear	N. W.	----	----	cleared 9 P. M.
	22	17	28	"	"	N. W.	----	----	
	23	18	29	Cloudy	Cloudy	S. W.	----	1.00	Partly clear part of A. M.; snow 3:30 to 9 P.M.; clear part of evening after 9 P. M
	24	24	30	"	Snow	N. E.	----	----	Commenced snowing 4 P. M.
	25	26	39	"	Cloudy	N. E.	0.06	4.00	Rain parts of day; snow
	26	29½	34½	"	most all day.	N. W.	----	----	squall in the evening.
	27	21	28½	Clear	Clear	N. W.	----	----	
S	28	15½	32	"	Cloudy	N. E.	----	----	Clouded over 10 A. M.
	29	27½	32	Cloudy	"	N. E.	----	----	
	30	30	37	"	"	S.	---	----	Cleared 10 P. M.
	31	28½	36½	Clear	Clear	W.		----	
							0.49	12.50	

Weather Record for New Brunswick, N. J.

February, 1866.

Date.	Thermometer. Lowest.	Thermometer. Highest.	Wind. Morning.	Wind. Afternoon.	Prevailing Wind.	Rain and Melted Snow in inches.	Snow in inches.	REMARKS.
1	27	28	Clear	Clear	N. W.			Cloudy part of evening.
2	19½	31	"	"	N. W., S. W.			Cloudy part of evening.
3	20	25½	"	"	N. W.			
S 4	10½	20½	"	"	W.			
5	11	19	"	"	N. W.			
6	14½	30	"	"	N. W.			
7	13	25½	Cloudy	Cloudy	N. E.			Light snow and rain during evening.
8	24	39	Misty	Rain	N. E.	0.65		Rain 5 to 11 P. M. and then snow.
9	32	36	Snow	Cloudy	N. E.	0.06	4.00	Snow till 10 A. M. and then light rain.
10	32	41	Cloudy	"	E.			
S 11	33	51¼	"	"	All points			Clear part of morning.
12	39½	44	Rain	Rain	N. E.	1.39		Rain till 8 P. M.
13	33	38½	Clear	Cloudy	N. W.			Clear part of evening.
14	33½	48½	Cloudy	most all day.	S. E.			Light sprinkle during day; steady rain 7:30 P. M.
15	21	21	Clear	Clear	N. W.	0.40		Grows colder all day; noon 17½°.
16	5	14	"	"	N. W.			
17	11	33½	"	"	N. W.			
S 18	22	37	"	Rain	S. E.			Clouded over 10 A. M.
19	34½	48½	Rain	Cloudy	W.	1.54		Rain part of afternoon; cleared 10 P. M.
20	34	43½	Clear	Clear	S. W.			Splendid Northern lights 11 P. M.
21	31	45	"	"	S. W.			
22	30	55	"	"	S. W.			
23	33	60½	"	"	S.	0.07		Foggy morning; clouded over 6 P. M.; misty after 8 P. M.
24	49½	62	Cloudy	Rain	S.	0.53		Partly clear part of morning; rain 2:15 to 11 P. M.
S 25	32½	37	Clear	Clear	N. W.			
26	15½	25½	"	"	N. W., S. W.			
27	22½	40	Cloudy	Cloudy	S. W.			Snow squall 7 A. M.; cleared 6 P. M.
28	30	40½	"	Clear	N. E., S. E.			Cloudy part of evening.
						4.64	4.00	

Weather Record for New Brunswick, N. J.

March, 1866.

Date.	Thermometer. Lowest.	Thermometer. Highest.	Weather. Morning.	Weather. Afternoon.	Prevailing Wind.	Rain and Melted Snow in inches.	Snow in inches.	REMARKS.
1	33	41½	Cloudy	Cloudy	E.			Clear part of morning.
2	37½	50	"	Clear	All points.			Cleared 3 P.M.; clouded over again 9 P. M.
3	38½	48	Misty	Cloudy	All points.	0.01		Sprinkle 10 A. M.
S 4	40	48	Clear	Clear	N. W.			Snow squall 6 P.M.; cloudy part of evening.
5	25½	35	"	"	N. W.			
6	26	37½	"	"	N. W.			
7	29	37	Cloudy	"	N. W.			Cleared 11 A. M.
8	22½	35	Clear	"	N. W.			
9	23	31½	"	Cloudy	N. W.			Clouded over 11 A.M.; snow squalls 1 to 3:30 P. M.; clear part of afternoon.
10	22	35	"	Clear	N. W.			For the last 6 days very high winds from N.W. and very dusty.
S 11	24	44½	"	Cloudy	S. W.	0.03		Clouded over 10 A.M.; light rain 4 to 5 P. M.
12	39	52	Cloudy	"	N. E.	0.05		Sun rose clear, rain 1 to 2 P. M.; partly clear during evening.
13	41	65	"	"	All points.			Clear 10 A.M. to 5 P.M. and part of evening.
14	42½	52	"	"	N. E.			
15	41½	60	"	most all day.	N. E.			Showers after 10:30 P. M.
16	52½	56	Rain	Cloudy	All points.	0.82		Clear part of afternoon.
17	28	31	Clear	Clear	N. W.			Very blustery & heavy snow squalls 4:15 to 5:45 P.M.
S 18	17	32	"	Cloudy	N. W., S. W.			
19	29	32	Cloudy	"	N. E.			Snow 9 A.M. to 1 P.M. but very light and melts as it falls.
20	31	37	"	Rain	N. E.			Drizzling rain after 3 P. M.
21	31½	44	Misty	Cloudy	All points.	0.28		
22	29	45	Clear	Clear	N. W.			
23	29	49	"	Cloudy	S. E.	0.22		Com. raining 5:30 P. M. and cont. till about 11 P. M.
24	41	46	"	Clear	N. W.			
S 25	30	32	Snow	"	N. W.		1.50	Snow till 8:30 A.M.; cleared 9 A.M.; very blustery.
26	15½	36	Clear	"	N. W.			Very blustery.
27	25	43	"	"	N. W.			
28	26½	48½	"	Cloudy	S. E.			Clouded over 2 P.M.; rain 11 P.M.
29	39	47	Rain	"	S. W., N. W.	0.37		Cleared 9 P. M.
30	34	45½	Clear	Clear	N. W.			Cloudy part of morning.
31	33½	50	Cloudy	Rain	S. W.	0.31		Rain 10 to 12 A. M. and part of afternoon and evening; cleared 11 P. M.
						2.09	1.50	

Weather Record for New Brunswick, N. J.

April, 1866.

Date	Thermometer Lowest	Thermometer Highest	Weather Morning	Weather Afternoon	Prevailing Wind	Rain and Melted Snow in inches	Snow in inches	REMARKS.
S 1	38½	51½	Clear	Clear	N. W.			
2	38	45½	Cloudy	Rain	N. W.	0.30		Sun rose clear; rain noon till 5 p. m.
3	39½	56½	"	Clear	N. E., S. W.			Cleared 9 a. m.
4	44	62	Clear	"	S. W.			
5	49½	73	Misty	"	S. W.			Cleared 8 a. m.
6	56½	71½	Cloudy	Show'rs	S. W.	0.25		Clear part of morning; showers 2:45 to 7 p. m.
7	40½	46	"	Rain	N. E.			Rain all day at intervals after 8 a. m.
S 8	34½	38	Rain Snow	Cloudy	N. E.	0.83		Rain till 8 a. m. and then snow till noon; melts as it falls; clear part of evening.
9	35	48	Clear	Clear	N. E.			Cloudy part of morning.
10	32	52½	"	"	S. E.			
11	38½	54½	Cloudy	most all day	S. E.			
12	41	63	Clear	Clear	S. W.			Foggy morning.
13	48½	69	Cloudy	"	S. W., N. W.			Clear part of morning.
14	46½	56	"	most all day	E.	0.01		Light rain 9 p. m.
S 15	45½	64½	C'y m'st all day	All points				
16	46	48½	Rain	Cloudy	N. E.	0.68		
17	45½	53	Cloudy	"	N. E.			
18	43½	54	"	"	E.			Clear part of evening.
19	48	73½	"	Clear	S. W.			Cleared 10:30 a. m.
20	54	77½	Clear	"	S. W.			
21	61	77½	"	Cloudy	S. W.	0.30		Cleared over 2 p. m.; thunder shower 4:15 p. m. Pears and cherries flowered.
S 22	64	76	Cloudy	Clear	S. W.			Clear part morning; cloudy evening.
23	55	70	"	Show'rs	E., S. W.	0.82		Rain before day and 8 to 10 a. m; terrible hail storm 4:45 with rain, .30 of an inch in 10 minutes, and showers till 10 p. m.; bar. 29.08; clear part of afternoon.
24	43	47	"	Cloudy	N. W.			
25	39	54½	Clear	Clear	S. W.			
26	37	45	Cloudy	most all day	N. W.			
27	38	60	Clear	Clear	S. W.			
28	40	66½	"	"	S. W.	0.01		Cloudy evening; shower 10:15 p. m.
S 29	42	64	"	"	N. W.			Violent wind all day.
30	41	60½	"	"	N. W.			
						3.20		

WEATHER RECORD FOR NEW BRUNSWICK, N. J.

May, 1866.

Date.	Thermometer. Lowest.	Thermometer. Highest	Weather. Morning.	Weather. Afternoon.	Prevailing Wind.	Rain and Melted Snow in inches.	Snow in inches.	REMARKS.
1	43	54	Cloudy	Rain	S. E.			Light rain at intervals during afternoon; steady rain after 8 P. M.
2	38½	56½	"	Clear	N. W.	1.33		Rain till 6 A. M.
3	41	49½	"	"	N. W.			Cleared 9 A. M.
4	37½	62	Clear	"	N. W.			High winds and very dusty.
5	43	61½	"	"	N. W.			High winds and very dusty.
S 6	43	66	"	"	N. W.			
7	45½	65½	"	"	N. E., S. W.			
8	42	70	"	Cloudy	S. W.			Foggy morning; clouded over 3 P. M.
9	53½	71½	"	"	S. W.	0.02		Light rain before day; cleared 10 P. M.
10	50	72	"	Clear	N. W., S. W.			Cloudy evening.
11	55½	71	Cloudy	Cloudy	S. W.			Clear 8 A. M. to 2 P. M.
12	53	73½	Clear	Clear	S. W.			
S 13	56	79	"	"	S. W.	0.39		Cloudy part of afternoon; shower 5 to 6 P. M.
14	44	61	"	"	N. W.			
15	41	64½	"	"	N. W., S. W.			
16	53½	75	"	"	S. W.			Cloudy evening; commenced raining 9:30 P M.
17	49½	54	Rain	Cloudy	N. E.	0.30		Misty evening.
18	51	59	"	"	N. E.	0.13		Rain till 10 A. M.
19	53	71½	Cloudy	Clear	N. E., S. W.			Cleared 10 A. M.
S 20	56	72½	"	"	S. E.			Cleared 8 A. M.
21	56	72½	Clear	"	N. W.			Light rain 3 P. M.; high winds during afternoon.
22	47	55	"	"	N. W.			High winds all day.
23	41	59	"	"	N W.			Cloudy evening; frost.
24	43½	65	"	"	N. W., S. W.			Frost.
25	48½	72	"	"	S. W.			
26	50½	72½	"	"	S. E.			Cloudy evening; rain 10:10 P. M.
S 27	61½	75½	Rain	"	S. W.	1.05		Rain till 10 A. M.; thunder storm 10 P. M.
28	62½	68½	C'r m'st all day.		S. W., N. W.			Ther. rose 68° and afternoon fell to 59°; blustering after 9 A. M., with heavy flying clouds.
29	52½	60½	Cloudy	Rain	S. W.	0.28		Sun rose clear; rain till 6 P. M.
30	47½	66½	Clear	Clear	W.			Cloudy part of morning.
31	56	72½	"	"	S. W., N. W.			Cleared 9 A. M.

4.50

WEATHER RECORD FOR NEW BRUNSWICK, N. J.

June, 1866.

Date	Thermometer Lowest	Thermometer Highest	Weather Morning	Weather Afternoon	Prevailing Wind	Rain and Melted Snow in inches	Snow in inches	REMARKS
1	54	65½	Clear	Clear	E.			
2	55	68	Cloudy	"	E.			
S 3	60	64	Rain	Misty	N. E.	0.22		
4	57	67½	Cloudy	Cloudy	N. E.			Partly clear part of afternoon.
5	61¼	71	"	Clear	N. E.	0.10		Showers 1 P M. and 11 P. M.
6	64	78½	"	"	S. W.	0.02		Cleared 10 A.M.; heavy blow and light rain 7 P. M.
7	61	76	Clear	"	N. W.			Cloudy parts of afternoon & evening, sprinkle 2:30 P.M.
8	62	75½	"	"	N.			Cloudy evening; with strong wind from N. E.
9	58½	67½	"	"	E.			Cloudy evening.
S 10	56	65½	Cloudy	Cloudy	S. W.			Clear evening.
11	58	78	Clear	Clear	N. W.			
12	60	76	"	"	S. W.			
13	62½	75½	C'y m'st all day.		S. W., N. E.	0.94		Slight shower 7:20 A.M and heavy shower 8 & 11 P M.
14	60	68½	Cloudy	Cloudy	N. E.	0.06		Light rain 4:30 to 8 P. M.
15	61	78	Clear	Clear	S. W.	0.33		Heavy shower 6:50 P. M. and light sprinkle during evening.
16	63½	77¼	"	"	N. E., S. W.			
S 17	61	71¼	"	Cloudy	S. E.	0.47		Clouded over 10 A.M.; light rain 11 A M.; showers 4:30 and 10:30 P. M.
18	67	74	"	Clear	S. W.			
19	57	69	"	"	S. W.			Cloudy part of afternoon
20	54	75½	"	"	S. W.			
21	59½	80½	"	"	S. W.			
22	65½	82	"	"	S. W.			
23	68	80	"	"	All points.	0.31		Cloudy part of morning and afternoon; light rain 7 A. M. and 6 P M. and heavy shower 4:10 P. M
S 24	67	81½	Cloudy	"	S. E.			Cleared 10 A. M.
25	70	88	Clear	"	S. W.			
26	74	89	"	"	N. W., S. E.			
27	74	87½	"	"	S. W.			Showery evening and steady rain 10:30 P. M.
28	68	72	Rain	Cloudy	N. W.	0.66		Rain till 10 A M.; clear part of evening; shower 10:30 P. M.
29	60	72	Clear	Clear	N. E.			Cloudy evening.
30	60	74	"	"	N. E.			
						3.10		

WEATHER RECORD FOR NEW BRUNSWICK, N. J. 121

July, 1866.

Date.	Thermometer. Lowest.	Highest.	Weather. Morning.	Afternoon.	Prevailing Wind.	Rain and Melted Snow in inches.	Snow in inches.	REMARKS.
S 1	56	74	Clear	Clear	N. E.			
2	57	79	"	"	S. W.			
3	63	84	"	"	S. W.			
4	64	83	"	Cloudy	S. W.	0.06		Clear part of evening; showery 5 to 8 P. M.
5	69	85½	"	Clear	S. W.			
6	71	91	"	"	S. W.			
7	75½	93½	"	"	S. W.			
S 8	74	93½	"	"	S. W.			Clouded over 6 P. M., with shower all around; few drops here.
9	74	78½	Cloudy most all day.		N.			Light sprinkle 1 to 2 P. M.
10	66½	76	"	Clear	E.			Clear part of morning.
11	56	80	Clear	"	E.			
12	62	88½	"	"	W.			Northern lights 10 P. M.
13	71	95	"	"	N. W.			
14	78	87	"	"	E.	0.26		Last night hottest I ever knew; shower 2:20 and 4:50 P. M.
S 15	71	92½	"	"	S. W.			
16	75½	97	"	"	S. W.			Ther. highest since July 18, '56; wind very variable.
17	79	98	"	"	S. W.			Partly clear part of evening, with showers all around; ther. 129½ in sun.
18	75	92½	"	"	S. W.	0.22		Shower 1:45 to 2 P.M.; ther. falls to 77° and rises again to 91°; shower after 8 P.M.
19	71	80½	Cloudy	"	N. E.			
20	70	78	"	most all day.	S. E.			
21	65	70½	Misty	Cloudy	N. E.	0.05		Light rain before day; misty evening.
S 22	65	79	Cloudy	Clear	S. W.	0.03		Shower 12:15 A. M.
23	68½	82	Clear	"	N. W.	0.33		Thunder shower 3:15 A. M.
24	64	81½	"	"	N. E.			
25	65½	85	"	"	S. W.	0.57		Shower 9 and 10 P. M.
26	64	79½	"	"	S. E.			
27	68	84	"	"	S. W.			Cloudy parts of morning and afternoon.
28	69½	85	"	"	S. W.	0.53		Light rain before day and 2 P.M.; shower 6 to 8:30 P.M.
S 29	65	82	"	"	N. E.			
30	67	82	"	"	N. E.	1.17		Shower 4:10 P.M., .23; heavy shower 6:45 P.M.; .94 in less than an hour.
31	64	80½	"	"	N.			
						3.22		

August, 1866.

Date.	Ther-mometer. Lowest.	Ther-mometer. Highest.	Weather. Morning.	Weather. Afternoon.	Prevailing Wind.	Rain and Melted Snow in inches.	Snow in inches.	REMARKS.
1	63	83	Clear	Clear	S. W.			Clouded over 8 P. M.; rain 9:15 P. M.
2	70	83	Cloudy	"	S. W.	0.24		Clear part of morning.
3	63	79	Clear	"	N. W.			
4	63	79½	"	"	S. W.	0.64		Shower 3 and 5:40 P. M.
S 5	57	75	"	"	N. W.			Cloudy part of evening.
6	61½	78	"	"	N. W.			
7	62	79	"	"	N. W.			
8	60½	79	"	"	N. E.			Cloudy part of afternoon.
9	64	69½	Rain	Cloudy	N. E.	1.80		Rain 1:30 to 8:30 A. M.; cleared 6 P. M.
10	58	74	Clear	Clear	N.			
11	56	76	"	"	All points			
S 12	58½	77	"	Cloudy	S. W.			Clear part of afternoon.
13	64	68	Rain	Rain	S. E.			Commenced raining 4 A. M.
14	62½	69	"	Cloudy	E.	1.90		Rain till 11 A. M.; rain part of evening.
15	67	76	Cloudy	Clear	N. E.	0.51		Rain 9:30 to 11 A. M.; cleared 2:30 P. M.; heavy shower 7:20 P. M.
16	60	69	Clear	"	N.			Cloudy part of morning.
17	53	74½	"	"	N. W.			
18	54½	77	"	"	S. W.			
S 19	61	75	Cy m'st all day		S. W.			Shower 5 A.M., 12:15 P. M., and rainy after 5 P. M.
20	62½	72	Clear	Clear	N.	0.74		Rain before day.
21	55	74	"	"	S. W.	0.38		Showery after 7:45 P. M.
22	62½	77	"	"	S. W.			Cloudy part of morning.
23	61	65½	Cloudy	Rain	N. E.	0.82		Rain 10:15 A. M. to 3 P. M.; light rain 5 P. M.; clear part of evening.
24	52½	67	Clear	Clear	N. W.	0.03		
25	49½	68	"	"	S. W.			
S 26	51½	69	"	"	S. W.			
27	53	74½	"	"	S. W.			
28	63	73	Cy m'st all day		S. W., S. E.	0.07		Shower 1:30 P. M.
29	63	71½	"	"	N. E.	0.02		Rain before day.
30	63½	75½	Clear	Clear	N. W.			
31	65	78	"	Cloudy	S. W.	0.65		Showers 4:30 to 8:30 P. M.; heavy shower 5:15 P. M.; ½ inch fell.
						7.80		

From June 1st to Aug. 31st ther. was 80° and above on 32 days.

September, 1866.

	Date.	Thermometer. Lowest.	Thermometer. Highest.	Weather. Morning.	Weather. Afternoon.	Prevailing Wind.	Rain and Melted Snow in inches.	Snow in inches.	REMARKS.
	1	68	80	Cloudy	most all day.	S.	0.16	....	Shower. The heat has been the more oppressive the 1st, 2nd and 3rd than the hot days in July, the air being so damp.
S	2	70½	81½	"	Clear	S. W.	....	....	
	3	70½	82	Clear	"	E.	....	....	Clouded over 8:30 P. M.; rain 9:30.
	4	70½	77	Cloudy	most all day.	N. E.	0.36	....	Rain before day.
	5	69	78½	Clear	Clear	All points.	....	....	Cloudy part of morning.
	6	67	75	"	"	N.	....	....	Cloudy part of morning.
	7	62	74½	"	Cloudy	S. E.	....	....	Cloudy part of morning; light sprinkle during the afternoon and showery evening.
	8	67	75	"	Clear	W.	0.43	....	Rain before day.
S	9	57	70½	"	"	N. W.	....	....	Cloudy part of morning.
	10	53	70½	"	"	N. W., S. W.	....	....	
	11	59½	69½	"	Rainy	S.	0.16	....	Clouded over 9 A. M.; rain 10 A. M., and at intervals during afternoon.
	12	67	75½	"	Clear	S. W.	....	....	
	13	60½	73½	"	"	N. W.	....	....	
	14	57	76½	Cloudy	most all day.	S. W.	0.24	....	Shower 5 and 7:45 P. M.
	15	56	62½	Clear	Clear	N. W.	....	....	
S	16	45	62	"	"	N. E., S., E.	....	....	Frost.
	17	50½	73½	Cloudy	"	S. W.	....	....	Cleared 9 A. M.
	18	63	80	"	"	S. W.	....	....	Cleared 10 A. M.; cloudy P. M., showers after 10:15 P. M.
	19	65½	78	"	most all day.	S. E.	0.58	....	Shower before day, and from 4 to 10 P. M.
	20	61	68	"	Cloudy	E.	....	....	Misty evening; thunder shower 12 P. M.
	21	65½	82½	Clear	Rainy	S.	0.38	....	Rain 3:45 to 11 P. M.
	22	50	61½	"	Clear	N.	....	....	
S	23	47	62½	"	"	N. E.	....	....	
	24	49	62	"	Cloudy	N. E.	....	....	Cleared 8 P. M.
	25	48	67½	"	Clear	N. E., S. W.	....	....	Foggy morning; clouded over 10 P. M.; misty 11:45 P. M.
	26	60½	77	Shower	Rain	All points.	....	....	Showers all day, till 4:10 P. M. and then steady rain; 1.18 in. 9:30 to 10:10 A. M.
	27	52	67	Clear	Clear	N.	2.83	....	Rain before day.
	28	49	67	"	"	S. E.	....	....	
	29	50	65	Cloudy	Cloudy	N. E.	....	....	Clear part of morning; rain 9 P. M.
S	30	58	70	Rain	"	N. E.	0.33	....	Rain till 9 A. M.; clear part of afternoon.
							5.47		

Weather Record for New Brunswick, N. J.

October, 1866.

	Thermometer.		Weather.		Prevailing Wind.	Rain and Melted Snow in inches.	Snow in inches.	REMARKS.
Date.	Lowest.	Highest.	Morning.	Afternoon.				
1	60	70	Cloudy	Clear	N. E.			Clear part of morning.
2	53	72	Clear	"	N. E., S. W.			Cloudy part of afternoon.
3	59	66½	"	"	N. W.			Cloudy part of morning.
4	41	54½	"	"	N. W.			
5	37	52½	"	"	N. W.			
6	36	58½	"	"	S. W.			
S 7	42½	66½	"	"	S. W.			
8	53½	72½	"	"	W.			
9	57	63	Cloudy	Cloudy	N. E.			Clear part of morning; misty part of afternoon and evening.
10	53	59½	"	"	N. E.			
11	50½	58	"	"	N. E.	0.01		Light rain 7 A. M.; com. raining again 6 P. M.
12	49	57½	Rain	"	N. E.			Rain part of evening.
13	50	61½	Cloudy	Clear	N. E.	0.64		Rain part of morning.
S 14	48	56½	"	Cloudy	N. E.	0.06		Rain 7 A. M.; clear part of morning; rain 5 to 9 P.M.; cleared 11 P. M.
15	49½	62½	Clear	Clear	N. E.			
16	48½	65½	"	"	N. E.			
17	49½	72½	"	"	N. W.			
18	49½	63½	"	"	N. E., S. E.			
19	45½	66½	"	"	S. W.			
20	47	67	"	"	S. W.			Cloudy part of morning.
S 21	51½	71½	Foggy	"	S. W.			Cleared 10 A. M.
22	57½	71½	Cloudy	Cloudy	S. W.	0.07		Clear part of morning; rainy parts of afternoon and evening.
23	55	63½	Clear	Clear	N. W.			
24	43	51½	"	"	N. W.			
25	41	48	"	"	N. W.			
26	34½	50	"	Cloudy	N. E., S. E.			Clouded over 8 A. M.
27	40	54	"	Clear	N. W.			Light sprinkle 10 P. M.
S 28	40	57½	"	"	All points.			
29	43½	66½	Cloudy	Cloudy	S. E.			Commenced raining 10 P. M.
30	61	63½	Rain	"	S., N. W.	3.10		Rained till 10 A.M.; cleared 6 P.M.; 3.10 rain—12 hrs.
31	41½	51½	Clear	Clear	N. W.			Cloudy part of afternoon.
						3.88		

Weather Record for New Brunswick, N. J.

November, 1866.

Date.	Thermometer. Lowest	Thermometer. Highest	Weather. Morning.	Weather. Afternoon.	Prevailing Wind.	Rain and Melted Snow in inches.	Snow in inches.	REMARKS.
1	34	48	Clear	Clear	W.			
2	40½	53	"	"	S. W.			
3	41	54	"	Cloudy	S. W.	0.08		Rainy evening after 6 P. M.
S 4	39¼	48	"	Clear	N. E.			Cloudy evening.
5	31	40½	"	"	N. E.			
6	30½	50	"	"	N. W.			
7	31½	55	"	"	N. W.			
8	36½	59½	"	"	W.			
9	43½	58½	"	"	S. W.			Cloudy 9 A. M. to 3 P. M.
10	41	57½	"	"	S. W.			Clouded over 9 P. M.
S 11	45½	62½	Cloudy most all day.		S. E.	0.27		Rain 8 to 12 P. M.
12	45	53	"	Clear	N. W.			Cleared 9 A M.
13	38	50½	Clear	"	N. E.			
14	36½	50	Cloudy most all day.		N. E.			
15	46	62	"	Cloudy	S. E.	0.01		Light rain 7 A. M.; misty part of afternoon and evening; steady rain 8 P.M.
16	44½	48½	"	most all day.	W.	1.66		
17	39	49	Clear	Cloudy	N. W.			
S 18	42	51	"	"	S. W.			Cleared part of afternoon.
19	44	57	Cloudy most all day.		S.			
20	51	59½	"	Clear	S. W., N. W.	0.02		Light rain 7 A. M.; cleared 4 P. M.
21	41½	48	"	"	N. W.			Cleared 8 A. M.; cloudy part of evening.
22	37	42½	"	Cloudy	S., N. E.			Few snowflakes (first) 11:30 A. M.; light rain part of afternoon
23	37	42	"	"	N. W.	0.12		Rain before day; clear part of afternoon
24	30	37½	Clear	Clear	N. W.			Cloudy part of evening.
S 25	32½	35	"	"	N. W.			
26	24	43½	"	"	S. W.			
27	31	48½	"	"	S. W.			
28	39	63	Cloudy	Cloudy	S. W.			Light rain 3 P. M; clear part of afternoon and evening.
29	56½	67½	"	most all day.	S. W.	0.02		Light rain part of morning.
30	56½	59	Rain	Clear	S. W., W.	0.64		Rain till 8 A. M.; cleared 10 A. M.; cloudy part of afternoon and evening.
						2.82		

December, 1866.

Date.	Thermometer. Lowest.	Thermometer. Highest.	Weather. Morning.	Weather. Afternoon.	Prevailing Wind.	Rain and Melted Snow in inches.	Snow in inches.	REMARKS.
1	34½	41½	Clear	Clear	N. W.			
S 2	25	38½	"	"	N. W.			
3	27	45	"	"	S. W.			
4	35	55	Rain	Cloudy	S. E., S. W.	0.64		Rain 8:30 A. M. to 12:30 P. M.
5	38	53½	Clear	Clear	S. W.			
6	36	54	"	Cloudy	S. W.			Light rain during evening.
7	45	55	"	Clear	W.			Cloudy part of morning.
8	40½	59½	Rainy	most all day.	S. E.	0.27		Com. raining 8:30 A. M.; cleared 7 P. M.
S 9	41½	44	Clear	Clear	N. W.			
10	29½	30½	"	"	N. W.			
11	19½	26½	"	"	W.			
12	20	29	"	"	N. W.			
13	17½	25½	"	"	N. W.			
14	22	25½	"	"	N. W.			
15	15	32	"	"	N. W.			
S 16	22½	41	Snow	Rain	N. E.		6.00	Snow 7:30 A. M till 2:30 P. M., and then rain.
17	30½	33½	Cloudy	Clear	N. W.	0.95		Rain before day; snow squalls during morning.
18	29	35	Clear	"	N. W.			
19	30	39	"	"	S. W.			
20	20½	23	"	"	N.			
21	2	17½	"	"	N. E.			Cloudy evening.
22	14	39½	Cloudy	Cloudy	N. E.	0.08		Partly clear part of morning; misty evening.
S 23	32	53	"	Rainy	S. W.			Misty part of morning
24	37½	45	Rain	Rain	S. W.	0.50		Cleared 7 P. M.
25	31½	37	Clear	Clear	W.			Partly clouded over part of afternoon.
26	24	37½	"	"	S. W.			Clouded over 6 P. M.
27	31½	35	{Rain, Snow}	Snow	S. W., N. W.	0.24	1.00	Rain and snow till 11 A. M, and then snow till 5 P. M.; cleared 10 P. M.; ther. 35° at 10 A. M.
28	19	24	Clear	Clear	W.			
29	20	26½	"	"	W.			Cloudy part of evening.
S 30	17	25½	"	"	N. W.			
31	20	29	Snow	Snow	N. E.		2.00	
						2.68	9.00	

Rain and melted snow for 1866, 46.59

Weather Record for New Brunswick, N. J.

January, 1867.

Date	Thermometer Lowest	Thermometer Highest	Weather Morning	Weather Afternoon	Prevailing Wind	Rain and Melted Snow in inches	Snow in inches	REMARKS
1	26¼	32	Snow	Snow	N. E.		0.50	Light snow most all day.
2	22½	30	Cloudy	Cloudy	N. E.			Clear part of morning.
3	12	26	Clear	"	N. W., S. W.			Clouded over 3 P.M.; partly clear part of evening.
4	16	30	"	"	N. W.			
5	17	40½	"	Clear	S. E.			Clouded over 3 P.M.; partly clear part of evening.
S 6	30	37½	Cloudy most all day.		N. W.		0.50	Snow before day.
7	27	30	Clear	Clear	N. W.			
8	19½	26	"	"	N. W.			
9	18	30	"	"	N. W.			Cloudy part of afternoon and evening.
10	26	31	Cloudy	Cloudy	N. E.			Light snow part of morning.
11	20	30½	Clear	Clear	W.			
12	16	26	"	"	W., N. W.			
S 13	15½	25	Snow	Cloudy	N. E.	1.25		
14	18	25	Cloudy	"	N.			Clear part of afternoon and evening
15	11	20	"	Clear	N.			Cleared 3 P. M.
16	5	22½	Clear	Cloudy	N. W., S. W.			Clear part of afternoon and evening; com. snowing 11 P. M.
17	14½	24	Snow	"	N. W.	7.00		Snow till 10 A.M.; then high winds and drifted very much and railroad travel interrupted for two days and the town filled with strangers.
18	13½	17	Clear	Clear	N. W.			
19	8	18½	"	"	W.			
S 20	4	28	Cloudy	Snow	N. W., N. E.			Snow 3 P. M.; light till 3 P. M. and then violently and drifted; ther 28° 10 P. M., 27° 11 P. M.
21	24½	34½	Foggy	Cloudy	N. E., S. W.	9.50		Snowed till 3 A M, and then light rain and misty morning; clear part of afternoon.
22	26	30½	Cloudy most all day.		W.			
23	20½	30	Clear	Clear	N. W.			
24	27	35	"	"	N. W.			
25	13	29	"	Cloudy	All points.		0.50	Commenced snowing 11 P.M.
26	27½	36	Cloudy	Clear	W.			Snow till 1 A.M.; cleared 10 A. M.
S 27	24½	27	Clear	"	W.			
28	15	25	"	"	S. W.			
29	13	19½	"	"	W.			
30	5¼	17½	"	"	W.		0.50	Snow till 11 A. M
31	5	27	Snow	Cloudy	N. E.. N. W.			
						19.75		

February, 1867.

Date.	Thermometer. Lowest.	Thermometer. Highest.	Weather. Morning.	Weather. Afternoon.	Prevailing Wind.	Rain and Melted Snow in inches.	Snow in inches.	REMARKS.
1	26	43	Cloudy	Cloudy	S. W.	----	----	Clear part of morning and evening.
2	34	38½	"	Rain	N. E.	----	----	Misty part of A.M. and most of afternoon; heavy rain after 8 P.M. with lightning.
S 3	33½	43½	"	Cloudy	S. W.	0.95	----	
4	35	45	Clear	"	S. W.	0.05	----	Clouded over 3 P. M.; light rain part of afternoon and evening.
5	37	43	Cloudy	most all day.	S.W., W.	----	----	Cleared 9 A.M.; clouded over 2 P.M.; cleared again 10 P. M.
6	33½	44½	Clear	Clear	S. W.	----	----	Cloudy part of afternoon.
7	29	42	"	"	S. W.	----	----	
8	29	49½	Cloudy	Rain	N. E.	----	----	
9	42½	53	"	"	S. W.	0.70	----	Commenced raining 5 P. M.
S 10	22½	24	Clear	Clear	N. W.	1.36	----	Snow squall at noon.
11	16	32½	"	"	S. W.	----	----	
12	26	43	"	"	S. W.	----	----	
13	32	48	Cloudy	Cloudy	S. W.	0.05	----	Rain 9 P. M.
14	40	51	"	Rain	S. W.	----	----	Rain part of morning.
15	38½	48	"	Cloudy	N. E.	0.88	----	Clear part P.M. and evening.
16	35	41½	"	Rain	N. E.	0.14	----	Clear part of evening.
S 17	36½	50½	Clear	Clear	W.	----	----	
18	35	48	"	"	N. W., S. W.	----	----	
19	37	45½	"	Cloudy	N.	---	----	Clouded over 3 P. M.
20	27	30	Snow	Snow	N. E.	----	8.00	Snow 7 A. M. to 4 P. M.
21	26	34	"	"	N. E.	---	10.00	Snow (light) 7 A. M. to 1 P. M., then heavy till 6 P.M. and then light to 12.
22	28	37	Cloudy	Cloudy	N. W.	----	----	Clear part of morning; cleared 7 P. M.
23	16	32	Clear	"	N. W.	----	----	Snow part of afternoon (melts), and rain part of evening.
S 24	28½	47	Cloudy	"	N. W.	0.08	----	Light rain 8 A.M.; clear part of morning and evening; light rain afternoon.
25	30½	35½	"	"	N. E.	----	----	Clear part of morning; snow and hail 9 P. M.
26	30	41½	"	Clear	W., N. W.	----	----	Cleared 8 A. M.
27	26	40½	Clear	"	W.	----	----	
28	26	47	"	"	S. W.	----	----	
						4.21	18.00	

Weather Record for New Brunswick, N. J.

March, 1867.

Date	Thermometer Lowest	Thermometer Highest	Weather Morning	Weather Afternoon	Prevailing Wind	Rain and Melted Snow in inches	Snow in inches	REMARKS
1	40¼	47	Rain	Cloudy	S. E., N. E.	0.57		
2	36½	54¼	Cloudy	"	W.	0.03		Light rain part of A. M.
S 3	25	35	Clear	"	N. E.			Clouded over 2 P. M.; snow 7:30 P. M.
4	25	35½	Cloudy	"	N. E., S.W.		2.50	Rain part of afternoon.
5	30½	38½	"	most all day	N. E.	0.10		Snow before day; cleared 7:30 P. M.
6	30	35	"	Cloudy	N. E.			Rain and snow after 5 P. M.
7	32	36¼	Rain	"	N. E.	0.88		Clear part of evening.
8	31	41	Clear	Clear	N. E.			
9	29	44	Cloudy	Cloudy	N. E.			Clear part of morning; rain 10 P. M.
S 10	35	40	Rain	Rain	N. E.			
11	37	51½	Cloudy	Clear	N.	0.44		Cleared 10 A. M.; clouded over 10 P. M.
12	38	41½	Rain	Rain	E.	0.48		Rain till 9 P. M.
13	37	41	Cloudy	Cloudy	S. E.	0.02		Light rain part of P. M.
14	25	28	"	Clear	N. W.			Snow squall 7 A. M.
15	17½	31	Clear	"	N. W.			
16	27½	32	Cloudy	Snow	N. E.			Com. snowing 10:30 A. M.
S 17	25	34¼	Snow	Cloudy	N. E., N. W.		10.00	Snowed till noon; light snow part of afternoon; cleared 6 P. M.; first stormy St. Patrick's day since I have kept daily record—11 years.
18	17½	27	Clear	Clear	N. W., S. W.			
19	15½	34	"	"	S. W.			
20	20	38½	"	"	N. E.			Clouded over 5 P. M.
21	33	38	Snow	Snow/Rain	N. E.	0.55		Snow till noon, but melts as it falls; rain and snow part of afternoon.
22	34	38½	Cloudy	Cloudy	N. E.	0.05		Light snow part of morning, and from 2 to 5 P. M.
23	33½	44	"	"	N. E.			
S 24	33	40	"	"	N E.			Rained at intervals after 8 P. M.
25	36½	47½	"	"	N.	0.38		Rain before day; clear part of A. M.; cleared 6 P. M.
26	30	43	Clear	Clear	N.			
27	33	38½	Cloudy	Cloudy	S. E.	0.01		Light snow part of morning; misty evening.
28	34	38½	"	"	N. W.			Cleared 6 P. M.
29	30	42¼	Clear	Clear	N. W.			
30	35	53	"	"	N. W.			
S 31	40	62½	"	"	N. W.			
						3.51	12.50	

59¼ inches of snow during December, January, February and March.

April, 1867.

Date	Thermometer. Lowest.	Thermometer. Highest.	Weather. Morning.	Weather. Afternoon.	Prevailing Wind.	Rain and Melted Snow in inches.	Snow in inches.	REMARKS.
1	44½	54½	Cloudy	Clear	W.	0.12		Rain 6 to 10 A. M.
2	40	56	Clear	"	W.			
3	35½	56½	"	"	N. W.			
4	39½	68	"	"	S. W.			
5	54¼	62	Cloudy	"	S. W., N. W.	0.08		Shower part of morning.
6	39	51½	Clear	"	N. W.			
S 7	37	61½	"	"	S. W.			
8	41½	67½	"	"	S. W.			Cloudy part of evening.
9	43	62	"	"	S. E.			
10	41	54	Cloudy	Cloudy	E.			Clear part of morning; rainy evening.
11	46	56½	"	Clear	N. W.	0.21		Rain before day; cleared 7 A. M.
12	37	59	Clear	"	S. E.			
13	40	67	"	"	N. W.			
S 14	42	55	"	"	S. E.			
15	44	71½	"	"	S. W.			Hazy evening.
16	57½	60½	Rain	Rain	S. W.	1.09		Rain till 4 P. M.; cleared 7 P. M.
17	52	59	Cloudy	Clear	N.	0.13		Rain part of morning after 9 P. M.; cleared 4 P. M.
18	43½	58½	Clear	"	N. W.			
19	38½	62	"	"	N. W., S. W.			Hazy evening.
20	46	67	Cloudy most all day.		S. W.	0.15		Shower after 7 P. M.
S 21	52	63½	"	Clear	N. W.			Cleared 9:30 A. M.
22	51	77½	Clear	"	S. W.	0.12		Cloudy part of morning with showers 6 to 9 A. M.; cloudy part of afternoon with shower 5 P. M.
23	41½	57	"	"	N. W.			Pears and cherries flowered —22nd.
24	41	43	Cloudy	Cloudy	N. E.	0.05		Light rain greater part of afternoon.
25	40	59	Clear	Clear	N. W.			
26	40½	61	"	"	S. E.			
27	40½	57	"	"	S. W., N. W.	0.20		Clouded over 10 A. M.; rain 11:30 A. M. to 2 P. M.; cleared 2:30 P. M.
S 28	34	50½	"	"	All points.			
29	37	45	Cloudy	Cloudy	S. E., E.	0.07		Light rain part of morning and afternoon.
30	43½	55½	"	"	N. E.	0.09		Light rain part of morning and afternoon.
						2.16		

WEATHER RECORD FOR NEW BRUNSWICK, N. J.

May, 1867.

Date.	Thermometer. Lowest.	Thermometer. Highest.	Weather. Morning.	Weather. Afternoon.	Prevailing Wind.	Rain and Melted Snow in inches.	Snow in inches.	REMARKS.
1	52	65	Foggy	Cloudy	S. W., N. W.	0.25		Shower all day; clear for a time at 5 P. M.
2	42	60½	Clear	Clear	N. W.			Clouded over 7 P.M., and showers after 10 P. M.
3	38	51½	Cloudy	"	N. E.	0.06		Rain before day and snow 4 to 5 A.M.; cleared 10 A.M.
4	35	53	Clear	"	S. E.			Frost.
S 5	39½	56	Cloudy	"	S. E.			Cleared 3 P. M.
6	44	70	Clear	"	S. E.			Cloudy evening.
7	53	59	Cloudy	Cloudy	N. E.	0.08		Showers part A.M.; rain 8 P.M.
8	49	54	Rain	Rain	N. E.	2.58		Rain till 9 A.M.; light rain parts of afternoon and evening; bar.1 P. M. 29.00.
9	44	57	Clear	Clear	N. W.			Cloudy part of morning.
10	43½	62	"	"	W.			Cloudy parts of morning and afternoon.
11	47	65	"	"	W.	0.03		Cloudy part of afternoon with shower 3:40 to 7:10 P. M.
S 12	45½	65	"	"	N. W.			
13	43½	64	"	"	S. E.	0.01		Cl'dy part of afternoon with shower 1 P.M., and heavy thunder shower 10:45 P.M.
14	51	69	Cloudy	"	All points.	1.04		Rain till 2 A. M.; sprinkle 1:30 P. M.; cleared 3 P.M.
15	48	64	Clear	"	S. W.	0.02		Cl'dy part A.M.; sh'wer 5 P.M.
16	46	63½	"	"	N. W.			Clouded over 8 P. M.
17	50½	63	Cloudy	"	N. W.	0.16		Rain till 9:15 A.M.; clear part of morning; light shower after 6 P.M.
18	47	59½	Clear	"	N. W.			
S 19	43½	64	"	"	N W., S. W.			Clouded over 6 P. M.
20	51	55	Rain	Cloudy	N. E.	0.44		Rain till 10 A. M.
21	51	52	Cloudy	"	E.	0.17		Rain 10 A. M. to 3 P. M.
22	50	59½	Rain	"	N. E., N. W.	0.24		Rain till 8 A. M.; clear 3 to 4 P. M.; sprinkle 4:30 P. M.; cleared 9 P. M.
23	47	61½	Clear	Clear	S. W.			Cloudy part of evening.
24	46	64	"	"	S. W.			
25	46½	71	"	Cloudy	S. W.			Clouded over 2 P. M.; light sprinkle part of evening.
S 26	58	71	Cloudy	"	S.	0.80		Light rain before day; sprinkle during day; steady rain 7 to 10 P. M.
27	53	69½	Clear	Clear	S. W.			Clear part of afternoon.
28	57	73	Cloudy	Cloudy	S. W.			
29	62	82	Clear	Clear	S. W.	0.02		Shower 2:30 A. M.; cloudy part of morning.
30	62	73½	Cloudy	Cloudy	S. E., S. W.	0.03		Clear part of aft'noon; shower 7:30 P.M.; cleared 9 P.M.
31	54	68	Clear	Clear	N. W.			

6.45

June, 1867.

Date	Thermometer Lowest	Thermometer Highest	Weather Morning	Weather Afternoon	Prevailing Wind	Rain and Melted Snow in inches	Snow in inches	REMARKS
1	51	73	Clear	Clear	S. W.			
S 2	53½	72½	"	Cloudy	S.			Commenced raining 6:30 P. M.
3	63	76½	"	"	S. W.	1.33		Rain before day and light shower 4:30 to 7 P. M.; cleared 9 P. M.
4	60	77	"	Clear	W.			
5	59	79	"	"	S. W.			
6	62	82	"	"	S. W.			
7	64	77	"	Cloudy	S. W.			
8	63	66½	Cloudy	"	N. E.	0.08		Rain before day, and 9 A. M. and 2:30 P. M., and steady rain 7:30 P. M.
S 9	49	58	Rain	"	N. E.	2.50		
10	51¼	66	Clear	Clear	N. E.			
11	46	70	"	"	S. W.			
12	53	72½	"	Cloudy	S. W.	0.05		Rain 10:45 P. M.
13	64	81	"	Clear	S. W.			
14	62	75½	"	"	S. E.			
15	60	77	Cloudy	most all day	S. W.	0.40		Shower 5 P. M.
S 16	67¼	82½	Clear	Clear	S. W.			Clouded over 6 P.M.; shower 7:50 P. M. and steady rain 9:20 P. M.
17	68½	76	Rain	Cloudy	S.	1.76		Rain till 10 A. M.; shower 11:30 A. M.; rain 5 to 9 P. M.
18	68¼	79½	Cloudy	Rain	S.	0.14		Shower 12:30 and 1:45 P.M.; steady rain after 3 P. M.
19	62	72	"	Clear	N. E.	1.22		Cleared 8 A. M.
20	57¼	74½	Clear	"	S. E.			
21	57	73	"	"	N. E.			
22	54½	72	"	"	E.			
S 23	58	74	"	Cloudy	E.			Cloudy part of morning and after 5 P. M.
24	67½	74	Cloudy	"	E.	0.03		Light rain part of A.M.; clear part of P. M. and misty part of evening.
25	67	68½	Rain	Rain	E.			Com. raining 12 M. 25th and continued with little intermission till 8 A. M. of 26th; 3.79 inches falling in 32 hours.
26	60	63	"	Misty	N. E.	3.79		
27	61	71	Cloudy	Cloudy	N. E., S. W.	0.12		Rain before day; cleared 9 P. M.
28	67	82	Clear	Clear	N. W.			
29	65	78½	"	"	N. E., S. W.			
S 30	64½	83½	"	"	S. W.			
						11.42		

Rain for February, March, April, May and June.................... 27.75
Snow for January, February and March, 50.25 inches 5.00
Total rain for six months... 32.75

July, 1867.

Date.	Thermometer. Lowest.	Thermometer. Highest.	Weather. Morning.	Weather. Afternoon.	Prevailing Wind.	Rain and Melted Snow in inches.	Snow in inches.	REMARKS.
1	70½	83½	Clear	Clear	N. W.	----	----	
2	67	80	"	"	N. E.	----	----	
3	65½	85½	"	"	S. W.	----	----	
4	70½	88	"	"	S. W.	----	----	Clouded over 9 P. M; light sprinkle 11 P. M.
5	72½	83	"	Rain	E.	1.51	----	Cloudy part of morning; shower 1:20 to 2:40 P. M.; 1.24 in. show'r 4 P.M., light steady rain after 10 P. M.
6	66½	79	Cloudy	Cloudy	N. E., S. E.	0.05	----	Clear part of afternoon; light rain 5:15 to 6:45 P. M.; cleared 10 P. M.
S 7	68	83½	Clear	Clear	N. W., W.	----	----	
8	68½	75½	Cloudy	most all day.	All points	----	----	
9	65	76	Clear	Clear	N.W.,E.,N.W	0.50	----	Shower 4 P. M.
10	58	74½	"	"	N. W.	----	----	
11	63½	80	"	"	S. W.	----	----	
12	68	77½	Cloudy	Cloudy	S. W.	----	----	Clear part A. M.; light rain 10 A. M., and 5:35 P. M.; steady 7:30 P. M.
13	62	73	"	Clear	N. E.	0.62	----	Rain before day; clear 9 A.M.
S 14	58	73½	Clear	"	N. E.	----	----	
15	56	74½	"	"	N. W., S. W.	----	----	Hazy evening.
16	59½	66½	Cloudy	Cloudy	All points	0.25	----	Shower all day; cleared 9 P.M.
17	57	76½	Clear	Clear	N. W.	----	----	
18	60	73	"	Cloudy	N. E., S. E., E	0.18	----	Showers 3:15, 4:00, 7:30 P. M.
19	58	69	Cloudy	Clear	N. E.	0.03	----	Clear part of A. M.; light shower at noon and 4 P. M.
20	58½	70	"	most all day.	N. E.	0.30	----	Shower 9, 11 A. M.; 1:35, 3:40, 4:45, 8 P. M. Last 3 days April showers, wind N. E.
S 21	60	75	"	Clear	N.	0.16	----	Partly clear part of A. M.; showers 2:10, 8:00 and 10 P. M.; cleared 11 P. M.
22	61	75	"	"	N. W., S. W.	0.01	----	Clear part of A. M.; shower 2:10 P. M; 15 showers in 5 days, with 0.68 rain.
23	63½	81	Clear	"	N., N. E.	----	----	
24	63	84½	"	"	S. W.	----	----	
25	69	85	"	Cloudy	S. W., N. W.	----	----	Clouded over 10 P. M.
26	69	77½	Cloudy	"	S. W.	1.08	----	Violent thunder storm 2 A. M.; light shower 7:30 A. M.; clear part of P. M.
27	71	74	"	"	E.	0.15	----	Rain before day.
S 28	70½	85½	"	Clear	E., S. W.	0.10	----	Cleared 11 A. M.; showers 7 to 8 P. M.
29	71	77½	Rain	"	S. W.	0.56	----	Light shower before day; rain 8 to 11:30 A. M.; cleared 4:30 P. M.
30	61½	75	Clear	"	N. E.	----	----	Brilliant Northern lights 12:30 A. M.
31	60	74	"	"	N. E., S. E.	----	----	
						5.50		

August, 1867.

Date	Thermometer Lowest	Thermometer Highest	Weather Morning	Weather Afternoon	Prevailing Wind	Rain and Melted Snow in inches	Snow in inches	REMARKS
1	60	74	Clear	Cloudy	N. E., S. E.			Com. raining 6:15 P. M.
2	69	76	Cloudy	"	N. E., N. W.	0.90		Rain before day; light rain 9 A.M.; clear part of P. M.
3	66½	70	Rain	Rain	All points	0.62		Rain till 5 P.M.; clear 6 P.M.
S 4	60	75	Clear	Clear	E.			Cloudy part of morning.
5	65½	79½	"	"	S. E.			
6	68½	79	Cloudy	Cloudy	S. E.	0.05		Light rain till 9 A.M.; clear part of A. M. and P. M.; heavy showers after 9 P.M.
7	70	78	"	Clear	S. E.	0.74		Shower before day and 7:45 A.M.; cl'dy part evening.
8	68	75	"	Cloudy	S. E.	0.13		Shower 11 A.M. and during P.M; clear part afternoon.
9	68	78½	"	Clear	S. E.	0.09		Rain 2 A.M., 1 P.M., 4:40 P.M.
10	69	82	Clear	Cloudy	S. W.	0.47		Clouded over 4 P. M., with stormy gale from N. W. 4:25 hard rain for 15 minutes and light rain to 7 P.M.
S 11	67½	77½	"	Clear	N. E.			
12	62	78½	"	"	S. W.			
13	63	80	"	"	S. W.			Cloudy part of A. M. & P. M.
14	71	82	Cloudy most all day.		S. W			Sprinkle night and 4:30 P.M.
15	71½	75½	Rain	Rain	N. E.	0.37		No rain 9 to 11 A. M.
16	69	76½	"	Cloudy	S. E.	2.75		Rain till 8 A. M., and light sprinkle during A.M. and P.M; sun out part of P. M.
17	67¼	78	"	Clear	S. W., N. W.	0.11		Light rain till 10 A. M. and shower 11:15 A. M.
S 18	65½	83½	Clear	"	S. W.			
19	68½	83	"	"	S. W.	0.07		Shower 4 A. M.
20	69	77	"	"	N. E.	0.05		Shower 8:35 A. M., cloudy P. M.
21	68	77½	"	"	N. E., S. W.			Cloudy part of morning.
22	66	69	Rain	Rain	N. E.	2.14		Steady rain till noon; heavy shower 4 P. M., and light rain at intervals till 11 P. M.
23	63	71½	Cloudy	Cloudy	N. E., N. W.			Clear part of afternoon.
24	65	80	"	Clear	S. W.			Cleared 10 A.M.; cloudy parts of afternoon and evening.
S 25	63½	75½	Clear	"	N.			
26	58	76½	"	"	N. E., S. E.			
27	60	76	"	"	E.			
28	67	80	Foggy	"	S. E., S. W.			Cleared 9 A.M.; cloudy evening with light sprinkle.
29	69	74½	Cloudy	Cloudy	S. W.	0.71		Light rain 7:45 A.M, and 1:30 P.M., and heavy shower, 2:30 P.M.; cleared 7 P. M.
30	60	68	Clear	Clear	N. W.			Bridget Dergan, aged 22, hung at 10:18 A.M. for murdering Mrs. Coriell New Market.
31	50	69	"	"	N. W., S.			
						9.20		

From March 1 to August 31 it has rained in measurable quantities on 91 days—39.49 inches. Rain for 3 Summer months, 26.12 inches.

WEATHER RECORD FOR NEW BRUNSWICK, N. J.

September, 1867.

Date.	Thermometer. Lowest.	Thermometer. Highest.	Weather. Morning.	Weather. Afternoon.	Prevailing Wind.	Rain and Melted Snow in inches.	Snow in inches.	REMARKS.
S 1	57½	73½	Cloudy	Clear	N. E., N. W.	----	----	Cloudy part of evening.
2	62	71	"	most all day.	E.	----	----	
3	64½	75½	Clear	Clear	S. E.	----	----	Cloudy part of morning and cloudy evening.
4	68	79½	Cloudy	"	S. E., S. W.	----	----	Cleared 9 A.M.; cloudy part of evening.
5	71	79	"	Cloudy	E., S. E.	0.08	----	Cleared 10 A. M.; thunder storm from E. passed to S. W. with little rain 2:10 P. M.
6	70½	79	"	Clear	S.	0.04	----	Light shower during morning; cleared 10 A.M.
7	67½	75	"	most all day.	N. E.	----	----	
S 8	64	71½	Clear	Clear	N. E.	----	----	Cloudy part of morning and afternoon.
9	62	67	Cloudy	Cloudy	N. E.	----	----	Light sprinkle 11:45 A.M. and 1:30 P. M.
10	64½	72	"	"	S. W., N. W.	----	----	Cleared 9:30 P. M.
11	52	65½	Clear	Clear	N. E.	----	----	
12	49	70	"	"	S. W.	----	----	
13	57	76	Cloudy	"	S. W.	----	----	Clouded 7 A. M. till noon. Aurora 8 P. M.
14	63	67½	Clear	"	N. E.	----	----	
S 15	51	66	"	"	N. E., S. E.	----	----	
16	54	69	Cloudy	most all day.	S. W.	----	----	
17	64½	80½	Clear	Clear	All points.	----	----	Sprinkle before day; partly clear part of afternoon.
18	69	78	Cloudy	"	S. W.	----	----	
19	68½	81	Clear	"	N. E., S. E.	----	----	Cloudy part of morning; clouded over 5 P. M.
20	67	74	Cloudy	Cloudy	S. W.	----	----	Clear part of evening; shower 10:30 P. M.
21	65	69	"	Clear	N. E.	0.22	----	Showers before day; clear part of morning; cleared 4 P. M.
S 22	53½	70	Clear	"	N.E., N.W. S. W.	----	----	
23	57	65	"	"	N. E.	----	----	Cloudy part of morning.
24	43½	67	"	"	N. E., S. W.	----	----	
25	48	72	"	"	S. W., N. W.	0.10	----	Shower 3:30 P. M. Aurora 10 P. M.
26	50	64	"	"	N. W.	----	----	
27	43½	64	"	"	N. W., S. W.	----	----	
28	46	70	"	"	S. W.	----	----	
S 29	54½	71	Cloudy	"	S. W.	----	----	Light rain before day; cleared 10 A. M.
30	46½	56	"	"	N. W.	----	----	Cleared 9 A. M.
						0.44	----	

Weather Record for New Brunswick, N. J.

October, 1867.

Date	Thermometer. Lowest.	Thermometer. Highest.	Weather. Morning.	Weather. Afternoon.	Prevailing Wind.	Rain and Melted Snow in inches.	Snow in inches.	REMARKS.
1	38½	62½	Clear	Clear	N. W., S. W.			
2	46	73	"	"	S. W.			Cloudy evening.
3	60½	66	"	"	N.			Clouded over 6 p. m.; rain 9:15 p. m.
4	49½	57	Cloudy	Cloudy	N. E.	0.26		Rain before day and parts of morning; commenced again 9 p. m.
5	53	68½	Rain	Rain	S. E., S. W.	1.44		Rain till 4:30 p. m.
S 6	46½	56½	Clear	Clear	N.			
7	40	57	"	"	N.			
8	36	57	"	"	S. W.			
9	41	64	"	Cloudy	S. W.			
10	55	67½	"	Clear	S. W.	0.03		Rain before day; cloudy part of morning; foggy evening.
11	56	65	Cloudy	most all day.	N. E.	0.39		Violent rain from east with lightning and hail 6:15 to 6:45 p. m.
12	52	60	"	" "	"	N. E.	0.08		Rain before day, 2:20 and 8 p. m.
S 13	46½	56½	Clear	Clear	N. W.			
14	46	62½	"	"	N. W.			
15	45	65	"	"	S. W.			
16	46	62½	"	"	N. W.			
17	45	68	"	"	S. W.			
18	53	73½	"	"	S. W.			
19	54	75	"	"	S. W.			
S 20	60	70½	"	"	E.			Hazy morning.
21	57½	62	Cloudy	Cloudy	E.			
22	58	67½	"	Clear	E., S. W.	0.16		Light sprinkle 8 and 9 a. m., and rainy evening after 6:45 p. m.
23	45	54½	Clear	"	N.			
24	37½	52½	"	"	N. E.			
25	35	55	"	"	N. W., S. W.			
26	36	57½	"	"	S. W.			
S 27	38	59	"	"	S. W.			
28	41	57½	Cloudy	Cloudy	E.			Com. raining 9:45 p. m.
29	52	62	Rain	"	N. E.	2.21		Rain till noon; clear part of afternoon.
30	49	57	Cloudy	"	N. E., W.	0.03		Rain before day.
31	51	57	"	"	N. W., N. E.			Clear part of afternoon.
						4.60		

November, 1867.

Date	Thermometer Lowest	Thermometer Highest	Weather Morning	Weather Afternoon	Prevailing Wind	Rain and Melted Snow in inches	Snow in inches	REMARKS
1	42	57½	Clear	Clear	N. W., S. W.			
2	46	66	"	"	S. W.			Cloudy part of evening.
S 3	45	60	"	Cloudy	S. E.	0.02		Clouded over 3 P. M.; light rain during evening after 7 P. M.
4	54	62	Cloudy	"	S. W., N. W.	0.01		Clear part of morning, light rain 2:15 P. M., cleared 7 P. M.
5	37	48	Clear	Clear	N. W.			
6	35½	49	"	"	N. W.			
7	32	48	Cloudy	Cloudy	N. E., S. E.			Clear part of morning.
8	40½	60	Clear	Clear	S. W.			
9	48	69	"	Cloudy	S. W.			Clear part of afternoon; rainy after 7 P. M.
S 10	59	65	Rain	Rain	S. W.			Rain till 7:45 A. M.; partly clear part of morning; com. raining 3 P. M.
11	49	61¼	Cloudy	Clear	S. W.	1.13		Cloudy and foggy morning; cloudy evening.
12	37	42	Rain	Cloudy	N. W.	0.25		Snow part of morning.
13	33½	40	Clear	Clear	N. W.			Cloudy part of afternoon.
14	31½	52	"	Cloudy	S. W.			Clouded over 2:30 P. M.; cleared 10 P. M.
15	34	41½	"	"	N. W.			
16	33½	51½	Cloudy	Clear	S. W., N. W.			
S 17	32½	44	Clear	Cloudy	S. W.	0.01		Cloudy part of morning; light rain 9:30 P. M.
18	26	31½	"	Clear	N. W.			
19	20	34	"	"	N. W.			Clouded over 10 P. M.
20	23½	45	"	"	S. W.			
21	33	48	"	"	All points			
22	33½	47	Cloudy	Cloudy	N. E.			
23	44	50½	Rain	"	N. E.	0.23		
S 24	46½	53	Cloudy	"	N. E.			
25	41¼	50½	Foggy	"	S. E.	0.02		Light rain 10 P. M.
26	49	59	Cloudy	Clear	S. W., N. W.			
27	38	50	Clear	"	N., S. W.			
28	43	47	Cloudy	Cloudy	N. E.	0.01		Light rain 11 A. M.
29	42	62¼	"	Rain	N. E., S. E.	0.38		Rain most of afternoon and evening till 11 P. M.
30	32	35	Clear	Clear	N. W.			Light snow squall 9:30 A.M.
						2.06		

WEATHER RECORD FOR NEW BRUNSWICK, N. J.

December, 1867.

Date	Thermometer Lowest	Thermometer Highest	Weather Morning	Weather Afternoon	Prevailing Wind	Rain and Melted Snow in inches	Snow in inches	REMARKS
S 1	18	26½	Clear	Clear	N. W., S. W.			Clouded over 10 P. M.
2	24	32½	Cloudy	"	S. W.			Snow 1 to 2 P. M.; cleared 4 P. M.
3	29	38	"	most all day	S. W.			
4	31	33	Clear	Cloudy	N.			
5	23	32½	"	"	N. W., S. W.			Snow squalls 8:30 A. M.
6	24½	46½	Cloudy	Rain	S. W.	0.10		Clear part of morning; rain 3:15 to 7 P. M.
7	36½	38	Clear	Clear	N. W.			Cloudy 1 to 3 P.M. with snow squalls.
S 8	20	26	"	"	N. W.			
9	20	24½	"	"	N. W.			Clouded over 7 P. M.
10	22½	37	Snow	"	S. W.		1.00	Snow till 9 A.M.; cleared 10:30 A. M.
11	27½	31	Cloudy	Cloudy	N. W.			
12	6½	16	Snow	Snow	N. E.			Ther. 16° 8 A.M.; 6° 2 P.M.; 8° 6 P. M high winds and snow drifted very much.
13	6	15	Cloudy	Clear	N. E.		10.00	Cleared 1:30 P. M.
14	4	18	"	Cloudy	N. E.		1.50	Ther. 16° 4 P.M.; 18° 3 P.M.; 20° 11 P.M.; light snow parts P.M. and evening.
S 15	16½	28	"	"	N. E.			Cleared 8 P.M.
16	17	30½	Clear	Clear	N. W.			Cloudy part of afternoon.
17	20½	33½	Cloudy	Cloudy	S. W.			Clear part of morning and part of evening.
18	27	32	"	Clear	N. W.			Cleared 9 A. M.
19	12	21½	Clear	"	N. W., S. W.			
20	10	28½	Snow	Cloudy	N. E., N. W.		1.50	Snow 7 A. M. till noon.
21	19	36	Clear	"	S. W., N. E.			Clouded over 2 P. M.; hail and rain 11 P. M.
S 22	33½	40½	Foggy	"	S. W.	0.27		Rain before day, 11:45 A. M. and 3 P. M.
23	37½	40	Clear	Clear	N. W.			Snow squall 11 A. M.
24	25	34	"	Cloudy	S. W.			Clouded over 8 A.M.; cleared 10:30 P. M.
25	26	48	"	"	All points			Clouded over 3 P. M.; rain 7 P. M.
26	36½	48	Cloudy	Clear	W.	0.22		Rain before day; cleared 8 A.M; cloudy part P. M.
27	34	48½	Clear	Cloudy	S.			Foggy evening.
28	43	47	Rain	Clear	N. W.	0.10		Rain till 8 A.M.; partly clear rest A.M.; cloudy even'g.
S 29	33	39½	Clear	"	N. W.			Cloudy evening.
30	26	29½	Cloudy	Cloudy	N. W.			Clear of part A.M.; cleared 7 P. M.
31	17½	27	"	"	N. E.			Com. snowing 7:30 P. M.
						0.69	13.00	

Rain and melted snow for 1867—56.56.

January, 1868.

Date.	Thermometer.		Weather.		Prevailing Wind.	Rain and Melted Snow in inches.	Snow in inches.	REMARKS.
	Lowest.	Highest.	Morning.	Afternoon.				
1	25	36½	Rain	Cloudy	N. E.	1.02		Snow till 12:30 A.M. then rain; clear part of even'g; 8 A.M. 4 in. snow on the ground.
2	34½	40½	Clear	Clear	S. W.			Clouded 5; rain 7:15 P. M.
3	32	40	Foggy	"	W.			Cleared 11 A.M.; cloudy P.M.
4	35	42	"	Cloudy	All points.	0.13		Rain before day; clear parts of afternoon and evening.
S 5	26½	31	Clear	Clear	N. W.			Cleared 7:30 A. M.
6	19½	31½	"	"	S. W.			Hazy evening.
7	26½	34½	"	Cloudy	All points.			Clouded over 8 A.M.; light sprinkle, noon; rain 10 P.M.
8	32	35½	Cloudy	"	N.	0.33		Rain before day; light snow 7:30 P. M.
9	31	32½	Clear	Clear	W.			Ther. 7:30 A.M. 31°; 10 A M.
10	7	18½	"	"	W.			32°; 12:30 P. M. violent
11	16	29½	"	"	S. W.			snow squall 25°; 3 P. M.
S 12	13½	20½	"	"	S. W., N. W.			20°; 10 P. M. 10°.
13	12½	21½	"	"	N. W.			
14	13	23	Cloudy	Cloudy	W.			Snow 5:15-11 P.M. about 1 in
15	20	29½	"	Clear	N. E., S. W.	2.00		Snow 7 to 8 A. M., 1 inch; cleared 2 P. M.
16	19	32	Foggy	"	S. W.			Cleared 9 A. M.
17	10½	22½	Cloudy	"	N. W.			Cleared 8 A. M.
18	13	24	Clear	"	W., S.W.			Clouded over 4 P. M.
S 19	13	25½	"	"	N. W., S. W.			
20	17	33	Cloudy	Cloudy	S. W., N. E.			Light snow 9:45 A.M. to 1 P. M.; rain part of evening.
21	32	34½	Rain	Snow	N. E.	0.72		Rain and snow (melts) till 2 P.M; light snow till 4 P. M.; cleared 7 P. M.
22	23	33½	Clear	Clear	N. W., S. W.			
23	20	45	Rain	Rain	S. E., S. W.	0.45		Rain 8:30 A.M. to 6 P.M.
24	35	39	Clear	Clear	N. W.			
25	20	27½	"	"	N. W.			
S 26	21	39	Cloudy	Cloudy	All points.			Partly clear part of P. M.
27	29	32	Snow	Snow	N. E.	0.20		Snow till 6 P. M. (2 in.), but so moderately that I collected it all in rain gauge.
28	19	25½	Cloudy	"	N. E.			Partly clear part of A.M.; snow 10 A M. to 5 P. M. (½ inch) in rain gauge.
29	23	33½	Snow	Rain	N. E.	0.38		Snow before day; 7:30 A. M to noon (2½ inches); rain to 5:30 P.M. (in rain gauge); heavy snow all night.
30	17	21	Clear	Clear	N. W.		4.50	Cleared 8 A M.
31	10½	23½	"	"	S. W.			
						3.23	6.50	

Weather Record for New Brunswick, N. J.

February, 1868.

Date	Thermometer Lowest	Thermometer Highest	Weather Morning	Weather Afternoon	Prevailing Wind	Rain and Melted Snow in inches	Snow in inches	REMARKS
1	2	25	Clear	Clear	S. W.			
S 2	3	26½	"	"	S. W.			Cloudy 2 to 7 P. M.
3	5	13½	"	"	N. W.			Coldest 9 to 10 A. M.
4	–1½	24	Cloudy	"	S. W.			Cleared 10 A. M.
5	3	30	"	Snow	N. E.	4.50		Partly clear part of morning; snow 1 to 10:30 P.M.
6	27	36	"	Clear	W.	0.04		Misty, partly clear part of morning; light snow 11 A. M. to noon, melts.
7	12	21	Clear	"	N. W.			
8	–1	18	"	"	W., S. W.			
S 9	12½	37	Snow	Rain	S. W.	0.43	3.00	Snow till 8:30 A. M., and then rain at intervals till 10 P. M.
10	14½	20½	Clear	Clear	N. W.			Clouded over 8:30 P. M.
11	9	19½	Cloudy	"	N. E., N. W.			Cleared 10 A. M.
12	–5	28½	Clear	"	N. W., S. W.			
13	19	37½	"	"	S. W.			Cloudy part of evening.
14	17	23	"	"	N. E., S. W.			Fine sleighing for last 16 days.
15	15	38½	Cloudy	"	S. W.			Cleared 8 A. M.; clouded over 6 P. M.
S 16	28½	34½	Clear	"	N. W., S. W.			Cloudy 7:30 A. M. to 3 P. M.
17	17	36	Cloudy	Snow	S. E., S. W.	0.16		Light snow at intervals all day, from 11 A. M. to 10 P. M., but melts.
18	21	27	Clear	Clear	N. W.			
19	20	41¼	Cloudy	"	S. W.	0.01		Snow squall 8:30 A. M.; cleared 9:30 A. M.
20	23	45¼	Clear	"	W.			Cloudy evening.
21	35	45	Cloudy	Cloudy	N. W.			Hazy about noon with sun partly out.
22	12	20½	"	Clear	N. E.			Cleared 9 A. M.
S 23	3	19	Clear	Cloudy	N. W., N. E.			Clouded 4 P. M.
24	10½	19	Cloudy	Snow	N. E.		4.50	Light snow 9 A. M to noon, and heavy 2:30 to 10 P. M.
25	17½	27	"	"	N. E.		2.00	Snow 2:30 to 5 P. M., and 8:30 to midnight.
26	22½	30	"	Cloudy	N. E.			
27	27½	31	Snow	Snow	N. E.	0.16		Snow 6 A. M. to 6 P. M., but melts.
28	27½	32½	Clear	Clear	W.			Cloudy parts of afternoon and evening.
29	19	25	"	"	N. W.			
						0.80	14.00	

March, 1868.

Date.	Thermometer. Lowest.	Thermometer. Highest.	Weather. Morning.	Weather. Afternoon.	Prevailing Wind.	Rain and Melted Snow in inches.	Snow in inches.	REMARKS.
S 1	10	27½	Clear	Snow	S. W., N. E.			Clouded 10 A M.; snow 12:15 P.M. Rev. S. B. How, D.D, died 2:30 A. M.
2	20½	24	Snow	"	N. E.		6.00	Snow till 9 A.M. and drifted very much again 2:30 to 5 P.M.; clear 5 to 6 P. M.
3	3½	11	Clear	Clear	N.W.			Very high wind; coldest day of the winter; snow squall 9 P. M.
4	2½	24	"	"	N. W., S. W.			
5	12	31	"	"	N. W., S. W.			
6	12	39	Cloudy	Cloudy	N. E., S. W.			
7	34½	38	"	Clear	S. W.			Clear 10 A.M. to 9 P. M., but hazy part of the time.
S 8	37½	50½	"	"	S. W.			Light sprinkle 9 to 10 A. M.
9	33	47	Clear	"	W.			Clouded over 6 P. M.
10	39	52	Cloudy	"	W.			Cleared 9 A.M ;cloudy ev'ng.
11	41	49	Clear	"	N. E.			Cloudy part of afternoon.
12	33	41	Cloudy	Rain	E.			Clear part of morning; com. raining 2:45 P. M.
13	35½	46	"	Cloudy	S. W.	0.29		Rain before day; foggy evening.
14	36	50½	Clear	"	S. W.			Clear part of evening.
S 15	44	61	Cloudy	Clear	S. W.			
16	38	48	"	Cloudy	N. E.	0.04		Light rain 3 to 4 P. M.
17	42½	74	"	"	All points			Clear 11 A.M. to 3 P.M.; com. raining 6:15 P. M.
18	51	56	"	Clear	N. W.	0.42		Cleared 10 A M.
19	31	48	Clear	"	N. E., S. E.			
20	32	42½	Cloudy	Cloudy	S. E.			Com. snowing 7:30 P. M.
21	27½	35	Snow	Snow	N.	0.07	6.00	Snow till 11 A. M. and drifted very much and again from 1 to 5 P.M ,but melts.
S 22	24	37	Clear	Clear	N. W.			
23	26	48½	"	"	S. W.			Cloudy evening.
24	38½	54½	"	"	N. E.			
25	31½	42	Cloudy	Cloudy	E.			Partly clear part of A. M.
26	34	46½	Clear	Clear	E.			
27	33½	46	Cloudy	most all day.	S. W.	0.03		Light rain afternoon and evening after 3 P. M.
28	40	52	"	Cloudy	S. W.			Cleared 9 P. M.
S 29	36	53	Clear	Clear	N. E., S. E.			
30	32	44	Cloudy	Cloudy	N. E.			
31	37	60	Clear	Clear	N. E.			Cloudy part of morning.
						0.85	12.00	

WEATHER RECORD FOR NEW BRUNSWICK, N. J.

April, 1868.

Date.	Thermometer. Lowest.	Thermometer. Highest.	Weather. Morning.	Weather. Afternoon.	Prevailing Wind.	Rain and Melted Snow in inches.	Snow in inches.	REMARKS.
1	38	67	Clear	Clear	N. W., S. W.			Cloudy evening
2	50	62½	Cloudy	Cloudy	S. W., N. W.	0.14		Shower 1½ P.M ; cleared 4 PM.
3	33½	49½	Clear	Clear	S. W.			
4	33	50	"	"	N. W.			Clouded over 6 P.M ; rain 9:30 and snow 11 P M.
S 5	27	34	"	"	N. W.	0.35		About 1 inch of snow on the ground ; snow squall during afternoon.
6	25½	42	"	"	N. W.			Cloudy evening
7	36	42	Rain	Rain	N. E.	1.25		Rain till 6:30 P M.; light sprinkle 9 A. M
8	33½	49	Clear	Clear	N. W.			Cloudy part of afternoon.
9	25	38	"	"	N. W.			Clouded over 6 P M.
10	32	38	Snow	Rain	S. E., N. E.	0.45	3.00	Snow till 9 A. M., and rain and snow till noon, and then rain till 6 P. M.
11	30	47	Clear	Clear	N. W., S. W.			Cloudy part of afternoon.
S 12	40	53	"	Snow	N., N. E.		4.50	Clouded over at noon; snow 3 to 6½ P M. and 8½ to 11 P.M.
13	22	41	"	Clear	N., S. W.			
14	29	48½	"	Cloudy	S. W.	0.12		Light rain 4:30 and during evening.
15	40	68½	Cloudy	"	S. W.			Clear parts of afternoon and evening.
16	54	64½	Rain	Rain	S. W.	0.58		Thunder shower 6 A. M.; showery 9 A M to 4 P.M.
17	60	63	Cloudy	Cloudy	N. W., S. W.	0.01		Clear part of morning; cleared 4½ P.M.; shower 8½ P.M.
18	46	51	Clear	Clear	N. W.			
S 19	36	57	"	Cloudy	S. W.			Clouded 10 A. M.
20	42	48	Rain	Misty	N. E.	0.30		Rain till 10 A M. and misty all rest of day.
21	46	54	Cloudy	Rain	S. E.	0.11		Cleared 8:30 P.M.; rain noon to 6 P. M.
22	40½	67	Clear	Clear	S. W.			
23	49	70½	"	"	S. W., N. W.	0.06		Ther. 70° 3:30 P.M., when wind came from N.W. and cloudy; shower 5:50 to 7:30 P. M.; 9 P M. 44°; clear evening.
24	34½	50	"	"	N., S. E.			A change of 36°; clouded over P. M. with a little hail 8 P M.
25	40	42	Rain	Rain	N. E.	0.75		Rain till 3 P.M.; light rain 6 P M.
S 26	36½	60	Clear	Clear	N. W.			
27	39	67	"	"	S. W.			
28	43½	56	Cloudy	"	N. E.			
29	43	51	"	Rain	N. E.	0.12		Rain after 1:30 P M.; during intervals P. M. & evening.
30	43½	67½	"	Clear	S. W.			

4.24 7.50

May, 1868.

Date.	Thermometer. Lowest	Thermometer. Highest	Weather. Morning.	Weather. Afternoon.	Prevailing Wind.	Rain and Melted Snow in inches.	Snow in inches.	REMARKS.
1	52	62	Clear	Clear	N.			Pears and cherries flowered.
2	46	52½	Cloudy	Rain	N. E.			Com. raining 8:30 A. M.
S 3	42½	59	"	Cloudy	N. E., S. W.	0.42		Clear part of morning; cleared 5 P. M.
4	42	63½	Foggy	Clear	S. W.	0.01		Cleared 9 A. M.; cloudy P. M.; shower 10:30 P. M.
5	50	62	Cloudy	Cloudy	S. W., S. E.			Clear part of morning; rainy after 4 P. M.
6	51	59	"	"	E., S. W.	0.20		Rain before day.
7	49	52	Misty	Rain	N. E.			Light rain afternoon and evening till 8 P. M; heavy rain with thunder and lightning rest of evening.
8	40	52	Cloudy	Clear	N. W.	0.90		Rain before day; cleared 10 A. M. with heavy flying clouds all day.
9	41	62½	Clear	"	N. W.			Cloudy evening.
S 10	50	65	"	"	N. W.			
11	43½	59	"	"	N. E.			
12	46	58	Cloudy	"	S. E.			Clear part of A. M.; cloudy part of evening.
13	49	59	Rain	Rain	N. E., S. E.	2.22		Rain 8:10 A. M. to 7 P. M.; rain at intervals till 11 P. M.
14	59	71½	Cloudy	Clear	S. W.			Clear 10 A. M.
15	52	59	"	Cloudy	N. E., S. E.			Light sprinkle during day.
16	52	60½	"	"	E.			
S 17	53	55	"	Rain	E.			
18	52½	62	Rain	Clear	N. W.	1.84		Rain till 7 A. M.; clear part of morning; shower part of P. M.; cloudy evening.
19	51	60	Cloudy	Cloudy	N. E.			
20	51	56½	"	Rain	N. E.			Com. raining 4 P. M.
21	51	62	Rain	Clear	N. W.	1.10		Rain till 10 A. M.; cloudy part of evening.
22	53	70	Clear	"	S. W.			
23	55½	60½	Cloudy	Rain	N. E.			Rain before day, and part of morning.
S 24	52	60	Misty	Cloudy	N. E., S. W.	0.77		Light rain 10 P. M.
25	53	68½	Clear	Clear	N. W.			Cloudy part of afternoon, with sprinkle 3 P. M.
26	55½	68½	"	"	E.			Cloudy part of P. M., and clouded over 6 P. M.
27	55	72	Cloudy	"	S. E.			Cleared 8 A. M.; cloudy P. M.
28	55	59	"	Cloudy	S. E.	0.07		Rain 10 P. M.
29	55	63½	"	"	N. E.	0.04		Rain 1:30 P. M.
30	60	67½	"	"	S. E.			Cleared 4 P. M.; clouded over 9 P. M.
S 31	59	70	Clear	Clear	N. W.			
						7.57		

June, 1868.

Date	Thermometer Lowest	Thermometer Highest	Weather Morning	Weather Afternoon	Prevailing Wind	Rain and Melted Snow in inches	Snow in inches	REMARKS.
1	51½	73½	Clear	Clear	N. W., S. W.			
2	59	66	Cloudy	Cloudy	N. E.			Light sprinkle during day; cleared 9 P. M.
3	52	65½	Clear	Clear	E.			Cloudy part of morning.
4	53	65	"	"	E.			Cloudy part of evening with light sprinkle near midnight.
5	51	66½	Cloudy	Cloudy	E.			Clear part of evening.
6	63	81	"	Clear	S. W.			Clear part A. M.; heavy showers after 10 P. M.
S 7	65	71	Rain	Cloudy	S. W., N. E.	1.54		Heavy shower before day.
8	62	70	Cloudy	"	E., S.			Clear part of afternoon.
9	60	71½	"	"	S. E., N. E.	0.43		Shower during A.M.; heavy shower 4 P. M.; cleared 5 P. M.
10	53	67	Clear	Clear	N. E.			Cloudy evening.
11	54	57½	Rain	Rain	N. E.	1.70		Heavy rain till 1 P. M., and misty rain rest of day.
12	54½	66	"	Cloudy	N. E., N. W.	1.83		Heavy rain till 2 P. M.; clear evening.
13	55	77	Clear	Clear	N., S. W.			
S 14	59	78	"	"	S. W., S. E			
15	59	79½	"	"	S. W.			
16	65	77	Cloudy	Cloudy	S. W., N. E.	0.21		Partly clear part of morning; shower 12:30 P. M.
17	68	78	"	Clear	E., S. W.			Cleared 4 P. M.
18	68	76	"	"	S. E.			Cloudy evening.
19	65	78½	"	"	S. W.			Cloudy part of afternoon.
20	67	87	Clear	"	S. W.			
S 21	70½	78½	"	Cloudy	N. E.	0.02		Shower before day; rainy evening after 6:10.
22	65½	69	Cloudy	"	E.	0.36		Rain before day; shower 6 P. M.; clear evening.
23	57½	75½	Clear	Clear	N. W., S. W.			
24	62	74	"	"	All points.	0.29		Cloudy part of A.M.; rain 11 A. M. to noon and 5:35 to 6:35 P. M.
25	59	71	"	"	E.			
26	59	74½	Cloudy	"	E., S. W.			
27	60	82	Clear	"	S. W., N.			Water in main pipe in George street first appearance.
S 28	67½	79½	"	"	N. E., S. E.			
29	63	78¾	"	"	S. E.			
30	63	77½	"	"	S. E.			Cloudy evening.
						6.41		

Weather Record for New Brunswick, N. J.

July, 1868.

Date.	Thermometer. Lowest.	Thermometer. Highest.	Weather. Morning.	Weather. Afternoon.	Prevailing Wind.	Rain and Melted Snow in inches.	Snow in inches.	REMARKS.
1	65½	78½	Cloudy	Clear	S. E.			
2	68	83½	"	"	E.			Cleared 10 A. M.
3	70½	88½	Clear	Cloudy	S. W.	0.63		Cloudy 3 P.M.; shower 5:30 and raining 7 to 8; clear 11 P.M.
4	70½	89	Cloudy	Clear	S. W.			Cleared 8 A. M.
S 5	74	91	Clear	"	S. W.	0.18		Shower 4:45 P. M.; cloudy evening.
6	71	80½	"	"	E.			Cloudy evening.
7	69	81	Cloudy	Cloudy	S. E.	1.85		Clear 12 to 3 P.M.; light sprinkle 4:15 P.M.; heavy shower 6:15 to 9 P. M.
8	69	82	"	most all day.	S. W.	0.21		Rain before day.
9	71	80	Clear	Cloudy	E.	0.23		Thunder shower 3 A. M.; clear part of afternoon.
10	70	77	Cloudy	Clear	E.			Cloudy part of afternoon.
11	67	85	Clear	"	S. W.			
S 12	71	88½	"	"	W., N.			
13	75	91	"	"	N.			
14	77	87½	"	"	E.			Cloudy evening.
15	74½	91½	Cloudy	"	S. W.			Cleared 8 A.M.; cloudy part of afternoon, with showers all around.
16	80	88	Clear	"	N., S. E.			15th and 16th warmest night since I have kept a record.
17	71	83	"	"	N. E., S. E.			Hazy part of evening.
18	69	85½	"	"	S. E.			
S 19	71	87½	"	"	S. W.	0.40		Cloudy part of afternoon and rain 6:30 to 8 P. M.
20	73	79	Cloudy	Cloudy	N. E.			Misty evening with rain 10:30 P.M.
21	69	75½	"	"	N. E., S. E.	0.64		Rain before day, and 8 A.M. and 2:30 to 4:30 P. M.
22	71	81½	"	"	S. W.			Clear part of afternoon and evening.
23	73	80	"	"	E.			
24	71	77½	"	"	S. E.	0.02		Rain before day, sprinkle during day; heavy rain 9:30 P. M.
25	69	81½	"	Clear	N. E.	2.10		Rain till daylight; cleared 9 A.M.; shower 6:45 P. M.
S 26	67	78	"	most all day.	N. E.			
27	66	75	"	most all day.	N. E.			
28	65	77½	Clear	Clear	N. E.			
29	64	78½	"	"	S. W., S. E.			
30	67½	80	Hazy	all day	S. E.			
31	70	82½	Clear	Clear	S. W.			For the last 6 days, there has been a dense haze over the sky.
						6.26		

August, 1868.

Date.	Thermometer. Lowest.	Thermometer. Highest.	Weather. Morning.	Weather. Afternoon.	Prevailing Wind.	Rain and Melted Snow in inches.	Snow in inches.	REMARKS.
1	71½	85½	Clear	Clear	S. W.			Cloudy part of P. M., with thunder storms all round.
S 2	73	81½	"	Cloudy	S. W.			Clear part of evening.
3	74	84	"	Clear	S. W.			Cloudy part of morning; cloudy evening.
4	68	77	Cloudy	Cloudy	N. W., S.	0.45		Rain 4 to 6 A. M., and light rain 11 A. M.; partly clear part of evening.
5	70½	77	"	"	N. E.	0.03		Rain before day; partly clear part of evening.
6	66	75	"	Clear	N. E., S. E.	0.30		Rain 12:15 A. M.; clear part of morning.
7	65	76	Clear	"	S. W.	0.02		Cloudy part of afternoon; shower 6:45 P. M.
8	68	80	Cloudy most all day.		S. W.	0.01		Light rain before day and 11:50 A. M.; shower all around.
S 9	70	81	Clear	Clear	S. W.	0.24		Shower 6 P. M.
10	64	77	"	"	N. W., S. W.			
11	68	75½	Cloudy most all day.		S. W.	0.02		Light sprinkle during day.
12	65	74½	Clear	Clear	N. W.	0.14		Rain before day.
13	56	73½	"	"	N. W.			
14	57½	76½	"	"	W.			
15	60	80	"	"	S. W., N.			
S 16	60	77	"	"	S. W., N.			
17	59½	72½	"	"	N. E., S. E.			
18	67½	83	Cloudy	"	S.			Clear part of morning.
19	70	83	Clear	"	S. W.			Cloudy part of morning.
20	73	81½	Cloudy most all day.		S. W.	1.29		Heavy shower 5:10 to 6:10 P. M.; (1.22 inches) and light rain 7 to 8 P. M.
21	70	76½	"	Cloudy	N. E.			Partly clear part of P. M.
22	66	78	Clear	Clear	N. E., S. E.	0.05		Rain before day.
S 23	63½	78	"	"	S. W., N. E.			
24	64½	77	"	"	All points.			Cloudy part of afternoon.
25	65	78	"	"	S. W.			Cloudy part of afternoon.
26	64½	76½	Cloudy most all day.		S. W.			
27	66	77½	Clear	Cloudy	N. E., S. E.			
28	62	73½	"	Clear	N. E., S. E.			Cloudy evening.
29	66	78	Cloudy	"	E., S. W.	0.10		Rain before day.
S 30	69	85½	Clear	"	S. W.			
31	70	81½	"	Cloudy	N. E., S. E.	0.90		Showers 2:50 and 4 P. M.; heavy showers 7 and 8:30 P. M.; cleared 9 P. M.
						3.55		

From June 1 to Aug. 31, ther. 80° and above on 56 days.

Weather Record for New Brunswick, N. J.

September, 1868.

Date	Thermometer Lowest	Thermometer Highest	Weather Morning	Weather Afternoon	Prevailing Wind	Rain and Melted Snow in inches	Snow in inches	REMARKS.
1	72	81½	Clear	Clear	N. W.	0.01		Rain before day.
2	67	76	C'y m'st all day		E.			
3	65	71½	Cloudy	Rain	E.			Clear part of morning; light rain during P.M., but heavy all night.
4	62½	74½	Rain	"	S. W.	2.84		Rain till 10 A.M. and 1 to 3 P.M., and steady after 5:30 P. M.
5	66	75	Clear	Clear	N. W.	1.01		Rain till 1:30 A. M.
S 6	59	75	"	"	N. W., S. W.			
7	67	76	Cloudy	"	S. W., N. W.	0.06		Light shower 8 to 10 A. M.
8	57	71	Clear	"	E.			
9	58¼	74½	Cloudy	Cloudy	S. W.			Light sprinkle part of A M.; clear part P.M.; misty evening, with rain 11 P.M.
10	69	79	"	"	All points	0.30		Rain before day and 4:50 to 6 P.M.; partly clear part of evening.
11	69	84½	"	Clear	S. W.			
12	73	84	"	"	S.			Cloudy even'g; warmest day, so late, since 1851.
S 13	72	84½	Clear	"	S. W.	0.20		Cloudy evening.
14	66	73½	Cloudy	Cloudy	N. E.	0.03		Shower 4 P.M.; cl'dy evening.
15	60	70½	Clear	Clear	N. E.			Rain before day & 4 to 5 P.M.
16	60	71½	Cloudy	"	S. W., N. W.			Cloudy part of afternoon
17	47	58¾	Clear	"	N.			Cleared 3 P. M; sprinkled 2 P. M.; cloudy evening.
18	43	62½	"	"	N, E.			Frost.
19	43½	64	"	"	S. E.			
S 20	52	67¼	"	Cloudy	S. W.	0.33		Rain 3:40 to 8:30 P. M.; cleared 10:30 P. M.
21	55	63¼	"	Clear	N. E.			
22	48	61	"	Cloudy	S. E.			Misty part of afternoon and com. raining 7:30 P. M.
23	56	72½	C'y m'st all day		S. W., N. W.	0.71		Rain till 5 A. M.
24	54½	58	Cloudy	Cloudy	N. E.	0.02		Rain 3:15 P.M.; misty even'g.
25	51	69	C'y m'st all day		S. W.	0.85		Rain before day; misty 10 A. M.; rain 7:30 P. M.
26	56	62	Cloudy	Cloudy	N. E.	0.57		Rain before day; sprinkle 9:30 A. M. and 3 P. M. and rainy evening after 7 P.M.
S 27	55	63½	Rain	"	N. E.	0.64		Rain before day & part A.M.
28	55	69	Cloudy	Clear	S. W.	0.02		Rain before day.
29	51	62½	Clear	"	N. W.			
30	46	67	"	"	S. W.			
						7.59		

WEATHER RECORD FOR NEW BRUNSWICK, N. J.

October, 1868.

Date.	Lowest.	Highest.	Morning.	Afternoon.	Prevailing Wind.	Rain and Melted Snow in inches.	Snow in inches.	REMARKS.
1	51	65	Clear	Cloudy	N. E.			
2	53	61	Cloudy	"	N. E.			
3	55	60½	"	"	N. E.	0.03		Rain parts of morning; cleared 8 P. M.
S 4	47½	62½	"	"	N. E., E.			Partly clear part of morning.
5	52½	63½	"	Clear	N. W., S. W.	0.25		Rain before day.
6	53	62½	Clear	"	N. W.			
7	45	63½	C'y m'st all day	All points.				
8	58	73	Cloudy	Cloudy	S. W., N. W.	0.06		Rain before day; clear part of morning; light rain part of afternoon; clear 9 P. M.
9	40	52½	Clear	Clear	N. E., S. E.			Clouded over 9 P. M.
10	43	61½	Cloudy	Cloudy	N. E., S. E.			Clear part of morning.
S 11	56	67	"	Clear	S. W.	0.03		Rain part of morning; cleared 10 A. M.
12	50½	64	Clear	"	S. W., N. W.			
13	41	58	"	"	N. W.			
14	48	52	Cloudy	Cloudy	N. E.	0.02		Light rain part of morning; steady rain 6 P. M.
15	52½	58½	"	"	N. E.	0.27		Rain before day; cleared 7 P. M.
16	51	62	"	most all day	N. W			
17	45	48	Clear	Clear	N. W.			
S 18	30½	48	"	"	N. W., S. W.			
19	40½	52½	Cloudy	Cloudy	S. W.			Misty part of morning.
20	42	52	Clear	"	N. E.			
21	46	48½	Cloudy	Rain	N. E.			Rain 10:30 A. M.
22	43½	47½	Rain	Cloudy	N. E.	0.66		Rain till 8 A.M., and light rain parts of afternoon and evening till 9 P. M.
23	36½	43	Clear	"	N. E.			Cleared 8 P. M.
24	31	48	"	Clear	N. E, S. W.			
S 25	36	53	"	Cloudy	S. W.	0.01		Cloudy part of morning; light rains parts of afternoon and evening.
26	47	59	"	Clear	S. W., N. W.			
27	39	59	C'y m'st all day	N. E, S. E.				
28	54	63	Cloudy	Clear	S. W., N. W.	0.01		Light rain part of morning.
29	38½	49	Clear	"	N. W.			
30	34	49	"	"	N. E, S. E.			
31	35	61	"	Cloudy	S. E.			Rain 9:30 P M.
						1.34		

WEATHER RECORD FOR NEW BRUNSWICK, N. J.

November, 1868.

Date.	Thermometer. Lowest.	Thermometer. Highest.	Weather. Morning.	Weather. Afternoon.	Prevailing Wind.	Rain and Melted Snow in inches.	Snow in inches.	REMARKS.
S 1	39	52	Rain	Rain	N. W.	1.86		7:30 A. M., 52°; 3 P. M., 45°; 6 P. M., 39°; 10:30 P. M., 42°; rain till 9 P. M.
2	37	40½	Cloudy	Clear	N. W.			Snow squalls 7 to 10 A. M.; cleared 5 P. M.
3	31	45½	Clear	"	N. W.			
4	35	57½	"	"	S. W.			
5	42	56½	Rain	"	S. W., N., W.	0.17		Rain 6:20 to 11 A. M.
6	39	48	Clear	"	W.			
7	32	48	Cloudy most all day.		S. W.			
S 8	39½	60	"	" "	E., S. W.	0.02		Rain 9:30 P. M.
9	54¼	66	Clear	Clear	S. W.			
10	54	63	Cloudy	Cloudy	S. W., N. E.			Partly clear part of morning; light sprinkle 11:30 A. M.; misty evening.
11	45	49	Rain	Clear	N. W.	0.64		Rain till 11 A. M.; cleared 3 P. M.
12	33	43	Clear	"	S. W., N. W.			
13	31	48	"	"	S. W.			
14	35	55	"	"	N.			
S 15	37	51½	"	"	S. E.			
16	36	44½	Cloudy	"	N. E., S E.			
17	34	49	"	Cloudy	N. E.			Rain 4:40 P M.
18	45	49	Rain	"	N. E.	1.85		Rain till 8 A. M.; clear part of evening.
19	36	47½	Clear	Clear	W.			
20	36	50	"	Cloudy	N. E.			Clouded over 8 A. M.
21	33	40	Cloudy	"	N. W.			Clear part of morning, and partly clear part of evening.
S 22	35	40	"	most all day.	N. W.			
23	32	43½	Clear	Clear	N. W.			
24	33	52	"	"	N. W.			
25	33	47½	"	Cloudy	All points.			
26	44	53½	Rain	Clear	S. E., N. W.	0.40		Rain till 10 A. M.; clear 11 A. M.
27	37	44½	Clear	"	N. W.			
28	31	49	"	"	S. W., S. E.			Cloudy evening.
S 29	38	45	Cloudy most all day.		N. W.			
30	34	48	Cl'y m't all day.		S. W., N. W.			

4.94

WEATHER RECORD FOR NEW BRUNSWICK, N. J.

December, 1868.

Date.	Thermometer. Lowest.	Thermometer. Highest.	Weather. Morning.	Weather. Afternoon.	Prevailing Wind.	Rain and Melted Snow in inches.	Snow in inches.	REMARKS.
1	26	30	Cloudy most all day.		N. W.			
2	25	34	Clear	Clear	N. W.			Cloudy part of afternoon.
3	27	35	"	"	N. W.			
4	27	35	Cloudy	Cloudy	S. W., N. E.			Snow 9:30 P. M.
5	31	33½	Rain } Snow }	"	N. E.	0.92		Heavy rain before day, but 3 in yet on ground at 7 A.M.; light snow part P.M.
S 6	30	37	Clear	Clear	All points			Clouded over 6:30 P. M.
7	32	40½	Rain	Cloudy	N. E.	1.48		Little snow before day and light rain till 9 A. M. and then heavy rain till 4 P. M.; clear part of evening.
8	35	38	Clear	Clear	S. W.			Cloudy part of morning.
9	26	30	"	"	W.			Snow squall 11:30 A. M.
10	20	27	Cloudy	"	S. W.			
11	17	25	Clear	Cloudy	N. E.			
12	16½	25	"	Clear	W.			
S 13	13½	24	"	"	W.			Cloudy evening.
14	19½	32½	"	Cloudy	S. W.			
15	27	36½	"	Clear	N. W.			
16	27	34	Cloudy	Rain	N. E.	0.50		Hail and snow 10 A.M. to noon; rain 3 to 9 P.M.
17	32	40½	"	Clear	S. W.			Clear part of morning.
18	35	40	Clear	"	N. W.			
19	21	27½	"	"	N.			
S 20	21½	37½	Rain	Misty	N. E.	0.24		Com. raining 7:30 A. M. and rained till 1 P. M.
21	34	44½	Clear	Clear	W.			Cloudy part of afternoon.
22	29	36	"	"	W.			Cloudy part of morning.
23	24	32	Cloudy	"	N. W.	0.03		Snow before day; ther. 32° 8 A. M.; cleared 9 A. M.; ther. 24° 3 P. M.
24	13½	18	Clear	"	N. W.			In the river with Dr. Morrogh's ice-boat; walked from 5-mile lock in 80 minutes, about noon, with clothes frozen on me.
25	8	21½	"	Cloudy	S. W.			
26	20	30½	"	Clear	N. W.			Cloudy part of morning.
S 27	20	32	Cloudy	Snow	N. E.	1.00		Snow 10 A. M. to 5 P. M.
28	30	39	"	Clear	S. W.			Cleared 8 A. M.
29	26½	34½	"	Rain	S. W.	0.05		Light rain part of afternoon; cleared 8 P. M.
30	29	32½	"	Cloudy	N. E., S. E.			Clear part of morning.
31	29	35	"	"	S. W.			Light rain part of evening; steady rain 11 P. M.
						3.22	1.00	

Rain and melted snow for 1868—54.10 inches.

Weather Record for New Brunswick, N. J.

January, 1869.

Date	Thermometer Lowest	Thermometer Highest	Wind Morning	Wind Afternoon	Prevailing Wind	Rain and Melted Snow in inches	Snow in inches	REMARKS
1	20	32	Hail Rain	Snow	N. E.	1.28		Hail and snow till 5 P. M.; 32° 8 A.M.; 26° 3 P.M.; 20° 10 P M ; about 3 inches on the ground.
2	20	31	Cloudy	Misty	N. E.	0.07		
S 3	27	34½	"	Cloudy	S. W.			
4	31	35½	"	"	S. W.			Rain part of evening.
5	35	41	Rain	Clear	S. W., N. W.	0.35		Rain part of morning; cleared 3:30 P. M.
6	34	39	Clear	"	S. W.			
7	33	48	"	"	S. W.			
8	34	50½	"	"	S. W.			Cloudy evening.
9	37	55½	"	Cloudy	S. E., S. W.			Cloudy part of morning.
S 10	40	42½	Cloudy	Clear	N. W.			Cleared 9 A M.
11	31½	37	"	Rain	N. E.			Snow and hail 9 to 11 A.M. and rain rest of day.
12	34	37	"	Cloudy	N. W.	0.72		Clear part of morning and part of afternoon.
13	28½	34½	Clear	Clear	N. W.			
14	28	41	"	"	S. W.			
15	35	39	Cloudy	Cloudy	S. W.	0.14		Rain 11 A.M. to 2 P.M , and part of evening.
16	33	37½	"	Clear	N. W.			Cleared 9 A.M.
S 17	26	39	Clear	Cloudy	S. E.			Snow 4 to 5 P M , and part of evening
18	31	32½	Cloudy	Snow	N. E.	0.03		Snow part of morning after 9 A.M.
19	23	31½	Snow	Cloudy	N. W.		4.00	Snow till 8 A.M.; cleared 9 A M.
20	26½	36	Cloudy	"	S. W.			Clear part of morning; cleared 6 P.M.
21	25	40	Clear	Clear	S. W.			
22	22	28	Cloudy	"	N. E.			
23	13½	37½	Clear	"	S. W.			
S 24	39	45½	"	"	S. W.			
25	33	37	"	"	N. W.			Cloudy part of morning; 33° before day; 37° 8 A M. and afterwards grows colder all day.
26	14	25½	"	"	N. W.			
27	20	36	Cloudy most all day.		S. W.			
28	32	44	Clear	Clear	S. W., N. W.			
29	30	49	"	"	All points.			Cloudy evening.
30	39	52	Cloudy	"	S. W., N. W.	0.50		Rain before day; thunder shower; cloudy evening.
S 31	35	37	"	most all day.	N. W.			
						3.09	4 00	

February, 1869.

Date	Thermometer Lowest	Thermometer Highest	Weather Morning	Weather Afternoon	Prevailing Wind	Rain and Melted Snow in inches	Snow in inches	REMARKS
1	24	31½	Clear	Clear	N. W.			
2	23¼	31	Cloudy	Cloudy	N. E.			Bar. 10 A. M., 30.50
3	30½	38	Rain	Misty	N. E.	0.95		Snow before day and then rain; shower with lightning after 8:30 P. M.
4	28	37½	Cloudy	most all	N. W.	0.57		Ther. highest 8 A. M., lowest at noon, with snow squalls; bar. 8 A. M. 29.16
5	19	28	"	Clear	N. W.	0.01		Snow squalls before day and 8 to 10:30 A. M.
6	21½	39½	Clear	"	N. W.			
S 7	29	37	"	"	N. W., N.			
8	19	37½	"	"	S. W.			Cloudy parts afternoon and evening.
9	33	41	Cloudy	Rain	S., N. E.			Light rain and mist all P. M.
10	35	29½	Rain	Cloudy	N. E.	0.57		Rain till 3 P. M.
11	37	49	Cloudy	Clear	S. W., N.	0.01		Rain before day.
12	33	47	Clear,	"	S. W.			
13	37	50	"	"	S. W.			
S 14	41	51½	"	Cloudy	N. E., E.			Com raining 8:30 P. M.
15	37	46½	Rain	Clear	N. E., N.	1.52		Rain till 9 A. M. and 10 to 11 A. M.; cleared 4 P. M.
16	34½	42½	Clear	"	S. W., N. W.			Cloudy evening.
17	32	42½	"	"	S. W.			Cloudy 9 A M to 3 P. M.
18	34	39	Cloudy	"	W.	0.59		Rain and snow before day; clear 9 A. M.
19	30	43	Snow	"	S. W., N. W.	0.09		Snow 7 to 11 A. M., but melts as it falls.
20	28	41½	Clear	"	S. W.			Cloudy 10 A. M. to 3 P M.; with snow squall at noon.
S 21	32	40½	Cloudy	Cloudy	E.			Clouded over 8 A. M., and misty part of afternoon.
22	39	45½	"	"	All points			Misty part of day and commenced raining 8 P. M
23	35	45	Rain	"	N. E., N. W.	0.72		Rain till 11 A. M and 1 to 3 P M
24	26	35½	Clear	Clear	S. W.			
25	23	36	"	Cloudy	S. W.			Clouded over 3 P. M.
26	33	35½	Snow	Snow	E., N. E.	0.81		Snow till 3 P. M., very wet and mostly melts; cleared 6 P. M.; snow squalls 11 P. M.
27	22	28½	Clear	Clear	W.			About 3 inches of snow on ground; cloudy part of evening.
S 28	13	24½	"	"	N. W.			

5.84

March, 1869.

Date.	Thermometer. Lowest.	Thermometer. Highest	Weather. Morning.	Weather. Afternoon.	Prevailing Wind.	Rain and Melted Snow in inches.	Snow in inches.	REMARKS.
1	7	26	Clear	Clear	N. E., W.	----	----	
2	10	32½	Cloudy	Cloudy	N. E., W.	----	----	Clear evening.
3	23	40	Clear	Clear	S. W.	----	----	
4	32	37½	Snow	Cloudy	S. W., N. W.	0.20	----	Snow till 1 P. M., but melts as it falls; cleared 7 P. M.
5	9	22	Clear	Clear	N. W., S. W.	----	----	
6	16½	28½	C'y m'st all day.		N. E., N. W.	----	0.50	Snow 5 to 7:30 A. M.
S 7	16½	27	Clear	Clear	N. W.	----	----	
8	21½	37	Cloudy	"	S. W.	----	----	
9	26½	42	Clear	"	S. W.	----	----	Cloudy 9 P.M. and com. raining 10 P.M.
10	34	57	Rain	Rain	S. E., S. W.	1.10	----	Rain steady 3 P.M. and then at intervals till 9 P.M.; cleared 10 P.M.
11	32	40½	Clear	Clear	N. W.	----	----	Cloudy evening.
12	27	37	Cloudy	"	N. W.	0.03	----	Snow till 9 A.M.; cleared 10 A.M.; clouded over 9 P. M.
13	33	52	"	"	S. W.	----	----	Cleared 8 A.M.
S 14	35	61	Clear	"	S. E., S. W.	----	----	
15	28½	34½	Snow	Cloudy	N. E., N.	0.38	----	Hail and snow 6:30 A. M. to 1 P.M.; cleared 5 P. M.
16	20½	30½	Clear	Clear	N., S. W.	----	----	
17	27	36½	"	"	W.	----	----	
18	22½	35½	"	"	N. W.	----	----	Striped bass caught below town weighing 42½ pounds.
19	25½	40½	"	Cloudy	S. W., S. E.	----	----	Snow 7:30 to 11 P. M. with rain.
20	35	47	Cloudy	Clear	All points.	0.14	----	Rain before day; cloudy part of afternoon.
S 21	23	31½	Clear	"	N.	----	----	
22	17	41	"	"	E.	----	----	Clouded 3 P.M.; snow 11 P.M.
23	31½	43	Rain	"	N. E., N. W.	1.04	----	Rain till 8:15 A.M.; clear 11 A.M.; cloudy part of P. M.
24	33	53	Clear	"	N. W.	----	----	
25	33½	49	"	"	All points.	----	----	
26	37½	56	Rain	Rain	S. E.	----	----	
27	51	61	Clear	Clear	W.	0.89	----	Rain before day.
S 28	39	58	"	Cloudy	E.	----	----	Clouded over 2 P. M.; clear 10 to 11 P. M.
29	43½	45½	Rain	Rain	N. E.	0.91	----	Rain 7 P.M. and misty afterwards.
30	40	56	Cloudy	most all day.	N. W.	0.13	----	Rain before 6 A.M., and light rain 7:30 P. M.
31	44	48	Clear	Clear	N. W.	----	----	Cloudy part of morning and part of evening.
						4.82	0.50	

WEATHER RECORD FOR NEW BRUNSWICK, N. J.

April, 1869.

Date.	Thermometer. Lowest.	Thermometer. Highest.	Weather. Morning.	Weather. Afternoon.	Prevailing Wind.	Rain and Melted Snow in inches.	Snow in inches.	REMARKS.
1	33	51	Clear	Clear	N. W.			Cloudy evening with light rain 7 to 8 P. M.
2	38	48½	Cloudy	Cloudy	E.	0.29		Rain 4 to 9 P. M.
3	39	44	"	Clear	N. W.			Cloudy part of afternoon with snow squalls at 3 P. M.
S 4	30	39	Clear	"	N. W.			Cloudy part of morning with snow squalls at noon.
5	33	53	"	"	W.			
6	41½	54	"	"	S. W., N. W.			
7	42	55	"	"	S. W., N. W.	0.03		Cloudy part of afternoon with shower 12:30 P. M.
8	35	54	"	"	S. W., N. W.			Cloudy part of afternoon.
9	33	58½	"	"	N. W.			
10	32	48¼	"	Cloudy	N. W.			Cloudy parts of afternoon and evening.
S 11	35	45	Cloudy	"	N. E.			Cleared 7 P. M.
12	32	48	Clear	Clear	All points			Cloudy part of afternoon.
13	35	48	"	"	All points.			Cloudy part of afternoon.
14	32	49½	"	"	N. W.			
15	32	54½	"	"	N. W., W.			
16	38	66	"	"	S. W.			
17	45	65	Cloudy	"	S. W.	0.13		Rain 10 A. M. till noon.
S 18	46	73	Clear	"	S. W.			
19	51	77	"	"	S. W.			Cloudy parts of morning and afternoon.
20	62	77	"	Cloudy	S. W.	0.25		Cloudy part of morning and clear part of afternoon; rain 8 to 9:30 P. M.
21	56½	64	Cloudy	Clear	W.	0.11		Rain till 7 A. M.; clear part of morning.
22	48	64½	Clear	"	N. W.			
23	43	64¼	"	Cloudy	N. E., S. E.			
24	49	71	"	Clear	S. W.			Cloudy part of afternoon; pears and cherries flowered.
S 25	53	57	"	"	N. W.			
26	46½	73	"	"	N. W., S. W.			Cloudy part of evening.
27	56	73½	"	"	N. S.			Cloudy evening.
28	56½	72½	"	"	N. W.			Clouded over 7 P. M., and com. raining 9 P. M.
29	48	56	Rain	Cloudy	W., N. E.	0.81		Rain till 8 A. M. and from 9 A. M. to 2 P. M.; cleared 8 P. M.
30	41	56	Clear	Clear	N. E., S.			Cloudy part of evening.

1.62

May, 1869.

Date.	Thermometer.		Weather.		Prevailing Wind.	Rain and Melted Snow in inches.	Snow in inches.	REMARKS.
	Lowest.	Highest.	Morning.	Afternoon.				
1	44	46½	Rain	Rain	S. E., N. E.			Steady rain till 6 P. M., and misty afternoon.
S 2	37½	43½	"	"	N. E., N. W.	1.88		Steady rain 7 to 9 A. M. and noon to 6 P. M ; cleared 11 P.M.
3	40	57½	Cloudy	Cloudy	N. W.			Sprinkle 2 P. M.; clear part of evening.
4	41	56	"	Clear	N. W.			
5	42	56½	Clear	Cloudy	N. E.			Clear part of evening.
6	42	60	"	"	N. E.			
7	47	55	Cloudy	"	N. E., S. W.			Cloudy evening with light sprinkle.
8	45½	64	Clear	Clear	N. E., S. E.			Cloudy with light sprinkles 5 to 7 P. M.
S 9	47	67	"	"	N.			
10	50	70	"	"	N., W., S.			
11	49	77	"	"	S. W.			
12	59	80½	"	"	S. W.			
13	61½	71	"	Show'rs	S. E.	0.28		Clouded over 10 A.M.; showers afternoon and ev'g.
14	54	70½	"	Rain	S. W.	0.20		Showers 2:15 and rain 3:15 to 6 P. M.
15	56	72½	"	Clear	S. W.			
S 16	55	68½	"	"	S. W.	0.44		Clouded 10 A.M. with sprinkle 10:30 and then rained to 2 P.M.; cleared 3 P. M.; thunder shower 4:15 P.M. with violent hail storm 2 miles north.
17	49½	61½	"	"	N. W.			Cloudy part of evening.
18	47	63	"	Cloudy	N. W., S. W.			Cloudy part of evening.
19	50	52	Cloudy	Rain	N. E., N. W.	0.58		Rain 8 A M. to 10 P. M.
20	48	65	Clear	Clear	N. W.			
21	50	63½	"	Cloudy	S. W., N. E.			Rain part P.M. and even'g.
22	49	61	Cloudy	most all day.	N. E.	0.32		Rain till 7:30 A.M ; clear evening.
S 23	46½	66	Clear	Clear	N. E., S. E.			
24	48	72	"	"	N. W.			Hazy evening.
25	53	77½	"	"	S. W.			
26	60	82	"	"	S. W.	0.53		Shower 5:40 to 6:45 P.M.and cloudy afterwards.
27	52	63	Cloudy	"	N. E., S. E.	0.12		Rain before day and 8 to 9 A.M ; cloudy evening
28	52½	58	"	Cloudy	N. E., S. E.	0.07		Rain to 7 A. M.; rainy evening after 8 o'clock.
29	52½	76	"	Clear	S. W.	0.17		Thunder shower 3 A. M.
S 30	60	69½	"	Cloudy	N. E., S. E.	0.25		Rain 6:30 to 7:30 A M.; partly clear part of afternoon.
31	60	78	Clear	Clear	S. W.	0.34		Cloudy evening with shower 9:20 to midnight.
						5.18		

Weather Record for New Brunswick, N. J.

June, 1869.

Date	Thermometer Lowest	Thermometer Highest	Weather Morning	Weather Afternoon	Prevailing Wind	Rain and Melted Snow in inches	Snow in inches	REMARKS
1	65	79	Clear	Clear	S. W.			Cloudy evening.
2	67	72¼	Cloudy	Rainy	N. E.	0.28		Light sprinkle during A. M., and showers P.M. till 6:30; cleared 9 P. M.
3	60	77	Clear	Clear	N. E., S. E.			Cloudy part of morning.
4	62½	73	Cloudy	Cloudy	S. E.	0.10		Showers 3:15 to 5 P. M.
5	67	80	"	"	S. W.	0.24		Clear part of P. M.; showers 3:40 to 5:40 P. M.
S 6	57	68	Clear	Clear	N. W.			
7	53	66	"	"	N. E., N. W.			
8	53½	66	"	"	N. W., N. E.	0.17		Cloudy 6 to 9 A. M., with sprinkle and shower 12:10 P. M.
9	48½	65	"	"	N. E., S. E.			
10	48	59	Cloudy	Rain	S. W.	0.12		Rain part of afternoon.
11	49	68½	Clear	Clear	W., N. W.	0.07		Cloudy part of evening with shower 7 P. M
12	50½	71	"	"	S. W.			
S 13	57	82	Cloudy most all day.		S. W.			
14	68	76	Show'rs	Cloudy	S. W.			Clear part of A. M. and P. M.
15	66	72	"	"	S. W.	0.11		Showers till 9 A.M.; cleared 4 P. M.
16	55	70	Clear	Clear	S. W.	0.97		
17	54½	74½	"	"	S. W.			
18	60	81½	"	"	S. W.			
19	70	83½	"	"	N.			
S 20	65½	84	"	Cloudy	S. E., S. W.	0.02		Light sprinkle 7 to 8 P. M.
21	71	82	"	"	S. W.			Rain before day and shower 4:50 P.M; rainy evening.
22	64	68½	Cloudy	"	N. E.	2.05		Rain before day and misty part of day.
23	64½	76	"	"	S. E., S. W.	0.23		Showers 7:30 A.M. and 4:40 P.M.; clear part of P.M.
24	66	75½	"	Clear	S. W.	0.01		Cleared 9 A.M, but hazy all day; rain before day.
25	64	78	Clear	"	All points.			
26	67½	77½	Cloudy	Cloudy	All points.	0.15		Rain before day; clear part of afternoon.
S 27	70	83	"	Clear	S. W.	0.82		Heavy shower (0.80) 12 to 1 A.M.; cloudy part of afternoon; sprinkle 7 to 8 P. M.
28	72	86½	Clear	"	S. W.			Cloudy part of afternoon, with light sprinkle 6:15 P. M.
29	67½	82	"	"	N. W., S. W.			
30	70	79	Cloudy	Cloudy	S. W., N.	0.23		Shower 6 to 7 A.M. and 11:30 to 11:45 A.M.; clear part of morning.

5.57

Weather Record for New Brunswick, N. J.

July, 1869.

Date.	Thermometer. Lowest.	Thermometer. Highest.	Weather. Morning.	Weather. Afternoon.	Prevailing Wind.	Rain and Melted Snow in inches.	Snow in inches.	REMARKS.
1	60	70½	Clear	Cloudy	N. W.			
2	57	76	Cloudy	Hazy	S. W.			
3	62½	83	Clear	Clear	S. W.	0.05		Cloudy part of morning; shower 1:45 P. M., and sprinkle 8:10 P. M.
S 4	74½	85	"	"	N. W.			Hazy evening.
5	64	75	"	"	N.			
6	59	72	"	"	N. E.			
7	57	75	"	"	S. W.			Cloudy evening.
8	61	80	"	"	S. W.			Cloudy evening.
9	68½	78	"	Cloudy	S. W.	0.70		Clouded over 9 A. M.; shower noon to 2 P. M.; clear evening.
10	64	81	"	Clear	S. W.			
S 11	70	89½	"	"	S. W.			
12	68	79	"	"	N. W.			
13	63½	78	"	Cloudy	N. E.			Cloudy part of morning; com. raining 5 P. M.
14	63	68	Cloudy	"	N. E.	1.04		Rain before day and misty morning; light rain 10:30 P. M.
15	66	82½	"	Clear	S. W.			
16	73½	90½	Clear	"	S. W.	0.02		Shower 12:30 A. M.; violent gust 5:15 P. M., with few drops of rain.
17	73	84½	"	"	N. W.			
S 18	70½	75	Cloudy	Cloudy	N.			Light rain at intervals after 6 P. M.
19	67½	73	"	"	N. E.	0.09		Rain till 1 A. M.; cleared 8 P. M.
20	65	72	Clear	"	E.			Clouded over 10 A. M.; clear part of evening.
21	66½	80	Cloudy	Clear	S. W., N. W.	0.53		Shower before day; cleared 10 A. M.
22	58	73	Clear	"	N. W.			
23	59	74	"	Cloudy	S. W.			
24	59	79	"	Clear	S. W.			
S 25	65	83	"	"	S. W.			Cloudy evening.
26	71	76½	Sh'rs	Cloudy	S. W.	0.58		Shower during morning and 2:30 P. M.; cleared 9 P. M.
27	72	83	Cloudy	"	S. W.	0.51		Clear part of afternoon; shower 2 P. M. (.04 in. 15 minutes); rain 5 to 6 and clear 7 P. M.
28	70	81	Clear	"	S. W.			Clear evening; light sprinkle 7 P. M
29	67½	78	Cloudy most all day.		S. W.	0.09		Rain 6 to 7 A. M.
30	61	75	Clear	Clear	N. W.			
31	58	73½	"	"	All points.			Hazy evening.

3.61

August, 1869.

Date.	Thermometer.		Weather.		Prevailing Wind.	Rain and Melted Snow in inches.	Snow in inches.	REMARKS.
	Lowest.	Highest.	Morning.	Afternoon.				
S 1	59	75	Clear	Clear	E.			
2	57½	77	"	"	S. W.			
3	69	84½	"	"	W.			
4	62½	79	"	Cloudy	N. W.			
5	65½	73	Cloudy	"	N. W.	0.38		Thunder shower 1:30 A.M. & rain 9 to 10 A. M.; cleared 6:30 P. M.
6	54	67	Clear	Clear	N.			Cloudy part of afternoon.
7	53½	68½	"	"	N.			Cloudy part of P.M., but clear during most of the eclipse.
S 8	51	72½	"	"	N. W.			Cloudy evening.
9	54½	76	"	"	S. W.			
10	57	79	"	"	S. W.			
11	61	82½	"	"	S. W.			Cloudy evening.
12	67	79	"	"	N. E., S. E.			
13	63	80½	F'ggy } Cl'dy }	"	S. W.	0.01		Cloudy part of afternoon; rain 5 to 6 P. M.
14	64	78½	Clear	"	E.			
S 15	65½	83	Cloudy	most all day.	S. W.	0.10		Rain before day; light sprinkle part of evening.
16	73½	81	Clear	Clear	N. W.			Cloudy part of morning.
17	66½	71	Cloudy	Cloudy	E.	0.02		Clear part of morning; light rain 1 A. M. and at noon.
18	66	75	Clear	Clear	N. E., S. E.			
19	65½	80½	"	"	S. W.			Cloudy party of morning.
20	71	92½	Cloudy	"	S. W.			Cleared 9 A.M.; warmest day since July, 1866.
21	75½	92½	Clear	Cloudy	S. W.			Cloudy most of afternoon and evening, after 3:30 with light sprinkle.
S 22	70	78	Cloudy	Clear	N. E., S. E.			
23	65	77½	Clear	"	E.			
24	61½	78½	"	"	N. E., S. E.			
25	60	80½	"	"	S. W.			Cloudy evening.
26	69	80½	"	"	N.			
27	56	76½	"	"	S. E.			
28	63	85	"	"	S. W.	0.19		Clouded over 8 P.M.; light sprinkle after 9:20; steady rain 10:30 to 11:30 P. M.
S 29	71	82	"	"	N. W.			Cloudy part of morning.
30	64	71	"	"	N. W.			Cloudy part of morning and part of afternoon.
31	56	68	"	"	N.			
						0.70		

Weather Record for New Brunswick, N. J.

September, 1869.

Date	Thermometer Lowest	Thermometer Highest	Weather Morning	Weather Afternoon	Prevailing Wind	Rain and Melted Snow in inches	Snow in inches	Remarks
1	41	62	Clear	Cloudy	N.			Clear part of afternoon.
2	50	63½	"	Clear	N. E.			Cloudy part of afternoon.
3	50	70	"	"	N. W.			
4	53	77½	"	"	S. W.			
S 5	54½	79½	"	"	S. W.			
6	61	79	Cloudy most all day.		S. E.	0.08		Foggy morning; clear 10 A. M. to 5 P. M.; light rain 9 to 11:30 P. M.
7	70½	80½	"	" "	S. E.	0.05		Clear 10 A.M. to 4 P.M.; rain at intervals 4:30 to 11 P.M.
8	73	77	C'y m'st all day.		S. E., S. W.	0.25		Light showers, at intervals from 9 A. M. to 9 P. M.
9	63	71½	Cloudy	Clear	W.			Cleared 9 A. M.
10	50	69	"	"	N. W.			Cleared 8 A. M.
11	54½	71½	Clear	"	N. W.			
S 12	53	75	"	"	N. E., S. E.			
13	55½	76	"	"	E.			
14	58½	73½	"	"	S. E.			
15	51½	71	"	"	S. E.			Foggy morning; clouded over 9 P. M.
16	64	74	Cloudy most all day.		S. E.			
17	66	69	"	Cloudy	E.	0.06		Misty and light rain parts of day till 11:30 P. M.
18	63½	68	"	"	E.	0.05		Rain before day; misty part of morning; clear part of evening.
S 19	62	77	"	Clear	S. W.			Cleared 10 A. M.
20	64	85½	Clear	"	S. W., N. W.			Hottest day so late since I have kept record.
21	60½	76	"	"	E.			Clouded over 5 P. M.; light sprinkle 8 P. M.
22	66	67½	Misty	Rain	E.	0.25		Misty most all day; rain 3 to 4 P. M.
23	67½	70½	Cloudy	Cloudy	S. E.			
24	61	73	Clear	"	S. E.			Partly clear part of evening.
25	60	75	"	"	S.			Clear part of afternoon.
S 26	68	74	Cloudy	Rain	S.	1.60		Light rain 9 A. M. to noon and afternoon; steady rain till 11 P. M.
27	51	58	Clear	Clear	N. W.			
28	43	58½	"	"	N. W., S. W.			Frost.
29	42½	65½	"	"	S. W.			
30	46	68	"	"	S. W.			
						2.34		

October, 1869.

	Date.	Thermometer. Lowest.	Thermometer. Highest.	Weather. Morning.	Weather. Afternoon.	Prevailing Wind.	Rain and Melted Snow in inches.	Snow in inches.	REMARKS.
	1	49½	73½	Clear	Clear	S. W.			
	2	52	72	Cloudy	Cloudy	S.	0.01		Foggy morning; clear 4 to 9 P. M.; rain 11 to 11:30 P. M.
S	3	64½	70	Rain	Rain	S., N. E.			Rain before day; 0.12 in. 9:15 A. M. to 4 P. M. 1.18 in., and com. again 10 P.M.
	4	62	65½	"	Cloudy	N. W.	3.60		Rain hard till 10 A. M.; (2.30 in.) and light till noon; (0.08 in.) misty 5:30 and cleared 7 P. M.
	5	52	60	Clear	Clear	N. W.			
	6	43½	59	"	"	N. W.			
	7	42	61½	"	"	All points			
	8	44½	66½	"	"	S. W.			
	9	46	66	"	"	S. W., E.			Clouded over 9 P. M.
S	10	57	63	Cloudy	Rain	N. W., N. E.	3.70		Rain 9:10 to noon; (heavy dashes) and then steady rain till 9 P. M.; cleared 11 P. M.
	11	51	60	Clear	Clear	N. W., S. W.			
	12	50½	68	Cloudy	Cloudy	S.			Partly clear part of A. M.
	13	50	53½	"	"	N. W.	0.19		Rain before day, and light rain 9 to 10 A. M.; cleared 6:30 P. M.
	14	41½	57	Clear	Clear	S. W.			Clear part of afternoon.
	15	45	60½	"	Rain	W.	0.29		Clouded over at noon; rain 2:15 P. M. to 6 and at intervals during evening till midnight.
	16	46½	53½	Cloudy	Clear	N. W.			Cleared 9 A. M.
S	17	39	57½	Clear	"	W.			English sparrows first seen this month in the streets. Supposed to have come from Jersey City.
	18	40½	52½	"	"	N. W.			
	19	43	49	Cloudy	Cloudy	S. W.	0.01		Rain 3:30 to 5:30 P. M.; clear but hazy 9 P. M.
	20	36	46½	Clear	Clear	N. W.			
	21	33	49½	"	Cloudy	S. W.	0.02		Rain from 4 to 10 P. M.
	22	45	55½	"	Clear	N. W., S. W.			
	23	45	63	Cloudy	Rain	S. E., S. W.	0.53		Rain 9 A. M. to 3 P. M., and 6 to 7 P. M.
S	24	47½	51½	Clear	Clear	N. W.			
	25	34	44	"	"	W.			
	26	31	40½	"	"	W., S. W.			Cloudy part of evening.
	27	32	40	"	"	N. W.			Coldest day in October since Oct. 27, 1859.
	28	31½	44½	Cloudy	Cloudy	S. W.			Light rain 3:15 to 4 P. M.
	29	39	45	"	"	W.	0.10		Rain 1:30 to 4 P. M.; cleared 9:30 P. M.
	30	33½	40	Clear	"	N. W.			
S	31	32½	41	"	Clear	N. W.			
							8.53		

WEATHER RECORD FOR NEW BRUNSWICK, N. J. 161

November, 1869.

Date.	Thermometer. Lowest.	Thermometer. Highest.	Weather. Morning.	Weather. Afternoon.	Prevailing Wind.	Rain and Melted Snow in inches.	Snow in inches.	REMARKS.
1	29	41½	Clear	Cloudy	S. W., W.			Clouded over 10 A. M.; partly clear 10 P. M.
2	36	50½	"	Clear	All points			
3	34	51½	"	"	S. W.			
4	38	58	"	"	S. W.			Cloudy part of evening.
5	41½	51	Cloudy	Cloudy	All points	0.16		Rain 9 to 11 A.M.; cleared 7 P. M.
6	37	47½	Clear	"	S. W., N. W.			
S 7	33	38½	"	Clear	N. W.			Snow squalls 10 A. M. to noon and 3:15 P.M; cloudy noon to 3:30 P. M.
8	30	38	Cloudy	most all day.	W.			
9	34	42	"	Clear	W.			Cleared 9 A. M.; cloudy part of afternoon.
10	30	42	Clear	"	W., N. W.			Cloudy part of afternoon.
11	32	48½	"	"	W.			
12	35½	44	"	"	N. W.			
13	30	45½	"	Cloudy	S. E.			
S 14	35	40½	Cloudy	"	N. E., N.	0.01		Snow part of A.M., but melts as it falls.
15	34½	38½	"	"	N. W.			Clear part of evening.
16	30	39	Clear	"	S. W.			Clouded over 8 A. M.; snow 6 to 7 P. M.
17	33½	61	Rain	Clear	S.E.,S.W.,W.	1.35		Rain till 11 A. M.
18	36	41½	Clear	"	S. W.			
19	29½	49	"	"	N. E., S. E.			Cloudy evening, with rain 10 P. M.
20	46	56½	Cloudy	Cloudy	S., S. W.	1.03		Rain till 6 A. M.; clear part A. M. and part of even'g.
S 21	35	43½	Clear	"	S. W., N. W.			
22	31½	39	"	Clear	W.			Clouded over 4 P. M.
23	35½	43	Rain	Cloudy	S. W.	0.13		Rain till 9 A. M.; light rain at 1 P.M. and steady rain at 10 P. M.
24	37	39	"	"	N., N. W.	0.74		Rain till 11 A.M.; cleared 6 P. M.
25	25½	37	Clear	Clear	N., N. E.			
26	28	39	"	Cloudy	N., S. W.			Clear part of evening.
27	36	44	Cloudy	Rain	S. W., N. W.	0.23		Clear sunrise; rain 10:30 A. M. to 6 P.M.; cleared 9 P.M.
S 28	34½	40	Clear	Clear	N. W.			
29	28½	40	"	Cloudy	S. W.			Cloudy 10 A.M; light sprinkle part of evening.
30	39	60½	Rainy	"	S. W.	0.11		Light rain parts of day and 11 P.M.
						3.76		

December, 1869.

	Date.	Thermometer. Lowest.	Thermometer. Highest.	Weather. Morning.	Weather. Afternoon.	Prevailing. Wind.	Rain and Melted Snow in inches.	Snow in inches.	REMARKS.
	1	46	47½	Clear	Clear	N. W., N.	----	----	Cloudy evening.
	2	30	34½	Cloudy	Cloudy	N. E.	0.63	----	Clear part of A. M. and part of P.M.; snow 2:15 to 6 P.M.
	3	24	31	"	Clear	N. W.	----	----	Light snow 8 A. M.; cleared 9 A. M.
	4	18½	36½	Clear	Cloudy	S. W.	----	----	Clouded 10:30 A. M.
S	5	34	39½	Rain	Rain	S. W.	0.10	----	Rain till 2 P.M.; rainy evening after 5 & 11 P.M. snow.
	6	24	33	Snow	"	N. E.	0.44	----	Rain and snow till 11 A.M.; regular snow storm 4½ P.M.
	7	15½	24	Clear	Clear	N. W., W.	----	4.00	Snow till 1 A.M.
	8	18	32½	Cloudy	"	W., N. W.	----	----	Cloudy part of afternoon.
	9	23	32	Clear	"	N. W.	----	----	
	10	10½	31½	"	"	N. W., S. W.	----	----	
	11	23½	42	"	"	W., S. W.	----	----	
S	12	31	44	Cloudy	"	E., S. W.	----	----	Light sprinkle part of A.M.; partly clear part of A.M.; cleared 4 P. M.
	13	35½	42½	Clear	"	N. W.	----	----	Clouded over 9 P. M.
	14	27	33½	"	"	N. E.	----	----	
	15	22	35½	Cloudy	Cloudy	N. E.	----	----	
	16	35	51	Rain	Clear	E., S. W.	0.45	----	Rain 7 A.M. to 2 P.M.; cleared 3 P. M.; foggy part of evening.
	17	34½	44	Clear	"	N. W., N. E.	----	----	Cloudy part of evening.
	18	35	40	Cloudy	Rain	N. E.	0.66	----	Rain 9 A.M. to 6 P. M.; clear part of evening; rain 9 P. M. to midnight.
S	19	34	35½	C'y m'st all day.		N. W., W.	----	----	
	20	28	33	Cloudy	Cloudy	S. W.	----	----	Cleared 7 P. M.
	21	25½	32	"	"	S. E.	----	----	Snow 2:15 P.M., just covered the ground; snow 8:30 to 10:30 P.M. and then rain.
	22	30½	57½	Rain	"	E., S. W.	1.02	----	Rain till 1 P. M.; light rain 9:15 P. M.
	23	34	36	Clear	Clear	N. W.	----	----	
	24	25½	37	"	"	W.	----	----	
	25	25½	38½	"	Cloudy	All points.	----	----	Com. raining 6:30 P.M.
S	26	35	47	Rain	Rain	N. E.	1.20	----	Heavy rain till 1 P.M.; light rain afterwards till 6 P.M.
	27	43	45	Cloudy	Cloudy	E.	----	----	Misty evening till 9, and then heavy rain till 11 P.M.
	28	4:	49½	"	"	N. E., N. W.	0.56	----	Rain before day and at intervals during day.
	29	37	39	"	"	N. W.	----	----	
	30	34	46	"	Clear	S. W.	----	----	
	31	36	46½	Clear	"	S. W.	----	----	
							4.46	4.00	

Rain and melted snow for 1869—50.37 inches.

January, 1870.

	Date.	Thermometer. Lowest.	Thermometer. Highest.	Weather. Morning.	Weather. Afternoon.	Prevailing Wind.	Rain and Melted Snow in inches.	Snow in inches.	REMARKS.
	1	34	47	Cloudy	Cloudy	N. E.	----	----	Com. raining 10 P. M.; bar. on 1st at noon 30.10, on 2d at 3 P. M 29.05.
S	2	41	57	Rain	"	E., S. E., S. W.	0.92	----	Rain till 1 P. M., and sprinkle 2 and 6 P. M.; clear 3 to 5:30 P. M.; gale after 5 P. M.; cleared 8 P. M.
	3	34	41	Clear	Clear	S. W.	----	----	Cloudy part of afternoon.
	4	27½	35	"	Cloudy	S. W., W.	----	----	Clear part of afternoon.
	5	27½	32½	"	Clear	W., N. W.	----	----	
	6	25½	42	"	Cloudy	S. W.	----	----	Clear part of afternoon; rain 9 P. M.
	7	24	27½	"	"	N. W.	0.20	----	Rain till 3 A. M.; clear part of afternoon.
	8	25½	31½	Snow	Clear	N. E., N. W.	0.10	----	Snow 7 to 10 A. M.; cleared at noon.
S	9	15½	22½	Clear	"	W.	----	----	
	10	18	31½	Cloudy	Cloudy	SW., NW, NE	----	----	Cleared 9 P. M.
	11	24	41	Clear	Clear	N. W.	----	----	Cloudy evening.
	12	36	49	"	Cloudy	S. W.	----	----	Hazy A M.; cleared 8 A. M.
	13	39	52½	Cloudy	Clear	S. W.	0.01	----	Light rain part of A. M.
	14	19½	29	"	Cloudy	N. E.	----	----	Partly clear part of A. M.; hail and snow 7 P. M.
	15	27	49	Rainy	Rainy	N. E.	0.30	----	Rain and misty all day.
S	16	36	46	Clear	Clear	W.	----	----	Blue birds and woodpeckers in town.
	17	35	62½	Rain	Cloudy	E., S.	0.48	----	Clear 3:30 to 8 P. M.; rain 8:30 to 10 P. M.
	18	43	45	Cloudy	Clear	W.	----	----	Cleared 2 P. M.
	19	30	37	Clear	"	N. E., E.	----	----	
	20	30	42½	"	"	N E., SW, NW	----	----	Cloudy part of evening.
	21	36	44½	"	"	S. W.	----	----	
	22	29	45½	"	"	N. E., S. E.	----	----	Cloudy evening.
S	23	39	56½	Cloudy	Cloudy	S. W.	----	----	Clear part of afternoon; rainy after 6 P. M.
	24	37	40½	"	"	N. E.	0.10	----	Misty and rainy evening.
	25	37½	48	Rain	"	N E., SW, NW	1.38	----	Rain till 2:30 P. M.; cleared 6 P. M.
	26	35½	52½	Clear	Clear	S. W.	----	----	
	27	38½	52½	"	"	S. W., N.	----	----	Cloudy evening.
	28	33½	42½	"	"	N. E.	----	----	
	29	31	42	Rain	Rain	N. E.	0.98	----	Rain 8 A. M. to 8 P. M.; clear part of evening.
S	30	36	42	Clear	Clear	N. W., S. W.	----	----	Cloudy evening.
	31	33½	34½	Cloudy	Cloudy	N. E.	0.06	---	Snow 9 to 10 P. M.
							4.53		

WEATHER RECORD FOR NEW BRUNSWICK, N. J.

February, 1870.

Date.	Thermometer. Lowest.	Highest.	Weather. Morning.	Afternoon.	Prevailing Wind.	Rain and Melted Snow in inches.	Snow in inches.	REMARKS.
1	28¼	37½	Cloudy	Clear	N. W.			Clear part of morning.
2	25	46½	"	"	S. E., S. W.			Sun rose clear.
3	29	39	Clear	"	N. E.			Cloudy evening.
4	17	29½	"	Cloudy	N. E.			Snow squall part afternoon.
5	22	32	Cloudy	"	N. E.			
S 6	25	34	"	most all day.	N. E.			
7	24½	38	Clear	Clear	N, E.			
8	32	32½	Snow	Hail, Snow	N. E.	0.54	6.00	Snow till 11 A.M. (6 in.); hail and snow till 8 P. M.; bar. 9 A. M. 30.10; bar. 3 P.M. 29.15.
9	27	34	Clear	Cloudy	N. W.			Clouded over 3 P. M.; partly clear part of evening.
10	29	36½	Cloudy	most all day.	W., N.W.	0.01		Snow squalls 10 A. M. and 4 P.M.
11	21½	33	Clear	Cloudy	S. W.			Clouded over 3 P. M.
12	31	43½	Cloudy	Clear	S. W.	0.02		Rain before day; cloudy part of evening.
S 13	22½	30	Clear	"	N. W.			
14	23	49	Cloudy	Rainy	S. E., S.	0.26		Rain 3 to 11 P. M.
15	39½	45	"	Rain	W., N. E.	0.74		Foggy morning; rain 2 to 10 P.M., with snow 9 P.M.; cleared 11 P. M.
16	32½	41½	Clear	Clear	N. W.			
17	29½	49	"	"	S.	0.02		Cloudy part of evening with rain 7 P. M.; bar. 30.29 9 A. M.
18	42	58	Rain	Rain	S.	1.88		Steady rain all A. M.; showers in P. M. till 9 P. M., with thunder and lightning 6:15 P. M.; bar. 29.30 7 P. M.
19	26	32	Cloudy	Clear	N. W.			
S 20	26	50½	Clear	Hazy	S., E., S.	0.55		Rainy evening.
21	15	16½	"	Clear	N. W.			
22	9	22½	"	"	W.			
23	18	34½	"	"	S. W., S. E.			
24	23	34½	"	"	N. W.			
25	14	32½	"	"	N. W.			First ice gathered this season—3 inches thick.
26	28½	40	"	"	N. W.			Clouded over 5 P. M.
27	30	33½	Cloudy	Rain	N. E.			Rain with hail 2:30 to 11 P.M., and then snow.
28	27½	36½	"	Cloudy	N. E., S. W.	0.26		Snow before day and light squalls during day.
						4.28	6.00	

Mildest winter I have known.

March, 1870.

	Date.	Thermometer. Lowest.	Thermometer. Highest.	Weather. Morning.	Weather. Afternoon.	Prevailing Wind.	Rain and Melted Snow in inches.	Snow in inches.	REMARKS.
	1	32	36½	Cloudy	Clear	N. W.	----	----	Cleared 8:30 A. M.; cloudy part of afternoon.
	2	25	32	Clear	"	N. W.	----	----	
	3	20½	32	"	"	N. W.	----	----	
	4	20	29½	Cloudy	Snow	N. E.	0.16	----	Snow 10:30 A. M. to 4 P. M. and again part of evening.
	5	23½	33	"	Cloudy	N.	----	----	Light snow part of morning; cleared 4 P. M.; cloudy part of evening.
S	6	20	30	"	Snow	All points	----	----	Com. snowing at noon.
	7	28	34½	Snow	"	N. E.	----	6.00	8 A. M. 6 inches on ground; after that melts as it falls.
	8	28	34½	"	Clear	N. W.	0.16	----	Snow till 10 A. M.
	9	21	34	Clear	"	N. W.	----	----	
	10	25	40½	"	"	S. W.	----	----	Cloudy part of afternoon.
	11	26½	37	"	"	N. E.	----	----	
	12	30	33½	Cloudy	Cloudy	N. E.	----	----	Misty and rainy after 4 P. M.
S	13	29	32	Snow	Snow	N. E.	0.70	----	Snow till 4 P.M.; partly clear part of evening.
	14	26	38½	Clear	Clear	N.	----	----	Cloudy part of afternoon.
	15	25	42	"	"	N. E., E.	----	----	Cloudy part of afternoon.
	16	35	45	Rain	"	E., SW., NW.	1.03	----	Rain till 10:30 A. M.
	17	19	32½	Clear	Cloudy	N. W.	----	----	Partly clear part of P. M.; light snow squalls part of afternoon.
	18	28	40½	Cloudy	Clear	N.	----	----	Cleared 9 A. M.
	19	28	43½	Clear	"	N. W.	----	----	
S	20	29	55½	"	Cloudy	S. W.	----	----	
	21	38½	57½	"	Clear	N. E., S. W.	0.05	----	Rain before day; cloudy part of afternoon.
	22	37½	48	"	"	W.	----	----	Cloudy parts of afternoon and evening.
	23	35½	41½	"	"	N. W.	----	----	
	24	31	42	"	"	N. W.	----	----	
	25	20½	44	"	"	N. W.	----	----	
	26	28½	41	"	Cloudy	N. E., S. E.	----	----	Clouded over 3 P.M.; partly clear part of evening.
S	27	37	44	Rain	Rain	E.	1.64	----	Rain 7 A. M. to midnight; very violent wind.
	28	40½	44½	Cloudy	Cloudy	S. W.	0.02	----	Partly clear part of A. M.; light rain 10 A.M. to 6 P.M.
	29	38½	52	"	Clear	N.	----	----	Cleared 9 A.M.; cloudy evening.
	30	40	51½	Clear	Cloudy	N. E.	----	----	Clouded over 8:30 A. M.; clear part of afternoon.
	31	41½	51	"	"	N. E., E.	----	----	Clouded over 3 P. M.
							3.76	6.00	

Weather Record for New Brunswick, N. J.

April, 1870.

Date.	Thermometer. Lowest.	Thermometer. Highest.	Weather. Morning.	Weather. Afternoon.	Prevailing Wind.	Rain and Melted Snow in inches.	Snow in inches.	REMARKS.
1	41	45	Cloudy	Cloudy	E.			
2	39	47	Rain	Rain	N. E.			
S 3	40	48	Cloudy	Cloudy	N. E.	1.70		Rain before day; com. again 6:30 P. M.
4	34	38	"	Snow	N. E., N. W.	0.15		Rain before day, with 5 to 6 A. M., and steady snow after 2:10 P. M.
5	33	40	"	Rain	N. W., N. E.	1.28		8 A. M. four inches snow on the ground; partly clear part of the afternoon and steady rain 5 P. M.
6	36	48	"	Cloudy	N. E., N. W.	0.15		Rain before day and part of A. M.; partly clear part of afternoon.
7	37	52	Clear	"	N. W.			
8	41½	61	"	Clear	N. W., S. W.			
9	40½	62	"	"	N. W., S. W.			
S 10	40	60	"	"	E.			
11	46½	49	Rain	Rain	N. E.	0.35		Rain 8 A. M. to noon, and 3 to 9 P. M.
12	45½	64½	Clear	Clear	N.	0.02		Rain before day.
13	43	67	"	"	N. W.			Clouded over 5 P. M.
14	51	73	"	Cloudy	S. W.			Partly clear part of P. M.
15	58	76	"	"	S. W., S. E.			Clear evening.
16	42½	49	Cloudy	"	S. E.			Clear part of afternoon.
S 17	41½	47	Rain	Rain	E.			
18	46	50	"	"	E., S. E.	1.77		Rain till 6 P. M.; cleared 9 P. M.
19	39½	49	Cloudy	Clear	N. E., S. E.			Clear part of morning; cleared 3 P. M.
20	40½	56	Clear	"	S. W.			
21	39½	57½	Cloudy most all day.		S. E.			
22	44	59	Clear	Clear	N., S.			
23	42½	62½	"	"	S. E.			
S 24	43½	70½	"	"	S. W.			Pears and cherries flowered.
25	50½	58½	Cloudy	"	N.			Cleared 2:30 P. M.
26	40	66½	Clear	"	N. W., S. W.			
27	46	72½	"	"	S. W.			
28	58½	77½	"	Hazy	S. W.			Clouded over 5 P. M.; shower 5:30 to 6 P. M., and steady rain after 8:15 P.M.
29	49	54	Cloudy	Cloudy	N. E., S. W.	0.45		Rain before day and part of morning.
30	43	63	"	"	E., S.			
						5.87		

May, 1870.

	Date.	Thermometer.		Weather.		Prevailing Wind.	Rain and Melted Snow in inches.	Snow in inches.	REMARKS.
		Lowest.	Highest.	Morning.	Afternoon.				
S	1	46½	70½	Clear	Clear	N. W.	----	----	
	2	45	67	"	"	N. E.	----	----	
	3	45	67½	"	Cloudy	S. W.	0.01	----	Light rain part of afternoon.
	4	55	80½	Cl'r but hazy all day.		S. W., N. W.	0.07	----	Rain before day. B. D. Stell died.
	5	54	60½	Cloudy most all day.		S. W.	----	----	
	6	53½	63½	"	Cloudy	S. W.	----	----	Clear part of morning; light rain part of P. M., and showery evening.
	7	56½	72½	Clear	Clear	S. W., N. E.	0.64	----	Rain before day; cloudy part A. M.; clouded over 6:30 P. M.
S	8	54	58	Cloudy	Cloudy	N. E.	0.07	----	Light rain 4 to 6 P.M., with thunder storm in the E.; misty evening.
	9	52	61½	"	"	N. E., S. E.	0.03	----	Partly clear part P. M.; rain 3:30 to 4 P. M.
	10	51½	53	"	"	E.	0.45	----	Rain noon till 1 P.M., and thunder shower from the E. 3:15 to 5 P. M.
	11	48½	53	Rain	Rain	N. E.	0.44	----	Rain till 8 P.M.; cleared 10 P. M.
	12	46	66	Clear	Clear	S. W.	----	----	
	13	49½	69	"	"	S. W.	0.03	----	Cloudy evening with light shower.
	14	52½	76½	"	"	N.	----	----	
S	15	57	79½	"	"	S. W.	----	----	
	16	59½	81½	"	"	S. W.	----	----	
	17	58½	66	Cloudy	Cloudy	N. E., E.	----	----	Clear part of morning.
	18	51	65½	"	most all day.	N. E., S.	----	----	Clear evening.
	19	50	73½	Clear	Clear	S. W.	----	----	
	20	61½	75	Cloudy	"	S. W.	0.05	----	Shower 5 A. M.
	21	62	75	"	"	S. E.	0.73	----	Cleared 9 A.M.; thunder shower 6 P.M. and showery evening.
S	22	56½	69	Clear	"	N. E., S.	----	----	
	23	54	68½	Cloudy	most all day.	S. W.	----	----	
	24	60	74½	"	most all day.	S. W.	0.20	----	Rain 3:30 to 6.20 P. M.
	25	65	76	"	Clear	N. W., W.	----	----	Cleared 9 A. M.
	26	57	71½	Clear	"	N. E.	----	----	Cloudy evening.
	27	55	59	Cloudy	Rain	N. E.	0.25	----	Rain part of A. M. and from 2 to 7 P. M.
	28	51	60	"	Cloudy	N. E.	0.03	----	Rain before day.
S	29	56½	60	Rain	Rain	N. E.	0.15	----	Rain nearly all day at intervals till 9 P. M.
	30	57½	65	Cloudy	Cloudy	N. E., S. E.	----	----	
	31	56½	68½	Clear	Clear	S. E.	----	----	Cloudy part of afternoon.
							3.15	----	

June, 1870.

Date.	Thermometer.		Weather.		Prevailing Wind.	Rain and Melted Snow in inches.	Snow in inches.	REMARKS.
	Lowest.	Highest.	Morning.	Afternoon.				
1	57	68	Clear	Cloudy	S. W.	0.03		Light rain part of afternoon.
2	61	69	Cloudy	most all day.	S.			
3	62½	69½	Cloudy	Cloudy	E.	0.04		Light rain before day and 3 P. M.; partly clear part of afternoon.
4	62	71½	"	Clear	E.			Clouded over again 5 P. M.
S 5	63	73	"	"	S. E.			Cloudy evening.
6	65	74	"	"	S. E.			Clouded over 10 P. M.
7	65½	73½	"	Cloudy	N. E., S. E.	0.23		Rain before day, and from 9 to 11:30 A.M.; clear part of afternoon.
8	67½	80½	"	Clear	All points.			Cleared 9 A. M.; cloudy part of evening.
9	67	73½	"	Cloudy	E.			Partly clear part of morning; misty evening.
10	59	62½	Rain	Rain	E.			Com. raining 7:30 A. M.; at 1 P. M. 2 in. had fallen; rest of day more moderate.
11	59	66	"	Cloudy	N. E.	3.47		Rained hard till 8:30 and then light till 10 A. M.; rain again 11 P. M.
S 12	58	74	Cloudy	Clear	S. E.	0.13		Rain before day; cleared 8:30 A. M.
13	63	79½	"	most all day.	S.E., S.W			Light sprinkle 9 A. M.
14	68½	80	"	Clear	S. W.			Cleared 9 A. M.
15	65½	81	Clear	"	S. W.	0.28		Clouded over 7 P. M., with shower.
16	67	78½	"	Cloudy	S. W.	0.10		Shower 9:45 to 11 P. M.
17	66	77	"	Clear	S. W., N. E.	0.85		Clouded over 10 A. M.; wind shifted to N. E. and shower 10:30 to 11:30 A. M.
18	65½	83	"	"	S. W.			
S 19	69	86	"	"	All points.			
20	69½	86	"	Cloudy	S. W.	0.73		Clouded over 4 P. M., with showers all around during afternoon and evening; rain 9:50 P. M. to midnight.
21	64	74	"	Clear	N.			
22	57	75½	"	"	N. W.			
23	63	81½	"	"	N. W.			
24	67	86½	"	"	N. W.			
25	69½	90	"	"	N. W.			
S 26	74	88	"	"	N. W., N. E.			Cloudy evening.
27	71	84	Cloudy	"	S. W., E.	0.05		Shower 5:20 P. M., and cloudy part of evening.
28	72	91	Clear	"	N. W.			
29	76	85½	"	"	N. E., S. E.			
30	71	87	"	"	S. W.			
						5.91		

July, 1870.

	Date.	Thermometer. Lowest.	Thermometer. Highest.	Weather. Morning.	Weather. Afternoon.	Prevailing Wind.	Rain and Melted Snow in inches.	Snow in inches.	REMARKS.
	1	76½	83½	Clear	Cloudy	S. W., N. E.	0.18	----	Clouded over 10 A. M. and wind to N. E.; light rain 10:30 to 11:30 A. M. and 1:30 to 2:30 P. M.
	2	64	70½	Cloudy	"	N. E., S. E.	----	----	Partly clear part of P. M.
S	3	59½	64	Rain	"	N. E.	0.23	----	Rain till 8 A.M. and from 11 to noon.
	4	59½	72½	Cloudy	Clear	S. E.	----	----	Cleared 8 A. M. Chimes in Catholic church (Somerset street) rung.
	5	60	77	"	"	S. W.	----	----	Clear part of morning.
	6	65	79	"	most all day.	S. W.	----	----	
	7	69	80	"	" " day.	S. W.	0.14	----	Shower noon to 3 P.M.
	8	66½	78	Rain	Clear	S. W.	1.88	----	Rain till 9:30 A. M.; cleared 10 A. M.
	9	64	77½	Clear	"	N. W., S. W.	----	----	
S	10	62½	80	"	Cloudy	S. W.	----	----	Clear morning.
	11	66½	82	"	Clear	S. W.	----	----	Cloudy evening, with sprinkle 11:30 P. M.
	12	72½	85½	"	"	S. W., N. W.	0.33	----	Cloudy evening, with rain 5:40 to 8 P. M.
	13	70	83	"	"	N. W., S. W.	----	----	
	14	69	86	"	"	S. W.	----	----	
	15	72	84	"	"	N.W.,W.	----	----	Cloudy evening.
	16	74	86	"	"	All points	0.38	----	Cloudy part of P. M. and evening, with shower 4:15 to 4:30 P. M.
S	17	78	92	"	"	S. W	0.62	----	Cloudy part of P. M. and evening, with sprinkle 5:15 & showers 9:30 P. M.
	18	75½	90	"	"	N. W., S. W.	----	----	Cloudy evening.
	19	77½	87½	"	"	N. E., S. E.	----	----	
	20	74	79½	Cloudy	Cloudy	S. E.	----	----	
	21	72	86½	Clear	Clear	N W.	0.42	----	Rain till 6:30 A. M.; cleared 7:30 A. M.
	22	67½	81½	"	"	E.	----	----	
	23	70	87½	Cloudy	"	S. W.	----	----	Cleared 9:30 A.M.
S	24	75	88½	Clear	"	S. W.	----	----	Cloudy evening.
	25	76½	90½	"	"	N. W.	----	----	
	26	77½	89	"	"	N. W.	----	----	
	27	78	86	"	"	N. W., S. E.	----	----	Cloudy evening.
	28	70	79½	Cloudy	Cloudy	E.	0.08	----	Rain before day; clear part of P. M.; shower after 9:50 P. M.
	29	72½	84	Clear	Clear	S. W.	0.40	----	Shower before day; cloudy part of morning.
	30	67½	78	"	"	N. W.	----	----	
S	31	63	80½	"	"	N. W., S. W.	----	----	
							4.66	---	

.1 days 80° and above and 12 days 85° and above.

August, 1870.

Date.	Thermometer. Lowest.	Thermometer. Highest.	Weather. Morning.	Weather. Afternoon.	Prevailing Wind.	Rain and Melted Snow in inches.	Snow in inches.	REMARKS.
1	65½	83½	Clear	Clear	S. W.	----	----	
2	68	86½	"	"	S. W., N. W.	----	----	
3	70	82	"	Cloudy	All points.	0.28	----	Cl'ded over 2:15 with shower 2:20 to 2:35 P.M. and light shower 5 to 8 P. M.
4	72	83½	Cloudy	"	All points.	0.02	----	Partly clear part of A. M.; light rain 7 P. M.; cleared 9 P. M.
5	65½	84	Clear	Clear	N. W.	----	----	
6	69½	88	"	"	All points.	----	----	
S 7	70	88½	"	"	S. W.	----	----	
8	70	87½	Cloudy	"	S., S. W.	----	----	Foggy A.M.; cleared 9 A. M.
9	74	89	"	"	S. W.	----	----	Cleared 9 A.M.; com. raining 11:45 P. M.
10	73½	81	Rain	Cloudy	S. W., S. E.	1.80	----	Rain till 8:30 A.M.; shower 4:30 to 5 P.M.; thunder showers all ev'g after 8.
11	73	80½	Cloudy	most all day.	S. W.	3.15	----	Heavy shower before day; light 7:30 A.M. and heavy again 5:45 to 11 P. M.
12	70½	85	"	Clear	S. W.	0.01	----	Cleared 8 A.M.; cloudy part ev'g with light rain 7 P.M.
13	71½	81½	Clear	"	All points.	0.79	----	Cloudy part of A. M., with showers 8 to 10 A.M.; cloudy evening with shower 6:40 to 9:40 P. M.
S 14	61	70½	Rain	"	N. E.	0.52	----	Rain till 11 A.M.; cl'red 2 P.M.
15	59½	75	Clear	"	NW, NE, SE	----	----	
16	61	78	"	"	S.	----	----	
17	64	79	"	"	S. W.	----	----	
18	66	83	"	"	S. W.	----	----	
19	68½	85½	"	"	S. W.	----	----	Northern lights at 9 P. M.
20	71½	85½	"	"	S. W., N.	----	----	
S 21	64	77	"	"	N. E.	----	----	Hazy morning.
22	60½	77	"	"	N.	----	----	Hazy evening.
23	61½	75½	"	Cloudy	N. E.	----	----	
24	68	76	Cloudy	"	E.	0.05	----	Rain 7:30 to 9 A.M.; clear part of evening.
25	70	87½	"	Clear	S. W.	0.08	----	Cleared 9 A.M.; clouded over 10 P.M., with sh'er 11½ P.M.
26	67	75½	Clear	"	N.	----	----	
27	57	71	"	"	N. E., S. E.	----	----	
S 28	55½	71½	"	Cloudy	S. W.	----	----	Clouded over 8 A. M.; cleared 9:30 P. M.
29	65	82½	Cloudy	Clear	S. W.	----	----	Cleared 9 A. M.; light rain 3:40 P. M. from one little cloud.
30	70	78½	"	"	N. W.	----	----	Cleared 8 A. M.
31	60	77	Clear	"	All points.	----	----	
						6.70	----	

June 1 to August 31 was 80° and above on 53 days.

Weather Record for New Brunswick, N. J.

September, 1870.

Date	Thermometer Lowest	Thermometer Highest	Wind Morning	Wind Afternoon	Prevailing Wind	Rain and Melted Snow in inches	Snow in inches	REMARKS
1	59	80½	Clear	Clear	S. W., S. E.			
2	62	80	"	"	S. E.			
3	66	79½	"	Cloudy	S. W., S. E.	0.22		Partly clear part of evening; rain 10 p. m. to midnight.
S 4	68	77½	"	Clear	S. W.			Cloudy part of morning, with light sprinkle about noon.
5	60½	73	"	"	N. W.			
6	55	75	"	"	N. W.			
7	55	76	"	"	S. W.			Cloudy part of evening.
8	61	74½	"	Cloudy	N. E., S. E.			
9	63½	70½	Cloudy	Clear	S. E.			Cleared 3 p. m.
10	57	75	"	"	S. W., S. E.			Clear 9 a. m. to noon; cloudy noon to 3 p. m.
S 11	53	69	Clear	"	N.			
12	49	69½	"	"	N. E., N. W.			
13	49	74	"	"	All points			
14	52½	76½	"	"	All points			
15	54	76	"	"	S. W.			
16	63	77½	"	"	S. W., S. E.			Cloudy evening; com. raining about midnight.
17	65½	67	Rain	Rain	N. E.	0.93		Heavy shower from S. E. to 6 a. m.; light rain till 8 a. m., steady rain all day after noon.
S 18	63	76½	Cloudy	Clear	N.		0.80	Rain before day; partly clear 10 a. m. till noon; cloudy part of afternoon.
19	56	70½	Clear	"	N. E.			
20	50½	72½	"	"	N. E.			
21	53	70	"	"	N. E., S. E.			Foggy morning.
22	48½	71	"	"	All points			
23	53	75	"	"	S. W.			
24	61¼	80	"	"	S. W.			Very brilliant Northern lights 10 to 10:30 p. m.
S 25	65	83	"	"	S. W.			
26	64	75	"	"	N. E., S. E.			Cloudy part of afternoon.
27	60	74	"	"	S. W.			Cloudy part of afternoon.
28	59	75½	"	"	N. E., S. E.			
29	64	72	Cloudy	most all	S. E.			
30	64½	72	"	Rain	N. E., S. E.	1.13		Light rain at intervals 7 to 9:45 a. m., and then steady storm till 4 p. m. and misty rest of day.
						3.08		

October, 1870.

	Date.	Thermometer. Lowest.	Thermometer. Highest.	Weather. Morning.	Weather. Afternoon.	Prevailing Wind.	Rain and Melted Snow in inches.	Snow in inches.	REMARKS.
	1	66	75½	Clear	Cloudy	W.	0.10		Rain before day; cloudy part of evening.
S	2	62	67½	Cloudy	"	N. E., E.			Clear part of A. M.; com. raining 9:15 P. M.
	3	60½	65	Rain	"	N. E.	0.07		Rain till 10 A. M.
	4	61	71	Clear	Clear	S. W.			Cloudy part of morning.
	5	54	68	"	Cloudy	N. W.			
	6	58	62	Cloudy	"	N. E.			
	7	50½	59	"	"	N. E.			Clear part of morning.
	8	48½	64½	Clear	Clear	N. E.			
S	9	45½	66	"	"	N. W.			Frost.
	10	48	68	"	"	S. W.			
	11	50	70	Cloudy	most all day.	S. W., S.			Rain 10 P. M.
	12	63	68½	Rain	Clear	S. W.	2.75		Rain till noon; cleared 12:30 P. M.
	13	55½	63	Cloudy	"	W.	0.05		Rain parts of A. M.; cleared 11 A.M.
	14	49	62	Clear	"	N. W.			Northern lights 7:30 P. M.
	15	45	66½	"	"	S. W.			
S	16	48½	70	"	"	S. W.			
	17	50½	66	"	"	S. W.			Cloudy part of afternoon.
	18	60	66	Cloudy	"	S. W., N. W.			Partly clear part of A. M.
	19	40	55½	Clear	Cloudy	All points			
	20	51	71½	Rain	Rain	S. W.	1.11		Rain till 8 A.M. and then at intervals till 3 P. M.; then steady rain till 8 P.M.
	21	47½	55½	Cloudy	Cloudy	W., S. W.			Cleared 4:30 P. M.
	22	43	60	Clear	Clear	S. W.			
S	23	42	59½	"	"	S. W.			
	24	42	65	"	"	S. W.			Northern lights all evening.
	25	49½	67½	Cloudy	"	S. W.			Cleared 9:30 A. M.; cloudy part of evening; Northern lights due West 9:15 .M.; blood red.
	26	55	57	"	"	N. E.	0.02		Rain before day.
	27	36½	56½	Clear	Cloudy	N. E., S. E.	0.04		Clouded over 8:30 A.M.; light rain part of afternoon and at 10 P. M.
	28	48	60½	"	Clear	N. W.			Cloudy part of evening.
	29	44½	56	"	"	N. W.			
S	30	36½	59	"	Cloudy	N. E., S. E.	0.08		Light rain 4 to 6 P.M.; com. raining 10 P. M.
	31	46	55	"	Clear	W.	0.78		Rain before day; cloudy 10 to 11 A. M., with light rain.
							5.60		

November, 1870.

	Date.	Thermometer. Lowest.	Highest.	Weather. Morning.	Afternoon.	Prevailing Wind.	Rain and Melted Snow in inches.	Snow in inches.	REMARKS.
	1	42½	56	Clear	Clear	N., S. W.			
	2	40	62½	Foggy	"	S. W.			Cleared 10:30 A. M.; cloudy part of afternoon.
	3	53½	61½	Cloudy	"	S. W., N. W.	0.12		Rain before day and at intervals from 9 A. M. to noon; cleared 1:45 P. M.
	4	40½	56	Clear	"	W.			
	5	46½	56	Cloudy	Cloudy	W., N. W.			Partly clear part of morning; light sprinkle part of afternoon; cleared 5:00 P. M.
S	6	41½	52½	Clear	Clear	N. E., S. E.			
	7	38½	56	"	"	N. W.			Hazy morning.
	8	38	58	"	"	N. E., S. W.			
	9	48½	67½	Cloudy	Rain	S. W., N. W.	0.21		Foggy morning; clear noon to 3 P. M.; rain 3:45 to 7 P. M.; cleared 8 P. M.
	10	40	45	Clear	Clear	N. W.			
	11	35	52	"	"	N. W.			
	12	41	56½	"	"	N. W.			
S	13	41	56	"	"	N. W.			
	14	39	57	"	"	N. E.			
	15	38	45½	"	"	N.			
	16	31	45½	"	"	N. W., W.			First real killing frost.
	17	31	46	"	"	S. W.			
	18	31½	42	Cloudy	Cloudy	S. W.	0.01		Partly clear part of morning; light rain part of afternoon; cleared 8 P. M.
	19	29	34½	Clear	Clear	N. W.			Cloudy part of afternoon.
S	20	30	43½	"	"	S. W.			Cloudy part of evening.
	21	36	49	Cloudy	Cloudy	S. W., N. W.			Clear part of morning and part of evening.
	22	38	49	Rain	Rain	N. E.	1.15		Rain till midnight.
	23	45½	48	Cloudy	most all day.	S. W.			
	24	39	43½	Clear	Clear	W., N. W.			Cloudy part of morning.
	25	35	46	"	"	S. W.			Clouded over 5 P. M., and com. raining 9:30 P. M.
	26	39	46½	Cloudy	"	W.	0.42		Light rain and misty till 8 A. M.; cleared 9 A. M.
S	27	38½	56½	Clear	"	W.			
	28	40	57½	"	"	S. W.			
	29	40½	61½	"	"	S. W.			Cloudy evening; mosquitoes about again.
	30	37½	46½	"	"	N.			Cloudy part of evening; D. A. C. Bowmonville's wife died 6 P. M.
							1.91		

December, 1870.

Date.	Thermometer. Lowest.	Thermometer. Highest.	Weather. Morning.	Weather. Afternoon.	Prevailing Wind.	Rain and Melted Snow in inches.	Snow in inches.	REMARKS.
1	32	49	Clear	Clear	S. W.			
2	36	52	"	"	S. W.			
3	43	47	"	"	N. W.			
S 4	40	54	"	"	S. W.			
5	41	54	"	Cloudy	E.			Cleared 10 P. M.
6	44½	48½	Cloudy most all day.		W.	0.05		Rain before day.
7	37	45½	Clear	Cloudy	All points.	0.04		Rain 8 to 10 P. M.
8	42	47	C'y m'st all day.		S. W., N. W.			
9	37½	43½	Clear	Clear	N. W.			
10	32	41	"	"	N. W.			
S 11	29	37½	Cloudy	Cloudy	N. E.			Com. raining 8 P. M.
12	36	52	Rain	Rain	E.	1.00		Heavy rain till 4 P M.; light rain and misty rest of day.
13	43½	48½	Clear	Cloudy	N. W.			
14	41	44	"	Clear	S. W.			Cloudy part of afternoon.
15	35	37	"	"	N. W.			A few snowflakes 7:30 A M.
16	26½	34	"	"	N. W.			
17	27	34	"	Cloudy	N. W.	0.03		Snowy evening after 7:45 P. M. to 11 P M.—¼ inch on ground.
S 18	31½	39½	"	Clear	S. W., N. W.			Snow squalls at noon.
19	26½	42½	"	Cloudy	S. W.			Com. hailing 7 P M. and at 9:30 turned to rain.
20	39½	43½	Cloudy	Clear	W.	0.67		Rain before day; cleared 8 A. M.; cloudy evening.
21	33½	35	Clear	"	N. W.			Ther falling steadily P. M.
22	17½	26½	"	"	N. W.			Cloudy evening.
23	20	25	Snow	"	N. E., N.			Light snow till 10 A.M.; cleared 10:15 A.M ; cloudy evening.
24	14	22	Clear	"	N. W.			
S 25	13½	27	"	"	N. W.			Farmers plowed in every month in 1870.
26	20	32	Cloudy	Cloudy	S. W.			Cleared 9:30 P.M.
27	21	32½	Clear	Clear	S. W.			Cloudy evening.
28	29	35	Snow	Snow	S. W., N. E.	0.25		Snow 8 A.M to 5 P. M. and part of evening.
29	25	26	Cloudy	Clear	N. E., N. W.			Ther. highest 8 A.M., grows steadily colder afterwards; 15° at 9 P M.
30	8½	34	Clear	Cloudy	W., S. E.	0.30		Snow 5:45 to 11 P. M.
31	30	40	"	Clear	S. W.			Cloudy part of A.M., with snow squalls; cloudy part of evening—4 in. snow on ground.
						2.34		

Rain and melted snow in 1870—52.99 inches.

January, 1871.

Date.	Thermometer. Lowest.	Thermometer. Highest.	Weather. Morning.	Weather. Afternoon.	Prevailing Wind.	Rain and Melted Snow in inches.	Snow in inches.	REMARKS.
S 1	29	38	Clear	Clear	W.			
2	27½	41½	"	Cloudy	S. W.			
3	24	34	"	Clear	S. W.			Cloudy part of afternoon.
4	20	27	"	"	N. W.			Cloudy evening.
5	23½	46½	Cloudy most all day.		S. W.			
6	42	44	"	Cloudy	S. W.	0.09		Rain 9:45 A. M. to 1 P. M.; clear part of evening.
7	26	29	Clear	Clear	N. W.			
S 8	17½	24	Cloudy	Snow	N. E.	0.10		Snow 1 to 4 P. M., and part of evening.
9	13½	23	Clear	Clear	N.			
10	10	26½	"	Cloudy	N., S. W.			
11	23½	35	Cloudy	Clear	S. W.			
12	32½	49	Clear	"	S. W.			
13	34	51	"	"	N. E., S. E.			
14	35	48	"	Cloudy	N. E.			
S 15	43	54	Cloudy	"	E.			Partly clear part of A. M.; rainy evening and steady rain after 9:30 P. M.
16	44½	49	Clear	Clear	N. W.	1.23		Rain before day; cloudy part of evening.
17	28½	40½	"	"	N. W.			
18	33	37½	Cloudy	Cloudy	N.			
19	22	35	Clear	"	N. E.			
20	30	35½	Cloudy	"	S. W.			
21	32½	42½	"	Clear	S. W.	0.10		Snow before day; clear 9 A. M. to 3 P. M.; rain 7 to 10 P. M.
S 22	22	24	Clear	"	N. W.			
23	7½	13½	Cloudy	Snow	N. E.		6.00	Snow 9:15 A. M. to 10 P. M.; ther. highest at noon; 8° at 3 P. M.
24	6	21	"	Cloudy	N. E., N. W.			Light snow 9 to 10 A. M.; cleared 5 P. M.
25	8	26	Clear	"	W., N.			
26	5	15	Snow	Snow	N. E.		11.00	5° 9 A.M., 7.5° at noon, 11.5° 3 P. M., 15°9 P.M.; snowed violently from 3 A.M. to 4 P. M., and moderately to midnight
27	20	29	Cloudy	Clear	N. W., S. W.			Cleared 10:30 A M; ther. on a steady rise from lowest on 26th to highest on 27th
28	15	27	"	Snow	N. E.			Commenced snowing 3 P M.
S 29	20	30	Snow	Cloudy	N. E., S. W.		5.00	Snow till 8 A M and lightly at intervals rest of A M.; clear part of afternoon.
30	23	35	Cloudy most all day.		S. W.			
31	31	38	"	Rain	S. W.	0.42		Rain 2 to 9 P. M.
						1.94	22.00	

February, 1871.

Date	Thermometer Lowest	Thermometer Highest	Weather Morning	Weather Afternoon	Prevailing Wind	Rain and Melted Snow in inches	Snow in in the	REMARKS
1	37	42	Cloudy	Cloudy	S. W.	0.03		Rain 2:30 to 4 P. M.; cleared 6 P. M.
2	23	40	"	"	S. W.			Cleared 8 P. M.
3	24	37	Clear	Clear	S. W.			Cloudy part of morning.
4	33½	39	"	"	S. W., N. W.			Cloudy part of evening.
S 5	2	10	"	"	N.			Ther. lowest 9 A. M.; very high wind all day. A. K. Cogswell died.
6	3½	23	"	"	N.			
7	12	29	"	"	N. E.			Cloudy evening.
8	26	35	Snow	Cloudy	N. E.	0.11		Snow till 10 A.M. and misty afterward.
9	34	38½	Cloudy	"	S. W.			Foggy morning; cleared 6 P. M.
10	29	33½	Clear	Clear	W.			
11	18	28½	"	Cloudy	S. W.			Clouded over about 4 P. M.
S 12	25	30	Snow	"	N. E.		6.00	Snow till noon.
13	23	30	Clear	"	N.			Clouded over 4 P. M.
14	22	26	Snow	Snow	N. E.		8.00	Snow 7 A. M. to 4:30 P. M.; clear part of evening.
15	15½	31	Clear	Cloudy	N. W., S. W.			Clouded over 3 P. M.
16	21	45	Cloudy	Clear	S. W., N. W.			Cleared 10 A. M.
17	26½	41	Clear	Cloudy	S. W.			Snow 8:30 to 9:30 P. M., but melts as it falls.
18	36½	52	Rain	Clear	S. W.	1.05		Rain 12:30 A. M. to 1 P. M.; cleared 4 P. M.
S 19	26½	36	Clear	Cloudy	S. W.			Clouded over 9 A. M.; cleared 9 P. M.
20	34	45	"	Clear	S. W.			Cloudy part A. M.; clouded over 7 P. M. and rain 8:30 P. M.
21	30	34	Snow	"	N. E.	0.18		Rain before day and snow 7 to 11 A.M.; cleared 3 P. M.
22	13	27½	Clear	"	N. E.			
23	17	36	"	Cloudy	All points	0.02		Misty and light rain after 8 P. M.
24	34	48½	Cloudy	"	S. W., N. E.			Partly clear part of A. M.
25	41	54	Clear	"	S. W.			Foggy morning and partly clear part of evening.
S 26	38½	41	Rain	Rain	N. E.			Steady rain 7:45 A. M. to 2 P.M., and at intervals rest of day and evening.
27	36½	45	Cloudy	Clear	S. W., N. W.	0.98		Rain before day; cleared 9 A.M., but heavy mist; cloudy parts of day and evening.
28	28½	37½	Clear	"	N. W., S. W.			Captain Isaac Fisher died.

2 37 14.00

Weather Record for New Brunswick, N. J.

March, 1871.

Date.	Thermometer. Lowest.	Highest.	Weather. Morning.	Afternoon.	Prevailing Wind.	Rain and Melted Snow in inches.	Snow in inches.	REMARKS.
1	34	57	Clear	Clear	S. W.			Rain part of morning.
2	35½	59½	"	"	E.			
3	52	64	Cloudy	Cloudy	S. W.	0.23		Rain 9:30 A.M. to 1 P.M. and from 6 to 6:30 P. M.
4	39	43	"	Rain	N. E.	0.12		Clear part of A. M.; rain part of P. M. and evening with snow; cleared 10 P. M.
S 5	33	50	Clear	Clear	N. W., S. W.			
6	37½	47½	Rain	"	S. W., N. W.	0.24		Rain till 10 A. M.; cloudy part of afternoon.
7	36	49½	Clear	"	All points.			
8	34½	47	"	Cloudy	E.			Clouded over 10 A.M.; misty afternoon 4:30 P. M
9	44	68	Cloudy	Clear	N. E., S. W.	0.04		Misty & light rain till 10 A.M.
10	51½	60	Rain	Cloudy	S. W.	0.44		Rain at intervals till 9 A.M.; cleared 11 A. M.; cloudy party of evening.
11	43	58	Clear	"	S. E.			Clear part of afternoon; light rain 6:15 P. M.
S 12	50	59	Rain	Rain	S.	0.60		Shower at intervals all day till 5 P.M ; cleared 10 P.M.
13	37½	51½	Clear	Clear	N. W.			Cloudy part of evening.
14	36	48	"	"	N. W.			Cl'y ev'ng with rain 10 P.M.
15	40½	44	Rain	Cloudy	E.	0.38		Rain till 10 A. M.
16	41	43½	Cloudy	"	E.	0.05		Misty all day with light rain at times.
17	40	54	Foggy	"	N. E.			Light rain 3:45 P. M.; rainy night after 6:15.
18	44	50	Rain	"	N. E., S.	0.75		Rain till noon; cleared about 9 P. M.
S 19	40	62	Clear	Clear	All points.			
20	41	47	"	Cloudy	N. E., E.			Clouded over 3 P. M. and com. raining 7 P. M.
21	40	48	Rain	"	N. W.	1.32		Rained hard till 6 A.M.; then light till 11 A. M.; cleared 6 P. M.
22	39	53½	Clear	Clear	N. W., W.			
23	41	51	"	Cloudy	N. E.			Clear part of evening.
24	34½	47½	"	Clear	N. E.			
25	34	48	"	"	N. W.			
S 26	34	47	Cloudy	Cloudy	S. E.			Clear part of A.M ; rain 4:30 P.M. & with sn'w aft'r 5 PM.
27	36	46	Rain	"	N. E., N. W.	0.76		Rain till 8 A.M. & misty rest of A. M.; clear part of P. M.
28	34	40	Clear	Clear	N. W.			
29	31	48	"	"	N., S. W.			Cloudy part of morning.
30	39	45	Rain	Misty	S. W., E.	0.16		Rained at intervals 7 A.M. to 2 P. M.
31	40½	54	Clear	Clear	N. E.			Cloudy party of evening.
						5.09		

April, 1871.

Date.	Ther-mometer. Lowest.	Ther-mometer. Highest.	Weather. Morning.	Weather. Afternoon.	Prevailing Wind.	Rain and Melted Snow in inches.	Snow in inches.	REMARKS.
1	41	44	Cloudy	Rain	E.			Light rain part of morning; steady rain after noon and after 8, with snow and hail.
S 2	34½	46½	"	Clear	N.	0.90		Snow and rain before day; ground covered with snow; cleared 3 P. M.
3	37	56½	"	most all day.	S. E.			Rain 9 P. M.
4	45	59½	"	Clear	N. W.	0.65		Rain till 6:30 A. M.; cleared 10 A. M.
5	45½	50	Clear	"	N. W.			
6	34	56	"	"	S. W.			
7	42½	67	"	"	S. W.			Cloudy part of morning.
8	55	82½	"	"	S. W.			Foggy morning; warmest day in April since 1847 except April 23, '61—83°.
S 9	56	80	"	"	S. W.			Hazy part of morning and afternoon. Northern lights.
10	59	76	"	"	N. W., S. W.			
11	56½	63	"	Cloudy	N. E.			Clouded 8 A. M., but clear part of afternoon; lightning in N. W. in evening.
12	48½	59	"	Clear	N. W.			Cherries flowered.
13	45	65	"	"	S. W., N. W.			Cloudy 10 A. M. to 4 P. M., with sprinkle 3:30 P. M.
14	40½	58½	"	"	N., S. E.			Northern lights.
15	41	58	"	"	All points			Cloudy part of morning with sprinkle 9:30 A. M.
S 16	41½	57	"	"	N. W.			Pears flowered.
17	37	55½	"	"	N. W.			Partly cloudy part of P. M.
18	39	60	"	"	N. W., S. W.			Northern lights.
19	48	56	Cloudy	Cloudy	E.			Light rain between 4 and 5 P. M.
20	48	67½	"	"	N. E., S. W.	0.13		Rain part of A. M., cleared 5 P. M.
21	53½	70	Clear	Clear	S. E., N. W.	0.01		Cloudy part of afternoon with rain 5 P. M.
22	53	58½	Cloudy	Cloudy	N. W.			Clear 5 P. M.
S 23	43½	56½	Clear	Clear	N. W.			
24	41	61½	"	"	N. W.			
25	44	68	"	"	S. W.			Cloudy parts of afternoon and evening.
26	52	67	"	"	All points.			
27	50	53	Cloudy	Rain	S. E.			Light rain part of morning; steady rain after 1 P. M.
28	44½	51	"	Cloudy	N. E.	1.50		Rain before day and part of afternoon.
29	49	62	"	most all day.	S. W.	0.03		Rain 1:30 P. M.
S 30	48	67½	Clear	Clear	N. W.			Cloudy part of evening.

3.22

27th Col. Joseph Warren Scott died.

Weather Record for New Brunswick, N. J.

May, 1871.

Date	Thermometer Lowest	Thermometer Highest	Weather Morning	Weather Afternoon	Prevailing Wind	Rain and Melted Snow in inches	Snow in inches	REMARKS
1	50	63	Clear	Clear	All points			Cloudy part of morning and part of afternoon.
2	48	67	"	"	N. E., S. E.			Cloudy evening.
3	54	60½	Cloudy	Cloudy	S. E., N. E.			Rain 7:30 P. M.
4	49	52	Rain	Rain	N. E.			Rain all day except from 1 to 3 P. M.
5	47	52	"	Cloudy	N. E.	2.16		Rain till 1 P. M.
6	48½	54	Cloudy	Rain	N. E., S.			Rain 3:30 P. M.
S 7	48	59	Clear	Clear	N. W.	0.98		Rain before day; cleared 6 A.M.; light rain (0.01) 7 P. M.
8	43	58½	"	"	N. W.			Northern lights.
9	40½	54	Cloudy	Cloudy	N. W.			Frost; clouded over at sunrise; partly clear part of evening.
10	46½	63	Clear	Clear	N. W.			
11	43	62½	"	"	N. E., S. W.			
12	46¼	65½	"	Hazy	S. W.			
13	50	72	"	Clear	N. W.			
S 14	41½	61	"	"	N. W.			Frost.
15	43	66	"	"	N. W., S. W.			
16	47	71	"	"	N. E., S. E.			Clouded over 8 P.M. and showery after 9 P.M. with lightning.
17	61	70	Rain	"	S. W., N.	0.16		Rain till 9:30 A.M.; cleared 1:30 P. M.
18	47½	65½	Clear	"	N. E., S. W.			
19	47	72	"	"	N. W., S. W.			
20	52½	78	"	"	S. W.			
S 21	56	76	"	"	S. W., S. E.			
22	56½	76	C'y m'st all day		S.E., S.W., N.			
23	60	71½	Clear	Clear	N. W.			
24	50	71	"	"	N. W., S. W.			
25	52	79	"	"	S. W.			
26	68	86	"	"	S. W., W.			Cloudy part of afternoon.
27	66	84	"	"	N. W., E.			Cloudy evening.
S 28	62	75	"	"	S. E.			Cloudy part of morning.
29	61	84	"	"	S. W.			Foggy morning.
30	68	87½	"	"	S. W.			Warmest day in May since May 28, 1851.
31	74	82½	C'y m'st all day		S. W., N. E.	0.20		Shower from N. E. 2:15 P. M. and rain 3:40 to 5 P.M.
						3.50		

Weather Record for New Brunswick, N. J.

June, 1871.

Date.	Thermometer. Lowest.	Thermometer. Highest.	Weather. Morning.	Weather. Afternoon.	Prevailing Wind.	Rain and Melted Snow in inches.	Snow in inches.	REMARKS.
1	65	73	Cloudy	Clear	S. E.			Cleared 3 P. M.
2	59	76	Clear	"	S. W.			Cloudy part of A. M., and part of evening.
3	67½	86½	"	"	S. W, N. W.			Cloudy part of A. M., and part of evening.
S 4	73	85½	"	Cloudy	N. W., N.	0.13		Clear part of afternoon; showery 6:50 to 9 P. M.; cleared 10 P. M.
5	66	83	"	Clear	N. E.			
6	63	81	"	"	S. E., S.			
7	66½	82½	C'y m'st all day	S. W., N. W.		0.82		Showers 5:30 to 7 P. M., and steady rain 8 to 11 P. M.
8	71	78	Cloudy	Clear	S. W.			Clear 4 P. M.
9	64	75¼	Clear	"	N. E.			
10	55	76	"	"	S. W.			
S 11	64	76½	Cloudy	Cloudy	S. W.	0.54		Northern lights 10 A.M.; showers 11:20 A.M to 4:30 P. M.; cleared 8 P. M.
12	60	69	Rain	Clear	N.E., N.W. S.W.	0.64		Rain 5 to 11 A. M.; cleared 2 P. M.; shower 4 P. M.
13	57	77	Clear	"	S. W.			
14	58	73¼	"	"	N. W., S. W.			
15	58	71	Cloudy	"	N., S. E.	0.53		Clear part A.M. and cloudy part P.M.; rain 5 to 8:30 A. M. and 4 to 4:20 P. M.
16	57	70	Clear	"	N. W.			
17	55	69½	"	Cloudy	N. E., S. E.	0.06		Clouded over 3 P. M. and rain 9:30 to 11 P. M.
S 18	62	75	Rain	"	S. E., N. W.	1.66		Rain to 11 A. M.; clear part P. M.; rain 4 to 6:20 P M.; clear part of evening.
19	61	74	Cloudy	Clear	N., S. W.			Clear part of morning.
20	64	82½	Clear	"	S. W., N. W.	0.36		Clouded over 6 P.M.; rain 6:30 to 10:30 P. M.
21	60½	73½	"	"	N.			
22	57	68½	"	"	N. E., S. E.			Cloudy 8:30 A.M. to 3 P. M.
23	62	78	"	"	N. W., S. W.			Cloudy evening.
24	61¼	66	Show'rs	Cloudy	N. E.	1.07		Shower till 1 P.M. and again 8 to 10 P. M., with thunder and lightning.
S 25	59	72½	Clear	Clear	N. E., S. E.	0.04		Rain 12 to 1 A. M.; cloudy part of morning
26	58	76	"	"	S. W.			Cloudy part of morning.
27	62	79	"	"	S. W., S. E.			Amos Robins died.
28	65	79	C'y m'st all day	S. W., S. E.		0.05		Light rain 9:30 to 11 A. M., and 4:30 to 5 P. M.
29	65	73½	Cloudy	Clear	N. W.			Cleared 10 A. M.
30	55	70	Clear	"	N. W.			
						5.90		

July, 1871.

Date.	Thermometer. Lowest.	Thermometer. Highest.	Weather. Morning.	Weather. Afternoon.	Prevailing. Wind.	Rain and Melted Snow in inches.	Snow in inches.	REMARKS.
1	55	68	Cloudy	Cloudy	S. E.	0.05		Clouded over 7 A. M.; rain 8:45 to 9:30 A. M.
S 2	63	77½	"	Clear	S. W.			
3	69	73½	"	most all day.	S. E.	2.50		Shower to 7 A.M. and noon to 1.15 P. M.—2.22 in 1 hour.
4	66	76	"	most all day.	S. E.			
5	68½	80½	Clear	Clear	S. W.			
6	68	84	Cloudy	most all day.	S. W.	0.10		Shower 5:15 to 6:30 P. M.; com. again 10:45 P. M.
7	71	84	Clear	Clear	S. W., N. W.	0.06		Rain before day.
8	64½	81	"	"	N. W.			
S 9	67	84½	"	"	S. W.			Cloudy part of A. M.; cloudy evening with rain 9:50 to 11 P. M.
10	71	84½	"	"	N. W.	0.14		Rain before day.
11	71	83½	"	Cloudy	All points.	0.18		Shower 2:15 P.M. and steady rain after 7:30 P. M.
12	72	83	Cloudy	Clear	S. W.	0.76		Rain before day.
13	70	82	Clear	"	N. E.			
14	71	79	Cloudy	"	E.	0.02		Rain 12:45 P.M.; cl'red 3 P.M.
15	69	84½	"	"	S. W., N. E.			Cleared 8 A. M.; cloudy part of afternoon.
S 16	69	83½	C'y m'st all day.		All points.	1.14		Heavy rain with hail 5:30 to 7 P. M (1.14) and com. again 10:15 P. M.
17	67	76	Clear	Clear	S. W., N. W.	0.38		Rain before day.
18	60	77	"	"	N. W., S. W.			
19	66	69	Cloudy	Cloudy	S. E., N. E.	0.17		Rain 10 A M. to 3 P. M
20	60	73	"	Clear	N. W.	0.12		Rain before day; cleared 8:30 A. M.
21	61½	72	Clear	Cloudy	N. W., S. W.	0.22		Clear part of P. M.; rain 6:45 to 7:15 P. M and 10 P. M. to midnight.
22	58	72	"	Clear	N. W.			Cloudy part of afternoon.
S 23	55	72	"	"	N. W., S.			
24	57	73½	Cloudy	most all day.	N. E.			
25	62	66½	"	Rain	N. E.			Com. raining 2 P. M.; northeast storm.
26	60	72	"	Cloudy	E., S. W.	0.78		Rain before day; cl'red 5 P.M.
27	62	78	"	most all day.	S. W.	0.17		Rain 10 P. M. to midnight.
28	65	78	"	most all day.	S. W.			
29	66	73	"	Cloudy	N. E.	0.07		Rain before day.
S 30	68	77	"	most all day.	S. E.	2.04		Rain 3:45 to 7 P. M.; .90 falling from 5 to 6 P. M.
31	65	76	C'y m'st all day.		All points.	0.01		Rain about 5 A. M.
						8.91		

The remarkable showers on 3rd and 30th were entirely local.

August, 1871.

Date.	Ther-mometer. Lowest.	Ther-mometer. Highest.	Weather. Morning.	Weather. Afternoon.	Prevailing Wind.	Rain and Melted Snow in inches.	Snow in inches.	REMARKS.
1	63½	76	Clear	Clear	E., S.			
2	62	80	"	"	S. W.			
3	66½	82	"	"	S. W.			
4	73	83½	Cloudy most all day.		S. W.	0.15		Shower 11 to 11:30 P. M.
5	75	83	"	Clear	W.	0.01		Light rain 10 to 10:30 A. M.
S 6	66½	82	Clear	"	N. W., S. W.			
7	65½	83½	"	"	S. W.			Cloudy evening.
8	73	81½	Cloudy most all day.		S. W.	0.38		Shower till 9 A. M.
9	71	80	Clear	Clear	N. W.			
10	62	78½	"	"	All points.			
11	63	81	"	"	S W.			
12	71½	84½	"	"	S. W.	0.02		Cloudy evening with shower 5 P. M.
S 13	69	78	C'y m'st all day.		N. E., S. E.			
14	69	77	"	most all day.	E., S. E.			
15	72	83	Clear	Clear	S. W.			Cloudy parts of morning and afternoon.
16	71	85	Cloudy most all day.		S. W.	2.02		Heavy rain before day (1.18); thunder shower 9 to 11 P. M. (0.84.)
17	71½	85½	C'y m'st all day.		N. W., S. W.			
18	65	77½	Clear	Clear	E., S. E.			
19	64	73	"	"	N.			
S 20	55½	72	"	"	N. E., S. E.			
21	58	74	Cloudy most all day.		E.			
22	65	72	Clear	Clear	E.			Cloudy part of morning.
23	61	71	Cloudy	Cloudy	E.			Misty parts of day.
24	69½	79½	"	most all day.	S. W.	0.33		Rain before day.
25	68	73½	"	Rain	All points.	1.20	4.70 in 31 hours.	Rain before day (1.20); clear part of morning; rain 10:30 A. M. to 12:15 P. M. *(0.80); 3 to 5 P. M. (0.10); 6 P. M. to 8 A. M. of 26th (2.60.)
26	68½	79½	Rain	Cloudy	S.	3.50		Rain till 8 A. M. (2.60); clear part of afternoon and evening.
S 27	74	84	Cloudy most all day.		S. W.			Light rain 6 to 8 P. M., and heavy shower after 10:30 P. M.
28	69	78	Clear	Cloudy	N., S. E.	1.35		Rain before day; clear part of afternoon.
29	71	84	Cloudy	Clear	S. E., S.	0.26		Rain before day; cloudy part of afternoon.
30	74	78	"	most all day.	S. W.	0.03		Light rain 6 to 6:30 P. M., and sprinkle afterwards.
31	64	73	Clear	Clear	N. W.			
						9.25		

*0.70 fell in 10 minutes, viz: 11:35 to 11:45 A. M.

September, 1871.

Date	Thermometer Lowest	Thermometer Highest	Weather Morning	Weather Afternoon	Prevailing Wind	Rain and Melted Snow in inches	Snow in inches	REMARKS
1	57½	71	Clear	Clear	N.			
2	57	73	"	"	N. W.			
S 3	58½	75	"	"	N. W., S.			
4	60	74½	"	"	E.			Cloudy part of afternoon.
5	58½	75	"	"	N.W.,E.,S.W.			
6	60	78	"	"	S. W.			
7	67½	72½	"	"	N.			Northern lights.
8	53	66½	"	"	N. E., S. E.			
9	49	68	"	"	N., E.			Cloudy part of morning.
S 10	57	71½	"	"	N. E.			
11	58	68½	"	"	N. E., S. E.			
12	58	69	C'y m'st all day.		S. E., S.			
13	61	65½	Rain	Cloudy	S. W., N. W.	0.54		Rain till 11 A. M.; cleared 6 P. M.
14	54	64	Hazy	Hazy	N. E.			Cloudy evening.
15	54	62	Rain	Rain	S. E.			
16	57	67½	C'y m'st all day.		N., N. W.	1.01		Rain before day.
S 17	56	70	C'y m'st all day.		W.			
18	50	62	Clear	Clear	N., S. W.			
19	49	65½	Cloudy	Cloudy	S. W.			Partly clear part of morning.
20	49	59	"	Clear	N. E., N.			Light sprinkle about noon; cleared 2:30 P. M.
21	42	57	Clear	"	N. E.			Frost.
22	41½	59	"	"	N. E., S. E.			
23	41½	66½	"	"	S. W.			
S 24	55	73½	"	"	S. W.			
25	55½	67	"	Cloudy	N. W.			
26	57	65	Cloudy	Clear	N. E., N. W.	0.84		Thunder shower 11 A. M. to 12:30 P. M.; cleared 2:30 P. M.
27	47½	62	Clear	"	W.			
28	46	60½	"	"	W.			
29	47	56½	Cloudy	"	N. W.			Cleared 8:30 P. M.
30	41	59½	Clear	"	N. W.			
						2.39		

October, 1871.

Date.	Thermometer. Lowest.	Thermometer. Highest.	Weather. Morning.	Weather. Afternoon.	Prevailing Wind.	Rain and Melted Snow in inches.	Snow in inches.	REMARKS.
S 1	42	59½	Clear	Clear	All points			
2	49½	67	"	"	W.			
3	50	60½	Cloudy	"	S. W.			Light sprinkle, noon to 2:30 P. M.; cleared 4 P. M.
4	53	68	Clear	"	S. W., N. W.			Cloudy part of afternoon.
5	47	69	"	"	S. E.			Hazy morning.
6	60	68	Rain	Cloudy	S. E., S. W.	2.12		Rain till 11 A. M. and from 6:30 to 11 P. M.
7	52	62	Cloudy	Clear	N. W.			Cleared 8 A. M.
S 8	42½	61	Clear	"	N. W., S. W.			
9	48	68	"	"	S. W.			
10	56	72	Cloudy	Cloudy	S. W.			Clear part of morning; light sprinkle 7 P. M.
11	65	73	Rain	Rain	S., S. E.	0.85		Rain till 7 A. M; clear part of P.M.; com. to rain 3 P.M.
12	42	56½	Cloudy	most all day.	N. W.	0.85		Rain before day; air filled with smoke all A. M.
13	53	60½	Clear	Clear	N. W., S. E.			
14	46	62	"	"	S. W.			Cloudy part of morning.
S 15	53	73	Cloudy	Cloudy	S. W.			Clear part of morning.
16	54	57	"	"	N., S. W.			Light sprinkle 11 A. M. to noon; clear evening.
17	45	62	Clear	Clear	S. W.			
18	46	56	"	"	N. W.			Cloudy part of afternoon.
19	40	55	Cloudy	"	S. W.			Cleared 10 A. M.
20	47	52	Clear	"	N.			
21	35	57	"	"	N., S. W.			
S 22	45	66	"	"	S. W.			Cloudy part of morning.
23	52	71½	"	"	S. W.			
24	60	63½	Cloudy	Cloudy	N. E.			Air filled with smoke all day.
25	50	54	"	Rain	N. E.	0.06		Rain before day and 9 A M.; steady rain after 1:45 P.M.
26	52	58	Misty	Misty	N. E.	0.50		Rain before day (0.50); mist (0.01) 11 P.M.
27	57	63	Cloudy	Cloudy	N. E., S. W.	1.13		Rain before day (1.09); light rain part of afternoon; cleared 5 P. M.
28	46	53	Clear	Clear	W.			Cloudy part of afternoon.
S 29	39	50	Cloudy	"	N. W.			
30	35½	53	Clear	"	S. W.			
31	44½	58½	"	Cloudy	S. W.			
						5.51		

WEATHER RECORD FOR NEW BRUNSWICK, N. J.

November, 1871.

Date.	Thermometer. Lowest.	Highest.	Weather. Morning.	Afternoon.	Prevailing Wind.	Rain and Melted Snow in inches.	Snow in inches.	REMARKS.
1	55	64	Rain	Clear	S. W., N. W.	0.63		Rain till 11 A. M. (0.62); cleared 3 P. M.; shower (0.01) 4 P. M.
2	42	52	Clear	"	W.			
3	40	52½	"	"	N. W.			
4	38	47	Cloudy most all day.		N. E.			
S 5	39	52½	"	Clear	N. E., N. W.			Cleared 9 A. M.
6	31	42½	Clear	"	N. W.			
7	31	45	"	"	N. W.			
8	32	50	"	"	S. W., N. W.			Cloudy part of evening
9	35½	46½	"	"	N. W., S. W.			Northern lights (blood red) N. and N. E. 6 to 9 P. M.
10	36½	48	Rain	Rain	N. E.	0.62		Rain till 5 P. M.
11	41½	45	Cloudy most all day.		N. W.			
S 12	33	43	Clear	Clear	N. W.			James V. Spader died.
13	31	44	"	"	N. E., S.			Cloudy evening.
14	38	54½	Cloudy	Rain	N. E., S E.			Com. raining 10 A. M.
15	49	51	"	most all day.	W.	1.65		Rain before day.
16	33	35	"	Snow	N. W.	0.05		Snow squall 7 A. M ; snow afternoon and morning, but melts as it falls.
17	33	46	"	Clear	N. W.			Cleared 9 A. M.
18	35	46	Clear	"	N.			
S 19	34	42½	Cloudy	Cloudy	N. E., S. E.			
20	41	53	Rain	Rain	S.			
21	43	48	Clear	Cloudy	W.	0.73		Rain before day.
22	37	42½	"	Clear	W.	0.05		Rain before day; cleared 7 A. M.
23	31	37½	"	"	N. W.			
24	34	53	Cloudy	Rain	S. E.	0.43		Rain 9 A. M. to 6 P. M.
25	39	46	Clear	Clear	N. W.			
S 26	34	51	Cloudy	Cloudy	S. W.			Misty part of morning and clear part of afternoon.
27	48	51	Clear	Clear	N. W.	0.03		Rain before day; cloudy part of morning.
28	20	30½	"	"	N.			Cloudy evening.
29	22	27	Cloudy	"	N. W.			Snow squalls 7 to 9:30 A.M.; cleared 10 A. M.
30	17	25	Clear	"	N. W.			

4.19

December, 1871.

Date.	Thermometer. Lowest.	Thermometer. Highest.	Weather. Morning.	Weather. Afternoon.	Prevailing Wind.	Rain and Melted Snow in inches.	Snow in inches.	REMARKS.
1	16	30	Clear	Clear	N. W.			
2	25	35	"	"	N. W.			
S 3	27	36½	"	Snow	S. W.			Clouded over 9 A. M.; snow 12:30 to 4 P. M. and misty afternoon.
4	35	43	Misty	Cloudy	S. W.	0.16		Clear part of afternoon;
5	14	19½	Clear	Clear	N. W.			snow and rain 6 to 7 P. M.
6	15	25	"	"	S. W.			Cloudy evening.
7	21	38	Cloudy	"	S. W., N. W.	0.07		Snow before day, (¾ in. on ground); cleared 2:30 P.M.
8	34	44	Clear	"	S. W., N. W.			Cloudy part of afternoon.
9	28	33½	"	"	N. W.			
S 10	21½	36	"	Cloudy	S. W.			Cleared 5 P. M.
11	31¾	41	"	Clear	S. W.			Cloudy part of morning.
12	35	41	"	"	N. W.			
13	30	41	Cloudy	Rain	S. E., N. E.	0.17		Rain at intervals during P.M.; clear part of evening.
14	27½	30	Clear	Clear	N. W.			Cloudy for an hour or two about noon, with snow squalls.
15	23½	28	Cloudy	Cloudy	N. E.			Cleared 6 P. M.
16	17½	33	Clear	Clear	S. W.			Cloudy part of afternoon.
S 17	29	37½	Cloudy	Cloudy	S. W.			Cleared 6 P. M.
18	32½	41	"	"	N. E, S. W.	0.07		Snow and rain 8:40 to 11 A. M.; cleared 5 P. M.
19	30	34	"	Snow	S. W.			Snow 11:30 A. M. to 5 P. M., and part of evening.
20	19	21	Clear	Clear	N. W.		2.50	Snow before day; cloudy part of afternoon; ther. 8 A.M., 19°; 11 A.M., 21°; 3 P. M., 15°.
21	1	9	"	"	N. W.			Coldest in December, since December 27th, 1851.
22	3	20	Cloudy	Snow	N. E.		2.50	Snow 10:30 A. M. to 10 P.M.
23	19	57	Misty	Rain	N.E,S.E,S.W			
S 24	41¼	49	Clear	Clear	S. W.	0.77		Rain before day.
25	35	47	"	Cloudy	S. W.			Clouded over 2 P. M.; foggy evening.
26	37	42	Cloudy	"	N. E.			Com. raining 9 P. M.
27	37	43	Rain	Clear	N., N. W.	0.20		Rain till 8 A. M.; cleared 9 A. M.
28	16½	22½	Clear	"	N. W.			
29	20	33	Cloudy	Cloudy	S. W., N. E.	0.17		Hail and rain 11 A. M. to 1:30 P. M.
30	31½	36	"	Misty	N. E.			Misty 2:15 to 7 P. M., and then rain.
S 31	34	40	Misty	Foggy	N. E.	0.20		Rain before day.
						1.81	5.00	

Rain and melted snow in 1871, 58.18 inches.

Weather Record for New Brunswick, N. J.

January, 1872.

Date.	Thermometer. Lowest.	Thermometer. Highest.	Weather. Morning.	Weather. Afternoon.	Prevailing Wind.	Rain and Melted Snow in inches.	Snow in inches.	REMARKS.
1	38	46½	Cloudy	Cloudy	N. W., N. E.	0.04	----	Rain before day; sun rose clear; sprinkle 2:15 P. M.; cleared 6 P. M.
2	28	38	Clear	Clear	N. E.	----	----	
3	29½	37½	Cloudy	M'sty } Rain }	N. E.	----	----	Snow part of A.M.; misty P.M. till 5 P.M., and then rain.
4	36	44	"	most all day.	N. W.	1.02	----	Rain before day.
5	37½	42	Clear	Clear	N. W.	----	----	
6	34	40½	"	"	N. W.	----	----	Cloudy part of afternoon.
S 7	16	23½	"	"	N. W.	----	----	
8	16	29	"	Cloudy	N. E.	----	----	Clouded over 9 A. M.
9	25½	38½	Cloudy	Clear	W.	----	----	Snow squall before day; cleared 8 A. M.
10	31½	41	Clear	"	N. W.	----	----	
11	29	45	"	"	W., S. E.	----	----	Clouded over 9 P. M.
12	36	47½	"	"	W.	----	----	
13	37	47	Cloudy	"	S. W.	----	----	Cleared 2 P.M.
S 14	23	26	"	"	N.	----	----	Cleared 10 A. M.
15	14	27	Clear	Cloudy	N. W., W.	----	----	Clear part of afternoon and part of evening.
16	24	31	Cloudy	"	N. E.	0.02	----	Snow 7:30 A. M. to 1 P. M.; clear part of afternoon.
17	24½	33½	Clear	Clear	N. W.	----	----	
18	21	32½	"	"	W.	----	----	Clouded over 9 P. M.; snow squall 11 P M.
19	28	44	"	Rain	S. E.	----	----	Clouded over 10 A M.; commenced raining 4:30 P. M.
20	37½	45	"	Clear	S. W.	0.47	----	Rain before day; cloudy part of afternoon.
S 21	34	41½	C'y m'st all day.		S. W., W.	----	----	
22	32	39	Clear	Clear	S. W.	----	----	Cloudy evening.
23	35	42	"	Cloudy	S. W., N. W.	----	----	
24	16	25½	"	Clear	N. W.	----	----	
25	19½	26	"	"	W.	----	----	
26	18	28	"	"	W.	----	----	
27	21	35	"	Cloudy	S. W.	----	----	Clouded over 10 A. M.
S 28	29	34	Snow	"	N. E., N. W.	0.10	----	Snow till noon; partly clear part of evening.
29	8	18	Clear	Clear	W.	----	0.05	Snow before day.
30	9	20½	"	"	N. W., W.	----	----	
31	10	21	"	"	W.	----	----	
						1.70	----	

February, 1872.

Date.	Thermometer.		Weather.		Prevailing Wind.	Rain and Melted Snow in inches.	Snow in inches.	REMARKS.
	Lowest.	Highest.	Morning.	Afternoon.				
1	12	25½	Clear	Clear	N. W., S. W.			
2	14	32	"	"	SW, N E, S E			Clouded 9 P. M.
3	23	30¼	Snow	Snow } Rain	N. E.	3.00		Snow till 10 A. M and then sleet rest of day; snow drifted.
S 4	27	35	Cloudy	Clear	N. W., W.	0.57		Snow before day; cleared 8 A.M.; deep red lights in South all evening.
5	23½	43	Clear	"	S. W.			
6	28	41	Foggy	Cloudy	S. W.	0.10		Clear part of morning; rain 3 to 6 P. M.
7	24½	32	Clear	Clear	N. W.			
8	19	34	"	"	N. E.			Cloudy part of morning and part of afternoon.
9	29	35	Cloudy	Cloudy	N. E.			
10	29	40	"	"	N. E.			Partly clear part of A M.
S 11	36	45	Rain	"	N. W., S. W.	0.24		Rain till 11 A M.; clear part of afternoon; cleared 8 P.M.
12	35	47½	Clear	Clear	S. W.			
13	34	45	"	Cloudy	N. E.			Com. raining 4 P. M and continued all the evening at intervals.
14	25	29	Cloudy	Clear	N. W.	0.43		Rain before day; snow squall till 9 A M; cleared 10 A.M.
15	13	22½	Clear	"	N. W.			Cloudy part of evening.
16	20	35	"	"	N. W.			
17	29	36	Cloudy	"	N. E.			Cleared 2:30 P. M.
S 18	18	37	Clear	"	N. E.			
19	21½	41½	"	"	N. E., S. E.			
20	26	47	"	"	N. W., S. W.			
21	34	46½	"	"	S. W., N. W.			
22	26	26	"	"	N. W.			Ther. at 26° at 7:30 A M.; falling all day
23	16	34	"	"	S. W.			Cloudy part of afternoon.
24	27	54	"	"	S. W.			
S 25	39	52	Cloudy	"	S. W., N. W.	0.02		Light rain before 7 A. M.; cloudy part of evening.
26	23	30	Clear	"	N. W.			
27	20	34	"	"	N. W.			
28	20	36	"	"	N. W.			
29	23	33	Cloudy	Cloudy	N. E.			Clear part of evening.
						1.36	3.00	

March, 1872.

Date	Thermometer. Lowest.	Thermometer. Highest.	Weather. Morning.	Weather. Afternoon.	Prevailing Wind.	Rain and Melted Snow in inches.	Snow in inches.	REMARKS.
1	15½	36	Clear	Clear	N. W.			
2	22	25	Cloudy	Snow	N. E.		1.50	Snow 12:15 to 6 P. M.
S 3	18	36½	Clear	Clear	N. W., S. W.			
4	24	39	Cloudy	Cloudy	S. W., N. W.	0.05		Snow 7:45 to 10 A. M ; clear part of P. M ; snow 5:45 to 7 P M.; cleared 10 P M.
5	3½	12½	Clear	Clear	N. W.			Cloudy part of afternoon.
6	7	25½	"	"	N. W.			
7	19	34	"	"	N. W.			
8	23	39½	"	Cloudy	N. W, S. W.			Clouded over 3 P. M.
9	30	35	Cloudy	Misty	E.	0.02		Light snow and hail till 9 A. M.; com. raining 10 P.M.
S 10	33	39	Rain	Rain	N. E., N. W.	1.23		Rain till 5 P.M.; cle'red 9 PM.
11	31	34	Clear	Cloudy	S. W., N. E.			Com. snowing 9:30 P. M.
12	29	37¼	Snow	"	N. E., N.	0.25		Snow till 9 A. M.; clear part of P.M.; cleared 7:30 P.M.
13	24	37	Clear	"	N. E., S. W.			
14	32	48	Cloudy	"	S. W., S. E.			Clear part of afternoon; com. raining 8:45 P. M.
15	28	31	Clear	Clear	N. W.	0.32		Rain before day.
16	19	34	"	"	N. W.			
S 17	26½	36	Cloudy	Cloudy	S. W.	0.23		Snow 9 A.M. to 3 P.M.; snow squall 8:30 PM.; cle'red 9 PM.
18	22½	36	Clear	Clear	N. W., S. W.			
19	32	50	"	"	S. W., N. W.			Cloudy part of morning.
20	20	24	"	"	N. W.			
21	15	28¼	"	"	N. W.			
22	20	36	"	"	N. W., S. W.			Cloudy evening.
23	31	36	Snow	Cloudy	All points.	0.04		Light snow nearly all day till 5 P.M.; cleared 7 P.M.
S 24	25	40¼	Clear	Clear	N. W.			
25	28	41	"	Cloudy	S. E.			Com. raining 9:45 P. M.
26	34½	36½	Snow } Rain	Rain	N. E.			Heavy snow before day, and then turned to rain.
27	33	46	Cloudy	Clear	N. E.	0.93		
28	34	54	Clear	"	N. W., S. W.			
29	41	60¼	Cloudy	"	{ S. W., N. W., N. E. }			Cleared 9 A.M. First morning of the month there was no ice.
30	36	47½	"	Cloudy	N. E., S. E.	0.02		Clear part of morning; rain 6:15 to 7:15 P. M.
S 31	36	39	Rain	Rain	N. E.	0.95		Rain till 3 P M, and from 8 to 10 P M ; cleared 11 P.M.
						4.04	1.50	

April, 1872.

Date	Thermometer Lowest	Thermometer Highest	Weather Morning	Weather Afternoon	Prevailing Wind	Rain and Melted Snow in inches	Snow in inches	REMARKS.
1	37	43½	Clear	Clear	N. W.			
2	34	51	"	"	N. W., S. W.			
3	40	51	Cloudy most all day.		N. W.			
4	33	49	Clear	Clear	N.			
5	34½	51	"	"	N. W., S. W.			
6	35	59	"	"	S. W.			Cloudy evening.
S 7	45	49	Rain	Rain	S. E., N. E.			
8	41½	56	Cloudy	Cloudy	N. E., S. E.	1.12		Rain before day.
9	45	63½	Rain	"	N. E.	0.38		Rain till 11 A. M.; ther. highest 9 P. M.; thunder shower 11 P. M.
10	54	62	Clear	Clear	W.			Cloudy part of morning, with sprinkle 9 A. M.; Northern lights.
11	42	61	"	"	W.			
12	44	60	"	Cloudy	E., S. W.			
13	52½	65½	Rain	Clear	N. W., S. W.	0.23		Rain till 9 A M.; cleared 10 A. M.
S 14	45	58	Clear	"	N. W.			
15	36	45	Cloudy	Cloudy	All points.			Partly clear part of afternoon; snow 5 to 6:30 P. M., and then snow and rain.
16	34	41	Clear	Clear	N.	0.08		
17	34	52½	"	"	N. W., S. W.			Cloudy part of afternoon.
18	37	53	"	Rain	E.			Clouded over at noon, and commenced raining at 3 P. M.
19	41	58	Cloudy	Clear	N. E., N. W.	0.30		Cleared 2 P. M.
20	44	66	Clear	Hazy	S. W.			
S 21	47	67½	"	"	S.			
22	49	57½	Cloudy	Clear	S., N. W.	0.04		Light rain till 9 A. M.; cleared 10 A. M.
23	33	51	Clear	"	N. W., S. W.			
24	42	66½	"	"	S. W.			Cloudy part of afternoon.
25	48	78	"	"	S. W.			
26	56½	80½	"	"	S. W.			
27	56½	69	"	"	N. W.			Cloudy part of morning.
S 28	52	67	Cloudy	"	N. W.			Cleared 9 A. M.; cherries flowered.
29	44	66½	Clear	"	All points.			
30	45	67½	"	"	All points.			Pears flowered.
						2.15		

May, 1872.

Date	Thermometer Lowest	Thermometer Highest	Weather Morning	Weather Afternoon	Prevailing Wind	Rain and Melted Snow in inches	Snow in inches	REMARKS
1	46	70	C'y m'st all day		S. E.			
2	58	70½	Rain	Clear	S. W.	0.60		Rain till 8 A. M.; cleared 11 A. M.; cloudy evening.
3	48½	61	Clear	"	N. W., S. W.			Cloudy evening with rain 9:30 P. M.
4	46	52	"	"	N. W.	0.13		Rain before day; cloudy part of afternoon.
S 5	42	60	"	"	N. W.			
6	50	72	"	"	N. W., N. E.			
7	48	77	"	"	S. W.			Cloudy part of evening with sprinkles 6 P. M.
8	61	83	"	"	N. W.			
9	63	85	"	"	S. W.			Cloudy part of afternoon.
10	66	87	"	"	S. W., N. E.			
11	58	65	"	"	E.			
S 12	57	79	"	"	S. W.			Hazy part of morning and afternoon.
13	57	71	"	"	N. W.			
14	51	69	"	"	N., S. W.			
15	50	74	"	"	S. W.			
16	54	70½	"	"	N. W.			
17	49	68	"	"	N. W., S. W.			
18	47	70	"	"	S. E.			Cloudy evening; com. raining 11 P. M.
S 19	58	66	Rain	Cloudy	SE, SW, NW	0.38		Rain till 9:30 A.M.; shower 3:30 P.M.; cleared 6 P. M.
20	57	73½	Clear	Clear	S. W., N. W.			
21	57	71½	"	"	N. W.			
22	56½	72	"	"	N. E., S.	0.45		Clouded over 6 P. M.; rain 7:45 to 10 P. M. and light rain 11 P. M.
23	62	76	Cloudy	"	S. W., N. W.			Clear part of morning.
24	58	74	Clear	"	S. W.			
25	63	74	Cloudy	Cloudy	S. W., N. W.			Light rain 7 A. M., clear part of afternoon.
S 26	60	67	"	"	N. E., S. W.			Cleared 5 P. M.
27	52	76½	Clear	"	SW, NW, NE	0.18		Showers 2:45 to 5 P. M.; cleared 9 P. M.
28	55	71	"	Clear	W., N. W.			
29	50	71	"	"	N. W.			
30	56	62	Cloudy	Cloudy	S. E.	0.68		Rain 9:30 A. M. to 2 P. M.; clear part of evening.
31	56	67	Clear	Clear	N. W.	0.03		Rain before day; cloudy part of afternoon.
						2.45		

Weather Record for New Brunswick, N. J.

June, 1872.

Date.	Lowest.	Highest.	Weather Morning.	Weather Afternoon.	Prevailing Wind.	Rain and Melted Snow in inches.	Snow in inches.	Remarks.
1	51	70½	Clear	Clear	N. W.	0.05		Clouded over 5 P. M.; rain 7:30 to 10 P. M.
S 2	56	67½	"	"	N. E., S. E.			
3	53	69	"	"	S. E.			
4	55	64	"	Cloudy	S., N. W.	0.17		Clouded over 9 A.M.; misty about noon; rain 4 to 5 P. M.; clear part of evening.
5	56	59	Rain	Rain	N. W., N. E.	0.45		Rain 6:30 to 10 A.M.; & 3 to 9:30 P.M.
6	54	76	Clear	Clear	NW, NE, SE			Cloudy part of evening, with light rain 7:15 P.M.
7	56	66	Cloudy	Rain	S. E., E.			Rain from noon to 6 P.M.; at intervals during ev'g.
8	59	78	"	Clear	S. E., S. W.	0.72		Rain till 6 A.M.; cl'red 8 A.M.
S 9	63½	81½	Clear	"	S. W.			
10	68½	80	"	Cloudy	S. W.	0.16		Rain before day; cl'red 7 PM.
11	64	80	"	Clear	N. W.			
12	63½	85½	"	"	S. W.			Cloudy evening.
13	69½	82	"	"	N. W., W.			
14	70	87½	"	Cloudy	S. W., N. E.	0.15		Light shower 2 P. M.; rain 4 to 6 P. M.
15	63	75½	"	"	N. W., S. E.			
S 16	65	74½	Cloudy	"	S. E.			Clear part of afternoon.
17	64	78	"	Clear	N. W., S. W.			Cleared 9 A. M.
18	63½	81	Clear	"	N. E., S. E.			
19	66	83½	"	"	N. W., S. W.			
20	67	86	Cloudy	"	S. W.			Cleared 9 A.M.; cloudy part of evening.
21	70½	87	"	"	S. W.			Cleared 7 A. M.
22	74	88	Clear	"	N. E.			
S 23	70	82	"	"	N. E., S. E.			
24	67	75½	Cloudy	Cloudy	S. E.			Clear part of afternoon.
25	65	67½	Rain	Rain	S. E., N. E.	1.73		Steady rain 5 A. M. till noon (1.57 in.) and at intervals till 11:30 P. M.
26	66	76	Cloudy	Cloudy	N. E.	0.10		Partly clear part of P. M.; rain 7:15 to 7:30 P. M.
27	70	77½	"	"	S. E.	0.32		Clear part of afternoon; shower 4:15 to 4:50 P. M.
28	69	85½	Clear	Clear	S. E., S. W.			
29	73	87	"	"	S. W.			Cloudy part of afternoon.
S 30	73	88½	"	"	N. W.			
						3.85		

July, 1872.

Date	Thermometer. Lowest.	Thermometer. Highest.	Weather. Morning.	Weather. Afternoon.	Prevailing Wind.	Rain and Melted Snow in inches.	Snow in inches.	REMARKS.
1	75	91	Clear	Clear	N. W., W.			
2	78	92½	"	"	N W.	0.03		Cloudy part of P. M. with thunder shower 2:50 P.M.
3	75½	93½	"	"	N. E., S. W.			
4	78	92½	"	"	S. W., N. E.			Clouded over 7 P. M., and com. raining 9:40 P. M.
5	74	87	"	"	S. W., N. E.	1.52		Rain before day (1.00), and shower 6 to 6:40 P. M. (0:52.)
6	71	83½	"	"	N, E., S.			
S 7	68	81½	Cloudy	"	S. E.	0.24		Rain till 7:30 A. M.; cleared 8:30 A. M.; cloudy part of afternoon.
8	70	81	"	"	N. E., S. E.			Cleared 10 A. M.
9	70	83	Clear	"	S. E.			
10	72½	86	"	Cloudy	S. W.	0.51		Cloudy part of morning; clouded over 3 P. M., and shower 4 to 9 P. M.
11	73	85	Cloudy	Clear	N. W., S. W.			Cleared 8 A. M.
12	74	80½	"	Cloudy	S. W.	0.60		Showers all day at intervals till 8 P. M.; cleared 9 P. M.
13	68	80	Clear	"	All points	0.01		Showers 5:45 P. M.; cleared 7 P. M.
S 14	71	84½	Cloudy	Clear	N. E., S. E.			Cleared 10 A. M.; cloudy part of evening.
15	75	84	"	Rain	S. W			Clear part of afternoon; shower 2:20 P. M. and at intervals after 4 P. M.
16	75	85	"	most all day.	S. W.	0.90		Showers 6 to 6:30 P. M. (0.20.)
17	75	86	Clear	Clear	S. W.	1.05		Showers noon and 4:30 P.M.; cloudy part of afternoon; heavy showers 8:30 to 9:30 P. M.
18	75	83½	"	Show'rs	S. E.	1.49		Clear part of afternoon; showers 3:30 to 4:30 (1.00 in 30 min.) and 8:40 and 11:30 P. M.
19	73	82	"	Clear	N.			
20	65	79½	"	"	N. E., S. W.			
S 21	64	80½	"	"	S. W.			Cloudy evening.
22	70	79	"	"	N. W.	1.00		Showers before day.
23	65	77	Cl'y m't all day.		N., S. W.			Light sprinkle 2:30 P. M.
24	68½	78	"	Clear	N. W.	0.22		Rain before day; cl'red 9 A.M
25	64½	78½	Clear	"	N. W.			Cloudy evening.
26	66	82½	Rain	"	S., N. W.	1.20		Rain till 10:30 A. M.; cloudy, light sprinkles 6:30 P. M.
27	77	78	Clear	"	N.			
S 28	65	81	"	"	S. W.			
29	67	83	"	"	S. W.			Cloudy evening.
30	72	80	"	"	N., N. E.			
31	67½	73	Cloudy	Cloudy	N. E., E.	0.20		Sun rose clear; clouded over 7 A. M., and rain 9 A.M to 4 P.M. at intervals.
						8.97		

24 days 80° and above, and 7 days 85° and above.

August, 1872.

Date.	Thermometer. Lowest.	Thermometer. Highest.	Weather. Morning.	Weather. Afternoon.	Prevailing Wind.	Rain and Melted Snow in inches.	Snow in inches.	REMARKS.
1	63	76	Clear	Clear	N. E., S. E.			
2	67½	74	Cloudy	Cloudy	S. E.	0.13		Light rain (0.01) before day; shower 2:45 P. M.; cleared 5 P. M.
3	68	78½	"	Clear	All points.			Northern lights.
S 4	66	77	"	"	N. E., E.			
5	67	78½	"	"	S. W., S. E.			Cleared 9 A. M.
6	68	77	"	"	S.			
7	70	83½	"	"	S. W.			Cleared 8 A. M.
8	67½	85	Clear	"	S. W.			Northern lights.
9	67½	85	"	"	S. W.			
10	70½	85	Cloudy	"	S. W.			Cleared 8 A. M.; cloudy part of evening.
S 11	71	87	Clear	"	S. W.			
12	75	89	"	"	S. W.			Clouded over 6 P. M., and com. raining 10 P. M.
13	74	87	Cloudy	"	S. W.	0.35		Rain before day; clear part afternoon; cloudy evening with rain 10:15.
14	74	88	Clear	"	S. W.	0.13		Rain before day (0.10); cloudy parts morning and evening with showers 5:50 and 11:15.
15	76	86½	"	"	S. W.			Cloudy evening with rain 11 P. M.
16	72	77	Rain	Rain	S. W., S. E.	1.10		Rain all day at intervals.
17	73	83½	Cloudy	Clear	S. W.	0.76		Rain till 6 A. M.
S 18	70	84	Clear	"	S. W.			
19	73	85	"	Hazy	S. W., N. W.			
20	72	84	Cloudy	Cloudy	S. E., N. E.	1.40		Rain before day (1.38);clear 8 A. M.; clouded over 3 P. M. with sprinkles afternoon and evening.
21	75	83	C'y m'st all day		N. E., S. W.			
22	73½	89	Clear	Clear	N. W., S. W.	1.10		Thunder shower 6:30 to 11 P. M.
23	72	83	"	"	N.			
24	68	81	"	"	N. W., S.			
S 25	69	81	"	"	W., S.			
26	68	82	"	"	N., S. E.	0.01		Rain before day.
27	72	83½	"	"	S. W., N.			Cloudy part of morning.
28	64	76	"	Cloudy	N. W., N. E.			
29	66½	71	Cloudy	Rain	N. E., S. E.			Commenced 4 P. M.
30	65½	73	Rain	Clear	N. W.	2.14		Rain till 6 A. M.; cleared 7 A. M.
31	57	70	Clear	"	N. W.			
						7.12		

June 1 to August 31, on 59 days, thermometer was 80° and above.

Weather Record for New Brunswick, N. J.

September, 1872.

Date.	Thermometer. Lowest.	Thermometer. Highest.	Wind. Morning.	Wind. Afternoon.	Prevailing Wind.	Rain and Melted Snow in inches.	Snow in inches.	REMARKS.
S 1	58	76	Clear	Clear	N. W.			
2	62	79	"	"	N. W.			Cloudy part of evening.
3	57	67	"	"	N.			
4	49	67	"	"	N. W.			
5	56½	68	Cloudy	Cloudy	All points			Clear part of afternoon.
6	56½	72	"	"	E., S. W.			Clear part of afternoon.
7	66	80¾	Clear	Clear	S. W.			
S 8	71½	88	"	"	S. W.			
9	73	85½	"	"	N. E., S. E.			Cloudy evening.
10	68	70	Cloudy	Cloudy	N. E., E.			
11	66	73	"	"	N. E., E.			Clear part of afternoon.
12	68	79	"	Clear	S. E.			Cleared 10 A. M.
13	70	74¼	Rain	Cloudy	S. W.	0.98		Rain till 10 A. M.
14	61	69½	Cloudy	Clear	N.			Clear 9 A. M.
S 15	56	68	"	Cloudy	N. E.			Rain at intervals after 7 P.M.
16	55	64	"	Clear	N. E.	0.24		Rain before day; cleared 2 P. M.
17	54	67½	Clear	"	N. W., S. E.			Cloudy 10 A. M. to 2 P. M.
18	61	71	Cloudy	"	S. W.			Cleared 10 A. M.
19	59½	70	"	"	W.	0.33		Rain 6:50 to 7:05 A. M. and 9:30 to 10 A. M.
20	55¼	67	Clear	"	N. W.			
21	50	72	"	"	S. W.			
S 22	58	81	"	"	W.			
23	64	79	"	"	E.			
24	63	72	Cloudy	"	N. E., E.			Foggy morning; cleared 2 P. M.; foggy evening.
25	64½	77¼	"	"	S. E.			Cloudy evening; rain 10 P.M.
26	66	72	Rain	"	S. E., S. W.	1.00		Rain before day (0.75); 9:30 A.M. to noon; cleared 2 P.M.
27	63	71	"	"	All points	0.46		Rain till 7.30 A. M.; cleared 2 P. M.
28	57	66	Clear	"	N., S. W.			
S 29	52	67	Cloudy	Cloudy	S. E.			Clear part of morning; clear evening.
30	59	70½	Clear	"	N. W.			
						3.01		

October, 1872.

Date.	Thermometer.		Weather.		Prevailing Wind.	Rain and Melted Snow in inches.	Snow in inches.	REMARKS.
	Lowest.	Highest.	Morning.	Afternoon.				
1	57	67	Cloudy	Clear	N. W.			
2	50½	63	Clear	"	N. W.			
3	52	64	Cloudy	Cloudy	S. W.			Light sprinkle before day; clear part of morning.
4	51½	65	Clear	Clear	N. W., N. E.			
5	51	63	Cloudy	Cloudy	N. E., S. E.			
S 6	60	76	"	Clear	S. E., S.			Clear part of morning.
7	60	73	"	Cloudy	S.			Clear part of morning; com. raining 5:40 P. M.
8	60	67	"	Clear	N.	0.37		Rained before day; cleared 8:30 A. M.
9	47	62½	Clear	"	N. W., S. W.			
10	50	70	"	"	S. W., N. W.	0.09		Foggy A. M.; shower 5:30 P. M. and cloudy evening.
11	46	55½	"	"	N. W.			Cloudy part of evening.
12	39	53	"	"	All points.			Cloudy part of afternoon.
S 13	45	54	Cloudy	Cloudy	N. E.			Light rain 3:40 P. M.; cleared 8 P. M.
14	44	53	Clear	"	S. W., N. W.			Light rain about noon; cleared 6 P. M.; Northern lights 6 to 8 P. M.
15	42	54	"	"	N. W., S. W.			
16	45	63	"	"	S. W., N. W.			
17	41	57	"	"	N. E., S. E.			
18	52	58	Cloudy	Rain	S., W.	0.28		Rain 9 A. M. to 6 P. M.; foggy evening.
19	49	58	Clear	Clear	N. W.			
S 20	40	55	"	"	N. W.			
21	40	64	"	"	S. W.			
22	46	66	"	Cloudy	S. W.			Cloudy part of morning.
23	57	65	Cloudy	"	S. W., N. E.			Clear part of A. M.; com. raining 6 P. M.
24	47	50	Rain	"	N. E.	0.57		Rain till 8 A. M.
25	48	54	"	Rain	N. E.			Rain all day at intervals.
26	53	69	"	Cloudy	E., S. W.	2.58		Heavy showers before day; rain at intervals till noon; cleared 8 P. M.
S 27	52½	62	Clear	"	S. W., W.			Clear part of afternoon.
28	49	53	Rain	Clear	N. E.	0.20		Rain till 10 A. M.
29	39	51	Clear	"	N. E.			
30	38	51	"	"	N. E.			
31	40	51	Cloudy	"	N. E.			Cloudy evening.
						4.09		

November, 1872.

Date.	Thermometer.		Weather.		Prevailing Wind.	Rain and Melted Snow in inches.	Snow in inches.	REMARKS.
	Lowest.	Highest.	Morning.	Afternoon.				
1	42	57	Clear	Clear	N. W.			
2	42	52½	"	Cloudy	N. W., S. W.			Clear part of afternoon.
S 3	45	48	Cloudy	Clear	N. E.			
4	42½	52	Clear	"	N. W.			
5	35	51	"	Cloudy	N., E.,			
6	46	54	Cloudy	Rain	S.			
7	50	55	Rain	Clear	N. W.	2.25		Rain till 9 A. M.
8	43	51	Clear	"	S. W., W.			Cloudy part of afternoon.
9	40	51	"	"	S. W., N. W.			Cloudy part of afternoon.
S 10	36½	51	"	"	N. W., S. W.			
11	35½	52½	"	Cloudy	S. W., S. E.			Rain 10 P. M.
12	49	59	Rain	Rain	S. E., S.	0.32		Rain at intervals till 6 P.M.; cleared 8 P. M.
13	41	49½	Clear	Clear	N. W., N. E.			Cloudy part of morning.
14	42	52½	Rain	Misty	S. E., N. W.	0.21		Rain till noon; clear part of evening.
15	37	40½	Clear	Clear	W.			
16	30	42	"	Cloudy	All points	0.07		Snow 3:45 to 9 P. M.
S 17	26	39	"	Clear	W.			
18	30	42	Cloudy	"	S. W.			Cleared 10 A. M.
19	30	43	Clear	"	S. W.			Cloudy part of evening.
20	37	43	Cloudy	"	S. W., N. W.			Cloudy part of afternoon, with snow squalls.
21	26	36½	Clear	"	S. W., W.			
22	28	37	Rain	Rain	N. E., N. W.	0.66		Rain 8 A. M. to 5 P. M.; cleared 6 P. M.
23	34	43½	Cloudy	Clear	S. W.			Cleared 9 A. M.
S 24	34	50	Clear	"	S. W.			
25	37	50	"	Cloudy	S. W.			Cloudy part of morning.
26	37	42	Snow Rain	Rain	N. E.			
27	34	43	Clear	Clear	N. W., S. W.	0.28		
28	29	37	"	"	N. W., E.			
29	29½	31	Snow	"	N. W.		2.50	Snow till 9 A. M.; cleared 4 P. M.
30	18	25½	Clear	"	S. W., W.			
						3.79	2.50	

December, 1872.

Date.	Thermometer.		Weather.		Prevailing Wind.	Rain and Melted Snow in inches.	Snow in inches.	REMARKS.
	Lowest.	Highest.	Morning.	Afternoon.				
S 1	18	36	Clear	Cloudy	S. W.	----	----	Hail and rain 10:45 P. M.
2	33	43	Cloudy	"	S. W.	0.12	----	Snow before day; rainy evening after 7:15 P. M.
3	38	45½	Clear	Clear	S. W.	0.10	----	Cloudy evening.
4	37	42	"	"	N. W.	----	----	Clear part of morning.
5	31½	37	Cloudy	Cloudy	S. W.	----	----	
6	30	43½	Clear	Clear	S. W., N. W.	----	----	
7	30½	40	Cloudy	"	N. E., S. E.	----	----	Cleared 9 A. M.
S 8	31	45	"	Rain	S. W.	0.12	----	Rain 12:30 to 5 P. M.; cleared 9 P. M.
9	37	38	"	Cloudy	S. W., N. W.	----	----	Snow squalls morning and afternoon; cleared 8 P. M.
10	17	27	Clear	Clear	N. W.	----	----	
11	23½	31	C'y m'st all day.		W., N. W.	----	----	
12	22½	25	Cloudy	Clear	N. E.	----	----	
13	17	34	Clear	"	W., S. W.	----	----	Cloudy part of morning; clouded over 10 P. M.
14	27	39½	"	"	S. W.	----	----	Cloudy part of morning.
S 15	27	47	Cloudy	"	S. W., N. E.	----	----	Cleared 10 A. M.
16	26½	36	"	{Snow Rain}	N. E.	----	----	
17	31	35	Clear	Clear	N. W., W.	0.24	----	
18	27½	33	Cloudy	Rain	N. E.	0.40	----	Snow 7:45 A. M. to 12:30 P. M., and misty rain to 5 P.M.
19	25	38	Clear	Cloudy	S. W., N. E.	----	----	Clouded over 2 P. M.; com. snowing 10 P. M.
20	29	41	Rain	"	N. E., S. W.	1.33	----	Rain till 9 A. M.; light sprinkles afternoon and evening with snow.
21	28	33	Clear	Clear	N. W., W.	0.04	----	Cloudy evening.
S 22	10½	15	"	"	N. W.	----	----	Snow squall before day.
23	7	33	Cloudy	"	N. E., S. W.	----	----	Cloudy part of evening.
24	12	18	"	"	N. W.	----	----	
25	7	16½	Clear	Cloudy	N. E.	----	----	
26	6½	15½	Snow	Snow	N. E.	----	20.00	Violent snow storm 2 A. M. to 7 P. M.; worst since Jan. 19, 1857.
27	10	16½	Cloudy	Clear	N. W.	----	----	Cleared 2:30 P. M.
28	9½	23	Clear	"	S. W.	----	----	
S 29	16	27	Cloudy	Cloudy	W.	----	----	Cleared 7:30 P. M.
30	4	23½	Clear	"	N. W., S. W.	----	----	Clouded over 4 P. M.; snow 10:30 P. M.
31	20½	34	{Rain Hail}	{Rain Snow}	N. E., N. W.	0.35	----	Hail, rain and snow till 10 P. M.; cleared 11 P. M.
						2.70	20.00	

Rain and melted snow for 1872, 47.93 inches.

January, 1873.

Date.	Thermometer. Lowest.	Thermometer. Highest.	Weather. Morning.	Weather. Afternoon.	Prevailing Wind.	Rain and Melted Snow in inches.	Snow in inches.	REMARKS.
1	17½	28½	Clear	Clear	All points.			
2	18	27	Cloudy	Cloudy	N. E.			Rain 9 P. M.
3	25	42	Rain	Foggy	N. E., S. W.	0.65		Rain till 8 A. M.; dense fog all day and evening.
4	36	40	Clear	Clear	W.	0.01		
S 5	24	40	Cloudy	Rain	N. E.	1.30		Rain 10 A. M. to 4 P. M. and misty after; cleared 10:30 P. M.
6	36	39	"	Clear	N. W.			Cleared 8 A. M.
7	16	29	Clear	"	N. E.			
8	16½	34½	Cloudy	Cloudy	N. E.			Rain part P.M. and even'g.
9	30	36	Clear	Clear	S. W.	0.08		
10	10½	27	"	"	S. W., W.			
11	8	16	"	"	N. W.			
S 12	11	24	"	Cloudy	N. W., N. E.			
13	22	37½	Cloudy	Clear	N. E., N. W.			Cleared 10 A.M.; clouded over 9 P. M.
14	33	45	"	"	S. W., N. W.	0.06		Rain before day; clear part A.M. and cloudy part P.M.
15	27½	33	"	Cloudy	N. E.			Light snow part of A. M.
16	32	53½	Foggy	Clear	N. E., S.	0.13		Rain before day; cleared 2 P. M.
17	46	46½	Cloudy	Cloudy	N. W., N. E.	1.15		Rain before day.
18	28	34	Rain	Misty	N. E.	0.44		Rain till noon; misty P. M., and snow 6:45 to 9:30 P.M.
S 19	21	25	Clear	Clear	W.			
20	18	34½	"	Cloudy	S. W.			Snow 3:30 P. M. to 4:30.
21	32	37	Cloudy	Rain	S. E., S. W.			
22	36½	40	Clear	Clear	N. W.	0.24		
23	28	33	"	Snow	N. E.			Clouded over 10 A. M.; snow 3 P. M.
24	23	32	Misty	Cloudy	N. E.	0.07	4.00	Snow before day; light snow part P.M.; cleared 11 P.M.
25	22	29	Clear	Clear	W., N. W.			Cloudy part of afternoon.
S 26	18	27	C'y m'st all day	All points.				Snow 7 to 8 A. M.; snow 11 P. M.
27	25½	31	Snow	Snow	N. E.		8.00	Snow till 8:30 P. M.; cleared 9 P. M.
28	21	31½	C'y m'st all day	W., S. W.				
29	3½	14	Clear	Clear	N., N. W.			Light snow before day.
30	−12	14	"	"	N. W., W.			Coldest morning I ever knew; bar. 30.19.
31	6½	29	"	"	W., S. W.			

4.13 12.00

February, 1873.

Date	Thermometer Lowest	Thermometer Highest	Weather Morning	Weather Afternoon	Prevailing Wind	Rain and Melted Snow in inches	Snow in inches	REMARKS
1	7½	29	Clear	Clear	N. W.			
S 2	10	19½	"	"	N. W., S. W.			
3	6	37	Cloudy	Snow Rain	S. W.			Snow 12:30 P. M. to 3 P. M.; then snow and rain to 5 P. M., and then misty.
4	35	46	Foggy	Clear	S. W.	0.40		Snow before day; cleared 9 A.M.; rain part of ev'ning.
5	37	40	Clear	"	W., N. W.			Cloudy part of morning and part of afternoon.
6	29	41	Cloudy most all day.		S. W.			
7	31	39½	"	Rain	N. E.			Rain 10 A. M.
8	36	46	Clear	Clear	S. W.	0.46		
S 9	28	31	"	"	N. W.			Cloudy part of morning.
10	13	24	"	"	N. W., W.			
11	22	37	Cloudy	Cloudy	All points.	0.03		Snow part of morning; rain part of evening.
12	35½	37	"	Snow	N. E.			Snow part of morning.
13	18½	28	Clear	Cloudy	N. E.		8.00	
14	15	28	Cloudy	"	N. E.			Cleared 8 A.M.; clouded over 3 P. M.
15	23	33	"	"	All points			
S 16	28	35	Snow	Rain	N. E.		3.50	Heavy snow till 10 A. M.; then rain to 4 P.M. and at intervals afterwards.
17	34	45	Cloudy	Clear	N., N. W.	0.78		Cleared 8:30 A. M.
18	27	40½	Clear	"	N. E., S. E.			Cloudy evening.
19	36½	42	Cloudy	"	S. E., S. W.	0.06		Rain 12 to 1 P. M.; cleared 3 P. M.
20	33	39	Clear	"	N. W.			
21	32	36½	Snow Rain	Cloudy	S. E., N. W.	1.24		Snow 7:15 A M. to 9:30 A.M.; then rain to 2 P.M.; cleared 8:30 P.M.
22	18	28	Clear	Clear	N. W.			
S 23	16	22	"	"	N. W.			
24	1	19	"	"	N. W., W.			Cloudy part of morning, with snow squall 10:40 A.M
25	17	32	"	"	W., N. W.			Cloudy part of morning.
26	27	38	"	"	N. W.			
27	28½	33½	Snow	Snow	N. E.			
28	27	35½	Cloudy	Clear	N. W.		6.00	Clear part of morning.
						2.97	17.50	

Weather Record for New Brunswick, N. J.

March, 1873.

Date.	Thermometer. Lowest.	Thermometer. Highest.	Weather. Morning.	Weather. Afternoon.	Previling Wind.	Rain and Melted Snow in inches.	Snow in inches.	REMARKS.
1	28	36½	Clear	Clear	N. W., S. W.			Cloudy part of morning.
S 2	21½	34	"	Snow	N.W.			Light snow afternoon and evening.
3	29	36	Snow	Clear	N. W.	1.00		Light snow till 8 A. M.; cleared 9 A. M.; cloudy part of evening.
4	13½	25	Cloudy	"	N. W.			Cleared 8:30 A. M.
5	12½	28	Clear	"	N. W.			
6	13	32½	"	"	N. W., S. W.			
7	20	40	"	"	S. W.			
8	26	46	"	"	S. W.			Cloudy part of morning, with light rain at noon.
S 9	40	49	"	"	S. W.			
10	33	42	Cloudy	"	N. W.	0.01		Snow before day; cleared 9 A. M.
11	33	46	Rain	Cloudy	S. E., S. W.	0.42		Rain 7 A. M. to 1 P. M., with hail 12:30 P. M.; clear part of afternoon.
12	38	40½	Clear	Clear	N. W.			
13	31	42½	"	"	N. W.			
14	35	47	"	"	N. W.			
15	36	55	Cloudy	Cloudy	S. W.			Clear part of afternoon.
S 16	38½	48	Clear	Clear	N. W.			
17	32	44½	"	"	N. W.			
18	32	54	"	Cloudy	S. W.	0.04		Clouded over 2:30 P. M.; rain 8:30 P. M. to 11 P. M.
19	43	51½	"	"	S. W., N. E.			Clear part of afternoon.
20	37	43	Cloudy	Rain	N. E.			Rain 9:30 A. M.; hail and snow in the evening.
21	31½	39	"	Clear	S. W.	0.50		Clear part of morning; snow squall 4 P. M.
22	34	43½	Clear	"	W., N. W.			
S 23	32	53½	"	"	S. W.			
24	32	37	Cloudy	Cloudy	N. E., S. E.			Light rain part of evening.
25	27	30	Misty	Misty	N. E.	0.12		Snow and rain before day; rain part of evening.
26	28	37½	"	Cloudy	N. E., N. W.	0.45		Rain 12 to 1:30 P. M.; clear part of afternoon.
27	24	37½	Clear	Clear	N. W.			
28	25½	50½	"	"	S. W.			
29	38	55	Rain	Rain	S., S. W.	0.72		Rain all day at intervals till 5 P. M.; bar. 29.10, 4 P. M.
S 30	41	52	Cloudy	Clear	N. W.			Cleared 8:30 A. M.; cloudy evening.
31	42	53	C'y m'st all day		S. W.	0.03		Rain before day; light showers morning and afternoon.
						2.29	1.00	

April, 1873.

Date.	Thermometer. Lowest.	Thermometer. Highest.	Weather. Morning.	Weather. Afternoon.	Prevailing Wind.	Rain and Melted Snow in inches.	Snow in inches.	REMARKS.
1	38	56	Clear	Clear	All points.			Cloudy evening.
2	43	65	C'y m'st all day	All points.		0.16		Rain before day; shower 4 P. M.
3	42	58	Clear	Clear	S. W.			Cloudy part of afternoon.
4	41½	56½	Cloudy	"	N. E., S. E.			Clear part of morning.
5	43	51	C'y m'st all day		E.	0.03		Rain before day; thunder shower after 8 P. M.
S 6	40½	46	Cloudy	Cloudy	E.	0.68		Thunder shower (0.03) 8:15 A. M.; thunder showers during evening.
7	41	52	"	"	S. E.	0.32		Rain before day.
8	46	59	"	Hazy	S. W.			
9	46	47	"	Cloudy	E.			Misty evening.
10	43½	57	Clear	Clear	N. W.	0.18		Rain before day.
11	42	62	"	"	S. W., E.			Cloudy part of afternoon.
12	35	39	Rain Snow	Rain Snow	N. E., N.			Rain till 8 A. M., and then violent snow storm till 11 A.M. and rain and snow rest of day.
S 13	36	51½	Clear	Clear	N.	1.71		Cloudy part A. M. and P. M.
14	42	54½	"	"	N. W.			
15	42½	57½	"	"	N. W., N. E.			
16	39	49	"	Cloudy	N. E., S. E.			Clouded over 10 A. M.; rain and snow after 9:30 P. M.
17	38	43	Rain	Rain	E.			
18	41½	51	Cloudy	Cloudy	N. W.	1.21		Rain before day; clear part of afternoon.
19	42	55	Clear	Clear	S. W., N. W.	0.01		Cloudy part of afternoon, with light showers.
S 20	38½	54	"	"	N. W.			
21	39	47	Cloudy	"	N. E., N. W.	0.04		Rain and snow part morning; cleared 2:30 P. M.
22	37	40½	"	Cloudy	S. W., N. E.	0.03		Rain part of morning; rainy evening.
23	35½	49½	C'y m'st all day		N. W., S. W.	0.35		Snow before day.
24	40	53	Clear	Clear	N. E., S. W.			Cloudy part of afternoon and evening.
25	39	51½	"	"	N. W., W.			Cloudy part of morning.
26	38	51½	"	"	N. W.			
S 27	38½	55½	"	"	N. W.			
28	37½	61	"	Cloudy	S. W.			
29	48	56	Cloudy	"	S. W.			Rainy evening after 9 P. M.
30	46	60	"	Clear	S. E., S. W.	0.40		Rain before day; clear part of morning.

5.12

May, 1873.

	Date.	Thermometer. Lowest.	Thermometer. Highest.	Weather. Morning.	Weather. Afternoon.	Prevailing Wind.	Rain and Melted Snow in inches.	Snow in inches.	REMARKS.
	1	45	64	Cloudy	most all day.	S. W.	----	----	Rain 10 P. M.
	2	48	55	Rain	Cloudy	E., N. E.	0.48	----	Rain till 2 P. M.; rain again 8 P. M.
	3	40½	44	Cloudy	"	N. E.	----	----	Rain before day; rain part of P.M. and part of ev'ing.
S	4	40	60½	Clear	Clear	N. W.	0.60	----	Rain before day.
	5	45½	69	"	"	S. W.	----	----	Cloudy evening.
	6	48½	62½	"	"	N. E., S. E.	----	----	
	7	42½	61½	"	Hazy	N. E., S. E.	----	----	Cherries partly in flower.
	8	49½	53½	Cloudy	Rain	E.	----	----	Rain 11 A. M.
	9	45½	51	Rain	"	N. E.	----	----	
	10	46½	58	Cloudy	Cloudy	N. E., S. E.	1.00	----	Clear part of evening.
S	11	49	60	"	"	N. E., S. E.	0.52	----	Thunder shower 1:45 A. M.; rain 10 A.M. to 1 P.M. and part of evening.
	12	49	64	Clear	Clear	N. W.	----	----	Pears and cherries flowered.
	13	50½	74	"	"	S. W., N.	0.20	----	Cloudy part of morning; shower 2:50 P. M.
	14	45	59	"	"	N. W.	----	----	Cloudy part of afternoon.
	15	45	65	"	"	N. W., S. W.	----	----	
	16	49	66½	Cloudy	most all day.	N. E.	----	----	
	17	50	65	Clear	Clear	N. W.	----	----	
S	18	48	68	"	"	N. W.	----	----	
	19	46½	66½	"	"	N. E., S. W.	----	----	
	20	48	64	"	Cloudy	E., S. E.	----	----	Clouded over 4 P. M.
	21	53	56	Cloudy	Rain	S. E.	----	----	Rain 2:15 P. M.
	22	50½	61	Rain	"	S. E.	----	----	
	23	55½	70	Cloudy	most all day.	S. E.	1.41	----	
	24	59	79	"	Clear	S. W.	----	----	
S	25	60½	78½	Clear	"	N. W.	----	----	
	26	60	77½	"	"	N. W., S. E.	----	----	
	27	58	78½	"	"	S. W., S.	----	----	
	28	66	85	"	"	S. W.	----	----	
	29	67	81	"	"	N. W., S. W.	----	----	
	30	66½	76	"	Cloudy	N. W., N. E.	0.05	----	Rain part of afternoon; cleared 7 P.M.
	31	50½	64½	"	Clear	N. E., S. W.	----	----	
							4.26	----	

Weather Record for New Brunswick, N. J.

June, 1873.

Date.	Thermometer. Lowest.	Thermometer. Highest.	Weather. Morning.	Weather. Afternoon.	Prevailing Wind.	Rain and Melted Snow in inches.	Snow in inches.	REMARKS.
S 1	50	74	Clear	Clear	W., S. W.			
2	55	78	"	"	All points			
3	59	67	"	"	E.			
4	56½	75¼	Cloudy	"	S. E., S. W.	0.14		Rain before day; showers after 10:30 P. M.
5	66	81	Clear	"	S. W., N. W.	0.14		Showers before day.
6	61½	82	"	"	All points	0.24		Cloudy part of P. M. and ev'ng with rain 4 to 6 P.M.
7	63	75½	"	"	N. W.			
S 8	57	74	"	"	N. E., S. E.			
9	55	77	"	"	All points			
10	60	80	"	"	S. W.			Clouded over 10 P. M.
11	70¼	81	Cloudy most all day.		S. W.			
12	65	78	Clear	Clear	N. E.			
13	58	72	"	"	E.			
14	54	70	Cloudy	"	N. E., S. E.			
S 15	60½	72½	"	Cloudy	S. W.			Light shower before day.
16	66	83½	"	Clear	S. W.			Cleared 8:30 A. M.
17	69	84	Clear	"	N.			
18	61	77	"	"	N. E., S. E.			
19	64	90	"	"	W.			
20	76½	90	"	"	N. W.			
21	65½	82	"	"	N. W.			
S 22	62	73½	Cloudy	Cloudy	N. E.			Partly clear part of P.M. and light sprinkle 6 P. M.
23	63	70	"	"	S. E.	0.05		Rain part of morning; com. raining 10 P. M.
24	62½	65	Rain	"	N. E.	0.55		Rain till 1:30 P. M.
25	55½	71	Clear	Clear	N. E., E.			
26	54	75	"	"	E., S.			Northern lights.
27	56	80	"	"	S. W.			
28	67	86	Cloudy	"	S. W.	2.76		Cl'red 8 A.M.; thunder shower with hail 4:15 to 6:15 P.M.; light rain aft'rwards.
S 29	68	82	Clear	"	S. W.			
30	68	82½	"	"	S. W., S. E.			Cloudy part of morning.
						3.88		

July, 1873.

Date	Thermometer. Lowest.	Highest.	Weather. Morning.	Afternoon.	Prevailing Wind.	Rain and Melted Snow in inches.	Snow in inches.	REMARKS.
1	70	81	Show'rs	Clear	S. E., N. W.	0.21		
2	69	86	Clear	"	S. W.			
3	73	90	"	"	S. W.	0.01		Light shower 5:30 P. M.
4	74	86½	"	"	S. W.			
5	72	79	Show'rs	"	S. W.	1.85		Showers till 1 P. M.; cleared 3 P. M.
S 6	69	79	Clear	"	N.			
7	61	75	"	"	N. E., S. E.			
8	63½	74½	Cloudy	"	S. E.			Cloudy evening; light sprinkle 6 P. M.
9	69	76½	Clear	"	N. E.	0.26		Cloudy part of evening; rain 8:40 to 9:40 P. M.
10	68½	79½	"	"	S. E.			
11	65	75	Cloudy	"	S. E., N. W.	0.54		Rain 5 to 6:30 A. M., and noon to 1:20.
12	60	75	Clear	"	N. E., S. E.			
S 13	62	78	"	"	S. W.			Cloudy part of afternoon.
14	65½	88	"	"	S. W.	0.08		Cloudy evening with shower 7:20 P. M.
15	73	87	"	"	N. E., N. W.			Cloudy part of evening.
16	69	83	"	"	N. E., S. W.			Cloudy part of afternoon.
17	68	79	Cloudy	"	E.	0.28		Shower 3 A. M.; showers after 10:30 P. M.
18	70	81	Clear	Cloudy	E.	0.30		Showers before day; shower during evening.
19	64½	70	Cloudy	"	N. E., S. E.			
S 20	63	78	Clear	Clear	N. W., S. W.			
21	65	78	"	"	N. W.			
22	61	82	"	"	N. E., S. W.			
23	65	85½	"	"	N. W.			
24	70	89	"	"	N. W.			
25	73	89	"	"	N. W., S. W.			
26	74	90½	"	"	S. W.			Clouded over 6 P. M.; rain 8 P. M.
S 27	72	82½	Show'rs	Show'rs	S. W.	0.66		Rain before day; showers all day and evening, after 8 A M.
28	71	80	C'y m'st all day	S. W.		1.64		Rain before day and 3:40 to 4:30 P. M.
29	73½	85	" "	" "	All points.	3.64		Heavy showers 4 to 7:30 P. M. (3.55) and light (0.09) till 10 P.M.
30	72	84	Clear	Clear	N. W., N.			
31	69½	83	"	"	N. E., S. E.			
						9.47		

Weather Record for New Brunswick, N. J.

August, 1873.

Date.	Thermometer. Lowest.	Thermometer. Highest.	Weather. Morning.	Weather. Afternoon.	Prevailing Wind.	Rain and Melted Snow in inches.	Snow in inches.	REMARKS.
1	73	85½	Cloudy	most all day.	S. W.	0.14	....	Shower 6 P. M.
2	72	86	Clear	Clear	S. W.	0.01	....	Cloudy part of afternoon, with shower 1 P. M.
S 3	73½	88	"	Cloudy	S. W.	0.35	....	Shower 3:30 to 4:30 P. M., and light rain part of evening.
4	69	80½	"	Clear	N.	....	....	
5	66	78	"	"	N. E.	....	....	
6	63½	79	"	"	N. W., S. W.	....	....	
7	65	84	"	"	S. W.	....	....	
8	72	81	Cloudy	"	S. W., N. W.	0.10	....	Shower 5:30 A. M.; cloudy part of afternoon.
9	69	80	Clear	"	N. E., N. E.	....	....	
S 10	68	77½	Cloudy	"	N. E., S. E.	....	....	
11	63	78	Clear	"	N. E., S. E.	....	....	
12	64	76	Cloudy	most all day.	S. E.	....	....	
13	63	66	Rainy	Rainy	N. E.	....	....	Rain all day at intervals, after 2 A. M.
14	63	67	Rain	Cloudy	N. E.	5.29	....	Rain till 2 P. M., from 9 to 11:15 P. M.; 3.00 in. fell; 5.29 in. in 36 hours.
15	63	71	Cloudy	"	N. E.	0.02	....	Rain before day; clear part of afternoon.
16	66½	80	"	most all day.	S. W.	0.12	....	Rain before day; rain part of evening.
S 17	65	72	"	"	" N. E., S. E.	0.05	....	Rain before day; rainy evening after 7 P. M.
18	63	68	Rain	Rain	N. E.	0.14	....	Rain before day; com. raining again 7 A. M.
19	66	74	Cloudy	Cloudy	N. E.	1.20	....	Rain before day; partly clear part of afternoon.
20	69	71	Rain	Rain	N. E.	0.29	....	Rain 7 A. M. to 4:30 P. M.; commenced again 7 P. M.
21	68	76	"	Cloudy	N. E.	2.01	....	Rain till 7:30 A. M., and showers 9:30 A. M. and 6:30 P. M.
22	71½	80	Cloudy	Clear	S. W.	0.04	....	Rain till 6 A. M.; shower 3 P. M.
23	70	83	Clear	"	N. W.	0.27	....	Shower 3:30 to 4 P. M.
S 24	58	71½	"	"	N.	....	....	
25	59	72	"	"	N. W., S. W.	....	....	Cloudy part of afternoon.
26	63	78	"	"	N. W., E.	....	....	Albany street paved with granite blocks.
27	63	73	"	"	E., S. E.	....	....	Cloudy part of afternoon.
28	59	72½	"	"	S. E., S.	....	....	Cloudy part of afternoon.
29	62½	73	"	Cloudy	N. E., S. E.	....	....	Rain 10:30 P. M.
30	67	77	Cloudy	Clear	N. E., S. W.	0.70	....	Rain before day.
S 31	66	81½	Clear	Cloudy	S. W., W.	0.06	....	Rain 3:45 to 5:30 P. M.

10.79 ...

September, 1873.

Date.	Lowest.	Highest.	Weather Morning.	Weather Afternoon.	Prevailing Wind.	Rain and Melted Snow in inches.	Snow in inches.	REMARKS.
1	70	87	Cloudy	Clear	S. W.	0.01		Rain before day; cleared 8 A. M.
2	64	78	Clear	"	W.			
3	59	76	"	"	N. W., S. W.			
4	67	82	Cloudy	"	S. W.	0.03		Rain before day; cloudy part of evening.
5	74	86	Clear	"	S. W.			
6	63	74	"	"	N.			
S 7	55½	70	"	Cloudy	N. E., S. E.			Rain 8 P. M.
8	61	70	Cloudy most all day.		N. E.	0.92		Rain before day.
9	56	70	Clear	Clear	N. E., S. E.			
10	55	66½	"	Cloudy	N. E.			
11	62	69	Cloudy	Clear	N. E., S. E.			
12	56	74	Clear	"	S. W.			
13	62	77	Cloudy	"	S. W.			Cleared 9 A.M.; rainy after 9 P. M.
S 14	56	62	Rain	"	N. W.	0.46		Rain till 8 A. M.
15	45	61½	Clear	"	N. W., S. W.			
16	50	71	"	"	S. W.			Cloudy part of morning.
17	53	65½	"	"	N. E.			
18	58	72	C'y m'st all day.		N. E., S.			
19	63½	69	Rain	Rain	S. E.	1.03		Rain till 3 P. M.; clear part of P.M.; rain again 9 P. M.
20	54	64	Cloudy	Clear	N. W.	0.20		Rain before day; cleared 9 A. M.
S 21	45½	62	Clear	"	N. W., S. W.			
22	46	63	"	"	N. E., S. E.			
23	54	69	Cloudy	Cloudy	S. E.	0.04		Light rain till 7:30 A. M.; rainy evening.
24	63	70	"	Clear	N. E.	0.55		Rain before day.
25	60	68	"	most all day.	S. E.			
26	61	73	"	Clear	S. W.	0.03		Rain before day; cleared 8 A.M.
27	58	76	Foggy	"	S. W.			
S 28	64	76	Cloudy	"	S. W.			Cleared 10 A. M.
29	67½	78	"	most all day.	S. W.			Rain 7:15 P. M.
30	59½	63	"	Clear	N., N. E.	0.32		Rain before day.
						3.59		

October, 1873.

Date.	Thermometer. Lowest.	Thermometer. Highest.	Weather. Morning.	Weather. Afternoon.	Prevailing Wind.	Rain and Melted Snow in inches.	Snow in inches.	REMARKS.
1	46	62½	Clear	Clear	N. E., N. W.			
2	50	64½	Cloudy	"	N. W., S. W.			Cleared 8 A. M.
3	49½	67	Clear	"	All points.			
4	50½	65¼	"	Cloudy	N. E.	0.06		Rainy evening.
S 5	61½	71	Cloudy	Clear	S. W.			Cleared 10 A. M.
6	58½	71½	"	Rain	S., N.			Light rain 8:20 A. M.; rain after 1:40 P.M. at intervals.
7	44	49	"	Clear	N.	1.34		Rain before day; cleared 4 P. M.
8	41½	66	Clear	"	N. E.			
9	49	63	"	"	N. E.			
10	44½	62	"	"	N. E.			
11	42	63	"	"	N. E., N. W.			
S 12	47	62	Cloudy	Cloudy	S. W., N. W.			Clear part of evening.
13	45	57	Clear	Clear	N. W., S. W.			
14	44	65	"	"	S. W.			
15	46	63½	"	"	N., N. E.			
16	43	66	Foggy	"	S. W.			Cleared 10 A. M.
17	54	65	Clear	"	All points.			
18	55	64	Cloudy	Cloudy	E., S. E.			
S 19	60	71	Cy m'st all day.		S. W., N. E.			Rain 8:30 P. M.
20	63	68½	Rain	Cloudy	N. E.	2.02		Rain till noon and 6 to 9 P. M.
21	50	56½	Clear	Clear	S. W.			
22	44	60	"	"	S. W.			
23	44	65	"	"	S. W.			Cloudy part of evening.
24	49	62	"	"	S. W.			Cloudy part of afternoon.
25	45½	59	"	"	N.			
S 26	39	56½	"	Cloudy	All points.			Clouded over 2 P. M.; rain 8:30 P. M.
27	52	63	Rain	"	S. W., N. W.	1.23		Rain till 3 P. M.; cleared 5 P. M.
28	44	55¼	Clear	Clear	W., S. W.			Cloudy evening with light sprinkle.
29	34½	48	"	"	S. W.			
30	32	46	"	"	N. W., N. E.			Cloudy part of afternoon.
31	38½	52½	"	"	N. E.			Cloudy evening.

4.65

November, 1873.

Date.	Thermometer.		Weather.		Prevailing Wind.	Rain and Melted Snow in inches.	Snow in inches.	REMARKS.
	Lowest.	Highest.	Morning.	Afternoon.				
1	35	48	Clear	Clear	W.			
S 2	33	54	"	"	S. W.			
3	43½	57½	Cloudy	"	S. W., N. W.			Cleared 9 A. M.
4	32	51	Clear	"	S. W.			Cloudy evening.
5	43½	55½	"	"	S. W., N.			
6	36	48	Cloudy	"	N. E.			Cleared 10 A. M.
7	32¼	49	"	Rain	N. E.			Rain 1 P.M.
8	45½	53	"	Clear	N. W.	0.82		Rain before day; showers 1 to 3 P.M; cleared 4 P. M.
S 9	43½	53	C'y m'st all day		W.			Light sprinkle morning and afternoon.
10	35½	40½	Cloudy	Clear	N. W.			Clear part of morning.
11	31	42	Clear	"	W., S. W.			Cloudy evening with rain 10 P. M.
12	38	46	Cloudy	Cloudy	W.	0.26		Rain before day and light rain part of afternoon.
13	34	39	Clear	Clear	W.			
14	26½	35	"	"	N. W.			
15	25½	40	"	"	S. W.			Cloudy part of morning.
S 16	30	49	C'y m'st all day		N. E., N. W.			
17	35½	37½	Cloudy	Misty	N. E.			Rain 7:30 P M. and snow 9 P. M.
18	34	40½	Snow	Cloudy	N. W.	0.97		Snow till 8 A.M.; clear part morning; 2 in. snow on ground; barometer, 7 A. M., 28.935.
19	32	38	Cloudy	"	N. W.			Clear part of morning; cleared 9 P. M.
20	28	36	Clear	Clear	N. W.			Cloudy parts of morning and afternoon with snow squall
21	23½	35	"	"	S W.			
22	27	42½	"	"	N. W.			
S 23	27	39½	Cloudy	Cloudy	N. W., N. E.			Rain 6 P. M.
24	37½	46	Rain	"	N. E., W.	2 29		Heavy rain till 1 P. M., and light rain till 3 P.M.; clear part of evening.
25	38	42	C'y m'st all day		N. W.	0.02		Rain before day and snow squalls during day.
26	26	34	Clear	Clear	N. W.			
27	27½	38	Cloudy	Cloudy	N. E			Cleared 6 P. M.
28	30	35	Clear	Clear	N. W.			Cloudy part of afternoon.
29	26	37½	"	"	N. W.			
S 30	25½	35	C'y m'st all day		N. W., N. E			
						4.36		

December, 1873.

Date.	Thermometer. Lowest.	Thermometer. Highest.	Weather. Morning.	Weather. Afternoon.	Prevailing Wind.	Rain and Melted Snow in inches.	Snow in inches.	REMARKS.
1	22	24	Snow	most all day.	N. E.			
2	20	34	Rain	Rain	N. E.	0.24		Snow before day; rain 8 A.M.
3	33½	43½	Foggy	Cloudy	S. E., N. E.	0.20		Rain before day; foggy evening.
4	42	67	Cloudy	"	S. W.	0.01		Rain before day.
5	40	42	"	"	N. W.			
6	31	38½	"	Clear	N. E.			Cleared 8:30 A. M.
S 7	26½	36	Clear	"	N. E.			Cloudy evening.
8	33	40½	Cloudy	Cloudy	N. E., E.			Rain part of evening.
9	37½	50	"	"	S. W.	0.06		Rain before day; cleared 9 P. M.
10	42	46½	C'y m'st all day.		N. W.			
11	35	45	Cloudy	Cloudy	S. W.	0.02		Light rain part of morning.
12	44	60½	Clear	"	S. W.			
13	46	51	Cloudy	Rain	N. E.	0.50		Rain 9 A.M. to 5 P.M.; clear part of evening.
S 14	31	41	Clear	Clear	N. W.			Cloudy part of afternoon.
15	35	45½	"	"	S. W.			
16	31	50	"	"	S. W.			
17	32	49	"	"	S. W.			Foggy morning.
18	34	51	Cloudy	"	N. W.			Cleared 10 A. M.
19	35	44	Rain	Cloudy	N. E.	0.40		Rain 7:30 A.M. to 2 P. M.; clear part of evening.
20	39	43½	Cloudy	Clear	S. W., N. W.			Cleared 8 A.M.; cloudy part of P. M. with snow squalls.
S 21	28½	35	Clear	"	N. W.			
22	22	33½	"	"	N. W., W.			
23	27	32	Cloudy	Snow	N. E.,	0.10		Snow 2 P.M. to 8 P. M.; cleared 10 P. M.
24	27	43	Clear	Clear	N. W.			
25	32½	42½	Cloudy	Cloudy	S. W., N. E.			Clear part of morning.
26	33	36	"	Snow Rain }	N. E.			Snow and rain all day after 7:30 A. M.
27	34	36	"	"	N. E.	0.42		Snow and rain after 9 A.M.
S 28	32½	41	C'y m'st all day.		W.	0.05	4.00	Snow before day.
29	29½	39	"	"	S. W.			
30	25½	30	Clear	Clear	N. W.			
31	21½	33	"	"	S. W.			
						2.00	4.00	

Rain and melted snow in 1873, 60.96 inches.

January, 1874.

Date.	Thermometer. Lowest.	Thermometer. Highest.	Weather. Morning.	Weather. Afternoon.	Prevailing Wind.	Rain and Melted Snow in inches.	Snow in inches.	REMARKS.
1	23	41	Cloudy	Cloudy	S. W.			Commenced raining 6 P. M.
2	35½	43½	Rain	"	S. W.	0.39		Rain till 10 A. M.
3	38	46	Foggy	Foggy	N. E.			
S 4	39	65½	Cloudy	Cloudy	S. W.			Clear part of afternoon; warmest day in January I ever knew.
5	45	46	"	"	N. E.	0.03		Rain 7 P. M.
6	33	39	Rain	Rain	N. E.	0.24		Rainy and misty all day.
7	37½	59	"	"	S. E.			
8	43	45½	Cloudy	Cloudy	S. W.	2.73		Rain before day, and light rain (0.02) 9 to 11 A. M.; cleared 8 P. M.
9	34	50	Clear	Clear	S. W.			
10	38	48	"	"	S. W.			
S 11	33	45	"	"	S. W., W.			
12	30½	38	"	"	W., N. W.			
13	26	34	Cloudy	Cloudy	N. E.			Clear part of morning; snow 10 P. M.
14	25	34	Snow	Clear	N. E., N. W.		4.00	Snow till 10 A. M.; cloudy part of evening.
15	16	25	Clear	"	W.			
16	13	26	"	"	N. W.			
17	13	26½	"	"	W.			
S 18	13	32	"	"	All points.			Ice 4 inches thick in Weston's pond; first of the season.
19	24½	40	Foggy	Rainy	N. W., S. W.	0.15		Rain part of afternoon; cleared 11 P. M.
20	35½	37	Clear	Clear	N. E.			Cloudy part of morning.
21	23½	38	Snow } Rain	Rainy	N. E., S. W.	0.13		
22	37	57	Cloudy	Cloudy	S. W.			Foggy morning; cleared 5 P. M.
23	54	64	Rain	Clear	S. W., N. W.	0.06		Rain till 7:30 A. M.; cleared 2 P. M.
24	34	41½	Clear	"	N. W., S. W.			Snow squall 7:40 P. M.
S 25	22	29	"	"	N. W.			
26	16	27½	"	"	N. W., S. W.			Cloudy evening.
27	26	41½	Cloudy	Cloudy	S. W.			
28	39	51	Rainy	Clear	S. W., N. W.	0.20		Cleared 2 P. M.
29	32	39	Clear	"	N. W., S. W.			Cloudy part of afternoon.
30	23½	28	Cloudy	"	N. E.			
31	19	31	"	Cloudy	N. E., N. W.			Snow squall before day; cleared 5 P. M.
						3.93	4.00	

February, 1874.

Date.	Thermometer. Lowest.	Thermometer. Highest.	Weather. Morning.	Weather. Afternoon.	Prevailing Wind.	Rain and Melted Snow in inches.	Snow in inches.	REMARKS.
S 1	17	24	Cy m'st all day		N. E.			
2	7	22	Cloudy	Snow	N. E.			Snow 11:45 A. M.
3	17	34	Snow Hail	Cloudy	N. E., N.	0.24	4.00	Snow and hail till 10 A. M., and then rain and snow till 2 P. M.; clear part of evening.
4	29	35	Clear	Clear	N. W.			
5	23½	32	"	"	N. W.			Light snow before day.
6	15	26	"	Cloudy	All points			Clouded over 8 A. M.; snow 5:45 P. M.
7	15	26	Cloudy	"	N. E.	0.01	8.00	Snow before day; snow flurries during day; cleared 10 P. M
S 8	7	31½	Clear	Clear	N. W., S. W.			Cutting ice yesterday at Weston's mill; 8 in. thick.
9	8	29	Cloudy	Cloudy	N. W.			
10	25	33	"	Clear	N. W., S. W.	0.01		Snow before day; cleared 8:30 A. M; cloudy even'g.
11	21½	34½	Clear	"	W.			
12	15	36	"	"	N. W., E.			
13	26½	52	Cloudy	Rain	S. E., S. W.			
14	41½	48	"	Clear	N. W.	0.31		Rain before day; cleared 7:30 A. M.
S 15	30	43	Clear	"	N. E., E.			Cloudy evening.
16	34½	49½	Cloudy	"	S. E., S. W.			
17	30	36	Clear	"	N. W.			
18	20½	35½	"	"	N. E.			
19	22	40	Cloudy	Rainy	N. E., S. E.			Rainy after 3 P. M.
20	38½	44½	"	Cloudy	S. W.	0.09		Rain before day.
21	40	62	"	Clear	NE, SW, NE	0.04		Rain before day.
S 22	41½	47	"	Cloudy	E.			
23	39	70½	Foggy	Clear	NE, SW, NW			Clouded 10:30 A. M.; cloudy part of evening.
24	35	38	Cloudy	Cloudy	N. W., N. E.			Clear part of evening.
25	27	29	"	Snow	N. E.			Snow 8 A. M. to 4 P. M. violently; rest of day moderately.
26	23	31½	Clear	Clear	N. W., S. W.		10.00	Snow before day.
27	25	39½	"	"	N. W.			
28	24½	39½	"	"	N. W., S. W.			Cloudy part of morning.
						0.70	22.00	

March, 1874.

Date.	Thermometer. Lowest.	Thermometer. Highest.	Weather. Morning.	Weather. Afternoon.	Prevailing Wind.	Rain and Melted Snow in inches.	Snow in inches.	REMARKS.
S 1	26½	45	Clear	Clear	S. W.			
2	31	51	"	"	S. W.			
3	36	57	Cloudy	"	S. E.			Hazy evening.
4	50	64	Rain	"	S. W., N. W.	0.10		Rain till 8:30 A. M.; cloudy part of afternoon.
5	33	49½	Clear	"	N.			
6	30½	36½	Cloudy	Snow Rain	N. E.			Snow 2:45 P.M. to 9 P.M. and then rain.
7	30	37	Rain	Misty	N. E.	1.05		Rain till 11 A.M., and misty rest of day.
S 8	33	43	Foggy	Clear	W.			Cleared 8 A. M.; cloudy part of P.M. with snow squalls.
9	29	36	C'y m'st all day.		W., N. W.			
10	24	35½	"	"	N. W.			
11	29	38	Clear	Clear	N. W.			
12	24	36	"	"	N. W.			
13	18½	28	C'y m'st all day.		N. W.			
14	23	39	Clear	Clear	N. W.			Every day since 8th P. M. the wind has been a gale from N. W.
S 15	28	44½	"	"	N. W.			
16	31	42	Cloudy	Cloudy	N. E., S. E.			Partly clear part of morning; rain 6:15 P. M.
17	35	49	Rain	Rain	N. E., S E.			Rain all day. First St. Patrick's day it has stormed all day in 18 years.
18	43½	57½	Cloudy	Cloudy	S. E.	0.73		Rain before day; clear part of P. M.; rain part of ev'g.
19	52	63	Foggy	"	S. W.			Partly clear part of P. M.
20	47½	50½	Cloudy	Clear	N. W.			Cleared 2 P. M.
21	35	52½	Clear	"	S. W.			
S 22	42	51½	"	"	S. W., N. W.			
23	35	41	"	"	N. W.			
24	21	35½	"	"	N. W.			
25	25	48½	"	"	S. W.			
26	38½	57	Cloudy	Cloudy	S. W.			Cleared 9 P. M.
27	36	49½	Clear	Clear	N., S. W.			
28	37	48	Cloudy	"	N. W.	0.13		Rain till 7:30 A.M.; cleared 8 A. M
S 29	36	45	"	"	N. W.			
30	33½	53½	Clear	"	S. W.			Rock fish caught in shad net weighing 52½ pounds.
31	35½	40	Cloudy	Cloudy	N.	0.05		Snow 10:45 A.M. till 4 P.M.

2.06

April, 1874.

Date.	Thermometer. Lowest.	Highest.	Weather. Morning.	Afternoon.	Prevailing Wind.	Rain and Melted Snow in inches.	Snow in inches.	REMARKS.
1	28	35	Cloudy	Cloudy	N. E., E.			
2	31½	45	C'y m'st all day	"	N. E., S. W.			
3	37	47	Clear	Clear	W.			
4	38	41½	Cloudy	"	N. W.			
S 5	22½	38½	Clear	Cloudy	S. W.			Hail and rain 7 P. M.
6	34	55	Cloudy	Clear	W.	0.25		Rain before day.
7	39	48	Rain	Cloudy	N. E.	0.14		Rain till 9:30 A. M.; cleared 9 P. M.
8	35	50	Cloudy	"	E.			Clear part of afternoon; rain 8 P. M.
9	41½	45	Rain	Rain	N. E.			Rain moderately all day till 9:30 P. M., and violently after that hour.
10	36	46	Cloudy	Cloudy	N. E., N. W.	2.05		Rain before day, and light rain (0.01) 8 A. M.; cleared 8 P. M.
11	35	56	Clear	Clear	S. W., N. W.	0.02		Cloudy part of afternoon, with rain and snow squalls.
S 12	25½	41	"	"	N.			
13	26½	46	"	"	N. W., S. W.			
14	34½	62	"	Cloudy	S. W.			Clear evening.
15	52	63	Cloudy	"	S. W.			Light sprinkles part of afternoon and evening.
16	45	50½	"	"	N. W., N. E.			
17	38	41	Rain	Rain	E., N. E.	0.50		
18	35	48	Cloudy	Clear	N. E., W.			Cleared 7:30 A. M.
S 19	37	52	"	Cloudy	S. W.			Clear part of morning; rain 7 P. M.
20	43½	46	Rain	Rain	E.			
21	42½	55	Clear	Clear	S. W., N. W.	2.02		Rain before day; cloudy part of morning.
22	40½	52	"	Cloudy	S. W., N. E.			Clouded over 10 A. M. to 8:30 P. M.
23	42	47	Cloudy	Rain	E., N. E.	0.35		Rain 9 A. M. to 9 P. M.
24	41	55	Clear	Clear	N. W.			Clouded over 5 P. M.
25	44	45	Rain	Rain	E.			Rain 7 A. M. John V. Henry died.
S 26	35½	46	C'y m'st all day	"	N. W.	1.32		Rain before day.
27	39	54½	Clear	Clear	N. W.			
28	35	*42	Snow	{ Snow Rain	N. E.			Clouded over 7 A. M.; snow 8:15 A. M. to noon (0.28), and then snow and rain.
29	33	40	{ Rain Snow	Clear	N. E., N. W.	1.60		Rain till 6:30 and then snow till 10 A. M. (0.20); cleared 4 P. M.
30	33	52	Clear	"	W.			
						8.25		

* 7 A. M.

Weather Record for New Brunswick, N. J.

May, 1874.

Date.	Thermometer. Lowest.	Thermometer. Highest.	Weather. Morning.	Weather. Afternoon.	Prevailing Wind.	Rain and Melted Snow in inches.	Snow in inches.	REMARKS.
1	42½	60	Clear	Clear	W.			
2	44	57½	"	"	W., N.			Cloudy part of morning and part of afternoon.
S 3	37½	61	"	"	N. W.			
4	42	61	"	Cloudy	S. W., S. E.			Rain 9 P. M.
5	46	59	Rain	"	N. E.	0.25		Rain till 9 A. M.; cleared 8:30 P. M.
6	43	61	Clear	Clear	N. E., S. W.	0.02		Cloudy 5 to 10 P. M., with light rain.
7	41½	55	"	"	N., N. W.			Cherries partly in flower.
8	42	69	Cloudy	"	S. W.			Cleared 10 A. M.
9	51	79	Clear	"	S. W.			
S 10	63	85	"	"	S. W.			Pears and cherries flowered.
11	53	60	"	"	N. E., S. E.			Clouded over 5 P. M. to 8 P. M.
12	42	61½	"	"	E., S.			
13	48	72	"	"	S. W.			
14	58	77	"	"	S. W.			
15	58	61	"	Cloudy	E.			Rain 5 P. M.
16	50	63	Rain	"	N. E., S. W.	0.82		Rain till noon; clear part of evening.
S 17	57	70	Clear	Clear	N. W., S. W.			
18	55½	63	Rain	"	S. W.	0.40		Rain at intervals till 3:30 P. M.; cleared 4 P. M.
19	48	66	Clear	"	N. W.			
20	50	64	"	Cloudy	S. W.	0.04		Clouded over 10 A. M.; rain part of afternoon; cleared 9 P. M.
21	50½	63	"	Clear	N. W.	0.04		Rain before day; cloudy part of afternoon.
22	50	67	"	"	N. W.			
23	47	68	"	"	W., S. W.			Cloudy evening.
S 24	52	64	"	Cloudy	S.			Clouded over 10 A. M.
25	56½	70½	Cloudy	Rain	All points.	0.28		Showers 8:15 A.M. to 4 P.M.; foggy evening.
26	58	68	Clear	Clear	W., N. W.			Cloudy part of afternoon.
27	52	70½	"	"	N. W., S. W.			
28	55	73½	"	"	N. E., S. E.			
29	57½	78	"	"	S. W., S. E.			
30	59	74	"	"	S. E.			
S 31	61	80	Cloudy	"	S. W.			Cleared 9 A.M.; cloudy evening with rain 10 P. M.

1.85

June, 1874.

Date	Thermometer Lowest	Thermometer Highest	Weather Morning	Weather Afternoon	Prevailing Wind	Rain and Melted Snow in inches	Snow in inches	REMARKS
1	65	75	Clear	Clear	N. W.	0.60		Rain before day.
2	53	67	"	"	N. E., S. E.			
3	53	63	"	Cloudy	S. E.			Clouded over 9 A.M.; rain 4 P.M.
4	57	66	Rain	"	N. E., S. E.	1.12		Rain before day and misty till 8 A. M.
5	62	75	C'y m'st all day		S. E.			
6	65	75	"	"	S. E.	0.02		Light rain 11:30 A. M. and 5 P.M.; foggy evening.
S 7	67	83	Cloudy	Clear	S. E., S. W.			
8	73	86½	Clear	"	W.			Cloudy evening.
9	70½	90	"	"	All points.	0.60		Cloudy evening with thunder shower 7:30 P. M.
10	71	81	"	"	N. E.			
11	66	69	Cloudy	Cloudy	N. E.	0.10		Showers 9 to 10 A.M.; misty evening.
12	62	81	"	Clear	N. E., S. W.	0.02		Rain before day.
13	61	70	Clear	"	N. W.			
S 14	53	70	"	"	W.			Cloudy 9 A.M. to 3 P.M.
15	53	75½	"	"	N. W., S. W.			Cloudy part of evening.
16	60	77¾	"	"	S. W.			Cloudy evening with light sprinkle.
17	68	80	Cloudy	"	S. W., N. W.	0.12		Rain before day; cleared 10 A. M.
18	66	79	Clear	"	N. W.			
19	64	73½	C'y m'st all day		N., N. E.			Light sprinkle 10 P. M.
20	57	67	"	"	N. E., S. E.			
S 21	60	73½	Cloudy	Clear	N. W., S. W.			Cleared 8:30 A. M.
22	63	80	Clear	"	N. W.			
23	67	89	"	"	S. W.			Cloudy part of evening.
24	74½	84	"	"	N. W.			
25	60	84	"	"	S. W., N. W.			
26	73	86	C'y m'st all day	All points.		0.38		Clear 9 A.M to 5 P.M.; shower 5:45 P. M.
27	67	78½	Cloudy	Clear	N. E., S. E.			Cleared 8 A. M.
S 28	65	86	Clear	"	S. W.			
29	72	94	"	"	S. W.	0.09		Warmest since July 17th, 1866; cloudy part of eve; shower 7 P. M.
30	72	85	Cloudy	"	N. W.			Cleared 9 A. M. Comet visible to naked eye.

3.05

Weather Record for New Brunswick, N. J.

July, 1874.

Date	Thermometer Lowest	Thermometer Highest	Weather Morning	Weather Afternoon	Prevailing Wind	Rain and Melted Snow in inches	Snow in inches	REMARKS
1	65	80	Clear	Clear	N. E., E.			
2	68	83½	C'y m'st all day.		S. W.	0.63		Shower 6:30 to 8:45 P. M.
3	66	80	Clear	Clear	N. E., N. W.			
4	62	81	C'y m'st all day.		N. E., S. W.	0.24		Sprinkle 9 A. M. and shower 4:30 to 5 P. M.
S 5	68	73½	"	"	" N. W., N. E.			Sprinkle 11:30 A. M.
6	63	73½	Cloudy	Clear	N. E., S. E.			
7	59	78½	Clear	"	S. W.			
8	67	88½	"	"	S. W.			Cloudy evening.
9	73	85	Cloudy most all day.		E.	0.09		Shower 8:25 to 8:40 A. M.
10	71½	89	"	"	" S. E., S. W.			Showers after 6:30 P. M.
11	72½	86	"	"	" S. W.	0.37		Showers before day; heavy showers after 6:50 P. M.
S 12	70	83	"	"	" S. W.	1.48		Showers before day; shower 11 A. M.
13	72	83	"	Clear	S. W., W.			Clear part of morning.
14	66	85	Clear	"	W.			
15	69½	89½	"	"	S. W.			
16	73	87	"	"	S. W., N. E.	0.21		Shower 12:50 P. M.; cloudy part of afternoon.
17	67	79	"	"	N.			
18	64	82½	"	"	All points.			
S 19	66	84½	"	"	S.			
20	67½	87	"	"	S. W.			Clouded over 5 P. M.; showers after 8:10 P. M
21	72½	77	Cloudy	"	S. W.	0.31		Rain before day; light rain (0.01) at noon; cleared 4 P. M.
22	63	79	Clear	"	N. E.			
23	63	80	"	"	N. W., S. E.			
24	62½	80	"	"	S. W., S. E.			
25	62	79	"	"	S. E.			
S 26	65	82½	"	Cloudy	N.			
27	70	84	"	Clear	S. W.			Cloudy part of afternoon.
28	69	84½	Cloudy	"	S. W.			Cleared 8 A. M.
29	70¼	75½	Rain	Cloudy	S. W., N. W.	0.69		Rain till 8:15 A. M (0.55); light rain till 10:30 A. M.; shower 3 P M.
30	64	80	Clear	Clear	N.			
31	62	82	"	"	S. W.			
						4.02		

WEATHER RECORD FOR NEW BRUNSWICK, N. J.

August, 1874.

Date.	Thermometer. Lowest.	Highest.	Weather. Morning.	Afternoon.	Prevailing Wind.	Rain and Melted Snow in inches.	Snow in inches.	REMARKS.
1	68	85	Clear	Cloudy	S. W.	1.04		Rain 3:10 to 7 P.M., and light sprinkle 8:30 P.M.
S 2	67	80	"	Clear	N. W.			
3	58	74½	"	"	N.			
4	57	74	"	"	N.			
5	57½	75	"	"	N. E.			
6	59	77	"	"	N. W., S. W.			
7	64	78	"	Cloudy	S. W.			Showers 4:50 P.M. and steady rain after 9 P. M.
8	66	71½	Cloudy	Show'rs	S. W., N. E.	0.59		Rain before day ; showers 3:30 to 9 P. M.
S 9	67	75	"	Cloudy	N.	0.33		Rain before day; rain 10 A.M. till 12:15 P. M.; clear ev'g.
10	63½	83	Clear	Clear	W., S. W.	0.04		Cloudy evening with rain 10:45 P. M.
11	67	81	"	"	S. W., S. E.			
12	69½	83	"	"	S. E., S. W.			Cloudy part of morning ; cloudy evening.
13	72½	83	C'y m'st all day.		S. W., N.			
14	69	73½	Cloudy	Cloudy	N. E.			Clear part of evening.
15	64	78	Clear	Clear	N. E.			
S 16	62½	78	"	"	N. E., S. E.			Mosquitoes first appeared.
17	62	77	"	"	N. E., S. E.			Cloudy part of morning.
18	59	84	"	"	S. W., N. W.			Cloudy part of evening.
19	62	80	"	"	N. W.			
20	65½	89	"	"	S. W.			
21	73	92	"	"	S W.			
22	65	72½	Rain	"	N. E.	0.18		Rain 6 A.M. to 1 P.M.; cleared 2:30 P.M.
S 23	58½	68	Cloudy	Cloudy	N. E., S. E.			Light rain 4 to 6 P.M.; partly clear part of evening.
24	62	72	C'y m'st all day.		N. E., S. E.	0.04		Rain before day; rain 10 P.M.
25	61½	70½	Clear	Clear	N. E., S. E.	0.13		Rain before day.
26	55½	71	"	"	N. E., S. E.			
27	55	70½	"	"	N. E., S. E.			
28	54	72	"	"	N. E., S. E.			
29	53½	72	"	"	N. E., S. E.			
S 30	55	75	"	"	S. W., S. E.			
31	57½	77	"	"	All points.			Cloudy part of morning.
						2.35		

Weather Record for New Brunswick, N. J.

September, 1874.

Date.	Thermometer. Lowest.	Thermometer. Highest.	Weather. Morning.	Weather. Afternoon.	Prevailing Wind.	Rain and Melted Snow in inches.	Snow in inches.	REMARKS.
1	63	78	Clear	Clear	N. W.			
2	60	81½	"	"	W.			
3	63	86	"	"	S. W.			
4	60½	66	Cloudy	Cloudy	N. E., S. E.			Light sprinkle before day.
5	64	73	C'y m'st all day.		S. E.			
S 6	66	77	Cloudy	Clear	S. W., N. W.			Clear part of morning.
7	64	83	Clear	"	N. W.			
8	63	80	"	"	All points.			
9	63	76	"	"	N. E., S. E.			
10	58½	82½	"	"	W.			
11	67	84	"	"	All points.			
12	70	78	"	"	N. E., S. E.			
S 13	64	70	Cloudy	Cloudy	N. E., S. E.			
14	66	74	"	"	S.			Partly clear part of afternoon.
15	63	75	"	"	S. E., S. W.			Partly clear part of morning; light sprinkle 3 P.M.
16	67½	70	Rain	Rain	N. E.			Rain 11:30 P. M. of 15th to 8:30 A.M. of 18th (57 hrs.) total 7.10; noon of 17th to 7 A. M. of 18th (19 hours), 5.02.
17	66½	67	"	"	N. E., S. E.			
18	63½	68½	"	"	S. E.	7.10		Rain till 8:30 A.M. and misty and rainy rest of day.
19	62	66	Cloudy	Cloudy	E.	0.38		Rain before day; misty evening.
S 20	64	68½	"	Rain	S. E., N.	0.67		Rain before day; raining again 2 to 11 P. M.
21	55½	67	Clear	Clear	N.			
22	50	65	"	"	N. W.			
23	50	71	"	"	W., S. W.			
24	56	72½	"	"	S. W.			Cloudy part of afternoon.
25	58	75	"	"	S. W.			
26	59½	75½	"	"	S. W., S. E.			
S 27	57½	71½	"	"	S. E.			Foggy morning.
28	59	68	C'y m'st all day.		S. E.			
29	60	65	Cloudy	Rain	N. E.	0.05		Light rain before day and 10 A. M.; steady rain after 3:30 P. M.
30	54	64	Clear	Cloudy	W.	0.41		Rain before day; light rain parts of afternoon (0.02).
						8.61		

October, 1874.

Date.	Thermometer. Lowest.	Thermometer. Highest.	Weather. Morning.	Weather. Afternoon.	Prevailing Wind.	Rain and Melted Snow in inches.	Snow in inches.	REMARKS.
1	47½	62½	Clear	Clear	W., S. W.			
2	52	69½	"	"	S. W., N. W.			Cloudy part of morning.
3	48	64	"	"	N. W., S. W.			
S 4	53	61	"	"	N. E.			Cloudy part of morning.
5	44	58½	"	"	N. E.			
6	45	60	C'y m'st all day.		E., S. E.			
7	55	67½	Cloudy	Cloudy	S. E.	0.06		Clear part of A. M.; shower 11:45 A.M.; rain after 6 P.M.
8	59	62	Rain	Rain	E., S. E.	0.35		Rain till noon; com. again 2:15 P. M.
9	55½	67	Cloudy	Clear	S. W.	1.43		Rain before day; cleared 7 A. M.
10	54	68	Rain	"	S. E., S. W.	0.82		Showers till 10:30 A. M.; clear part of morning.
S 11	55	68	Clear	"	N. W., W.			Cloudy part of morning.
12	49	61	"	"	N. W.			
13	42	50	C'y m'st all day.		N. E., N. W.			
14	40	48	Cloudy	Cloudy	N.			Cleared 6 P. M.
15	36	57	Clear	Clear	N. W., S. W.			
16	42	63	"	"	S. W.			
17	43	63½	"	"	S. W.			
S 18	52½	60	"	"	N.			Cloudy part of morning.
19	45	50½	"	"	N. W.			Cloudy part of morning.
20	41	62½	"	"	N. W., S. W.			
21	45½	62	"	"	S. W., N. W.			Cloudy part of morning.
22	44	64	"	"	N. W., S. W.			
23	49	59	"	"	N. E., E.			Foggy morning; cloudy part of A. M.; cloudy evening.
24	54	61	Cloudy	Cloudy	N. E., S. E.			Clear part of evening.
S 25	54	62	"	Clear	N. E., S. W.			
26	47	66	Clear	"	S. W.			
27	47½	69	"	"	S. W.			
28	52½	64½	"	"	N. W.			Cloudy part of evening.
29	50	72	"	"	N. E., S. W.			Cloudy part of morning.
30	56	61½	Cloudy	"	N. W.			Sprinkle before day; cleared 8 A. M.
31	40	52	Clear	Cloudy	W.			Clear part of evening.
						2.66		

Weather Record for New Brunswick, N. J.

November, 1874.

Date.	Lowest.	Highest.	Weather. Morning.	Weather. Afternoon.	Prevailing Wind.	Rain and Melted Snow in inches.	Snow in inches.	REMARKS.
S 1	35½	50	Clear	Cloudy	S. W.			Clear part of afternoon.
2	36	50½	"	Clear	W.			
3	33	52½	"	"	S. W., S. E.			Cloudy part of afternoon.
4	34	55	"	"	All points			
5	35½	56	Foggy	"	S. W.			Cloudy evening.
6	46½	65½	Clear	"	S. W.			
7	44	58	"	"	All points.			
S 8	37	58	"	"	S. W			
9	48	57	Cloudy	"	S. W., W.	0.06		Foggy morning; rain 11:45 A. M. to 2 P. M ; cleared 4 P. M.
10	37½	59	Clear	"	S. W.			Foggy morning; cloudy part of evening.
11	50	63	"	"	S. W., N. W.			Cloudy part of afternoon.
12	39	47½	"	"	N. W.			
13	30	41	"	"	N. W.			
14	23	35½	"	"	N.			
S 15	24½	42½	Cloudy	Cloudy	S. W.			Cleared 7:30 P. M.
16	32	52	Clear	Clear	W.			Cloudy evening.
17	40	54½	Cloudy	Cloudy	N. E., S W.			Light rain during evening.
18	50	56	"	Clear	S. W, N. W.	0.12		Rain before day; cleared 8 A. M.
19	35	42	Clear	"	N. W., S. W.			Cloudy part of afternoon.
20	33	41	{ Rain Snow	Cloudy	N. E., N. W.	0.38		Snow before day and then rain to 3 P. M.; clear part of evening.
21	35	38½	Clear	Clear	W.			Cloudy part of morning.
S 22	31	40	"	Cloudy	N. W., S. E.			Rainy evening after 8 P. M.
23	37	59	Rain	Rain	S. E.,S.W.,W.	1.32		Rain till 7 P. M. at intervals; thunder shower 3:40 P. M.
24	38½	42½	Clear	Clear	W., N. W.			
25	28	38	"	"	W., N. W.			Cloudy part of evening.
26	27½	40	"	"	N. W.			
27	28	47	"	"	S. W.			
28	35	48½	Cloudy	Cloudy	E.			Foggy evening.
S 29	38	56	Rain	Clear	S. W., N. W.	0.55		Rain with snow till 10:15 A. M.; cleared 3 P. M.
30	26½	32	Clear	"	N. W.	0.01		Light snow before day.
						2.44		

December, 1874.

Date.	Thermometer. Lowest.	Thermometer. Highest.	Weather. Morning.	Weather. Afternoon.	Prevailing Wind.	Rain and Melted Snow in inches.	Snow in inches.	REMARKS.
1	21½	34	Clear	Cloudy	N. E.	0.01		Snow 2:15 to 4 P. M.; clear evening.
2	28	44	"	Clear	S. W.			
3	33	49	"	Cloudy	S. W.	0.01		Light rain part of evening.
4	36½	40	Cloudy	Clear	N.			Cleared 7:30 A. M.
5	25½	40	Clear	"	N. E., S. W.			Cloudy evening.
S 6	33	44	"	Cloudy	S. W., S. E.			Rain 7:30 P. M.
7	38	44	Cloudy	"	N. E.	0.47		Rain before day; clear part of afternoon.
8	36½	39	"	Clear	N. W.			Clear part of morning.
9	26	40	Clear	Cloudy	S. W.			Clear part of evening.
10	32½	41½	"	Clear	N. W.			Cloudy evening with snow 10:40 P. M.
11	34	40½	"	"	W.	0.15		Snow before day; cloudy part morning and part even'g.
12	29	38	"	"	S. W., N. W.			Snow squall about noon.
S 13	29	38	Cloudy	Cloudy	N. E., S. W.			Rain 10:15 P. M.
14	36	46½	Rain	Clear	S. W., N. W.	0.21		Rain till 9 A. M.
15	14½	25	Clear	"	N. W.			
16	17	33½	"	"	S. W.			Cloudy part of evening.
17	31	41	Cloudy	Cloudy	S. W.			Light rain part of morning.
18	28	36	Clear	Clear	N. W.			Cloudy part of evening.
19	33	42½	"	"	S. W.			
S 20	32	35	Rain Snow	Rain Snow	N. E.	1.60		Rain and snow till 9 P. M.
21	29½	35	Clear	Clear	N., W.			
22	19	39	Cloudy	Cloudy	N. E.	0.11		Clear part of morning; rain 3:30 P. M. to 7 P. M.
23	35	43	Clear	Clear	W.			
24	33	42	Cloudy	"	W.			Cleared 9:30 A. M.
25	27	35	Clear	"	S. W., W.			
26	19	37½	C'y m'st all day.		N. E.			Misty evening.
S 27	35	42½	Clear	Cloudy	All points.	0.03		Rain before day.
28	37	45	Foggy	Foggy	S. W.	0.16		Rain before day and part of evening.
	1	46	Cloudy	Clear	W., N. W.	0.03		Rain part of morning; cleared 3 P. M.
30	24½	30½	Clear	"	N. W.			
31	12½	22½	"	"	N.			
						2.78		

Rain and melted snow 1874, 15.32 inches.

Weather Record for New Brunswick, N. J.

January, 1875.

Date	Thermometer. Lowest.	Highest.	Weather. Morning.	Afternoon.	Prevailing Wind.	Rain and Melted Snow in inches.	Snow in inches.	REMARKS.
1	13	23	Clear	Clear	N. W.			Cloudy ev'g, with hail 9:45
2	22	38	Snow/Rain	Cloudy	E., S. W.	0.50		Clear part of P.M.; cleared 7:30 P.M.; ice 7 in. thick on Weston's pond.
S 3	27	34½	Clear	Clear	S. W.			
4	30	36	Snow	Rain	N. E.	0.05		Light snow and rain all day after 7 A. M. to 9 P.M.
5	29	33½	Cloudy	Clear	N. W., S. W.			Cleared 2 P. M.
6	18	30	Clear	"	N. E.			Cloudy evening with light snow 10:45 P. M.
7	26	36	Snow/Rain	Rain	N. E.	0.15		Snow before day and rain till noon; com. rain again 4 PM.
8	30	34	Clear	Clear	N. W.	0.63		Rain before day; cloudy part of evening.
9	27	35½	Cloudy	"	N.E.,S.,N.W.			Cleared 4 P. M. with heavy wind from N. W.
S 10	½	13	Clear	"	W.			
11	10	24	"	"	W.			
12	16	25½	"	Cloudy	N. E.			Cloudy part of morning; hail and rain 10 P. M.
13	22	34	Cloudy	"	N. E.	0.22		Hail and snow before day.
14	29	31	Clear	Clear	W.			
15	16	25½	"	"	W., N. W.			
16	20	26¼	Cloudy	Cloudy	S. W., W.			Cloudy part of evening.
S 17	20½	28	Clear	Clear	N. W.			
18	17½	20½	Snow	Snow	N. E.		8.00	Snow till 5:30 P.M.; cleared 6:30 P. M.
19	-9	20	Clear	Clear	N. W., S. W.			
20	3½	20	"	"	N. W., W.			
21	8½	27½	Cloudy	Cloudy	N. E.			
22	25	30	"	Clear	N. E., S. W.	0.16		Rain 9 to 11:30 A. M.
23	23	32	Clear	"	S. W.			
S 24	17½	30	Cloudy	Rain	N. E.	0.65		Snow 10 A.M. to 1 P.M. & rain till 6 P.M.; cleared 10 P.M.
25	28	32	Clear	Clear	W., N. W.			
26	17½	30	"	"	N. W.			
27	16	28½	"	"	N. W., S. W.			Cloudy part of afternoon.
28	26	37	Cloudy	Cloudy	N. E., S. E.	0.24		Snow before day; rain 3:30 P.M. to 6:30 P.M.
29	33	36½	"	Snow	N. E.	0.08		Snow part of morning, and at intervals rest of day.
30	25	35½	Clear	Clear	W.	0.16		Snow before day; cleared 7:30 A. M.
S 31	22	32½	Cloudy	Snow	N. E.			Light snow part of A. M.
						2.84	8.00	

February, 1875.

Date.	Thermometer. Lowest.	Thermometer. Highest.	Weather. Morning.	Weather. Afternoon.	Prevailing Wind.	Rain and Melted Snow in inches.	Snow in inches.	REMARKS.
1	21½	26	Clear	Clear	N. W., S. W.		3.50	Snow before day.
2	14	35	"	"	N. W., S. E.			Cloudy part of afternoon.
3	26	50	Cloudy	Rain	N. E., S.	0.56		Rain 8 A. M. to 4 P. M.
4	23	26	"	Clear	W., N. W.			Cleared 8 A. M.
5	12	21	Clear	"	N. W., S. W.			
6	17½	32	"	"	S. W., N. W.			Cloudy part of morning.
S 7	8	12½	Cloudy	Cloudy	N. E.			Snow squall 6:30 P. M.
8	7	20	"	Clear	N. W.			Light snow part of morning; cleared 9 A. M.
9	4	8	Clear	"	N. W.			Ther. lowest 1 P. M.; cloudy part of afternoon.
10	3	21	"	"	N. W., N. E.			
11	15½	45	{ Snow Rain	Snow Rain }	N. E., S. W.	0.70	3.00	Snow till 8 A. M. and then rain to 3:45 P. M., and snow to 5 P. M.; cleared 8 P. M.
12	13	24	Clear	Clear	W.			Cloudy 8 P. M., and snow 9:30 P. M.
13	20	29	Cloudy	"	S. W.	0.03		Snow before day; cleared 10 A. M.
S 14	18	28	Clear	"	N. E., N. W.			Light snow before day.
15	7	17½	"	"	N. W.			
16	9	19½	"	"	N. W.			
17	11	37	Cloudy	"	S. W., N. W.			Clear part of morning.
18	12	22½	Clear	"	N. W.			
19	16	30	Cloudy	Snow	N. E.	0.04		Snow 8:20 A. M. to 5 P. M.
20	27½	30½	Snow Rain }	Rain	N. E., W.	0.57		Snow before day, and rain till 6 P. M.
S 21	27	34	Clear	Clear	W.			
22	25½	40½	Cloudy	"	N. E., S. E.			Cleared 9 A M.
23	33	49	Clear	Cloudy	S. W.			Clouded over 3 P. M.; rain 10 P. M.
24	41½	50	Foggy	"	S. W.	0.14		Rain before day, and light at 9:30 A. M.
25	40	53	"	Rain	S. W.	1.06		Rain before day, and from 1:30 to 9 P. M.
26	33	42½	Clear	Clear	S. W., W.			Northern lights.
27	30	36	Cloudy	Cloudy	N. E., N. W.	0.06		Clear part of morning; snow 1:30 to 4 P. M.; cleared 5 P. M.
S 28	18	24	Clear	Clear	N. W.			
						3.16	6.50	

Weather Record for New Brunswick, N. J.

March, 1875.

Date.	Thermometer. Lowest.	Thermometer. Highest.	Weather. Morning.	Weather. Afternoon.	Previling Wind.	Rain and Melted Snow in inches.	Snow in inches.	REMARKS.
1	13	29½	Snow	Snow / Rain	N. E.	0.58	4.00	Snow 8 A.M. to 5 P. M., and then rain to 11 P. M.
2	27½	40	Cloudy	Clear	S. W., N. W.			Cleared 11 A. M.
3	20	28½	"	Snow	N. E.			Snow 7:45 A. M. all day and drifted very much.
4	23½	34	Clear	Clear	N. E.		6.00	Snow before day.
5	19	30½	Cloudy	Snow	N. E.			Snow 12:30 P. M.
6	28	39	"	Clear	All points		2.50	Snow before day.
S 7	31	34	"	Snow / Rain	N. E.			Snow 1:45 P.M. to 5 P.M., and then rain and hail.
8	30	40	Snow	Clear	N. E., N. W.	1.20		Rain before day and snow till 9 A. M.; clear part of morning; cleared 2 P. M.
9	25	36	Clear	Cloudy	N. W., W.			Clear part of evening.
10	32½	42	Cloudy	Clear	N. E., S. W.	0.01		Rain and snow before day; cleared 10 A. M.; cloudy part of afternoon.
11	30	42½	Clear	"	S. W.			
12	35½	51½	"	"	S. W.			
13	32	36	Rain	Cloudy	N. E.	0.24		Cleared 10 P. M.
S 14	28½	36½	Cloudy	"	S. W., S. E.			Foggy morning and evening.
15	34	40½	Foggy	Foggy	N. E.	0.15		Rain 10:45 A. M. to 1 P. M. and 3:30 to 4 P. M.
16	38	48	Cloudy	Cloudy	S. W.	0.02		Light rain before day; foggy A. M.; clear part of P. M.
17	36	37	Clear	Clear	N. W.			
18	17	30	"	"	W.			
19	25	31	Cloudy	Cloudy	N. W., S. W.			
20	25	27½	Snow / Hail	"	N. E.	0.55		Snow and hail till noon.
S 21	20½	32	Cloudy	Clear	N. E., N. W.	0.03		Snow before day; cleared 3 P. M.
22	18	30½	Clear	"	N. W.			
23	16½	31½	"	"	N. E., S. W.			
24	25	35½	Snow	Cloudy	S. W.	0.20		Snow 7:45 A. M. to 3 P. M.
25	30	37	Clear	Clear	N. W.			
26	28½	41½	"	Cloudy	S. W.	0.07		Hail and rain 1 to 3:30 P.M.
27	35	51	"	Clear	N. W.			
S 28	36	44	"	"	N. E., W.			
29	35	47	"	"	N. E., S. E.			
30	34	55	"	"	S. W., N. W.			
31	43	56½	Cloudy	Cloudy	S. W., S. E.			Clear part of afternoon.
						3.05	12.50	

April, 1875.

Date.	Thermometer.		Weather.		Prevailing. Wind.	Rain and Melted Snow in inches.	Snow in inches.	REMARKS.
	Lowest.	Highest.	Morning.	Afternoon.				
1	40	67½	Cloudy	Clear	N. E., S. W.			Rain 8 to 10 P. M.
2	54	70	C'y m'st all day		S. W.	0.12		Rain till 11 A. M.; clear part of afternoon.
3	45	50	Rain	Cloudy	N. W., N.	0.28		
S 4	39	52	"	Clear	N. E., N.	0.10		Rain till 9 A. M.; cleared 2 P M.
5	40	59	Clear	"	N. E., N. W.			
6	39	57	"	"	All points.			
7	36	40	Cloudy	Cloudy	N. E., S. E.			Clear part of evening.
8	36½	55	C'y m'st all day		S.			
9	40	44	Cloudy	Cloudy	N. E., S. E.	0.05		Rain part afternoon; Mich'l Sullivan hung 11 A. M.
10	40	61	"	Clear	N. W., S. W.			Cleared 7:30 A. M.; cloudy part of evening.
S 11	43½	65	Clear	"	All points.			Cloudy evening, with rain 10:30 P. M.
12	42	47	Cloudy	Cloudy	E.	0.08		Rain 6:30 to 8 A M.; rainy after 5 P M.
13	32½	35½	Rain } Snow	Snow	N. E.	1.16		Rain before day and snow all day till 11 P.M., but mostly melts as it falls.
14	33	50	Clear	Clear	N. W.			
15	38	56	"	"	S. W., S.			Cloudy part of morning.
16	45	51	Cloudy	Cloudy	All points.	0.11		Light rain before day and 9 to 11:30 A.M. and 5 to 6 P. M.; snow squalls in even'g.
17	31	36½	Clear	Clear	N. W.			Snow squalls A. M. and P. M.
S 18	26½	35½	"	"	N.			Cloudy part of afternoon, with snow squalls.
19	24	41½	"	"	N. W.			Cloudy part of day, with snow squalls in the morning.
20	33	46	"	"	N. W.			
21	29	46	"	"	N. W.			
22	30½	51	"	"	N. W.			
23	35	56	"	"	N. W.			
24	38	57	"	{ Rain { Snow	All points.			Cloudy 2 P.M.; rain 3:20 till 10:30, and then snow.
S 25	35	53½	Cloudy	Clear	N. W.	0.42		Snow before day cleared 7 A. M.
26	40	60	Clear	"	N. W.			Cloudy evening.
27	46	58	"	"	N. E., S. E.			Cloudy evening.
28	41½	47	Rain	Rain	N. E.	0.48		Rain till 6 P. M.; cleared 8 P. M.
29	38	60	Clear	Cloudy	N. E., S.			Clear parts of afternoon and evening; rainy after 9 P. M.
30	39½	63	"	Clear	N. W., S. W.	0.04		Cloudy part of afternoon.
						2.84		

May, 1875.

Date.	Thermometer.		Weather.		Prevailing Wind.	Rain and Melted Snow in inches.	Snow in inches.	REMARKS.
	Lowest.	Highest.	Morning.	Afternoon.				
1	40½	50	Clear	Cloudy	E.			Light rain 12 to 2:30 P. M. and 11 P. M.
S 2	44½	55½	"	Clear	N. W.	0.05		Rain before day.
3	39	56	"	"	N. W.			
4	40½	47	Rain	Cloudy	N. E., S. W.	0.40		Rain till 12:30 P.M.; cleared 5:30 P.M.
5	41	61½	Clear	Clear	N. W., S. W.			
6	47½	54½	Rain	Cloudy	S., N. E.	0.09		Rain till 10 A.M.; clear part of evening.
7	43½	56	Clear	Clear	N. W., N. E.			Cloudy part of afternoon.
8	44	57	Cloudy	Cloudy	S. E.	0.10		Rain till 6 A.M.; clear part of morning.
S 9	47	73	"	Clear	N.E., S.W., E.			Cleared 10 A. M.
10	50	73½	Clear	Cloudy	S. W.			Clouded over 9:30 A. M.; cleared 6 P. M. Cherries flowered.
11	51½	70½	"	Clear	N. W., S. W.			
12	58	75	"	"	S. W., N. W.	0.12		Cloudy parts of morning & afternoon; shower 3 P. M.
13	48	67	"	"	N. W., S. W.			Pears flowered.
14	46½	66	"	"	N. E., S. E.			
15	50½	71	Cloudy	Cloudy	All points.	0.02		Clear 10 A.M. to 5 P.M.; light rain part of evening.
S 16	46	62	Clear	Clear	N.			
17	42	63	"	"	N. E., S.			
18	42½	62	"	"	N. E., S. E.			
19	49	64	C'y m'st all day		S. W.			
20	54	79	"	"	S. W.			
21	61	84	Clear	Clear	S. W.			Cloudy evening.
22	68	82½	C'y m'st all day		S. W., N. W.			
S 23	65	84	Clear	Clear	All points.			Cloudy part of afternoon.
24	63½	81½	C'y m'st all day		E., S. W.			
25	66	68	Rain	Rain	S. E., N. E.	0.99		Rain all day at intervals till 6 P. M.
26	64½	80½	Clear	Clear	N. E.			
27	59	73½	"	"	N. E., S. W.			
28	56	78½	"	"	S. W.			
29	58	80	"	"	S. W.			Cloudy evening.
S 30	61	78	"	"	N. E., N.			
31	58½	75½	"	"	All points.			
						1.77		

Weather Record for New Brunswick, N. J.

June, 1875.

Date	Thermometer Lowest	Thermometer Highest	Weather Morning	Weather Afternoon	Prevailing Wind	Rain and Melted Snow in inches	Snow in inches	REMARKS
1	56	71	Clear	Clear	E., S. E.			
2	51½	70½	Cloudy	"	S. E.			Cleared 8:30 A. M.
3	56½	67	"	Cloudy	S. E.			Light sprinkle 7:30 P. M.
4	57	77½	Clear	Clear	S. W.			
5	60	80	"	Cloudy	S. W.			
S 6	67	77	C'y m'st all day	All points				
7	66	78½	Cloudy	Cloudy	S. W., N. W.	0.50		Light rain before day; partly clear part of morning; shower 1:30 to 3:40 P.M.; light rain part of evening; cleared 10 P. M.
8	56½	71½	Clear	Clear	N. W., S.			Cloudy evening.
9	59	64	Cloudy	Rain	N. E.			Misty rain after 2:45 P. M.
10	57½	74½	"	Clear	All points	0.05		Misty rain before day; cleared 10 A. M.
11	60½	80	Clear	"	S. E.			
12	60	79	Cloudy	"	S. W.			Cleared 8 A. M.; cloudy evening with rain 10 to 11 P. M.
S 13	56	67	Clear	"	N. W.	0.18		Rain before day.
14	47½	69	"	"	N. W., S. W.			
15	54	74	"	"	N. W, S. W.			
16	60	77½	"	"	All points			
17	59	77½	"	"	E.			Cloudy evening.
18	62	70½	Rain	"	S. E, N. W.	0.60		Rain till 9 A.M.; cl'red 4 P.M.
19	57	75	Clear	"	N. W.			Hazy morning.
S 20	55	75	"	"	N. W., S. W.			
21	56	80½	"	"	S. W.			
22	61	82½	"	"	S. W.			
23	68½	80	Cloudy	"	S.	1.00		Showers 5:30 to 9 A. M.
24	71	88	Clear	"	S. W.			
25	73½	91½	"	"	S. W.			
26	73	80½	"	"	N. E., S. E.	0.30		Cloudy part of afternoon, with rain 3:10 to 4 P. M.; rain 11 P. M.
S 27	71	88	"	"	S. W.	0.38		Rain before day; cloudy evening, with light sprinkles.
28	74½	90½	"	"	S. W.			
29	69½	72	Cloudy	Cloudy	E.	0.10		Rain before day; showers after 8 P. M.
30	66	82½	"	Clear	W.	0.85		Rain till 6 A. M.; cleared 8:30 A. M.
						4.56		

July, 1875.

Date.	Lowest.	Highest.	Weather Morning.	Weather Afternoon.	Prevailing Wind.	Rain and Melted Snow in inches.	Snow in inches.	REMARKS.
1	70	78	Clear	Clear	W., N. W.			Cloudy part of morning.
2	61	75½	"	"	All points.			
3	61½	77	"	"	W., S.			Albany St. bridge bought by the county and made free.
S 4	63½	80	"	"	S. W.			Cloudy parts of A.M. and P.M.
5	72	85	"	"	S. W.			Cloudy part of morning.
6	73½	90	"	"	S. W.	0.55		Shower 8 to 9:30 P. M.
7	73	82	C'y m'st all day		All points.			
8	70	82	Clear	Clear	N. E., S. E.			
9	67	79	"	"	S. E.			Cloudy part of evening.
10	68	77	C'y m'st all day		S. E.			
S 11	71	85½	Cloudy	Clear	N. W.	0.02		Rain before day; cleared 8 A. M.
12	62½	73	C'y m'st all day		N. E., S. W.			
13	60	81½	Clear	Clear	S. W.			Light rain about 2 P. M.
14	68½	82	"	"	N. W., W.			
15	68	84½	"	Cloudy	S.	0.05		Clear part of P. M.; showers 12:10 and 2:30 P. M.
16	69	73½	Rain	Clear	E., N. E.	1.26		Heavy rain till 7:30 A. M.; showers till 1 P.M.; cleared 4 P. M.
17	66	83	Clear	"	N. W.			
S 18	68	84	Cloudy	"	E.,S.W.,N.W.	0.22		Light rain 6 A. M.; cleared 8 A.M.; shower 1 P.M.
19	61	75	Clear	"	N. W.			
20	59	74	"	Cloudy	S. W.			
21	64	80	"	Clear	S. W.			
22	65½	80	"	Cloudy	All points.			Rain 11 P. M.
23	72½	85½	Cloudy	Clear	S. W., N. W.	0.11		Rain before day; cleared 10 A. M.
24	70½	80½	Clear	"	N. E., N. W.			
S 25	64	83	"	"	N. W., S. W.			
26	68½	83½	C'y m'st all day		S. W.	0.74		Shower 11:55 A. M.; and heavy shower 3:35 P.M. to 4:05 P. M.
27	71¼	85	Clear	Clear	S. W.	0.07		Shower 8:15 P. M.
28	67	77	Cloudy	"	N. W.	0.04		Rain 9:30 to 11:30 A. M.
29	65½	70½	"	Rain	S. W., N. E.	0.88		Rain 8:15 A. M. to 9 P. M.
30	63	81½	Clear	Clear	W., S. W.			
31	69	77	"	Cloudy	N. E.			Clear parts of afternoon and evening.

3.94

August, 1875.

Date	Thermometer Lowest	Thermometer Highest	Weather Morning	Weather Afternoon	Prevailing Wind	Rain and Melted Snow in inches	Snow in inches	REMARKS
S 1	64	71	Clear	Cloudy	N. E., S. E.	----	----	Clear part of afternoon.
2	61½	62½	Rain	Rain	N. E.	1.15	----	Rain till 5 P. M., and misty part of evening.
3	57	73½	Cloudy	Cloudy	All points	0.54	----	Rain before day; partly clear part of afternoon; shower 8 to 9 P. M.
4	67½	81	C'y m'st all day	"	S. W., S.	0.08	----	Shower 4:40 P. M. and light rain during evening.
5	69	80	Cloudy	Clear	N. E., S. W.	0.10	----	Rain before day; cleared 8 A. M.
6	66	82	Clear	"	S.	0.04	----	Shower 12:45 P. M.; rain 11:15 P. M.
7	66½	79	C'y m'st all day	S. W.		0.52	----	Showers till 5 A.M.; showers 6:35 and 8:40 P. M.
S 8	69	78½	Cloudy	Clear	S. W.	----	----	
9	66	81	Clear	"	S. W.	----	----	
10	64	81½	"	"	S. W.	----	----	
11	69	76½	Rain	Cloudy	All points	3.68	----	Showers 6 A.M. to 1:30 P.M.; clear part of afternoon.
12	71½	82	Cloudy	Rain	S. W., S. E.	0.47	----	Clear part A. M.; rain 12:25 to 5:30 P.M.;cleared 6 P.M.
13	72	83	C'y m'st all day	S. W.		0.53	----	Clear 9 A. M. to 4 P. M.; rain 5:15 to 9 P. M.
14	71	81	Clear	Cloudy	W.	0.05	----	Rain before day; clear part of afternoon.
S 15	70	81	"	"	S. W., S. E.	----	----	Foggy morning; clear part of afternoon.
16	72	81½	Cloudy	Clear	All points	----	----	Cleared 10 A. M.
17	72½	80½	"	"	S. E.	----	----	Foggy morning; cleared 10 A. M.
18	72	80	Show'rs	"	SE, SW, NW	0.50	----	Showers till 12:30 P. M.; cleared 1 P. M.
19	70½	82	Cloudy	"	S. E., S. W.	----	----	Foggy morning; cloudy parts of afternoon.
20	69½	81½	Clear	"	S. W.	----	----	
21	66½	80½	"	"	S. W.	----	----	
S 22	65	78	Cloudy	Cloudy	S. W.	0.15	----	Clear part of A. M.; rain 5:15 to 6:45 P. M.
23	62½	67	"	Rain	N. E.	0.27	----	Rain part of morning and 1 to 7 P. M.
24	62	69	Clear	Cloudy	N. E., S. E.	----	----	Light rain 6:30 P. M.
25	61½	72	"	Clear	N. E., E.	----	----	
26	60	73	"	"	N. E., S. E.	----	----	
27	59	73½	"	"	N. E.	----	----	
28	61	75	"	"	N. E., E.	----	----	
S 29	64	77	"	"	S. E., S. W.	----	----	Cloudy part of morning and part of afternoon.
30	65½	81	"	"	W., N. E.	----	----	
31	67	82	"	"	N. E., S. E.	----	----	
						8.08	----	

Weather Record for New Brunswick, N. J.

September, 1875.

Date.	Thermometer. Lowest.	Thermometer. Highest.	Wind. Morning.	Wind. Afternoon.	Prevailing Wind.	Rain and Melted Snow in inches.	Snow in inches.	REMARKS.
1	67	80	Clear	Clear	N. E., S. E.			
2	64	80	"	"	N. E., S. E.			
3	68	85	"	"	All points			
4	73	87	"	"	S. W., N. W.			Cloudy part of morning.
S 5	66	80½	"	"	N. W.			
6	66¼	83½	"	"	S. W., N. W.			
7	63	77	"	"	N. W.			
8	56	80	"	"	N. W., S. W.			
9	63	81½	"	"	S. W.			
10	69	80	"	Cloudy	S. W., N. E.	0.30		Cloudy part of morning; rain 2:45 to 5:15 P.M.; cleared 7 P. M.
11	50¼	63	"	Clear	N. E., S. E.			
S 12	50	66	"	Cloudy	N. E., S. E.			Light sprinkle 8:20 P. M.
13	61	70½	Cloudy	"	N. E.	0.34		Rain 6:30 to 8 A. M.; clear part of A.M.; cleared 9 P.M.
14	63½	72½	C'y m'st all day		N. E., S. E.			
15	64	73½	Cloudy	Cloudy	S. W., S. E.	0.30		Clear part of A.M.; rain 4:45 to 7 P.M.; cleared 8 P.M.
16	59½	68½	"	Rain	S. W., S. E.	0.10		Foggy morning; light rain P.M and ev'g till 10 P. M.
17	63	70	Clear	Clear	W., N. W.			Cloudy part of afternoon.
18	48½	61	"	"	N. W.			Clouded over 6 P. M.; rain 10 P. M.
S 19	47	52½	Rain	Cloudy	N. E.	1.05		Rain till 11 A. M.
20	50	65	Cloudy	Clear	N. E., S. W.			Cleared 8:15 A. M.
21	48	61	Clear	"	N. W.			
22	46	57½	"	"	N. W.			Cloudy part of afternoon with light rain 4 P. M.
23	41½	60	"	"	N. W., S. W.			Frost.
24	41	62½	"	"	W., N. W.			
25	46	65½	"	"	S. W.			Cloudy evening.
S 26	55	63½	Rain	"	N. W.	0.10		Rain till 8:30 A.M.; cleared 11 A. M.
27	47	70	Clear	"	S. W.			
28	53	71	"	"	S. W.			
29	57	70½	Cloudy	"	N. E., S. E.			Cleared 10 A. M.
30	57½	75	C'y m'st all day		S. W.			
						2.19		

October, 1875.

Date	Thermometer Lowest	Thermometer Highest	Weather Morning	Weather Afternoon	Prevailing Wind	Rain and Melted Snow in inches	Snow in inches	REMARKS
1	57	68	C'y m'st all day.		N. E., N. W.	0.05	---	Rain before day; shower 3 P. M.
2	44½	61½	Clear	Clear	N. W.	---	---	
S 3	42	65	"	"	S. W.	---	---	
4	50	69½	"	"	S. W.	---	---	Cloudy part of afternoon.
5	55	72	Cloudy	"	S. W.	---	---	Foggy morning.
6	56	60	Rain	Rain	E.	---	---	Rain 7 A. M.
7	58½	64	"	Clear	N. E., N.	0.79	---	Rain till 9 A. M.; cleared at noon.
8	43	63	Clear	"	N. W., S. W.	---	---	Cloudy part of afternoon.
9	45	58	"	"	N. W., N. E.	---	---	
S 10	43½	58½	C'y m'st all day.		N. E., S. E.	---	---	Rain 9 P. M.
11	47	50	Cloudy	Cloudy	N. W.	0.12	---	Light rain at intervals till 9 A. M.
12	43	52	"	Clear	N.	---	---	Cleared 8 A. M.
13	34	49½	Clear	"	N. W., S. W.	---	---	
14	34½	55	"	"	N. E.	---	---	Cloudy part of morning; cloudy evening.
15	50	56	C'y m'st all day.		N. E.	0.04	---	Misty and rainy parts of afternoon and evening.
16	53	58½	Rain	Cloudy	SE, SW, NW.	0.32	---	Rain till 10 A. M. and from 1 to 4 P.M.; clear parts of afternoon and evening.
S 17	41½	54	Clear	Clear	N. W., S. W.	---	---	
18	41	59	"	"	All points.	---	---	Cloudy evening.
19	48	54	C'y m'st all day.		N.	---	---	
20	41	58½	Clear	Clear	N. W., S. W.	---	---	
21	47	66½	"	"	S. W.	---	---	
22	48	68	"	"	S. W.	---	---	
23	48	68½	"	Hazy	S. W.	---	---	
S 24	53	69	"	Clear	S. W.	---	---	Cloudy parts of morning and afternoon.
25	52½	70½	"	"	S. W., N. W.	---	---	
26	49	60	C'y m'st all day.		N. E., S. E.	---	---	Rain 9:30 P. M.
27	48½	56	Clear	Clear	S. W., N. W.	0.45	---	Rain before day; cloudy part of afternoon.
28	42	53	"	"	N. W., S. W.	---	---	Cloudy part of afternoon.
29	46	62	"	"	All points.	---	---	Cloudy evening.
30	52½	62	Cloudy	Rain	S. E.	0.85	---	Rain 12:40 P. M. to 11 P. M.
S 31	40	47	Clear	Clear	W.	---	---	Cloudy part of afternoon with snow squall 3:35 P. M.

2.62 ---

November, 1875.

Date.	Thermometer.		Weather.		Prevailing Wind.	Rain and Melted Snow in inches.	Snow in inches.	REMARKS.
	Lowest.	Highest.	Morning.	Afternoon.				
1	38	44	C'y m'st all day.		W.	0.03		Snow after 9 P.M. to 11 P.M.
2	34	44½	Clear	Clear	N. W.			Snow squall 11:15 A. M.
3	32	44	"	"	N. W., S. W.			
4	35	40	Rain	"	N. E.	0.35		Rain till noon; cleared 4 P. M.
5	33½	42	Clear	"	N. W., E.			Cloudy parts of morning and afternoon.
6	31½	47½	"	"	N. W., S. W.			
S 7	32	49½	"	Cloudy	S. W.			Clouded over 3 P. M.
8	39	47	"	Clear	N. E.			Cloudy part of morning.
9	31	45	"	"	N. E., S. E.			
10	37½	43	Rain	Rain	N. E.	1.23		Rain 6 A. M. to 3:30 P. M., misty till 6 P. M.; cleared 8 P. M.
11	40½	49	Clear	Clear	N. W.			Cloudy part of morning.
12	37½	57	"	"	S. W.			
13	40	60	"	"	S. W.			Cloudy evening.
S 14	45	55	C'y m'st all day.		All points	0.06		Rain 7 to 9 P. M. and misty afterwards.
15	38	44	Cloudy	Cloudy	N. E., E.			
16	42	47	"	Clear	N. E., N. W.	0.23		Rain 8:30 A. M. to 3:30 P.M.; cleared 4 P. M.
17	34½	38	Clear	"	N. W.			Snow squall 11:15 A. M.
18	29½	41	"	"	S. W.			Cloudy evening.
19	38	51	Cloudy	"	S. W.	0.10		Rain before day.
20	42	44	"	Cloudy	N.E.,S.,N.W.	0.10		Rain 10 A. M. to 1 P M; cleared 7 P. M.
S 21	34	42	"	"	N. E., N. W.	0.03		Rain 9 to 11 A. M.; cleared 5.30 P. M.
22	29	37	Clear	Clear	All points			
23	27	50	Cloudy	Rain	N. E., S. W.	1.42		Light snow before day; rain 8 A. M. to 11 P. M.
24	41	47½	Clear	Clear	W., N. W.			
25	32	40½	"	"	N. E., S. E.			
26	31	54	Cloudy	Rain	N. E., S. W.	0.77		Rain 10 A. M. to noon, and 2 P. M. to 8 P. M.
27	42½	48	Clear	Clear	N. W.			
S 28	30	45	"	Cloudy	N. E., S. E.			Clouded over 8 A. M.
29	42	47	"	Clear	W., N. W.			
30	12	19½	"	"	N.			River frozen over; cloudy evening.
						4.37		

December, 1875.

Date.	Lowest.	Highest.	Weather. Morning.	Weather. Afternoon.	Prevailing. Wind.	Rain and Melted Snow in inches.	Snow in inches.	REMARKS.
1	14	23	Cloudy	Cloudy	N.			Cleared 6 p. m.
2	15	30	Clear	Clear	N.			
3	15½	34	"	Cloudy	N. E., S. W.			Clouded over 4 p. m.
4	33	38	Cloudy	"	All points			Light sprinkle before day; clear part of evening.
S 5	30	37	"	Rain	N. E.			Clear part of morning; light rain during afternoon and steady rain after 7 p m.
6	33	36½	Rain	Cloudy	N. E.	0.95		Rain till 7:30 a. m.
7	35½	39½	Cloudy	Rain	N. E.			Com. raining about noon.
8	34	38	{Rain Snow}	{Rain Snow}	N. E.	0.70		Rain and snow till 7:30 a.m.; clear part of morning; rain & snow noon to 7 p.m.
9	35½	43½	Cloudy	Cloudy	N., W.			Foggy morning.
10	35½	39½	"	Clear	N. W.			Cleared 9 a. m.
11	32	38½	"	Cloudy	S. W.			
S 12	35½	44	"	Clear	N. W.			Cleared 10 a. m.
13	34½	43	Clear	"	S. W., W.			Cloudy parts of a. m. and p. m. with snow squalls.
14	30	33½	"	"	W., N. W.			Cloudy parts of a. m. and p. m. with snow squalls.
15	23	34½	"	Cloudy	N. W., S. W.	0.01		Light snow part of evening.
16	31	43	"	"	N. W., S. W.			Light rain after 8:30 p.m.
17	35	36	"	Clear	W., N. W.	0.02		Light rain before day; cloudy part of afternoon.
18	16	23½	"	"	N. W.			
S 19	17½	24	"	"	W., N.			
20	5½	29	"	"	N. E., S. E.			Cloudy part of afternoon.
21	21	45	"	"	S. W.			Cloudy evening.
22	40	56	"	"	W.	0.21		Rain before day.
23	42	60	"	"	S. W.			Cloudy part of evening.
24	37	39	"	{Snow Rain}	E.			Cloudy part of morning.
25	35½	42	Cloudy	Cloudy	N. E., W.	0.47		Rain before day and part of morning; cleared 6 p. m.
S 26	34	41½	"	"	N. E., E.			Misty and foggy evening.
27	37½	49	Rain	Clear	N.	0.21		Rain till 7:30 a. m; cleared 10:30 a. m.
28	28	35	Cloudy	Rainy	N. E.			Rain 11 a. m.
29	33	38	Rain	Cloudy	N. E.	0.10		Light rain till 9 a.m.; rainy evening.
30	35½	43½	"	Foggy	N. E., S. E.	0.09		Light rain till 8 a.m.; misty evening.
31	40	44½	Cloudy	Cloudy	S. W.	0.01		Light rain before day; foggy evening.
						2.77		

Rain and melted snow for 1875—44.89 inches.

Weather Record for New Brunswick, N. J.

January, 1876.

Date.	Thermometer. Lowest.	Thermometer. Highest.	Weather. Morning.	Weather. Afternoon.	Prevailing Wind.	Rain and Melted Snow in inches.	Snow in inches.	REMARKS.
1	43	54	Cloudy	Cloudy	S. W.			Clear part of A. M.; foggy and misty evening.
S 2	47	66	Foggy	"	S. W.	0.09		Clear 8 A. M. to 3 P.M.; rain 4 to 6:30 P. M.; clear part of evening.
3	45	50½	Clear	Clear	N. W.			January 2 warmest day in January I ever knew.
4	30½	35	"	"	N. W.			
5	21	41	"	"	N. E., S. W.			
6	38	48	C'y m'st all day		S. W., N. W.			Light sprinkle part of A. M.
7	31	40½	Cloudy	Clear	N. W., S. W.			Clear part of morning.
8	32	46	Clear	Cloudy	S. W.			Light rain part of evening.
S 9	43½	57	Cloudy	"	S. W.			Partly clear part of evening.
10	39	42	"	Clear	S. W., N. W.			
11	21	29	Clear	"	W.			
12	20	31	Cloudy	"	S. W., N. W.			Light snow part of afternoon; cleared 4 P. M.
13	19	27	Clear	"	W., N. W.			
14	15	31	"	Cloudy	S. W.			Clear part of evening.
15	25	40	"	"	S. W.			Clear part of evening.
S 16	35	48½	C'y m'st all day		S. W.			
17	37	47	Cloudy	Cloudy	S. W.	0.25		Rain before day; clear part afternoon; foggy evening.
18	35½	58½	Foggy	"	E., S. W.	0.01		Light rain part of A. M.; clear part of evening.
19	55	59	Cloudy	Rainy	S. W.			Light rain during P. M. and heavy rain after 6 P. M.
20	34½	41	Clear	Clear	N. W.	0.38		Rain before day.
21	34	43	"	"	S. W., N. W.			
22	27	30½	Cloudy	Cloudy	N. E.			Light snow after 4:15 P. M., and misty after 9 P. M.
S 23	25	42	"	"	S. W.	0.19		Rain before day and from 8 A. M. to 1 P. M.
24	35	38½	C'y m'st all day		N. W.	0.03		Rain and snow before day.
25	29	37½	Cloudy	Cloudy	S. W.			Clear part of morning and part of evening.
26	25½	33	Clear	Clear	N. W., W.			
27	26½	41½	Snow Rain	Cloudy	S., S. W.	0.22		Snow before day and rain till 11:30 A. M.; clear part of evening.
28	40	47½	Cloudy	"	N. E.			Clear part of morning; foggy evening.
29	37	57	"	"	S. E., S. W.	0.04		Light rain part of afternoon; clear evening.
S 30	25	31	Clear	Clear	N., N. E.			
31	21½	35	Cloudy	Cloudy	N. E.			
						1.21		

Weather Record for New Brunswick, N. J.

February, 1876.

Date	Thermometer Lowest	Thermometer Highest	Weather Morning	Weather Afternoon	Prevailing Wind	Rain and Melted Snow in inches	Snow in inches	REMARKS.
1	33	43½	Cloudy	Cloudy	S.			Misty part of afternoon; rain 9 P. M.
2	26	30	"	Clear	N. W.	0.56		Rain before day; cleared 9 A. M.
3	15½	25	Clear	Cloudy	N. W., S. W.			Light snow 3:30 to 4 P. M., and steady snow storm after 6:30 P. M.
4	21½	32	Snow	"	W., N. W.		10.00	Snow till 9 A. M.; cleared 5:30 P. M.
5	11½	23½	Clear	Clear	N., N. E.			
S 6	8	32	"	Cloudy	N. E., S. E.			Clouded over 8 A. M.; rain after 5 P. M.
7	31	46½	"	Clear	S W., W.	0.57		Rain before day.
8	31½	43½	"	"	N. W.			
9	33	47½	Foggy	Cloudy	S. W., S. E.	0.07		Light rain 2 P. M.; rain 10:30 P. M. to 11:30 P. M.
10	42	47½	Clear	"	N. W., S. E.			Cleared 6 P. M.
11	37	50	Cloudy	"	S. E., S. W.	0.01		Light rain part of afternoon; partly clear part of afternoon.
12	42	53	Clear	Clear	W.			
S 13	36	55	"	Cloudy	S. W.			Rain at intervals after 7 P.M.
14	42	44	Rain	Misty	E., N. E.	0.70		Rain till 1 P. M., and misty rest of day with thunder shower 10:30 P. M.
15	35½	56½	"	Cloudy	N. E., S. W.	1.28		Rain till 3 P. M.; clear part of evening. Bar. 12:30 P. M., 28.975.
16	30	36	Clear	Clear	W.			Cloudy part of afternoon and part of evening.
17	29½	35	Cy m'st all day.	W., N. W.				Snow squalls all day.
18	32	39	"	"	"	N. W.		
19	28	46½	Clear	Clear	S. W.			Cloudy part of evening.
S 20	36½	44	"	"	N. W.			
21	27½	39	"	Cloudy	All points.			Snow and rain 9:30 P. M.
22	34	40½	"	Clear	N. W., S. W.	0.00		Rain before day. Seal, 4 feet long, caught below town in frost fish net.
23	19½	24	"	"	N. W.			
24	12	28	"	"	N. W.			
25	19	36	"	"	N. W.			
26	26	39	Cloudy	"	All points.			Cleared 10 A. M.
S 27	27	34	"	Cloudy	N. E.			Rainy evening.
28	28	32	Rainy	Misty	N. E.	0.23		Rainy morning till 11; light snow after 9:30 P.M.
29	28½	36	Cloudy	Cloudy	N. E., N. W.	0.05		Snow before day, and part of morning; clear parts of afternoon and evening. No ice crop gathered here this Winter.
						4.07	10.00	

March, 1876.

Date.	Lowest.	Highest.	Morning.	Afternoon.	Prevailing Wind.	Rain and Melted Snow in inches.	Snow in inches.	REMARKS.
1	30½	35	Cloudy	Cloudy	W.			Light snow part A. M., and snowy evening after 5:20.
2	26	34	C'y m'st all day		N. E.		2.00	Snow before day.
3	21½	35	Clear	Clear	N. W.			
4	23	40	"	"	W., S. W.			
S 5	30½	52	"	"	S. W.			
6	37	57½	"	"	S. W.			Cloudy part of morning, with sprinkles of rain.
7	43	65½	"	"	S. W.			Cloudy part of evening.
8	54	55	Cloudy	"	S. W., N. W.	0.09		Rain before day and part of morning; cleared 4:30 P. M.
9	31	46	Clear	"	N.			
10	31½	48½	"	"	N. E., S. E.			
11	35½	41½	Cloudy	"	E.			Light rain 8:30 to 9 A. M.; cloudy evening.
S 12	35	39	"	Cloudy	E., S. E.			Misty after 5:30 P. M.
13	37½	48	Rain	Clear	N. E,. N. W.	0.42		Thunder showers before day; rain till 6:30 A. M; cleared at noon.
14	23	39	Clear	"	N. W.			
15	24½	42	"	"	N. W.			
16	28½	39	Cloudy	Rain	N. E., E.	0.85		Rain 9:30 at intervals till 9:30 P.M.; clear part eve'g.
17	34	46	C'y m'st all day		N. E,. N. W.	0.07		Foggy A. M.; snow and rain 7:40 to 10:30 A. M.
18	29	32	Clear	Clear	N. W.			Cloudy part of morning and part of afternoon.
S 19	15	32½	"	"	N.			
20	18	32	Cloudy Rain		N. E., E.			Snow 3 P.M. to 9 P.M., and then heavy rain; bar. 30.33
21	30	47	Rain	Cloudy	W.	1.80		Rain till 7:20 A. M.; clear part of morning; bar. 29.24.
22	26½	38	Clear	Clear	W.			
23	30½	40	Cloudy	"	W.			
24	30	47	Clear	Cloudy	S.			
25	35	50	Snow Rain	Rain	E., S. E.			Snow before day and heavy rain till 3:15 P.M.; light rain rest of day.
S 26	40½	49	Clear	Cloudy	W.	3.33		Rain before day; clear part of evening.
27	37	44½	"	Clear	W., N. W.			Cloudy part of afternoon.
28	33	55	Cloudy	Rain	E.			Sprinkle 11 A.M.,and steady rain 3:40 P. M., with high wind.
29	30½	47	C'y m'st all day		W.		0.75	Rain before day.
30	33	42	" "	" "	W.			Snow squalls morning and afternoon.
31	34½	47½	" "	" "	W.			
						7.31	2.00	

April, 1876.

Date.	Thermometer.		Weather.		Prevailing Wind.	Rain and Melted Snow in inches.	Snow in inches.	REMARKS.
	Lowest.	Highest.	Morning.	Afternoon.				
1	38	44	Clear	Clear	N.			Cloudy part of morning and part of afternoon.
S 2	32	48	"	"	All points.			
3	34	42½	Rain	Rain	S. E., N. E.			
4	39	46	"	Cloudy	N.	1.47		Rain till 6 A. M. and misty rest of morning and part of evening.
5	40	54	Clear	"	All points.			Clear part of evening.
6	39½	53	"	Clear	N. W., S. W.			
7	39½	59	"	"	S. W., N. W.			Cloudy part of afternoon.
8	37½	52	"	"	N. W.			
S 9	32½	49	"	"	N.			
10	33½	56	"	"	N. W.			
11	39	61	"	"	N. W., S. W.			
12	44	67	C'y m'st all day.		All points.			Rain 9 P. M.
13	49	63	Cloudy	Cloudy	E.	0.38		Rain before day.
14	50	70	"	"	N. W.	0.07		Rain 10:15 to 11:30 A. M.
15	51	60	Clear	Clear	S. W.			
S 16	49½	61½	"	"	S. W.	0.01		Cloudy part of morning with light rain 8 A M. and part of evening.
17	42½	53	"	"	N. W.			Light rain part of aft'noon.
18	38	50	"	"	N. W.			Cloudy part of afternoon.
19	40	49	"	"	N. W.			Cloudy part of afternoon.
20	36	56	"	"	N. W., S. W.			Cloudy evening with light rain.
21	45½	66½	"	"	N. W.			
22	43	58	"	"	N. W., S. W.			
S 23	45	62	"	Cloudy	S. W., N. W.			Clear part of evening.
24	46½	52½	Cloudy	"	E.			
25	41½	46½	"	"	N. E.			
26	39½	56½	C'y m'st all day.		N. E.			
27	40	64	Clear	Clear	N. W., S. W.			
28	50	67	Cloudy	Cloudy	All points.	0.40		Clear part of morning; rain 2:15 to 6 P. M.
29	48	61½	Clear	Clear	All points.			Cloudy part of evening. Pears and cherries flowered.
S 30	49	59	Rain	"	S. W., N. W.	0.26		Rain till 7 A.M.; clear part of morning and cloudy part of afternoon.

2.59

May, 1876.

Date.	Lowest.	Highest.	Weather Morning.	Weather Afternoon.	Prevailing Wind.	Rain and Melted Snow in inches.	Snow in inches.	REMARKS.
1	37½	54	Clear	Clear	N. W.			
2	42	59	"	Cloudy	All points			
3	47	54	Cloudy	"	N. E., S. E.			Clear part of evening.
4	42½	59½	C'y m'st all day.		S. W.			
5	45	70	Clear	Cloudy	S. W.			Clear part of afternoon.
6	54	74	Cloudy	Clear	S. W.	0.12		Rain before day; clear part of morning.
S 7	59	84	Clear	"	S. W.			Cloudy part of evening.
8	68	82	"	Cloudy	S. W.	0.03		Shower 5:20 P. M.
9	56	59½	Rain	Rain	N. E.	0.99		Rain till 12:30 P. M., and com. again 5:30 P M.
10	56	67½	"	Cloudy	S. W.	0.71		Rain till 8:15 A. M.; cloudy most all day; rain 6 to 8 P. M.
11	50	65	Clear	Clear	N. W.			
12	54	62	Cloudy	Cloudy	All points	0.12		Showers part of morning and afternoon; clear evening.
13	47	63	Clear	Clear	N. W.			
S 14	46½	63½	"	"	N. W., S. W.			Cloudy part of evening.
15	52	68	C'y m'st all day.		S. W., E.	0.01		Rain part of evening.
16	49	57	Cloudy	Cloudy	N. E., S.			Clear evening.
17	49	56½	"	"	N. E.			Clear part of morning.
18	52	63	"	"	S. W.	0.16		Rain 8:40 to 11 A. M.; clear part of evening.
19	54	74½	Clear	Clear	All points.			
20	57	71	"		N. E., S. E.			
S 21	57	82½	"	"	S. W.	0.24		Clouded over 6 P. M., and rain 8:15 to 10:30 P. M.
22	66½	80	C'y m'st all day.		S. W.	0.55		Light shower 3:15 P.M., and showers 6:15 to 10 P. M.
23	52½	63½	Clear	Clear	N.			
24	47½	69	"	"	All points.			
25	54	76½	"	"	S. W.			
26	53	65	"	"	S. E.			
27	52	77	"	"	S. W.			Cloudy part of morning.
S 28	58	79½	"	"	S. W.			Cloudy evening.
29	66	83	"	"	S. W., N. W.			Cloudy part of evening.
30	58	67½	"	"	N. E., S. E.			
31	49½	65	"	"	E.			
						2.93		

June, 1876.

Date.	Thermometer. Lowest.	Thermometer. Highest.	Weather. Morning.	Weather. Afternoon.	Prevailing Wind.	Rain and Melted Snow in inches.	Snow in inches.	REMARKS.
1	47	72½	Clear	Clear	All points.			
2	54	77	"	"	All points.			Cloudy evening.
3	64	83	"	"	S. W.			Cloudy evening.
S 4	70	82	C'y m'st all day.		S. W.	0.33		Shower 5 P. M. and rainy 6:15 to 8:30 P. M.
5	66	74	" "	" "	N. W.			
6	57½	72	Clear	Clear	N.			Cloudy part of afternoon.
7	54	75	"	"	N. W., S. W.			
8	61	82½	"	"	S. W.			
9	67	84	"	"	S. W.			
10	67	85½	"	"	S. W.			Cloudy part of afternoon.
S 11	70½	85	"	"	S. W.	0.30		Cloudy parts A.M. and afternoon; shower 2:40 P. M.
12	60½	69	Cloudy	Cloudy	N. E.			
13	66	77	C'y m'st all day.		S.	0.75		Showers at noon, 3 P.M. and 5 P. M.
14	66	78½	Clear	Clear	S. W., S.			Cloudy part of morning.
15	64	80	Cloudy	"	S. W., N. E.			Cleared 10 A. M.
16	64	77	"	"	N. E.			
17	65½	81	"	"	S. E., S.			Light rain before day.
S 18	69½	77	"	Cloudy	S. E.			Rain 11 P. M.
19	69	82	Rain	Clear	N. W.	0.34		Showers till 7 A.M. and light one at 12:50 P. M.
20	68	78½	Cloudy	"	S. W.	0.17		Showers till 7:30 A. M.
21	66	78	Clear	"	S. W., W.	0.02		Cloudy part of morning, with light showers.
22	61½	77	Cloudy	"	N. W.			Clear part of morning.
23	60	80	Clear	"	N. W., S. W.			
24	66	86	"	"	S. W.			
S 25	70½	89½	"	"	S. W.			
26	73	90	"	"	All points.			
27	72½	92	"	"	S. W.			Cloudy part of afternoon.
28	75	88	"	"	N. W., S. W.			Cloudy evening.
29	73	84	"	"	N. E., S. E.			Cloudy part of evening.
30	72	87½	"	"	All points.			Cloudy part of morning.
						1.91		

July, 1876.

Date.	Thermometer.		Weather.		Prevailing Wind.	Rain and Melted Snow in inches.	Snow in inches.	REMARKS.
	Lowest.	Highest.	Morning.	Afternoon.				
1	70	85	Clear	Clear	All points.			Cloudy part of morning.
S 2	76	93½	"	"	S. W.			Cloudy part of afternoon.
3	79	90	"	"	S. W., N. W.			Cloudy part of morning.
4	73	92	"	"	S. W.			Cloudy evening.
5	76	91	"	"	S. W.			
6	75	86	"	"	N. W.			
7	68½	87	"	"	All points.			
8	72	94½	"	"	N. W.			Hottest day since July 17, 1866.
S 9	80½	96	Hazy	"	N. W.			Highest minimum I have ever known; maximum 5:30 P. M.
10	73½	93½	Clear	"	N. E., S. W.			
11	78	94	"	"	S. W.	0.02		Light shower 4 P. M.; cloudy evening; showers all around us.
12	75½	92	"	"	S. W., S. E.			
13	78	94	"	"	All points.			Cloudy evening.
14	78	87½	C'y m'st all day.		N. E., S. W.			
15	75½	91	Clear	Clear	N. E., S. E.			
S 16	72	87	"	"	N. E., S. E.			
17	70	90	"	"	S. W.			
18	74	91½	"	"	S. W.	0.10		Cloudy evening with light rain 9 to 11 P. M.
19	76	91	"	"	N. W., S. E.			
20	76	96	"	"	S. W.	0.05		Cloudy evening with shower 10:30 P M.; maximum 2:30 P. M.
21	76	86	"	"	N. W., N.			
22	69½	80½	"	"	N. E., S. E.			
S 23	72	82	"	"	S. W., N.	0.04		Cloudy part of morning and part of afternoon, with shower 3 P. M.
24	63	77	"	"	N. W.			
25	61½	77½	"	"	N. W., S. W.			Cloudy part of afternoon and evening.
26	63	78	"	"	N. W.			Light rain 6 A. M.
27	59	81	"	"	N. E., S. W.			
28	67	86	"	"	S. W.			Clouded over 5 P. M., and light showers after 8 P.M.
29	71	83½	"	"	N. W.	0.21		Rain before day; cloudy evening.
S 30	65	70½	Rain	Rain	N. E.	1.28		Rain 7 A. M. to 12:30 P. M. and 3:45 to 11:30 P. M.
31	62	68	Cloudy	Cloudy	N. E.			
						1.70		

Weather Record for New Brunswick, N. J.

August, 1876.

Date	Thermometer Lowest	Thermometer Highest	Weather Morning	Weather Afternoon	Prevailing Wind	Rain and Melted Snow in inches	Snow in inches	REMARKS
1	63½	78½	Clear	Clear	N. E., S. E.			
2	65	76½	"	"	N. E., E.			Cloudy part of afternoon.
3	65	73½	C'y m'st all day.		N. E., S. E.			
4	67	76½	Cloudy	Cloudy	S. E.			Clear evening.
5	68½	81	"	Clear	S. W.			Clear part of morning and cloudy part of afternoon.
S 6	69	87	Clear	"	S. W.			
7	73	90	"	"	S W.			
8	75	86½	"	"	N. W.			
9	68½	85	"	"	N. E., S. E.			
10	66	86	"	"	N. E., S. E.			
11	67	85½	"	"	S. W., S. E.			
12	67	85	"	"	S. E.			Foggy morning.
S 13	70	84½	"	"	S. E.			Foggy morning.
14	71½	83	C'y m'st all day.		N. E.			Foggy morning; light rain 7 P. M.
15	71	88	Cloudy	Clear	S. W.			Clear part of morning and cloudy part of afternoon.
16	75	86	Clear	"	N. E., S. E.			
17	71	80	Show'rs	Cloudy	All points.	1.06		Showers till 10:40 A. M.; clear part of afternoon.
18	68½	77½	C'y m'st all day.		N. E., S. E.			
19	67½	76	"	"	N. E., S. E.	0.02		Shower 7 A. M.
S 20	70	84½	Cloudy	Clear	W., N. W.			Light rain before day; cleared 8 A. M.
21	56	74	Clear	"	N. W.			
22	55	78	"	"	N. W.			
23	66	80	"	"	N. W., S. E.			Cloudy part of morning.
24	66	83	"	"	S. E., S.			
25	70	84	"	"	S. W.			Cloudy evening.
26	70½	81	Cloudy	"	N. W.			Cleared 8 A. M.
S 27	63	78	Clear	"	N. W.			
28	58	78	"	"	N. W.			
29	60	81	"	"	N. W., S. W.			
30	66½	79	C'y m'st all day.		S. W., S. E.			
31	67	80	Cloudy	Clear	N. W., S. E.			
						1.08		

June 1 to Aug. 31, ther. was 80° and above on 63 days—hottest and dryest summer I have known.

September, 1876.

Date	Thermometer. Lowest.	Thermometer. Highest.	Weather. Morning.	Weather. Afternoon.	Prevailing Wind.	Rain and Melted Snow in inches.	Snow in inches.	REMARKS.
1	67	87½	Clear	Clear	S. W.			Cloudy part of afternoon.
2	70	78	"	"	N. W.	0.15		Rain before day; cloudy part of morning.
S 3	56½	75	"	"	W., S. W.			
4	57	78½	"	"	S. W.	0.15		Cloudy part of evening, with rain 7 to 9 P. M.
5	58½	71	"	"	N. W.			
6	53½	72	"	"	N. W., S. W.			Cloudy part of afternoon.
7	60	66½	Cloudy	Cloudy	S. E.	0.02		Misty 6:30 to 8:30 A. M.
8	63	75	Rain	"	S. W.	0.57		Rain till 7 A. M.; clear part P. M.; shower 6:15 to 6:45 P. M.
9	61	75	Clear	Clear	N. W.			
S 10	57	66	"	Cloudy	N. E., S E.			Rainy evening.
11	55	62	Rain	"	S. E., N. E.	0.46		Rain till noon.
12	58	65	Cloudy	"	N. E., S. W.	0.05		Light rain part of morning.
13	55	70	"	Clear	N. E., S. E.			Clear part of morning
14	59½	74	C'y m'st all day.		S. E.			Rain 11 P. M.
15	62	74½	Cloudy	Clear	S W., W.	0.27		Rain before day; clear part of morning.
16	59	66	"	Cloudy	N. E., E.			Partly clear part morning.
S 17	53	71	Rain	Rain	N. E., S. E.	2.57		Steady rain till 8 P.M., with high winds and light rain 10:30 to 11 P. M.
18	63½	73	Clear	Cloudy	S. W.			
19	61	72	"	Clear	N. W.			Cloudy part of afternoon.
20	60	69	"	Cloudy	N. W., N. E.			
21	58	66	C'y m'st all day.		N. E., S. E.			
22	56	61	Cloudy	Cloudy	N. E.			
23	57½	62	"	Rain	N. E.	0.58		Rain 8 to 9 A.M. and 3 to 10 P. M.
S 24	58	62	"	Rainy	N. E.	0.06		Rain before day; raining after 3 P. M.
25	58	68½	"	Clear	N. E., S. E.	0.52		Rain before day.
26	56	64	"	"	S., N.	0.20		Showers 11:30 A. M. to 3:00 P.M.; cleared 3:30 P. M.
27	49	61	Clear	"	S. W.			
28	48½	64	"	"	S. W.			
29	49½	68½	"	"	S. W.			Cloudy part of afternoon.
30	54	59	Cloudy	Rainy	All points.	0.22		Light rain all day after 7:45 A. M.
						5.82		

Weather Record for New Brunswick, N. J.

October, 1876.

Date.	Thermometer. Lowest.	Thermometer. Highest.	Weather. Morning.	Weather. Afternoon.	Prevailing Wind.	Rain and Melted Snow in inches.	Snow in inches.	REMARKS.
S 1	49½	61	Clear	Clear	N. W.	0.35		Rain before day.
2	48	62	"	"	N. W.			Cloudy part of evening.
3	46	63	"	"	S. W.			
4	50	62	C'y m'st all day.		S. W., N. W.			
5	50	52½	Cloudy	Cloudy	N. E.	0.03		Light rain part of morning.
6	49	72	C'y m'st all day.		S. W.	0.13		Rain part of evening.
7	51	59	Clear	Clear	W., N. W.			
S 8	40½	58½	"	"	S. W., N. W.			
9	40	52	"	"	N. W., S. W.			
10	41	62½	"	"	S. W.			Cloudy part of morning; cloudy evening.
11	44	53	"	"	N. W.			
12	35½	52	"	"	All points			
13	38	59½	"	"	S. W.			
14	42	65	"	"	S. W.			Cloudy evening, with rain 11 P. M.
S 15	35	41	Cloudy	"	N. W.	0.28		Rain and snow before day.
16	34	49½	Clear	"	W.			
17	42	57	Cloudy	"	S. W., N. W.			Clear part of morning and cloudy part of afternoon.
18	37¼	56	Clear	"	N. W., S. W.			
19	37	60½	"	"	S. W.			
20	43	58	Cloudy	Cloudy	E.			
21	56	62	Rainy	Rainy	N. E.			Misty rain all day.
S 22	58¼	62½	Cloudy	Cloudy	N. E., S. E.	0.20		Rain before day; foggy morning and evening.
23	57	62	"	"	S. E.	0.02		Rain before day.
24	57	64	"	Clear	N. W.	0.48		Rain before day; cleared 8 A. M.
25	48	55	Clear	"	W.			
26	41½	51¼	"	"	S. W., N. W.			Cloudy part of morning and part of evening.
27	43	48	Cloudy	"	N. W.			
28	37¼	44	"	Misty	N.W.,S., N.E.	0.04		Light rain part of evening.
S 29	36	49	Clear	Clear	N. E.			
30	33½	53	"	"	All points			Cloudy part of afternoon.
31	46	56	Cloudy	Cloudy	S. W.	0.01		Light rain before day; cleared 8 P. M.

1.54

November, 1876.

Date.	Thermometer.		Weather.		Prevailing Wind.	Rain and Melted Snow in inches.	Snow in inches.	REMARKS.
	Lowest.	Highest.	Morning.	Afternoon.				
1	48	69	Clear	Clear	S. W.	----	----	
2	54½	72	"	"	S. W.	----	----	
3	57	61	Cloudy	"	S. W., N. W.	0.17	----	Rain before day and at 10 A. M.; clear part of A. M.
4	43	56	Clear	"	N. W.	----	----	
S 5	43½	52½	Cloudy	"	N. W., N. E.	----	----	Clear part of morning.
6	38	54	Clear	Cloudy	N. E., S. E.	----	----	Cloudy part A. M. and clear part P.M.; rainy after 7 P.M.
7	52	55½	Rain	"	S. W., N. W.	1.73	----	Rain till 9:30 A. M. and part of afternoon and evening.
8	46½	53¼	Cloudy	"	N. W., N. E	----	----	Clear part of morning.
9	45½	54½	Clear	Clear	N. W.	----	----	
10	41	44	Cloudy	Rain	N. E., N. W.	0.18	----	Rain 11 A. M. to 4 P. M. and part of evening.
11	41	47½	C'y m'st all day		N. W.	----	----	
S 12	40	52	Cloudy	Clear	N. W.	----	----	Cleared 9 A. M.
13	40½	60	Clear	"	N. W., S. W.	----	----	Cloudy evening.
14	52½	60½	"	Cloudy	S. W., N. E.	0.02	----	Cloudy part A. M.; light rain part P. M. and evening.
15	41	42	Rain	Rain	N. E.	0.44	----	Rain till 5:30 P. M.
16	39	45	Cloudy	Clear	N. E.	----	----	
17	37	48	"	Cloudy	N. E., E.	----	----	Clear part of afternoon.
18	42½	50	"	"	N. E., E.	0.02	----	Light rain before day; rain 11 P. M
S 19	44	45	Rain	Rain	N. E.	0.02	----	Light rain before day and rain all day after 8 A. M.
20	42½	47	"	"	N. E.	----	----	Heavy rain till 4:45 P. M.; light rain rest evening.
21	42	50	Cloudy	Cloudy	N. E.	2.61	----	Rain before day; partly clear part of morning.
22	44	48½	"	"	E., S. E.	0.02	----	Light rain before day; clear part of evening.
23	40	45	Clear	"	N. W., W.	----	----	
24	37	45	"	Clear	N. W.	----	----	Cloudy part of evening.
25	35	43	"	"	N. W., S. W.	----	----	Cloudy evening.
S 26	37	39	Cloudy	Snow	S., N. W.	0.14	----	Snow 10:30 A. M. till 4 P. M., and part of evening.
27	34	39	Clear	Snow / Rain	N. W., S. W.	0.10	----	Cloudy part A.M.; snow 1:15 to 5 P. M. and misty till 8 P. M.
28	34	42½	"	Clear	S. W.	----	----	
29	31½	42	"	"	N. W.	----	----	
30	31	34½	Cloudy	Cloudy	N. E., N. W.	----	----	Clear evening.
						5.45	----	

Weather Record for New Brunswick, N. J.

December, 1876.

Date	Thermometer. Lowest	Thermometer. Highest	Weather. Morning.	Weather. Afternoon.	Prevailing Wind.	Rain and Melted Snow in inches.	Snow in inches.	REMARKS.
1	20	25½	Cloudy	Clear	N. W.			Cleared 8 A. M.
2	19	26	Clear	"	N. W.			Cloudy part of morning and part of afternoon with snow squalls.
S 3	23	35	"	"	N. W.			
4	28	36	"	"	N. W.			Cloudy part of morning.
5	25	38	"	"	N. W.			
6	25½	39	"	"	S. W.			
7	29	43½	"	"	S. W.			Cloudy part of morning and part of afternoon.
8	32	40	C'y m'st all day.		S. W.			
9	12	16	Clear	Clear	N. W.	0.03		Snow before day.
S 10	5	17½	"	"	N. W., W.			Cloudy evening.
11	15	22½	Cloudy	Cloudy	N. E.	0.07		Snow before day.
12	18½	36	"	Clear	N., N. W.	0.02		Snow before day; cloudy evening.
13	30	47½	Clear	"	S. W.			
14	36	46	"	Cloudy	S. W.			Cloudy part of morning.
15	31	35	"	Clear	N. W.			Cloudy part of morning.
16	25½	38	"	"	S. W., N. W.			
S 17	10	19	"	Cloudy	All points.			
18	15	32½	Snow Rain / Rain Snow		All points.	0.94	3.00	Light snow till 7:30 A. M., and then rain to 2:15 P. M., and then snow to 6 P. M.; clear 9 P. M.
19	13½	24	Clear	Clear	S. W.			Cloudy part of morning.
20	14½	22½	"	"	S. W.			Cloudy evening.
21	13½	23	Cloudy	Cloudy	N. E.	0.50		Snow 10:45 A. M. to 1:30 P. M.; clear part of afternoon and evening.
22	12	32	"	Snow	N. E.			Snow and sleet afternoon and evening.
23	29	31	Clear	Clear	N. W.	0.47		Sleet before day.
S 24	18	23	Cloudy	Cloudy	N. W.			Clear part of evening.
25	17	25½	"	"	N. E.			
26	22	33	Snow	"	N. E.	0.02	1.00	Light snow till 9 A. M., and light snow and mist part of afternoon.
27	25½	33	Clear	Clear	N. W.			
28	14½	26	Cloudy	Cloudy	N. W., N. E.			
29	22½	37	Snow	Snow / Rain	N. E.	0.62		Snow 8 A. M. to 1 P. M., and then rain till 8 P. M.
30	23	31	Clear	Clear	W.			Cloudy part of morning.
S 31	19	28	Cloudy	"	W.			Cleared 8:30 A. M.
						2.17	4.00	

Rain and melted snow for 1876, 39.43 inches.

January, 1877.

Date.	Thermometer. Lowest.	Thermometer. Highest.	Weather. Morning.	Weather. Afternoon.	Prevailing Wind.	Rain and Melted Snow in inches.	Snow in inches.	REMARKS.
1	14	23½	Clear	Snow	W., N. E.			Clouded over 9 A. M. and snow 2:15 P. M.
2	19½	27	Cloudy	Clear	N. W.		15.00	Snow before day; drifted badly; cleared 10 A. M.; heaviest snow storm since 1867.
3	12	22½	Clear	"	W., S. W.			Cloudy part of afternoon.
4	9	21	"	"	S. W., N. W.			
5	10	22	"	"	W.			Cloudy part of evening.
6	6	40	Cloudy	Cloudy	N. W., N. E.			Partly clear part of morning; rain 7 P. M.
S 7	36	41	"	Clear	S. W., W.	0.72		Rain before day; cleared 3 P. M.
8	32	42	Clear	Cloudy	S. W.			
9	16½	23	"	Clear	N. W.			
10	13	26	"	Cloudy	N. E.		0.75	Cloudy part of A. M.; snow part of evening; cleared 10:30 P. M.
11	18½	35	"	"	S. W.			Cloudy part of morning.
12	29½	31	"	"	N., N. E.	0.05		Light snow and misty after 4 P. M.
13	17	29	Cloudy	Clear	N. W.			
S 14	20	30½	Clear	"	W.			
15	21½	32½	Snow	Mist Rain	N. E.	2.50		Snow till 11:15 A.M.; misty P. M. and rainy evening.
16	30	44	Cloudy	Clear	All points.	0.64		Cleared 10 A. M.; cloudy part of afternoon.
17	25	29	"	Cloudy	N. E.		0.25	Clear part of morning; snow 5 to 7 P. M.
18	26	35	"	Clear	W., S. W.			
19	31	40	Clear	Cloudy	S. W.			Clouded over 3 P. M.; fine sleighing since Dec. 18th.
20	36	42½	Rain	Clear	S. W.	0.14		Foggy and rain till 1 P. M.; cleared 4 P. M.
S 21	27	30½	Cloudy	Cloudy	N. W., S. W.			
22	25	30	Snow	"	N. E., N. W.		3.00	Snow till 4 P. M.
23	18½	31½	Cloudy	Clear	N. W.			
24	6	29	Clear	"	S. W., N. W.			Cloudy part of morning.
25	17	26	"	"	W., S. W.			
26	17	34	Cloudy	"	S. W.			
27	26	41	Clear	"	S. W., N. W.			Cloudy evening.
S 28	27½	34½	"	"	N. E., S. E.			Cloudy evening.
29	26	39	"	"	S. W.			
30	26	42	"	"	W., N. E.			
31	26½	43	"	"	W., S. W.			Cloudy and misty evening.
						1.55	21.50	

Weather Record for New Brunswick, N. J.

February, 1877.

Date	Thermometer Lowest	Thermometer Highest	Weather Morning	Weather Afternoon	Prevailing Wind	Rain and Melted Snow in inches	Snow in inches	Remarks
1	37	50	Cloudy	Clear	S. W.			Cleared 8 A. M.
2	37	45	"	Rain	N. E., S. E.			Partly clear part morning.
3	37	43	"	Cloudy	W.	0.55		Rain before day.
S 4	38	43	Clear	Clear	N.			
5	33	42½	"	Cloudy	S. W.			
6	35	42	"	Clear	N. W.			Cloudy part of afternoon.
7	32	45¼	"	"	S. W.			
8	33	41	"	"	N.			
9	28	39	"	"	N. W.			
10	26½	40½	"	"	N. E., S. W.			
S 11	32¼	47	"	"	All points			
12	33	53	C'y m'st all day		S. W., N. W.	0.02		Rain 5 to 6 P. M.
13	21	32	Clear	Clear	N. W.			
14	19	37½	"	"	N. W., W.			
15	25	44	"	"	S. W.			
16	35½	48	C'y m'st all day		S. W.			Light rain part of evening.
17	31¼	35	Cloudy	Clear	N. W.			Cleared 7:30 A. M.; cloudy part of afternoon, with snow squalls.
S 18	26	38½	Clear	"	N. W.			
19	33	39½	Snow	"	S. W., N. W.	0.10		Snow before day and from 9 A. M. till 12:15 P. M.; cleared 2 P. M.
20	23½	36¼	Clear	"	N. W.			
21	31	48	"	"	N. W., S. W.			
22	33	55	"	"	S. W., W.			Cloudy part of afternoon.
23	33	45	"	Cloudy	N. E.			Cloudy part of morning; rain 11:30 P. M.
24	32½	36	{Rain Snow}	{Rain Snow}	N. E.	1.01		Rain, snow and mist till 11 P. M.
S 25	34	44	C'y m'st all day		N.			
26	35	40	Cloudy	Cloudy	N.			
27	34½	42	"	"	All points			
28	35	46	Clear	Clear	S. W., N. W.			Cloudy part of morning.
						1.68		

Weather Record for New Brunswick, N. J.

March, 1877.

Date.	Thermometer. Lowest.	Thermometer. Highest.	Weather. Morning.	Weather. Afternoon.	Prevailing Wind.	Rain and Melted Snow in inches.	Snow in inches.	REMARKS.
1	33	49	Clear	Clear	S. W.			
2	36	54	Cloudy	Rain	S. E., S. W.			Rain 8 A. M.
3	43	50	Clear	Clear	S. W.	0.78		Rain before day; clouded over 10 P. M.
S 4	43	54	Cloudy	"	S. W., N. W.	0.10		Clear part of A. M.; rain before day and 7 to 9 A. M.
5	32	39	"	"	S. W.			
6	27½	36	Clear	"	N. W., S. W.			Cloudy evening.
7	32	50	C'y m'st all day.		W., N. E.			
8	35	61	"	"	N. E., S. W.			Light rain 10 P M.
9	55	59	Cloudy	Clear	S. W., N. W.	0.65		Rain before day and shower 10:15 A. M.
10	26	32½	Clear	"	N. W.			
S 11	25	39½	"	"	S. W.			
12	34	43	Cloudy	Cloudy	All points.			Light rain part of afternoon; rain 11 P. M.
13	36	41	Rain	"	N. E.	0.30		Rain till 8:45 A. M.; clear part of afternoon.
14	35	39	Cloudy	Misty	S. E.			Misty P. M. and rainy eve'g.
15	26½	37	Clear	Clear	N. W.	0.13		Rain before day.
16	29	36	"	Snow	N. W., S. E.			Clouded over 11 A. M. and com. snowing 1 P. M.
17	28	30	Cloudy	Cloudy	N. E.	0.38		Snow and rain before day; 3 in. of snow on ground.
S 18	17	29	"	Clear	N. E., N. W.			Cleared 10 A. M.
19	15	25	Clear	Snow	All points.			Light snow after 3 P. M.
20	19	33	"	Clear	All points.		1.25	Snow before day.
21	27	47½	Cloudy	Cloudy	All points.	0.04		Light rain about 6 A. M; rain after 6:15 P. M.
22	41	49	"	"	N., N. E.	0.63		Rain before day.
23	41	59	"	Clear	N. W., S. W.			
24	44	60½	Clear	"	All points.			Cloudy part of afternoon.
S 25	39	42½	"	Cloudy	E.			Clouded over 8 A. M.; rain 10:30 P. M.
26	38	50	Rain	Rain	N. E.			
27	42	53	Foggy	"	N. E., N. W.	1.78		Rain before day and after 11 A. M.
28	32	36	Rain } Snow }	Cloudy	N. W.	1.44		Rain before day and heavy snow till 10:30 A. M. and snow squalls till 5 P. M.
29	30½	36	Cloudy	"	N. W.			Clear part of afternoon.
30	32	50	Clear	Clear	N. W.			
31	34½	50	"	Cloudy	N. E., S.			
						6.23	1.25	

April, 1877.

Date.	Lowest.	Highest.	Morning.	Afternoon.	Prevailing Wind.	Rain and Melted Snow in inches.	Snow in inches.	REMARKS.
S 1	38½	50½	Cloudy	Cloudy	S. E.	0.01		Clear part of A.M. and sprinkle during day and light rain 10 P. M
2	43	51½	"	Rain	N. E., N. W.	0.36		Rain 10 A. M. to 6:30 P. M.; cleared 10 P. M.
3	34	50	Clear	Clear	N. E.			Cloudy part of evening.
4	40	46	Cy m'st all day.		N. E., S. E.			
5	37	46	Cloudy	Cloudy	N. E., N. W.			Clear part of evening.
6	39	54½	Clear	Clear	N. W.			Cloudy part of afternoon.
7	41	57	"	"	N. W., N. E.			
S 8	34	53½	"	"	N. E., S. E.			Cloudy part of afternoon.
9	36	47	Cloudy	"	E.			Cloudy part of afternoon.
10	37	56	Clear	"	N. E.			
11	39	61	"	"	N. E			
12	42	57½	"	"	N. W., N. E.			
13	34	48½	"	Cloudy	N. E., S. E.			Clouded over 3 P. M.
14	36	52	Cloudy	Clear	N. E., S. E.			
S 15	35	58½	Clear	"	All points.			
16	37½	64	"	"	S. W.			Cloudy part of afternoon.
17	44	62½	"	Cloudy	S. E.			Cloudy after 3 P.M., with light sprinkle 7:15 P.M.
18	46	49½	Rain	Rain	N. E.			
19	41	47½	Cloudy	"	N. E.	1.47		Rain before day and from noon till 11 P. M.
20	45½	54	Rain	Cloudy	N. E., N. W.	0.22		Rain 7 A. M. to 3 P. M.; cleared 6 P. M.
21	41	52	Clear	"	N. W.			Clear part of afternoon.
S 22	42½	66	"	Clear	N. E.			
23	44	74	"	"	N. W., N. E.			
24	48	76	"	"	N. W., N. E.			
25	56	67	"	"	N. W.			
26	47	66	"	Cloudy	N. W., S. W.			Clouded over 5 P. M.; cherries flowered.
27	53½	63	Cloudy	"	All points.			Partly clear part of morn'g; light rains after 3 P. M.
28	48	52	Rain	Rainy	E.			Pears flowered.
S 29	46	61	Cloudy	Cloudy	N. E., S. E	0.62		Rain before day; clear part of P.M.; heavy rain 9:30 P.M.
30	48	62	"	"	N. E., S. W.	0.70		Rain before day; clear part of P.M.; cleared 8:30 P.M.

3.38

May, 1877.

Date	Thermometer Lowest	Thermometer Highest	Weather Morning	Weather Afternoon	Prevailing Wind	Rain and Melted Snow in inches	Snow in inches	REMARKS
1	47	59	Clear	Cloudy	N. W., W.	0.04		Light rain part of afternoon and evening.
2	45	53½	"	Clear	N. W.			Cloudy part of evening.
3	35½	58½	"	"	N. W.			Cloudy part of afternoon.
4	46	61	"	"	S. W., N.			Cloudy part of afternoon.
5	40½	59	"	"	N. E., S. E.	0.01		Cloudy evening with light rain at 10 P. M.
S 6	46	59½	Cloudy	"	N. E., S. E.			Clear part of morning, and cloudy part of afternoon.
7	42	65	Clear	"	All points.			
8	49	56	Cloudy	Cloudy	N. E.	0.02		Light rain part of morning.
9	47	55	"	"	{ N.E.,N.W., S. W.	0.02		Light rain part of afternoon; rain 10 P. M.
10	46	52½	"	"	N. W., N.	0.06		Light rain before day.
11	45	58	C'y m'st all day.		N. W., S. W.			
12	48	60	Cloudy	Clear	All points.			Clear part of morning.
S 13	45	68	Clear	"	N. W., S. W.			
14	52	73	"	"	W., S. W.			
15	55	79	"	"	S. W.			
16	62	82	Cloudy	"	S. W.			Cleared 9:30 A. M.; light sprinkle part of morning.
17	66	83½	Clear	"	S. W.			Cloudy parts of morning and afternoon, with light rain 5:30 P. M.
18	66	87	"	"	S. W.			Bathing 11 A. M.
19	71½	86	"	"	N.			
S 20	66	87½	"	"	All points.			
21	63	68	Cloudy	Cloudy	N. E., S. E.	0.08		Partly clear part of morning; rain part of P. M.
22	57	77	"	Clear	S. W., N. W.	0.38		Shower before day; cleared 8 A. M.; shower 1 P. M., and sprinkle 5 P. M.; rain 9:30 P. M.
23	55½	70	Clear	"	N. W.	0.10		Rain before day.
24	48	59	"	Cloudy	N. W.			Cloudy part of morning, and clear part of evening; sprinkle 5 P. M.
25	47	61	"	"	All points.	0.03		Light rain 11:50 A. M., and 3:30 P. M.; clear evening.
26	50	63½	"	Clear	W.	0.20		Cloudy part of afternoon, with showers.
S 27	50	64	"	"	N., S E.	0 05		Cloudy part of afternoon with showers.
28	49	71½	Cloudy	"	All points.			Cleared 7:30 A. M.; northern lights 9 P. M.
29	53	76½	Clear	"	S. W.			
30	56½	78	"	"	S. W.			
31	61	82	"	"	S. W.			
						0.99		

June, 1877.

Date.	Thermometer. Lowest.	Thermometer. Highest.	Weather. Morning.	Weather. Afternoon.	Prevailing Wind.	Rain and Melted Snow in inches.	Snow in inches.	REMARKS.
1	63¼	83	Clear	Clear	All points			Cloudy part of afternoon.
2	63½	86	"	"	S. W.			
S 3	67	86	"	"	S. W.	0.17		Cloudy part of P.M. and ev'g with showers 4:15 & 7 P.M.
4	68½	82½	"	"	S. W.	0.01		Rain before day; cloudy part of morning.
5	66¼	74	C'y m'st all day		N. E., S. E.			Rain 10:50 P. M.
6	64	69	Rain	Rainy	N. E.	1.47		Rain till 7 A.M.; rainy 12:45 to 7 P. M.
7	63½	70	"	Cloudy	E.	0.07		Rainy till 10:15 A.M.; partly clear part of afternoon.
8	64½	78	Cloudy	Clear	S. W., N. E.			Clear part of morning.
9	65	79	C'y m'st all day		S. W., S.			
S 10	71	79	"	"	S. W., N. W.	0.02		Light sprinkle part of P. M.
11	60	67	Cloudy	Clear	N. E., S. E.			
12	57	70¼	"	Cloudy	S. W., S. E.			Clear part of morning.
13	61	75½	"	Clear	S. W., S. E.			
14	65	81	"	"	S. W.	0.08		Cloudy part of afternoon, with shower 5:15 P. M.
15	66	83½	"	"	S. W.			Clear part of A. M.; light shower 3:15 P.M.; cloudy evening.
16	69½	77	"	Cloudy	S. W.	0.31		Rain before day and shower 10 A.M. and 12:30 P. M.; cleared 6 P. M.
S 17	68	79½	Clear	Clear	N. W.			
18	61½	80½	"	"	S. W.			Cloudy part of afternoon.
19	66	84½	Cloudy	"	S. W.	0.62		Rain before day; clear part of morning.
20	64½	72	Clear	"	N. E., S. E.			
21	60	79	C'y m'st all day		S. W.			Rain 8 P. M.
22	67	73	Clear	Clear	N. W.	0.72		Rain before day.
23	54	71	"	"	N., S. W.			
S 24	55	78	"	"	S. W.			
25	65½	82	"	"	S. W.			Cloudy part of afternoon.
26	69	86½	"	"	S. W.	1.02		Cloudy part of A. M., with light showers 7 to 9 A.M.; cloudy evening, with rain 9 to 11 P. M.
27	66	73	C'y m'st all day		N. E., S. E.			
28	61½	72½	"	"	S. E.			
29	61	75	Clear	Clear	S. E.			Cloudy part of evening.
30	60	79	Cloudy	"	S. E., S. W.			Cloudy part of afternoon.
						4.49		

July, 1877.

Date.	Thermometer. Lowest.	Highest.	Weather. Morning.	Afternoon.	Prevailing Wind.	Rain and Melted Snow in inches.	Snow in inches.	REMARKS.
S 1	68½	85¼	C'y m'st all day.		S. W.	0.37		Showers 5:30 to 7:30 A. M., and 6:45 to 8 P. M.
2	67	80½	Clear	Clear	N. W.			Cloudy part of afternoon.
3	63	75	Rain	Cloudy	S. E.	0.41		Rain till 7:15; clear part A. M.; and shower 10 P. M.
4	68	78½	Clear	Clear	N. W., N. E.	0.02		Cloudy part morning, with light shower 11:30 A.M.
5	64	82	"	"	N. W., S. W.	0.02		Cloudy part evening, with light shower 8:15 P. M.
6	65	79	"	"	N. E.	0.03		Rain before day; cloudy part of afternoon.
7	64	78	"	"	N. E., S. E.			
S 8	63	80½	"	"	S. W.			Cloudy part A.M. and P.M.
9	68	84	C'y m'st all day.		S. W.	1.01		Shower 4:15 P. M.; nearly 1 inch in 15 min.; light shower 10 P. M.
10	70	83	"	"	S. W.			Light rain 8 P. M.
11	68	80	"	"	N. E.			
12	66½	80	Clear	Clear	N. E.			
13	64	81½	"	"	N.			
14	62	76	"	"	N.			
S 15	62½	83½	"	"	S. W.			Cloudy part A.M. and P. M.
16	68½	87	"	"	S. W.			
17	72	86	Cloudy	"	S. W.			Clear part of morning and cloudy part of afternoon.
18	69½	86	Clear	"	S. W.			Cloudy part afternoon, with sprinkle 5:15 P. M.
19	72½	78	Cloudy	Show'rs	S. W.	0.42		Sprinkles part of A.M;show'rs during P. M. till 5 P. M.
20	69	78	"	Cloudy	S. W.	0.69		Heavy showers before day; clear part of A.M.; light showers 3:30 to 8 P. M.
21	70½	78	"	"	All points.			Clear part of evening.
S 22	70	80	"	Clear	N. E., S. E.			Clear part of morning and cloudy part of afternoon.
23	71	79	"	Cloudy	All points			Clear part P.M. and even'g.
24	71	85	Clear	Clear	N.			Cloudy part of morning.
25	68	87½	"	"	N. W.			
26	70	90½	"	"	N. W., W.			Cloudy evening.
27	76	83	"	Cloudy	S. E.	0.38		Clouded over 5 P.M. and rain 6:45 to 11 P. M.
28	69	78	Cloudy	"	S. E.			Rain 8 P. M.
S 29	71	81	"	"	S. E.	1.18		Rain before day; clear part P. M.; rain 7:30 to 8:30 P.M.
30	73	83	"	Clear	N. E.	0.07		Rain before day; clear part A.M. and cloudy part P. M.
31	71	83	Clear	"	N. E., E.			Cloudy evening.

4.60

Weather Record for New Brunswick, N. J.

August, 1877.

Date	Thermometer. Lowest.	Thermometer. Highest.	Weather. Morning.	Weather. Afternoon.	Prevailing Wind.	Rain and Melted Snow in inches.	Snow in inches.	REMARKS.
1	69	76	Cloudy	Cloudy	N. E.	0.03		Light rain before 6:30 A.M.; misty part of morning;
2	66½	76	C'y m'st all day.		N. E., E.			clear part of evening.
3	67½	81	Cloudy	Clear	N. E., S. W.			Clear part of morning;
4	69	79	Clear	"	N.			sprinkle 11 P. M.
S 5	61	79	"	"	N. W.			
6	61	81	"	"	N. W., S. W.			
7	70	83	C'y m'st all day.		S. W.			
8	71	87	Clear	Clear	S. W.			Cloudy part of evening.
9	72½	78	Cloudy	Cloudy	All points.	0.24		Showers 9:30 to 11 A. M., and 2 to 3 P. M.; clear part of evening.
10	69½	84	"	Clear	N. W., S. W.			Cleared 9 A. M.; light
11	66	83	Clear	"	N. W., S. W.			sprinkle 6:30 P. M.
S 12	66½	84	"	"	S. W.			Clouded over 11 P. M.
13	70	79	C'y m'st all day.		All points.	0.51		Rain before day, and light rain 8 to 9 A. M., and 8 to
14	69	81	C'y m'st all day.		N. E.			9 P. M.
15	70	74	Cloudy	Cloudy	E.	0.29		Rain 9:45 to 11 A. M., and 11:50 A.M. to 3 P.M.; partly clear part of evening.
16	68	79	Foggy	Clear	All points.	0.41		Clear part of morning, and
17	66	80	Clear	"	S. W.			cloudy part of afternoon
18	66	80½	"	"	N. W.			and evening with showers
S 19	65	82½	"	"	All points.			3 and 10:45 P. M.
20	66	81	"	"	S. E., N. E.			Cloudy part of afternoon and hazy evening.
21	67	80	"	"	N. E., S. E.			Cloudy part of morning, and part of afternoon.
22	66	82	Cloudy	"	S. W.			Foggy A.M.; clear part A. M.
23	65½	82½	Clear	"	S. W.			
24	69	79	C'y m'st all day.		S. E.			Shower 10:30 P.M. till noon; showers 4 to 6 and 7:30 to 8:15 P. M.; 1.72 in. 4 to 4:45 P. M., and 9:30 P. M. steady rain.
25	69½	79½	Cloudy	Cloudy	All points.	3.19		Rain before day; clear part of morning; rain 12:05 to 1 P. M.; clear part of evening.
S 26	70½	83	"	Clear	N. W.			Foggy A.M.; clear part A.M.
27	65	83½	Clear	"	N. W.			
28	68½	86	"	"	N. W., S. W.			
29	71	88½	"	"	S. W., N.			Cloudy part of afternoon.
30	70½	82	"	"	N. W.			
31	64½	82½	"	"	All points.	0.18		Cloudy part of morning and part of afternoon with shower 3:25 P. M.
						4.85		

WEATHER RECORD FOR NEW BRUNSWICK, N. J.

September, 1877.

Date	Thermometer. Lowest.	Highest.	Weather. Morning.	Afternoon.	Prevailing Wind.	Rain and Melted Snow in inches.	Snow in inches.	REMARKS.
1	70½	80½	C'y m'st all day.		S. W., N. W.	0.01	----	Light rain 6:40 A. M.
S 2	64½	74½	Cloudy	Clear	N. W.	----	----	Clear part of morning.
3	58	71	Clear	"	N. W.	----	----	
4	56½	76	"	"	S. W.	----	----	Cloudy part of morning.
5	59	76½	"	Cloudy	S. W.	----	----	Clouded over 3 P. M.
6	65½	71	Cloudy	Rain	N. E., S. E.	0.19	----	Rain 10:45 A.M. to 9 P. M.
7	56	61	Rain	Rainy	N. E.	0.70	----	Steady rain till 7 A.M. and at intervals rest of day till 10 P. M.
8	53½	61½	Cloudy	Cloudy	N. E.	0.05	----	Light rain 2 to 6 P.M.; made fire in my office.
S 9	55	71½	Clear	Clear	N. W.	----	----	
10	55	72½	"	"	N. W., S. W.	----	----	Cloudy part of morning and part of evening.
11	58	72½	C'y m'st all day.		N. E., S.	----	----	
12	64	74	"	"	S. E.	----	----	
13	65	77	"	"	All points	----	----	
14	65½	81	"	"	All points	----	----	Foggy morning.
15	68	78	Cloudy	Cloudy	N. E., S. E.	0.15	----	Partly clear parts of A. M. and P. M.; showers 10:15 A. M. and 12:05 P. M.
S 16	60½	79	"	Clear	S.	----	----	Clear part of A. M, & cloudy part of P. M., with sprinkle 2:30 P. M.
17	67	80	C'y m'st all day.		S. W.	0.15	----	Foggy morn'g; showers 3:20 to 5:40 P.M.; rain 9:30 P.M.
18	61	71	Cloudy	Clear	N.	0.55	----	Rain before day; clear part of morning.
19	54½	64½	C'y m'st all day.		N. W.	----	----	
20	51½	68	"	"	All points	----	----	
21	52	68½	Clear	Clear	N.	----	----	
22	48	66½	"	"	N.	----	----	
S 23	49	71	"	"	N. W., S. W.	----	----	
24	52	74	"	"	S. W.	----	----	
25	55	75	Cloudy	"	S. W.	----	----	Foggy A. M.; clear'd 10 A.M.
26	61	76½	Clear	"	S. W.	----	----	Foggy A. M.; cleared 7:15 A. M.
27	61	77¾	"	"	S. W.	0.05	----	Foggy A. M.; cleared 8:30 A. M.; cloudy evening, with light rain 5:50 P. M.
28	67½	74	Cloudy	Cloudy	S. E.	----	----	
29	67½	73	"	"	S. E.	----	----	Clear evening.
S 30	56	70½	Clear	Clear	N. E., S. E.	----	----	
						1.94	----	

October, 1877.

Date	Thermometer Lowest	Thermometer Highest	Weather Morning	Weather Afternoon	Prevailing Wind	Rain and Melted Snow in inches	Snow in inches	REMARKS
1	53	73	Clear	Clear	N. E., S. W.			
2	55	73½	Foggy	"	S. W.			Cleared 10 A. M.
3	60	72½	"	"	N. E., S E.			Cleared 11 A.M.; cloudy P.M
4	66	72	Cloudy	Rain	S. E			Light rain part of morning and steady rain 2:30 P. M., and very heavy after 6 P. M.; bar. 29.40 7 P. M
5	54¼	61½	Clear	Clear	N.	4.30		Rain till 1 A. M.; great freshet in the river; 0.9 of rain in 6 hours.
6	45	59	"	"	N.			
S 7	42	59	"	"	N. W., S. E.			
8	47	61	Cloudy	Cloudy	S. E.			Rainy evening.
9	59	68	Rain	Clear	S. W., N. W.	1.71		Rain till 7:45 A. M.; cleared 9 A. M.
10	51	66	Clear	"	All points.			Cloudy 11 P. M.
11	54	62	"	"	W.	0.10		Rain before day; cloudy part of after day.
12	49	61	"	"	N. W.			Cloudy part of afternoon.
13	48½	62	"	"	N. W.			
S 14	46½	68½	"	"	N. W., S. W.			Cloudy part of morning.
15	53	74	"	"	S. W.			
16	57½	76	"	"	S. W., N. W.			
17	47	62	"	"	N. E., W.			Cloudy part of evening.
18	51	64	"	Cloudy	All points.			Cloudy part of morning.
19	59½	67	Cloudy	"	S. W.			Partly clear part P. M.
20	56	57	"	"	S. W., N. E.	0.03		Light rains (0.03) during morning; ther. 7 A. M., 63°; 9 A. M., 56°; 11 A. M., 57°, falling after.
S 21	46½	50	"	"	N. E.	0.11		Light rain before day, and 7:30 A. M. to 8:30 A. M.; rainy evening.
22	42½	51	Rain	Clear	N. E., N. W.	0.40		Rain till 11 A. M.; cleared 4 P. M.
23	39	61	Clear	"	S. W.			First frost.
24	47	66½	"	"	S. W.			Cloudy evening.
25	52	66½	"	Cloudy	S. W.			Clear part of afternoon.
26	42	43½	Cloudy	Misty	E., N. E.	0.03		Misty afternoon and part of evening.
27	39½	48	"	Cloudy	N. E.			
S 28	46½	55½	"	"	S. W.			
29	54½	60	"	Clear	S. W.			Cloudy part of afternoon.
30	51	56	"	"	N. W., S. W	0.05		Light rain 7 to 10:30 A. M.; cloudy part of afternoon.
31	42	54	"	"	All points.	0.10		Rain 12:30 to 3 P. M.; cleared 5 P. M.
						6.83		

November, 1877.

Date.	Thermometer. Lowest.	Thermometer. Highest.	Weather. Morning.	Weather. Afternoon.	Previling Wind.	Rain and Melted Snow in inches.	Snow in inches.	REMARKS.
1	41	54	Clear	Clear	N. W., S. W.			Cloudy evening.
2	46	65	Rain	Rain	S. E., S. W.	1.24		Rain till 5:45 P. M.; cleared
3	45	51	Clear	Clear	S. W.			6 P. M.
S 4	36	50½	"	"	S. W.			
5	37	57	"	Rain	S. E., S. W.	1.23		Clouded over 7:30 A. M.; rain 4:15 P. M. to 11:15 P. M.
6	38½	44	"	Clear	N.			
7	33	48	"	"	All points			
8	34	61	"	Cloudy	N. E., S. E.			Cloudy part of morning; misty part of afternoon with rain 8 P. M.
9	59	68	Rain	Clear	W.	2.01		Heavy rain before day, and misty till 8:45 A. M.; cleared 9 A. M.
10	41	43	"	Rain	N. E.	0.37		Light rain before day, and 7:30 A. M. to 6:30 P. M. with some snow.
S 11	36	43	Cloudy	Cloudy	N. E., N. W.			Cleared 6 P. M.
12	34	51	Clear	Clear	N. W., S. W.			
13	38½	50	"	"	N. W., S. W.			
14	35	55½	"	"	S. E., S. W.			
15	41	62½	"	"	S. W.			Cloudy evening.
16	56	64½	Rain	"	S. W., W.	0.15		Light rain till 7 A. M.; clear part of morning and cloudy part of P. M.
17	43	57	Clear	"	N. E., S. E.			Cloudy part of morning; foggy evening.
S 18	48	52	"	"	N. W.			
19	35	44½	"	"	N. W.			
20	30½	40½	"	"	All points.			
21	26	38½	"	Cloudy	N. E.	0.01		Misty and rainy evening.
22	35	48½	Cloudy	"	N. E., S. E.			Clear part of morning.
23	45	52	"	"	N. E., S. E.			
24	45	49½	"	"	E. N., E.			Misty part of day; after 5 P. M. steady rain with strong winds from S. E.
S 25	47	52½	Rain	"	E., N. E.	1.80		Heavy rain before day and light rain till 9 A. M.; foggy evening.
26	48	57	Foggy	"	E., S. E.	0.11		Light rain before day and part of morning; shower 1 P. M.; cleared 6 P. M.
27	47½	53	Clear	"	S. W.			Cloudy 11 A. M.
28	45½	53	"	Clear	S. W.	0.01		Light rain before day; cloudy part of afternoon.
29	42	45	Rain	Rain	N. E., N. W.	0.31		Rain till 5 P. M.; cleared 5:30 P. M.
30	29	36	Clear	Clear	N. W.			
						7.29		

WEATHER RECORD FOR NEW BRUNSWICK, N. J.

December, 1877.

Date.	Lowest.	Highest.	Weather. Morning.	Afternoon.	Prevailing. Wind.	Rain and Melted Snow in inches.	Snow in inches.	REMARKS.
1	26	38	Clear	Clear	N. W.			Cloudy part of evening.
S 2	24	35	"	"	N.			
3	24	39	"	"	S. W.			
4	30	41	"	Cloudy	All points			Cloudy part morning; rain 7:40 P. M.
5	38	60	Rain	Rain	N. E., S. W.			
6	41	45	C'y m'st all day	W.		1.03		Rain before day.
7	36	41	Clear	Clear	W.			Cloudy part of morning.
8	32	45	"	"	S. W.			
S 9	31	39	"	"	N. W.			
10	28	40½	"	"	S. W.			Cloudy parts A. M. and P. M.
11	34	45½	"	"	S. W.			Cloudy parts A. M. and P. M.
12	37	49	"	"	S. W.			
13	36	55½	"	"	S. W.			Cloudy part of evening with sprinkles of rain.
14	34	43	"	"	N. W.			
15	33	50½	"	Cloudy	S. W.			Clear part of afternoon.
S 16	44½	58½	"	Clear	S. W., N. W.			
17	35	52	"	"	N. E., S. W.	0.01		Cloudy parts A.M. and P. M., with light rain 3 P. M.
18	31½	38½	"	Cloudy	N. E., S. E.			Clouded over 4 P. M.
19	33	47½	Cloudy	"	All points			Clear parts P.M. and even'g.
20	44	59	C'y m'st all day	S. W., N.				Light rain before day.
21	30½	41	Clear	Cloudy	N. E., S. E.			Clouded over 4 P. M.
22	38	48	Cloudy	"	N. W.			Clear part of morning; clear evening.
S 23	36	42	"	Clear	N. E., N. W.			Cloudy part of afternoon; cloudy evening.
24	33	45	"	"	N. E., N. W.			
25	29	42½	Clear	"	All points			
26	31½	42	Cloudy	Cloudy	N. E.			
27	37	46½	"	"	N. E.			Clear part of afternoon.
28	35½	49½	Clear	Clear	N. E.			
29	32	45½	"	"	N. E.			Cloudy part of afternoon.
S 30	32	36	Cloudy	Rainy	N. E.	0.15		Light rain 8:30 A. M. till 1 P.M. and 2 to 6 P.M.; clear part of evening.
31	29	37½	Clear	Clear	N.			
						1.19		

Rain and melted snow for 1877—47.28 inches.

January, 1878.

Date.	Thermometer. Lowest.	Thermometer. Highest.	Weather. Morning.	Weather. Afternoon.	Prevailing Wind.	Rain and Melted Snow in inches.	Snow in inches.	REMARKS.
1	23	36½	Clear	Clear	N. W.			
2	26½	38	Cloudy	Cloudy	S. W.			Snow squall 7 P.M.; cl'red 10 P.M., with wind from N.W.
3	14½	25	Clear	Clear	N. W., N. E.			
4	13½	41½	Snow Rain / Rain Mist		N. E.	0.87		Snow 6:45 to 9:30 A. M.; then rain and mist till 5:45 P. M.; cleared 9 P. M.
5	30	36	Clear	Clear	S. W., W.			
S 6	19	27	"	"	S. W., W.			
7	15	23	"	"	N. W.			
8	12½	28	"	"	S. W.			
9	22	35½	Cloudy	Cloudy	N. E.	0.01		Partly clear part of A. M.; light rain part of P. M.
10	32	42	Rain	Rain	N. E.	0.11		Rain before day and 9:15 A. M. and all day and even'g.
11	37	43½	"	Cloudy	W., N. W.	0.68		Rain till 9:15 A. M.; clear part of evening.
12	40	49	Clear	Clear	N. W.			
S 13	32	45	"	Cloudy	All points			C'dy part of A.M.; light rain 7½ to 9½ P.M. & then heavy.
14	37	47	Foggy	"	S. W.	1.12		Rain before day and misty 7:30 to 8:30 A. M.; clear part of afternoon and ev'g.
15	30½	43	C'y m'st all day		N. W.			
16	27	31	Clear	Clear	N.			
17	21	32	Cloudy	Cloudy	N. W., S. E.			
18	28	38	"	Clear	N. E., S. E.			Cleared 10 A. M.
19	29	42	"	"	S. W.			
S 20	33	42	"	Rain	All points	0.39		Clear part of A. M.; rain 1 to 11 P. M.
21	40	47½	"	Cloudy	S. W.			
22	41	49	"	"	S. W.			Clear part of A. M. and part of P. M.; rain 11 P. M.
23	23	25½	"	Clear	N. W.	0.12		Rain and light snow before day; cleared 8 A. M.
24	17	33	Clear	"	W., S. W.			
25	20	44	"	"	S. W., S. E.	0.02		Cloudy 6 P.M. and light rain 7 P. M. to 11 P. M.
26	38	50½	Foggy	Cloudy	S. W.	0.50		Rain before day; cleared 10 A.M.; cleared 7 P. M.
S 27	36	44½	Clear	"	S. W.	0.10		Cl'dy part of A.M.; light rain 3:40 to 4:30 & 7 to 9:30 P.M.
28	38½	42½	Cloudy	Clear	N. W.	0.09		Rain before day; clear part of morning.
29	19	31	Clear	"	N. W.			
30	23½	30	"	"	N. E.			Cloudy evening.
31	21½	32½	Snow	Snow	N. E.			Snow 6 A. M. violently all day.
						4.01		

Weather Record for New Brunswick, N. J.

February, 1878.

Date	Thermometer Lowest	Thermometer Highest	Weather Morning	Weather Afternoon	Prevailing Wind	Rain and Melted Snow in inches	Snow in inches	Remarks
1	27	32	Snow	Cloudy	N. E.		10.00	Heavy snow before day and drifted badly and light snow till 1 P. M.; snow 4 to 5:30 P. M.; cleared 9 P. M.
2	23	31	Cloudy	"	All points			Clear 10 A. M. to 3 P. M.; clear evening.
S 3	10	25½	Clear	Clear	All points			
4	10	34	"	"	N. W., W.			
5	22	36	"	"	N. W., W.			
6	23	38	"	"	N. W., S. W.			
7	26½	42½	"	"	S. W.			
8	30	40	Cloudy	Rainy	N. E.	0.33		Rainy and foggy P. M. and evening till 11 P. M.
9	38	48	"	Cloudy	S. W., N. E.	0.06		Rain before day; clear part A. M. and part afternoon.
S 10	34	38½	Rain	"	N. E.	0.49		Rain till 8 A. M., and misty till 11 A. M.
11	28½	35	Clear	Clear	N. W.			
12	23	34	"	Cloudy	N. W., S. W.			Clear part of afternoon.
13	32½	40	C'y m'st all day		N. W.			
14	30	35	Cloudy	Clear	N. E.			
15	24	35½	C'y m'st all day		N. E., S. E.			
16	33	43	"	"	S. W., N. W.			
S 17	34	49	"	"	All points			Light snow before day and light rain 11 A. M.
18	30½	33½	Clear	Clear	N. E.			Cloudy part of morning.
19	18	33	"	"	All points			
20	26	42	Cloudy	Cloudy	S. W.			Light snow 7 A. M.
21	36	46	"	"	N. E.			Light rain before day and at noon; partly clear part afternoon; rain 8 P. M.
22	37	43	Rain	Rain	N. E.			Steady rain till 2 P. M., and at intervals rest of day and night
23	40	46	Cloudy	Cloudy	All points	1.68		Rain before day; foggy A. M.
S 24	38	44½	Clear	Clear	N. W.			Cloudy part A. M. and P. M.
25	35½	44	C'y m'st all day		N. W.			
26	31	43	Clear	Clear	N. W.			Cloudy part of morning.
27	35	54	"	"	N. W.			
28	37½	54½	Cloudy	"	N. W., S. W.			Clear part of morning.
						2.56	10.00	

WEATHER RECORD FOR NEW BRUNSWICK, N. J.

March, 1878.

Date.	Thermometer.		Weather.		Prevailing Wind.	Rain and Melted Snow in inches.	Snow in inches.	REMARKS.
	Lowest.	Highest.	Morning.	Afternoon.				
1	35	42	Clear	Clear	N. E., S. E.	----	----	
2	30	53	"	Cloudy	S. E.	0.08	----	Clear part of afternoon; light rain 7:15 to 11 P. M.
S 3	45	60½	Rain	Clear	S. W.	0.21	----	Light rain till 10 A. M.; clear part of morning
4	45	46½	C'y m'st all day.		S. W., N. W.	----	----	and cloudy part of P. M.;
5	32	47	Clear	Clear	N. W.	----	----	rain 4:30 to 5 P. M.
6	35	57	"	"	S. W.	----	----	
7	40	68½	"	Cloudy	S. W.	0.20	----	Shower with thunder and lightning 6:50 P. M.; clear evening.
8	44	62	"	Clear	W.	----	----	
9	41	60	"	"	All points	----	----	
S 10	39	66	"	"	S. W.	----	----	
11	46	48	Cloudy	Cloudy	E.	----	----	Misty part of day.
12	34½	38	Rain	Rain	N. E.	0.75	----	Rain before day, and from 7 A. M. to 2 P. M.; misty afternoon and rain after 8 P. M.
13	36½	55	C'y m'st all day.		N. E., S. W.	0.78	----	Rain before day.
14	48	56	Cloudy	Cloudy	N. W.	0.18	----	Rain 1:30 to 3:30 P. M., and 4:45 to 6 P. M.; cleared 11 P. M.
15	41	52	Clear	Clear	N. W.	----	----	Cloudy part of afternoon.
16	36	51½	"	"	N. E.	----	----	Cloudy evening.
S 17	39	42	Rain	Rain	N. E.	0.98	----	Rain till 11 A. M., and 3 to 7 P. M., and 10:30 P. M. to 11:30 P. M.
18	37	48½	Cloudy	Cloudy	N.	----	----	Cleared 6 P. M.
19	40½	57	Clear	Clear	N. W.	----	----	Cloudy part of afternoon.
20	41	51	"	"	N. W.	----	----	
21	35½	44	C'y m'st all day.		N. W.	----	----	
22	37	50	Cloudy	Clear	All points.	----	----	Cleared 10 A. M.
23	37	59	Clear	"	S. W.	----	----	Cloudy part of evening.
S 24	45	53	Cloudy	Cloudy	S. W., N. W.	0.11	----	Rain 9 A. M. to 12:30 P. M.; clear part of afternoon and evening; snow squall 11 P. M.
25	17	35	Clear	Clear	N. W.	----	----	Ground covered with snow; cloudy part of afternoon.
26	30	47	"	"	N. W., S. W.	----	----	Cloudy part of morning.
27	37	57	C'y m'st all day.		S. W., N. W.	0.04	----	Rain before day.
28	43	64	Cloudy	Cloudy	S. W.	----	----	Clear part of morning.
29	43	55	"	Clear	N. E.	0.03	----	Rain 7 to 7:30 A. M.
30	37	54	Clear	Cloudy	N. E., S. W.	----	----	
S 31	42	55	"	"	All points.	0.03	----	Clear part of afternoon; light rain parts of P. M. and evening.
						3.39	----	

9th, railroad bridge burnt at 3:45 A.M., and passengers go by stage via Albany street bridge. First train over new bridge at 2:15 P. M. on 14th.

April, 1878.

Date.	Lowest.	Highest.	Weather. Morning.	Weather. Afternoon.	Prevailing Wind.	Rain and Melted Snow in inches.	Snow in inches.	REMARKS.
1	45	60	Cloudy	Clear	N. W.			Clear part of morning.
2	45	63	Clear	"	N. W.			
3	42	62½	"	"	S. W.			
4	43½	50	Cloudy	Cloudy	N. E.			Partly clear part of morning and clear part of ev'g.
5	44	60	"	Clear	N.			Clear part of morning and cloudy part of afternoon.
6	43	63	Clear	"	N. W.			Cloudy part of evening.
S 7	47½	56	C'y m'st all day.		N. W.			
8	46	62	Clear	Clear	N. W.			
9	44	54	Cloudy	Cloudy	S. E.			Partly clear part of A. M.; light rain part of even'g.
10	44½	52	Rain	"	S. E.	0.23		Rain till 10:30 A. M. and part of evening.
11	50	58½	Cloudy	"	S. W., N. E.	0.50		Rain 12 to 1 P. M.
12	51½	65	Clear	Clear	W., N. W.	0.01		Cloudy part of afternoon, with light showers.
13	48	61½	"	"	N. W.	0.01		Light rain before day.
S 14	45½	65½	"	"	N. W.			Cherries flowered.
15	44½	60	"	"	N. E., S.			Cloudy part of afternoon.
16	47	56	Cloudy	"	N. E., S. E.	0.15		Rain 8:30 to 11 A.M.; cloudy part of P M.; pears flowered.
17	42	58	"	"	N. E., S. E.			Clear part of morning.
18	42½	61	Clear	"	All points.			
19	47	68	"	"	S. W.			
20	55½	63	Cloudy	Cloudy	S. W., S. E.	0.05		Showers part of A.M.; partly clear part of evening; sprinkle 11:30 P. M.
S 21	54	75	Clear	Clear	N. W.			
22	52	70	"	Cloudy	N. W., N. W.			Clear part of afternoon.
23	51	60	Cloudy	"	N. E., S. E.	0.20		Rain before day; clear part of afternoon.
24	48	65	"	"	E., S.			Partly clear part of P. M.
25	62	64	"	"	S., S. E.	0.23		Rain 8 to 11:30 A. M. and 12:30 to 1 P. M.
26	57	64	"	"	N. E.			
27	52	64	"	"	N. E.			
S 28	54	62½	"	"	N. E.			Light rain before day.
29	53	63	"	"	N. E.			Light rain before day; clear part of afternoon.
30	51	61½	"	"	N. E., S. E.			Clear part of afternoon; foggy evening.
						1.38		

Weather Record for New Brunswick, N. J.

May, 1878.

Date	Thermometer Lowest	Thermometer Highest	Weather Morning	Weather Afternoon	Prevailing Wind	Rain and Melted Snow in inches	Snow in inches	REMARKS
1	50	69	Cloudy	Clear	S. W., S. E.			Clear part of morning and cloudy part of afternoon.
2	53	75	"	"	All points.			Cleared 7:30 A. M.
3	57½	80½	Clear	"	S. W.			
4	65	78½	C'y m'st all day	S. W.				N. Y. Coaching Club with "Tally-ho" to Phila.; rain 9 P. M.
S 5	57	63	Rain	Clear	All points.	1.22		Rain till 11 A.M.; cleared 3 P. M.
6	49	67	Clear	"	S. W., N. W.			
7	50½	66½	C'y m'st all day	N. E., S. E.				
8	53	73½	Clear	Clear	E.			Cloudy evening.
9	55	59½	Cloudy	"	N. E.	0.37		Rain 7:40 to 11 A. M.; cleared 5 P. M.
10	53	66	Clear	"	N. W.			Cloudy part of afternoon, with light sprinkle.
11	47	56	"	"	N. W.	0.05		Cloudy parts of day; showers 10 A. M. and 12:30 P. M., with hail.
S 12	41	57	"	Cloudy	N. W., W.			Clear evening; frost.
13	41	55	"	Clear	N. W.			Cloudy part afternoon; frost.
14	39	56	"	Cloudy	All points.			Frost.
15	47	53	Cloudy	"	N. E., E.			Partly clear part of afternoon; light sprinkles.
16	44	63	Clear	Clear	N. W., S. E.			
17	50	65½	"	Cloudy	S. E., S.			Clear part of afternoon.
18	50	69½	"	Clear	S. W., S.			
S 19	51	71	C'y m'st all day	S. W.				
20	56	57	Rain	Rain	S. E.			Misty rain all day.
21	53	72½	Cloudy	Clear	W.	0.72		Heavy shower before day; clear part of morning.
22	55	67	Clear	"	N.			
23	48	71	"	"	N. W.			
24	51	68	"	Cloudy	S. E., S.			Cloudy part of A. M., and clear part of afternoon.
25	59	73	C'y m'st all day	S. W.				
S 26	63	78	Clear	Clear	S. W.			Cloudy part of afternoon and evening.
27	60	75	"	"	S. W.			Cloudy part of evening.
28	60	75	"	"	N. W.			Cloudy part of afternoon.
29	57	71	"	"	N. W., S. W.			Cloudy part of afternoon.
30	59	61	Cloudy	Cloudy	S. E., N. E.	2.04		Heavy showers 2 to 4 P. M., and light rain till 6 P. M.
31	53½	56	Rain	Rain	N. E.	1.31		Raining at midnight.
						5.71		

Weather Record for New Brunswick, N. J.

June, 1878.

Date.	Thermometer. Lowest.	Thermometer. Highest.	Weather. Morning.	Weather. Afternoon.	Prevailing Wind.	Rain and Melted Snow in inches.	Snow in inches.	REMARKS.
1	54	61	Cloudy	Rain	N. E.	0.45		Light rain before day; rainy after 11:50 A.M. till 11 P.M.
S 2	57	63	"	Cloudy	N. E., S. E.	0.04		Light and misty rain at intervals all day.
3	57	66	"	Clear	E.			Cleared 2:45 P. M.
4	56	76	"	"	S. W.			Foggy A.M.; clear part of A. M.; cloudy part of even'g.
5	65	75½	Clear	"	N. W., N.			
6	50	68	"	"	N. W.			
7	50½	66½	"	"	N. E., S. E.			
8	54	65½	Cloudy	Cloudy	S., S. W.	0.05		Light rain during day at intervals.
S 9	60½	70	"	Clear	N. W.			Clouded over 10:30 P. M.
10	53½	57½	Rain	Misty } R'iny }	N. E.	1.00		Rain till 8 A. M.; misty and rainy P. M. and evening.
11	51	63	C'y m'st all day		N. W., S. W.	0.23		Rain before day and showers 2:40 and 4 to 5 P. M.
12	52	69	Clear	Clear	N. W.			Cloudy part of evening.
13	53	72	"	"	N. W.	0.07		Cloudy part of afternoon, with light showers.
14	55½	74	"	"	N. E., S. E.			
15	57	78	"	"	S. W.			
S 16	61	77	"	"	S. W.			
17	64	76	Cloudy	Cloudy	S. W.			Clear part of afternoon.
18	61½	64	Rain	Rain	N. E.	0.88		Rain till 3:50 P. M. and cleared off 6:50 P. M.
19	55	74	Clear	Clear	N. E.			
20	58½	77½	"	"	All points			
21	62	76½	"	"	S. W.			Cloudy part of morning and part of evening.
22	64	76	Rain	"	N. E., S. W.	1.40		Rain till 8:30 A.M.; shower 7:45 to 8:45 P. M.
S 23	60½	73½	Clear	"	S. W.			Cloudy part of morning.
24	61	75	"	"	S. W.	0.22		Cloudy part of A.M. & part of P. M., with shower 7 to 7:15 P. M.
25	63½	77	"	"	N. W., S. W.			Cloudy part of evening.
26	62	81	"	"	N. W., S. W.			
27	64	85	"	"	S. W.			Cloudy part of evening; first warm night.
28	70	86	"	"	N. W.			First bath in the river.
29	71	84	"	"	N. E., E.			
S 30	67	84	"	"	S. E.			
						4.34		

July, 1878.

Date.	Thermometer. Lowest.	Thermometer. Highest.	Weather. Morning.	Weather. Afternoon.	Prevailing Wind.	Rain and Melted Snow in inches.	Snow in inches.	REMARKS.
1	68	85	Clear	Clear	S. W., S. E.			
2	70	86½	"	"	S. W.			
3	72	87½	"	"	S. W.			
4	73	80	"	Cloudy	S. W., N. W.	0.31		Shower 12:35 P. M., and light rain 6:50 to 9 P. M.
5	71	87	"	Clear	N.			
6	70½	83½	"	"	N., S. E.			
S 7	65	83	"	"	N. E., S. W.			
8	67¼	87½	"	"	S. W.	0.71		Cloudy evening with shower 8:50 to 11 P. M.
9	73¼	86	C'y m'st all day		S. W.	0.07		Shower 2:20 P. M., and light sprinkles afterwards.
10	74¼	90	Cloudy	Clear	S. W.			Clear part of morning, and cloudy part of afternoon.
11	72	83	Clear	"	N. E., S. E.			Cloudy evening.
12	70	73¼	Cloudy	Rain	N. E., S. E.	2.71		Rain before day, and 9:30 A. M. to 8 P. M., and light shower 11:30 P. M.
13	68	77	"	Clear	N. E., S. E.	0.02		Cloudy part of afternoon; shower 1 P. M.
S 14	66	82	Clear	"	S. W.			Cloudy part of morning.
15	70	87	"	"	N. W., S. E.			Cloudy evening.
16	66½	74	Cloudy	"	N. E., S. E.			Cloudy part of evening.
17	67	81	"	"	S. W.			
18	73	92	Clear	"	S. W.			
19	77½	90	"	"	N. W.			Cloudy part of morning, and part of afternoon.
20	75	86	"	"	N. E., S. E.			
S 21	71½	83	C'y m'st all day		All points.	0.78		Foggy morning; shower 9:30 A. M., and 3:30 and 4:30 P. M.
22	68½	79	Clear	Clear	N. W.			Partly cloudy evening.
23	64	81	"	"	N. W.			
24	65	80½	"	"	N. W., W.			
25	65½	83	"	"	S. W.			
26	69	86½	"	"	S. W.			Cloudy part of morning, and part of evening.
27	73½	81	Cloudy	Cloudy	S. W., N. W.			Clear part of afternoon, and part of evening.
S 28	66	82½	Clear	Clear	All points.			Cloudy evening.
29	68	82	"	Cloudy	All points.			Rain after 8:30 P. M.
30	67	70	Rain	"	N. E.	1.63		Rain till 6 A. M., and from 10:30 A. M. to 1 P. M
31	63½	72	Cloudy	"	N. E., S. E.			Clear part of evening.

6.23

Weather Record for New Brunswick, N. J.

August, 1878.

Date.	Thermometer. Lowest.	Thermometer. Highest.	Weather. Morning.	Weather. Afternoon.	Prevailing Wind.	Rain and Melted Snow in inches.	Snow in inches.	REMARKS.
1	66	78	Cloudy	Cloudy	All points	0.49		Shower 6 A.M. and rain 8 to 11 A. M.; clear part P. M.; showery evening.
2	67	83	Clear	Clear	N. W.	0.22		Rain before day.
3	69	84½	"	"	N. W.			
S 4	70	85	"	"	All points			Cloudy part of afternoon.
5	69	79	Cloudy	Cloudy	All points	0.17		Shower 2 P.M.; clear even'g.
6	71	80	"	"	All points	0.68		Clear part P.M.; shower 12:20 P. M., and rain 6:35 to 8:45 P. M.
7	66½	80½	Clear	Clear	N. W.			Cloudy part of evening.
8	67	83	"	"	S. W.			Cloudy part of morning.
9	70	86½	"	"	S. W.			
10	72	75½	Cloudy	Cloudy	All points	0.04		Sprinkles during day and light rain part evening.
S 11	69½	79½	"	Clear	S. W.	0.01		Light rain 6 to 7 A. M.
12	67	79½	Clear	"	N. W.			
13	65	80	"	"	S. W.			Cloudy evening.
14	68	79	Cloudy	"	N. E., S. E.			Clear part of morning.
15	68½	75	"	Cloudy	N. E., S. E.			Light sprinkle morning and evening.
16	71	76	"	Rain	N. E., S. E.			Rain 11:30 A. M. & rest day.
17	70	80	"	Cloudy	S. W.	0.90		Light rain before day; clear part P. M. and evening.
S 18	72½	81½	Clear	Clear	N. W.			
19	67	81	"	"	N. W.			Cloudy part P.M. and eve'g.
20	65	79½	Cloudy	"	N. W.			Clear part of morning.
21	67	79½	Clear	"	N. W., N. E.	0.34		Cloudy evening; shower with hail 5:12, and light shower 8:30 P. M.
22	64½	73	C'y m'st all day		N. E., E.	0.01		Shower 3 P. M.
23	62	72½	Clear	Clear	N. E., S. E.			
24	56½	74	"	"	N. E., S.			
S 25	64	72	Cloudy	"	S. W.	0.16		Shower 11:50 A. M. to 12:10 P.M., and light rain after; cleared 4 P. M.
26	56	72½	Clear	"	All points			
27	58	76	"	"	S. W., S. E.			
28	61	76	"	"	All points			Cloudy part of evening.
29	60	74	"	"	N. E., S. E.			Cloudy part of evening.
30	63	80	"	"	All points			
31	64	76	"	Cloudy	S. E.			Cloudy part of morning.
						3.02		

September, 1878.

Date	Thermometer Lowest	Thermometer Highest	Wind Morning	Wind Afternoon	Prevailing Wind	Rain and Melted Snow in inches	Snow in inches	REMARKS
S 1	71	83½	Cloudy	Clear	S. W.	0.32		Rain till 6 A. M.
2	72½	84	Clear	"	S. W.			Cloudy part of evening.
3	72	83	"	Cloudy	All points	0.10		Showers 12:10 and 2:10 P.M.; clear part of evening.
4	70	72	Cloudy	Rainy	S. E.			Shower 5:15 and 10 A.M. and rainy P.M. and evening.
5	68½	75	Clear	Clear	N. E.	0.37		Light rain before day; cloudy part of evening.
6	67	76½	Cloudy	"	N. E., S. E.	0.05		Light rain before day; clear part of morning.
7	65½	72½	"	Cloudy	N. E.	0.01		Clear part of morning; misty rain part of evening.
S 8	57½	69	Clear	Clear	N. E., S. E.			Cloudy part of morning.
9	58	71	Cloudy	"	N. E., E.			Clear part of morning.
10	62	73	"	Cloudy	N. E., S. E.	0.15		Rain 3:45 to 6:30 P.M.; partly clear part of evening.
11	66	76	"	"	N. E., S. E.			Clear part of afternoon and misty part of evening.
12	68	76	"	"	N. E., S. E.	0.06		Rain before day & 9:30 to 10 A.M.; clear part of P. M.
13	70½	78½	"	"	S. E., S. W.	0.52		Shower 9:30 to 9:45 A.M. and rainy afternoon till 4 P.M.; cleared 8 P. M.
14	59	71½	Clear	Clear	S. W.			
S 15	56	71½	"	"	S. W., N. W.			
16	53	67	"	"	N. E., S. E.			
17	51	72	"	"	S. E., S. W.			
18	58	78	"	"	S. W.			
19	63	77	"	"	N. E., S. E.			
20	61	80	"	"	S. W.			
21	67½	77	"	Cloudy	S. W.			Cloudy part of A. M.; clear part of afternoon; misty part of evening.
S 22	56	67	"	Clear	N. W., N.			
23	48	64	"	Cloudy	N. E., S. E.			Clear part of afternoon.
24	58½	70	Cloudy	"	S. E., S.	0.13		Clear part of morning; rainy parts of P. M. and even'g.
25	63	74	Clear	Clear	All points			Foggy morning; cloudy part of evening.
26	65	77	C'y m'st all day	S. W., N. W.		0.42		Shower 4:05 to 4:30 P. M.
27	51½	65	Clear	Clear	N.			
28	43½	59	"	"	N. E., S. E.			
S 29	48	62½	C'y m'st all day	N. E., S. E.				Light rain 6 P. M.
30	54	65½	Cloudy	Cloudy	N. E., S. E.			Clear evening.
						2.22		

October, 1878.

Date.	Thermometer.		Weather.		Prevailing Wind.	Rain and Melted Snow in inches.	Snow in inches.	REMARKS.
	Lowest.	Highest.	Morning.	Afternoon.				
1	52	69	Clear	Clear	N. E., S. E.			
2	61	75	Cloudy	"	S. W.			Clear part of morning; cloudy evening.
3	65	75	"	"	All points.			Clear 7:30 p. m.
4	55½	74	Clear	"	N. W.			
5	54	66	"	"	All points.			Cloudy evening.
S 6	56	64	Cloudy	"	N. W.	0.01		Clear part of morning; light rain before day.
7	43½	62	Clear	Cloudy	All points.	0.05		Light rain part of evening.
8	54	66½	Cloudy	Clear	S. W.			Clear part of morning.
9	56½	77	"	"	S. W.	0.90		Clear part of morning, and cloudy part of evening with heavy showers 7 to 8 p. m.
10	55	64½	Clear	"	S. W., N. W.			
11	46	59½	Cloudy	Cloudy	N. E.			Clear part of morning; misty part of evening.
12	50	60	Clear	"	N. E.			Clear part of afternoon.
S 13	50	68	Cloudy	Clear	N. W.			
14	49	68½	"	"	N. W., S. W.			
15	53	72½	Clear	"	S. W.			
16	56	73	"	"	S. W.			
17	58	76½	"	"	S. W.			
18	58½	63	"	Rain	All points.	0.97		Rain 8:15 to 10 a. m., and from 2:15 to 8 p. m. and cloudy rest of evening.
19	46	54½	"	Clear	N. W.			Clear part of morning and cloudy part of afternoon.
S 20	43	61	Cloudy	"	N. W., S. W.			
21	45	67	"	"	S. W.			
22	42	63	Clear	Cloudy	S. W., S. E.			Foggy morning; cleared 8 a. m.; clouded over 4 p. m.
23	55	66½	"	"	S. E., S. W.	0.88		Rain till 11 a. m. with violent wind; clear part of evening.
24	47½	61	"	Clear	N. W.			
25	45	58½	Rain	"	N. E., S. E.			
26	41	61	Clear	"	All points.			
S 27	44	65	"	Cloudy	S.			Clear part of afternoon; rain at intervals after 10 p. m.
28	43	52½	"	Clear	N. W.	0.10		Rain before day.
29	36	51	"	"	All points.			Cloudy evening with rain 10:30 p. m.
30	43	57½	Rain	"	All points.	0.50		Rain till 10:30 a.m.; cloudy part of afternoon.
31	48	54	Cloudy	"	W., N. W.	0.01		Light sprinkles till 8 a m.; clear part of morning and cloudy part of evening.
						3.42		

November, 1878.

Date.	Thermometer. Lowest.	Thermometer. Highest.	Weather. Morning.	Weather. Afternoon.	Prevailing Wind.	Rain and Melted Snow in inches.	Snow in inches.	REMARKS.
1	38	48	Clear	Clear	N. W.			Cloudy part of morning.
2	37	56	"	"	S. W.			
S 3	41	49½	"	"	N. W.			
4	32½	48	"	"	S. W., N. W.			
5	30	42½	"	"	N. W.			
6	33½	40	Cloudy	Cloudy	All points			Rainy after 7 P. M.
7	35	45	"	Clear	S. W., N. W.	0.16		Rain and snow before day; clear part of morning and cloudy part of afternoon.
8	39	42½	Clear	"	N. W.			
9	33	44	"	"	N. W.			Cloudy evening.
S 10	38½	54½	"	"	N. W.			
11	40	56	"	Cloudy	S. W., S. E.			Light sprinkle 8 P. M.
12	48	60	"	Clear	S. W.	0.08		Rain before day; cloudy parts morning and P. M.
13	41	56	"	"	S. W., N. W.			Cloudy; light sprinkle 1 P.M.
14	36	47	"	"	N. W.			
15	28	44	"	"	E.			Cloudy part of afternoon.
16	32½	50	Cloudy	Cloudy	E.			
S 17	46	50	Mist, Rain	Rain	N. E.			Misty and rainy during A. M. and rain rest of day.
18	43	47	Rain, Mist	Misty	N. E.	0.70		Rain before day; misty till 5:30 P.M.; clear evening.
19	43½	56½	C'y m'st all day.		N. E.			
20	44	48½	Cloudy	Cloudy	N. E., N. W.	0.03		Light rain part A. M.; clear part of evening.
21	46	51	"	"	S. W., S. E.	0.02		Light rain part A. M.; rain 10:35 P. M.
22	46	55½	Rain	"	N. E., S. E.	1.06		Rain till 11 A.M.; clear parts of afternoon and evening; bar. 29.015.
23	42½	47	Clear	"	W.			Cloudy part of morning;
S 24	39	52½	"	Clear	S. W.			clear evening.
25	40	53	Cloudy	Cloudy	N. E., S. E.			Partly clear part P.M.; misty rain part of evening.
26	41	44	"	"	N.			Clear parts of afternoon and evening.
27	33½	59	"	Rain	N. E., S. E.			Rain 11:30 A. M.; very hard from 6:30 to 9 P. M., and light rest of evening.
28	46	48	"	Cloudy	S. W., N. W.	1.60		Light rain before day; clear evening.
29	42	49	"	Clear	W.			Cleared 10 A. M.
30	36½	48½	Clear	"	N. W.			
						3.65		

December, 1878.

Date.	Thermometer. Lowest.	Thermometer. Highest.	Weather. Morning.	Weather. Afternoon.	Prevailing Wind.	Rain and Melted Snow in inches.	Snow in inches.	REMARKS.
S 1	33	45½	Clear	Cloudy	N. E., E.			Clouded over 2 P. M.
2	39	59½	Rain	Clear	N. E., S. W.	0.88		Rain till 1 P.M.; cl'red 2 P.M.
3	42	48	Clear	"	S. W.			Cloudy evening.
4	41	49½	Cloudy	"	S. W., N. W.	0.26		Rain before day; clear part of A.M.; cloudy part of P.M.
5	35½	37½	C'y m'st all day.		N. W.			Snow squall 10:40 A. M.
6	32	41½	Cloudy	Clear	S. W.	0.01		Light snow before day; clear
7	30	41	Clear	"	N. W.			part A.M.; cloudy part P.M.
S 8	30	39	"	Cloudy	N. W.			Clear part of afternoon.
9	33	46	Snow Rain }	Rainy	S. E., N. E.			Snow before day; rain till 3 P.M.; rainy at intervals afterwards; bar. 9 A.M.—30.16; bar. 7 P.M —28.85, lowest bar. I've ever known.
10	44	60	Rain	Rain	S. E.	2.32		Rain till 6:45 P.M.; partly clear part of evening.
11	41	43	Cloudy	Cloudy	W.	0.05		Rain before day; clear part of evening.
12	37	40½	"	"	S. W., N. W.			Clear part of morning.
13	35	41	"	Clear	N. W.			Clear part of morning.
14	32	41	"	"	All points.			Clear part of morning; cl'dy evening with light rain.
S 15	36	42	Rain	Cloudy	N. W.	0.31		Rain before day & at int'vals till 2 PM; light snow 7½ PM.
16	29	34½	Clear	Clear	N. W.			
17	25	36	"	Cloudy	N. W.			Clear part of evening.
18	29	37	"	Clear	N. W.			Cloudy part A.M. and P. M.
19	25	35	"	"	N. W.			
20	24	33½	"	"	"			
21	27	47½	Cloudy	Rain	S.E., N.E., S.E	1.25	3.00	Snow 8:45 A.M. to 2 PM; then rain till 10 PM.; cl'r 11 PM.
S 22	36½	38	"	Clear	S. W., W.			Clear part A. M. and cloudy part P. M.
23	20	25	Clear	"	W.			Cloudy part of evening.
24	16	23	"	"	W., S. W.			
25	15	22½	"	"	W.			
26	16	26½	"	Cloudy	W.			Clear part of afternoon.
27	21	30	Cloudy	"	N. W.			Clear part A.M.; light snow part P.M.; clear evening.
28	25½	32	"	Clear	S. W., N. W.			Clear part of A.M.; cloudy part of P.M.; light snow part of morning.
S 29	17	30	Clear	"	W.			
30	24	33½	Cloudy	"	S. W., N. W.	0.50		Snow before day; clear part of morning.
31	19½	32	Clear	"	W.			Cloudy part of evening.
						5.08	3.50	

Total rain-fall for 1878—46.56 inches.

January, 1879.

Date.	Thermometer. Lowest.	Thermometer. Highest.	Weather. Morning.	Weather. Afternoon.	Prevailing Wind.	Rain and Melted Snow in inches.	Snow in inches.	REMARKS.
1	28½	32	Cloudy	Cloudy	All points.	----	----	Snow 10:30 A. M., and at intervals rest of day, but very light.
2	27	34	Snow	Clear	N. E., N. W.	----	3.00	Snow till 1 P. M.; cleared 2 P. M.
3	-1½	11	Clear	"	-- W.	----	----	Violent wind all day; cloudy evening.
4	6½	23	"	"	N. W.	----	----	Cloudy part of evening.
S 5	15	23	"	"	N. W.	----	----	Cloudy part of evening.
6	16½	29½	"	"	W.	----	----	Cloudy evening.
7	21½	30	"	"	W., S. W.	----	----	Cloudy part of afternoon.
8	22	37½	Cloudy	Cloudy	S. W.	----	1.00	Light snow before day; clear part of morning; snow and rain after 7 P.M.
9	34	35	Rain	Rain	N. E.	1.47	----	Rain till 4 P. M., and light snow part of evening; cleared off 10 P. M.
10	23	31	Clear	Clear	N. W., W.	----	----	Cloudy part of morning.
11	22	33	"	Cloudy	S. W.	----	----	Cloudy part of morning.
S 12	23½	29½	Cloudy	"	N. E.	----	----	
13	26½	37	"	Clear	N. W., S. W.	----	----	Cloudy part of afternoon.
14	27	36	Clear	"	S. W., N. W.	----	----	
15	24½	28	Cloudy	Cloudy	N.	----	----	Clear part of morning; snow 9 P. M.
16	13	23½	Snow	"	N. E.	----	8.00	Snow till noon; clear evening after 8 P. M.
17	14	25	Clear	"	N.	----	----	
18	23	38	Cloudy	Clear	S. W., N. W.	----	----	Light snow before day.
S 19	15	30	"	"	N. W.	----	----	Clear part of morning.
20	18	24	Clear	"	N. W.	----	----	Cloudy part of morning.
21	4½	25	"	Cloudy	W., S. W.	----	----	Clear part of evening.
22	19	40	"	Clear	All points.	----	----	Cloudy part of afternoon.
23	28½	41½	Cloudy	"	S. W., N. W.	0.08	----	Foggy morning; rain part of morning.
24	19	35	C'y m'st all day		S. E., S. W.	----	----	
25	29½	46	Clear	Clear	N. W., S. W.	----	----	
S 26	18	27	"	Cloudy	N. W.	----	----	
27	19	38½	Cloudy	"	S. W.	----	----	Clear part of morning.
28	37	49	"	"	S. W.	0.06	----	Clear part of afternoon; light rain before day; clear evening.
29	35	40	"	Clear	N.	----	----	Clear part of morning.
30	25½	38½	Clear	"	N. W.	----	----	
31	29	40	"	"	N W., W.	----	----	
						1.61	12.00	

February, 1879.

Date.	Thermometer. Lowest.	Thermometer. Highest.	Weather. Morning.	Weather. Afternoon.	Prevailing Wind.	Rain and Melted Snow in inches.	Snow in inches.	REMARKS.
1	28	33½	Clear	Clear	N. W.			Cloudy part of P. M., with snow squall at 2 o'clock.
S 2	16	26½	Cloudy	"	N. W.			Clear part A. M. and cloudy part of afternoon.
3	24	35½	C'y m'st all day.		N. W.			
4	29	38½	Cloudy	Clear	N. W.			Clear part of morning.
5	26½	35	"	Snow Rain	S. E.	0.27		Snow 11:20 A.M. to 3 P.M. and misty rain till 7 P.M.
6	28½	37	"	Cloudy	N. W., S. W.			Clear part of morning and part of afternoon.
7	28	38	Clear	Clear	W.			
8	24	35	"	"	N. W.			
S 9	22	38	"	"	S. W., N. W.			Cloudy part of morning.
10	20	32	"	"	N. W., S. W.			Cloudy evening.
11	30	50	Cloudy	Rain	S. W., S.			Clear part A.M.; rain part A. M.; steady rain after 3 P.M.
12	40½	42½	Rain	Clear	S. W., W.	0.72		Rain till 7:30 A.M.; clear part A.M.; cloudy part P. M.
13	33	36½	C'y m'st all day.		W.			
14	18	27	Clear	Clear	N. W.			Cloudy part A. M.; cloudy part evening with snow squalls at 7 P. M.
15	12	24	"	"	N. W., S. W.			
S 16	15	34½	"	Cloudy	S. W.			Clear part of evening.
17	28	31	Cloudy	Snow	N. E.			Snow 11:30 A. M. and rest of day and night.
18	26½	30	"	Cloudy	N. E.		4.00	Snow before day; clear part of evening.
19	20	29	"	"	N. E., E.			Light snow part A.M.; clear part of P. M.; snow part of evening.
20	21	31½	Snow	"	N. E.		2.00	Snow till 11 A. M., and part P.M. and evening; clear part of evening.
21	18	27	Clear	Clear	N. W.			
22	10	25	Cloudy	Cloudy	S. W., N. E.		1.00	Clear part A. M.; light snow part P.M.; clear part eve'g.
S 23	18½	40	"	Clear	S. W.			Clear part A. M. and cloudy part of afternoon.
24	22½	29	Clear	Cloudy	N. W.			
25	21½	32	Cloudy	"	N. E.		1.50	Light snow before day and from 11 A. M. to 3 P. M.
26	26	50½	Foggy	"	S. W., N. W.	0.22		Clear part A. M.; rain 3:15 to 6 P. M., and light sprinkle afterwards.
27	23½	30	Clear	Clear	N. W.			Light snow before day; cloudy part of evening.
28	10½	24	"	"	N. E.			
						1.21	8.50	

Weather Record for New Brunswick, N. J. 273

March, 1879.

Date.	Lowest.	Highest.	Weather. Morning.	Weather. Afternoon.	Prevailing Wind.	Rain and Melted Snow in inches.	Snow in inches.	REMARKS.
1	17	38½	Clear	Clear	N. E., S. W.			Cloudy part A.M. and eve'g.
S 2	33	39	Cloudy	Cloudy	N. E., S. E.			Clear part of morning.
3	30	41	Clear	Clear	N. E., S. E.			Cloudy part of morning.
4	28½	40	Cloudy	Cloudy	All points	0.08		Rain 10:45 P. M.
5	38	49	"	Clear	N. W.			Cleared 8 A. M.
6	27	40½	"	Cloudy	N. E., S.	0.05		Snow and rain 12:40 to 3 P. M.; clear evening.
7	36	42	Clear	Clear	N. W.			
8	23	38	"	"	All points			Snow and rain after 8 P. M., with thunder and light'ng
S 9	30	45	Cloudy	"	S., N.	0.40		Rain before day; clear part A. M.; cloudy part eve'g.
10	36	61½	Clear	"	W.			
11	41½	63	Cloudy	"	S. W., N.			Light rain 8:15 A. M.; clear part of morning.
12	36	48	Clear	"	N. W.			
13	34	57	Cloudy	"	S. E., S. W.			
14	38½	49	"	Cloudy	N. E., N. W.	0.08		Rain 2 to 4 P. M.; clear evening.
15	35	44½	Clear	Clear	N. W., W.			
S 16	33	46	"	"	S. W.			Cloudy part of evening.
17	36½	46	Rain	Rain Snow	SE, NE, NW.	0.45		Rain till 7 A.M.; light rain at intervals 11 A. M. to 9 P. M., with snow.
18	28	40	Clear	Clear	N. W.			
19	26	38½	"	"	N. W.			Snow squall 10:50 A. M., with sun shining.
20	30	45	"	Cloudy	S. W.			Rain 10 P. M.
21	37	48½	Cloudy	Clear	N. E., N. W.	0.13		Rain before day; cloudy part of afternoon.
22	30	37	Clear	Rain	S. E.			Cloudy part A.M., with light rain P.M. and heavy eve'g, with thunder and light'ng
S 23	34	43	C'y m'st all day.		N. W.		1.25	Rain before day.
24	30	45	Clear	Cloudy	N. W., S. W.			Clear part P. M and even'g.
25	36½	45	"	Clear	S. W., N. W.			Cloudy part morning and part of afternoon.
26	30	45	"	"	All points			Clouded over 5 P. M., and snow 10 P. M.
27	33	47½	Rain	Cloudy	S. E., N. E.	0.71		Rain till 8:15 A.M., and light rain part of evening.
28	38	52	Cloudy	Clear	S. E., N. E.			Clear part of morning.
29	38	47½	"	Rain	S. E.			Rainy after 4:15 P. M.
S 30	39½	53	Clear	Clear	N. W., N.	0.51		Rain before day; cloudy part of morning.
31	33½	39	Cloudy	"	N.			Cloudy part of afternoon.
						3.66		

April, 1879.

Date.	Thermometer.		Weather.		Prevailing Wind.	Rain and Melted Snow in inches.	Snow in inches.	REMARKS.
	Lowest.	Highest.	Morning.	Afternoon.				
1	33½	55½	Clear	Clear	N. W.			
2	39	40½	"	"	N. W.			
3	31	44	"	Cloudy	All points.	0.09		Cloudy A.M.; light rain 12:30 P. M. and snow storm 4:15 to 5:15 P. M., with ther. again registering 31°; clear part of evening.
4	28	36½	C'y m'st all day.		N. W.			Snow squalls part of A. M.
5	27½	35	"	"	N. W.			
S 6	27	46	Cloudy	Clear	N. W., S. W.			Clear part of morning.
7	36	52	"	Cloudy	S. W., N.	0.09		Rain 8 to 11 A.M.; clear ev'g
8	36	53	Clear	Clear	W., N.			
9	36	63	"	"	S. W.			
10	46	50	Cloudy	Rain	S. E., N. E.	1.30		Clear part of A.M.; rain 9:20 A.M. to 9 P.M.; com. again 10:30 P. M.
11	37	43	"	Cloudy	N. E., N. W.	0.02		Light rain 10:30 A.M. to 1:30 P. M.
12	35	50	Clear	Clear	N. W.			
S 13	36	53½	"	Cloudy	S. W.	0.06		Rain 6 to 8 P.M.; cl'red 9 PM.
14	40	51½	Cloudy	"	S. W.	0.04		Light rain part A. M. & ev'g.
15	44½	49½	"	"	N. E.	0.06		Light rain part of afternoon; foggy evening.
16	42½	58	Clear	Clear	N. W., S. W.			Cloudy evening with light sprinkle.
17	39	42½	Rain	Rain	N. E.			Rain at intervals all day & very hard in the evening and night.
18	37	43	"	Cloudy	N. E., N. W.	1.02		Rain till 1 P. M.
19	39½	43	Cloudy	"	N. E	0.07		Rain part A.M. and P.M. with light light snow 3 P. M.; clear evening.
S 20	37½	57½	Clear	Clear	N. W., N.			
21	40	63½	"	"	N. W.			
22	45	68½	"	"	N. W.			
23	49½	68	"	Cloudy	W., N.			Cloudy part of morning and clear evening.
24	44	64	"	Clear	All points.			
25	49	64½	"	Cloudy	S. W.			Cloudy part of morning and clear evening.
26	51	73	C'y m'st all day.		All points.			
S 27	44	55	Cloudy	Cloudy	E.			
28	47½	64½	"	Show'rs	All points.			Clear part of afternoon; showers after 2:30 P.M.
29	55	66½	"	Cloudy	N. E., S. E.	1.55		Rain before day; clear part of A.M.; clear part of P. M.
30	53½	72	Clear	Clear	N. W.			
						4.90		

May, 1879.

Date.	Thermometer. Lowest.	Thermometer. Highest.	Weather. Morning.	Weather. Afternoon.	Prevailing Wind.	Rain and Melted Snow in inches.	Snow in inches.	REMARKS.
1	47	59	Clear	Clear	N. W.			
2	41½	52	"	"	N. W., N.			Cloudy part of morning, and part of afternoon; frost.
3	40	60	"	"	N. W., S. W.			Cloudy part of afternoon; frost and ice.
S 4	46½	58½	Cloudy	Cloudy	S. W.	0.02		Light rain part of morning and part of afternoon; cherries flowered.
5	53½	72½	Clear	Clear	S. W.			
6	55½	68½	"	"	N. W.	0.16		Shower between 12 and 1 A. M.; cloudy part of morning; pears flowered.
7	48½	64½	"	"	All points.			
8	48	65	"	"	N. E., S. E.			
9	45½	66	"	"	N. E., S. E.			
10	44	64	"	"	N. E., S. E.			
S 11	41	65	"	"	N. E., S. E.			Clouded over 10 P. M.; frost.
12	48	74½	"	"	S. E., S. W.			Cloudy part of morning.
13	60	76½	Cloudy	"	S. W.			Clear part of morning.
14	59	77½	Clear	"	S. W.			
15	60	76	C'y m'st all day.		S. W., S. E.			Misty part of evening.
16	62½	78½	" "	" "	All points.	0.64		Light rain 6:30 to 8 A. M.; 10:30 A. M.; heavy shower 6 to 7 P. M.; and light rain to 7:30 P. M.
17	59½	68	Cloudy	Cloudy	N. E., S. E	0.36		Rain 4:45 to 6 P. M.; rainy after 9:45 P. M. till midnight.
S 18	62	73	"	Show'rs	All points.	0.25		Partly clear part of morning; shower 1:30 P. M.; 3 to 4 P. M.; 10 P. M.
19	62½	75	Rain	Clear	S. E., S. W.	0.83		Rain till 7 A.M.; clear part of morning; cloudy evening with rain 6 to 7 P. M.
20	63	74	Cloudy	"	S. E.	0.35		Shower 2 to 2:10 P. M.
21	65	78	"	"	S. W., N. W.	0.05		Clear part A.M. and cloudy part P. M. with showers 3:30 and 4:50 P. M.
22	55	67½	Clear	"	N. E.			
23	49	62	"	"	N. E.			
24	47	68	"	"	S. W.			Frost.
S 25	56	75	"	"	S. W., N. W.	0.18		Cloudy part of morning; cloudy evening with rain 7 to 8:30.
26	60	69	"	"	N.			
27	48	67½	"	Cloudy	N. E., S	0.01		Light rain 8:30 P. M.; clear part of evening; frost.
28	55	72	"	Clear	N.W.E.,S.W.			Cloudy part of evening.
29	56½	77	"	"	S. W., S. E.			
30	58½	79½	"	"	S. W.			Cloudy part of afternoon.
31	65	86½	"	"	N. W.			
						2.85		

June, 1879.

Date.	Thermometer. Lowest.	Thermometer. Highest.	Weather. Morning.	Weather. Afternoon.	Prevailing Wind.	Rain and Melted Snow in inches.	Snow in inches.	REMARKS.
S 1	71	89½	Clear	Clear	S. W.	----	----	
2	71½	84	"	Cloudy	All points.	0.40	----	Rain 7:10 P.M. till midnight.
3	67½	69½	Cloudy	"	N. E., S. E.	0.62	----	Rain 8:15 to 10:30 A.M.; light sprinkles part of aft'noon; rainy evening after 6.
4	62½	73	Rain, Cl'dy	Clear	N. W., S. W.	1.14	----	Rain till 6 A. M.
5	63	80	Clear	"	S. W.	0.17	----	Cloudy evening with rain 8:50 to 10:30 P.M.
6	64½	80	"	"	S. W., N. W.	0.12	----	Rain before day; cloudy part P.M. & shower 5:45 to 6 P.M.
7	51	66	"	"	S. W.	----	----	
S 8	52½	72½	"	"	N. W.	----	----	
9	59	71½	"	"	N. W., S. W.	----	----	Cloudy part of A.M. and P.M.
10	60	83	"	"	S. W.	0.05	----	Cloudy evening with shower 9 P. M.
11	69	82½	"	Cloudy	S. W.	0.87	----	Heavy shower 6 to 6:40 P. M.; clear evening.
12	67	78	Cloudy	"	SW.,N.E.,SE.	0.62	----	Clear part of afternoon and showers 4:25 to 6:20 P.M.
13	65½	78	Clear	Clear	N.	----	----	
14	57	75	"	"	N. E., S. W.	----	----	
S 15	65½	83½	"	Cloudy	S. W.	0.67	----	Cloudy part of A.M.; showers 4:15 to 6:30 P.M.; clear ev'g.
16	70	80	"	Clear	S. W., N. W.	----	----	Cloudy part of afternoon, with light sprinkles.
17	57	71	"	"	N. W.	----	----	
18	54	68½	"	"	N. W.	0.08	----	Cloud part P.M. & ev'g, with rain 8:30 to 9:30 P. M.
19	55	68	"	"	N. E., S. E.	0.01	----	Cloudy part of afternoon, with light rain 2:15 P.M.
20	53	72	"	"	N. W., S. W.	----	----	
21	57	76½	"	"	S. W.	----	----	
S 22	59	70	Cloudy	Cloudy	S. W., S. E.	----	----	Clear part A. M.; clear ev'g after 9 o'clock; sprinkle 6:15 P. M.
23	61½	81	Clear	Clear	S. W., N. W.	----	----	
24	66	83½	"	"	S. W., S. E., S.	----	----	
25	66½	77	Cloudy	Cloudy	N. E., S. E.	0.10	----	Cl'r part A.M.; rain 8 to 11 P.M.
26	66	81	"	Clear	S. W.	0.06	----	Light rain before day & 7:10 A.M.; cloudy part of P. M.
27	69½	87	Clear	"	S. W.	----	----	Cloudy part of evening.
28	73	88½	"	"	S. W.	0.10	----	Cloudy part of evening, with shower 8:30 P. M.
S 29	73	85	Cloudy	Cloudy	S. W., N. E.	0.09	----	Cl'r part A.M.; show'r 1:45 P.M.
30	64½	78	Clear	Clear	N., S. E.	----	----	Cloudy part of afternoon, with sprinkle 3 P. M.
						5.10	----	

July, 1879.

Date	Thermometer. Lowest	Thermometer. Highest	Weather. Morning.	Weather. Afternoon.	Prevailing Wind.	Rain and Melted Snow in inches.	Snow in inches.	REMARKS.
1	60	77	Clear	Clear	N. W., S.			
2	60½	82½	"	"	S. W.			
3	67	88½	"	"	S. W.			Cloudy part of afternoon.
4	72	92	"	"	S. W.	0.70		Cloudy evening, with light shower at 7 and heavy shower 8:30 P. M.
5	65	72½	Cloudy	"	N. E., S. E.			Clear part of morning.
S 6	60	74	Clear	"	S. E.			
7	80	76½	Cloudy	Cloudy	S.			Clear part of morning and part of evening.
8	65	81	"	Clear	S. W.	0.25		Rain before day.
9	68	83	Clear	"	N. W.			
10	68	86	"	"	N. W.	0.18		Cloudy evening with sprinkle 7:20 and shower 8 P.M.
11	71	84	"	"	S. W.	0.31		Cloudy part of A.M. and part of P M. and evening, with rain 7:25 to 9 P. M.
12	69½	78½	Cloudy	"	N., N. E.			Clear part of morning and cloudy part of afternoon.
S 13	63½	80½	Clear	"	S. E.			
14	64½	85	"	"	S. W.			
15	69½	91	"	"	S. W.			
16	76	94½	"	"	S. W., N. W.	0.20		Cloudy part of evening with shower 8:15 to 8:35 P. M.
17	71½	82	"	"	N. W.	0.26		Showers before day
18	64	76	"	"	N. W., S. E.			Cloudy part of afternoon.
19	61	75½	"	"	N. E., S. E.			
S 20	60	75	"	"	N. E., S. E.			Cloudy part of evening.
21	59	79	"	"	S. E., S. W.			Cloudy part of afternoon.
22	65	85½	"	"	S. W., S.			Cloudy evening.
23	69	83	C'y m'st all day.		S. W.			C. started for San Francisco at 2 P.M.; left Phila. 11:55 P. M.
24	70½	80½	Cloudy	Clear	N. E., S. E.	0.26		Shower before day; clear part A. M; cloudy part of P.M.
25	67	75	"	Cloudy	N. E.	0.80		Clear part of morning; rain 8 to 10 P.M.
26	63	73	"	Rain	N. E., S. E.	2.20		Rain before day; heavy rain 4 to 7:30 P. M. and light rain till 11 P. M.
S 27	68	83½	Clear	Clear	S. W.			
28	70	84	"	Cloudy	All points.			
29	71	84	"	Clear	S. W.			Cloudy evening.
30	72½	80	C'y m'st all day.		N. W.			
31	71	83½	Cloudy	Clear	N. E., S. E.			Clear part of morning and cloudy evening.
						5.16		

Weather Record for New Brunswick, N. J.

August, 1879.

Date.	Thermometer. Lowest.	Thermometer. Highest.	Weather. Morning.	Weather. Afternoon.	Prevailing Wind.	Rain and Melted Snow in inches.	Snow in inches.	REMARKS.
1	70	85	Clear	Clear	S. W.			
2	73	89	"	"	S W.			
S 3	74	89½	"	"	S. W., N. W.			Cloudy part of afternoon.
4	73½	82	"	Cloudy	All points	0.63		Cloudy part of morning; rain 3:45 to 7 P. M.
5	69	84	"	Clear	S. W.			Cloudy evening.
6	75	85	"	"	N. W., S. W.			Cloudy part of afternoon.
7	71	73	Cloudy	Cloudy	N. E.			
8	67½	78½	"	Clear	N.	1.05		Heavy rain before day; cloudy evening.
9	64	69	"	Cloudy	N.			Partly clear part of morning, and part of evening.
S 10	55½	72	Clear	Clear	N.			
11	56½	76½	"	"	N. W., S. W.			
12	63½	80	"	"	S. W.			
13	63½	79	"	"	S. W.			Cloudy part of evening.
14	66½	82½	Cloudy	"	S. W.			Clear part of morning, and cloudy part of afternoon.
15	66	75	"	Cloudy	N. E., S. E.			Clear part of morning.
16	65½	68½	"	"	E., N. E.	0.44		Rain at intervals before day, and till 4:30 P. M.; thunder shower 10:45 P. M.
S 17	64	76½	"	Rain	S. W.	0.43		Rain before day, and 8:30 to 11 A. M., and 4 P. M., rest of day and night.
18	67½	69½	Rain	"	S.W,S.E,N.E.	3.27		Heavy rain till 8:30 P. M., and light till 9:30 P. M.; clear 10:15 P. M.
19	60½	76	Clear	Clear	W., N. W.			
20	61	75	"	"	N. E., S.			
21	62½	78	Cloudy	"	S. W.			Clear 9 A. M.
22	67	82	"	"	S. W.			
23	71	83½	Clear	Cloudy	S. W.	0.51		Shower 7 P. M.; heavy till 7:30 and light till 8:30.
S 24	70½	76	Cloudy	"	S. W.	0.05		Clear part of afternoon; shower 6:45 P. M.; clear part of evening.
25	66	70	"	Rain	N. E.	0.10		Rain at intervals after 5 P. M., and steady rain after 10 P. M.
26	59	67	"	Cloudy	N. E.	0.82		Rain before day; clear evening.
27	56½	69	Clear	Clear	N. E.			Cloudy part of afternoon.
28	56	72	"	"	N. E, S. E.			Cloudy part of evening.
29	60	78½	"	"	S. W.			
30	67½	77½	"	"	N.W,N.E,SE.			
S 31	60½	77	"	"	All points.			
						7.30		

September, 1879.

Date	Thermometer Lowest	Thermometer Highest	Weather Morning	Weather Afternoon	Prevailing Wind	Rain and Melted Snow in inches	Snow in inches	REMARKS
1	65	83	Clear	Clear	S. W.			
2	69	80¼	Cloudy	Cloudy	S. W.			Clear part of morning
3	67	70	Misty Rain	Rain	E., S. E.	0.88		Misty rain till 6 P.M. & then heavy rain till 9:15 P. M.; partly clear part of ev'ng.
4	69	79	Cloudy	Clear	S. W., W.			Clear part of morning.
5	63	75½	Clear	"	N. W.			
6	56½	72½	"	"	N. E., S. E.			Cloudy part of evening.
S 7	65	79	C'y m'st all day.		N. E., S. E.	0.28		Rain before day; clear 8 A.M. to 4 P.M. & part of even'g; shower 10:50 P. M. with hail.
8	67½	76	Cloudy	Clear	S. W., N. W.	0.06		Light rain till 6 A M.; clear part of morning.
9	57	69	Clear	"	N. W.			Partly cloudy 4 P. M. with light sprinkle.
10	54	67	"	"	N. W., N. E.			Cloudy parts of P.M. & ev'g.
11	55	69½	"	"	N. E., S. E.			
12	52½	69	"	"	S. E.			
13	53½	69	Cloudy	Cloudy	S. W., S.			Partly clear part of morning; rainy after 6 P. M.
S 14	61	65	Rain	Clear	S. W.	0.75		Rain till 7 A.M.; showers 8¼ to 9 A.M. and 2:40 to 3 & 6:15 to 7 P. M; clear rest of afternoon and evening.
15	52	67	Clear	"	N.W,SW,SE.			
16	52	67	"	"	N. E., S. E.			
17	60	72	"	"	SW,NW,SW.			
18	51½	70¼	"	"	S. W.			Cloudy parts P.M. and ev'g.
19	58	66	C'y m'st all day.		NW,NE,SE.			
20	52	67	Clear	Clear	N. E.			Cloudy part of evening.
S 21	51½	62	Cloudy	Cloudy	N. E.			
22	55	61	"	Clear	N. E.	0.01		Light rain before day; cloudy part of afternoon.
23	50½	70	Clear	"	N. W., S. W.			Cloudy part of afternoon.
24	60	70¼	Cloudy	"	S. W., N. W.	0.02		Clear part A.M. & cloudy part P.M , with shower 3:30 PM.
25	47	56½	Clear	"	N. W., N. E.			
26	40½	58	"	"	NW,N E,S.E.			Frost.
27	42½	62	"	"	S. E.			Frost.
S 28	47½	66	Foggy	"	S. E.			Cloudy part of evening.
29	55	65	Cloudy	Cloudy	S. W.			Cleared off 6 P. M.
30	57	73½	"	Clear	S. W.			
						2.00		

Weather Record for New Brunswick, N. J.

October, 1879.

Date.	Thermometer. Lowest.	Thermometer. Highest.	Weather. Morning.	Weather. Afternoon.	Prevailing Wind.	Rain and Melted Snow in inches.	Snow in inches.	REMARKS.
1	58½	81	Clear	Clear	S. W.			Warmest day since October 6, 1861.
2	62	78	"	"	S. W., S. E.			
3	64	83½	Foggy	"	S. W., N. W.			Clear part of morning.
4	58½	72	Clear	"	N. W., S. W.			
S 5	53	76	"	"	S. W.			
6	61	71½	"	"	All points			Cloudy part of evening.
7	59	70	Cloudy	"	N. E., N. W.			Cloudy part of afternoon.
8	56	73	Clear	Cloudy	S. W.			Cloudy part of morning and clear part of afternoon and evening.
9	64½	80	"	Clear	All points.	0.02		Cloudy evening, with light rain 7 to 9 P. M.
10	64	74½	"	"	N. E., S. E.			Clouded over 5 P. M.
11	61	67	Cloudy	Cloudy	N. E., S. E.			Misty part of afternoon.
S 12	61½	71	"	Clear	S. W.			
13	61½	74½	Clear	"	N.W., N.E., E			Cloudy part of afternoon.
14	52	69½	"	"	All points			
15	52½	74	"	"	S. W., N. W.			
16	62	80	"	"	N. W.			
17	61	76	Fgy Cl'dy	"	S. E.			Clear part of morning; cloudy evening.
18	64½	77	Cloudy	Cloudy	S. W.			Clear part of morning.
S 19	59½	67	"	Clear	N. W.	0.07		Light rain 1:30 A.M.; cleared 8 A. M.
20	44	60	Clear	"	N. W., S. W.			
21	43½	60	"	Cloudy	S. W.	0.04		Misty rain after 8 P. M. to 11:30 P. M.
22	55	65	Cloudy	"	S.	0.02		Misty rain 8 P. M. to 10:15 P. M.
23	61½	70½	"	Clear	S. W., N. W.	0.01		Clear part of morning; cloudy evening with light rain 7 P. M.
24	45	50	Clear	"	N. W.			
25	32	45	"	"	N. W.			
S 26	28½	52	"	"	N. E., S. W.			Bar. 30.64 7 A. M.
27	33	52	"	Cloudy	S. W.			Clouded over 10 A. M.; clear part of evening.
28	42	60	C'y m'st all day.		NE, SW, NW.	0.11		Shower 12:15 to 2 P. M.; clear evening, bar. 29.50 4 P. M.
29	45	60½	Clear	Clear	W., S. W.			
30	47	59	"	"	S. W., N. W.			
31	41	51	"	"	N. W.			
						0.27		

November, 1879.

Date.	Thermometer.		Weather.		Prevailing Wind.	Rain and Melted Snow in inches.	Snow in inches.	REMARKS.
	Lowest.	Highest.	Morning.	Afternoon.				
1	35	47	Clear	Clear	N. W.			
S 2	30½	45	"	Cloudy	S. W., S. E.			Light rain 10 P. M.; clear part of evening.
3	35	39	Cloudy	Clear	W., N. W.	0.13		Rain and snow before day; clear part A.M.; cloudy part P. M.; snow squalls 2 P. M.
4	29	39	Clear	Cloudy	N. W.			Cloudy part A. M.; clear part P. M. and evening.
5	24	39	"	Clear	N. W.			Clouded over 8 P. M., and snow 11:30 P. M.
6	31	39	Cloudy	Cloudy	S. E., N. E.	0.29		Snow before day; rain part P. M. and evening.
7	35	48½	Clear	Clear	N. W., S. E.			
8	33½	52	"	Cloudy	N. E., S. W.			Cloudy part of morning.
S 9	50	68½	Cloudy	Clear	S W.			Clear part of morning.
10	56½	66	Clear	"	S. W., N. W.			Cloudy part of evening.
11	44	51	Cloudy	Cloudy	N. E., S. E.	0.01		Clear part of morning; light rain 11 A. M. to 1 P. M.; foggy evening.
12	49	71½	Clear	Clear	S. W.	0.01		Clear part of morning, and part P. M. with light rain
13	57	65½	"	"	SW.N.W,S.E.			Cloudy evening.
14	50½	58	Cloudy	Cloudy	S. E.	0.04		Light rain before day; 2 to 2:20 P. M.; clear 10 P M.; C. home fr.San F. 3:30 P.M.
15	55	71½	Clear	"	S. W.			Cloudy part of morning; sprinkles during afternoon; cleared 8 P. M.
S 16	53	61	"	Clear	S. W., N. W.			
17	41½	54½	"	"	N. W., S. W.			Cloudy part of evening.
18	43	46	Rain	Cloudy	N. E.	0.69		Rain till 11 A.M.; 2:30 to 5; 6:30 to 7 P. M.; cleared 10:30 P.M.; first heavy rain since Sept. 14—64½ days.
19	35	41	Clear	Clear	N. W., W.			Cloudy part of afternoon.
20	32½	38½	Cloudy	"	N. W.			Cloudy part of afternoon.
21	18½	29	Clear	"	N. W.			
22	19	35	"	"	S. W.			Cloudy part of evening.
S 23	30	50	Cloudy	"	S. W., N. W.			Clear part of morning, and cloudy part of afternoon.
24	28	41	Clear	"	S. W.			
25	29	47	"	"	S. W.			Cloudy part of morning.
26	30½	45	"	"	N. W.			
27	31	48	Cloudy	"	N. E., S. W.			Clear part of morning.
28	39	60½	"	Cloudy	E., S. W.	0.09		Light rain 7:30 A. M. to 2 P. M. at intervals; steady rain after 7 P. M.
29	45	48½	Rain	Clear	N. W.	0.87		Rain before day, and 7 to 9 A. M.; clear part of A. M.
S 30	29	36½	Clear	"	N. W.			

2 13

December, 1879.

Date.	Thermometer.		Weather.		Prevailing Wind.	Rain and Melted Snow in inches.	Snow in inches.	REMARKS.
	Lowest.	Highest.	Morning.	Afternoon.				
1	24	42	Clear	Clear	S. W.			
2	32½	49	"	"	S. W.			Cloudy part of evening.
3	36	53½	"	Cloudy	S. W.			Foggy A.M.; clear part P. M.
4	46	60	Cloudy	Clear	S. W., N.			Clear part of morning and cloudy part of evening.
5	35	46½	Clear	Cloudy	N. E.,			Cloudy part of morning and clear part of afternoon.
6	41½	58½	Cloudy	Rain	N. E., S. E.	0.87		Light rain at intervals after 6:30 A. M.; heavy showers during ev'g till 10:30 P.M.
S 7	50	55	Clear	Clear	W., S. W.	0.08		Rain before day; cloudy part of evening.
8	42½	52½	C'y m'st all day.		S. W., N. E.			
9	36½	46	Clear	Cloudy	N. E., S. E.			Clouded over 3 P. M.; light rain 10:30 P. M.
10	40	54	Cloudy	"	E., S. E.			Light sprinkles part of ev'g.
11	52	61	"	Rainy	S. W., N. W.	0.24		Light rain at intervals 9 A.M. to 9 P. M.
12	38	41½	"	Clear	N. W., N.			Cleared 9:30 A. M.
13	27	36	Clear	"	N. E., S. E.			
S 14	29	43	Rain	Rain	N. E.	1.41		Heavy rain till 12:30 P. M. and light till 2 P.M.; rest of day after 4 P. M.
15	40½	47½	Cloudy	Clear	S. W., N. W.			Clear part of morning.
16	29½	35	Clear	"	W.			Cloudy part P.M. and even'g.
17	31½	45½	Cloudy	"	S. W., N. W.			Clear part of A. M.; cloudy part of P. M. and evening.
18	23	33	Clear	"	N., S. W.			
19	27	32½	Snow	Cloudy	N. E.	0.17		Snow till 1 P. M. and light snow part of evening.
20	30	39½	Snow } Rain	"	S. W.	0.10		Snow and rain till 7:30 A.M.
S 21	20	22½	Clear	Clear	N. E.			Ther. 20° at 10 A.M.; 22½° at 1 P. M. and falling all day; cloudy 5 P.M.; snow 9½ P.M.
22	11	36	Snow } Rain	Cloudy	N. E.	0.96		Snow & rain till 1 P.M. about 4 in. of snow on ground.
23	32	36	Cloudy	"	S. W., N. E.			Rain 9 P. M.
24	32	40	Rain	"	N. E., S. W.	0.85		Rain till 9 A.M.; light rain part of evening.
25	37	40	"	"	N.	0.37		Rain till noon; snow 7:30 to 9:30 P. M.
26	16	25	Clear	Clear	N. W., S. W.			
27	12	30	Cloudy	"	W., S. W.			C'ar part of morning; cloudy part of evening.
S 28	24	39	Clear	Cloudy	S. W., N. W.			Clear part of afternoon.
29	30½	42	Cloudy	"	N. W., S. W.			Clear part of morning.
30	39	48	"	Clear	S. W., N. W.			Clear part of morning.
31	18½	33	"	Cloudy	N. E., N. W.	0.29		Snow 9:15 to 11:45 A.M.; sleet part P. M.; cleared 11 P.M.
						5.34		

Rain and melted snow for 1879, 43.57 inches.

January, 1880.

Date	Thermometer Lowest	Thermometer Highest	Weather Morning	Weather Afternoon	Prevailing Wind	Rain and Melted Snow in inches	Snow in inches	REMARKS
1	30½	39	Clear	Clear	W.			
2	32	43½	Cloudy	"	S. W.			Clear part of morning and cloudy part of afternoon.
3	35	40	Clear	"	N. E., S. E.			Cloudy evening.
S 4	37	49	"	Cloudy	S. W.			Cloudy part A. M., and clear part of afternoon.
5	39	48	"	"	N. E.			Clear part of afternoon.
6	34½	44	Rain	"	N. E.	0.30		Light rain till 3 P. M., and part of evening.
7	39	45	Clear	Clear	N. E.			Cloudy part A. M. and P. M.
8	31½	44	"	"	N. E.			Cloudy part of morning; cloudy evening.
9	37	41	Misty	Misty	N. E.			
10	39½	52	Clear	Clear	W., N.	0.04		Light rain before day.
S 11	31	47½	"	Cloudy	N. E., E.			Clouded over 3 P. M., misty part of evening.
12	43	51¼	Cloudy	"	S. W., N.			Clear part of morning; rain 6 P. M.
13	23½	31½	Snow	Clear	N. E., N.	0.37		Snow till 11 A. M.; drifted very much.
14	11	30	Clear	"	N. W.			
15	17	36	"	Cloudy	S. W.	0.01		Cloudy part morning; light rain part of evening.
16	24	37	"	"	N. W.			Cloudy part of morning; clouded over 4 P. M.
17	31	36	Cloudy	"	S. W., W.			Foggy morning; partly clear part of afternoon.
S 18	33	45	"	Clear	S. W., N. W.			Cleared 2 P. M.
19	37	50	Clear	"	W., S. W.			Cloudy part of evening.
20	38	47	Cloudy	Cloudy	N. E.	0.07		Light rain part of A.M. and part even'g; cl'red 10 P.M.
21	35	43	Clear	Clear	N. W.			
22	28½	53	Cloudy	Rain	N. E., S. E.	0.61		Partly clear part of morning; rain 12 to 10 P. M.
23	40	46	Clear	Clear	W., N. W.	0.06		Rain before day; cloudy part of evening.
24	36½	44	"	"	S. W., N. W.			Cloudy part of morning.
S 25	29½	43	"	"	S. W.			Cloudy part of afternoon.
26	28½	47	"	"	W., S. E.			
27	35	53½	Misty	Rain	N. E., S. E.	0.64		Rain 11 A. M. to 11:30 P. M.
28	48	61½	Clear	Clear	S. W., N. W.			Cloudy part of morning.
29	34	39	"	"	N., N. E.			
30	22	48	Cloudy	Cloudy	N. E., S.			
31	44	50	Rain	Clear	S. W., N. W.	0.10		Light rain till 10 A. M.; cleared 2:30 P. M.
						2.20		

February, 1880.

Date	Thermometer Lowest	Thermometer Highest	Weather Morning	Weather Afternoon	Prevailing Wind	Rain and Melted Snow in inches	Snow in inches	REMARKS
S 1	32	40	Clear	Clear	S. W., N. W.			
2	10	23	"	"	N., E.			Cl'dy eve'g; bar. 30.34 9 A.M.
3	18	34	Snow Rain	Cloudy	N. E., N. W.	0.22	6.00	Snow till 9 A. M. & then rain to 1 P.M.; snow drifted very much; clear ev'g; bar. 29.13-1 P. M.
4	25	36	Clear	Clear	S. W., W.			Cloudy with snow squall 4:15 P. M.
5	19	30½	"	"	W., S. W.			Cloudy part of evening.
6	26	38	"	"	W.			
7	25½	41	"	"	S.E,S W,NW,			Cloudy part of P. M., with snow squall 4:30 to 4:50 P.M.
S 8	20	35	"	"	S. W.			
9	27	35	"	"	N. W.			
10	9	30	Cloudy	Cloudy	N. E.			Clear part of morning and part of evening.
11	24	41	Clear	Clear	N. W., S. E.			Cloudy part of P.M. and ev'g.
12	33	53	Rain	Cloudy	S. W.	0.12		Light rain till 6:30 A. M.; partly clear part of P.M.
13	44	60	"	"	N.E., S.,N.W.	0.88		Rain till 8:30 A. M.; partly clear part of afternoon; rain 6:30 to 11:45 P. M.
14	46	50	Clear	Clear	N. W.			Cloudy part of morning.
S 15	32	36½	Cloudy	Cloudy	N. E., N. W.	0.06		Snow 10:15 A. M. to 4 P. M.; clear part of evening.
16	32	47	Clear	Clear	W., S. W.			
17	32	56	"	"	S. W.			
18	40	64	Cloudy	Cloudy	S. W.	0.33		Clear part A.M. and part P.M.; rain 4 to 10:30 P. M. at intervals.
19	35	39½	Clear	Clear	N. W.			
20	22	34	"	"	N. W., W.			
21	26	38	Cloudy	"	S. W.	0.09		Snow 10:20 A. M. till 1:30 P.M.; cleared 2 P. M.
S 22	29½	43	Clear	"	W., S. W.			Cloudy evening.
23	37	47	Cloudy	"	W., N. W.	0.04		Light rain 7 to 7:30 A. M.; clear part of morning and cloudy part of afternoon.
24	26	41	Clear	"	N. W.			
25	31	47	C'y m'st all day	S. E.				
26	40	53½	Cloudy	Cloudy	All points.	0.08		Light rain part of evening; cleared 9:30 P. M.
27	38	63	Clear	Clear	S. W.			
28	43½	58	Cloudy	Rain	S. E			Rain after 4:30 P. M.
S 29	48	65	"	Cloudy	S. W., N. W.	0.21		Rain before day; clear part of afternoon.
						2.03	6.00	
								No ice crop gathered here this winter.

By Mr. Whitehead's (Newark) record this has been the warmest winter in 36 years.

Weather Record for New Brunswick, N. J.

March, 1880.

Date.	Lowest.	Highest.	Weather. Morning.	Afternoon.	Prevailing Wind.	Rain and Melted Snow in inches.	Snow in inches.	REMARKS.
1	39	46½	Cloudy	Clear	N. W.			Cleared 8 A. M.
2	32	45	Clear	"	W., S. W.			
3	33	52½	"	Cloudy	S. W.	0.18		Rain 4:45 to 10 P. M.
4	44	66	Cloudy	Clear	S. W., N. W.			Clear part of morning.
5	51½	71	Rain	"	S. W.	0.22		Rain till 6:30 A. M., and 7:45 to 8:30 A. M.; clear part of morning.
6	43	49½	Clear	"	N. W.			Telephone put in my house.
S 7	36	40½	Cloudy	Rain	N. E., S. E.	0.34		Rain 12:15 P. M. to 10 P. M.
8	35½	42	Clear	Clear	N. W.			Cloudy part of morning.
9	23	29	Cloudy	Cloudy	N. E.	0.10		Snow 10:20 A.M. to 3:45 P.M.
10	28	44	"	Clear	N. W.			Clear part of morning.
11	22½	26	Snow	Cloudy	N. E.		3.00	Snow till 4:30 P. M.
12	23	35	Cloudy	"	N. W.			
13	24	31	"	"	N. E.			Snow squalls part of afternoon and evening.
S 14	28	39	"	"	N. E., S., W.	0.10		Light snow before day, and light rain part of morning; clear part of evening.
15	33	40	"	"	N.E.,S., N.W.			Partly clear part of morning; rainy after 7:45 P.M.
16	32½	39	Rain	"	N. E., N. W.	0.87		Rain till 1:30 P.M.; clear part of evening.
17	34½	42	Clear	Clear	N. W.			
18	28	40	"	"	All points.			Cloudy evening.
19	34	40	Cloudy	Snow	N. E.	1.21		Rain 8:30 A. M. to 1 P. M., and then snow till 9:30 P. M.
20	33	48	"	Clear	S. W.	0.05		Cleared 7:30 A. M.; cloudy part of evening with rain 8:30 to 9:30 P. M.
S 21	32	44	Clear	"	N. W.			
22	32	54	"	"	S. W., N. W.			Cloudy part of afternoon.
23	34	55½	"	"	S. W.	0.05		Cloudy part of evening with shower 8:15 P. M.
24	34	38	"	"	N. W.			
25	18½	38	"	"	N. W.			
26	26	47	"	"	N. W., S. W.			Cloudy part of evening.
27	37	47	Rain	Rain	S. W., N. E.	1.23		Rain till 11 P. M.
S 28	30½	38½	Cloudy	Cloudy	N. E.	0.13		Rain before day, and mist and rain 9:30 A. M. to 2 P. M.; snow after 6:15 P. M.
29	30	39	"	"	N. E.	0.09		Snow before day and part of morning.
30	34	47	Clear	Clear	N.			
31	33½	54	"	"	N.			

4.57 3.00

April, 1880.

Date.	Thermometer. Lowest.	Highest.	Weather. Morning.	Afternoon.	Prevailing Wind.	Rain and Melted Snow in inches.	Snow in inches.	REMARKS.
1	37½	59	Clear	Clear	N. W., W.			
2	38	61	"	"	N. E., S.			Cloudy evening.
3	51	66½	Cloudy	Cloudy	S. W., S.	0.36		Shower 2 P.M., and showers 4:30 to 9 P.M.
S 4	54	64	C'y m'st all day.		S. W.	0.30		Rain 2 to 3 P.M., and shower 8 P.M.
5	53	69	Clear	Clear	S. W., N. W.			Cloudy part of afternoon, with sprinkle; Ed. Waldron died at Macon, Ga.
6	45	58	Cloudy	"	NW,SW,NW	0.03		Clear part of morning and cloudy part of afternoon, with shower 3:45 P. M.
7	37	44	Clear	"	N. W.			
8	31	45	"	"	N. W., W.			
9	32	50	"	"	S. W.			
10	37	63	"	"	S. W.			
S 11	40	45½	"	"	N. W.			
12	28½	45	"	"	W.			
13	34	61½	"	"	S. W.			
14	48	75	"	"	S. W.			
15	52½	78	"	Cloudy	S. W.			Clouded over 3 P. M.
16	57	61½	C'y m'st all day		N. E., E.	0.05		Rain before day.
17	47	56	"	"	S. E., N. W.	0.12		Rain before day with lightning.
S 18	41½	59½	Clear	Clear	All points.			Cherries flowered.
19	41	57	Cloudy	Cloudy	S. E.			Misty rain 9 to 10 A. M.; clear part of afternoon.
20	55	60	"	Clear	N. W., S. W.	0.08		Light rain before day and 11 A.M. to 1 P. M.; cleared 3 P. M.
21	39½	66½	Clear	"	N. W., S.			
22	44	68	"	"	S. W.			
23	47½	53	C'y m'st all day		N. E., S. E.			Snow and rain 11 P. M
24	40	45	Cloudy	Cloudy	N. E., E.	0.26		Rain before day; misty part of evening.
S 25	41	52	"	"	N. E., S. E.			Clear part of morning; misty evening.
26	44	60	"	"	S. E., S. W.	0.05		Rain before day and 8 to 9 A.M.; foggy A. M.; clear part of evening.
27	50	60	Clear	Clear	N. W.			Cloudy part of P.M. & ev'g.
28	44	62	"	"	N. W., S. W.			
29	47	60	"	Rain	S. W., S.			Clouded over 8 A. M.; rain 3:30 P. M.
30	54	59	"	Clear	N. W.	1.11		Rain before day; cloudy part of afternoon and evening.

2.36

My pear trees failed to put forth any flowers.

May, 1880.

Date	Thermometer. Lowest.	Thermometer. Highest.	Weather. Morning.	Weather. Afternoon.	Prevailing Wind.	Rain and Melted Snow in inches.	Snow in inches.	REMARKS.
1	37	54	Clear	Clear	N. W., S. W.			Cloudy part of evening; frost and ice.
S 2	47	67½	"	"	S. W.			Cloudy part A. M. and P. M.
3	53	76	"	"	S. W.			
4	55	76½	"	"	S. W.			
5	53	68½	"	Cloudy	N. E., E.			Cloudy part of morning; clear evening.
6	54	81	"	Clear	S. W., N. W.			Hazy part of afternoon.
7	55	65	"	"	N. E., S. E.			N. Y. Coaching Club with "Pioneer," to Jobstown; cloudy part of morning.
8	51	70	"	"	N. E., S. E.			Cloudy part A. M. and eve'g.
S 9	57	82	Cloudy	"	S. E., S. W.			Foggy A. M.; clear part A. M.
10	64	85½	Clear	"	S. W.			
11	66	81½	C'y m'st all day		S. W., N. W.			
12	62	73	Clear	Clear	N. W.			Sun obscured by smoke during afternoon.
13	52½	60	"	"	N. W.			Cloudy part of afternoon.
14	48	56½	C'y m'st all day		N. E.			
15	42½	64½	Clear	Clear	N. E., N.			Cloudy part of evening.
S 16	49	74	"	"	N. W., S. W.			Sun obscured by smoke part of afternoon.
17	60	81	"	"	S. W., W.			Sun obscured by smoke part of afternoon.
18	61	70½	"	Cloudy	N. E., E.			Clouded over 4 P. M.; sprinkle 6:30 P. M.
19	54	62½	Cloudy	"	E.			
20	57	83	"	Clear	E., S. W.			Cleared 10 A. M.
21	64	84	Clear	"	S. W.			
22	64	79	"	Cloudy	S. W.			Clear part of afternoon.
S 23	66	79	C'y m'st all day		S. W.			Sprinkle before day and 6 P. M.
24	68	83	Cloudy	Clear	S. W.			Cleared 8 A. M.
25	69	90	Clear	"	S. W., W.			Hottest day in May in my records.
26	72	91	"	"	N. W., E., S. W.			Cloudy part of evening.
27	73	92	"	"	W., S. W.			
28	73	88	"	Cloudy	S. W., N. W.			Sprinkle 4 P. M.
29	60	75	"	"	N. E., S. E.			Clouded over 4 P. M.
S 30	61½	74	Cloudy	"	S. E., S. W.	0.19		Rain till 6:40 A. M. and showers 4 and 10 P. M.; clear part of evening.
31	67	76	Clear	Clear	N. W.	0.48		Rain before day; cloudy part of morning.
						0.67		

The smallest rain fall for any month in my records except October, 1870, (0.27) and September, 1867, (0.44).

June, 1880.

Date	Thermometer Lowest	Thermometer Highest	Weather Morning	Weather Afternoon	Prevailing Wind	Rain and Melted Snow in inches	Snow in inches	REMARKS
1	64	83½	Clear	Cloudy	S. W., N. E.			
2	48½	62	Rain	"	N. E.	0.32		Rain till 7:45 A. M.; clear part of evening.
3	53	70	Clear	Clear	N.E., S., S.W.	0.02		Cloudy part of afternoon, with rain 5:30.
4	54	72	"	"	All points.			
5	59	75½	"	Cloudy	S.			Clouded over 3 P. M.
S 6	63	79	Cloudy	Clear	S. W.			Sprinkle 6 A. M.; clear part of morning and cloudy part of evening.
7	66	83½	Clear	"	S. W., W.			
8	63½	69	"	Cloudy	N. E.			
9	57	69	Cloudy	"	N. E., S. E.			Clear part of evening.
10	57	73	Clear	"	S. W., S.			
11	63	79	Cloudy	Clear	S. W.			
12	71	89½	Clear	Cloudy	N. W., S. W.	0.10		Clear part of afternoon and evening; shower 8:20 P.M.
S 13	72	86½	"	Clear	N. W., W.	0.70		Cloudy part of morning, and afternoon with shower 4:55 to 5:10 with gale.
14	67	75½	"	"	N. W., N.			Cloudy part evening.
15	63	66	Cloudy	Rain	E., S. E., N. E.	0.69		Rain 6:15 to 7:15 A. M., and 11:30 A. M. to 9:30 P. M.
16	58	73½	Clear	Clear	N. E., S. E.			
17	57	78	"	"	N. E., S. E.			
18	59	80	"	"	All points.			
19	58	81	"	"	All points.			
S 20	63	84½	"	"	S. W., N. W.			
21	66½	86	"	Cloudy	N. W., S. W.			Clouded over 3 P. M.; sprinkle 5:15 P. M.
22	68½	78	Cloudy	"	N. W., N.	0.02		Light rain before day; partly clear part of afternoon.
23	64	82½	Clear	Clear	N. W., S. W.			
24	69	90	"	"	N. W.			
25	73	90½	"	Cloudy	N. W., S. W.			Cloudy part of morning, and clear part of afternoon.
26	76	90	"	"	N. W.			Clear part of afternoon.
S 27	72	88	"	Clear	S. E.			
28	74	90½	"	"	S. W.			
29	74	86	"	"	N. W., S. W.			Cloudy part of afternoon.
30	74½	84	"	"	N. W., S. W.			

1.85

July, 1880.

Date.	Thermometer. Lowest.	Thermometer. Highest.	Weather. Morning.	Weather. Afternoon.	Prevailing Wind.	Rain and Melted Snow in inches.	Snow in inches.	REMARKS.
1	66	86	Clear	Cloudy	S. W.			Clouded over 3 P. M.; sprinkles after 5 P. M.
2	66½	78½	Cloudy	Clear	All points	0.42		Rain before day; cloudy part P.M.; shower 10 P.M.
3	66½	79½	Clear	"	N.			
S 4	64	82	"	"	N., S.			
5	67½	82	"	Cloudy	S. W.			Rain 2:50 to 7:30 P.M. (1.66) clear part of evening; rain again 10:30 P. M.
6	68½	80	C'y m'st all day		All points	2.98		Rain before day (1.30;) light rain 3:30 P. M. (0.02.)
7	70	84	Clear	Clear	N. E.			
8	69	85½	"	"	S. W.			
9	71	87½	"	"	S. W.			Cloudy part of A.M. and P.M.
10	75	88	"	"	SW, N W, W.	0.17		Cloudy part of evening with shower 10 P. M.
S 11	73	85	"	Cloudy	All points	0.03		Clear part of afternoon and evening; showers 4:15 and 6:15 P. M.
12	68	83½	"	Clear	N. E., S. E.	0.11		Cloudy &rainy after 8:20 P.M.
13	73½	89	"	"	S. W., N. W.			Cloudy before day.
14	71	85½	"	"	All points			
15	70	78½	C'y m'st all day		S. W.	0.40		Rain 7 to 9 A. M.
16	72	84	"	"	S. W.			Sprinkle 7 P. M
17	69	83	Clear	Clear	NW,SW,NW			
S 18	66½	81½	"	"	All points			
19	66	82½	"	"	S. E.			
20	68½	76	C'y m'st all day		S. E.	2.02		Rain 5 to 7:15 A. M. (0.75,) and part of morning (0.07) and 7:35 to 9:30 P.M.(1.20) 1 inch in 15 minutes.
21	66	74	Clear	Cloudy	All points.	0.02		Clouded over 9 A. M.; rain 9:30 to 10:30 A. M.; clear part of evening.
22	67	71	Cloudy	Rain	N. W., N. E.	2.38		Light rain before day and part of morning (0.02;) heavy rain 1 to 9P.M.(2.36)
23	60	72	"	Cloudy	NW,S.W,S.E.			Clear part of afternoon.
24	67	78	"	Clear	S. W.	0.01		Light rain before day; clear part A.M. and part P.M.
S 25	68½	82	Clear	"	S. W., S.			Cloudy evening.
26	69	84	Cloudy	"	S. W.			Cleared 9 A. M.; cloudy evening with sprinkles.
27	69	82½	Clear	"	All points.	0.29		Cloudy part of afternoon with showers 3 to 3:15 (0.26,) and 3.55 to 4 P. M. (0.03.)
28	63	75	"	"	N. E., N. W.			
29	60	74½	"	"	N. W.			
30	59	76½	"	"	N. W.			
31	62	80	"	"	S. W.			
						8.83		

August, 1880.

	Date.	Thermometer. Lowest.	Thermometer. Highest.	Weather. Morning.	Weather. Afternoon.	Prevailing Wind.	Rain and Melted Snow in inches.	Snow in inches.	REMARKS.
S	1	65½	83½	Clear	Clear	S. W.	----	----	
	2	67½	85	"	"	S. W.	----	----	Cloudy part of evening.
	3	71½	73½	Cloudy	Cloudy	N. W., N. E.	0.39	----	Showers 11 A.M. to 4:15 P.M.; partly clear part evening.
	4	65½	74½	"	"	SW, NW, NE.	0.52	----	Rain before day and 7 A.M., and 12:30 to 2 P. M.
	5	64	74	C'y m'st all day		N. E., S.	0.22	----	Rain before day.
	6	62½	75	" "	" "	N. E., S. E.	----	----	
	7	61	78½	Clear	Clear	N. W., N. E., S.	----	----	
S	8	63	80	"	"	S. W.	----	----	
	9	66	81½	"	"	S. W.	----	----	
	10	68	84½	"	"	S. W., S. E.	----	----	Cloudy part of morning; cloudy evening.
	11	71	80½	C'y m'st all day.		All points.	0.82	----	Shower 1:50 P. M. (0.04); shower 7:35 to 9:15 P.M. (0.78), greater part in 10 minutes.
	12	65½	76	Clear	Clear	N. E., S. E.	----	----	Cloudy part of afternoon.
	13	63	80½	"	"	N. W., S. W.	----	----	
	14	64½	78	"	Cloudy	S. W., N. W.	0.03	----	Cloudy part of A.M.; shower 5:45 P.M. (0.03); clear part of evening.
S	15	66	75	"	Clear	N. W., N.	----	----	
	16	53	70	"	"	All points.	----	----	
	17	54	73	"	"	S. W.	----	----	
	18	56	74	"	"	S. W., S.	----	----	Cloudy part of afternoon.
	19	64½	76½	C'y m'st all day.		S. W.	----	----	
	20	69	80½	Clear	Clear	S. W.	----	----	Cloudy part of morning.
	21	71½	85	"	"	S. W., W.	0.35	----	Shower 5:40 to 6 A.M.; cloudy part of A. M. and evening.
S	22	70	81	"	"	N. E., S. E.	----	----	
	23	68	84	"	"	N. E., S. E.	----	----	Cloudy part of afternoon.
	24	72½	84½	"	"	S. W.	----	----	Foggy morning.
	25	75	88	"	Cloudy	S. W., N. E.	1.58	----	Shower 2 to 3:15 P.M. (1.58), mostly in 30 minutes.
	26	60	68½	Cloudy	Clear	N. E., S. E.	----	----	Cloudy part of afternoon.
	27	59	71½	Clear	"	N. E., S. E.	----	----	Cloudy part of morning.
	28	63½	79	Cloudy	"	S. W.	----	----	Clear part of morning.
S	29	70	85	Clear	Cloudy	S. W., N. W.	0.14	----	Cloudy part of A.M. and clear part of afternoon; shower 5:15 to 7 P. M.
	30	62	66	Cloudy	"	N. E.	0.03	----	Rain before day (0.02), and 11.30 to 1 P. M. (0.01).
	31	59	71	"	Clear	N. E., S. E.	----	----	Clear part of morning and cloudy part of evening.
							4.08	----	

Weather Record for New Brunswick, N. J.

September, 1880.

Date.	Thermometer. Lowest.	Thermometer. Highest.	Weather. Morning.	Weather. Afternoon.	Prevailing Wind.	Rain and Melted Snow in inches.	Snow in inches.	REMARKS.
1	61	73½	Clear	Clear	E., S. E.			Cloudy part of morning.
2	64	78½	Cloudy	"	S. E., S. W.			Clear 9 A. M.
3	67	82	"	"	S. W., S.			Clear part of morning.
4	72	87	"	"	S. W.			Clear part of morning.
S 5	73½	87½	Clear	"	S. W.			Cloudy part of afternoon.
6	73	85	C'y m'st all day.		S. W.	0.11		Shower 7:15 to 8 A. M.
7	66	70	Cloudy	Cloudy	N. E., S.	0.16		Rain before day (0.02) and 8:30 to 11:30 A. M. (0.14.)
8	50½	62½	"	"	N. E.			
9	56	60½	"	Rain	N. E.	0.01		Rain part of morning (0.01); rain after 12:30 P. M.
10	55	66	"	Clear	N. W.	1.05		Rain before day (1.04) and 7 to 8:30 A. M. (0.01); cloudy part of afternoon.
11	53	71	Clear	"	N. W., S. W.			
S 12	53	73½	"	"	S. W.			
13	58	75	"	Cloudy	S. W., N. W.			Rain 6:30 P. M.
14	57	69	"	Clear	N. W.	0.45		Rain before day.
15	53	66	"	"	N. W.			Cloudy part of morning and part of afternoon.
16	55	71	"	"	N. W., S. W.			
17	58	76	"	"	S. W.			Cloudy part of morning.
18	62	82	"	"	S. W.			Saw 4 mile heats at Sheepshead Bay; Ferida wins 7.23½—7.41 best on record (Glenmore & Irish King.)
S 19	63	75½	"	"	N. E., S. E.			Cloudy evening.
20	65¼	78¼	Cloudy	Cloudy	S. E.			Clear part of afternoon.
21	65½	75	"	Clear	N. W., S. W.	0.01		Clear part of morning; rain before day.
22	55	69	Clear	"	W., N. W.			
23	50	65	"	"	N. W., S. W.			
24	47½	68½	"	"	N. E., S.			
25	58	70	Cloudy	"	S. W., S. E.			Clear part of morning.
S 26	54	73	Clear	"	N. E., S. E.			Cloudy 10:15 P. M.
27	65	76	C'y m'st all day.		S. W.			
28	67	73	Cloudy	Clear	S. W., N. W.	0.02		Partly clear part of morn'g; rain 10:15 to 11:15 A. M. (0.02); cleared 5:15 P. M.
29	52	68½	Clear	"	S. W., W.			
30	50	62½	"	"	W.			
						1.81		

October, 1880.

Date.	Thermometer. Lowest.	Thermometer. Highest.	Weather. Morning.	Weather. Afternoon.	Prevailing Wind.	Rain and Melted Snow in inches.	Snow in inches.	REMARKS.
1	42½	60½	Clear	Clear	N. W., S. W.	----	----	Frost.
2	45	65	"	"	N. E, S E.	----	----	Frost.
S 3	47	70	"	"	N. E., S.	----	----	
4	55½	75½	Cloudy	"	S. W.	0.25	----	Clear part of A. M.; cloudy evening with rain 6:35 to 8 P. M. and 11:30 P. M.
5	53	60	Rain	Cloudy	N. E., S	0.42	----	Rain till 10:15 A. M.; partly clear part of afternoon; clear evening.
6	54½	68	Clear	Clear	S. W., N. W.	----	----	Cloudy part of morning.
7	46	62	"	"	W., N. W.	----	----	
8	41	60	"	"	N. E., S. E.	----	----	
9	44	64	"	"	N. E, S. E.	----	----	
S 10	45½	68	"	"	All points.	----	----	Foggy morning.
11	47½	73	"	"	S. W.	----	----	
12	57	75	"	"	S. W., N. W.	----	----	Cloudy part of afternoon.
13	47½	60½	"	"	N.	----	----	
14	42	62	"	"	N. E., S. W.	----	----	
15	46	68	"	"	S. W.	----	----	Cloudy part of morning.
16	52	76½	"	"	S. E., S. W.	----	----	Cloudy part of morning.
S 17	65	70	"	Cloudy	S. W., N. W.	0.12	----	Cloudy part of morn'g; light rain at intervals 11 A. M. to 6:30 P.M.; clear'd 7 P.M.
18	40	52½	"	Clear	S. W., N. W.	----	----	
19	33½	51	"	"	W.	----	----	Cloudy evening.
20	41	52½	"	"	N. W., S. W.	0.02	----	Light rain before day.
21	38	63	"	Cloudy	N. E., S.	----	----	
22	53	57½	Rain	Rain	S. E., N. E.	0.50	----	Rain 5:30 A. M. to 6:15 P. M.
23	52½	56½	Cloudy	Cloudy	S. W., N. W.	0.03	----	Rain before day and 8 to 9 A.M. (0.03); clear part ev'g.
S 24	42	50½	Clear	Clear	W., N. W.	----	----	
25	38	50½	"	"	W., N. W.	----	----	
26	35	57½	"	Cloudy	S. E., S. W.	0.04	----	Cloudy part of morn'g; rain at intervals 4 to 8 P. M.; clear part of evening.
27	49	56½	"	Clear	N. W.	----	----	
28	37	43½	Cloudy	Cloudy	N. E., S. E.	0.02	----	Hail and rain 8:30 A.M. (0.02); sprinkles part of aft'noon.
29	42	46½	"	Misty Rain	N. E.	0.06	----	Misty rain 11:30 A.M. to 8 P.M.
30	44½	61½	Rain	Rain	N. E., S. E.	----	----	Rain 7 A. M. to noon and 2 P. M. rest of day.
S 31	51	55	Cloudy	Clear	N. W.	0.64	----	Rain till 6:30 A. M.; clear part of morning.
						2.10	---	

WEATHER RECORD FOR NEW BRUNSWICK, N. J.

November, 1880.

Date.	Lowest.	Highest.	Weather. Morning.	Weather. Afternoon.	Previling Wind.	Rain and Melted Snow in inches.	Snow in inches.	REMARKS.
1	38	53	Clear	Clear	W., S. W.			Cloudy part of evening with sprinkle 8:30.
2	38½	52	"	"	N. W.			
3	36	56	"	"	N. E., S. E.			Cloudy part of evening.
4	45	57	Cloudy	Cloudy	N. E., S. E.			Sprinkles P.M. and evening.
5	54	62½	Rain	"	S. E., S. W.	0.47		Rain 5:45 A. M. till noon (0.47); clear evening.
6	53½	68	Cloudy	"	S. E.	0.11		Foggy A. M.; rain part eve'g.
S 7	45½	51½	Clear	Clear	N. W.	0.09		Rain before day.
8	36	52½	"	"	N. W., S. W.			
9	42	58	"	"	S. W.			
10	39½	58½	"	Cloudy	All points.			Cloudy 3 P. M.
11	52	64½	Rain	Clear	S. E., W.	0.81		Rain till 9 A.M.; heavy rain before day.
12	45	57	Clear	"	S. W., N. W.			
13	39½	45	Cloudy	Cloudy	W.			
S 14	36½	43½	"	"	N. W.			Partly clear at noon and part of evening.
15	35½	42½	"	Clear	N. W.			Cloudy part of evening.
16	32	47	Clear	"	S. W.			
17	33	48	Cloudy	Cloudy	N. E., E.			Clear part of afternoon.
18	40	48½	"	"	S. W., N. W.	0.03		Foggy A. M.; cleared 5:30 P. M.; rain 12:30 to 2 P. M.
19	25	34½	Clear	Clear	N.W., E., S.E.			Cloudy part of evening.
20	29	40	Cloudy	Rain	N. E., N. W.	0.23		Rain noon to 5 P.M.; cleared 5:30 P. M.
S 21	27	33	Clear	Clear	N. W., S. W.			Cloudy part of morning.
22	16	27½	"	"	W., N. W.			River frozen over this A. M.
23	16	30	"	"	N. W.			
24	16	30½	"	Cloudy	All points			Snow 10 P. M.
25	27	33	Snow	"	N. W.		3.00	Snow till 10 A.M., 1 in., and 1:15 to 5 P. M., 2 in.; clear part of evening.
26	14	26	Clear	"	N. E.		1.00	Snow 5:30 P.M. to 9 P. M. at intervals.
27	21	32	Cloudy	Clear	N., W.			
S 28	19½	34	"	Rain	N. E.	0.31		Rain 10:30 A. M. to 7 P. M.
29	32	41	"	Cloudy	S. W., N. W.			Clear part of evening.
30	29	36	Clear	Clear	N. W., W.			Cloudy 10 P. M.

2.05 4.00

December, 1880.

Date.	Thermometer. Lowest.	Thermometer. Highest.	Weather. Morning.	Weather. Afternoon.	Prevailing Wind.	Rain and Melted Snow in inches.	Snow in inches.	REMARKS.
1	27	40	{ Snow Rain	Cloudy	N. E., N. W.	0.64	----	Snow and rain till 11:45 A. M. (0.64;) clear part P.M.
2	35	41	Clear	Clear	S. W., N. W.	----	----	Cloudy part of afternoon.
3	34½	40½	"	"	N. W.	----	----	Cloudy part of evening.
4	30½	40	"	"	N. W., S. W.	----	----	Cloudy part of evening.
S 5	34	47	Rain	Cloudy	All points.	1.00	----	Rain till 1:30 P. M.; misty evening.
6	38	44	Cloudy	"	S. W., N.	----	----	Clear evening.
7	27½	30½	Clear	Clear	W., N. W.	----	----	
8	18½	30	Cloudy	"	W., SW., NW.	0.02	----	Snow 7:30 to 9:30 A.M.(0.02;) cleared 3 P.M.
9	16	24½	Clear	"	N. W., W.	----	----	
10	13	15	"	"	N. W.	----	----	Coldest 10 A. M.
11	11	24	"	Cloudy	N. W., W.	----	----	Clear evening.
S 12	21	38½	C'y m'st all day	S. W.		----	----	
13	33½	40½	Cloudy	Clear	S. W.	0.10	----	Snow and rain before day; cleared 4 P. M.
14	33	42½	C'y m'st all day	S. W., S. E.		0.06	----	Rain 5:30 P.M. till 7 P.M.
15	35	41½	Clear	Cloudy	S. W.	----	----	Cloudy part of A. M., and clear part of afternoon; snow squalls 1:20 P.M.
16	35½	40	Cloudy	Clear	S. W., N. W.	----	----	Clear part of A.M., and cleared 3 P. M.
17	25	34	Clear	"	N. W.	----	----	
18	27	34	"	"	N. W.	----	----	Cloudy part A. M. and P. M.
S 19	22	36½	"	"	N. W.	----	----	
20	24	32	Cloudy	Cloudy	N. E.	----	----	Light snow after 8:30 P. M.
21	28	34	Snow	"	N. E.	2.00		Snow till 10 A. M., drifted, and 3 to 4:15 P. M.
22	23½	35½	Clear	Clear	N.	----	----	
23	19½	36	"	"	N. W., S. W.	----	----	Cloudy part of afternoon.
24	26	30	Cloudy	Cloudy	N. E.	1.00		Snow at intervals after 8:45 A. M. till midnight.
25	28	35	Misty	"	N. E.	----	----	
S 26	30	34	Snow	Snow	N. E.	6.00		Snow till 4:15 P. M. (4 in.,) and after 8:30 P. M.
27	29	36	Cloudy	Cloudy	N. W., W.	----	----	Snow before day.
28	17	20	"	"	N. W., W.	----	----	Light snow before day; clear part of morning; snow 9 P. M.
29	14	16½	Snow	Snow	N. W.		6.00	Snow till 9 P.M.; cleared 10 P. M.
30	-3½	6	Clear	Clear	W.	----	----	
31	0	11	"	"	W., S. W.	----	----	
						1.82	15.00	

Rain and melted snow for 1880—37.17 inches; smallest in my records.

WEATHER RECORD FOR NEW BRUNSWICK, N. J.

January, 1881.

Date.	Thermometer. Lowest.	Thermometer. Highest.	Weather. Morning.	Weather. Afternoon.	Prevailing Wind.	Rain and Melted Snow in inches.	Snow in inches.	REMARKS.
1	-6½	15	Clear	Clear	S. W.			Dec. 30, 31, 1880, and Jan. 1, 1881, coldest "spell" I ever knew.
S 2	9	24	Cloudy	"	N. W., S. W.			
3	13½	34	Clear	"	S. W.			Cloudy part of morning.
4	19	29	Cloudy	Snow	N. E., E.			Snow 11:45 A. M. to 2 P. M., and remainder of day after 4 P. M.
5	25	34	"	Cloudy	N. E.		8.00	Snow before day; rain 7:40 P. M.
6	31½	37	Rain	"	NE,NW,SW.	0.90		Rain till 9 A.M.; clear part of evening.
7	29	39	Clear	Clear	S. W., W.			
8	17½	28	"	Cloudy	W., S. W.			Clear evening.
S 9	14	24	Cloudy	Snow Rain	N. E.		3.50	Snow 10:40 A. M. to 5 P. M., and then rain.
10	22	39	Rain	Cloudy	N. E., N. W.	2.42		Rain till 8:30 A. M. (2.40), and 9 to 10 A. M. (0.02); clear part P.M. and eve'g.
11	25	28	Cloudy	"	N. E.		0.50	Snow 8:30 to 10:30 P. M.
12	19	26½	Clear	Clear	N. W., S. W.			
13	17	38	"	"	S. W.			Cloudy part of A. M. & P. M.
14	34½	38½	Rain	Cloudy	S. W., N. W.	0.32		Rain 6 to 11:45 A.M. (0.27), and then snow till 1:30 P. M. (0.05); clear evening.
15	11	19	Clear	"	N. W., N.			Clear part of afternoon.
S 16	12	20½	C'y m'st all day		N. E., N. W.			
17	23	38	Cloudy	Clear	N. W., N.			Clear part of morning.
18	21	30	Clear	"	N. W., W.			Cloudy evening.
19	24½	33	Cloudy	"	N. W., S. W.			
20	19	34	Clear	"	N. W., N. E			Cloudy evening after 9.
21	25	35½	Rain	Rain	N. E., S. W.	1.23	0.50	Rain (freezing as it fell) till 3 P.M. and at intervals rest of day till 10:30 and then snow till 11:30 P. M.; bar. 29.30.
22	31	38	Cloudy	Cloudy	S. W., N. W.			Partly clear part P. M. and clear part of evening.
S 23	30	33	Clear	Clear	W., N. W.			Cloudy part of morning and part of afternoon, with snow flurries.
24	22	28	"	"	N. W., W.			
25	15	24	"	"	N. W., W.			
26	17½	30½	"	"	W., S. W.			Cloudy part of evening; snow squall 10:30 P. M.
27	15	21	"	"	N. W.			
28	12	24½	"	"	N. W.			Cloudy part of afternoon.
29	16	26	"	"	W.			Cloudy part of morning.
S 30	18½	30	Snow	Cloudy	S.E.,N.E., W.		1.00	Snow till 10 A. M.
31	25	30½	Cloudy	"	N., W.			Clear part of evening.
						4.87	13.50	

February, 1881.

Date.	Thermometer. Lowest.	Thermometer. Highest.	Weather. Morning.	Weather. Afternoon.	Prevailing Wind.	Rain and Melted Snow in inches.	Snow in inches.	REMARKS.
1	10	13	Snow	Snow	N. E.		4.00	Snow till 11:45 A.M. and rest of day after 1:30 P. M. (drift'g badly) till 11¼ P.M.
2	0	14	Clear	Clear	N. W.			
3	5½	21	"	"	N. W.			
4	11	26	"	"	N. W.			Cloudy part of morning.
5	11½	30½	"	"	N. W.			
S 6	18	31½	"	"	N. E.			Cloudy part of morning.
7	14	34	"	"	N. E., N. W.			
8	20	36	C'y m'st all day.		N. E., E.			44 days sleighing.
9	31	41½	Cloudy	Cloudy	N. E., E.			
10	38	48½	Rain	Foggy	S. E., S. W.	0.36		Foggy morning; rain 6:30 A. M. to 12:15 P. M.
11	34	47	Clear	Clear	N. W., S. W.	0.04		Rain before day; cloudy part of evening.
12	37	53½	Rain	Foggy	S. E., S. W.	0.85		Rain 6 to 11 A.M. (0.80) with thunder and lightning; shower 11:50 A.M. (0.03); 5 P.M. (0.02); clear part of evening.
S 13	29	35	Clear	Clear	W.			Cloudy part A.M. & part ev'g.
14	23½	31	"	"	N. W.			Cloudy part of morning.
15	22½	34	"	"	N. W., S. E.			Cloudy part of evening.
16	27	40½	Snow	"	N.E.,S.W.,W.		3.00	Snow till 6:30 A. M.; cloudy part of P. M. with snow squall 5:20 P.M.
17	26	37	Clear	"	N. W., W.			
18	27	42	Cloudy	Cloudy	All points			Clear part P.M ; rain 6:30 PM.
19	35½	42	Rain	Clear	N. E., N. W	1.53		Rain till 7 A. M.
S 20	25	34½	Clear	Cloudy	N E., E.			Clouded over 4 P. M.; partly clear part of evening.
21	31	40½	Rain } Snow }	Clear	N. E., N. W.	0.20		Rain and sleet till 8:45 A M. and then snow till noon; cloudy part of afternoon.
22	31½	42	Clear	"	N. W , S. W			Cloudy part of evening.
23	34½	40	"	"	S. W., N. W.	0.08		Clouded over 7:30 A.M.; rain & snow 8:10 to 10:30 A.M.; cloudy part of afternoon.
24	11	22	"	"	N. W.			Cloudy evening.
25	18	32½	Snow	"	N. W.		2.00	Snow till 9 A. M.; clear part of morning.
26	15	30	Clear	"	N. E., S. E.			Partly cloudy part of morning; cloudy evening.
S 27	27	40	Cloudy	Cloudy	N. E., S. E.			Rain 7 P. M.
28	35	53	Foggy	"	S. W.	1.15		Rain before day (0.75) and from 3:15 to 6 P.M. (0.40), with thunder and light'g.
						4.21	9.00	

Weather Record for New Brunswick, N. J.

March, 1881.

Date	Thermometer Lowest	Thermometer Highest	Weather Morning	Weather Afternoon	Prevailing Wind	Rain and Melted Snow in inches	Snow in inches	REMARKS
1	32	34	Cloudy	Snow	W., N. W.	0.19		Rain and snow before day, and snow 10 A.M. till 6 P.M.
2	24	32	"	Cloudy	N. W.			Clear part of afternoon.
3	27	39	Clear	"	N. E., S. E.			Misty part of evening.
4	33	41	Snow } Rain }	"	N. E.,S.,S. W.	0.66		Snow before day, and rain till 11 A.M.; clear part of evening.
5	29	38	Clear	Clear	S. W.			
S 6	30	43	"	"	N. W.			
7	35	50	"	"	N. W.			
8	33	50½	"	"	All points.			Cloudy evening.
9	35½	44	Rain	Rain	N. E.			
10	39	49	Cloudy	Cloudy	N. E., N. W.	1.53		Rain before day.
11	32	41½	Clear	Clear	N. W.			
12	29½	36	Cloudy	Rain	N. E.			Light rain 2:30 P. M., and sleet and rain after 5 P.M.
S 13	32	42	"	Cloudy	All points.	0.63		Rain before day (0.58,) and from 5:15 to 6:30 P. M.; partly clear part of P. M.
14	38½	44	"	Clear	N. W., N.			Clear part of morning, and cleared off 5 P. M.
15	33½	47½	Clear	"	N. E., S. E.			
16	34½	58	"	"	S. W., N. W.			Cloudy part of afternoon.
17	38	42½	Cloudy	Cloudy	E.	0.08		Sleet & rain 8 P.M. to 11 P.M.
18	35	42	"	"	N. E.			
19	36	42	"	Rain	N. E., E.			Rain 10 A. M.
S 20	37	45	"	Cloudy	N. E., N. W.	1.74		Rain before day (1.72,) and part of afternoon (0.01,) and part of evening (0.01.)
21	37	47	Clear	Clear	S. W., W.			Cloudy part of evening.
22	35	45½	"	"	S. W., N. W.			Cloudy part of morning, and part of evening.
23	34½	42½	"	"	N. W.			Cloudy part of morning, and part of evening.
24	32	46	"	Cloudy	S. W., N. W.			Snow squall 12:20 P. M.; clear part of afternoon.
25	36	49½	"	Clear	S. W., N. W.			Cloudy part of A. M., with light snow and rain 10:35.
26	34	39½	Cloudy	Cloudy	N. W.			Clear part of evening.
S 27	30½	44	Clear	Clear	N. W.			Cloudy part of morning.
28	32	49	"	"	S. W., N. W.			
29	36½	45½	Cloudy	"	N. E.			
30	33½	38	Rain	Cloudy	N. E.	0.54		Rain 5 to 8:30 A. M. (0.33,) and 9.40A.M to 1 P.M.(0.16) and misty part of P. M. (0.05;) bar. 29.12.
31	34	42	Cloudy	Rainy	N. W., N. E.	0.20		Snow till 8:30 A.M. (0.08,) and rain and snow 12:30 till 1 P. M. (0.03,) and at intervals rest of day (0.09.)
						5.57		

April, 1881.

Date.	Thermometer. Lowest.	Thermometer. Highest.	Weather. Morning.	Weather. Afternoon.	Prevailing Wind.	Rain and Melted Snow in inches.	Snow in inches.	REMARKS.
1	36	41½	Cloudy	Cloudy	S. W., N. W.	0.06	----	Clear part of morning; light rain 11 A.M. and 4 P. M.; clear evening.
2	34	42	Clear	Clear	N. W.	----	----	
S 3	28½	41½	"	"	N. W.	----	----	Cloudy part A.M. and eve'g.
4	30½	40	"	"	W., N. W.	----	----	Cloudy part of afternoon.
5	24	34	"	"	N. W.	----	----	Snow squall 5:30 A.M.; cloudy part of evening.
6	27½	35	C'y m'st all day		N. W.	----	----	Snow flurries part of A. M.
7	25	50½	Clear	Clear	N. W.	----	----	
8	33½	51½	"	"	N. E., S. E.	----	----	Cloudy part of afternoon.
9	37½	53½	C'y m'st all day		N. E., S. E.	----	----	
S 10	40	59½	Clear	Clear	N. E., S. E.	----	----	
11	42	61½	"	"	S. W., N. W.	----	----	Cloudy part of evening.
12	39	41	Rain	Cloudy	S. E., N. E.	0.26	----	Rain at intervals till noon (0.26).
13	37	40½	Rainy	Rainy	N. E.	0.19	----	Rain at intervals all day till 7 P.M.; partly clear part of evening.
14	38½	45½	Cloudy	Cloudy	N. E.	0.02	----	Clear part of morning; rain 8 to 11:30 P. M.
15	41	56½	Clear	Clear	N. W.	----	----	Cloudy part A.M. and eve'g.
16	38	60	"	"	S. W., N. W.	----	----	
S 17	43	59½	"	"	N. W.	----	----	
18	46	55	Cloudy	"	S. W.	----	----	Light rain part of morning; cloudy part of afternoon.
19	38	58	Clear	"	NW, NE, SW.	----	----	
20	42	52½	Cloudy	"	S. E.	----	----	
21	36½	63	Clear	"	S. W.	----	----	
22	49	59	"	"	All points	----	----	Cloudy evening.
23	42	65	"	"	All points	----	----	Cloudy part A. M. and P. M.
S 24	44½	76½	"	"	S. W.	----	----	
25	56½	75	"	"	N.W., N.E., E.	----	----	Cloudy evening.
26	47	70½	Cloudy	Cloudy	N. E., S. E.	0.02	----	Rain before day (0.02), and misty 8 to 9 A. M.; clear part of afternoon.
27	56	66	"	"	N. E., S. E.	----	----	
28	53	72	"	Clear	S. W., N. W.	----	----	Clear 9 A. M.; cherries flowered.
29	57	70	"	"	SE, SW, NW.	----	----	Cloudy part of afternoon; light sprinkles during A.M.
30	45	64	Clear	"	N. W., N. E.	----	----	
						0.55	----	

May, 1881.

Date.	Thermometer. Lowest.	Thermometer. Highest.	Weather. Morning.	Weather. Afternoon.	Prevailing Wind.	Rain and Melted Snow in inches.	Snow in inches.	REMARKS.
S 1	40	62	Clear	Clear	N. E., S. E.			Frost.
2	49	64	Cloudy	Cloudy	S. W., W.	0.11		Rain before day (0.01); rain at intervals 11 A.M. to 4 P.M. (0.10); clear evening.
3	45	60	Clear	Clear	N. E., S. E.			Cloudy part of morning and part P. M.; pears flowered.
4	40½	62	"	"	N. E., S. E.			Frost.
5	40½	59½	"	Cloudy	S. E.			Frost.
6	47	56½	Rain	"	All points.	0.82		Rain till 9:30 A.M. (0.80) and 2 to 2:30 P.M. (0.02.)
7	52	63	Cloudy	Clear	E., S.			Clear part of morning and cloudy part of afternoon.
S 8	48	72	Clear	"	S. W.			
9	52½	76½	"	"	S. W.			
10	59	81	"	"	S. W.			
11	64	86	"	"	S. W.			
12	71	88½	"	"	N. W.			Cloudy part of afternoon.
13	59	80	Cloudy	"	S. E.			Clear part of morning.
14	56	70½	C'y m'st all day.		S. E.			
S 15	59	77½	Cloudy	Clear	S. W.	0.50		Showers with thunder and light'ng before day (0.50); misty part of morning.
16	58	61½	"	Cloudy	N. E.	0.24		Sh'wer before day (0.22); rain 11:50 to 12:30 P. M. (0.02.)
17	50	53	"	"	N. E.			
18	46½	54	"	Rain	N. E.			Rain 2 P. M. to 10:45 P. M. (0.24) and still raining.
19	51	60	"	Cloudy	N. E., S. E.	0.27		Rain before day (0.03); clear part of afternoon.
20	52	59	"	"	S. E.	0.15		Rain before day (0.12); 9 to 10 A.M. (0.01) and 2:30 P.M. (0.02.)
21	51½	64½	"	"	N. E., S.			Clear part of afternoon.
S 22	57	70½	C'y m'st all day.	All points.		0.13		Shower 5:30 to 5:40 P. M. (0.10) & 6 to 6:30 P.M. (0.03.)
23	55	68	"	"	N. E., S. E.	0.01		Shower 2:30 P. M.
24	56½	70	Cloudy	Clear	N. E., S. E.			
25	56	74	Clear	"	S. E.			Cloudy part of evening.
26	57	72	Cloudy	"	N. E., S. E.			Clear part of morning.
27	55	81½	Clear	"	S. W.			
28	64½	75	"	"	S. W., S. E.			Cloudy part of morning with sprinkle 9 A.M.
S 29	58½	80	"	"	S. W.			Cloudy part of morning.
30	65	83	"	"	S. W.			Cloudy part of evening.
31	69	83	"	Cloudy	All points.	0.07		Clear part of P. M. and part ev'g; rain 3:30 to 5 P. M.
						2.30		

June, 1881.

Date	Thermometer Lowest	Thermometer Highest	Weather Morning	Weather Afternoon	Prevailing Wind	Rain and Melted Snow in inches	Snow in inches	REMARKS.
1	68	77	Cloudy	Cloudy	N. E., S. E.	0.30		Clear part of afternoon; rain 7:45 P. M. to 12 A. M.
2	59	68	"	"	N. E., S. E.			Clear part of afternoon.
3	55	58	"	"	N. E.	0.34		Rain before day (0.02); 3 to 6 (0.32); rain 10:15 P. M.
4	50	66	"	Clear	NE, NW, SW	0.07		Rain before day; cloudy part of afternoon.
S 5	54½	72	Clear	"	N. W., S. W.			Cloudy evening.
6	56	68	Cloudy	"	N. E., S. E.			Cleared 9:30 A. M.
7	50½	61½	Clear	Rain	S. E.	0.08		Cloudy 9; rain 9:30 A. M. to 3 P. M. (0.08): rain 7:30.
8	55	72	Cloudy	Cloudy	All points.	0.79		Rain before day (0.77); clear part of morning; rain 3 to 6 P. M. (0.02).
9	60	66	"	Rain	E.			Rain 3 P. M.
10	50	58	Rain	Cloudy	N. E.	1.69		Rain till 7 A. M. (1.65); part of morning (0.02); part of afternoon (0.02).
11	51	64	Cloudy	Clear	N. E., S. E.	0.01		Rain before day; cleared 3 P. M.
S 12	53½	75½	Clear	"	N. E., S. E.			
13	57	66	Cloudy	Cloudy	S. E.			Clear part of afternoon.
14	56	70½	"	"	All points.	0.24		Shower 5:30 A. M. (0.04); showers 4:35 to 6:30 P. M. (0.20); clear part of P. M.
15	59½	78	Clear	"	N. W.			Clouded over 4 P. M.
16	57	72	"	"	N. W.			
17	57	65½	Cloudy	"	N. E., S. E.	0.15		Rain 6 to 7 and 8 to 9:30 A. M. (0.14); clear part P. M.; rain 10 to 10:15 P.M. (0.01).
18	62	80	Clear	"	N. W., W.			
S 19	63	84½	"	Clear	S. W.			Cloudy part A. M. and ev'g.
20	63½	80	"	Cloudy	N., S.			Clear part of afternoon.
21	66½	76	Cloudy	Clear	N. W.			Cleared 7 A. M.
22	55	71	Clear	"	N. W.			
23	56	70	"	Cloudy	All points.			Clear part of afternoon.
24	55	70½	"	Clear	All points.			Cloudy evening.
25	59	73½	"	"	All points.			Cloudy part of afternoon.
S 26	60	74	Cloudy	Cloudy	N. E., S. E.	0.13		Partly clear A. M., shower 1:40; clear 2:30 to 8:30 P.M.
27	63	68	"	"	N. E., S. E.			Rainy evening after 8.
28	65	82	Clear	Clear	S. W.	4.95		Rain before day (0.85); shower 2:40 to 3 P. M. (0.78); 3:25 P. M. (0.01); showers 9:30 to 10:45 P. M. (0.31).
29	68½	84½	Cloudy	"	S. W.	0.13		Clear part A. M. and P. M.; showers 7:10 A. M., 2 P. M.
30	66	79	Clear	"	N. W.			Cloudy part of evening.
						5.88		

July, 1881.

Date.	Lowest.	Highest.	Weather. Morning.	Weather. Afternoon.	Prevailing Wind.	Rain and Melted Snow in inches.	Snow in inches.	REMARKS.
1	64	78½	Clear	Clear	N., N. E.			Cloudy part of evening.
2	61	78	"	"	N. E., S. E.			
S 3	62	83	"	"	S. W.			Cloudy part of morning.
4	69½	86	"	"	All points.	0.01		Cloudy part of P. M. and evening, with light rain 6:50 to 7:15 P. M. (0.01.)
5	69	84	Cloudy	"	S. W.			Clear part of morning.
6	72	89¼	Clear	"	N. W.			
7	69	81	"	Cloudy	N. E., S. E.	0.06		Clouded over 4 P. M. and rain 8:30 to 11:30 P. M.
8	70	76	Cloudy	"	All points.			
9	64	78	"	Clear	N. E., S. E.			Clear part of morning.
S 10	65	82	"	"	S. E.			
11	70	81	C'y m'st all day	All points.		0.30		Shower 11:45 A. M. (0.01) & 12:15 to 1:30 P.M. (0.09) & 8:45 to 9:30 P.M. (0.20)
12	64½	74½	Cloudy	Clear	N. E., S. E.			Cloudy part of afternoon.
13	67	88	C'y m'st all day	All points.				
14	73½	87	Clear	Clear	N. W., N. E.			Cloudy evening
15	70	81	"	"	N. E., S. E.			Cloudy part of afternoon.
16	66	83	"	Cloudy	S. W.			Cloudy part of morning and clear part of evening.
S 17	71	84	"	Clear	N. W.			Cloudy part of morning.
18	62½	77½	"	"	N. W.			Cloudy part of afternoon.
19	65	82	"	"	N. W.	0.22		Showers 4:25 & 4:45 to 5 P.M.
20	64	81½	C'y m'st all day		S. W.			
21	72	86½	Clear	Clear	S. W., N. W.			
22	66	79	"	Cloudy	W.			
23	66	79½	Cloudy	Clear	N.			
S 24	63	84	Clear	"	All points.			
25	67	86	"	"	S. W.			
26	72	84	C'y m'st all day.		S. W., W.			
27	69	80	"	"	All points.			
28	65	79	Clear	Clear	All points.			Cloudy part of afternoon.
29	64	78	C'y m'st all day.		N. E., S. E.			
30	66	70	Cloudy	Cloudy	N. E., E.	0.07		Rain 4 to 6 P.M. and rest of evening after 8 P. M.
S 31	66	73	"	"	N. E.	0.20		Rain before day (0.17) and 2:30 P. M. (0.02) and 8 P. M. (0.01.)
						0.86		

August, 1881.

Date.	Thermometer.		Wind.		Prevailing Wind.	Rain and Melted Snow in inches.	Snow in inches.	REMARKS.
	Lowest.	Highest.	Morning.	Afternoon.				
S 1	68	82	Cloudy	Clear	S. W.	----	----	Clear part of morning.
2	70	83½	"	"	S. W., N. W.	0.43	----	Cleared 8 A.M.; shower 7:45 to 8:45 P.M.
3	68	85½	Clear	"	All points.	----	----	Foggy morning.
4	72½	90	"	"	All points.	----	----	Cloudy part of evening.
5	75	91	"	"	All points.	----	----	Cloudy evening.
6	77	90½	C'y m'st all day.		S. W.	----	----	
S 7	73	81	Cloudy	Cloudy	S. W.	1.09	----	Light rain 7 to 8 A.M. (0.01;) show'r *1 to1:15 P.M.(0.26;) 6 to 7 P.M. (0.47;) 7:30'to 8 P.M. (0.35;) clear part of afternoon.
8	67	79	Clear	Clear	N. W.	----	----	Cloudy part of morning.
9	63	81	"	Cloudy	S. W.	----	----	Clear part of afternoon.
10	72½	88	"	Clear	S. W., N. W.	----	----	
11	64	80	"	"	N W, N E, S E.	----	----	
12	64	83	"	"	S. W.	----	----	Cloudy part of afternoon.
13	69	95	"	"	S. W.	----	----	Cloudy evening; hottest day since July 20, 1876, and hottest day in August since 1854; bar. 29.61.
S 14	71	80½	"	"	N. W., N.	----	----	
15	65	77	"	Cloudy	N. E.	----	----	Clear part of afternoon.
16	62	73	C'y m'st all day.		N. E.	----	----	
17	57	68	Clear	Cloudy	N. E., S.	0.01	----	Sprinkles during afternoon.
18	59	67	Cloudy	"	N. E.	0.01	----	Rain before day (0.01.)
19	64	72½	"	"	N. W., N. E.	0.02	----	Clear part of morning; rain 5 to 6 A.M. (0.01,) and 11:30 A.M. to 2 P.M.(0.01.)
20	67	79	"	Clear	N. E.	----	----	
S 21	68	86	Clear	"	N.	0.17	----	Cloudy part of morning; cloudy evening with rain 8:10 to 9, and 10 to 10:30 P.M.
22	68	81	"	"	N. W., N.	----	----	
23	63	82	"	"	N. W., N.	----	----	
24	61½	82	"	"	N. E., S. E.	----	----	
25	62	78	"	"	S. E.	----	----	Cloudy part of morning.
26	62	83	"	"	S. W.	----	----	Foggy morning.
27	63	83	"	"	S. W., S. E.	----	----	
S 28	64	87	"	"	S. W.	----	----	
29	66	85	"	"	S. W., S. E.	----	----	
30	68	91	"	"	S., N. E., S.W.	----	----	
31	70	92	"	"	S. W.	----	----	
						1.73	----	

* Shower 1 P.M. on 7th which deposited 0.26 in. at my house did not extend south beyond New street—5 blocks.

September, 1881.

	Date.	Thermometer. Lowest.	Thermometer. Highest.	Weather. Morning.	Weather. Afternoon.	Prevailing Wind.	Rain and Melted Snow in inches.	Snow in inches.	REMARKS.
	1	72	86	Clear	Cloudy	S. W.	----	----	Cloudy part of morning.
	2	73	80	Cloudy	“	N. E., S. E.	----	----	Partly clear parts of morning and afternoon.
	3	67½	76½	“	Clear	N. E., S. E.	----	----	Cloudy part of evening.
S	4	64½	72	“	Cloudy	S. E.	----	----	
	5	68	83	“	Clear	S. W.	----	----	Clear part of morning.
	6	72	93½	“	“	S. W.	----	----	Clear part of morning; hottest day in Sept. since Sept. 13, 1851.
	7	75	97½	Clear	“	S. W., N. W.	----	----	Hottest day since July 17, 1866, and hottest day in Sept. in my records.
	8	76	90	“	Hazy	N.W., E.,S.E.	----	----	
	9	67	79	Cloudy	Cloudy	NE, SW, SE.	----	----	
	10	71	78	“	“	N. E.	0.34	----	Rain at intervals 7:45 to 11 A. M. (0.06) and 5:20 to 8 P. M. (0.28).
S	11	66	79	“	“	N. E., S. E.	----	----	Clear part P.M.; rain 9:40 P.M.
	12	64	77	“	Clear	N. E., N.	0.23	----	Rain before day (0.23); clear part of morning.
	13	57½	78½	Clear	“	N. W., S. W.	----	----	
	14	59	74½	“	“	N. E., S. E.	----	----	
	15	60	70	Cloudy	Cloudy	N. E., S. E.	0.20	----	Partly clear part afternoon; showers part of evening.
	16	65	67	“	“	N. E., S. E.	0.10	----	Rain 11 A.M. to 1 P.M. (0.09); sprinkle 2 to 5 P.M. (0.01); partly clear part of eve'g.
	17	60	68	“	Clear	N. E., S. E.	----	----	Clear part of morning and cloudy part of afternoon.
S	18	51½	76½	Clear	“	N. E., S. E.	----	----	
	19	64	82½	“	“	N. E., N.	----	----	
	20	63	81	“	“	All points	----	----	
	21	62½	72½	“	“	N. E., S. E.	----	----	
	22	58½	73	Cloudy	Cloudy	N. E., S.	----	----	Clear part of evening.
	23	67	83½	“	Clear	S. W.	----	----	Clear part of morning and cloudy part of evening.
	24	66	86	Clear	“	S. W.	----	----	
S	25	69	87	“	“	S. W.	----	----	
	26	70½	90	“	“	S. W.	----	----	
	27	71½	89	“	“	S. W.	----	----	Cloudy part of morning and part of afternoon with sprinkle 4:30 P. M.
	28	74	87½	“	“	S. W., N. W.	0.07	----	Cloudy part of morning and evening, with rain 8 to 9 P. M.
	29	68	73	“	Cloudy	N. E., S. E.	----	----	Clear part of afternoon; misty part of evening.
	30	66	86	Cloudy	Clear	N. E., S. W.	----	----	Clear part of morning.
							0.94	----	

October, 1881.

Date	Thermometer Lowest	Thermometer Highest	Weather Morning	Weather Afternoon	Prevailing Wind	Rain and Melted Snow in inches	Snow in inches	REMARKS
1	71	86½	Clear	Clear	S. W.			Cloudy part of A M.; hottest day in Oct. in my records.
S 2	69	73	Cloudy	Cloudy	N. E., S. E.			Partly clear part of A. M.
3	65	80	"	Clear	N. W., S. W.	0.25		Rain 5 to 8:45 A. M.; cloudy part of evening.
4	66½	78	C'y m'st all day		S. W., N. W.			
5	38½	51½	Clear	Clear	N.			Frost.
6	37	60	"	"	N. W., S. W.			Frost.
7	43½	67½	C'y m'st all day		S. W.			
8	56	77	Clear	Clear	S. W.			Cloudy part of afternoon.
S 9	67	70	Cloudy	Rainy	N. W.	0.11		Partly clear part of morning; rain 1 to 6 P. M.; cleared 7:45 P.M.
10	52	66½	Clear	Clear	N. W.			
11	35½	52½	"	"	N. E., S. E.			
12	37	59	"	Rainy	S. W.	0.10		Cloudy part of morning; rain 1 to 6 P. M.
13	54	71	C'y m'st all day		S. W.			
14	49	57½	Clear	Clear	N. E., S. E.			Cloudy part of evening.
15	49½	70	Cloudy	"	S. W.			Cloudy part of evening.
S 16	60	76½	Clear	"	S.W.,N.,N.E.			Cloudy part P. M. and eve'g.
17	58	64	Cloudy	Cloudy	N. E.			Clear part of morning.
18	62½	78½	Clear	"	S. W.			Cloudy part of morning and clear part of evening.
19	48	58	"	Clear	N.			Cloudy part of afternoon.
20	47	58½	Cloudy	"	N. E., S. E.			
21	43	63	Clear	"	N. W.			
22	42½	65½	"	"	S. W.			
S 23	47	67	"	"	S. W.			Cloudy part A.M.; cl'dy ev'g.
24	56	58	Rainy	Misty	S. W.,N.,N.E.	0.21		Rain till 6 A.M. (0.08) & 8:15 A. M.) till 12:15 P.M. (0.13.)
25	54	67	Cloudy	Clear	S. W., N. W.	0.02		Rain before day (0.02); cloudy part of evening.
26	48½	55½	Clear	"	N. W.			
27	35	58	"	"	W., S. W.			
28	41	57	"	"	S. E.			Cloudy part A.M ; cl'dy ev'g.
29	54	62	Rainy	Cloudy	S. E., S.	0.32		Rain 5 to 6:45 A.M. (0.08) 9½ to 10 A.M. (0.02) 11:15 A. M. to 12:15 P. M. (0.07) 7:30 to 9 P. M. (0.15.)
S 30	59	68	Cloudy	"	All points	0.74		Rain before day (0.04); clear part of A. M.; rain 3:50 to 4:50 P.M. (0.04) 7:15 to 9 P. M. (0.06.)
31	65	68½	"	"	S. W.	0.50		Rain before day (0.22), 8:30 to 11 A.M. (0.21) and 8 to 11 P. M. (0.07)
						2.25		

WEATHER RECORD FOR NEW BRUNSWICK, N. J.   305

November, 1881.

Date.	Thermometer.		Weather.		Prevailing Wind.	Rain and Melted Snow in inches.	Snow in inches.	REMARKS.
	Lowest.	Highest.	Morning.	Afternoon.				
1	56	59½	Cloudy	Cloudy	N. E.	0.06		Shower 6:30 A. M., 0.03, and rain 8:30 to 9:30 A.M., 0.03.
2	53	57¾	"	"	N. E.			
3	56½	60½	"	Rain	S. W., N. W.	0.03		Rain before day, 0.03; rain 4:15 P. M.
4	40½	48	"	Clear	S. W., W.	0.58		Rain before day, 0.58; cleared 9 A. M.
5	36	58	Clear	"	S. W., S.			Cloudy part of afternoon.
S 6	45	59	"	"	S. W., N. W.			
7	42	52	Cloudy	Cloudy	N. E., S. E.			Clear part A.M.; rain 5¼ P.M.
8	50	61	Rain	"	N. E.	0.43		Rain till 6 A. M., 0.41, and 10:30 to 11 A.M., 0.02.
9	58½	68	Cloudy	"	S. W., N. W.	0.56		Rain before day, 0.06; 10 A. M., 0.04, 11 A. M., 0.03, 5:05 to 5:45 P.M., 0.43.
10	45½	54	Clear	Clear	N. W.			Cloudy part of afternoon.
11	41	48	C'y m'st all day		N. W., N. E.			Cloudy part of morning.
12	43	60	Cloudy	Rain	S. E., S. W.	0.60		Misty 7 to 11 A.M., and then rain til 6 P. M., 0.52, and 8:30 to 10 P.M., 0.08.
S 13	52½	59	Clear	Clear	S. W., N. W.			
14	41	55	"	"	S. W., N. W.			
15	39	47	"	"	N. W.			
16	34	46	"	"	W.			
17	35	56	"	"	S. W.			Cloudy evening.
18	50	60½	Cloudy	Cloudy	S. W.			
19	55	64	"	"	S. W., N. W.	0.10		Partly clear part of morning; rain 5 to 9 P. M.
S 20	38½	45	Clear	Clear	N. W.			
21	33½	46½	"	Cloudy	S. W.			Cloudy part of morning.
22	41	42	Cloudy	Clear	N. W.	0.03		Rain before day, 0.03.
23	26	38	"	Rain	N. E.			Snow flurry 8:45 A.M.; rain and sleet 11 A. M.
24	35	42½	"	Clear	N. W.	0.73		Rain before day, 0.73; clear part of morning and cl'dy part of afternoon.
25	26	34	Clear	"	W., S. W.			
26	27	43	"	"	S. W.			
S 27	33½	49½	"	"	S. W.			Cloudy part of evening.
28	29	37	"	"	N. E., S. E.			
29	27	50	"	"	NE,NW,SW.			Cloudy part of afternoon.
30	35½	53	Foggy	Cloudy	S. W.	0.01		Clear part of aft'noon; misty rain part of evening.
						3 13		

December, 1881.

Date.	Thermometer. Lowest.	Thermometer. Highest.	Weather. Morning.	Weather. Afternoon.	Prevailing Wind.	Rain and Melted Snow in inches.	Snow in inches.	REMARKS.
1	49	57	Rain	Cloudy	S. W., W.	0.63	---	Foggy A.M.; light rain till 7 A.M., 0.04; 8 to 11:15 A. M., 0.50, and 1 to 2 P.M., 0.09; clear evening.
2	38	46	Clear	Clear	All points.	---	---	
3	34½	42	Cloudy	Cloudy	N. E.	---	---	Partly clear part of morning; misty evening.
S 4	37	39	Rain	Rain	N. E.	0.30	---	Rain at intervals till 7:30 P. M.
5	35½	45½	Clear	Clear	N. E.	---	---	Cloudy part of evening.
6	34	46	"	Cloudy	All points.	---	---	Cloudy part of morning and clear part of evening.
7	41	46	Rain	Clear	S. W., W.	0.31	---	Rain till 9:10 A.M., 0.27 and 12:20 to 1 P. M., 0.04; cleared 3 P. M.
8	33	39½	Clear	"	N. W., W.	---	---	
9	31½	45	C'y m'st all day.		S. W., W.	---	---	
10	30	35	Clear	Clear	N.	---	---	
S 11	23	34	"	Cloudy	N. W., S. W.	---	---	Clear part of evening.
12	30½	44½	Cloudy	"	S. E., S. W.	0.08	---	Rain at intervals 5 to 10 P. M., 0.08.
13	41	50	"	"	S. W.	---	---	Clear part P. M. and even'g.
14	56½	67	"	"	S. W., N. W.	0.02	---	Rain 8 to 8:30 A.M., 0.01, and 12 to 12:30 P. M., 0.01; steady rain 5 P. M.
15	33½	36½	"	Clear	N. W.	0.80	---	Rain and snow before day, 0.80.
16	22	33	Clear	"	N., S. W.	---	---	
17	26	42	"	"	S. W.	---	---	
S 18	32½	48	"	"	S. W.	---	---	
19	34	45	"	"	N. W., S. W.	---	---	
20	33½	47	C'y m'st all day.		S. W.	---	---	
21	38	45	Cloudy	Cloudy	N. E., S. E.	---	---	Clear part of A.M.;misty ev'g.
22	38½	57	Rain	Rain	S. E.	0.26	---	Rain till 2 P. M., 0.26; rain after 7 P. M.
23	53	56½	Cloudy	Cloudy	S. W., N.	0.49	---	Rain before day, 0.43; clear part A. M.; 4:30 to 6:30 P. M., 0.04; 7 to 8 P. M., 0.02; cleared 10 P. M.
24	28	36½	Clear	Clear	N. W.	---	---	
S 25	30	45	"	"	N. W.	---	---	
26	35	47	Cloudy	Cloudy	S. W.	---	---	Partly clear part of morning; rainy evening.
27	44	59	Rain	"	S. E.	0.32	---	Rain till 10:30 A.M., 0.32.
28	46	50½	Cloudy	"	N. E., S. W.	0.05	---	Rain before day, 0.05.
29	47	56	"	"	S. E., S. W.	0.66	---	Rain 12 to 4:30 P. M , 0.65, and part eve'g,0.01; partly clear part of evening.
30	40	44	"	Clear	N. W., W.	---	---	Cleared 8 A.M.; cloudy eve'g.
31	25	33½	Clear	"	W., S. W.	---	---	Cloudy evening.
						3.92	---	

Rain and melted snow for 1881, 38.46 inches.

January, 1882.

Date.	Thermometer. Lowest.	Thermometer. Highest.	Weather. Morning.	Weather. Afternoon.	Prevailing Wind.	Rain and Melted Snow in inches.	Snow in inches.	REMARKS.
S 1	26	33	Clear	Cloudy	S. W., N. E.			Cloudy part of morning; light snow during even'g.
2	16	25	"	Clear	N. W.			
3	15	32	"	"	S. W.			Cloudy part of afternoon.
4	12½	22½	"	"	N. W., N. E.			Cloudy part of afternoon.
5	11	25½	Cloudy	Cloudy	N. E.			Clear 11 A. M. to 3 P. M.; snow squalls A.M.and P.M.
6	24	37½	Misty	"	N. E.	0.08		Light snow before day; foggy part of afternoon and rainy ev'g till 10.
7	34	41	Cloudy	"	S. W., N. W.			Clear evening.
S 8	33	41½	"	{M'sty / Rain}	S. E., N. E.	0.11		Rain 7:30 to 8:30 A.M., 0.01, & rainy ev'g till 10:30, 0.10
9	39	48½	"	Clear	S. W., N. W.			Foggy morning.
10	33½	41	Clear	Cloudy	N. W.			Snow 8:30 P. M.
11	33	42½	Rain	Clear	All points.	0.86		Snow before day, and rain till 10 A. M., 0.86.
12	37	44	Clear	Cloudy	N. W.			
13	33½	42	{Snow / Rain}	"	S. E., S. W.	0.80		Snow till 10:30 A. M., and then rain till 3 P.M., 0.80.
14	36	42½	Clear	Clear	N. W.			Violent snow squall 2:40 P.M.
S 15	26	40	"	Cloudy	S. W.			
16	37	47	Cloudy	"	S. W.	0.05		Rain before day; clear part A.M; rain P.M. and ev'g.
17	29	31½	{Rain / Snow}	"	N. W.	0.33		Rain before day; snow till 10:30 A.M.; clear part P.M.
18	17	32	Cloudy	"	N. E.			Rain 6:30 P. M.
19	31	39	"	Clear	N. W.	0.38		Rain before day, 0.38; clear part of morning.
20	23½	33½	"	Cloudy	N. E.			Partly clear part of A. M.
21	32	40	Rain	"	N. E.	0.59		Rain till 4:30 P.M. and ev'g.
S 22	37	40	Clear	Clear	W., N. W.		1.00	Cloudy part of A. M.; snow squalls 6 to 7 P. M.
23	14½	19	"	"	N. W.			
24	1	13	"	"	N. W.			Bar. 10 A. M., 30.75.
25	8	29	"	{Snow / Rain}	N. E., E.			Light snow 1:30 to 6 P. M., and then rain.
26	33½	38½	Cloudy	Cloudy	S. W.	0.97		Rain before day, 0.92, and 10 A. M. to 4 P. M., 0.05.
27	37	47	Clear	Clear	S. W., N. W.	0.02		Rain before day, 0.02.
28	31½	37	Cloudy	Cloudy	N. E.	0.40		Snow 8:30 A. M. to 2 P. M., 0.37, and rain part P. M.
S 29	29	32	"	Clear	N. W.			Cleared 8 A. M.
30	18	30	Clear	"	W., S. W.			
31	23	28½	Cloudy	Snow	S. W., N. E.		8.00	Snow 7:45 A.M. to 10 P.M.
						4.59	9.00	

February, 1882.

Date	Thermometer. Lowest.	Thermometer. Highest.	Weather. Morning.	Weather. Afternoon.	Prevailing Wind.	Rain and Melted Snow in inches.	Snow in inches.	REMARKS.
1	26	36	Clear	Clear	N. W., S. W.	----	----	
2	23½	39	"	"	S. W.	----	----	
3	31½	39	"	"	W., N. W.	----	----	
4	17	19	Cloudy	Snow	N. E.	----	----	Snow 10 A. M.
S 5	13	33½	"	Clear	W.	----	12.00	Snow before day; drifted badly; cleared 8 A. M.
6	18	36	Clear	"	S. W., N. W.	----	----	
7	17	40	"	"	All points	----	----	Cloudy part of morning and part of evening.
8	35	44½	Cloudy	"	S. W.	0.02	----	Rain before day.
9	26	36	"	Rain	N. E.	0.83	----	Rain 10 A. M. to 10 P. M.
10	34½	42	Clear	Clear	N. W.	----	----	Cloudy part of morning.
11	29	38	"	"	All points	----	----	
S 12	30	45	C'y m'st all day		S. W., N. W.	----	----	
13	37	53	Cloudy	Rain	S. W.	0.29	----	Rain part of morning, 0.03, and 12:15 to 7 P. M., 0.26.
14	41½	49	"	Clear	N. W., W.	----	----	Clear part of morning.
15	35	52	Clear	"	S. W.	----	----	
16	36½	50	Cloudy	Cloudy	S. W., E.	----	----	Rain 7 P. M.
17	44½	51	Clear	Clear	N. W.	0.54	----	Rain before day, 0.54.
18	19	29½	"	"	N. E.	----	----	
S 19	21	36	Cloudy	Rain	E., S. E.	0.24	----	Sleet 10:30 A. M. to 2 P. M., and rain till 5:30 P. M.
20	35	46½	"	Cloudy	S.W., N., N.E.	----	----	Clear 11 A.M. to 2 P.M ; rain 7 P. M.
21	36½	39	Rain	Rain	S. E., N. E.	1.10	----	Rain till 6:30 P M., 1.08, 9 to 10 P. M., 0.02; at 5 P. M. shower from N. W. with thunder and lightning.
22	32	36	Cloudy	Clear	N. W.	----	----	Clear part of morning and cloudy part of evening with snow flurries.
23	29	35½	C'y m'st all day		N. W.	----	----	Snow squalls part of aft'noon.
24	22	32	Clear	Clear	N. W., N.	----	----	
25	23	37	"	"	N., N. W., S W.	----	----	
S 26	29	44½	"	"	S. W.	----	----	
27	32½	54	"	"	S. W.	----	----	
28	35	46	"	Cloudy	E.	0.02	----	Cloudy part of morning; light rain part of evening.
						3.04	12.00	

March, 1882.

Date.	Thermometer. Lowest.	Highest.	Weather. Morning.	Afternoon.	Prevailing Wind.	Rain and Melted Snow in inches.	Snow in inches.	REMARKS.
1	39	58	Rain	Cloudy	S.	0.72		Rain till 3 P. M., 0.70; part of evening, 0.02.
2	49½	63	Cloudy	Clear	N.			Cleared 9 A. M.
3	46	58	Clear	"	N. W.			
4	39	53	"	"	N. W.			
S 5	36	49	"	Cloudy	All points.	0.01		Light rain 5 to 6 P. M.
6	42	51	Rain	Clear	All points.	0.14		Rain till 12:30 P.M.; cloudy part of afternoon.
7	40	45	Clear	"	N. W.			Cloudy part of morning.
8	25½	38½	"	"	All points.			
9	30	51	Snow Rain	Cloudy	N. E., S. E.	0.41		Rain till 12:30 P. M., 0.27; part of afternoon, 0.09; part of evening, 0.05.
10	49	51	C'y m'st all day.		W., N. W.			
11	36½	44	" "	" "	N. W.			
S 12	36	54	Cloudy	Clear	S E., S. W.			Light sprinkle part of A.M.; cloudy evening and light rain after 10 P. M.
13	39	45	"	"	N. W.	0.02		Rain before day; clear part A.M.; Dr. C.Morrogh died.
14	27	37	Clear	"	N. W.			
15	20	32	"	Cloudy	N. E., S. E.			
16	28	37	Snow	"	N. E.		3.00	Snow till 8 A. M.; clear part of A. M.; clear evening.
17	30	44	Clear	Clear	N. E			Mrs.M. K. How, widow Rev. D. S. B. How, died.
18	29	40	"	Cloudy	N. E, S. E.			Clear part of afternoon.
S 19	35	54	Cloudy	Clear	S. W., N. W.	0.02		Rain before day; cleared 9 A. M.
20	39	52	"	Cloudy	N. W., S. W.			Clear part of morning.
21	42	45	Rain	"	S. E.	0.37		Rain till 10 A.M., 0.28, part of evening, 0.09.
22	36½	44	Clear	Clear	S. W., N. W.	0.02		Rain before day, 0.01; snow squall 2:40 P. M. and 4 P. M., 0.01, and 7 P. M.
23	31	43	"	"	N. W., S. W.			Cloudy part of morning.
24	35	44½	Cloudy	"	S. W., N. W.			Clear part of morning and cloudy part of afternoon.
25	24½	37	Clear	"	N. W.			
S 26	31	53	Cloudy	"	S. W.			Clear part of morning.
27	38	57	"	Cloudy	S. W.	0.28		Rain 7:30 A. M. to 1 P. M., 0.27; 2:30 to 3 P.M., 0.01; rainy after 10 P. M.
28	43	49	"	Clear	N.	0.29		Rain before day, 0.24, and 6:45 to 9 A.M., 0.05; clear part of morning.
29	31	47	Clear	"	N. E., S. E.			Cloudy part of afternoon.
30	38½	57	Cloudy	"	S. W., N. W.	0.04		Rain 9:20 to 10:40 A.M., 0.04.
31	34½	42	Clear	"	N. W.			
						2.32	3.00	

Weather Record for New Brunswick, N. J.

April, 1882.

Date	Thermometer. Lowest	Thermometer. Highest	Weather. Morning	Weather. Afternoon	Prevailing Wind	Rain and Melted Snow in inches	Snow in inches	REMARKS.
1	30	54	Cloudy	Clear	S. W.			Cloudy evening.
S 2	42	72½	Clear	"	S. W.	0.19		Cloudy part of morning, and part of afternoon with shower 3:30 to 4 P. M.
3	36	47	"	"	N. E., S. E.			Cloudy part of afternoon.
4	38	56½	Cloudy	"	S. W.			Cloudy evening.
5	45	46	"	Cloudy	N. E., S. E.	0.09		Rain 8:30 to 11:40 A.M.,0.04, and 1 to 3:30 P. M., 0.05.
6	37	42	"	"	N. E., S. E.	0.04		Rain till 8:30 A. M.
7	38	56	"	Clear	N.E.,E.,S.W.	0.03		Rain till 8 A. M.; cloudy parts of afternoon and ev'g
8	48	63	Clear	"	N.E.,E.,S.W.			
S 9	43	55	Cloudy	Cloudy	S. W., S. E.			Rain 7 P. M.
10	30½	37	Rain, Snow	"	N. E.	0.32		Rain and snow till 6:30 A.M., 0.31; snow squalls all day, 0.01, to 5 P. M.
11	29	39	Clear	Clear	N. W.	0.01		Snow before day, 0.01; cloudy part of afternoon with snow flurries.
12	30	44	"	"	S. W., N. W.			
13	35	51½	"	"	N. W.			
14	37½	51	"	"	N. W.			Cloudy part of evening.
15	37½	53	"	"	N. W.			Cloudy part of afternoon.
S 16	36½	57	"	"	N. W.			Northern lights 11 P.M.
17	42½	65	"	"	N. W.			
18	47	68½	"	"	N. W.			
19	47	69½	"	Cloudy	S. W.	0.15		Shower 3:10 to 6:30 P. M., 0.15; thunder shower after 10 P. M. with hail.
20	53	60	"	Clear	S. W., N. W.	1.00		Rain before day, 1.00.
21	43½	51	"	Cloudy	N. W.			
22	43	56	"	Clear	N. W.			
S 23	39	52½	"	"	All points.			Cloudy part of afternoon.
24	38	56	"	"	N.			
25	37	53	"	"	All points.			
26	36	49	Cloudy	Cloudy	N. E., S. E.			Rain 5:30 P.M.
27	39	46	"	"	N. E.	1.00		Rain before day, 0.98; rain part of evening, 0.02; cleared 10 P. M.
28	42	56½	"	"	N. E., S. E.	0.02		Clear part of morning; rain 6 to 6:30 P. M., 0.02; cleared 8 P. M.
29	47	60	Cy'm'st all day.		N. W., S. W.			
S 30	47	61	"	"	N. E., N. W.			
						2.85		

May, 1882.

Date	Thermometer. Lowest.	Thermometer. Highest.	Weather. Morning.	Weather. Afternoon.	Prevailing Wind.	Rain and Melted Snow in inches.	Snow in inches.	REMARKS.
1	43	64	Clear	Clear	S. W.			
2	46½	58	"	"	S. W., N. W.			Cloudy part of morning; cherries flowered.
3	37	56½	"	"	N. W., S. W.			Frost.
4	44	66	"	Cloudy	S. W., W.			Pears flowered.
5	46½	50	Rain	"	N. E.	0.22		Rain till 2 P. M.; clear part of evening.
6	42	46	Cloudy	Rain	N. E.	0.41		Rain 10:30 A.M. to 10 P. M.; clear part of evening.
S 7	38	56½	Clear	Clear	N. E., S. E.			Cloudy part of A. M.; frost.
8	38½	60½	"	Cloudy	S. W.	0.15		Rain 7 to 10:30 P. M.; frost.
9	50	71¾	"	"	S. W., N. W.			Clear part of P.M.; rain 7 P.M.
10	57	61	Cloudy	"	N. E., S. E.	0.43		Rain before day, 0.42; cleared 7:30 A.M.; rain part of afternoon, 0.01.
11	46	51	"	"	N. E.	0.14		Rain 5:30 to 7 A. M., 0.14; rainy after 9 P. M.
12	41	44	Rain	"	N. E.	0.75		Rain till 2 P.M.; misty ev'g.
13	40	49	Misty	"	N. E.	0.02		Misty till 7 A.M.; misty ev'g.
S 14	44	49	Cloudy	Rain	N. E.	0.08		Rain before day, 0.04; part of morning, 0.04; steady rain after 11:45 A. M.
15	46	56	C'y m'st all day.		N. E., S. E.	1.00		Rain before day, 1.00.
16	44	60	Clear	Clear	All points			
17	45	63¼	Cloudy	Cloudy	N.W.,NE.,S.E			Clear part of morning.
18	46½	57	Clear	Clear	N. E.			Cloudy part of morning.
19	41	52	C'y m'st all day.		N. E., E.			
20	48	67½	Clear	Clear	W., S. W.			
S 21	52	74	"	Cloudy	S. W.			Partly clear part of evening.
22	61	74	C'y m'st all day.		E.	0.06		Thunder shower 3:05 P. M.
23	55	67	Cloudy	Clear	N. W.	0.18		Rain before day; cleared 7:30 A. M.
24	54	65	Clear	"	N. W.			
25	51	53	Rain	Cloudy	S. E., N. E.	0.84		Rain till 4 P. M.
26	43	63	Clear	Clear	N. W., S. W.			Foggy early morning.
27	48½	69	C'y m'st all day.		S. W., S. E.			Rain 10:45 P. M.
S 28	58	78	"	"	S. W., N. W.	0.55		Rain before day, 0.55; shower after 8:30 P. M.
29	60	71	Cloudy	Clear	N.	0.46		Rain before day, 0.46; cleared 8:30 A. M.
30	50	70¼	Clear	"	W., S. W.			
31	56	79½	"	"	S. W.			Cloudy evening.
						5.29		

June, 1882.

Date.	Thermometer. Lowest.	Thermometer. Highest.	Weather. Morning.	Weather. Afternoon.	Prevailing Wind.	Rain and Melted Snow in inches.	Snow in inches.	REMARKS.
1	65	73	Rain	Clear	S. W., N.	0.27		Rain till 11 A. M.; cleared 3 P. M.
2	52	69½	Clear	"	N. W., S. W.			
3	54	76	"	"	S. W.			Cloudy part of A. M.; cloudy evening.
S 4	64	74½	Cloudy	"	S. W., N. W.	0.08		Showers 8:30 and 10 A. M.; clear part of morning.
5	54½	66½	Clear	"	W., N. W.			Cloudy part of afternoon, with sprinkles.
6	54	70	"	"	N. W.			Cloudy part of afternoon.
7	52	77½	"	"	W., S. W.			
8	60½	80½	"	"	S. W.			
9	63½	80	"	"	S. W.			Cloudy part of morning.
10	60	68	"	Cloudy	N. E., S. E.	0.04		Cloudy part of A. M., with rain 10:30, 0.02, and part P.M. and evening, 0.02.
S 11	61	71	Cloudy	Clear	N. E., S. E.			
12	55	71	Clear	"	N. E., S. E.			
13	55½	76	"	"	S.E.,N.W.,S.E			
14	56½	78	"	"	S. W.			Cloudy part of evening.
15	58	83	"	"	S. W., N. W.	0.03		Cloudy part of evening, with shower 8.35.
16	69	82	"	"	S. W., N. W.			Cloudy part of evening.
17	66	88½	"	"	N. E., S.			Hazy evening.
S 18	65½	82	Cloudy	"	S. E., S. W.	0.14		Rain before day, 0.14.
19	70	88½	Clear	Cloudy	All points.	0.49		Shower 1:30 P. M., 0.22; 3:15 to 4:15 P.M., 0.17, and 9:30 to 11 P. M., 0.10; clear part of evening.
20	60½	74	"	Clear	N.			
21	61	75½	Cloudy	"	W., N. W.			Cleared 8 A. M.
22	58	79½	Clear	"	All points.			
23	63	84	"	"	S. W.			
24	70	88½	"	"	S. W.			
S 25	75	92½	"	"	S. W.			Cloudy part of evening, with sprinkles 9:45.
26	74½	87½	"	"	S. W., N. W.	0.15		Shower 2:40 to 3 P.M., 0.03; 3:30 to 4 P. M., 0.12.
27	67	83	"	"	N. W.			
28	63½	81	"	"	All points.			Cloudy part of morning.
29	68	79	"	"	N.			
30	60	74	"	Cloudy	N. E., S. E.	0.28		Cloudy part of A.M.; showers 9:40 to midnight and still raining.
						1.48		

July, 1882.

Date.	Thermometer. Lowest.	Thermometer. Highest.	Weather. Morning.	Weather. Afternoon.	Prevailing Wind.	Rain and Melted Snow in inches	Snow in inches	REMARKS.
1	64	83½	Rain	Clear	S. W.	0.94		Rain till 7 A. M., 0.92, and shower 7:20 P. M., 0.02.
S 2	66½	75	Clear	"	N. W.			
3	60	71½	"	Cloudy	W., S. W.			Partly clear part of evening.
4	62	70½	Cloudy	Rain	N. E.	0.31		Clear part of A.M.; rain 1:30 to 5:30 P.M., 0.25, and part of evening, 0.06; coolest 4th of July since 1859.
5	56½	62	Rain	Cloudy	N. E., N.	0.93		Rain till 7 A. M., 0.72; 1 to 5 P. M., 0.21.
6	56	73	Clear	Clear	N. W., S. W.			
7	59½	77	"	"	All points.			
8	63	81½	"	"	S. W			Cloudy part of morning.
S 9	70	84½	"	"	S. W.			Cloudy part A.M. and eve'g.
10	70	88½	"	"	S. W.			
11	74½	90	"	"	S. W.			
12	69	86½	"	"	S. W., S. E.	0.49		Showers 9 to 10:30 P. M.
13	72	83	"	"	W.	0.13		Rain before day.
14	68	82	"	"	All points.			Cloudy part of afternoon.
15	67	81	"	"	N. E., S. E.			Cloudy part of morning.
S 16	64	81	Cloudy	"	N. E., S. E.			Foggy morning; cleared 9:30 A. M.
17	65	80	"	"	S. E.			Cleared 8 A. M.; cloudy part of evening.
18	70½	81½	"	"	S. E.			Cleared 7:30 A. M.
19	71½	85	Clear	"	S. W.	0.11		Rain before day; cloudy part of afternoon.
20	71½	84½	"	"	N. W., S. W.			
21	68	79	C'y m'st all day.		N. E., S.			
22	67	77½	" "	" "	N. E., S.			
S 23	64½	84	Clear	Clear	N. W., N.			
24	66½	80½	"	"	N. W.			
25	69	89	"	"	S. W.			
26	71	90½	"	"	S. W.			
27	73	91	"	"	S. W.			
28	75	92	"	"	S. W., N.	0.10		Shower 5:30 to 5:45 P. M.; cloudy part of evening.
29	74	87	C'y m'st all day.		All points	0.03		Shower 8 P. M.
S 30	69	83	Clear	Clear	N. E., S. E.			
31	69	79½	"	"	E., N. E.			Cloudy part of morning.
						3.04		

Weather Record for New Brunswick, N. J.

August, 1882.

Date	Thermometer Lowest	Thermometer Highest	Weather Morning	Weather Afternoon	Prevailing Wind	Rain and Melted Snow in inches	Snow in inches	REMARKS
1	63	77	C'y m'st all day.		N. E., S. E.			
2	64	72	Rain	Cloudy	N. E., S. E.	0.64		Rain till 12:45 P. M., 0.48, 2:25 to 3:40 P. M., 0.15, and 8 P. M., 0.01; clear part of evening.
3	65½	79	Cloudy	Clear	N. E., S. E.			Clear part of morning.
4	63½	80	Clear	"	N. E.			Northern lights 8:30 P.M.
5	66½	83	Cloudy	"	N. E., S. E.			Clear part of morning.
S 6	70	87½	"	"	S. E.			Foggy morning; clear part of morning.
7	73	87¼	C'y m'st all day.		All points.	0.41		Shower 3:42 to 4:20 P. M, 0.34 in 10 minutes.
8	71	85	Clear	Clear	S. W.	0.06		Cloudy part of afternoon and evening, with rain 5 to 6 P. M.
9	71	83	"	"	S. W.			
10	68	81	"	"	S. W.			Cloudy part of afternoon.
11	63	79	"	"	N. W., S. W.			
12	65	75	Cloudy	Cloudy	S. W.			Clear evening.
S 13	66	82½	Clear	Clear	S.W., N., N. E.			
14	66	83¼	"	"	N. E., S.			
15	69	85½	"	"	S. W.			Cloudy part of afternoon.
16	72	81	Cloudy	"	N.E., S. W.			Cloudy part of afternoon.
17	72	86	Clear	"	S. W., N. W.			Partly cloudy part of A. M.
18	68	79	"	"	N. W.			
19	56	75½	"	"	N.			
S 20	55½	77½	"	"	N. E., S. E.			
21	60	77½	"	"	N. E., S. E.			
22	65	72	Cloudy	"	S. W., S. E.			Sprinkle 6 to 8 A.M.; cloudy part of afternoon.
23	62½	77½	C'y m'st all day.		All points.			
24	69	84	Clear	Clear	N. W.			
25	65	83	"	"	All points.			
26	66	78	C'y m'st all day.		N. E., S. E.			
S 27	67½	69	Rain	Rain	E.			Com. raining before day.
28	60	70½	Cloudy	Clear	N. E., S. E.	2.09		Rain before day; cleared 11 A. M.
29	57	73	Clear	"	N. E., S. E.			
30	54½	75	"	"	S. W., S. E., N.			
31	55	73½	"	Cloudy	S. W., S. E.			Sprinkles part of evening.
						3.20		

WEATHER RECORD FOR NEW BRUNSWICK, N. J.

September, 1882.

Date.	Thermometer. Lowest.	Thermometer. Highest.	Weather. Morning.	Weather. Afternoon.	Prevailing Wind.	Rain and Melted Snow in inches.	Snow in inches.	REMARKS.
1	67	79½	Cloudy	Clear	S.E., S.W., W.	0.55		Rain 2 to 5:30 A.M.
2	69	83	Clear	"	All points			Cloudy part of evening.
S 3	71	83½	Cloudy	"	S.			Cleared 8 A.M.; cloudy part of evening.
4	72	81	"	"	All points	0.31		Rain before day, 0.31; clear part of morning.
5	66½	80	Clear	"	N. W., N. E.			
6	65½	75½	Cloudy	"	N. E., E.			Clear part of morning and cloudy part of afternoon.
7	62	76½	Clear	"	N. W., S. W.			
8	63	80	"	"	S. W.	0.01		Cloudy evening with shower 10:30 P. M., 0.01.
9	63	73½	Cloudy	Cloudy	N. E., S. E.			Clear part of evening.
S 10	63	71	"	"	N. E.			Clear part of morning.
11	63	66	Rain	Rain	N. E.			Rain before day, 0.70; 7:15 A. M. to 1:30 P. M., 0.87 ; partly clear part of afternoon; rain again 5:30 P.M.
12	58	71	Cloudy	Clear	N.	2.40		Rain before day, 0.83; cleared 8 A. M.
13	52	68	Clear	"	N. E., S. E.			Cloudy part of evening.
14	59	77	"	"	S. W.	0.04		Cloudy part of morning and cloudy part of evening, with shower 9 P. M.
15	65½	75	"	"	N. W.			
16	59½	75	"	"	N. W.			
S 17	60½	74	"	"	N. W., S. W.			
18	63	78½	Cloudy	"	S. W.			Clear part of morning.
19	67	85	Clear	"	S. W.			
20	71	84	"	"	SW, NW, N.E	0.62		Rain 8:20 to 10:40 P.M., 0.62.
21	67½	70	Cloudy	Cloudy	N. E.	0.61		Rain before day, 0.60; light rain part of evening, 0.01.
22	63	72	Rain	Rain	All points	4.12		Rain till 3:30 P.M., 3.90, and 9 to 10:15 P. M., 0.22.
23	59	61	"	"	N. E.	0.49		Rain before day, 0.04; 7 A.M. to 11:30 P. M., 6:45.
S 24	56	68½	Clear	Clear	N., N. E.			Cloudy even'g; great freshet; no trains till 10 P. M.
25	58	61	Cloudy	Cloudy	N. E.	0.09		Rain 10:45 to 11:15 A. M., 0.04, and part of ev'g, 0.05.
26	55	62½	"	"	N. E.	0.17		Rain before day, 0.06, and 8:30 to 10:30 A. M., 0.11.
27	55½	60½	"	"	N. E.			Partly clear part of even'g.
28	48½	55	"	"	N. E.			Sun sets clear with a perfect rainbow; rain 6:30 PM.
29	48	64	"	Clear	N. E.	0.11		Rain before day, 0.11; clear part of morning.
30	48½	68½	Clear	"	N. W.			
						15.52		

Weather Record for New Brunswick, N. J.

October, 1882.

Date.	Thermometer.		Weather.		Prevailing Wind.	Rain and Melted Snow in inches.	Snow in inches.	REMARKS.
	Lowest.	Highest.	Morning.	Afternoon.				
S 1	53	73	Clear	Clear	N. W.			
2	52	71	"	"	N. W., S. W.			Great comet, largest since 1843, 4 to 5 A.M. in the E.; cloudy part evening.
3	52¼	62½	Cloudy	"	N. E., S. E.			Clear part of morning.
4	49	66½	Clear	"	All points.			Saw comet second time.
5	52	72½	"	"	S. W., S. E.			Foggy A. M.; cloudy even'g.
6	61	68	Cloudy	Cloudy	S. E., N. E.			Clear part of A. M. and ev'g.
7	58	69½	"	Clear	S. W.			Foggy morning.
S 8	56½	73	Clear	"	S. W.			Saw comet third time.
9	57	72	"	"	S. W.			Foggy and cloudy part A.M.; saw comet fourth time.
10	59	69	"	"	N. W.			Cloudy 10 P.M.; at 4:30 A.M. a rarely clear sky, wind N.W., no moon, comet unequalled in my time.
11	48	50	Cloudy	Rain	N. E.	0.18		Rain before day, 0.04; misty rain 9 A.M. till noon, 0.02; 3:30 to 10:45 P. M, 0.12.
12	46	53	"	Cloudy	N. E.	0.02		Rain before day, 0.02.
13	51	60	"	"	N. E., E.			Clear part A. M.; misty ev'g.
14	52	69	"	Clear	N. E.	0.04		Rain before day; clear 9 A.M.
S 15	50½	69	Clear	"	N. W., N. E.			Saw comet sixth time.
16	58	65	Cloudy	Cloudy	N. E.			Misty rain after 6:30 P. M.
17	61	68	"	"	N. E., E.	0.11		Rain before day; foggy.
18	62	69	"	"	N. E., S. E.			Foggy A.M.;partly clear part of P. M. and evening.
19	63	67	"	Rain	S. W., N. W.	0.20		Rain before day, 0.05; partly clear part A.M.; rain 12:30 to 5:30 P. M., 0.15.
20	48	55½	C'y m'st all day.		N., N. E., E.			
21	42	55	Cloudy	Clear	N. E., E.			Clear part of morning.
S 22	44	53	"	Cloudy	N. E.			Misty evening.
23	50	55	"	"	N. E., S. E.	0.04		Misty rain 10 A M. to 2 P.M.
24	52	60	"	Clear	N. E., N. W.	0.01		Rain before day, 0.01.
25	14½	58	Clear	"	N. W., W.			Comet merely visible.
26	45	66½	Cloudy	"	S. W., N. W.			Cleared 8 A. M.
27	42	56	Clear	Cloudy	NW.,SW.,SE			Rain 5:30 P.M.; thunder and lightning at midnight.
28	45	54	Cloudy	"	N. E., S. E.	0.63		Rain before day; clear part of afternoon.
S 29	51	62	"	"	S. W.	0.01		Rain before day, 0.01; foggy A. M.; clear part evening; rain 10:30 P. M.
30	55	60	"	Clear	All points.	0.18		Rain before day; foggy A.M.; clear part A. M. and P. M.
31	49	62¼	Foggy	Cloudy	S. E., S. W.			Partly clear part afternoon.
						1.42		

WEATHER RECORD FOR NEW BRUNSWICK, N. J.

November, 1882.

Date.	Thermometer. Lowest.	Highest.	Weather. Morning.	Afternoon.	Prevailing Wind.	Rain and Melted Snow in inches.	Snow in inches.	REMARKS.
1	59½	70	Cloudy	Clear	S. W., N. W.			Cleared 8 A. M.; cloudy part of evening.
2	52	58	"	"	N. W.	0.11		Rain before day.
3	32	45½	Clear	"	N., S. E.			First frost.
4	38	47	Cloudy	"	N. E.			
S 5	31	43	Clear	"	N. E.			
6	28	44½	"	"	N. E., S. E.			Cloudy part of evening.
7	37	46½	Cloudy	Cloudy	N. E.			Partly clear part of P. M
8	40½	50	"	Clear	N. E., N. W.			
9	41½	57½	"	"	S. W.			Cloudy evening.
10	47½	52	"	Cloudy	All points.	0.01		Rain part of morning.
11	51	59	"	"	N. E., S. E.			Clear part of afternoon; clear evening.
S 12	51	59	"	"	S. W.			Clear part of evening.
13	51	68	"	"	S. W., N. W.	0.22		Foggy morning; clear part of afternoon; rain 5 to 8:30 P. M.
14	38	43	"	"	W., N. W.			Clear part of morning; and part of evening, comet still visible.
15	35	47	"	Clear	N. W., W.			Cleared 8 A. M.
16	35	50	Clear	"	W., S. W.			
17	39½	41½	Rain	Rain	All points.			Snow part of evening.
18	32	37	Cloudy	Clear	N. E.	0.40		Rain before day, 0.40; cleared 8 A. M.; cloudy part of afternoon.
S 19	26½	38	Clear	"	N.			
20	28	41	"	"	N. W.			
21	27½	41	"	"	N. W., S. W.			Cloudy part of afternoon.
22	31½	44½	"	"	N. W., W.			
23	33	47	"	"	S W.			
24	34	44	"	"	S. W., N. W.			
25	34	43	"	"	N. W.			
S 26	29	37	"	Snow	S. W., S. E.	0.37		Clouded over 10 A. M.; snow 12:45 to 7 to P. M.; over 3 inches on ground.
27	31	38	Cloudy	Clear	W., N. W.	0.02		Snow 7:15 to 9 A. M., 0.02; clear 10 A. M.
28	21	31	Clear	Cloudy	N. W., N. E.			Cloudy part of morning.
29	25	32	Snow	Snow	N. E., N.			
30	26½	31	Cloudy	Clear	N. W.	0.47		Snow before day; clear 8 A. M; over 4 inches snow on ground.
						1.60		

December, 1882.

Date.	Thermometer. Lowest.	Thermometer. Highest.	Weather. Morning.	Weather. Afternoon.	Prevailing Wind.	Rain and Melted Snow in inches.	Snow in inches.	REMARKS.
1	23	37	C'y m'st all day		S. W.			
2	22½	40	Clear	Clear	S. W., N. W.			Cloudy evening.
S 3	25	29	Cloudy	"	N. W.			Cleared 8 A. M.
4	11	35	Clear	"	All points.			Cloudy evening.
5	24	41	"	Cloudy	S. W., N. E.			Light snow before day.
6	37	48½	Cloudy	Clear	W.	0.04		Rain before day, 0.04; cleared 8 A. M.
7	34½	42	"	"	S. W., N. W.			Cleared 3 P. M.
8	12	22½	Clear	"	N. W.			
9	13½	28	"	"	S. W.			Cloudy evening.
S 10	26	36	Snow } Rain	Cloudy	N. E., S.	0.27		Snow before day and rain 8 to 11:45 A. M., 0.24, and part of evening, 0.03.
11	33½	40	Rain	Clear	S. W., N. W.	0.07		Rain till 8:45 A. M., 0.07; cloudy part of evening.
12	30	37	Clear	"	N. W.			
13	28	44½	Cloudy	Cloudy	E., S., S. W.	0.47		Rain 8:30 A. M. to 1 P. M., 0.47; clear evening.
14	29	34½	Clear	Clear	W.			Cloudy evening.
15	27	31	"	"	W., N. W.			Cloudy part of afternoon.
16	20	28	"	"	N. W.			Cloudy part of afternoon, with snow squalls.
S 17	22½	34	"	"	N. W.			
18	26	33½	Cloudy	"	N. W., N.			Clear part of morning and cloudy part of afternoon.
19	20½	33½	Clear	"	N., N. E.			
20	16½	34	"	Cloudy	N. E., E.			
21	30	38	Cloudy	Rain	N. E., S. E.			Light snow before day; rain at noon.
22	34	39	Rain	"	N. E.	0.65		Rain till 7:15 A.M.; rain 3 PM.
23	35	45	Cloudy	Cloudy	N. W.	0.41		Rain before day; clear part of morning.
S 24	37	41	"	"	N. W.			Clear part of morning; clear part of evening.
25	36	44½	"	Clear	S. W., N. W.			Clear part of morning.
26	35	42½	C'y m'st all day	S. W.				
27	34	40	Clear	Clear	W., N. W.			Cloudy part of morning.
28	31½	37	"	"	N. W.			
29	26	37	"	"	S. W.			
30	30	35½	Cloudy	"	N. W., N. E.			
S 31	30	38½	Clear	"	N. W., S. W.			Cloudy evening.
						1.91		

Rain and melted snow for 1882—48.66 inches.

WEATHER RECORD FOR NEW BRUNSWICK, N. J.

January, 1883.

Date.	Thermometer. Lowest.	Highest.	Weather. Morning.	Afternoon.	Prevailing Wind.	Rain and Melted Snow in inches.	Snow in inches.	REMARKS.
1	32½	38	Clear	Cloudy	N. W., S. W.			0.50 Snow 8:15 to 11:30 P. M.
2	30¼	38	"	Clear	S. W., N. W.			Cloudy part of morning.
3	24	38	"	Cloudy	W., S. W.			Cloudy part of morning; clear evening.
4	27½	30	Cloudy	"	N. W.			Clear part of morning; snow 10:30 P. M.
5	14	18½	Snow	"	N. E.		3.50	Snow till noon; snow part of evening.
6	15	27	Cloudy	"	N. E.			Misty part of evening.
S 7	26	37	"	Clear	S. W.	0.06		Rain before day; cloudy part of afternoon.
8	23	33	Clear	Cloudy	N., E.			
9	23	27	"	"	N. E.			Cloudy part of morning.
10	12½	19	Snow	"	N. E.		6.00	Snow till noon, drifted very much; clear part of P. M.; snow part of evening.
11	11	20	Cloudy	Clear	N. E., N.			
12	9	24½	Clear	"	N. W.			
13	6	35	"	Sleet } Rain	S. W.			Cloudy part A. M.; sleet and rain 3:40 P. M.
S 14	34	38	Rain	Clear	S. W., N. W.	0.70		Rain till 8 A. M.; cleared at noon.
15	16	27	Clear	"	N. W., S. W.			
16	18	27½	Cloudy	Cloudy	N. E.	0.06		Snow 7:30 till noon.
17	25	37	"	Rain	N. E., E.	0.44		Rain 8 A.M. to 6 P. M., with sleet part of morning.
18	35	40½	"	Clear	N. W.			Clear part A. M.; hazy eve'g.
19	23½	27	"	Cloudy	N. E.	0.12		Snow 8:40 A. M. to 1 P. M.; misty part of afternoon.
20	24	38	"	Rain	N. E.			Rain 1:30 P. M.
S 21	35	42	"	Cloudy	S. W., N. W.	0.80		Rain before day, 0.80; clear part afternoon and partly clear part of evening.
22	17½	22½	Clear	Clear	N. W.			Cloudy part of afternoon.
23	5¼	19	"	"	N. W.			
24	8	23	"	"	N. W., S. W.			Cloudy evening.
25	20½	28½	Cloudy	Cloudy	N. W., N. E.	0.02		Light snow part of even'g.
26	17	28	"	"	N. E.			Light snow part of morning
27	23	35	"	Misty	S. E., S. W.	0.06		Misty afternoon and light rain part evening, 0.06.
S 28	34	38	"	Cloudy	S. W., N. E.	0.26		Rain before day, 0.04; rain 10 A. M. to 3 P. M., 0.21; part of evening, 0.01.
29	33	35	"	"	N. E.			Snow squalls part of morning and evening.
30	32½	42	Clear	Clear	N. W., S. W.			Clouded over 10:30 P. M.
31	34	47	Cloudy	"	S. E., S. W.	0.19		Rain before day, 0.01, and 8:45 to 10:45 A. M., 0.18; cleared 2 P. M.
						2.71	10.00	

February, 1883.

	Date.	Thermometer. Lowest.	Thermometer. Highest.	Weather. Morning.	Weather. Afternoon.	Prevailing Wind.	Rain and Melted Snow in inches.	Snow in inches.	REMARKS.
	1	27½	33½	Clear	Clear	N. W.			Cloudy part of morning.
	2	17	28	"	"	N. W, S. E.			Cloudy part A.M. and P.M.
	3	24	38	Rain	Cloudy	N. E.	0.08		Misty rain till 10 A.M., 0.07, partly clear part of afternoon; rain part P.M., 0.01.
S	4	34½	55	Cloudy	"	S. W., N. W.	0.03		Rain 8:30 to 9 A. M., 0.03; partly clear part of ev'g.
	5	29	34½	Snow	"	S. W., W.	0.16		Snow till 11:30 A.M.; cleared 6:30 P. M.
	6	15	30	Clear	"	S. W.			Rain and sleet 9 P. M.
	7	28	44	Rain	Clear	S. W.	1.04		Rain till 10:30 A. M., 1.04; cleared 2 P. M.
	8	28	35½	Clear	"	W.			
	9	28	39	"	"	S. W.			
	10	22½	30	"	"	N., N. E., S. E.			Clouded over 5 P.M.; snow 9:30 P. M.
S	11	25	41	Snow / Rain	Rain	N.E,S.E,SW.	1.02		Snow till day, then rain (5 in. snow on ground 7 A.M.) till 3 P.M., 0.99, part P.M., 0.03.
	12	32½	36½	Clear	Clear	N. W.			Cloudy part of morning.
	13	23	32½	Cloudy	"	N. W, S. W.			Clear part of A.M., and cl'dy part of afternoon.
	14	22½	34	"	Rain	S. W., S. E.	0.23		Sleet 9:30 A.M. to 7 P.M.
	15	32	35	Rain	"	N. E.	0.83		Rain till 7 A.M., 0.24; 12.30 to 5 P. M., 0.58, part of evening, 0.01.
	16	31½	37	Foggy	Cloudy	N. E., S. E.	0.05		Rain before day, 0.01; part ev'g, 0.04; foggy even'g.
	17	34	46	"	"	N. W., S. W.	0.07		Misty rain till 10 A.M., 0.06, 4:20 to 4:30 P.M., 0.01, rain 11 P. M
S	18	27	32½	Rain / Snow	Clear	N. W., W.	0.16		Rain before day and snow 5 to 10 A.M., 0.16, cl'd 2 P.M.
	19	18½	37½	Clear	"	N. W., S. W.			Cloudy part of morning.
	20	26½	38	"	Cloudy	N.E,S.E.,SW			Cloudy part of morning.
	21	29	34½	"	Clear	N. W.			
	22	29½	37½	Cloudy	Cloudy	S. W.			Partly clear part of A. M.
	23	29	35	Clear	Clear	N. W.			
	24	16	33	"	Cloudy	N. E., S. E.			Snow 8 P.M., and rain 10 P.M.
S	25	32	46	Rain / Fog	Clear	S. W., N. W.	0.94		Heavy rain before day, and misty till noon; cleared 4 P. M.
	26	32	36	Clear	"	N. W.	0.06		Cloudy part evening; snow squalls 7:15, 0.02; 10 P.M., 0.04.
	27	18	27	"	"	N. W.			Cloudy part of evening.
	28	24½	40	Cloudy	"	S. W., N. W.			Clear part of morning.
							4.67		

Weather Record for New Brunswick, N. J.

March, 1883.

Date	Thermometer Lowest	Thermometer Highest	Weather Morning	Weather Afternoon	Prevailing Wind	Rain and Melted Snow in inches	Snow in inches	REMARKS
1	27	45	Clear	Clear	S. W.			Cloudy part of morning.
2	36	57	Cloudy	"	SW, N.W, NE			
3	32½	36½	"	"	N. W.			Cleared 10 A. M.; clouded over 9 P. M.
S 4	26¼	39	"	"	S. W., N. W.	0 02		Clear part of A. M. & cloudy part of afternoon, with snow 2 to 3 P. M, 0.02.
5	15	26	Clear	"	N. W.			
6	21½	37	Snow	Rain	N. E., S. W.	0.51		Snow 6 A.M. to 2 P. M., 0.25 and then rain till 6 P. M. 0.26; partly clear part of evening.
7	32	36	Cloudy	Clear	N. W.			Clear part of of morning.
8	10½	22½	Clear	"	W.			Cloudy part of evening.
9	14	36	"	"	All points.			Bar. 3 P. M. 30.23°
10	28½	38	Rain	Cloudy	NE., NW, S.W	0.45		Rain till 1 P.M., 0.42 & part of P. M, 0.03; cleared 7 P.M. Bar. 2 P.M. 29.28°
S 11	33	39	Clear	Clear	S. W., N. W.			Cl'dy at intervals from 10:15 A.M. till 2 P.M. with snow squalls.
12	22	37	"	"	S. W.			Cl'dy part P.M. & part ev'g.
13	32½	45½	"	"	S. W.			
14	28	52	"	"	All points.			Cloudy part of morning.
15	42	55	"	"	S. W., N. W.			Cloudy part of morning; cloudy evening.
16	23	33½	"	"	N. W.			
17	28	43½	"	"	S. W.			Cloudy part of morning and parts of P M. and evening.
S 18	36	60	"	"	S. W.			
19	36½	56	"	Cloudy	N. E., E., S.	0.08		Clouded over 4 P. M. & rain 9:30 P. M. to 11:30 P. M.
20	27	34	"	Clear	N. W.			Cloudy part of morning.
21	21	33½	"	"	N. W.			
22	20½	33½	"	"	N. W., S. W.			
23	24	34½	"	Cloudy	S. E.	0.01		Light snow part of evening.
24	26	40	"	Clear	N. W.			
S 25	27½	47	"	"	N. W.			
26	30½	49	"	Cloudy	N. E., S. E.			Clouded over 3 P. M.
27	37	47½	Rain	"	N E., E.	0.04		Light rain till 11 A. M, 0.04; clear parts P. M. and ev'g.
28	33	43	Clear	Clear	N. W.			Cloudy part of evening.
29	30½	37½	Cloudy	Cloudy	All points.			
30	30½	33½	Snow	"	N. E.	0.85		Snow till 3 P.M.; cleared 7:15 P.M.; 6 inches snow on ground at noon.
31	23½	37½	Clear	"	N.W, N.E, S.E			Clear part of evening.
						1.96		

21

Weather Record for New Brunswick, N. J.

April, 1883.

Date.	Thermometer. Lowest.	Thermometer. Highest.	Weather. Morning.	Weather. Afternoon.	Prevailing Wind.	Rain and Melted Snow in inches.	Snow in inches.	REMARKS.
S 1	24½	38	Clear	Clear	N.E,NW,SW.			
2	29	42	Cloudy	"	N. E., S. E.			Cloudy part of evening.
3	33	48½	Clear	"	N. W.			
4	33½	53½	"	"	N. W., S. W.			Cloudy evening.
5	43½	67½	Cloudy	"	S. W.			Cleared 9 A.M.; cloudy ev'g.
6	58	61½	C'y m'st all day.	All points				
7	42½	45½	Rain	Cloudy	N. E.	0.09		Rain till 7 A. M.; clear part of evening.
S 8	37½	51½	Clear	Clear	N.			
9	38	60	"	"	N. W.			Cloudy part of evening.
10	45	57½	Cloudy	Cloudy	S. W., S. E.	0.02		Partly clear part P.M.; misty rain 10 to 11 P. M.
11	48	58	"	"	N. E., E.			Clear part of afternoon.
12	42½	49	"	"	E., N. E.	0.39		Shower 8 A. M., 0.02; 10 to 11 A.M., 0.31, with thunder and lightning; noon, 0.02, and 7 P. M., 0.04.
13	45½	60	Clear	Clear	N. E., S. E.			
14	42	56	"	"	N. E., S. E.			Cloudy part of evening.
S 15	40	56	Cloudy	"	S. W., S. E.			Cloudy part of evening.
16	44	50	"	Cloudy	N. E.	0.81		Foggy A.M.; misty rain part P.M. and eve'g, and heavy showers 9 to 11 P. M.
17	46	56	"	"	N. E.	0.20		Rain before day, 0.02; 7:30 to 10 A. M., 0.17; 2 P. M., 0.01; cloudy part P. M.
18	47½	65½	Clear	Clear	N.W.,N.E.,E.			
19	46	68	"	"	S. W.			Cloudy parts P.M. and eve'g.
20	47½	53½	Cloudy	"	S.W.,N.W.,N	0.12		Thunder showers 5:30 A. M., 0.05; rain 7:45 till 11 A.M., 0.07; cloudy part aftern'n
21	41	59½	Clear	"	N. W., S. W.			
S 22	42½	48	Cloudy	Rain	E., N. E.			Rain 8:30 A. M.
23	37	39	Rain	Rain/Snow	N. E.	0.56		Rain before day, 0.56; rain 8 A. M., all day with hail; snow after 10 P. M.
24	33	43½	Cloudy	Cloudy	N. W., S. W.	0.69		Snow and rain before day, 0.59; roofs covered with snow; rain and hail part P.M.; 0.10; cleared 8 P. M.; Northern lights.
25	33½	47	Clear	Clear	N. W., N.			Cloudy evening.
26	35½	52½	"	"	S. W., S. E.			Cloudy part of evening.
27	40½	63	"	"	S. W., N. W.	0.10		Hazy part A.M.; cloudy part of evening, with shower.
28	46½	61	"	Cloudy	All points	0.50		Showers 2:40 to 7 P.M.; clear part of evening.
S 29	34	46	Rain/Snow	Clear	N. E.	0.55		Rain till 8:30 A.M.,0:40, and then hail and heavy snow (0.14) till 1:30; light rain till 1 P.M.,0.01; cl'rd 4 P.M.
30	37	55	Clear	"	N., S.E., SW.			
						4.03		

May, 1883.

Date.	Ther-mometer. Lowest.	Highest.	Weather. Morning.	Afternoon.	Prevailing Wind.	Rain and Melted Snow in inches.	Snow in inches.	REMARKS.
1	39½	55½	Clear	Cloudy	S. E.	----	---	Clear part of afternoon.
2	44	58½	"	Clear	S. E., E.	----	----	Cloudy parts A. M. and ev'g.
3	48	67½	Cloudy	"	N. E., S. E.	----	----	Clear part of morning; cloudy part of evening.
4	53	72	"	Cloudy	S. W., S. E.	----	----	Clear 8 A. M. to 4 P. M.
5	47	54	"	"	E.	0.02	----	Light showers 6 to 7 P. M.; cherries flowered.
S 6	47½	66	"	Clear	N.	0.04	----	Rain before day, 0.04; cleared 9 A. M.
7	48	64½	Clear	Cloudy	N. W., S. W.	----	----	Cloudy part of morning.
8	53½	78	"	Clear	All points.	0.47	----	Thunder showers with hail 4:50 to 7 P. M., 0.33 in 10 min.; pears flowered.
9	55	69	"	"	N. E., S. E.	----	----	
10	48½	66	Cloudy	"	E.	0.06	----	Th'nder show'r 2½ A. M. 0.06.
11	54	68½	Clear	Cloudy	All points.	0.03	----	Clouded over 7 A. M.; light rain parts of day; clear part of evening.
12	47	66	"	Clear	N.E.,S., S.W.	----	----	Cloudy part of evening.
S 13	50	63	"	"	N.	----	----	
14	43	57	"	Cloudy	N. E., S. E.	0.06	----	Cl'y part A.M.; rain part P.M.
15	48	66½	Cloudy	Clear	All points.	0.45	----	Rain before day, 0.04; 9 to 11 A. M., 0.02; cloudy even'g with rain 7 to 7:30 P. M., 0.38; 9 P. M., 0.01.
16	51	66	Clear	"	N. W.	----	----	
17	44	65	"	"	NE,NW,S.W.	----	----	
18	47½	71	"	"	All points.	----	----	
19	48	70	"	"	NW.,N.E,SE.	----	----	Cloudy part of evening.
S 20	55	68½	Cloudy	"	S. E.	----	----	Partly clear part of morning; cloudy evening.
21	55	64	"	Cloudy	S. E.	----	----	Thunder showers after 6:45 P.M. (at 10½ A.M. 0.97 had fallen) and still raining; bar. 29.50° 10 P. M.
22	56	74	Rain	Clear	S. E.	1.24	----	Heavy rain after midnight and then light till 6 A.M.; c'y ev'g; bar. 29.45° all day.
23	55½	60	Cloudy	Cloudy	S. W., W.	----	----	A. B. V.
24	51½	72	Clear	Clear	N. W.	----	----	Cloudy part of morning.
25	51	76	"	"	S. W.	----	----	
26	57	81	"	"	S. W.	----	----	Cl'd'd over 5 P.M.; rain 10 P.M.
S 27	64	74½	Rain	"	S. W.	0.23	----	Rain till 5:30 A. M., 0.23; cleared 8 A. M.
28	58½	73½	Clear	"	N. W., S. W.	----	----	Cloudy evening.
29	61½	74	Cloudy	"	S. W., N. W.	0.01	----	Clear part A. M; light rain 11:15 A.M.; cl'dy part P.M.
30	53	68½	Clear	Cloudy	N W.,N E,SE.	0.03	----	Cloudy part A.M.; light rain about noon; cl'r part P. M.
31	60	72½	C'y m'st all day.		S. W., W.	0.18	----	Rain before day.
						2.82	----	

June, 1883.

Date.	Lowest.	Highest.	Weather. Morning.	Afternoon.	Prevailing Wind.	Rain and Melted Snow in inches.	Snow in inches.	REMARKS.
1	54	72	Clear	Clear	N. W.			
2	53	72	"	"	N. E., S. E.			
S 3	51½	64	Cloudy	Cloudy	N. E., S. E.			Sprinkles P. M. and evening; partly clear part evening; rain 11 P. M.
4	61	79	"	Clear	S. W.	0.20		Rain before day; clear part of morning.
5	66½	84	Clear	"	S. W.			Cloudy part A.M. and eve'g.
6	71	87	"	"	S. W.	0.07		Cloudy part A. M. and P. M., with showers 4:15 P. M.
7	70	85	"	Cloudy	S. W., W.	0.29		Clouded over 3 P. M ; rain 6 to 10 P. M.
8	68½	81½	"	Clear	S. W.			Cloudy part of morning.
9	65	82	"	"	S.			Cloudy part of evening.
S 10	69½	87	"	"	S. W.			Cloudy part A. M.; cloudy eve'g; rain 10:45 P. M.
11	72	85	"	"	S. W., N. W.	0.50		Rain before day,0.46; cloudy part A.M;sh'w'r 2 P.M.,0.04
12	62	81	"	"	W., S. W.			
13	66	85	"	Cloudy	S. W., N. W.	0.36		Shower 1:30 P.M.,0.30; light rain 6 to 10 P. M., 0.06.
14	59½	72½	"	Clear	N. E.			
15	54	75	"	"	NW.,N.E,SE			
16	55½	72½	"	Cloudy	S. W., S. E.	0.10		Clear part of afternoon; shower 10 P. M., 0.10.
S 17	60½	73½	Cloudy	"	S. E.			Clear part P.M. and even'g.
18	63½	68½	"	"	S. E.	0.31		Rain 11:30 A. M. to 3 P. M., 0.30;shower 4:30 P.M.,0.01; partly clear part of eve'g.
19	63	78½	Rain	Clear	S. E., S. W.	1.43		Rain till 5:30 A. M, 1.43; clear part of morning; cloudy part of afternoon.
20	65	78½	Clear	"	N. W., S. W			Cloudy evening.
21	65	77	"	"	W., S. W.			Cloudy part A.M. and eve'g.
22	63½	78	"	"	N. E., N.			Cloudy part of afternoon.
23	64	81½	"	"	N. E.			
S 24	66	83	"	"	All points.			
25	64	80	"	"	S. E.			Foggy morning.
26	68	74	Cloudy	Cloudy	S. E.			Sprinkle about noon; partly clear part of afternoon.
27	67	70	Rain	Rain	S. E., N. E.	1.90		Rain before day, 0.08; at intervals 8:30 A.M. to 6:40 P. M. and then steady till 10:30, 1.82;cleared 11 P.M.
28	63½	80	Clear	Clear	S. W.			
29	69½	80	Cloudy	"	S. E., S. W.	0.06		Clear part A.M.; shower 1:30 P.M., 0.04; 6:30 P.M., 0.02.
30	67½	79	Clear	"	All points.	0.02		Shower 11:15 A. M., 0.02; cloudy part of afternoon.
						5.24		

July, 1883.

Date.	Thermometer.		Weather.		Prevailing Wind.	Rain and Melted Snow in inches.	Snow in inches.	REMARKS.
	Lowest.	Highest.	Morning.	Afternoon.				
S 1	57	73	Clear	Clear	N E., N W, S W			
2	61	85	"	"	S. W., N.	0.01		Cloudy part of P. M., with shower 6:20 P. M.
3	69	85	"	"	All points.			Cloudy part of afternoon.
4	70	90	"	"	S. W.			
5	74	87½	"	"	S. W.	0.53		Cloudy part of A.M.; cloudy part of P.M., with shower 6:45 to 7:10 P.M.
6	73½	89	"	"	S. W.			Cloudy part of P.M., with sprinkle 8:30.
7	75	91	"	"	S. W.	0.07		Showers 7:10 and 7:35 P. M.
S 8	76¼	80½	"	Cloudy	S. W., N. E.	0.92		Cloudy part of A.M.; shower at noon, 0.03; 12:40 to 1:30 P.M., 0.45; steady rain 6 to 11:30 P M.
9	59	71	Cloudy	"	N. E., S. E.			
10	64	77	"	Clear	S. W.			Clear part of morning.
11	63	81	Clear	"	S. W.			
12	68	79½	"	"	S. W., S.	0.23		Light rain 10:15 to 11:30 A. M., 0.03; shower 2:20 to 2:25 P M., 0.20.
13	68½	82½	"	"	S. W.			Cloudy part A.M.; cloudy P.M.
14	67	81½	Cloudy	"	N., W.			
S 15	69	84	Clear	Cloudy	S. W., S.	0.32		Clouded over 2 P. M.; rain 7:30 to 9:15 P M.
16	69½	83	"	Clear	N. W.			
17	69	88	"	"	S. W.	0.03		Cloudy part of afternoon; light rain 4:30 to 5:30 P.M.
18	68	80	"	"	N. W.			
19	64½	77½	"	"	N. W., N.			
20	62	76	"	"	N. W.			
21	60	79	"	Cloudy	S. W., S.	0.19		Clear part afternoon; rain 10:45 P.M. to 11:45 P.M.
S 22	70	86	C'y m'st all day.		S. W.	0.45		Shower 4 P.M., 0.07, and 6 to 6:20 P.M., 0.38.
23	74	86	"	"	N. W., S. W.	0.13		Shower 3:15 to 4 P.M.; a gale with little rain.
24	66	70	Rain	Cloudy	N. W, N. E.	0.41		Rain till 8:45 A M., 0.37, and 5 to 6 P. M., 0.04.
25	63	76	Clear	Clear	N. E., S. E.			Cloudy part of morning.
26	63	79	"	"	All points	0.04		Shower 5:20 P. M.
27	62½	81½	Cloudy	"	All points	0.05		Clear part of morning, and cloudy part of afternoon with rain 6:15 to 6:45 P.M.
28	68½	83	Clear	Cloudy	S. W.	0.06		Cloudy 3 P.M.; shower 4:45 to 5:10 P.M., 0.04; and 7:10 to 7:30 P.M., 0.02.
S 29	66½	77	"	Clear	N, N. W.			
30	59	75½	"	"	N. W.			
31	62	79	"	"	W., S. W.			

3.44

August, 1883.

Date.	Thermometer.		Weather.		Prevailing Wind.	Rain and Melted Snow in inches.	Snow in inches.	REMARKS.
	Lowest.	Highest.	Morning.	Afternoon.				
1	63½	83½	Clear	Clear	S. W.			Cloudy part of morning.
2	68	71	Cloudy	Cloudy	S W,S.E,N.E.	3.50		Rain 8:20 A.M. till 3 P. M.; mostly from 10:30 A. M. to 1:30 P. M.
3	63	78½	Clear	Clear	S. W., W.			Cloudy part of morning.
4	60	74½	"	"	S.W,NW,SW			
S 5	58½	76	"	"	W.,N.W., W.			
6	59	76	"	"	N. W., W.			
7	57	76	"	"	N. W., N. E.			
8	58	76	"	"	All points.			
9	58½	77	"	"	N. E., S. E.			
10	62½	73½	Cloudy	"	N. E., E.			
11	60	77	Clear	"	N. E., S. E.			
S 12	60	79	"	"	N. E.			
13	62½	84	"	"	S. W., W.			Cloudy part of afternoon.
14	65½	76	"	"	N. W., N.			Cloudy part of morning.
15	60	70	"	Cloudy	N. E., E.	0.04		Cloudy part of morning; light rain 3 to 7 P. M., 0.04 ; rain 10 P. M.
16	59	65	Rain	"	N. E.	0.44		Rain till 11 A. M.; clear part of evening.
17	57	75	Clear	Clear	N, W , S. W.			
18	64	81	Cloudy	"	S. W.	0.16		Foggy morning; cloudy ev'g with shower 7:50 P. M.
S 19	67	83	Clear	"	N. W., S. W.	0.15		Cloudy part of morning and cloudy part of afternoon with shower 2:35 P. M.
20	68	86½	"	"	S. W.			
21	72½	85½	"	"	N. W., S. W.	0.11		Shower 1:35 A. M.
22	65	85½	"	"	N. W.,S.W,S.			
23	66	86½	"	"	S. W.			Cloudy evening.
24	69½	79	"	"	N.			
25	58½	77	"	"	N. W.			
S 26	59	80½	"	"	W,S.W.,NW.			Cloudy part of afternoon.
27	56½	73	"	"	NW,NE,SE.			
28	53	72	"	"	N. E., S. E.			Cloudy evening.
29	59½	72	Cloudy	Cloudy	N. E.			Clear part of afternoon.
30	60	72½	"	Clear	N. E., S. E.			Cloudy part of afternoon.
31	54½	77½	Clear	"	N. E., S. E.			
						4.40		

Weather Record for New Brunswick, N. J. 327

September, 1883.

Date.	Lowest.	Highest.	Weather. Morning.	Weather. Afternoon.	Prevailing Wind.	Rain and Melted Snow in inches.	Snow in inches.	REMARKS.
1	57	76	Clear	Clear	N. E., S. E.			
S 2	58	81	"	Cloudy	S. W.	0.12		Clouded over 3 P. M., and rain 7:45 P. M. to 10:45 P. M.
3	64½	70	"	Clear	N.			
4	48	71	"	"	N.W.,E.,S.W			
5	60	73	"	"	W., N.			Cloudy part of morning.
6	48	70	"	"	N.W,E.,S.E.			
7	49	74	"	"	S. W., S.			
8	57½	78	"	Cloudy	S. W.	0.12		Cloudy part A.M.; clear part P.M.;rain 5:45 to 6:20 P.M.
S 9	51	65	"	Clear	N. W., N.	0.10		Rain before day, 0.10.
10	43	63½	"	"	N. E., S. E.			Cloudy part P.M.; light frost.
11	48	63	Cloudy	Cloudy	N. E.			Partly clear part A. M.; rain 8:15 P. M.
12	53½	61	"	Rain	N. E.	0.07		Rain before day, 0.07; misty rain 3 to 10 P. M., and then heavy rain.
13	59	67½	"	Cloudy	S. E., S. W.	0.77		Rain before day, 0.76; light rain parts A. M. and P. M.
14	63½	77	C'y m'st all day.		S. W.			
15	66	77	Clear	Clear	All points.			Cloudy part of morning.
S 16	61	74½	"	"	N. E., S. E.			Cloudy evening.
17	66	79½	Cloudy	Cloudy	S.W.,N.,N.E.	0.08		Clear part P.M.; shower 6:40 P. M., 0.08; rain 9 P. M.
18	55	67½	"	Clear	N. E., S. E.	0.41		Rain before day.
19	52	70	Clear	"	N. E., E.			Cloudy part of afternoon.
20	53	72	"	"	N. E., S. E.			Cloudy parts A. M. and P. M.
21	55½	73	"	"	N. E., S. E.			Cloudy evening.
22	55	64	C'y m'st all day.		N. E., S. E.			
S 23	55	64	Cloudy	Cloudy	N. E., S. E.			Partly clear part afternoon.
24	60	67½	"	Rain	N. E.,S.,S.W.	0.99		Rain 6 to 10:30 A. M., 0.11; 11:30 A.M. to 10 P.M.,0.88.
25	55	67½	Clear	Clear	S. W., W.			Cloudy part of afternoon.
26	48	61½	"	"	N. W.			
27	45	67	"	"	S. W.			Cloudy part of morning; cloudy evening.
28	56	71½	Hazy	"	S. W.	0.04		Foggy A. M.; cloudy evening with showers, 0.04.
29	50	59½	C'y m'st all day.		N. E., S. E.	0.16		Rain before day.
S 30	57	70	Cloudy	Cloudy	S.W.,N., N.E.	0.49		Clear part P. M.; showers after 6:30 P. M; and raining at midnight.
						3.35		

October, 1883.

Date	Thermometer. Lowest	Thermometer. Highest	Weather. Morning	Weather. Afternoon	Prevailing Wind.	Rain and Melted Snow in inches.	Snow in inches.	REMARKS.
1	49	59	Cloudy	Clear	N E,N W,S W.	0.33		Rain before day; clear part of morning.
2	50	70½	Rain	"	S.E,S.W,N W	0.61		Rain till 12:15 P. M., 0.61; cloudy part of evening.
3	48	64½	Clear	"	W.			
4	43½	55	"	"	N. W.			
5	38	55	"	"	N. W.			Frost.
6	38	54½	"	Rain	N.E.,S.E,N.E			Clouded over 11 A.M.; rain 2 P. M.
S 7	46	58	Cloudy	Clear	N. E., S. E.	0.46		Rain before day, 0.46; cleared 8 A. M.
8	42½	60½	Clear	"	N. E., S. E.			
9	46½	64	"	"	N. E., S. E.			
10	45	67½	"	"	N. E., S. E.			
11	49	72	"	"	N.W,N.E,S.E			Cloudy 10:30 P. M.
12	59½	63½	Misty	Misty	N.E.,S.E,N.E	0.14		Rain before day, and rainy at intervals all day.
13	60½	70½	"	"	N. E., E.	0.29		Misty and foggy, with showers at intervals.
S 14	69	79	Cloudy	Clear	S. W., N. W.	0.08		Rain before day, 0.08; cleared 10 A. M.; warmest since October 10, 1865.
15	48	55½	Clear	"	N., N. E.			
16	35	49	"	"	N. E., S. E.			
17	34½	50½	"	"	N. E., S. E.			
18	35	55	"	"	N. E., S. E.			Cloudy 5 P. M.
19	48½	63½	Cloudy	Cloudy	S. W.			Clear part of afternoon.
20	58	63½	{ M'sty / Rain	"	S. W., N. W.	0.18		Misty before day and rain 8 A. M. to 12:30 P. M., 0.18; partly clear part of afternoon.
S 21	41	48	Cloudy	"	N. E.			
22	40	49½	"	"	N. E.			Partly clear about noon.
23	43½	45	"	Rain	N. E.			Rain 9 A.M.
24	40	49½	"	Cloudy	N. E.	1.40		Rain before day; cleared 5 P. M.
25	39	52½	Clear	Clear	N.W., N. E.			Cloudy part of morning.
26	44	52	Rain	Cloudy	N. E., E.	0.10		Rain till 12:30 P. M.; clear part of evening.
27	43½	54½	C'y m'st all day.		N. W.			
S 28	47½	55	Cloudy	Cloudy	N. E., S. E.			
29	52½	65½	Rain	"	S., S. W.	0.70		Rain 6 to 11:45 A. M., 0.41; 2 to 2:40 P. M., 0.13; 7 to 9 P. M., 0.16; cleared 10 P. M.
30	55	64	Clear	Clear	W.			
31	47½	65½	"	"	S. W., N. W.			Cloudy part of afternoon.

4.29

November, 1883.

	Date.	Thermometer. Lowest.	Thermometer. Highest.	Weather. Morning.	Weather. Afternoon.	Previling Wind.	Rain and Melted Snow in inches.	Snow in inches.	REMARKS.
	1	42	52	Clear	Clear	S. W., N. W.	----	----	Cloudy part of afternoon.
	2	39	47	"	"	W., N. W.	----	----	Cloudy part of afternoon.
	3	34	47½	"	"	N. W., S. W.	----	----	
S	4	39	58	"	"	S. W.	----	----	
	5	38½	62	"	"	S. W.	----	----	
	6	44½	61½	"	Cloudy	S. W.	----	----	Cloudy part of morning and clear parts of afternoon and evening; rain 11 P. M.
	7	47	54	"	Clear	N. W.	0.25	----	Rain before day.
	8	37	55	"	"	N. W., S. W.	----	----	Cloudy evening.
	9	49	59	Cloudy	Cloudy	S., S. W.	0.15	----	Rain 9 to 10 A.M., 0.04, 12:15 to 2 P.M., 0.11; partly clear parts of aft'rnoon & eve'g.
	10	53	55	Rain	Rain	All points.	0.27	----	Rain at intervals till 4 P. M.; clear part of evening and foggy afterwards.
S	11	49	55	Cloudy	Cloudy	All points	0.07	----	Rain part of afternoon, 0.01, and part of evening, 0.06.
	12	38½	41	Clear	Clear	N. W.	----	----	Snow squalls 9:15 and 10:30 A. M. and 2:30 P. M.
	13	32½	40½	"	Cloudy	W., S. W.	----	----	Cloudy part of morning and clear part of evening.
	14	39	47	Cloudy	Clear	S. W., N. W.	----	----	
	15	26	38½	Clear	"	S. W.	----	----	
	16	23	35	"	"	N. W.	----	----	
	17	21½	38½	"	"	S. W.	----	----	
S	18	28	47½	"	"	S. W.	----	----	At noon clocks set back 3 min. 58½ sec.
	19	32	53½	"	"	S. W.	----	----	
	20	33	53	"	Cloudy	S. W., S. E.	----	----	Clear part of afternoon.
	21	45	55½	Foggy	"	S. E., E.	0.04	----	Rain 12:20 to 1:30 P. M.; clear part of evening.
	22	52	68	C'y m'st all day		S. W.	0.01	----	Light rain 9 A. M.
	23	61	64	Cloudy	Cloudy	S.W.,N.,N. E.	----	----	Light rain after 9:40 P. M.
	24	47	53½	"	Clear	N. E., N., W.	0.09	----	Rain before day, 0.09; cleared 3 P. M.
S	25	43	50½	C'y m'st all day		N. E.	----	----	
	26	39	48	Cloudy	Rain	N. E	0.60	----	Rain 9:40 A. M. to 10 P. M.
	27	40½	43½	Clear	Clear	N.	0.01	----	Rain before day.
	28	30½	46	"	"	NW,SW,NW	----	----	
	29	30	37½	"	"	N. W., S. W.	----	----	
	30	33	45	C'y m'st all day		S. W., N. W.	----	----	
							1.49	----	

December, 1883.

Date.	Thermometer. Lowest.	Thermometer. Highest.	Weather. Morning.	Weather. Afternoon.	Prevailing. Wind.	Rain and Melted Snow in inches.	Snow in inches.	REMARKS.
1	28½	37	Clear	Clear	N. E., S. E.			Clouded over 8 P. M.; light sleet 9 P. M.
S 2	33	45	Cloudy	"	N.E., S., N.W.	0.02		Light rain parts A.M., 0.02; cloudy part even'g, with snow squall.
3	28½	36	Clear	"	N. W.			
4	23½	45	"	"	N.E., S., S.W.			Cloudy part of evening.
5	35	48	Cloudy	Cloudy	W.	0.15		Rain before day; clear evening.
6	37	46	Clear	Clear	NW., NE., SE			
7	33	51	Cloudy	Cloudy	S.W., S. E., S.			Partly clear parts A.M.& P.M.
8	45	55	"	Rain	S. W.	0.45		Rain before day, 0.01; 10:30 A.M. to 12:15 P.M., 0.11, and 1 to 11 P. M., 0.33.
S 9	44½	48	"	Clear	N., N. W.			
10	34	49	Clear	"	S. W.			Cloudy part P.M. and eve'g.
11	33½	40	"	Cloudy	N. W., S. W.			Clear part P. M. and eve'g.
12	36	43	"	Clear	N. W.			Light rain before day; cloudy part of afternoon.
13	31½	47½	"	"	S. W.			Cloudy part of evening.
14	41	51½	Cloudy	Cloudy	S. W., N. W.	0.06		Shower 7 A. M., 0.02; light shower during eve'g, 0.04.
15	20½	26½	Clear	Clear	N. W.			
S 16	15½	29	"	Cloudy	S. W.			Light snow 10 P. M.
17	23	32½	Cloudy	Clear	N. E., N. W.		1.00	Snow before day, 1 inch; cleared 9 A. M.
18	23	38	"	Cloudy	S.W.			Light snow part morning.
19	25	32	Snow	"	N. E.		6.00	Snow 5:30 A.M. to 3 P.M., 6 in.
20	22½	26½	Cloudy	"	N. E.			Light snow after 6:30 P. M.
21	21½	30	Snow	Clear	NE, NW, SW.		3.00	Snow till 8:45 A.M., 3 inches; cloudy part of evening.
22	21	26	Clear	"	N. W.			
S 23	2	10	"	Cloudy	N. E.			Snow 7 P. M.
24	5	32	Snow } Sleet }	"	NE., N., S.W.		10.00	Heavy snow and light sleet before day, 4 inches.
25	25	32	Cloudy	Snow	N. E.		5.00	Snow 2 P.M. to 8 P. M., 5 in.
26	16	32½	Clear	Cloudy	N. W., N. E.			Partly clear part evening.
27	27	45	Cloudy	"	N.E., S., S.W.	0.41		Rain 2:40 to 5 P. M., 0.41; heavy fog part afternoon; partly clear part of eve'g.
28	26	31½	Clear	Clear	N. W., W.			
29	23	33½	"	"	N. W., S. W.			
S 30	16½	36	"	"	N.E., W., S.W.			Cloudy evening.
31	32½	39	Cloudy	Cloudy	N. E.	0.02		Rain before day, 0.02.
						1.11	25.00	

Rain and melted snow for 1883—43.01 inches.

January, 1884.

Date.	Thermometer. Lowest.	Thermometer. Highest.	Weather. Morning.	Weather. Afternoon.	Prevailing Wind.	Rain and Melted Snow in inches.	Snow in inches.	REMARKS.
1	33	35½	Cloudy	Cloudy	N. E.	0.18		Rain before day and part of A. M., 0.18; rainy ev'g.
2	33¼	40	Rain	"	N. E.,S.,N.W.	0.80		Rain till 1 P. M., cleared 5 P. M.
3	23¼	30	Clear	Clear	S. W.			
4	16	24	"	"	W.			
5	13	18½	Cloudy	Cloudy	N. W.			Cleared 5 P. M.
S 6	9	17½	Clear	Clear	W.			
7	8	20	"	"	N. W., S. W.			
8	13½	*40	Cloudy	Snow Rain	N. E, S. E.			Snow 1 to 3:30 P. M., 0.17; and then rain; ther. rising all day; bar. 7 A.M.,30.31
9	†26	‡45¼	"	Cloudy	S., S. W., W.	1.94		Rain before day, 1.77.; cleared 6 P.M.; ther. falling all day; bar. 7 A.M., 29.14.
10	23	31	Clear	Clear	W., S. W.			Clouded over 5 P.M.; sleet 8:30 P M.
11	29	38	Rain	Rain	S. W.	0.41		Rain before day, 0.04, and 7 A. M. to 7 P. M., and snow till 9 P. M, 0.37.
12	23½	27½	Clear	Clear	N. W., W.			Cloudy part of morning.
S 13	22	36	"	Cloudy	S. W			Clear part of evening.
14	31	43½	"	"	S. W., N			
15	23½	27	Snow	Snow	N. E.		4.50	Snow till 8 A. M, 3 in., and 2 P.M. to 11 P.M., 1.50.
16	12	21	Clear	Clear	N. W., S. W.			Cloudy part of evening.
17	5	25½	"	"	S. W.			
18	22	38	Cloudy	Cloudy	S. W.			Clear 8 A. M. to 3 P. M.
19	30½	34	Snow	"	N. E.	0.28		Snow and sleet 8:15 A. M., 0.12; heavy snow till noon, 0.15; and light till 3:30 P M., 0.01.
S 20	17½	24	"	"	N. E., N. W.	0.10		Snow till 2 P M., 0.10; cleared 6 P.M.
21	8	21	Clear	Clear	W., S. W.			
22	7	31	"	"	S. W.			Cloudy evening.
23	21	37	"	"	S. W., N. E.			Cloudy part P. M. and part of evening.
24	22½	36	Cloudy	Rain	N. E.	1.07		Rain 7 A.M. to 10 P M.
25	17	23	"	Cloudy	N. W.			Clear part of A. M; clear evening.
26	10	24	Clear	Clear	N. W., W.			
S 27	13	27	"	"	N. W., N. E.			Cloudy evening.
28	21	33½	Cloudy	Snow	N. E.			Snow 12:15 P. M.
29	26	32½	Snow	Cloudy	N. E.		3.00	Snow till 7:30 A. M., 3.00; cleared 6:30 P.M.
30	15	36	Cloudy	Rainy	S. W.			Foggy morning; rain at intervals after 4:40 P.M.
31	35	41	"	Cloudy	S. W.	0.10		Rain before day, 0.10; foggy evening.
						4.88	7.50	

*11 P. M. 8th   †7 A. M. 9th   ‡11 P. M. 9th.

February, 1884.

Date.	Thermometer. Lowest.	Thermometer. Highest.	Weather. Morning.	Weather. Afternoon.	Prevailing Wind.	Rain and Melted Snow in inches.	Snow in inches.	REMARKS.
1	38	41	Cloudy	Clear	S. W., N. W.	0.02		Rain before day, 0.02; cleared 10:30 A. M
2	20	36	Clear	"	S. W.			Cloudy part of afternoon; 45 days sleighing.
S 3	23½	39½	"	"	N.W.,N.E.,E.			Cloudy evening.
4	32	34	Cloudy	Cloudy	N. E.	0.04		Rain before day, 0.04; rainy after 9:30 P. M.
5	30	41	Rain	"	N. E., N. W.	0.43		Rain till 8 A. M.; 0:43; clear part of evening.
6	38	54	Cloudy	"	All points			Partly clear part afternoon; light rain at intervals during evening.
7	41	45	Rain	Rain	W., N., N. E.			Rain all day at intervals.
8	32	34½	"	Misty	N. E.	0.40		Rain till 7 A.M., 0 38; light rain parts of P. M., 0.02.
9	32	38	"	"	All points	0.11		Rain till 8 A. M., 0 08, and part P. M., 0 03; partly clear 10:45 P. M.
S 10	36	42	Clear	Clear	N.			Cloudy part of evening.
11	30	37½	Snow	Cloudy	N. E.		4.00	Snow till 7:30 A.M., 4 inches; rainy evening.
12	31	41	Cloudy	"	N. E.	0.18		Rain before day, 0.18; foggy A M; rainy evening.
13	35	57	Rain	Foggy	S. W.	0.10		Rain parts A. M. and P. M.
14	43	59	Cloudy	Cloudy	S. W., N. W.	0.11		Showers part of A. M., with thunder and lightning 0.10; part P. M., 0.01.
15	25	31	"	Clear	N. E., N.			Cleared about noon.
16	21	35½	Clear	"	N. E., S. E.			Cloudy part of afternoon.
S 17	30	44	Cloudy	Rain	N. E.			Rain 9 A. M.
18	40	49½	"	Cloudy	S. W., N. W.	1.00		Rain before day,0.99;7 to 7:30 A.M.,0.01; sprinkle 7 P. M.
19	39	42	"	"	S. E.			Rainy evening.
20	38	52½	Rain	Clear	S. W., N. W.	0.54		Rain till 7 A.M.,0.53;9 to 9:30 A.M.,0.01;cleared 11:15 A.M.
21	26	40	Clear	"	N. W., S. W.			Cloudy part of morning.
22	28	41	"	"	N. E., S. E.			Clouded over 5 P. M.
23	35	41½	Rain	Cloudy	N. E., N. W.	0.77		Rain till noon; snow squalls part P.M.; cleared 5 P. M.
S 24	20½	30	Clear	Clear	N. W., S. W.			Cloudy part of evening.
25	27½	41	C'y m'st all day.	S. E., E.				Rain 10:30 P. M.
26	33½	39	Rain	Cloudy	N. E.	0.21		Rain with light snow till 7 A.M., 0.17; part ev'g, 0.04.
27	36	43½	Clear	"	S. W., N. W.			Clear part of afternoon.
28	33	38	Snow	"	E., N.E., N.W.	0.97		Heavy wet snow till 10 A. M., and light till 11:30 A. M.; cleared 7:30 P. M.
29	6	16	Clear	Clear	N. W.			
						4.88	4.00	

WEATHER RECORD FOR NEW BRUNSWICK, N. J.   333

March, 1884.

Date	Thermometer. Lowest	Highest	Weather. Morning.	Afternoon.	Prevailing Wind.	Rain and Melted Snow in inches.	Snow in inches.	REMARKS.
1	7	20½	Clear	Clear	W.			River frozen over again.
S 2	15	23	Snow	Snow	N. E.		1.00	Light snow all day.
3	13	28	Cloudy	Clear	N. W.	0.02		Clear part A. M. and cloudy part P. M. and evening,
4	13	22½	Clear	"	W.			with heavy snow squalls.
5	11	32	Cloudy	Snow	SW, SE, NE		2.00	Snow 10:45 A. M. to 8 P. M.
6	28	38	"	Clear	NE,NW,SW.			Cloudy part of afternoon.
7	29	32	"	Cloudy	N. E.			Rainy evening.
8	30½	36	Rain	Rain	N. E.	0.83		Rain till 4 P.M.; rainy eve'g.
S 9	28½	34	Cloudy	Cloudy	N. E.	0.51		Rain before day, 0.07; 11:45 to 2, 0.29; thunder and lightning 12:30 P.M.; rain and snow 5 to 8 P.M., 0.15.
10	28	36	Clear	Clear	N., N. W.			Cloudy part of afternoon.
11	27	47	C'y m'st all day.		S. E., S.	0.02		Shower between 8 and 9 P.M.
12	38½	62	Cloudy	Cloudy	S. W.	0.05		Clear part of A.M. and eve'g; sh'w'r between 2 and 3 PM.
13	38¼	40	"	"	S. W., N. W.			Clear part of morning.
14	37	39	Rain	Rain	N. E.			
15	35½	45½	Cloudy	Clear	N., N. W.	0.38		Rain before day, 0.37; rain and snow part of A. M., 0.01; cleared 10:30 A. M.
S 16	33½	42	"	"	S. W., N. W.			Cleared 7:30 A. M.
17	30	51	Clear	Cloudy	S. W.			Cloudy part of morning.
18	36	48	"	"	All points.			Clear part of afternoon.
19	37	43	Rain	Rain	E.	0.96		Rain 6 A. M. to 8 P. M.
20	38	44	"	Cloudy	N. E., N. W.	0.40		Rain till 10:30 A. M., 0.37; part of evening, 0.03.
21	38	47	"	"	N. E., S. E.	0.03		Light rain till 7 A. M., 0.03.
22	34	56	Cloudy	Clear	S. W.			Cleared 8 A. M.
S 23	39½	53	Clear	Cloudy	S. W., S. E.	0.02		Cloudy part of A. M.; light rain 2 to 4 P. M., 0.02; rainy evening.
24	49	60	Cloudy	"	S.W.,N.W.,N	0.11		Rain before day; cl'rd 7 P.M.
25	41½	56½	Clear	Clear	N.E.,W.,S.E.			Cloudy 6 to 10 P. M. and partly clear after.
26	43½	56	Rain	Cloudy	E.,N.E.,N W	0.60		Rain till 11.15 A. M., 0.56; part of P. M., 0.04.
27	46	56	Cloudy	Clear	N. W.			Clear part of morning.
28	42	59½	Clear	Cloudy	N. W., S. W.			Clouded over 3 P. M.; light rain 10:40 P. M.
29	42	59	"	Clear	N. E., N. W.			Cloudy part of morning; first dusty day.
S 30	25½	37½	"	"	N. W.			Violent gale set in on 29th at 8:30 P.M., and continued until Monday morning.
31	27	47½	"	"	N. W.			
						3.93	3.00	

April, 1884.

Date.	Lowest.	Highest.	Weather. Morning.	Weather. Afternoon.	Prevailing. Wind.	Rain and Melted Snow in inches	Snow in inches.	REMARKS.
1	36	49	C'y m'st all day		N. W., S. W.			
2	37½	39½	Rain	Rain } Snow	SE, NE, NW.			Rain nearly all day with heavy snow 4 to 6 P. M.
3	34½	44	Cloudy	Cloudy	N. W.	0.81		Rain before day, 0.81; partly clear part A.M. and P.M.
4	38	52½	Clear	Clear	N. W.			Cloudy part of evening.
5	38	47	"	"	N. W.			Cloudy part of evening.
S 6	34½	48	"	"	N. W.			
7	35½	51½	"	"	N. W.			Cloudy part of afternoon.
8	36	52	"	Cloudy	All points.	0.05		Rain 3 to 8 P. M.
9	38	40½	Cloudy	"	N.E.,N.E.N.E	0.62		Rain 6:30 to 10:45 P.M., 0.19; noon to 4 P. M., 0.43, with snow and hail.
10	36½	52	C'y m'st all day		N. W.	0.06		Rain before day, 0.03; showers 5 to 5:20 P.M., 0.03.
11	42	54½	Clear	Clear	N W.			
12	37½	56	"	"	W., S. W.			
S 13	41	58	"	"	N. E., S. E.			Cloudy part A. M. and eve'g.
14	39½	61½	"	"	S. W.			Cloudy part of evening.
15	42½	51	Cloudy	Rain	E.			Rainy after 8:30 A. M.
16	48	68	Rain	Clear	S. E., S. W.	0.60		Rain before day and show'rs 5:50 to 7:30 A. M., 0.60, with thunder; cleared 8 A. M.; cloudy evening.
17	51	57	Clear	"	N. W.			Cloudy part A. M. and P. M.
18	44	58½	"	Cloudy	N. W., N.			Cloudy part of morning, and clear part afternoon.
19	48	61	C'y m'st all day		N. E., S. E.			
S 20	49	62	Cloudy	Clear	All points.			Cloudy evening.
21	50	59½	"	"	N. W., N. E.			
22	37	56	Clear	"	All points.			
23	41	60	"	"	N. E., S. E.			Cloudy evening.
24	48	56	Cloudy	Cloudy	N. E., S. E.	0.02		Clear part of A. M.; rainy part of evening.
25	47	56	"	"	N.E.,SE.,SW.	0.04		Rain part of evening.
26	50½	60	"	Clear	N. W., N. E.			Cloudy part of afternoon.
S 27	48	67	Clear	"	S. E.			Cherries flowered.
28	44	68½	"	"	SE.,S.W.,N.E.			Cloudy part of evening.
29	44	56	"	"	N. E., N.			Cloudy part of morning.
30	41	67	"	"	N. E., S. E.			
						2.20		

Weather Record for New Brunswick, N. J.

May, 1884.

Date.	Thermometer. Lowest.	Thermometer. Highest.	Weather. Morning.	Weather. Afternoon.	Prevailing Wind.	Rain and Melted Snow in inches.	Snow in inches.	REMARKS.
1	50½	67	Clear	Clear	S. E.			
2	50	83½	"	"	N E, S.W, N W			C'dy part of A. M and part P.M.; during ev'g sky hid by smoke; pears flowered.
3	51½	66½	"	"	N. W., S. W.			Cloudy part of afternoon.
S 4	54	62	Cloudy	Rainy	S. W., S. E.	0.02		Light rain 10:30 A. M. to 6 P. M., 0.02.
5	51	68½	"	Cloudy	S. E., S. W.	0.12		Thunder showers with hail 5:30 to 7 A. M.; clear part of morning.
6	53	55	Rain	Rainy	E., N. E.	0.70		Rain 7:30 A. M. to 1 P.M., 0.70; misty afternoon and rainy evening.
7	47	50	"	Rain	N. E.	0.71		Heavy rain before day, 0.53, and misty rain all day, 0.18, till 11:15 P. M.
8	44½	50½	Misty	Cloudy	N. E.	0.01		Light rain part of afternoon.
9	48½	64	Cloudy	"	S. E., S. W.	0.27		Clear part of afternoon; rain 8:45 to 10:45 P. M.
10	53	63	"	Clear	S. W., N. W.	0.07		Rain before day, 0.07; clear part of morning.
S 11	48	67	"	"	S. W., N. W.			Cleared 10 A. M.
12	47½	67	Clear	"	N. W.			
13	48½	69	"	Cloudy	N. W., S. W.	0.11		Clouded over 2 P M.; rainy evening 7:15 to 10 P. M.
14	50	67	Cloudy	Clear	N. W., W.	0.58		Rain before day, 0.58; clear 7:30 A. M.
15	49½	70	Clear	"	S. W.			
16	54	64	Cloudy	"	S. W., N. W.			Cleared 9 A.M.; light rain 7 A. M.
17	47	65	Clear	"	N. W.			
S 18	48	70	"	"	S. W.			
19	53½	76	Hazy	"	S. W., S.			Cloudy part of afternoon.
20	59½	74	Cloudy	"	S. W.	0.03		Rain before day, 0.03; cleared 8 A.M.; cloudy part P.M.
21	58	77½	Clear	"	N. W.			
22	60	81	"	"	N. W., S. W.			Cloudy evening.
23	66½	85	Cloudy	"	S. W.			Cleared 9 A.M.; cloudy ev'g.
24	68¼	85	Clear	"	S. W.			Cloudy evening.
S 25	67	78½	"	"	All points.			
26	58	67	Cloudy	"	E.			Clear part of morning, and cloudy part P.M. & ev'g.
27	56½	73½	"	"	N. E., S. E.			Cleared 8 A. M.
28	51	58	Rain	"	N. E.	0.55		Rain till 1 P.M, 0.50; 2 to 3:15 P.M., 0.05; cleared 4 P. M.
29	45	55	Clear	"	N. W.			Cloudy part of evening.
30	44	58	"	"	N. W., S. W.			
31	47	65½	"	"	S. W., S.			

3.17

Weather Record for New Brunswick, N. J.

June, 1884.

Date.	Thermometer. Lowest.	Thermometer. Highest.	Wind. Morning.	Wind. Afternoon.	Prevailing Wind.	Rain and Melted Snow in inches.	Snow in inches.	REMARKS.
S 1	48	67	Clear	Clear	S. W., S. E			
2	49½	73	"	"	All points.			Cloudy part of evening.
3	56½	81½	"	"	All points.			Cloudy part of afternoon.
4	63	82	"	"	All points			
5	63	84	"	"	S.			
6	63	83	"	"	S. W.	0.07		Cloudy part of morning and part of afternoon with shower 4:15 P. M.
7	65½	84½	"	"	S. W.			
S 8	65½	83	"	"	S. W.	0.42		Cloudy 2 to 5 P. M., with shower 2:10 to 2:40 P. M.
9	64	79	Cloudy	"	S.			Foggy morning; clear part of morning.
10	64½	73½	"	Cloudy	E.			Clear part of afternoon.
11	56½	61½	"	"	N. E., S. E.			Rainy evening.
12	.57	71	"	"	All points	0.19		Rain before day, 0.19; clear part of afternoon; new town clock strikes 6:00 P. M., and hands all placed 11:30 A. M.
13	64½	68	"	"	NW, N E, S E.	0.25		Rain 8:40 to 10:15 A.M., 0.24, and part of evening, 0.01.
14	54½	62	C'y m'st all day	"	N. E., S. E.	0.01		Rain before day, 0.01.
S 15	45	66	Clear	Clear	N. E., S. E.			Coldest A. M. since June 11, 1859.
16	46	78	"	"	W.			
17	60	83½	"	"	NW, N E, S E.			
18	63	85½	"	"	S. W.			
19	64	88	"	"	S. W., S.		0.08	Cloudy ev'g with shower 8:50 P.M., 0.08.
20	69	85½	"	"	N. E., S. E.			Cloudy part of morning.
21	70	89	"	"	All points.			Cloudy part of evening.
S 22	72½	86½	"	"	N.W, N E, S.E.			
23	60½	77	"	"	E., S. E.			
24	65	87	Cloudy	"	S. W.			Clear part of morning.
25	73	83	"	Cloudy	SW, SE, N.E.	0.03		Shower 6:40 P.M., 0.03; rainy after 9 P.M.; very heavy after 10:15 P.M.
26	56½	64	Rain	"	N. E.	4.29		Very heavy rain till 10:15 A. M., and light till noon, 4.29 mostly in 12 hours; cleared 5 P. M.
27	52½	72	Clear	Clear	N. E., E.			
28	56	74	"	"	N. E., E.			
S 29	55	77½	"	"	N. E., S. E.			New post-office in Opera House building open 9 A. M.
30	62½	79½	Cloudy	"	S. W.			Clear part A.M.; cloudy part of afternoon and ev'g.
						5.34		

July, 1884.

Date.	Thermometer. Lowest.	Thermometer. Highest.	Weather. Morning.	Weather. Afternoon.	Prevailing Wind.	Rain and Melted Snow in inches.	Snow in inches.	REMARKS.
1	70	81½	Cloudy	Clear	S. W.	0.69	----	Rain before day, 0.66; cleared 7:30 A. M., cloudy part of evening with shower 5:10, 0.03.
2	72	86½	Clear	"	S. W.	----	----	
3	72½	83	"	"	N. E., S. E.	----	----	
4	66	76	Cloudy	Cloudy	N. E., S. E.	0.05	----	Clear part of morning; showers 11:15 A. M. and 1 P.M., 0.05; clear part of afternoon.
5	68	84	"	Clear	S. W.	0.71	----	Rain before day, 0.44; clear part of A.M.; cloudy ev'g with shower 8:45, 0.27.
S 6	67	80½	Clear	"	W.	0.43	----	Rain before day, 0.43.
7	63	75	"	"	N.	----	----	Cloudy part of afternoon.
8	60	73	C'y m'st all day.		N.	----	----	
9	62	74½	Clear	Clear	N., N. W.	0.03	----	Shower 2 P. M.
10	63	78	"	"	N. W., S. W.	----	----	
11	64	83	"	"	S W, S E, N E.	----	----	Cloudy part of afternoon.
12	68	81½	C'y m'st all day.		S. W.	0.09	----	Showers 9:30 and 10:45 P. M., 0.09.
S 13	65½	81½	Cloudy	Clear	S. W., N. W.	1.20	----	Rain after midnight, 1.18; 7 A. M., 0.02.
14	62½	74½	Clear	"	N. W.	----	----	
15	59	73½	"	"	N. W.	----	----	
16	62	74	"	"	N. W.	----	----	
17	59	73	"	"	N. W.	----	----	Cloudy part of afternoon.
18	61	76½	"	"	N. W., S. W.	----	----	
19	64	81½	"	"	S. W.	----	----	Cloudy part of A. M, and part of afternoon.
S 20	62	77	"	"	N. W.	----	----	
21	59	77½	"	"	N. W.	----	----	Cloudy evening.
22	63	83	Hazy	"	N. W., S. W.	----	----	
23	65	88½	Clear	"	S. W.	0.42	----	Showers 8 to 11:30 P. M.
24	70	86	"	"	All points	----	----	Cloudy evening.
25	68	75½	Cloudy	Cloudy	S. W., S. E.	0.21	----	Rain 6 to 7:15 A.M., 0.01; 10 A.M. to 2:30 P.M., 0.20; clear part of evening.
26	63	74	"	Clear	E., S. E	----	----	
S 27	62½	71½	"	Rain	E., N. E.	0.54	----	Rain before day, 0.02; 10:10 A.M. to 9 P.M., 0.52.
28	60	71	"	Cloudy	N., E., S. E.	----	----	Clear parts of A.M. and P.M.
29	63	67½	"	"	N. E.	0.12	----	Rain before day, 0.09; 10:30 to 11:30 A.M., 0.02; 8 to 9 P.M., 0.01.
30	59½	75	"	Clear	N. W., S. W.	0.11	----	Rain before day, and 6:45 to 7:45 A.M., 0.11; clear part of morning.
31	64	74½	"	Cloudy	S. W	0.20	----	Partly clear part A.M. & P.M; shower 2, 4 & 8:45 to 10:15 P.M., 0.20.
						4.80	----	

August, 1884.

	Date.	Thermometer. Lowest.	Thermometer. Highest.	Weather. Morning.	Weather. Afternoon.	Prevailing Wind.	Rain and Melted Snow in inches.	Snow in inches.	REMARKS.
	1	64	79	Clear --	Clear --	N. W., S. W.	----	----	
	2	66	78½	" --	" --	N. E., S. E.	----	----	Cloudy part of evening.
S	3	66	77½	Cloudy	Cloudy	S. E.	----	----	Partly clear parts AM. & PM.
	4	70½	83½	"	Rain --	S.	0.88	----	Clear part of A. M. and part of P.M.; showers 11:25 A.M. to 6:30 P. M , 0.63; steady rain 8 to 11 P.M., 0.25.
	5	68	76½	"	" --	S.E.,S.W.,S.E	1.34	----	Clear part of A.M.; rain 11:45 A.M. to 3:30 P.M., 1.33; 6 P. M., 0.01.
	6	66½	78	Clear --	Clear --	N. W., S. W.	----	----	
	7	65	71	Cloudy	Cloudy	S. E., N. E.	0.05	----	Rain 6 to 7:30 A. M., 0.01; 11:45 A.M. to 2 P. M., 0.04; clear evening.
	8	63	80	"	Clear --	All points.	0.80	----	Clear part of morn'g; cloudy evening with rain 8:10 to 8:40 P. M.
	9	63½	73	"	Cloudy	N. E.	0.18	----	Clear part of morning; rain 2:30 to 3:45 P. M.
S	10	61½	70	"	"	N. E.	----	----	Partly clear part of A. M. & part of evening; earthquake 2:07 P. M.
	11	61	75	Clear --	Clear --	All points.	0.02	----	Rain before day, 0.02.
	12	61	71½	Cloudy	Cloudy	N. E., E.	----	----	
	13	60	76	Clear --	Clear --	N. E., S. E.	----	----	Cloudy part of morning.
	14	61	80	" --	" --	All points	----	----	
	15	65	83	" --	" --	All points.	----	----	
	16	67	80	" --	" --	N. E., S. E.	----	----	
S	17	66	82	" --	" --	N. W., S. W.	----	----	
	18	67	81½	C'y m'st all day.		S. W.	----	----	
	19	70	85½	Clear --	Clear --	All points	----	----	
	20	69½	89½	" --	" --	S. W.	----	----	Cloudy part of evening.
	21	75	86	Cloudy	" --	S. W.	----	----	
	22	73	85	"	Cloudy	S.W, N.W., E.	0.49	----	Clear parts of A. M. and P. M.; rain 4:40 to 7:30 P.M.
	23	68	80	"	Clear --	S. W.	----	----	Clear part of morning.
S	24	67½	74½	Clear --	" --	N.	----	----	
	25	51	70	" --	" --	N. E., S. E.	----	----	Cloudy evening.
	26	61	76	Cloudy	" --	S. W	0.20	----	Rain 6 to 10 A. M.
	27	63½	78	Clear --	" --	All points	----	----	
	28	59	76½	" --	Hazy --	S. W., S. E.	----	----	
	29	65	74½	Rain --	Cloudy	S. W.	0.58	----	Showers till 2 P.M., 0.51; part ev'g, 0.07; clear part ev'g.
	30	70	81½	Cloudy	Clear --	All points	0.38	----	Shower 5:40 to 6 P. M , 0.14; rain 6:30 to 9 P.M., 0.24.
S	31	67½	78½	"	" --	N. W.	0.11	----	Rain before day, 0.11; cleared 7:30 A. M.
							5.03	--	

September, 1884.

Date.	Thermometer. Lowest.	Thermometer. Highest.	Weather. Morning.	Weather. Afternoon.	Prevailing Wind.	Rain and Melted Snow in inches.	Snow in inches.	REMARKS.
1	60	75½	Clear	Clear	N. W.			
2	58	76	"	"	All points.			
3	61	80½	"	"	S. W.			
4	66	85	"	"	S. W.			Charles S. Hill died about 6 A. M.
5	68	87½	"	"	S. W.			
6	70	87	"	"	All points			
S 7	69	87	"	"	S. W.			
8	68½	86	"	"	S. W.			Mahlon Runyon (suicide) between 9 and 10 A. M.; bank closed.
9	73	88	"	"	S. W.			
10	74½	90	"	"	All points			
11	72	88	"	"	S. W.			Cloudy part of evening.
12	65	77	"	"	N.			Cloudy part of morning.
13	56	70	"	"	N.			
S 14	48	64½	"	"	All points.			
15	47	70	"	"	All points.			
16	56	77½	"	"	S. W.			Cloudy part of evening.
17	63½	80	"	"	S. W.			Cloudy part of evening.
18	62½	74	C'y m'st all day.		N. W., N.			
19	53	68½	Clear	Clear	All points.			
20	57½	71½	Cloudy	"	S. W., N. W.			Partly clear part of morning and cloudy part of afternoon.
S 21	50	67½	Clear	"	N. E., S. E.			
22	49	73	C'y m'st all day.		S. W.	0.01		Shower 9:35 P. M., 0.01.
23	63	73½	" "	" "	W., N., E.			
24	61½	81	Cloudy	Clear	N. E., S.			Cleared 7 A. M.; cloudy part of afternoon; bank resumed.
25	69½	81	Clear	Cloudy	S.W.,N.W.,N			Clear part of evening.
26	57	70½	"	Clear	N. E., S. E.			
27	49½	72	Cloudy	"	E., S.			
S 28	63	81	"	"	S. W.			Cleared 7:30 A. M.; cloudy part of evening.
29	68	80	Clear	"	S. W., N. W.	0.21		Shower before day, 0.21.
30	65	72	Cloudy	Cloudy	N. E., S. E.	0.15		Rain 2:40 to 4 P. M., 0.15; clear part of evening.
						0.37		

WEATHER RECORD FOR NEW BRUNSWICK, N. J.

October, 1884.

Date.	Thermometer. Lowest.	Thermometer. Highest.	Weather. Morning.	Weather. Afternoon.	Prevailing Wind.	Rain and Melted Snow in inches.	Snow in inches.	REMARKS.
1	63½	79	Clear	Clear	N. W.			
2	55	63	"	Rain	N. E.			Clouded over 7:30 A. M.; rain 11:45 A. M.
3	52	58	Cloudy	Cloudy	N. E., S. E.	0.38		Rain before day, 0.37; 8 to 9 A. M., 0.01; misty evening.
4	56½	78	"	Clear	S. W.	0.02		Rain before day, 0.02; cleared 9 A. M.
S 5	68½	75½	Clear	"	N. W.			Cloudy part of morning.
6	56	79	"	"	N. W., S. W.			Cloudy part of morning.
7	61	73	"	"	N. W.			
8	53	71	"	"	N.E., S., S.W.	0.02		Cloudy evening with rain 7:30 to 8 P. M.
9	48½	58½	"	"	N. W., N.			Cloudy part of morning.
10	39	63	"	"	S. E., S. W.			Frost.
11	45	69	"	"	S. W.			Cloudy at noon.
S 12	60	75	"	Cloudy	S. W.	0.02		Light rain part of afternoon; clear evening.
13	61½	70	"	Clear	S. W., N. W.			
14	48½	56½	"	"	N. W.			
15	37	52½	"	"	N.			
16	43	60	Cloudy	Cloudy	S. W.			Clear part of afternoon.
17	53½	68	"	"	S. W., N. W.	0.04		Rain before day, 0.01; clear parts A. M. and P. M.; rain 9 to 10 P. M., 0.03.
18	49	58	"	Clear	N. W.	0.01		Rain 7 A. M., 0.01; cleared 8 A. M.
S 19	39	58	Clear	"	N. W., S. W.			
20	47	69½	"	"	S. W.			
21	52½	73	"	"	S. W.			
22	58½	74½	"	Cloudy	S. W., N. W.	1.09		Cloudy part of morning; rain 5:20 P. M. to 10:40 P. M.
23	51	55	"	Clear	N. W.			Cloudy before day.
24	37½	50	"	"	N. W.			Cloudy part of evening.
25	42	53	Cloudy	"	S. W., N. W.			Clear part of morning.
S 26	33	48	Clear	"	All points			Cloudy part of evening.
27	40	59	Cloudy	Cloudy	S. E.			Partly clear part afternoon.
28	57½	61½	"	Rain	S. W., N. W.	0.25		Rain 8:30 A. M. to 5 P. M.
29	41	52	Clear	Cloudy	N. E., E.			Rain 5:30 P. M.
30	44	49	Rain	Rain	N. E.			
31	44	47	Cloudy	Cloudy	N. E.	1.33		Rain before day, 1.31; misty parts of day, 0.02.
						3.16		

November, 1884.

Date.	Thermometer. Lowest.	Thermometer. Highest.	Weather. Morning.	Weather. Afternoon.	Prevailing Wind.	Rain and Melted Snow in inches.	Snow in inches.	REMARKS.
1	44	57½	Cloudy	Clear	S. W.			Clear part of morning and cloudy part of evening.
S 2	52½	54½	"	Cloudy	S.W.,N.W.,N.	0.03		Partly clear A. M.; rain 2 to 2:30 P.M.; cleared 6 P. M.
3	38	52	Clear	"	N.W.,N.E.,S.E.			Clear parts of afternoon and evening.
4	43	60	Cloudy	Rain	N. E., S. E.			Rain 2 P. M.
5	45½	52	Clear	Clear	N. W.	0.43		Rain before day, 0.43.
6	37	43½	"	"	N. W.			
7	32	48	"	"	S W.			Cloudy part of evening.
8	39	52	"	"	N. W.			Cloudy part of morning.
S 9	31	48	"	"	N. E., S. E.			
10	31	55	"	"	N. W., S. W.			
11	39	59	"	"	S. W., N. W.			Foggy morning; cloudy part of ev'g; W. Coulter died.
12	44½	54	"	"	N. W.			
13	37	54	"	"	N. W., S. W.			
14	42	53½	"	"	N. W., S. W.			
15	40	57	"	"	S.W., N., S.E.			
S 16	35½	53	"	"	N. E.			Cloudy parts of afternoon and evening.
17	42	60	"	"	N. W.			Cloudy parts of morning and evening.
18	34	39½	"	Cloudy	N. E.			Cloudy part of morning; rain and snow 10:30 P. M.
19	29	34	Cloudy	Rain	N. E.	0.08		Snow & rain before day, 0.08.
20	33	42	"	Clear	N. E., N. W.	0.33		Rain before day, 0.33; clear part of morning and cl'dy part of afternoon.
21	33½	48	Clear	"	S. W.			
22	32	51½	"	"	S.W.,N.,N.E.			
S 23	38½	64	Cloudy	Rain	S. E., S.			Partly clear part A.M.; misty parts of day; heavy rain during evening; 7:30 to 10 P. M.—1 33 inches.
24	39½	42	Clear	Clear	N. W.	1.83		Rain before day, 1.83.
25	23	36	"	Cloudy	S. W.			Cloudy part of morning.
26	34	46	Cloudy	Clear	S. W., N. W.			
27	29	41	"	Cloudy	S. W., S. E.			
28	37½	46	"	Rain	N. E.			Rain 10 A. M.
29	41	45	Rain	Clear	N. W.	0.87		Rain till 5 A. M., 0.87.
S 30	33½	40	Cloudy	Cloudy	S.W.,NW.,N.	0.03		Snow 4:10 P.M. to 9:30 P. M.
						3.60		

December, 1884.

Date	Thermometer Lowest	Thermometer Highest	Weather Morning	Weather Afternoon	Prevailing Wind	Rain and Melted Snow in inches	Snow in inches	REMARKS
1	34	41	Cloudy	Cloudy	W., N.			Clear part of afternoon.
2	31	39½	Clear	Clear	N. E.			
3	29½	44	"	"	S. W., N. W.			Cloudy part of A. M. and
4	35	50	"	"	W., S. W.			part of evening.
5	34	52½	"	"	S. W.			
6	35	63	Cloudy	Rain	N. E., S. E.	1.40		Foggy morning; rain 12:30 P.M. till midnight, 1.40.
S 7	51	60	Clear	Clear	S. W.			Cloudy part of afternoon, and part of evening.
8	46	49	Cloudy	"	W.			
9	39	48	Clear	"	S. W., N. W.			Cloudy with snow squall 3 P. M.
10	35	43½	"	"	N. W., S. W.			Cloudy evening.
11	39½	50	Cloudy	Cloudy	S. W.			Rain 10 P. M.
12	34	36	Rain	"	N. E.	0.79		Rain till 3 P. M., 0.79.
13	32	39	Cloudy	"	N.			Clear part of morning.
S 14	30	34	Clear	"	N. E., S. E.			Clouded over 10 A.M.; rain 8:30 P. M.
15	33	48	Rain	Clear	S. W., N. W.	1.25		Rain till 7 A.M., 1.25; cleared 10 A. M.; cloudy part of evening.
16	34	40½	Clear	"	W., S. W.			
17	35	40	Cloudy	Cloudy	All points			
18	27	29½	"	Snow	N. W., N.		1.00	Snow 11:45 A. M. to 7 P. M., 1.00.
19	7	14	Clear	Clear	N. W.			
20	2½	12½	"	"	N. W., N. E.			Cloudy evening with snow 10:30.
S 21	8	36	Snow Rain	Rain	N. E., N. W.		3.50	Snow 10 A.M., and then rain.
22	31½	39	Cloudy	"	S. W., N. W.	1.29		Rain before day, 1.22; part of afternoon, 0.07, and part of evening, 0.02.
23	24	28	"	Cloudy	N. W., W.			Clear part of morning.
24	19	28	Snow	"	N. E.		2.00	Snow till 11:20 A.M., 2 in.
25	22	26	Clear	"	N. W., N. E.			Cloudy before day; clear part of afternoon.
26	13	21	Cloudy	Clear	N. E.		2.00	Snow before day, 2 inches; cleared 10 A.M.
27	12	31½	"	Cloudy	N. E.			
S 28	31	37	"	Foggy	N. E.	0.02		Misty rain part of morning, 0.02.
29	35	42	Foggy	Cloudy	N. W., S. W.	0.02		Rain before day, 0.02; partly clear part of evening.
30	39	47	"	"	S. W.			
31	43	60	"	"	S. W.	0.01		Rain before day, 0.01; clear part of afternoon.
						4.78	8.50	

Total rain fall for 1884, 48.44 inches.

January, 1885.

Date	Thermometer Lowest	Thermometer Highest	Weather Morning	Weather Afternoon	Prevailing Wind	Rain and Melted Snow in inches	Snow in inches	REMARKS
1	44	50	Cloudy	Cloudy	N. W.	0.03		Rain before day, 0.03; snow squall 4:15 P. M.; partly
2	22	26	Clear	Clear	N. W.			clear part of evening.
3	13½	25½	"	"	S. W.			Cloudy evening.
S 4	21	31½	Cloudy	Cloudy	All points.	0.04		Snow part A. M.; and sleet part A.M.,0.04; cl'rd 8 P.M.
5	25	37	Clear	"	S. W.			Clouded over 3 P. M.; rain 9 P. M.
6	34	51½	Rain	"	S. E., S. W.	1.23		Rain till 2 P. M., 1.20; part of evening, 0.03.
7	44	50	Cloudy	"	S. W., W.			Partly clear part of A. M.; cleared 9 P M.
8	37	46	Clear	Clear	S. W.			Cloudy part A.M. and eve'g.
9	34	51½	"	"	S. W.			Cloudy part of evening.
10	31	35½	"	"	N. W.			
S 11	25	48	Cloudy	Cloudy	S. E., S.			Clear 9 A.M. to 2 P.M.; sprinkles part of afternoon.
12	45	61½	Rain	"	S. W., N. W.	0.83		Rain till 6 A. M., 0.74; 8 A. M., 0.01; thunder shower 12:50 P.M., 0.07; 2:30 P.M., 0.01; clear part of A. M.; cleared 5:30 P. M.
13	34	39	Clear	Clear	W., N.			R. J. Hannah died.
14	23½	34	"	"	N. W., S. W.			
15	29	38	Snow Rain	Cloudy	SE, NE, NW.	0.64		Snow 7 to 9:30 A. M., and then rain till 3:30 PM.0.64.
16	35½	38½	Rain	Rain	N. E.			Misty rain all day.
17	35	60	Cloudy	Clear	S. W., N. W.	0.36		Rain before day, 0.36; cl'rd 9 A.M.;max.60° before day.
S 18	22	28	Clear	"	W.			Cloudy part A. M. and eve'g.
19	19½	25½	"	"	N. W.			Cloudy part of afternoon.
20	19	31½	Cloudy	Cloudy	S. W.			Clear 9 A. M. to 3 P. M.
21	27	36	"	Clear	S. W., N. W.			Cleared 9 A. M.
22	12	20	Clear	"	N. W.			
23	10½	28½	"	Cloudy	S. W.			Clouded over 10 A. M.; snow 9 P M.
24	22½	36	Snow Rain	"	NE,NW,SW.	0.47		Snow and rain till 7 A. M.; clear part of afternoon.
S 25	34	39	Cloudy	"	S. W.			
26	30	32	Clear	Clear	S. W., N. W.			Cloudy part of morning.
27	11	19	"	Cloudy	NW,SW,SE.			Clouded over 2 P. M.
28	16	30	Cloudy	Clear	N. E., N. W.	0.12		Light rain 9:15 A. M., and then snow till 1:30 P. M.; cleared 2 P. M.
29	7	20	Clear	"	W.			
30	14	31½	Cloudy	Cloudy	All points.			Clear part of evening.
31	24	35½	Clear	Clear	N. E., S. E.			Cloudy part of evening.
						3.72		

29th year of my daily observations.

February, 1885.

Date.	Lowest.	Highest.	Weather. Morning.	Afternoon.	Prevailing Wind.	Rain and Melted Snow in inches.	Snow in inches.	REMARKS.
S 1	28½	37	Cloudy	Clear	N. E., N. W.	0.03	----	Light snow and rain part of A.M.; cleared 3 P M.; snow squall 5:15 P. M.
2	14	20	Clear	"	N. W., S. W.	----	----	Cl'ded over 8 PM.; snow 9 PM.
3	14	24½	Cloudy	Cloudy	NE,NW,NE.	----	2.00	Snow before day 2 in.; clear part of morning.
4	22	34½	"	"	N. E.	0.08	----	Rain part of evening, 0.08.
5	32½	40	"	Clear	N. W., N. E.	----	----	Clear part of morning and cloudy part of afternoon.
6	23	27	"	"	N. E., N. W.	----	----	Clear part of morning.
7	11	28	Clear	"	N. W.	----	----	Cloudy part of even'g; collision on railroad bridge 2:50 A. M.; great oil fire.
S 8	23	38	Cloudy	"	N. E., N. W.	----	----	Cleared 2 P. M.
9	22	40	"	Rain	N. E.	----	----	Rain 2:30 P. M.; light till 6 P. M. & heavy afterwards.
10	36	42	"	Clear	S. W., N. W.	1.84	----	Rain before day, 1.82; part of morning, 0.02.
11	1	10	Clear	"	N. W., W.	----	----	C., New Orleans 6 P. M.
12	7	25½	"	"	S. W.	----	----	
13	17	29	"	Snow	N. W., N. E.	----	2.00	Cloudy part of morn'g; snow 2:40 till 9 P. M.
14	15	27½	Cloudy	"	N. E.	----	----	Snow 4 P.M.; partly clear part of morning.
S 15	19	32½	Clear	Clear	N.,N. E.,S. E.	----	3.00	Snow before day; cloudy part of evening.
16	25	41	Rain	Rain Cl'dy	N,E,S.,N. W.	1.51	----	Light rain till 9 A. M., 0.11, and heavy till 3 P.M., 1.38; 3:45 P.M., 0.02; cl'red 6 PM.
17	6½	18	Clear	Clear	N. W., W.	----	----	Coldest 9:30 A. M.; cloudy part of evening.
18	13	25	Snow	"	N.E.,N.W.,W	----	1.50	Snow till 9 AM.; cl'red 11 AM.
19	10¾	22	Clear	"	W., N. W.,W.	----	----	Cloudy part of evening.
20	9	20	"	"	N. W.	----	----	
21	11	26	"	"	N. W.	----	----	
S 22	13	24½	"	"	N. W.	----	----	
23	16	30	"	"	N. W.	----	----	
24	15½	28	"	Cloudy	All points.	----	----	Clouded over at noon; snow 10 P. M.
25	21½	34	Snow	Clear	N. E.	----	6.00	Snow till 8 A. M. 6 in.; cleared 10 A. M.
26	8½	32½	Clear	Cloudy	N. E., E.	----	----	Clouded over 9:30 A. M.
27	28	35	Cloudy	"	All points.	0.02	----	Light snow at intervals, 7:15 A. M. till 9 P. M., 0.02.
28	31	41	"	Clear	N. W., S. W.	----	----	Cleared 8 A. M.

3.48 14.50

WEATHER RECORD FOR NEW BRUNSWICK, N. J. 345

March, 1885.

Date.	Thermometer.		Weather.		Prevailing Wind.	Rain and Melted Snow in inches.	Snow in inches.	REMARKS.
	Lowest.	Highest.	Morning.	Afternoon.				
S 1	30	46½	Cloudy	Rain	N. E., S.,S W.	0.35		Partly clear part A.M.; rain 2:30 to 8 P. M.
2	35	40½	Clear	Clear	N. W.			Cloudy part A. M. and P. M.
3	26	40	"	"	W., S. W.			Cloudy part of afternoon.
4	33	48	"	"	N. W., S. W			Cloudy part of afternoon.
5	37	45	"	"	N. W., N			Cloudy part of morning.
6	30	39½	"	"	All points.			Cloudy evening.
7	30½	35	Snow	Cloudy	N. E., S. E.	0.08		Snow 5 to 10 A. M., 0.08.
S 8	27	31½	Cloudy	Clear	N., N. W.	0.03		Snow before day, 0.03; clear part of morning.
9	16	37	Clear	Cloudy	N. W., S. W.			Clouded over 4 P. M.
10	33	37	Cloudy	Clear	N. W.			Cleared 7 A. M.
11	19½	30	Clear	"	N. W., W.			Cloudy evening.
12	27¼	40½	Cloudy	Cloudy	N. W., N. E.			Partly clear parts of day.
13	8	30½	"	"	N. E., E.			Cleared 7 A. M. to 2 P. M.; light snow 9 P. M.
14	26	37½	"	Clear	N., W.			Cl'red 8 A.M.; C. home 1 P.M.
S 15	28½	42	{ Snow Rain	Cloudy	S. W.	0.16		Light snow 6:30 A. M., and rain at intervals till 4 P.M.
16	20	39	Clear	"	N. W., S. W.			Clouded over 3 P M., light snow part of evening.
17	14	24½	"	Clear	N. W.			Cloudy part of afternoon.
18	10	28	"	"	N. E., S. E.			
19	17½	29	Cloudy	"	S.E,S.W,NW.	0.02		Clear part A.M.; snow 10:30 A.M. to 2 P.M., 0.02; cleared 3 P. M.
20	10	23½	Clear	"	N. W.			
21	8½	23½	"	"	N. W.			
S 22	11	23½	Cloudy	Cloudy	N E.			Partly clear parts of day and evening; very high winds for 6 days.
23	16½	28	"	Clear	N.			Cleared 4 P. M.
24	16	39	Clear	Cloudy	S. W.			Clouded over 5 P.M.; partly clear part of evening.
25	32	40	Cloudy	Clear	N. W.			Cleared 7:30 A. M.
26	26	49½	Clear	"	N. E., S., S.W.			
27	35	56	Cloudy	Cloudy	S. W., N. W.			Clear part A.M.; light sprinkles part of afternoon.
28	40½	50	Clear	"	N. W., N. E.			Cloudy part of A.M.; clouded over 4 P.M.; rain and snow after 7 P. M.
S 29	28½	39½	Cloudy	Clear	N. E., N. W.	0.44		Snow before day, 0.44; cloudy part of afternoon.
30	27	45	Clear	"	N. W., W., S.			Cloudy evening.
31	36½	58½	C'y m'st all day.		S. W.			Light sprinkle part of ev'g.

1.08

April, 1885.

Date	Thermometer Lowest	Thermometer Highest	Weather Morning	Weather Afternoon	Prevailing Wind	Rain and Melted Snow in inches	Snow in inches	REMARKS
1	44	61½	Clear	Clear	S. W., N. W.	0.03	----	Rain before day, 0.03; light sprinkle 9:30 A. M.
2	37	43	Cloudy	Cloudy	N. E., E.	0.03	----	Rain before day, 0.03; clear part of morning.
3	38½	68½	"	Clear	S. E., S. W., S.	0.01	----	Rain before day, 0.01; cleared 7:30 A.M.; cloudy ev'g.
4	40½	45	Rain	Cloudy	N. E., N. W.	0.67	----	Rain 6 to 11:15 A. M., 0.67.
S 5	32½	52½	Clear	Clear	S. W.	----	----	Light shower 4:15 P.M.; cl'dy 10 P. M.; rain 11 P. M.
6	42½	53½	"	"	N. W.	0.04	----	Rain before day, 0.04.
7	35	51½	"	Cloudy	N. W., W., S.	----	----	Rainy evening after 7:30; 0.01 at 10:15.
8	42	63	Cloudy	"	N.E., S.,N.W.	0.16	----	Rain before day, 0.06; partly clear part A.M.; light rain 2:45 to 6:45 P. M., 0.10.
9	29	43½	Clear	Clear	N. W., N. E.	----	----	Cloudy evening.
10	32½	43½	Cloudy	Cloudy	N. E., S. E.	----	----	Clear part of A. M.; partly clear part of evening.
11	34	44½	Clear	"	E., S.	0.06	----	Rain and snow 2:30 to 9 P. M., 0.06; Dis. Tel. and Fire Alarm put in.
S 12	35½	47½	Cloudy	Clear	S. W., W.	0.03	----	Rain before day, 0.03; cloudy part of afternoon.
13	35½	49	Clear	"	W., N. W.	----	----	Cloudy part of evening, with sprinkles.
14	32	48	"	"	N. W.	----	----	
15	34	43	Cloudy	Cloudy	N.W.,S.,N.E.	0.07	----	Clouded over 6:30 A.M.; rain 11 A. M to 2 P. M., 0.07.
16	39	56	Clear	Clear	N.	----	----	Cloudy part of evening.
17	35	60	"	"	All points.	----	----	
18	40½	56	"	"	N. E., S. E.	----	----	
S 19	36	63	"	"	All points.	----	----	
20	42	69	"	"	W., S. W.	----	----	
21	46	76	"	"	S. W., W.	----	----	
22	57	80	"	"	All points.	----	----	
23	53	76	"	"	S. E.	----	----	
24	54	77	"	Hazy	S. W.	----	----	
25	60	72	"	Clear	N. E	----	----	
S 26	45	50	Rain	Cloudy	E., N. E.	0.48	----	Light rain 6 to 7 A.M., 0.01; rain 8 A.M. to noon, 0.35; 12:45 to 2 P. M., 0.12; partly clear evening.
27	42	68	Clear	Clear	W.	----	----	Cherries flowered, young tree
28	48	58	"	Rain	N. E., S. E.	0.54	----	Thunder shower 2:30 P. M., 0.02; rain 3:45 to 7 P. M., 0.44; 9:50 to 11 P M.,0.08.
29	38	56½	Cloudy	Clear	N.	0.02	----	Snow 7:20 to 8:40 A.M., 0.02.
30	43½	67½	Clear	"	N. W., S. W.	----	----	Cloudy part morning; cloudy evening.
						2.14	----	

Weather Record for New Brunswick, N. J.

May, 1885.

Date	Thermometer Lowest	Thermometer Highest	Weather Morning	Weather Afternoon	Prevailing Wind	Rain and Melted Snow in inches	Snow in inches	REMARKS
1	42	48	Cloudy	Rain	N. E.			Rain 8:30 A. M.
2	45	59	"	Clear	N.	0.45		Rain before day, 0.45; cleared 10 A. M.
S 3	39	54½	Clear	"	N. W.			Frost.
4	40½	56	Cloudy	"	E., N., S. W.			Cl'r part A.M.; cl'dy part P.M.
5	42	63½	"	"	E., S. E.			Cleared 9 A. M.
6	48	65	"	Cloudy	N. E., E.			Clear 10 A. M. to 4 P. M.; pears flowered.
7	46	55	"	Rain	N. E.	0.32		Rain 6 to 7 A.M., 0.02; light 11 A.M. to 3:30 P.M.; then heavier till 9 P.M., 0.30.
8	47	57	Rain	Cloudy	N. E., E.	0.46		Rain till 1 P.M., 0.46; clear part P. M.; cleared 8 P.M.
9	40	59½	Clear	"	All points	0.16		Clear part P.M. & ev'g; rain 5:30 to 8 P. M.; frost.
S 10	44	58	"	Clear	S. W., W.			
11	43	56	Cloudy	"	N. W.			Cl'r part A.M.; cl'dy part P.M.
12	40	62¼	Clear	Cloudy	S.			Clear part of evening; frost.
13	48	56	Cloudy	"	N.E.,E.,N.E.			Sprinkle part of evening.
14	49	61	"	"	N. E., N. W.	0.01		Rain before day, 0.01; clear evening.
15	51	78	Clear	Clear	N.			
16	55½	72½	"	"	N. E., E.			
S 17	48	65	"	"	N. E., E.			Cl'dy part A.M.; cl'dy 9 P. M.
18	46½	69½	Cloudy	Cloudy	N. E.			Partly cl'r parts A.M. & ev'g.
19	52½	80	Clear	Clear	S. W.			Cloudy evening.
20	64	75	Hazy	Cloudy	N. E., E.			
21	54	64½	Cloudy	"	N. E., S. E.			Partly clear about noon.
22	53½	63½	"	"	E.	0.01		Light rain part of evening.
23	53½	60	Rain	"	N. E., S. E.	0.39		Heavy rain before day and light till 7 A.M., 0.37; part A.M., 0.02; clear part P. M.
S 24	57	65½	Cloudy	"	N. E., E.			Partly clear at noon; clear part of evening.
25	57	66½	"	"	S. E.	0.03		Rain 9 to 11 A.M.; clear part P M; partly cl'r part ev'g.
26	61	77½	Clear	Clear	N. W.			
27	59	76	"	Cloudy	All points			Cloudy 10 A M.; partly clear part of evening.
28	62	70	Cloudy	Clear	All points			Cleared 9 A. M.
29	48½	66	Clear	Cloudy	N. E., E.			
30	50½	62½	Cloudy	"	N. E., S. E.	0.03		Rain noon to 3 P. M., 0.03.
S 31	58	69	"	"	S. E.	0.15		Rain before day, 0.12, 7:15 to 7:30 A. M., 0.02, 3:30 to 4:30 P.M., 0.01; cl'ed 9 P.M.
						2.01		

June, 1885.

Date.	Thermometer. Lowest.	Thermometer. Highest.	Weather. Morning.	Weather. Afternoon.	Prevailing Wind.	Rain and Melted Snow in inches.	Snow in inches.	REMARKS.
1	59	76½	Clear	Clear	S. W.			
2	57	74½	"	"	N. W.			
3	54½	71	"	"	N.E., S. E.,S.			Cloudy part of evening.
4	54	71	Cloudy	"	S., S. E.	0.01		Shower 2 P. M.
5	64½	84	Clear	"	SW., N., N.E.	0.09		Cloudy part of morning and part of afternoon, with showers 3:45 & 4:15 P. M.
6	54	73½	"	"	NE,NW,SW.			
S 7	55	76½	"	"	S. W.			Cloudy parts of morning and afternoon and of evening.
8	65	79	Rain	Cloudy	S. W., N. W.	0.83		Rain till 6:30 A. M.; clear evening
9	54½	68	Clear	Clear	N. W.			
10	50½	71½	"	"	W., S. W.			
11	54½	75	"	"	S., W., S.			
12	56	79	"	"	S. W.			
13	58½	80½	"	"	S. W.			Foggy morning.
S 14	66	88	"	"	S. W.			
15	66	80½	"	"	S. E.			Cloudy part of morning and part of evening, with sprinkle 9:15 P. M.
16	66	90	"	"	S. W.			Cloudy evening, with rain 10:40 P. M.
17	63	74½	Cloudy	"	N.	0.31		Rain till 5 A. M.
18	57	76	Clear	"	N. W., S. W.			
19	59	80	"	"	S. E.			
20	61	83	"	"	S. W., S.			Cloudy part of evening.
S 21	61½	85	"	"	S., S. W.			
22	71	83	"	"	S W.,N.,N.E.			Cloudy part of morning.
23	58	73	"	"	N. W.			Cloudy part of morning.
24	58½	79	"	"	N. W., S. W.			
25	61	78	"	Hazy	S. W.			Cloudy evening.
26	67	80½	Cloudy	Clear	S. W., S.			Clear part of morning.
27	68	80	"	"	S. E.			Cloudy part of evening.
S 28	69	76	"	Rainy	S. E.	0.42		Rain before day, 0.01; 8 to 11 A.M., 0.09; clear part of afternoon; 5 to 6:45 P.M., 0.24, 10 to 10:40 P.M., 0.08.
29	69	81	"	Clear	S. W., N. W.	0.01		Rain before day, 0.01; cleared 8:30 A. M.
30	61½	73½	Clear	Cloudy	N. W.			Cloudy part of morning; clear part of afternoon.
						1.67		

July, 1885.

Date.	Thermometer. Lowest.	Highest.	Weather. Morning.	Afternoon.	Prevailing Wind.	Rain and Melted Snow in inches.	Snow in inches.	REMARKS.
1	57½	74	Clear	Clear	N. W.			
2	56½	72	"	"	W.			
3	60½	75	Cloudy	"	S. W., W.			Sprinkle 7 A. M.; clear part of morning.
4	62	80	Clear	"	S.W., N., S.E	0.11		Cloudy part P. M., with showers 1:10 to 2:10 P. M.
S 5	63	80½	"	Cloudy	NE.,S.E.,N.E	0.81		Cloudy 2 to 8:30 P.M.; shower 2:20 to 2:50 P. M., 0.62; 5:10 to 7 P. M., 0.18; 8 P. M., 0.01.
6	64	78	C'y m'st all day	S. E.		0.05		Rain noon to 1:15 P.M., 0.04; 3:30 P. M., 0.01.
7	68	81	Cloudy	Cloudy	S. E., N. E.	1.37		Partly clear part A.M.; rain 3:40 to 4 P. M., 0.03; 5 to 6:10 P.M., 1:34; cleared 10 P. M.
8	68	84	Clear	Clear	W., S. W.			
9	71	90	"	"	S.W., N., S.E			Cloudy with sprinkle 7 P.M.; rain 10:35 P. M.
10	71	85	"	"	S. W., N. W.	0.10		Rain before day, 0.10; cloudy part of morning.
11	67	79	"	"	N.			
S 12	62	77½	"	"	N. E., S. E.			
13	61	75	C'y m'st all day	N. E., S. E.				
14	65	73	Rain	Clear	S. W., S.	1.48		Rain till 11:30 A. M., 1.48; cleared 3 P. M.
15	64½	79	Clear	"	N. W., S. W.			
16	66	86	"	"	S. W., S. E.			
17	72	90½	"	"	S. W.			
18	74½	90	"	"	S.W.,N., N.E.			
S 19	69	80½	"	"	N. E., S. E.			
20	71	86	"	"	All points.			Foggy A.M.; cl'dy part P.M.
21	74	94	"	"	S. W., N. W.	0.08		Showers 2 P. M. and 8:30 P. M , 0.08.
22	76½	88	"	"	N. E., S. E.			
23	72½	86	"	"	N. E., S. E.			
24	72	86	"	"	S. W., S. E.			
25	75½	89	"	"	S. W.			Cloudy part of evening with sprinkles.
S 26	76½	90	"	Cloudy	All points.	0.05		Clouded over 5 P. M.; light rain 7:30 to 10:30 P. M.
27	66	77	Cloudy	Clear	N. E., S. E.	0.01		Rain 7 to 7:30 A. M., 0.01; cloudy part of afternoon.
28	65	81	Clear	"	N. E., S. E.			Cloudy part of morning.
29	67½	84	"	"	S. W.	0.23		Cloudy part A. M.; shower 2:20 to 2:50 P. M., 0.23.
30	68	81	"	"	N. E., S. E.			
31	69	83	Cloudy	"	S. E.			Clear part of morning and cloudy part of afternoon.
						4.29		

August, 1885.

Date.	Ther-mometer.		Weather.		Prevailing Wind.	Rain and Melted Snow in inches.	Snow in inches.	REMARKS.
	Lowest.	Highest.	Morning.	Afternoon.				
1	69	87	Clear	Cloudy	S. W.	0.15		Clouded over 4 P.M.; shower 5:15 to 5:35 P.M., 0.13; 7 P. M., 0 02.
S 2	68½	81	Cloudy	"	All points.	0.16		Clear part of A M.; rain 4:20 to 7 P.M., 0.15; part of evening, 0.01.
3	70	75	"	Rain	S. E., S. W.	3 30		Shower 7:15 to 11 A.M., 0.11; 1 to 6:10 P.M., 1.16; 9:20 to 11 P.M., 2.03; last from S. W.; bar. 29.68.
4	67½	81½	Clear	Clear	S. W.			
5	67½	81	"	"	N. W., N.	0.01		Cloudy with shower 4:15 P.M.
6	62	74½	"	"	N., W.			
7	60	70	Cloudy	Rain	N.E.,S. E	0.18		Rain 2:30 to 7 P. M., 0.17; part of evening, 0.01.
8	62½	75½	Clear	Clear	N. E., S. E.			
S 9	59	74	"	"	N. E., S. E.			
10	65	80½	"	"	S. W., S. E.			
11	70½	83	Cloudy	"	S. W., S.			Cleared 10 A.M.
12	72½	82½	"	"	S. W., S. E.	0.04		Cleared 9 A.M.; shower 2 P. M., 0.04.
13	75	86	"	Cloudy	S. W.	0.78		Clear 8 A.M.; shower 1 P.M., 0.09; 2 P.M., 0.01; 7:35 to 11 P.M., 0.68.
14	73	84	Clear	Clear	S. W., N. W.			Cloudy part of morning.
15	63	75	"	"	N. E., N. W.			
S 16	60	73½	"	"	N., N. E.			
17	57½	76	"	"	S. E., S.W., S.			Cloudy evening.
18	64	82	"	"	S. W.			
19	70	82½	"	"	All points.	0.05		Shower 6:45 P.M., 0.05.
20	62	75½	"	"	All points.			
21	61	80½	"	"	N. E., S.			Cloudy part A.M., and P. M.
22	72	84½	C'y m'st all day	S. W.		0.08		Shower part of ev'g, 0 03; 10 to 10:30 P.M., 0.05.
S 23	68½	75	Cloudy	Cloudy	N. E., E.	0.04		Shower 11:10 A.M , 0.01; 6:10 P.M., 0.03.
24	70	88½	"	Clear	S. W.			Cleared 8 A. M.
25	71	74	Clear	Cloudy	N. E.	0.38		Cloudy 9 A.M.; light rain about noon, 0.02; 4 to 9 P. M., 0.36.
26	54½	68	"	Clear	N. E., N. W.	0.01		Rain before day, 0.01.
27	52	65	"	"	N. W.			Cloudy part of afternoon.
28	50½	68	"	"	N. W., S. W.			Coldest days Aug. in my records; fire in my office.
29	57	70	"	Cloudy	N. E., S. E.			Cloudy part of A.M.; clear part of evening.
S 30	62½	74	Cloudy	Clear	S. E., S. W.	0.11		Rain before day, 0.08; 7:15 to 7:45 A.M., 0.03; cloudy part of afternoon
31	67	79	Clear	"	S. W., N. W.	0.01		Shower 5:30 A M., 0.01.

September, 1885.

Date	Thermometer Lowest	Thermometer Highest	Weather Morning	Weather Afternoon	Prevailing Wind	Rain and Melted Snow in inches	Snow in inches	REMARKS.
1	59	78	Clear	Clear	S. W., W.			
2	57	67	"	"	N. W.			
3	48	71½	"	"	N.W., N.E., S.			
4	58	79	"	"	S. W.	0.06		Cloudy part of evening, with shower 6:25 P. M., 0.06.
5	66	70	Cloudy	Cloudy	N. W., N.	0.07		Partly clear part of morning; rain noon to 2 P. M., 0.01, and 4 to 6½ PM., 0.06.
S 6	51	67	Clear	Clear	N. W.			
7	54	68	Cloudy	"	All points			Clear part of morning and cloudy part of afternoon.
8	54½	70½	Clear	Rain	S. E.			Clouded over 4 P. M.; rain 6 P. M.
9	62½	79½	Cloudy	Clear	S. W.	0.49		Rain before day, 0.44; clear part AM.; show'r 11:25 AM., 0.05; cl'dy parts PM. & eve.
10	60	66	Clear	Cloudy	N. W., N. E.	0.04		Cloudy part of morning; rain noon till 3 P. M., 0.04.
11	52	64	Cloudy	Clear	N. E., S. E.			Cloudy part of afternoon.
12	54	67	Clear	"	N. W., S. W.			Cloudy part of morning and part of afternoon.
S 13	56	74	Cloudy	"	S. W.			Cleared 10 A. M.
14	63½	81	"	"	S. W.			Cleared 8 A.M.; cloudy part of evening.
15	65½	83	Clear	"	S. W.			
16	64	76	"	"	N. W.			
17	54	71	"	"	N. W., S. W.			
18	53	76	"	"	S. W.			
19	62½	79	"	"	S.W., N., S.W.			
S 20	56	69½	"	"	N. E., S. E.			
21	51	65½	"	"	N. E., S. E.			
22	52	64	Cloudy	Cloudy	N. E.	0.14		Rain 4 to 6 P.M., 0.07; shower 9:45 P. M., 0.07.
23	51	57	Clear	Clear	N. W.			Cloudy part of morning; bar. 7 A. M. 29.50.
24	44	67	"	"	S. W.			
25	51	69	"	"	All points			
26	49½	71½	"	"	N.E., S., S.W.			Foggy morning.
S 27	56½	78½	"	"	W., N., S. E.			
28	59	74½	"	"	N. E., S. E.			Cloudy part of morning.
29	55	75	"	"	All points			Foggy morning.
30	61	77	"	"	All points			
						0.80		

October, 1885.

Date.	Thermometer.		Weather.		Prevailing Wind.	Rain and Melted Snow in inches.	Snow in inches.	REMARKS.
	Lowest.	Highest.	Morning.	Afternoon.				
1	58	72	Clear	Clear	N. E., S. E.			
2	54	61	Cloudy	M'sty Rain	N. E., S. E.	0.02		Misty rain parts A. M. and P. M., 0.02; rain during ev'g.
3	59½	71	Rain	Clear	N. E., S. E.	0.55		Rain till 7 A. M., 0.35; 7:45 to 8:30 A. M., 0.18; 10 to 11 A. M., 0.02; cloudy part of evening.
S 4	63½	75	Cloudy	"	S. W., N. W.	0.03		Clear part A. M.; shower 12:15 to 12:35 P. M., 0.03; cleared 4 P. M.; bar. 11 A. M., 29.52.
5	46½	59	Clear	"	S. W.			
6	47½	51	Rain	Cloudy	N. W.	0.56		Rain 6:30 A.M. to 3:30 P.M., 0.56; cleared 8 P. M.
7	40	52½	Clear	Clear	N. W.			Cloudy part P. M.; frost.
8	39	48½	Cloudy	Cloudy	N. E.	0.05		Rain 9 A. M. till noon, 0.01; part of afternoon, 0.04.
9	42	54	Clear	"	N. E., N. W.			Cleared 6 P. M.
10	42	63	"	Clear	W.			
S 11	45	65½	"	"	All points.			
12	46½	56	Cloudy	Cloudy	N. E., E.			
13	51	61½	Rain	"	E., S. E.	1.45		Rain till 3 P. M., 1:45; clear part of evening.
14	56	63	Clear	Clear	S. W.	0.02		Rain before day, 0.02; cl'dy parts P. M. and evening; bar. 7 A. M., 29.60.
15	51½	60	"	"	S. W., N. W.			Cloudy 11 A.M. to 5 P. M.
16	50	63	"	"	N. W., S. W.			
17	44	63	"	"	S. W., S. E.			
S 18	50	60	Cloudy	"	S. W.			Foggy A.M.; cl'dy part P.M.
19	49	65	Foggy	Cloudy	S. W., S. E.			Clear parts A. M. and P.M.
20	56	71½	C'y m'st all day	S.		0.01		Shower 7 A. M., 0.01.
21	62½	64½	Cloudy	Rain	S., N., N. W.	0.84		Rain 7:45 A.M. to 4:10 P.M., 0.84; cleared 7 P. M.
22	41½	53	Clear	Clear	N. W.			
23	36	54	"	"	All points			Cloudy part of afternoon.
24	40	57½	"	"	N. W.			
S 25	39	56	"	"	All points			
26	38½	59	"	"	S. W.			
27	44	63	"	"	S. W.			
28	44½	64	Foggy	"	S. W., S. E.			Clear part A.M.; cloudy parts of afternoon and eve'g.
29	54	61	Cloudy	Rain	S. E., N. E.			Rain 11:40 A.M., at intervals rest of day; bar. 10 P. M., 29.175.
30	51	53	"	Cloudy	N. E., N.	0.47		Rain before day, 0.44; partly clear part A.M.; rain and snow 6 to 9 P. M., 0.03.
31	36½	48	Clear	Clear	N.			Cloudy part of morning.
						4.00		

November, 1885.

Date.	Lowest.	Highest.	Weather. Morning.	Weather. Afternoon.	Prevailing Wind.	Rain and Melted Snow in inches.	Snow in inches.	REMARKS.
S 1	30	51	Clear	Cloudy	N. E., S. E.			Clouded over at noon and rainy after 6:15 P. M.
2	46	51	Rain	Clear	N.E., N.W., W.	1.52		Heavy rains before day and light till 9 A. M.; cleared 10 A.M.
3	39	49	Clear	"	W., N.W.			Cloudy evening.
4	42	51	"	"	W., S. W.			Cloudy part of morning.
5	44	63	"	"	S. W.			Cloudy part A.M.; cl'y eve'g.
6	54	67	"	Cloudy	S. W.			Cloudy part of morning.
7	60	68	Cloudy	"	S. W.	0.01		Light sprinkles part of A. M.; clear evening.
S 8	64	70½	Rain	Rain	S.W, N., N.E.	0.82		Rain till 9 A.M., 0.08; 11:15 to 11:30 A.M., 0.02; partly clear at noon; rain 2:30 to 10:30 P.M., 0.72.
9	50	55	Cloudy	Cloudy	N. W.			Clear part A. M. and eve'g.
10	45½	50½	Clear	Clear	N. W.			Cloudy part of morning.
11	40	54½	"	"	N. W., S. W.			
12	46½	64	"	"	S. W.			Cloudy part of afternoon.
13	47½	66½	"	Cloudy	S. W.	0.02		Light rain part P.M., 0.02.
14	39	50	"	Clear	N. W., S. W.			Cloudy part of afternoon.
S 15	35½	44½	"	"	W., N. W.			Cloudy part of evening.
16	34½	46	"	Cloudy	S. W., N. W.			
17	37	50	"	Clear	W., S. W.			
18	37	58	"	Cloudy	S. W.			Cloudy part A.M. and partly clear part of evening.
19	49½	58	Cloudy	"	SW., N., N.E.	0.01		Clear part A. M.; light rain parts of P. M. and eve'g, 0.01; cleared 10 P. M.
20	34	43	Clear	Clear	N. E.			
21	33	42½	Cloudy	Cloudy	N. W.			Cleared off 6 P. M.
S 22	35	45	"	"	S. W., S. E.			Rain 6 P. M.
23	33	36	Rain / Snow	M'sty / Rain	N. E.	1.02		Rain till 5:30 A.M. and then heavy snow till 10:15 A. M., 1.02; misty rain afternoon and evening.
24	33	38	Snow / Rain	Cloudy	N. E.	0.47		Snow before day and rain and snow till 3 P.M., 0.47.
25	36	38½	Rain	"	N. W.	0.12		Rain till 7 A. M., 0.10, and part of afternoon, 0.02.
26	35	39	Cloudy	"	N. E.	0.01		Rain before day, 0.01.
27	32	40½	Clear	Clear	N. E., N.W.			
28	28	40	"	"	N. W.			Cloudy part A. M. and ev'g.
S 29	30	41	"	Cloudy	N. W., N. E.	0.04		Snow and rain 5 to 8 P. M., 0.04; cleared 9:30 P. M.
30	33½	40	Cloudy	"	N. E.			Clear part of evening.
						4.04		

Weather Record for New Brunswick, N. J.

December, 1885.

Date	Thermometer Lowest	Thermometer Highest	Weather Morning	Weather Afternoon	Prevailing Wind	Rain and Melted Snow in inches	Snow in inches	REMARKS
1	35½	38½	Cloudy	Cloudy	N. E.			
2	33	43	Clear	Clear	N. E., N.			
3	34	43	Cloudy	"	S. W., N. W.			Snow squall 11:30 A. M. and cloudy part of P. M., with snow squall 3:15 P. M.
4	33½	40½	Clear	Cloudy	S. W., S. E.			
5	37½	48	Cloudy	"	S. W., N. W.	0.07		Rain 7:30 to 9:30 A.M., 0.07; cleared 7:30 P. M.; bar. 11 A. M. 29.20.
S 6	26	35½	Clear	Clear	W., S. W.			Cloudy part of evening.
7	16½	23	"	"	W., N. W.			Snow squall before day.
8	15	33	"	Cloudy	S. W.			Clouded over 2 P. M.
9	31½	60	Cloudy	"	N. E., S.	0.74		Rain 6 to 7 A. M., 0.01, 10 to 11 A. M., 0.09, 1 to 4 P. M., 0.64.
10	47½	49	"	"	N. W.	0.01		Rain before day, 0.01; clear evening.
11	32	38½	Clear	Clear	W.			
12	27	35½	"	"	W.,N.W,S.W.			Cloudy evening.
S 13	28	53½	Cloudy	Rain	N. E., S. E.	1.05		Rain 11 A.M. to 6 P.M., 1.05.
14	42½	44	"	Cloudy	S. W., W.	0.33		Rain before day, 0.27; part of afternoon, 0.06.
15	30	35½	Clear	Clear	N. W.			Cloudy evening.
16	30½	41½	"	"	S. W., N. W.			
17	28	38	"	"	N. E.			Cl'dy part A.M. & part P. M.
18	32½	41	Cloudy	"	NE,NW,SW.			Cleared 2 P. M.
19	34½	44½	"	"	S. W., N. W.			Light rain before day; cl'dy part PM.; sn'w squall 10 PM.
S 20	29½	34	Clear	"	N. W.			Cloudy part of morning.
21	29	43½	Cloudy	"	N. W.			Clear part of morning and cloudy part of afternoon.
22	36	45	Clear	Cloudy	N. W., S. W.			Cloudy part of morning and clear part of evening.
23	33½	53	"	"	S. W.			Cloudy part of morning and clear part of afternoon.
24	46	49	Cloudy	Clear	N. W., N.			Cleared 9 A.M.; cloudy part of evening.
25	25	33	Clear	"	N. E.			
26	21	30	"	"	N. E.			
S 27	19	36	"	"	N. E., N. W.			
28	31	40½	"	Cloudy	W.			
29	38½	45	Cloudy	Clear	N. W.			Cleared 10 A. M.
30	28	44	Clear	"	All points			Clouded over 8 P. M.
31	35½	52	Rain	Cloudy	E., S., N. W.	0.52		Rain till noon, 0.52.
						2.72		

Rain and melted snow for 1885—36.70 inches.

January, 1886.

Date	Thermometer Lowest	Thermometer Highest	Weather Morning	Weather Afternoon	Prevailing Wind	Rain and Melted Snow in inches	Snow in inches	REMARKS
1	39½	47	Clear	Clear	N. W.			Cloudy part of evening.
2	30	44	"	"	N. E., S. E.			
S 3	34	43½	Cloudy	Cloudy	N. E., E.	0.03		Misty rain part of P. M.
4	40	56½	"	Rain	S. E.			Rain 4 P. M.
5	48	52	"	Clear	S. W., W.	1.12		Rain before day; cleared 8 A.M.; cloudy part of P M.; bar. 1 P.M., 29.49
6	33	38	Clear	Cloudy	W., N. W.	0.01		Heavy snow squalls 12.05 to 12:15 P. M., 0.01; parts P. M. and evening.
7	18	29	"	Clear	N. W.			
8	14½	27½	"	Cloudy	N.W.,N.E.,E.			Clouded 2 P. M.; snow 10:45 P. M.; bar. 8 A. M., 30.01.
9	16	22½	Snow	"	N.E.,N.W.,W		8.00	Snow till 10:45 A.M., drifted badly; clear part A. M.; cleared 8 P.M.; bar. 8 A.M., 28 81; lowest I ever saw.
S 10	11	19	Cloudy	"	S. W., W.			Clear part of A.M., and P.M.
11	10	18½	"	Clear	N. W.	0.04		Snow before day, 0.04; clear part of morning.
12	2½	13½	Clear	"	N. W., W.			
13	0	16½	"	"	W., N. W.			
14	1½	21½	"	"	N., N. E.			Bar. 8 A. M., 30.72
15	6	27½	"	"	N. W., W.			
16	12½	32	Cloudy	Cloudy	N. E.			Partly clear part of A. M.
S 17	30	38	Clear	Clear	N. W.	0.06		Sleet before day, 0.06; cloudy part of morning.
18	22	31½	"	Cloudy	N. W., W.			
19	26	37½	Snow Rain	"	S. W., N., W.	0.78		Heavy snow before day; rain till 3 P.M.; clear part ev'g.
20	26	32	Clear	Clear	N. W., S. W.			Cloudy part of morning; hazy evening.
21	23½	39	Cloudy	Rain	N. E., N.	0.42		Rain 10 A.M. to 7 P. M.
22	34½	37½	"	Cloudy	N. E., N. W.	0.02		Rain before day, 0.01; part of A. M., 0.01; clear ev'g.
23	20½	25	Clear	Clear	N.			
S 24	8	14	Snow	Cloudy	N. E.	0.10		Snow till 10 A. M., 0.05; 11:30 A.M. to 2 P.M., 0.05; partly clear part of ev'g.
25	9	30	Cloudy	"	N. E.			
26	28	42½	"	Clear	N. W., N. E.			Cleared 10:30 A. M.
27	32	35	"	Rain	N. E.			Rain 9 A.M.; light all day but heavier in the ev'g.
28	33	38	Rain	Misty	N. E.	0.48		Rain till 7 A. M., 0.45; misty afternoon and ev'g, 0.03.
29	35	40½	Cloudy	Rainy	N., N. W.	0.07		Rain after 10 A.M., and part of afternoon, 0.07.
30	36	38	"	Snow	S. W., N. W.	0.23		Clear part of A.M.; snow 10 A. M. to 5:15 P. M.
S 31	21	35½	Clear	Cloudy	S. W.			Clouded over 9 A.M.; cleared 9 P. M
						3.36	8.00	

Thirtieth year of daily observations, and twenty-fifth of rain fall

February, 1886.

Date.	Thermometer. Lowest.	Thermometer. Highest.	Weather. Morning.	Weather. Afternoon.	Prevailing Wind.	Rain and Melted Snow in inches.	Snow in inches.	REMARKS.
1	22	27½	Clear	Clear	N. W.			
2	17	31	"	"	S. W.			
3	13	17	Cloudy	Snow	N. E.			Light snow 7:30 A. M. till noon & heavy afterwards.
4	3½	13	Snow	Cloudy	N. E., N.		6.00	Snow till 10 A.M.; clear part of aft'rnoon; coldest 9 A.M.
5	-1	13	Clear	Clear	N. W.			
6	5	20½	"	Cloudy	S. W.			
S 7	18	31	Cloudy	"	S. W.	0.02		Light snow before day, 0.02.
8	25	39	Clear	Clear	N. W.			
9	29	47½	"	"	S.W., N,N.E.,			
10	30	41	Cloudy	Cloudy	N. E.			
11	35	37½	Rain	Rain	N. E.			Light rain till 10 A.M; then very heavy till 8 P.M. and light afterwards till 10 P. M., 0.10.
12	36	50	"	Rainy	N. E.	2.51		Light rain till 11:30 A.M., 2.40; light rain afternoon and eve'g till 10 P.M.,0.11.
13	40½	48	"	Cloudy	S. W.	0.41		Rain till 8 A.M., 0.34; 8:30 to 11:30 A.M., 0.05; part of eve, 0.02; cleared 9 P. M.
S 14	36½	52	Clear	Clear	S. W.			Cloudy part of morning.
15	37¼	62½	"	"	S. W.	0.03		Cloudy part of A.M.; cloudy part of evening with light rain, 0.03.
16	32½	38½	"	"	W., N., W.			
17	21	31½	Cloudy	"	N. W., S. W.			
18	28	47	Clear	"	S. W.			
19	34½	47	"	Cloudy	S. W., N. W.	0.01		Cl'ded over 10 A. M.; light rain noon to 1 P. M., 0.01; clear part of evening.
20	25	32	"	Clear	N. W.			Cloudy part A.M., with snow squall; cl'dy part of P. M.
S 21	15½	32	"	Cloudy	N. W., S. W.			Clouded over 8 A. M.; electric light 20th.
22	30½	40	Cloudy	Clear	N. W., S. W.			
23	31¼	47½	"	"	S. W., N. W.			Cl'r part A.M. & c'y part P.M.
24	25	36½	Clear	"	N. W., S. W.			
25	27¼	49¼	Cloudy	Rain	S. E., S.	0.99		Rain 7:20 A.M. to 5:30 P. M.
26	20	24	"	Clear	N. W.	0.37		Rain and snow before day, 0.37; clear part of A. M.
27	11	25	Clear	"	N. W.			
S 28	13	30½	"	"	N. W.			
						4.34	6.00	

WEATHER RECORD FOR NEW BRUNSWICK, N. J.

March, 1886.

Date	Thermometer. Lowest	Thermometer. Highest	Weather. Morning	Weather. Afternoon	Prevailing Wind.	Rain and Melted Snow in inches.	Snow in inches.	REMARKS.
1	12	22½	Clear	Clear	N. W.			
2	12	28¼	"	"	N. W.			
3	21½	38	"	"	N. W.			6th day of violent North West winds.
4	27½	41	"	"	N. W.			Cloudy part of morning.
5	30	39¼	Cloudy	"	N. W.			
6	29	43½	Clear	"	N. W.			
S 7	25	43	"	"	N. W., S. W.			
8	33	40	Cloudy	Cloudy	S. W.	0.04		Clear part A. M.; light snow P. M.; clear part ev'g.
9	33¼	43	Clear	Clear	N. W.			Cloudy part of evening.
10	29	41¼	Cloudy	"	N. E., N.			Light snow before day; partly clear part morning.
11	29	46	Clear	"	N. W., S. W.			
12	35	43½	Cloudy	Cloudy	S. W.	0.06		Rain 1 to 4 P.M., 0.06; clear part of evening.
13	36	46½	"	"	S. W., N. W.	0.06		Partly clear part A.M.; rain 9:05 A.M. to 1 P. M., 0.05; rain and snow part of evening, 0.01
S 14	34	49	Clear	Clear	S. W.			Cloudy part of evening.
15	33½	53½	"	"	N. E., S. E.			Cloudy part of afternoon.
16	32	60	"	"	S.E., S.W., N.			Foggy morning.
17	33½	50	"	"	N.W, NE, SE			
18	34	54	"	Cloudy	S. W., S. E.			Clear part of afternoon.
19	39¼	43	Cloudy	"	S.E., N.E., E	0.05		Light rain before day, 0.01; hail, rain, thunder and lightning 4 P. M., 0.04.
20	34¼	41½	"	Rain	N. E.	0 02		Misty till 7:15 A. M., 0.02; misty P.M.; rain after 6 PM.
S 21	37	49¼	Rain	"	N. E., S. E.	0.91		Rain till 7:15 A. M., 0.88; part A.M., 0.03; clear part P. M.; rain 6:45 P. M.
22	40	47	C'y m'st all day.		S. W.	0.49		Rain before day, 0.49.
23	34	40½	Cloudy	Clear	W., N. W.			
24	30	44	Clear	"	N. W.			
25	33	56	"	Cloudy	S. W.			
26	47¼	55¼	Cloudy	Clear	W., S. W.			Cloudy evening.
27	44	46	"	Rain, Snow	S.W., S.E., N E			Rain 10 A.M., and after 4 P. M. with snow.
S 28	33½	50½	"	Clear	N. E., S. E.	0.67		Rain and snow before day, 0.67; clear 6 A. M.
29	35	40	"	Rain	S. E., N. E.			Misty part A.M.; rain 3 P.M.
30	37	44½	Rain	"	S. E.	1.35		Rain before day, 0.69; 9 to 11:30 A M., 0.21; part P.M., 0.05; sh'r 7 to 9 P.M., 0.40.
31	43	66½	Cloudy	Cloudy	S.	0.30		Rain before day, 0.03; rain 7:45 to 10 P. M., 0.27.
						3 95		

April, 1886.

Date.	Thermometer.		Weather.		Prevailing. Wind.	Rain and Melted Snow in inches.	Snow in inches.	REMARKS.
	Lowest.	Highest.	Morning.	Afternoon.				
1	48	57	Cloudy	Clear	S. W.			Cleared 7 A. M.
2	43	53	Clear	"	S. W., N. W.			Cloudy evening.
3	35½	41	Cloudy	Cloudy	N. E.			Clear part of afternoon.
S 4	29	35	"	Snow	N. E.	0.21		Snow before day, 0.05; snow 2 to 9 P. M., 0.16.
5	32	37½	Rain } Snow	Rain	N. E.	0.08		Rain and snow till 11 A. M., 0.08; rain 3:50 P. M.
6	35	47½	Rain	Cloudy	N. E.	2.74		Rain till 10:30 A. M., 2.41; 4:50 to 8 P. M., 0.33.
7	39½	47	Clear	"	S.W.,N., S E.	0.04		Cleared at sunrise; rain parts of afternoon and evening, 0.04; cleared 8 P. M.
8	38	47	"	Clear	N. W.			Cloudy part of afternoon.
9	35½	61	"	"	N. W., S. W.			
10	44	67½	"	"	S. W.			
S 11	42½	48	Cloudy	Cloudy	N. E., S. E.			Partly clear part of morning; light rain 3 P. M.; partly clear part of ev'g.
12	41½	62½	"	"	N. E.,S. E., S.	0.02		Shower 8:15 A.M., 0.02; cle'r parts of aft'noon & even'g.
13	52	67	Rain	Clear	S. W.	0.36		Sh'rs till 8 A. M., 0.30; show- 5 P.M., 0.05; 8 P. M., 0.01.
14	49	67	Clear	"	NW.,NE,SE.			Cloudy evening.
15	47	64½	Cloudy	"	S. E.			Foggy morning.
16	41½	46½	"	Cloudy	N. E., S. E.			
17	41½	56	"	Clear	N. E., S. E.			
S 18	39	64½	"	"	N. E., S. E.			Cleared 7:30 A. M.
19	46½	74	Clear	"	N. W., S. W.			
20	56	66½	"	"	N. E., S. E.			
21	45½	70½	Cloudy	"	E., S., S. W.			Cleared 10 A. M.
22	54½	76½	Clear	"	All points.			Cherries flowered.
23	53	79	"	"	NE,NW.,SW			
24	60	79	"	Cloudy	S. W.			Light shower 4 P. M.; pears flowered.
S 25	51½	57½	Cloudy	Clear	N. E., E.			Cleared 4 P. M.
26	48½	65½	"	"	E., S. E.			Cleared 10 A. M.
27	50	52	"	Cloudy	E.	0.12		Rain 8:20 to 10:40 A.M., 0.11; 1 to 1:30 P. M., 0.01.
28	46	66½	"	Clear	S. W.			Clear part of morning.
29	50	55	"	"	E.			Clear part of morning.
30	40	55½	Clear	"	N. E., E.			Cloudy evening.
						3.57		

Weather Record for New Brunswick, N. J.

May, 1886.

Date.	Thermometer. Lowest.	Thermometer. Highest.	Weather. Morning.	Weather. Afternoon.	Prevailing Wind.	Rain and Melted Snow in inches.	Snow in inches.	REMARKS.
1	43	55½	Clear	Cloudy	N. E.			Clear part of afternoon.
S 2	47	67½	"	Clear	N. E., S. E.			
3	45	67	"	"	S. E.			Cloudy part of afternoon.
4	50	73	"	"	S. W.			Cloudy part of afternoon.
5	60½	79	"	"	S. W.	0.05		Cloudy part of P.M.; shower 4 to 5 P.M, 0.02; 6 to 6:30 P. M., 0.03.
6	53½	69	Cloudy	"	All points	0.15		Rain before day, 0.01; clear part of A.M.; shower 9:30 P. M., 0.14.
7	50	65½	"	Rain	N. E.			Foggy A.M.; clear part of A.M.; rain 3:30 P. M.
8	50	53	Rain	Cloudy	N. E.	2.43		Rain till 7 A.M., 1.90; 8:30 to 11:15 A. M., 0.35; 12:30 to 2 P.M, 0.12; part of evening, 0.06.
S 9	49	70	Clear	Clear	N. W.			Cloudy part of evening.
10	53	59	Cloudy	Cloudy	N. E., E.	0.03		Partly clear part of P. M.; rain 1:30 to 2:30 P.M.
11	50	60½	"	"	N. E., S. E.			Clear part of afternoon.
12	50	57	"	"	S. E.			Clear part of afternoon.
13	48	51½	"	Rain	S E., N. E.	1.36		Rain 10:30 A.M. to 8:45 P.M.
14	49	62	C'y m'st all day		N. E., S. E.			
15	49	61¾	Cloudy	Cloudy	S. E.	0.03		Misty part of A M., 0.02; part P. M., 0.01; rainy evening after 9 P. M.
S 16	56	66½	Rain	Clear	N W.	0.24		Rain till 5:30 A. M., 0.24; cleared 7:30 A.M.
17	45½	64	Clear	"	N. W., W.			
18	48½	66	"	Cloudy	W., S.			
19	53	64½	Rain	"	S. W.	0.25		Rain till 9:30 A.M., 0.25.
20	56	65½	Cloudy	"	S. W.	0.07		Partly clear part of P.M.; then shower 9:30 P. M.
21	53½	72½	Clear	Clear	N., W., S. W.			
22	58	78	"	"	S. W.	0.26		Shower 7:15 to 10 P.M., 0.26.
S 23	63	80	"	"	N. W., S. W.			Cloudy before day; cloudy part of evening.
24	65	70½	Cloudy	Rain	W., N., S. E.	0.15		Rain 12:15 to 5:15 P. M.; clear part of evening.
25	55	63½	"	Clear	N.	0.02		Rain 6 to 8 A.M., 0.02; clear part of A.M., and cloudy part of afternoon.
26	45½	59	Clear	"	N. W.	0.01		Shower 11:45 A.M., 0.01.
27	47	62	Cloudy	Cloudy	S. W.	0.25		Shower 8:45 to 10:15 A.M., 0.03; 5:40 to 8 P.M., 0.22; cleared 9 P.M.
28	50½	70	Clear	Clear	N. W.			
29	52	72½	"	"	N. W., S. W.			
S 30	58	79	"	"	S. W.			
31	64	70	"	Cloudy	N. E.			Cloudy 9 A.M.; sprinkles part of morning; clear ev'g.
						5.30		

June, 1886.

Date	Lowest	Highest	Wind Morning	Wind Afternoon	Prevailing Wind	Rain and Melted Snow in inches	Snow in inches	REMARKS
1	56	74	Cloudy	Clear	N. E., S. E.	----	----	Cleared 8 A. M.
2	57	73	"	Cloudy	S. E., S. W.	----	----	Clear part of evening.
3	62	71	"	"	S. W., N. W.	0.11	----	Light rain 6 A.M. to 1 P.M., 0.11; clear part of afternoon and evening.
4	53	68	Clear	Clear	N. W., E., S.	----	----	
5	53	70½	"	"	S., S. E.	----	----	
S 6	54	76½	"	"	S.E., S. W.,S.	----	----	Cloudy evening.
7	59½	71	Cloudy	Cloudy	S. E.	----	----	Clear part of afternoon.
8	62½	76	Clear	Clear	N., W., S. W	----	----	
9	57	77½	"	Cloudy	S.E., S., S. E.	0.33	----	Rain 5 to 8 P. M., 0.33.
10	58	76	Cloudy	Clear	N. W., S. W.	0.16	----	Rain before day, 0.14; shower 7 P. M., 0.02.
11	63	78½	Clear	"	N. E.	----	----	
12	61	75	"	"	N. E., S. E.	----	----	Cloudy part of evening.
S 13	61	75	Cloudy	"	S. E., N. E.	----	----	Partly clear part morning; cloudy part of evening.
14	59	61½	Rain	Misty	N. E.	0.45	----	Rain 5 to 6:45 A. M., 0.22; 7:15 A. M. to 12:45 P. M., 0.23; misty rest of day.
15	56	70½	Cloudy	Cloudy	N. E., S. E.	0.05	----	Misty rain before day, 0.05; clear evening.
16	60	74½	"	Clear	S. E., S. W.	----	----	Foggy morning; clear part morning; cloudy evening.
17	67½	79	"	Cloudy	S. W.	1.73	----	Shower 1 to 2:15 P. M., 1.70; 2:45 to 3:15 P. M., 0.03; clear part of evening.
18	66	71	"	Clear	N. W., N.	----	----	
19	53	71½	Clear	"	N. E.	----	----	
S 20	55	75	"	"	All points	----	----	
21	58	76	"	"	S. W., S.	----	----	
22	60	69	Cloudy	Rain	N. E., S. E.	0.23	----	Rain parts A. M., 0.03; 2 to 6:15 P.M., 0.20; rain 10:30 P. M.
23	60	65½	Rain	Cloudy	S. E., N. E.	0.97	----	Rain till 9:30 A. M., 0.94; part of afternoon, 0.03.
24	58½	67½	Cloudy	"	N. E., S. E.	----	----	
25	61½	76	"	"	S. E., S. W.	0.03	----	Rain before day, 0.02; clear part P. M.; shower 7 P. M., 0.01; clear part evening.
26	61½	78	Clear	Clear	N. W.	----	----	Cloudy with light shower 4:45 P. M.
S 27	62½	78	"	"	N. W.	----	----	
28	58½	73	"	"	N. E.	----	----	
29	58	79½	"	"	S. W.	----	----	
30	62½	74	"	"	N. E., S.	----	----	

4.06

Weather Record for New Brunswick, N. J.

July, 1886.

Date	Thermometer Lowest	Thermometer Highest	Weather Morning	Weather Afternoon	Prevailing Wind	Rain and Melted Snow in inches	Snow in inches	REMARKS
1	56½	75½	Clear	Clear	S. E.			
2	58	71½	"	Cloudy	N.E., E., N.E.			Cloudy part of morning.
3	63	83½	"	Clear	N.W., NE, SE			Cloudy before day.
S 4	65½	85	"	"	N.W., NE, SE			
5	65	82½	Cloudy	"	All points.			Foggy morning; cleared 9 A.M.; cloudy 10 P. M.
6	68½	86	Clear	"	S. W.			
7	71	90½	"	"	S. W.			Cloudy part of evening.
8	76	84	C'y m'st all day.		N. E., S. E.			
9	66	81	Clear	Clear	N. E., S, E.			
10	62½	77	Rain	"	N. E., S., N.	0.89		Rain with thunder till 8 A. M., 0.82; 8:50 to 9:40 A.M.; 0.07.
S 11	66	82	Clear	"	S, W., N. W.			
12	62	75	"	"	N. E., S. E.			
13	58	76½	"	Cloudy	S. W., S. E.			Clouded over 3 P. M.
14	65	75	"	"	N. E., S, E.	0.75		Cloudy part A. M.; rain 3:50 to 4:45 P. M., 0.04; 6:40 to 8 P. M., 0.71.
15	67	79½	Cloudy	"	S. E., S.	1.12		Rain 5:15 to 6:15 A.M , 1.12; clear part of afternoon.
16	67	77	Rain	"	S.	0.84		Rain till 6:30 A. M., 0.81; clear part P.M.; rain 10:30 P. M., 0.03.
17	66	81	Clear	Clear	NW, NE, SE			
S 18	67	82½	"	"	S. W.			Shower after 10:40 P. M.
19	65	76½	"	"	N. W.	0.28		Shower before day, 0.28.
20	63	78	"	"	N. W., N.			
21	64½	70½	Cloudy	Cloudy	N., E., N. E.	0.12		Rain 7 to 11:30 A. M., 0.42; clear part of evening.
22	62	79½	Clear	Clear	N. W.			
23	63½	78	"	"	N. E., N.			
24	60	78½	"	"	N., W., S. W.			
S 25	64	74½	Hazy Cl'dy	most all day.	S. W.			
26	66	79	Cloudy	Cloudy	All points.	0.18		Foggy morning; rain 6 to 7:30 P. M., 0.18.
27	70	80½	"	Clear	S. W., N. W.	0.05		Rain 8:15 to 10 A. M., 0.05; cloudy evening.
28	67½	83	Clear	"	N.E., N.W., W.			
29	68½	87	"	"	S. W.			Cloudy evening.
30	74	88	C'y m'st all day.	All points.				
31	71	80	Cloudy	Cloudy	All points.	0.08		Showers 5:15 to 9:30 A. M., 0.08; clear parts of afternoon and evening.
						4.61		

August, 1886.

Date.	Lowest.	Highest.	Weather. Morning.	Weather. Afternoon.	Prevailing Wind.	Rain and Melted Snow in inches.	Snow in inches.	REMARKS.
S 1	69	80	Cloudy	Cloudy	S. E., S.	0.01		Clear part of morn'g; shower 2 P. M., 0.01.
2	73	83	"	Clear	N. W.			Cleared 8 A. M.
3	60	73	Clear	"	N. W.			
4	57½	74½	"	"	N. W.			
5	58	78	"	Cloudy	N. W., S. W.			Clouded over 3 P. M.
6	62	72	Cloudy	"	N. E.	0.03		Rain before day, 0.03; cl'r part P.M. and part eve'g.
7	63	66	"	Rain	N. E.	0.86		Rain 7:20 A.M. to 7 P.M., 0.83; 9 to 11 P. M., 0.03.
S 8	60	77	"	Clear	N. W., S. W.			Cleared 7 A. M.
9	64	80½	Clear	"	S. W., S.			Hazy part of morning.
10	65	78	Cloudy	"	S. W.			Clear part of morning and cloudy part of afternoon.
11	70	84	Clear	"	S. W.			Cl'dy part P.M.; digg'g up before my house for city rail'y.
12	73	84	Cloudy	"	W., N. W.			Cl'r part A.M.; putting down the rails for city railway.
13	66	83	Clear	"	N., E., S.			
14	72	86	Cloudy	"	S. W., N.			Cleared 9 A. M.
S 15	63	77½	Clear	"	N. E., S. E.			
16	61	78	"	Cloudy	S.			Foggy AM.; cl'ded over 2 PM.
17	72	80½	"	Clear	W., N., N. E.			
18	62	72	"	Cloudy	N. E., E.			Cl'dy part A. M.; clear eve'g,
19	58	75	"	Clear	N. E., S. E.			Cloudy part of afternoon.
20	58½	73½	"	"	N. E., S. E.			
21	56	73	"	"	N. E., E.			
S 22	54½	73½	"	"	N. E., S. E.			
23	58	76	"	"	N. E., S. E.			Cloudy part of morning.
24	61	77½	C'y m'st all day	All points.				
25	66	80	Clear	Cloudy	N. E., E.			Cloudy part of morning and clear part of afternoon.
26	65½	84	"	Clear	S. W., W.			Cloudy part of morning.
27	65	82	C'y m'st all day	All points				
28	68	85½	Clear	Clear	S. W., N. W.			Cloudy part of afternoon.
S 29	71	86½	Cloudy	"	S. W., S.			Cleared 10 A.M.; cloudy 3 to 4 P.M., with sprinkles.
30	71½	78	"	"	S. E.	0.77		Sprinkle before day; shower 8 to 11:50 A.M., 0.75; 1 P. M., 0.02; cleared 2 P. M.
31	71	74½	Clear	Cloudy	S. W., N. W.	0.23		Rain before day, 0.02; 9:45 A. M., 0.08; 1 P. M., 0.02; 5:30 P. M., 0.11; cleared 9:30 P. M.
						1.90		

September, 1886.

Date.	Thermometer Lowest.	Thermometer Highest.	Weather Morning.	Weather Afternoon.	Prevailing Wind.	Rain and Melted Snow in inches.	Snow in inches.	REMARKS.
1	60	71½	Clear	Clear	N. W.	----	----	
2	54	70½	"	"	N. E., S. E.	----	----	
3	53	72	"	"	All points.	----	----	
4	55	69	"	"	N. E., S. E.	----	----	Cloudy evening.
S 5	60	72	Cloudy	"	N. E., E.	----	----	Cleared 11 A. M.
6	60½	74½	Clear	"	N. E., S. E.	----	----	Cloudy part of morning and part of evening.
7	67	79	Cloudy	"	N. E., S. E.	----	----	Misty and foggy before day; cloudy part of evening.
8	69	78½	"	"	N. E., S. E.	----	----	Clear part of morning, and cloudy part of evening.
9	68	73	"	Cloudy	N. E., E.	0.75	----	Rain 8 A.M. to 4:30 P.M., 0.75.
10	69	80	"	Clear	N., S. E.	0.01	----	Rain before day, 0.01.
11	69½	79	Clear	"	N. W.	----	----	
S 12	58½	79	"	Cloudy	S. W.	0.39	----	Cloudy part of morning; clear part of afternoon; shower 6 to 7 P. M., 0.39.
13	58½	69½	"	Clear	W., N. W.	0.01	----	Rain before day, 0.01; cloudy part of afternoon.
14	53	73	"	Cloudy	S. W.	----	----	
15	60	72½	"	"	S. W., S. E.	----	----	
16	64	75½	Cloudy	"	S. E	0.16	----	Rain before day, 0.09; 8:30 to 11:30 A. M., 0.07; clear evening.
17	68	84	Clear	Clear	S. W.	0.05	----	Cloudy part of morning; showers 8:50 to 9:20 P.M., 0.05.
18	66	75	"	"	N. E., S. E.	----	----	
S 19	56	75	"	Cloudy	N. E., S., S. W.	----	----	
20	62	68½	"	Clear	N. W.	----	----	Cloudy before day.
21	49	67	"	"	N. W.	----	----	
22	47½	59½	Cloudy	Cloudy	N. E.	----	----	
23	57	75	"	Clear	S.W., N., N.E.	0.12	----	Rain before day, 0.12; cleared 8 A. M.
24	51	70½	"	"	All points.	----	----	Cleared 10 A. M.
25	59	69½	C'y m'st all day.		S. W., S. E.	----	----	
S 26	62½	79	"	"	S. W.	----	----	
27	67½	80½	"	"	"	----	----	
28	67	85½	Clear	Clear	S. W.	----	----	
29	59½	68	Cloudy	"	N. W.	0.01	----	Rain before day, and 7:45 A. M.
30	50	67	Clear	"	N. E., S. E.	----	----	
						1.50	----	

October, 1886.

Date.	Thermometer. Lowest.	Thermometer. Highest.	Weather. Morning.	Weather. Afternoon.	Previling Wind.	Rain and Melted Snow in inches.	Snow in inches.	REMARKS.
1	51	67	Clear	Clear	S. W., N. W.			
2	41	58	"	"	N. W.			Frost.
S 3	38½	60½	"	"	N. W., S. W.			
4	42	67	"	"	S. W.			Cloudy evening.
5	47	68	"	"	N. E., S. E.			
6	50½	67½	"	"	N. E.			
7	50	68½	"	"	N. E., S. E.			
8	49	69	Cloudy	"	N. E., S., S. W.			Cleared 10 A. M.
9	51	76	Clear	"	S. W., N. W.			Hazy part of morning.
S 10	53	73	"	"	NW, NE, SE.			
11	51½	73	"	"	All points.			
12	54	77	"	"	S. W., N. W.			
13	60	71½	"	Cloudy	NW, NE, SE.			Clouded over 3 P. M.
14	59	67	Cloudy	"	S. E.			Light rain 6 P. M.; city railroad opened.
15	61	71	Clear	Clear	S. W., N. W.			
16	46	51	"	"	N. W., N.			
S 17	30½	49½	"	Cloudy	N. W., S. W.			
18	47	66	"	Clear	All points.			Cloudy part of morning and part of afternoon.
19	50	58	Cloudy	Cloudy	N. E., N E.			
20	52½	65	"	Clear	E., S., S. W.			Cleared 4 P. M.
21	55½	67	"	"	S. W., N. W.	0.02		Rain 8:30 to 9:30 A. M., 0.02; cleared 11 A. M.
22	43	63	Clear	"	S. W.			
23	50	67	"	"	All points.			
S 24	42	58	"	"	N. E., S. E.			
25	44	65	C'y m'st all day		N. E., N. W.			
26	50	56½	Cloudy	Cloudy	S.W., N., N. E.			Foggy morning; rainy after 5:15 P. M.
27	46½	50½	Rain	"	N. E.	1.62		Rain till 11 A. M., 1.41; 2 to 3 P. M., 0.18; part of evening, 0.03.
28	45	53	Cloudy	Misty	N. E.	0.54		Rain before day, 0.48; part of evening, 0.06.
29	50	55½	"	Cloudy	N. E.	0.01		Light rain part of afternoon.
30	49½	53	"	"	N. E.			Rain 9:30 P. M.
S 31	50	55	Rain	"	N. W., N. E.	0.29		Rain till 7 A. M., 0.28; 11 A. M. till noon, 0.01; clear evening.
						2.48		

November, 1886.

Date	Thermometer. Lowest.	Thermometer. Highest.	Weather. Morning.	Weather. Afternoon.	Prevailing Wind.	Rain and Melted Snow in inches.	Snow in inches.	REMARKS.
1	47	65	Clear	Clear	N. W., N.			
2	49	68	"	"	N. W., S. W.			
3	50	67	"	"	S. W.			
4	52	59	"	"	S. W., N. W.			
5	37	60½	"	"	S. W.			
6	44½	62½	"	Cloudy	S. W.			Foggy A. M.; rain 6 P. M., with thunder and light'g,
S 7	36½	44	Cloudy	Clear	N. W.	1.02		Snow and rain before day, 1.02: cleared 8 A.M.; cl'dy part P.M.,with snow squall
8	30	40½	Clear	"	S. W., N. W.			Cloudy part of afternoon, with snow squall.
9	32	47	"	"	S. W.			Cloudy evening.
10	40	50½	Cloudy	"	S. W.	0.01		Rain parts A. M.; cloudy parts P.M. and evening.
11	45½	58½	Clear	"	S. W., N. W.			Cloudy part of afternoon.
12	43	45½	Cloudy	Rain	N. E.	0.02		Light rain parts A.M., 0.02 ; rain 3 P. M.
13	39	42½	Rain	Cloudy	N. W.	1.69		Rain till 6:30 A. M., 1.69; cleared 11 P. M.
S 14	31½	45	Clear	Clear	N. W.			
15	34½	49½	"	"	S. W., N. W.			
16	32	44½	"	"	N. W., S. W.			
17	34	58†	Rain	Rain	N. E., S. E.	0.14		Rain 7 A. M. to 6 P.M., 0.14.
18	67*	67½	Cloudy	Clear	S.E., S., N.W.	0.54		Rain before day, 0.01 ; 10 to 11 A. M., 0.53, with thunder and lightning.
19	39	44	Clear	"	S. W., W.			
20	36	53	"	"	S. W.			Cloudy part of morning.
S 21	38	50	"	"	N. W., S. W.			
22	34	49	"	"	N. W., N., E.			Cloudy evening.
23	41	63	Rain	Cloudy	S. E., S. W.	0.86		Heavy rain till 9 A.M., 0.80, and light till 11 A. M., 0.04; part evening, 0 02.
24	53	54	Cloudy	Clear	W.			Clear part of A. M.; cloudy part of evening.
25	37	41	"	Rain	N. E.	0.48		Rain before day, 0.02 ; 9 A. M., 0.02 ; 1 to 5:30 P. M., 0.28; 7 to 10 P. M., 0.16; cleared 11 P. M.
26	30	38½	Clear	Clear	N. W.			
27	27	37½	"	"	S. W., W.			
S 28	27½	43½	"	"	S. W.			
29	31	54	"	"	S. W., S.			Cloudy part of evening.
30	36	49	Cloudy	Cloudy	S. E., N. E.	0.05		Clear part A. M. ; rain 4 to 5:30 P. M.
						4.81		

* 7 A. M. † 10 P. M.

December, 1886.

Date.	Thermometer. Lowest.	Thermometer. Highest.	Weather. Morning.	Weather. Afternoon.	Prevailing Wind.	Rain and Melted Snow in inches.	Snow in inches.	REMARKS.
1	35	43	Cloudy	Cloudy	W.	0.01		Clear part A. M.; light rain part of afternoon.
2	17	22½	Clear	Clear	N. W.	0.01		Snow squall before day, 0.01.
3	17½	28	"	"	N. W.			
4	18	26½	"	Cloudy	N. W.			
S 5	10	22	Snow	"	N. E.		6.00	Snow till 4 P. M. and drifts badly.
6	19	29	Cloudy	"	N. E.			Clear 11 A. M. to 2 P. M.; snow 9 P. M.
7	21	31	Snow	"	N. E.		3.00	Snow till 7 A. M., 3 inches.
8	20	35	Clear	Clear	W., S. W.			
9	19	39	"	"	N. W.			
10	15	39	"	"	N. W., S. W.			
11	27	43½	"	"	S. W.			
S 12	31	41	Cloudy	Cloudy	N. E.	0.07		Rain 10 A.M to 3 P.M., 0.07.
13	36	40	Rain	Rain	N. E.	0.20		Misty rain all day and part of evening.
14	37	41	Cloudy	Clear	N. W.			Cleared 10 A. M.; cloudy part of evening.
15	32	39	"	Snow, Rain	S. W., S. E.			Snow and rain 7:30 A. M. to 5 P.M., and then snow.
16	15	22	Snow	Clear	N. E., N. W.	0.45		Snow before day, 0.44; part of morning, 0.01.
17	11	27	Clear	Cloudy	S. W.			Clouded over 3 P. M.
18	24½	40½	Snow, Rain	Rain	S. W., S.	1.31		Snow before day and then rain till 9 P. M.
S 19	33½	36½	Cloudy	Cloudy	S. W.			Clear part of evening.
20	31	38	"	Clear	N. W.			Clear part of morning.
21	25	39	Clear	"	S. W.			
22	30	38	Cloudy	Cloudy	S. W., W.			
23	32	39	Clear	"	N., E.	0.07		Clouded over at noon; rain 4:40 to 8 P. M.
24	36	53	Foggy	"	All points.	0.13		Rain before day, 0.06; shower 9 A. M., 0.02; part ev'g, 0.05; clear part morning.
25	33	37½	Clear	Clear	N. W.			
S 26	21	30	Cloudy	Cloudy	N. E.	0.01		Snowy evening.
27	28	39½	"	Clear	S. W., N. W.			Cleared off at noon.
28	23	28	C'y m'st all day.		N. W.			
29	20	28	Clear	Cloudy	N. W., N. E.			
30	15	20†	Snow	Snow	N. E.			Light snow all day.
31	25*	33	Snow, Rain	Rain	N. E.	0.57		Snow and rain till 8 P. M.
						2.83	9.00	

* 7 A. M. † 10 P. M.   Rain and melted for 1886, 45.04 inches.

January, 1887.

Date	Thermometer. Lowest.	Thermometer. Highest.	Weather. Morning.	Weather. Afternoon.	Prevailing Wind.	Rain and Melted Snow in inches.	Snow in inches.	REMARKS.
1	29	37½	Rain	Cloudy	S. W., N. W.	0.77		Heavy rain before day, 0.70; 8 to 11 A.M. cl'r part ev'g.
S 2	17	20½	Clear	Clear	N. W.			Cloudy before day.
3	10	19	"	"	W., N. W.			
4	8	24	"	"	N., N. E.			Cloudy part of evening.
5	20	35	Cloudy	Rain/Snow	N. E.			Rain 4 P. M., snow afterw'd.
6	28	33½	Clear	Clear	N. W.	0.66		Snow before day, 0.66.
7	20	30½	C'y m'st all day		W., N., N. E.			
8	6	16	Clear	Clear	N. E.			
S 9	7	20	Cloudy	Snow	N. E.			Light snow 8 A.M. to 2:30 P. M., and then heavy.
10	18	24	"	Clear	W., N. W.		5.00	Snow before day, 5 in.; clear part of morning.
11	10	21	Clear	"	W., S. W.			
12	9	34	"	Cloudy	S. W.			Clear part of evening.
13	22	40	"	"	N. W., S., E.			Rain 9 P. M.
14	34	39½	Rain		N. E., S., W.	0.99		Rain till 11 A. M.
15	35	39	Cloudy	"	S. W., W.			Clear part of afternoon, and part of evening.
S 16	26	36	Clear	"	S. W.			
17	31	40½	Cloudy	Rain	E., S., N. W.	0.35		Rain before day, 0.02, and 8:15 A. M. to 7 P. M., 0.33; cleared 10:30 P. M.
18	23	26	Clear	Clear	N. W.			
19	9	27	"	Cloudy	S. W.			Clear part of evening.
20	23	39	Cloudy	"	S. W.			Clear part of morning.
21	38	50	"	Clear	S. W., N.			Cleared 8 A. M.
22	30	38	"	Cloudy	N. E.			Clear part of evening.
S 23	36	60	Clear	Clear	S. W.			
24	52	56	Rain	Rain/Snow	S. W., N. W.	0.45		Rain till 2:45 P. M., and then snow till 4 P. M.; cleared 6:30 P. M.
25	31	49½	Clear	Clear	S. W.			
26	42	43½	"	Rain/Snow	S. W., N. W.	0.12		Clouded over 7:30 A M.; rain 9:45 A.M. to 1:30 P.M., and then snow till 4:30 P. M.; cleared 6 P. M.
27	15	27½	"	Clear	N. W., S. W.			
28	23	49	C'y m'st all day	S. W.				
29	46	54	Cloudy	Rain	S., W., N.	0.88		Rain 10 A. M. to 7:15 P. M.; clear part of evening.
S 30	36	43	"	Cloudy	N. E., S., S.W.	0.02		Rain part of A. M., 0.02; partly clear part of ev'g.
31	35	39	"	Clear	N. W., N., E.			Cleared 7:30 P. M.

4.24 5.00

February, 1887.

Date	Thermometer Lowest	Thermometer Highest	Weather Morning	Weather Afternoon	Prevailing Wind	Rain and Melted Snow in inches	Snow in inches	REMARKS
1	25	31	Clear	Cloudy	N., N. E.			Cloudy part of morning.
2	19	27	Snow } Sleet }	"	N. E.	0.41		Snow & sleet to 11 A.M., 0.32; sleet part of evening, 0.09
3	24	36	Cloudy	"	N E., S., N.W.	0.28		Rain 1:30 to 4.30 P.M., 0.28.
4	30	34	Clear	Clear	N. W.			Cleared before day.
5	18	26	Cloudy	Cloudy	N. E., S. E.	0.04		Clear part A. M.; snowy ev'g; bar. 8 A. M., 30.87.
S 6	23	39	"	"	S. W.	0.02		Rain parts of P.M. and ev'g, 0.02; partly clear part of evening.
7	31	36½	Rain	Rain	N. E.	0.30		Rain till 8:30 A.M., 0.13; 11:30 A.M. to 8:30 P.M., 0.17.
8	30	39	"	Cloudy	N. E.	0.24		Rain till 9 A.M.; foggy afternoon and evening.
9	38	47	Clear	Clear	W., N. W.			Cleared before day.
10	30	49½	"	Cloudy	S.			Clear part P.M.; rain 10 P.M.
11	44	63	Cloudy	"	S. W.	0.11		Rain before day, 0.07; 2.45 to 4.15, 0.04; cleared 8 P.M.
12	24½	32	Clear	Clear	N. W.			
S 13	19	29	"	"	N. W., N			
14	16	34	"	"	N. E., S. E.			Cloudy evening.
15	32	43½	Rain	Cloudy	S. W.	0.60		Rain till 11 A. M., 0.60.
16	39	48	C'y m'st all day		S. W.			
17	37	46	Clear	Clear	S. W., N. W.			
18	35	56	Cloudy	Rain	S. E., S.	1.52		Rain 1 to 4.30 P. M., 0.73; 6 to 8:45 P.M, 0.79; thunder and lightn'g; clear 9 P. M.
19	42	53½	Clear	Clear	W., S. W			
S 20	34	37½	Cloudy	Cloudy	N., N. E.			Snow 7 P. M.
21	28½	38	"	"	All points.	0.11		Snow before day, 0.11; clear part of morning.
22	33½	44	"	"	SE, SW, NW.	0.10		Rain 8 to 11 A. M., 0.10; clear evening.
23	33	40	Clear	"	N., E., S. E			Snow 10 P. M.
24	34	49	Rain	Clear	S. W., N. W.	0.40		Rain till 7 A. M.
25	23	34	Clear	"	N. W., N			
26	25	38	Cloudy	Snow } Rain }	E., S.E., N. E.	1.97		Snow 8:30 A.M. to 2:45 P.M. and then heavy rain till 8 P. M.
S 27	32	35	Clear	Clear	S. W., N. W	0.05		Rain before day, 0.05; snow squall 1 P. M.
28	19	30	"	"	N. W.			
						6.15		

Weather Record for New Brunswick, N. J.

March, 1887.

Date.	Lowest.	Highest.	Weather. Morning.	Weather. Afternoon.	Prevailing Wind.	Rain and Melted Snow in inches.	Snow in inches.	REMARKS.
1	22½	29	Cloudy	Cloudy	All points	0.02		Snow 6 to 10 A. M., 0.02; clear part of evening.
2	22	41½	C'y m'st all day.		All points			
3	31	36	Cloudy	Cloudy	N. E.			
4	29	35	"	Clear	N. E.			Cleared 2:30 P. M.
5	20½	35	Clear	Cloudy	N. E., E.			Snow 5 to 10 P.M., 0.30, and then rain.
S 6	32	35½	Rain	"	N. E.	0.55		Rain till 7 A. M., 0.22; part of P.M. and evening, 0.03.
7	33½	40	Cloudy	"	S. E., E.			
8	33	49	Clear	Clear	N. W.			
9	30	45½	"	Cloudy	S. E			Rain 7:30 D. M.
10	38	49	Rain	Clear	N. W.	0.38		Rain till 10 A. M., 0.38.
11	27	38½	Clear	"	N. W.			
12	28	46	"	"	N. W.			
S 13	32	47½	"	"	All points.			Cloudy part P.M. and eve'g, with sprinkle 4 P. M.
14	38½	47	"	"	N. W.			Cloudy parts A. M. and P M.
15	20	37	"	"	N. W.			
16	26	35	"	Cloudy	N. W.			Clear evening.
17	27	37½	"	"	N. W.			Clouded over 10 A. M.; snow squalls P. M. and eve'g.
18	26½	42	Cloudy	"	N. W.	0.07		Snow before day, 0.07; clear part of morning.
19	34	46½	"	Clear	N. W.			
S 20	35	46½	"	Cloudy	N. W.			Clear 7:30 to 11:30 A. M.; clear part of evening.
21	34	49½	Clear	"	All points.			Rain 9:15 P. M.
22	33½	40	Rain } Snow }	"	N. E., N. W.	1.06		Rain and snow till 8 A. M.; 0.99; rain part A.M., 0.07 ; clear part of evening.
23	30	39	Clear	Clear	N. W.			Cloudy part of morning.
24	27	48	"	Cloudy	S. W., S.			Clear part of afternoon.
25	40	48	"	Clear	W., N. W.	0.01		Rain before day, 0.01.
26	32	43	Cloudy	"	N. E., N. W.			Cleared 8 A. M.
S 27	25½	36½	"	Cloudy	N. E., S. E.			Clear 11 A. M. to 2 P. M.; min 7:45 P. M.
28	33	47	Rain	"	S. W., N. W.	1.47		Rain till 7:45 A.M., 1.45; part of evening, 0.02.
29	27	33½	Clear	Clear	N. W.			
30	19	37½	"	"	N. W.			
31	26	37	"	Cloudy	N. E., S. E.	0.03		Snow 8:30 to 11 P. M., 0.03, and still snowing.
						3.59		

April, 1887.

Date.	Thermometer. Lowest.	Thermometer. Highest.	Weather. Morning.	Weather. Afternoon.	Prevailing Wind.	Rain and Melted Snow in inches.	Snow in inches.	REMARKS.
1	29	35	Snow	Cloudy	N. E.	0.06		Light snow till 11 A.M., 0.06.
2	31	42	"	"	N. E., N. W.	0.15		Snow till noon, 0.15; cleared 5:30 P. M.
S 3	35½	58	Clear	Clear	S. W.			
4	44	72	"	"	S. W.			Cloudy evening.
5	46	50	Cloudy	"	N. W.	0.02		Rain before day, 0.02; clear 7:30 A.M.; cloudy ev'g.
6	30	46	Clear	"	N. W.			
7	32	50	"	"	N. W., N.			
8	32	52	"	"	N. E., S. E.			
9	37	63	"	"	S. W.			
S 10	47½	77	"	"	S. W., N. W.			Cloudy part of morning.
11	54	79	"	"	W., N.			Cl'dy part P M.; cloudy ev'g.
12	46	56	"	Cloudy	N. E., S. E.			Cloudy part of A. M., and clear part of afternoon.
13	41	46	Cloudy	"	N. E., S. E.			
14	37	51	"	"	N. E., S. E.			
15	44	53	Clear	"	E., S. E.			Clouded over 10 A. M.; sprinkles during P. M.; rain 10 P M.
16	43	57½	C'y m'st all day		N. E., N. W.	0.11		Rain before day, 0.11.
S 17	39	50	Clear	Clear	N. W.			Cloudy part of afternoon.
18	31	34	{Snow Hail}	Rain	N. E.	0.93		Snow and hail 6:30 A. M. to 1:30 P. M., 0.62; rain till 4 P.M., 0.22; part of evening, 0.09.
19	30	47	Cloudy	Clear	N.	0.02		Snow before day, 0.02; cleared 10 A. M.
20	34	54	Clear	"	N. W., N. E.			Cloudy part of evening.
21	39	61	"	"	S. W.			
22	44	65	"	Cloudy	S. W.			Clouded over 4 P. M.
23	47	56	Rainy	"	S. E.	1.19		Rain before 6 A. M., 0.08; part of A.M., 0.09; 7:10 to 9:15 P.M., 1.02.
S 24	49	61	Clear	Clear	N. W., W.			Cloudy before day.
25	44	58	"	Cloudy	N. E., S. E., E.			Rain 7:20 P. M.
26	43	60	Rain	Clear	N. W., S. W.	0.62		Rain till 7 A. M., 0.62.
27	47	63½	Cloudy	"	S. W., N. W.			Cleared 7:30 A. M.; cloudy part of evening.
28	48	60	"	Cloudy	S., E., S.	0.18		Clear parts of morning and afternoon; rainy evening.
29	53	58	Clear	"	S. W., N. W.	0.03		Light rain part of morning, 0.03; clear evening; cherries flowered.
30	45	58	"	Clear	N. W.			Cloudy part of afternoon.
						3.31		

May, 1887.

Date.	Thermometer. Lowest.	Thermometer. Highest.	Weather. Morning.	Weather. Afternoon.	Prevailing Wind.	Rain and Melted Snow in inches.	Snow in inches.	REMARKS.
S 1	47½	70	Clear	Clear	N. W., S. W.			Cloudy part of evening.
2	57	76	"	"	S. W., S. E.			Cloudy part of evening.
3	49	67½	Cloudy	Hazy	E.			
4	53	78	Hazy	"	All points.			Foggy morning.
5	59	70	Cloudy	Clear	E.			Clear part of A. M.; cloudy evening
6	53	62	"	Cloudy	N. E., S. E.			Clear part of afternoon.
7	51	59½	"	"	N. E., S. E.	0.04		Rain before day, 0.03; part of afternoon, 0.01.
S 8	50	58	"	"	N. E , E.	0.54		Rain 9 to 11:45 A. M., 0.47; part of afternoon, 0.07.
9	55	69	"	"	E.			Clear part of morning and part of afternoon.
10	53	71	"	Clear	N. E., S. E.			Cleared 10:30 A. M.
11	57	81	Clear	"	S. W., N. W.	0.03		Shower 7 P. M., 0.03.
12	58½	78	"	"	N. W.			
13	55	71	"	"	N. E.			
14	48	69	"	"	N. E , S.			
S 15	51	72	"	"	S. E.			
16	51	71	"	"	S. E.			
17	52	72½	"	"	S. E.			
18	54	73	Cloudy	Cloudy	All points.			Clear part of afternoon.
19	56	79	Clear	Clear	All points.			
20	59	83	"	"	S. W.			
21	62½	82	"	"	S. W.			Foggy morning.
S 22	61	79¼	Cloudy	"	E., S.			Foggy morning.
23	62¼	80½	Clear	"	N. W.			
24	67	78½	Cloudy	"	S. W.	0.03		Clear part of morning; shower 11:15 A. M.
25	67½	80½	"	"	S. W.	0.02		Clear part of A. M.; cloudy eve'g, with shower at 8.
26	63	78	Clear	"	S. W., N. W.			Cloudy part of A.M.; cloudy evening, with sprinkle.
27	57	72½	"	"	N. W., S. W.			
28	55	65½	Cloudy	Show'rs	N. E.	0.42		Clear part of A. M.; showers 11:20 A.M. to 8 P.M., 0.42.
S 29	52	65	"	Cloudy	N. E., S.	0.06		Rain before day, 0.05, clear part of evening; shower 8:30 P. M., 0.01.
30	56	71	"	Clear	S.			
31	58	61	"	Cloudy	S. E.			Rain 10 P. M.
						1.14		

June, 1887.

Date.	Thermometer.		Weather.		Prevailing Wind.	Rain and Melted Snow in inches.	Snow in inches.	REMARKS.
	Lowest.	Highest.	Morning.	Afternoon.				
1	52	77½	Rain	Clear	N. E., S. E.	1.55		Rain till 8 A. M.; cleared at noon; hazy evening.
2	63½	76½	Cloudy	"	S. E., S. W.	0.02		Clear part of A. M.; showers 12:20 P. M., 0.02; rain 10 P. M.
3	61½	74	Clear	"	W.	0.11		Rain before day, 0.11.
4	61½	78	"	"	NW.,N.E.SE.			Cloudy evening.
S 5	58	64	Cloudy	Cloudy	S. E.			
6	57	63½	"	"	S. E.	0.01		Sprinkles P.M. and ev'g,0.01
7	59	66	Rain	"	S. E., E.	0.30		Rain till 8 A. M.
8	61½	72	Cloudy	"	N. E., N. W.			Cleared 6 P. M.
9	65	83½	Clear	Show'rs	N. W., N. E.	0.48		Shower 2:30 P. M., 0.01; shower 6:30 P. M., 0.47.
10	60	67	Cloudy	Clear	N. E., S. E.			Cleared 2:30 P. M.
11	52	69	Clear	"	N. E., S. E.			
S 12	51	74	"	"	N. E., S. E.			
13	56	82½	"	"	N. E., S. E.			
14	64	77½	"	"	N. E., S. E.			Cloudy evening.
15	57	70½	"	"	N. E., S. E.			
16	55	80	"	"	S. W.			
17	68	86	"	Cloudy	All points.	0.58		Shower 2 to 2:20 P.M, 0.58.
18	66	72½	Cloudy	"	All points.	0.03		Rain before day, 0.03.
S 19	60	79½	Clear	Clear	All points.	0.04		Cloudy evening; rain before day, 0.04; thunder shower 11:30 P. M.
20	66	83½	Cloudy	"	S. W., S. E.	0.24		Rain before day, 0.24; cleared 7 A. M.
21	67½	86½	Clear	"	S. E., S. W.			
22	69	79	Cloudy	Show'rs	S. W.	1.13		Thunder storm 1:30 A. M., 0.59; P.M. and eve'g, 0.54, till 10:30.
23	67	70½	Rain	Rain	S. W., E.	1.79		Rain till 9 A.M , 0.94; rain 1 to 11 P. M., 0.85.
24	63	78½	Cloudy	Clear	S. W.			Cleared 7 A. M.; cloudy part afternoon and evening.
25	63½	75	"	"	N. W., N. E.			Cleared 7 A. M.
S 26	62	76	Clear	"	All points.			Cloudy part of afternoon.
27	61	76	"	"	N. E.			
28	61	79	"	"	S. W.			
29	63	84½	"	"	W., S. W.			
30	69	88	"	"	S. W.			
						6.28		

WEATHER RECORD FOR NEW BRUNSWICK, N. J.

July, 1887.

Date.	Lowest.	Highest.	Weather Morning.	Weather Afternoon.	Prevailing Wind.	Rain and Melted Snow in inches.	Snow in inches.	REMARKS.
1	70	88½	Clear	Clear	S. W			
2	70	88½	"	"	S. W.			
S 3	71	88	"	"	S. W.			
4	72	85½	"	"	S. W.			
5	70½	76	Cloudy	Rain	S. E.	0.35		Showers 10 A. M. to 9 P. M.
6	72	84	"	Clear	S. W.	0.29		Rain before day, 0.09; cl'dy ev'g with sh'er 8:30, 020.
7	73	87	"	"	S. W.			Cleared 7:30 A. M.
8	74	88½	Clear	"	N. W., N. E			
9	74	83	"	Cloudy	S. W., S. E.	0.16		Sh'er 11:15 A.M., 0.08; rainy part of evening, 0.08.
S 10	72	82½	Cloudy	Clear	S. W., N. W.	0.06		Cleared 7:30 A.M.; shower 1:45 P.M., 0.06; cl'dy ev'g.
11	68	82½	Clear	"	N. W.			
12	66½	85½	"	"	N. W.			
13	70	91	"	"	N. W., S. W.			
14	74½	87	"	"	N.			
15	68	83	"	Cloudy	N. W., W.			
16	69	94½	"	Clear	S. W.	0.08		Shower 7 to 8:30 P.M.
S 17	75	88½	"	"	N. W., S. W.	0.15		Shower at noon, 0.02; shower 10:30 P. M., 0.13.
18	75	90	"	"	S. W., N. W.			
19	68	76	Rain	"	N. E., S. E.	0.11		Rain till 7 A.M., 0.11; cleared at noon.
20	65½	80	Cloudy	"	N. E., S. E.			
21	68½	75½	"	{ M'sty / Rain }	S E.	0.16		Misty rain part P. M., 0.02; part of evening, 0.14.
22	72	83	"	Clear	S. E.	0.39		Shower 1 P.M., 0.36; 3.15 P. M., 0.03.
23	73	82	Rain	Show'rs	S. W, NW, NE	0.88		Rain till 6 A. M., 0.46; shower P.M., 0.42; steady rain after 4:15 P. M.
S 24	72	76	"	Cloudy	S. E., N. E.	1.80		Rain before day, 1.07; showers 7:30 A.M. to 2:15 P.M, 0.73; clear evening.
25	73	84	Clear	Clear	S. E.	0.07		Rain before day, 0.07.
26	73	86	"	"	N. W., N. E.	0.03		Cloudy ev'g with shower at 7, 0.03; rain 11:30 P. M.
27	71	84	Cloudy	"	N. E., S. E.	1.60		Rain before day, 1.60; clear part of morning.
28	71½	83½	Clear	"	S. E.			Cloudy part of morning.
29	75	86	Cloudy	"	S. W.	0.01		Clear part A.M; show'r 1:30 P.M.; cloudy evening.
30	75½	87½	"	"	N. E., S			Clear part of morning.
S 31	76½	89	"	Cloudy	All points.	0.07		Clouded over 3 P. M.; rain part of evening, 0.07.
						6.20		

August, 1887.

Date	Thermometer Lowest	Thermometer Highest	Weather Morning	Weather Afternoon	Prevailing Wind	Rain and Melted Snow in inches	Snow in inches	REMARKS
1	72½	85½	Cloudy	Cloudy	S. W.			Clear 8 A. M. to 3 P. M.
2	75½	83	"	"	S. W., S. E.	4.73		Clear part A.M.; light shower 1 P.M.; great shower 2 to 3.15 P.M., 4.62; part of P. M. and evening, 0.11.
3	69	80¼	"	Clear	N. E., S. E.			Clear part of morning.
4	69	78	"	"	S. E.			
5	68	81	Clear	"	S. E.	0.05		Showers 10:15 A.M., 2 and 6 P. M.
6	75	84	Cloudy	Cloudy	S. W., N. W.	0.76		Clear part of A.M.; shower 2 to 3 P. M.; clear evening.
S 7	65½	76½	Clear	Clear	N.			
8	58½	74	"	"	N. E., S. E.			
9	59	76	"	"	S. E.			
10	61	80	"	"	S. W.			Cloudy evening.
11	69	83	Cloudy	"	S. W.	0.52		Clear part of A. M.; shower 6 P. M., 0.52.
12	69	85	Clear	"	S. W., N.			Cloudy part of morning.
13	63	75	"	"	All points.			
S 14	63	77	"	"	N. E., S.			Cloudy evening.
15	66½	70	Cloudy	Cloudy	SW.,S.E.,N.E	0.02		Rain before day, 0.01; 2 P. M., 0.01.
16	65	77½	"	Clear	N. E., N. W.			Clear part of morning.
17	65½	79	Clear	Cloudy	N. E., S. E.			Clear part of afternoon.
18	70	83	Cloudy	Clear	S. W., N. W.	0.25		Rain before day, 0.24; 11 A. M., 0.01; clear part A. M.
19	67	83½	Clear	"	S. W.			
20	70	74	Cloudy	Cloudy	N. E.			Foggy A.M.; clear part ev'g.
S 21	62	78	Clear	Clear	S. W.			Cloudy evening.
22	69	84	Cloudy	Rain	S. W.	0.73		Rain before day, 0.01; clear part A. M.; rain 4 P. M. to 10:30 P. M.
23	68½	81	"	Clear	S. W.	0.21		Shower 5 P.M.; cloudy ev'g.
24	70	76	"	Cloudy	N. E.	0.07		Misty part of A. M., 0.01; shower 12 to 1 P. M., 0.06.
25	63½	73½	"	Clear	N. E.			Cleared 8 A. M.
26	58	71	Clear	"	N. W.			
27	53	71	"	"	N. W.			
S 28	55	71	"	"	N. W., N.			
29	58	72½	"	"	N., N. E.			
30	56½	73	"	"	N. E.			
31	56	71	"	"	N. E., S. E.			
						7.34		

WEATHER RECORD FOR NEW BRUNSWICK, N. J. 375

September, 1887.

Date	Thermometer Lowest	Thermometer Highest	Weather Morning	Weather Afternoon	Prevailing Wind	Rain and Melted Snow in inches	Snow in inches	REMARKS
1	55	72½	Clear	Clear	All points			
2	59	73½	C'y m'st all day		S. W.			
3	64	73½	Clear	Clear	N. W., N.			
S 4	53½	74	"	"	N. E.			
5	59	76½	"	"	N. W., S. W.			
6	59	75½	"	Cloudy	S. W.			
7	66½	82½	Cloudy	"	S. W.	0.06		Rain before day, 0.06; clear part of evening.
8	63	71	Clear	Clear	N. W.			
9	52	71¼	"	Cloudy	N. W., S. W.			
10	63	75½	"	Clear	S. W., W., N.	0.02		Rain before day, 0.02.
S 11	55	64½	Cloudy	Rain	N. E., S. E.			Rain 4 P. M.
12	59	63	Rain	Cloudy	E., N. E.	1.63		Rain till noon.
13	58½	66	Cloudy	"	N. E., S. E.	0.03		Rain part of afternoon.
14	64	72	"	"	S. W.			Clear part of evening.
15	65	75	"	Clear	All points			Cleared 7:30 A. M.
16	57	67	Clear	"	N.			
17	47	64	"	"	All points			
S 18	47½	67½	"	"	All points			
19	55	74	"	"	S. W.			
20	57	68	Hazy	Hazy	N. E.			
21	51	71½	"	"	S. W.			Foggy morning.
22	62	67	Cloudy	Cloudy	S. W., N. W.	0.01		Rain part of afternoon.
23	56	61	Clear	"	N., N. E.	0.28		Rain before day, 0.28.
24	46½	55½	C'y m'st all day		N.			
S 25	41	57	Clear	Cloudy	N. W.			Frost.
26	42	59	"	Clear	W., S. W.			
27	43	61½	Cloudy	"	N. W., S. W.			Rain 11 A. M.
28	53½	59	"	Rain	S. W., S. E.			Rain before day, 0.93.
29	56	66	"	Cloudy	S. E, N.E.,N.	0.93		Rain before day, 0.02; part of morning, 0.02; part of evening, 0.07.
30	62	64	"	"	E., S. E.	0.11		
						3 07		

Weather Record for New Brunswick, N. J.

October, 1887.

Date.	Thermometer. Lowest.	Thermometer. Highest.	Weather. Morning.	Weather. Afternoon.	Prevailing Wind.	Rain and Melted Snow in inches.	Snow in inches.	REMARKS.
1	60	63	Cloudy	Cloudy	N. E.	0.48		Rain before day, 0.05; showers 12:30 to 1:30 P.M., 0.43; clear part of evening
S 2	58	68½	C'y m'st all day		S. W., W.	0.01		Shower 11:30 A. M.
3	54½	70	" "	" "	S. W.	0.01		Rain at noon, 0.01.
4	51	69	Clear	Clear	S. W., N. W.			Cloudy part of afternoon.
5	51	61	Cloudy	"	S. W., N. W.			
6	49½	65	Clear	"	N. W., S. W.			
7	53½	75	"	"	S. W.			
8	56	75	"	"	All points			
S 9	62	74½	"	Cloudy	S. W.	0.03		Cloudy part morning; rain 5:45 P. M. to 10 P. M.
10	64	75	Cloudy	Clear	S. W., N. W.			Clear part morning; cloudy part of evening.
11	55	58	"	Cloudy	N. W.	0.03		Rain part of morning, 0.03.
12	42	53½	Clear	Clear	N. W.			
13	38	61	"	"	S. W.			
14	45	56½	"	"	N. W.			
15	38½	53	"	"	N. W., N. E.			
S 16	35	58	"	"	S. E., S. W.			
17	43	65	Cloudy	"	S. W., S. E.			
18	53	66½	"	Cloudy	S. W.			Clear part A.M.; rain 7:30 P.M.
19	50½	55½	"	"	N. E.	0.08		Rain before day, 0.08; clear evening.
20	43	58	"	Rain	N. E., S. E.			Rain 3 P. M.
21	53	60	Rain	Clear	N. E., N. W.	1.73		Rain till 6 A. M., 1.73; clear part A.M.; cloudy part P.M.
22	39	46	Clear	Cloudy	N. W.			Clouded over 10 A. M.; clear evening.
S 23	35	54	"	Clear	N. W., S.			Cloudy part of evening.
24	52	63	Cloudy	Cloudy	S. W., N. W.			Clear part of morning.
25	44	48	"	"	All points			
26	35½	48	Clear	"	N. E., S. E.			
27	43	52½	Cloudy	"	N. E.			Rainy evening.
28	46	52½	Rainy	"	N. E.	0.07		Misty rain till 7 A. M., 0.07.
29	48	58½	Cloudy	Clear	N. W., S. W.			Cleared 8 A. M.
S 30	42	49	Clear	"	N.			Cloudy part of morning.
31	30½	50	"	"	N. E.			
						2.44		

November, 1887.

Date.	Thermometer. Lowest.	Thermometer. Highest.	Weather. Morning.	Weather. Afternoon.	Prevailing Wind.	Rain and Melted Snow in inches.	Snow in inches.	REMARKS.
1	38½	47	Rain	Clear	N. E.	0.27		Rain before day, 0.27; cleared 10 A. M.
2	33	54	Clear	"	N. E., S. W.			
3	40	58½	"	"	S. W.			
4	40	64	"	Cloudy	S. W., N. W.			Clouded over 3 P. M.
5	36	45½	"	Clear	N. W.			Cloudy evening.
S 6	32½	52½	"	"	S. W.			
7	40	56	"	Cloudy	S W.			Clear part of evening.
8	43½	60	Hazy	Clear	S. W., N. W.			
9	32	44	Clear	"	N. E., S. E.			
10	36	51	Cloudy	Rain	All points	0.50		Rain 10 A. M. to 5 P. M.; cleared 7 P. M.
11	36	41¼	Clear	Cloudy	S. W., N. W.	0.08		Cloudy part of morning, and clear part of ev'g; snow squall 12 to 12:45 P. M.
12	36	42½	"	"	N. W.			Cloudy part of A. M., and clear part of evening.
S 13	38½	48	"	Clear	N. W., N.			
14	34	51	Cloudy	Cloudy	N. E., S.			Clear part of morning.
15	45	50	"	"	N. W., W.	0.25		Rain before day, 0.24; part of morning, 0.01.
16	44	50½	"	Clear	N. W.			Cleared 9 A. M.
17	42	55	"	"	S. W., N. W.			Cleared 8 A. M.
18	37	45½	Clear	"	S. W.			Cloudy part of morning.
19	30	43	Cloudy	Rain	N. E.	0.70		R'n 9:30 A M. to 6 P.M., 0.69; part of evening, 0 01.
S 20	35	39½	"	Cloudy	W.	0.06		Rain before day, 0.06; clear evening.
21	27	38	"	Clear	S. W., N. W.			Cloudy part of evening.
22	30	43	Clear	"	S. W.			Hazy evening.
23	32	44	Cloudy	Cloudy	All points.			
24	39	46½	"	"	N. E.			
25	43	50	"	"	N. E.			Foggy morning.
26	43	57	"	Clear	N. E.			Clear part of A. M., and cloudy part of afternoon.
S 27	43	66	Clear	Cloudy	E., S. W.			Foggy morning.
28	60½	62	Cloudy	Rain	S. W., N. W.	0.49		Shower 7 A M., 0.02; rain 9 A.M. to 3:30 P. M., 0.47; cleared 8:30 P. M.
29	28	36	Clear	Clear	N.			
30	26	34¼	"	"	N., N E.			
						2.30		

Weather Record for New Brunswick, N. J.

December, 1887.

Date.	Thermometer. Lowest.	Highest.	Weather. Morning.	Afternoon.	Prevailing Wind.	Rain and Melted Snow in inches.	Snow in inches.	REMARKS.
1	13½	25½	Clear	Clear	N. E.			
2	18	34	Cloudy	Cloudy	N. E.			
3	32½	45½	"	"	N. W.			Cleared 8:30 P. M.
S 4	37	45	"	"	N. E., E.			
5	44	51	Rain	Clear	S. W., N. W.	0.25		Rain till 9 A.M., 0.25; cleared 11 A. M.
6	34½	45	Clear	"	N., S. W.			
7	30	47	"	Cloudy	S. W.			
8	42	50	Cloudy	Clear	N. W.	0.01		Light rain part A. M., 0.01.
9	32	44	Clear	Cloudy	N. E., S. E.			
10	39	57	Rain	Rain	N. E., S. E.	0.03		Rain before day, 0.03; 8:30 A. M.
S 11	55	57½	Cloudy	Cloudy	S. W.	1.05		Rain before day, 0.99; part P.M., 0.05; part ev'g, 0.01.
12	48	51	Clear	Clear	N. W.			Cloudy part A. M. and P. M.
13	34½	44	"	"	W.			
14	33½	47½	"	Cloudy	S. W.			Clear part of evening.
15	39	42	Rain	Rain	S., E., N.	0.86		Rain 7 A.M. to 5 P.M.; cleared 8 P. M.
16	34	39	Clear	Clear	N. W.			
17	29	35	Cloudy	Cloudy	N. W., N. E.			Snow 6 P. M.
S 18	28½	36	"	"	W., N. W.	0.95		Snow before day, 0.95.
19	34½	39	"	Clear	N. W.			Cleared 9 A.M.; ground covered with snow; wind N. W. and does not freeze.
20	23	38	"	Hail / Rain	All points			Hail and rain 4:45 P. M.
21	33	41	"	Cloudy	W., N. W.	0.31		Rain before day, 0.31; clear part A. M. and P. M.
22	27	32½	Clear	Clear	S. W., N. W.			Cloudy part of morning.
23	21	30½	"	"	S. W.			
24	24	32	Cloudy	Cloudy	N. E.			
S 25	25	35	Clear	Clear	N. E.			
26	22	32	Cloudy	Cloudy	N. E.	0.10		Snow 5 to 11 P. M.
27	24	34	"	Clear	N. W., S. W.			Cleared 8 A. M.
28	23½	50	Rain	Rain	S. E., S. W.	1.52		Rain till 3 P.M., 1.52; cleared 4 P. M.
29	15	26	Clear	Clear	W.			
30	18	27	"	"	W., N. W.			
31	15½	26	Cloudy	Snow	All points	0.20		Snow 2:30 P. M. to 11 P. M., 0.20; still snowing 11 P.M.
						5.28		

Rain and melted snow for 1887—51.84 inches.

January, 1888.

Date	Thermometer Lowest	Thermometer Highest	Weather Morning	Weather Afternoon	Prevailing Wind	Rain and Melted Snow in inches	Snow in inches	REMARKS
S 1	23	56	Rain	Rain	S.	2.10		Heavy rain till 3.45 P.M., 1.90, and light till 11 P.M., 0.20.
2	34	37½	Cloudy	Clear	N. W.			Cleared 9 A. M.; cloudy part of evening.
3	29	35	"	"	N. W.			Light snow part of morning; cleared 10 A.M.; cl'dy ev'g.
4	28	35	"	Cloudy	N.W., S., S.E			Clear part of morning; light sleet 8 P. M.
5	32	37	"	Clear	N.			Cleared 8 A. M.
6	25	31	"	Sleet	N. E., S. E.	0.21		Misty 9 A. M. to noon, and then sleet till 5 P. M.
7	33½	42½	"	Cloudy	S. W.	0.06		Misty before day and rain part of evening, 0.06.
S 8	37½	41	"	"	N. E., N. W.	0.07		Rain before day, 0.07; clear part of evening.
9	28	34	Clear	"	N. W., N. E.			Clouded over 10:30 A. M.
10	29	38	Snow / Rain	Clear	N. E., N. W.	0.19		Snow and rain till 8 A. M., 0.19; 10 A. M.
11	23	26	Clear	"	N. W.			
12	14	25	"	"	N. W., N. E.			Cloudy part of evening.
13	19	43	Snow	Rain	N.E., S., S.W.	1.05		Snow till 8 A.M., and then rain till 3 P. M., 0.05; cleared 9 P. M.
14	33½	38	Clear	Clear	N.W.,E.,S.E			
S 15	28	39	Misty	Cloudy	N.E., S., S.W.	0.03		Rain 5 to 6 P. M., 0.03.
16	17	23	Clear	Clear	N.			
17	16	33	Cloudy	Snow	N. E.	0.27		Snow 11 A. M. to 4:30 P. M., 0.27, and then misty.
18	26¼	30	"	Clear	N. W.	0.15		Light rain before day, 0.15; clear part of morning.
19	18	25½	Clear	"	N. W.			
20	17	28½	"	"	W., N. W.			
21	18	20½	Cloudy	"	N. W.			Clear part of morning.
S 22	4	15½	Clear	"	N. W., S. W.			
23	4½	21	"	Cloudy	All points.			
24	23½	25	"	Clear	N. W.			
25	5	34	"	Snow / Rain	N., N. E.	0.31		Clouded over 11 A. M.; snow noon to 8:30 P. M., 0.31; and then sleet.
26	23½	27	Cloudy	Clear	N. W.	0.63		Rain before day, 0.63; cleared 8 A. M.
27	15	20	Clear	"	N. W.			Cloudy part of morning.
28	5	14	"	"	N. W.			Cloudy part of afternoon.
S 29	8	22	"	"	S. W., N. W.			Cloudy part of evening.
30	20	30½	Cloudy	Cloudy	S. W.			
31	27½	31½	Snow	"	N. E., S. E.	0.15		Snow till 8 A. M., 0.13; part of afternoon, 0.02.
						5.22		

February, 1888.

Date.	Thermometer. Lowest.	Thermometer. Highest.	Weather. Morning.	Weather. Afternoon.	Prevailing Wind.	Rain and Melted Snow in inches.	Snow in inches.	REMARKS.
1	15	31	Clear	Clear	N., N. W.			Cloudy part of morning.
2	24	34½	"	"	N. W., W.			
3	20	39	"	"	S. W., N. E.			
4	26	38	Cloudy	Rain	E.			Misy rain 8 A.M.; foggy ev'g.
S 5	36	45	"	Cloudy	S. W., W.	0.37		Rain before day, 0.37; clear part A. M., and part P. M.
6	30	34	Clear	Clear	N.			
7	22½	37	Cloudy	Cloudy	E.			Light snow part A.M., 0.03; rainy evening.
8	33	36	Foggy	Snow-Rain	S. W., N. W.	0.34		Rain before day, 0.20; snow and rain noon to 3:30, 0.14; cleared 4:30 P. M.
9	20	25	Clear	Clear	N. W.			
10	6	15	Cloudy	Snow	N. E.	0.12		Light snow till 7 A.M., 0.03; snow noon to 8 P M., 0.09
11	12	32	Sleet Snow	Snow Sleet	N. E.	0.72		Snow before day, 0.12; sleet and snow 8 A.M. to 7 P.M., 0.60.
S 12	23	31½	Clear	Cloudy	N. E.	0.08		Cleared 7:30 A.M.; snow 4:30 to 10 P. M.
13	27	38	Cloudy	Clear	N., W., S. W.			Cleared 8 A. M.
14	26½	45½	Clear	"	S. W.			Cloudy part of evening.
15	15	30	"	"	N. W.			Max. 7 A.M.; min. 6 P. M., and still falling.
16	4	17	"	"	N.W., W.			
17	15	41	"	"	S. W.			
18	32	41	Cloudy	"	N.E., N., S.W.			Light snow part of morning.
S 19	27½	41	Clear	"	S. W., N. E.			Cloudy evening.
20	35	53	Rain	Rain	S. E., S.	0.47		Rain all day at intervals, till 10:30 P. M.
21	42	46½	Clear	Cloudy	N. W., W.			Cloudy part of A.M.; clear part of afternoon.
22	34	44	"	Clear	N.			
23	31	44	"	"	N. E., S., N. E.			Cloudy part of morning.
24	32	43½	"	"	N. E., S. E.			Cloudy evening.
25	35	43½	Rain	Rain	E., N. E.	1.60		Rain till 1:30 P. M., 1.58; misty till 4 P. M., 0.02.
S 26	39	43½	Cloudy	Clear	S. W., N. W.	0.20		Rain before day, 0.20; partly clear part of morning.
27	30	34½	Clear	"	N. W.			Cloudy part of A. M., and part of afternoon.
28	13½	26	"	"	N. W.			Cloudy evening.
29	21	33½	Cloudy	Cloudy	All points.			Clear evening.
						3.90		No ice crop gathered this season.

WEATHER RECORD FOR NEW BRUNSWICK, N. J.

March, 1888.

Date.	Thermometer. Lowest.	Highest.	Weather. Morning.	Afternoon.	Prevailing Wind.	Rain and Melted Snow in inches.	Snow in inches.	REMARKS.
1	26	41½	Cloudy	Cloudy	S. W.	0.02		Rain 5:30 to 6 P. M., 0.02.
2	28	32	Misty	"	N E.			
3	30	43½	Cloudy	Clear	S. W., N. W.	0.03		Rain before day, 0.03; cleared 9 A. M.
S 4	17	30	Clear	"	N.			
5	16	26½	Cloudy	Cloudy	N. W., N. E.	0.02		Snow 5 to 8 P.M., 0.02; clear part of evening.
6	13	29	Clear	Clear	N. W.			
7	20	35	"	"	S. W., N. W.			Cloudy part of morning, with snow squall.
8	25	36½	"	"	N. W.			
9	27½	43½	"	"	N. W., N.			
10	29	46	"	"	N. E., S. E.			Cloudy evening.
S 11	35	41½	Cloudy	Rain	S. E.			Rain 12:40 P. M.
12	12	20	Snow	Snow	N.			Violent storm all day; ther. 7 A. M., 20°; noon, 17°; 9 P. M, 12°.
13	5	14½	"	Cloudy	N. W.	2.02		Continued storm till 7 A.M.; rain from 12:40 P. M. of 11th to 1 A M. of the 12th, and then snow with violent wind till 7 A. M. of the 13th, being between 2 and 3 feet on level; drifts 6 to 10 ft. in streets; worst snow storm in my records.
14	12	39	Cloudy	"	N. W., N. E.	0.07		Clear part A. M.; snow 1? A. M. to 1 P.M.; clear eve'g.
15	30	40	Clear	Clear	N. W.			
16	34	48	Cloudy	Cloudy	S. W., W.	0.02		Clear part A.M.; rain 4:30 to 6:30 P. M.
17	34	38½	Clear	Clear	N. W.			Cloudy part of morning.
S 18	19	37	"	"	N. W.			
19	24	43	"	"	S. E.			
20	35	50	Cloudy	Cloudy	S. W.	0.20		Rain parts A.M. & P.M., 0.20.
21	45	59	Rain	Rain	S. W., N. W.	1.22		Rain till 9:30 A. M., 0.75; 4 to 11 P.M., 0.47.
22	37	42	Cloudy	Cloudy	S. W., N. W.			Clear part A.M.; snow squall 11:30 A. M.
23	18	26	Clear	Clear	N. W.			Cloudy part of afternoon.
24	18	32	"	"	N. W.			
S 25	19	34	"	Cloudy	N. E., S. E.			Snow 8 P. M.
26	28	36	Snow } Rain	Rain	E., N. E.			
27	33	42	Cloudy	Cloudy	N. E.	1.35		Rain before day, 1.35.
28	38	49	"	"	N.E., S., S. W.	0.13		Rain before day, 0.13.
29	40	46	"	Clear	N. W.	0.35		Rain before day, 0.32; part A.M., 0.03; cleared 3:30 P.M.
30	36	58	Clear	"	S. W.			Cloudy part of afternoon.
31	42	64	"	"	W., N.			
						5.43		

Weather Record for New Brunswick, N. J.

April, 1888.

Date.	Lowest.	Highest.	Morning.	Afternoon.	Prevailing Wind.	Rain and Melted Snow in inches.	Snow in inches.	REMARKS.
S 1	37	51½	Clear	Cloudy	N. W., S. E.	0.03		Rain 3 to 4 P. M.; clear part of afternoon.
2	40	64	Cloudy	Clear	N. W., N. E.			Sprinkle 9 A. M.; cleared 10 A. M.
3	40	49	Clear	"	N. W., N.			
4	36	56	"	"	N.E., S., S.W.			
5	39	51	Cloudy	Rain	S. E., S., W.			Rain at noon; thunder and lightning in evening.
6	57	62½	"	Clear	W., N. W.	2.15		Rain before day, 2.15; cleared 10 A. M
7	46	58½	Clear	"	N. W.			
S 8	34	45½	"	"	N., N. W.			
9	33	51	"	"	N W., S., S.E			
10	35	53	Cloudy	Rain	S. E.	1.45		Rain 9 A.M. to 9:30 P.M.,1:45.
11	46	56	Foggy	Clear	W., N. W.	0.07		Rain before day, 0.07; cleared 7:30 A. M.
12	40	50	Clear	Rain	W., N.	0.11		Clouded over 9 A. M.; rain 10 A. M. to 3:30 P. M.; cleared 4 P. M.
13	32¼	49	"	Clear	N. W., W.			
14	40	53¼	Cloudy	Cloudy	S. W., N. W.	0.09		Rain 9 to 10 A. M., 0.07; 3 P. M., 0.02.
S 15	40	52	Clear	"	N. W.			
16	36	51½	Rain, Snow	Clear	N. E., N. W.	0.39		Rain and snow till 7 A.M., 0.39; cleared 8 A. M.
17	37	53½	Clear	Cloudy	N. W., S. W.			
18	44	57½	Cloudy	"	N. W., N. W.			Clear part of morning and part of evening.
19	41	59	Clear	"	S. W.			Clear part of evening.
20	43	49	Rain	"	S. W., N. W	0.19		Rain till 8:30 A.M., 0.17; part of A.M., 0.02; clear even'g.
21	37	48	Clear	Clear	N. W.			
S 22	36	53	"	"	W., S. W.			
23	39	52	Cloudy	Cloudy	N. E., N.		0.09	Rain before day, 0.06; part of A. M., 0.03; clear evening.
24	37	51	Clear	Clear	N. W., N.			
25	36	56	"	"	N. W., S. W.			
26	40	67	"	"	S. W.			
27	48	67	"	"	N.W.,N.E., S.			
28	48	76	"	"	All points.			Cloudy evening.
S 29	62	83	"	"	All points.	0.11		Cherries flowered; showers 4:15 to 5:45 P. M.
30	52	75½	"	"	N. E., S. E.			Cloudy evening.
						4.68		

Weather Record for New Brunswick, N. J.

May, 1888.

Date	Thermometer Lowest	Thermometer Highest	Weather Morning	Weather Afternoon	Prevailing Wind	Rain and Melted Snow in inches	Snow in inches	REMARKS
1	53	62	Cloudy	Cloudy	All points	0.06		Light rain part of A. M.
2	46	52	"	"	N., N. E.			Clear part of evening.
3	40	56½	Clear	"	NW,N.E,S.E.			Cloudy part of A. M., and clear part P. M.; frost.
4	46	54	Cloudy	"	S. E.	0.01		Light sprinkles part A. M.
5	50	75	Clear	Clear	S. W., N. W.	0.04		Rain before day, 0.04.
S 6	52	75	"	"	All points			
7	57	72½	"	"	N. W.			Cloudy part of evening.
8	53	58½	Cloudy	Cloudy	S. E., E.			Rainy 5 P. M.
9	51½	73	"	"	All points	0.30		Rain 6 A.M., 0.02; clear part of P.M.; sh'ry ev'g, 0.28.
10	63¼	77	"	"	S. W.	0.03		Clear part of morning; showery 3 P. M., 0.03.
11	60	65	Rain	Rain	S. E.	1.71		Rain till 8 P.M., 1.71; mostly 1 to 6 P. M.
12	57	71	Cloudy	Cloudy	S. E.	0.26		Rain before day, 0.07; clear part of afternoon; rain 6 to 8 P. M., 0.19.
S 13	59	65	"	"	N., E., S.	0.05		Rain 6 to 7 A.M., 0.05; clear parts of P. M. and ev'g.
14	53	65	Clear	"	N. E., S. E.	0.55		Cloudy part of A. M.; shower 2:15 to 3:15 P.M., 0.30; 5 to 9 P. M., 0.25.
15	47	53	Cloudy	"	N., N. W.	0.31		Rain 8 to 11 A.M., 0.31.
16	45	52½	"	"	S. W., N. W.	0.02		Clear part of P. M., and sprinkles during day, 0.02,
17	42	60	Clear	Clear	N. W.			Cloudy part of afternoon.
18	50	58	Cloudy	Cloudy	S. W., S. E.	0.05		Rain 2:30 to 4:30 P.M., 0.03; part of evening, 0.02.
19	50	68	"	"	All points	0.31		Rain before day, 0.31; clear part of morning.
S 20	52	64	Clear	Clear	N.			Cloudy part of morning.
21	46	68½	"	"	N. W., S. W.			Cloudy part of evening.
22	49	68	"	"	S. E.			Hazy evening.
23	50	60	Cloudy	Cloudy	N. E.	0.05		Clear part of A.M.; rain 3:30 to 7 P.M., 0.05.
24	54	61½	"	Rain	N. E.	0.08		Rain before day, 0.08.
25	56	64	"	Cloudy	N. E., E.	0.26		Rain before day, 0.26.
26	54	58½	Rain	"	N. E.	0.14		Misty & rainy till 3:30 P. M.
S 27	56	71	Clear	"	All points			Cl'dy part A.M.,cl'r part P.M.
28	56	64	Cloudy	"	S. E., E.			Heavy thunder showers after 9 P. M.
29	56	82	"	Clear	S. W.	0.62		Rain before day, 0.62.
30	65	75	"	Cloudy	S. W.	0.36		Thunder showers before day, 0.36; clear part of A. M.
31	67	69	"	"	S. W., S. E.	0.04		Rain before day, 0.02; part of morning, 0.02.
						5.25		

June, 1888.

Date	Thermometer. Lowest.	Thermometer. Highest.	Weather. Morning.	Weather. Afternoon.	Prevailing Wind.	Rain and Melted Snow in inches.	Snow in inches.	REMARKS.
1	62	74	Clear	Clear	N. W.			Cloudy part of morning.
2	53	70	"	Cloudy	N. E., S.	0.01		Light shower during eve'g.
S 3	55	68½	"	Clear	N.			
4	53	72	"	"	N. W., S. W.			
5	57	79	"	"	N. W., S. W.			
6	60	86	"	"	S. W.			
7	69	78½	"	"	N. W., N.			
8	62	75½	Cloudy	"	N.E., N., S.W.			Cleared 11 A. M.
9	60	80	"	"	S. W.			Cleared 9 A. M.
S 10	58½	80½	"	"	S. W.	0.01		Clear part A. M.; showers at noon, 0.01; cloudy eve'g.
11	67	79	Clear	Cloudy	S. W., N.			Cloudy part of morning and clear part of afternoon.
12	56	73	"	Clear	N. W., S. W.			
13	56	75½	"	"	S. W., S. E.			
14	56½	82	Cloudy	"	S., W., N.			Cloudy ev'g, with sprinkles.
15	67	87½	"	"	S. W.	1.19		Showers before day and 7 A. M., 0.05; clear part A. M.; shower 9:30 P. M. to 11:30 P. M., 1.14.
16	68	82	Clear	Cloudy	S. W.	0.03		Cloudy part A. M.; shower 1 P. M.; clear evening.
S 17	67	83	"	Clear	N. E., S. E.			
18	67	86½	"	"	S. W., N. E.			
19	68	79	"	"	N. E., S. E.			
20	62	86	"	"	S. W.			
21	69	86	"	"	All points.			
22	68½	91	"	"	S. W.			
23	76	93	"	Cloudy	S. W.	1.11		23d was hottest day in June since 1864; thunder shower 2:40 to 3:30 P. M., 1.07; rain 4:15 to 5:15 P.M., 0.04.
S 24	72	90½	"	Clear	S. W.			Cloudy part of morning.
25	74	88	"	"	N. W.			
26	73	86½	Cloudy	"	S. W., N.			Clear part of morning and cloudy part of evening.
27	68	79	Clear	"	N.W., N., S.E.	0.05		Cloudy evening with rain at 10, 0.05.
28	58	65	Cloudy	Rain	S. E., N. E.	0.93		Rain 7 A.M. to 3 P. M., 0.93; misty rain after 5 P. M.
29	52	65	Mis'y Rain	Cloudy	N. E.	0.17		Misty rain till 11 A. M.; cleared 6 P. M.
30	56	76½	Clear	Clear	N. W., S. W.	0.01		Cloudy part of evening with shower, 0.01.
						3.51		

July, 1888.

Date.	Thermometer. Lowest.	Thermometer. Highest.	Weather. Morning.	Weather. Afternoon.	Prevailing Wind.	Rain and Melted Snow in inches.	Snow in inches.	REMARKS.
S 1	62	70½	Clear	Clear	N. W., N. E.			Cloudy part of morning.
2	56	72½	"	"	N. E.			
3	59	79	"	"	All points			
4	60	83	"	"	S. W.			
5	66	86	"	Cloudy	S. W.	1.30		Cloudy part of A. M.; terrible shower with hail 2 to 2:50 P. M.; clear evening.
6	68	83	"	Clear	N. W.			
7	68	88½	"	"	S. W., N. W.			
S 8	66	81	"	"	N. W.			Cloudy part of evening.
9	66	69	Rain	Rain	S., N E.			Rain 6 A. M.
10	63	73½	Cloudy	Cloudy	N. E., S. E.	0.87		Rain before day, 0.87; partly clear parts A. M. and P. M.
11	62	84	Clear	Clear	S. W.			Cloudy evening.
12	66	75	"	Cloudy	N. W.	0.03		Shower 2:30 P. M., 0.03.
13	56	73	"	Clear	N. W.			
14	59	78½	"	"	N. W.			
S 15	62	78	"	"	N. W., N. E.			
16	61	78½	"	"	N. E., S. E.			
17	62	75½	"	"	N. E.			Cloudy part of morning.
18	58	76½	"	"	N. E., S. E.			
19	65	74	Cloudy	Rain	S. W., S.	0.17		Rain 10 A.M. to 1 P.M., 0.04; part of P. M., 0.12; part of evening, 0.01.
20	67	78	"	Cloudy	S. W.	0.04		Rain before day, 0.04; partly clear parts A.M. and ev'g.
21	65	77	Hazy	Hazy	N. E., S. E.			
S 22	68	80	Cloudy	Clear	N. E., S. E.			Clear part of morning.
23	66	87	Clear	"	S. W.			
24	71	86½	"	"	S. W., N. W.			Cloudy part of evening.
25	66	82	"	"	N., S.			
26	65	83	"	"	S. W.			Cloudy evening.
27	69	78½	Cloudy	Cloudy	S. W., S. E.	0.25		Rain part A. M., 0.07; clear part P. M.; showery evening, 0.18.
28	63	77½	Clear	Clear	N. E., S. E.			
S 29	63	71	Cloudy	Cloudy	N. E., S.			Partly clear part of morning; clear part of evening.
30	63½	77½	"	"	S. W.			Partly clear part of afternoon; clear evening.
31	67	83	"	Clear	S. W.			Clear part of morning; showery after 9:30 P. M.
						2.66		

August, 1888.

Date	Thermometer Lowest	Thermometer Highest	Weather Morning	Weather Afternoon	Prevailing Wind	Rain and Melted Snow in inches	Snow in inches	REMARKS
1	73	83	Cloudy	Clear	S. W., N.	0.43		Rain before day, 0.42; part morning, 0.01; clear part of morning.
2	64	79	Clear	Hazy	N. W., N.			
3	65	84½	Hazy	"	S. W.			
4	69	91	"	Clear	S. W.	0.72		Sh'er 9:30 P.M. to 11:30 P.M.
S 5	72	85½	Cloudy	"	All points			Clear part A.M.; cl'dy ev'g.
6	74	86	C'y m'st all day		S. E., N. E.			
7	71	83	Cloudy	Clear	S. E.			
8	73	87	"	"	S. E.	0.46		Cleared 9 A.M.; shower 9 to 10:30 P. M.
9	71	86	Clear	"	S. W., N. W.			Cloudy part of morning.
10	66	79	"	"	N.			
11	62	79	"	"	N., S. E.			Cloudy part of evening.
S 12	65	71	Cloudy	Cloudy	S. E.	0.89		Clear part of A. M.; rain 8:30 A. M. till noon, 0.88; part of evening, 0.01.
13	67	73½	"	Clear	S. W., N. W.	0.03		Rain before day, 0.03; clear part of morning.
14	57½	77½	Clear	"	W., S. W.			
15	63	83½	"	"	S. W.			Cloudy part A.M.; cl'dy ev'g.
16	72	91½	Cloudy	"	S. W.			Cleared 8 A. M.
17	76	87	"	Cloudy	S. W.	0.17		Clear part A. M.; showers 3:30, 0.05; 5 P.M., 0.12.
18	74	80	"	"	S. W.			Clear part of morning.
S 19	72	82	"	Clear	N. W, S. W.			Clear part of morning.
20	66	81	"	"	All points			Clear part A.M.; cl'dy ev'g.
21	66	72	"	Rain	S. E., N. E.			Rain 9 A.M. to 9 P. M., 2.31, and still raining.
22	63	71½	Clear	Clear	N. W.	2.98		Rain before day, 0.67
23	54	71	"	"	N. W.			
24	60	80	"	"	S. W.			
25	62	82½	"	"	S. W.			
S 26	64	83½	"	"	N. W.			
27	68	80	"	Cloudy	S. W., N. W.	0.21		Cloudy part of morning; shower 1:20 P. M., 0.21; clear evening.
28	57	72	"	Clear	N. W.			
29	55	76½	"	"	S. W.			
30	60	80	"	"	S. W.			
31	64½	82	"	Cloudy	S. W., S.	0.04		Foggy morning; light rain part of evening, 0.06.
						5.93		

Weather Record for New Brunswick, N. J.

September, 1888.

Date	Thermometer Lowest	Thermometer Highest	Weather Morning	Weather Afternoon	Prevailing Wind	Rain and Melted Snow in inches	Snow in inches	REMARKS
1	71	78	C'y m'st all day.		S. W., N. W.	0.07	----	Rain before day, 0.03; shower 11 P. M., 0.04.
S 2	66	76	Clear	Clear	N. W.	----	----	Cloudy part of morning.
3	60	74	"	Cloudy	N. E., S. E.	----	----	
4	63	72	Cloudy	"	N. E., N.	----	----	Clear 8 A.M. till noon; clear part of evening.
5	65	75½	Clear	Clear	S. W., N.	----	----	
6	52	62	"	Cloudy	N. E.	----	----	
7	48	61	"	"	N. E., S. E.	----	----	Cloudy part A. M.; light sprinkles part of even'g.
8	56	77½	Rain	Rain	S. E., S. W.	2.87	----	Rain till 8 A. M., 0.24; 3 to 5 P.M., 1.69; 8 to 10:15 P. M., 0 94, and still raining.
S 9	67	71	"	Misty	All points.	0.55	----	Rain before day, 0.40; 8 to 11:30 A. M., 0.13; misty till 10 P. M., 0 02.
10	66	73	Cloudy	Cloudy	W., N.	----	----	Clear part of morning.
11	61	71	"	Rain	N. E.	1.60	----	Clear part of morning; rain 12:30 to 11 P. M.
12	58	77	"	Clear	N. W., S. W.	----	----	
13	65	72	"	"	W., N. W.	0.62	----	Rain before day, 0.62; cleared 8 A. M.
14	51½	67	Clear	"	N. W., S. W.	----	----	
15	51	69½	"	"	S. W., N. E.	----	----	Foggy A. M.; cl'dy part P.M.
S 16	57	75	Rain	Cloudy	N. E.	0.71	----	Rain 6 to 11 A M., 0.14; 3 to 3:30 P. M., 0.02; 6 to 10 P. M., 0.55.
17	68	73½	Misty	Rain	S. E.	0.63	----	Rain part A.M., 0.03; part P. M., 0.09; 6 to 9:30 P.M., 0.51.
18	70	78½	Cloudy	Cloudy	S. W.	0.44	----	Rain before day, 0.44; clear parts P. M. and evening.
19	65	72	"	Clear	N. E., S. E.	----	----	
20	63	74	C'y m'st all day.		S. W., S. E.	0.05	----	Rain before day, 0.01; shower 7 P. M., 0.04.
21	64	72	Cloudy	Clear	S. W., N. W.	0.39	----	Rain before day, 0 39; cleared 8 A. M.
22	57	68	Clear	Cloudy	All points.	----	----	
S 23	57	67	C'y m'st all day.		N. E.	----	----	
24	54	65	Clear	Clear	N. E., E.	----	----	
25	51	57½	Cloudy	Cloudy	N. E.	----	----	Rain 6:30 P. M.
26	54	68	Clear	Clear	N. W., W.	0.24	----	Rain before day, 0 24.
27	55	70	"	Cloudy	S. W., W.	----	----	Clear part of evening.
28	51½	63	"	Clear	N. W.	----	----	
29	47	58	"	"	N. W.	----	----	
S 30	42	53	"	"	N. W.	----	----	Frost.
						8.17	----	

October, 1888.

Date.	Thermometer. Lowest.	Highest.	Weather. Morning.	Afternoon.	Prevailing Wind.	Rain and Melted Snow in inches.	Snow in inches.	REMARKS.
1	45	60	Cloudy	Clear	S.	0.05		Rain 6:30 to 10:30 A.M.,0.05; cleared 2:30 P. M.
2	55	65	"	"	S. W., N. W.	0.01		Rain before day, 0.01; clear-9 A.M.; cloudy part P. M.
3	42	51	Clear	"	N. W.			Cloudy part P. M.; frost.
4	38	56	"	"	S. W.			Cloudy part of morning.
5	42½	65½	"	"	S. W.			Cloudy part of evening.
6	54	61	Cloudy	Rain	N. E., S.	2.74		Rain before day, 0.02; rain 8:30 A.M. to 10 P.M., 2.72.
S 7	52	61	"	Clear	N. W.			Clear part morning; cloudy part evening.
8	47	57	Clear	"	N. W.			Cloudy part of afternoon.
9	40	48	"	"	N. W.			
10	38	54	"	"	N. W.			
11	37	48	Cloudy	Cloudy	N. E.			Partly clear part of even'g.
12	46	54	Rain	"	N. E., S.	0.28		Rain till 10 A. M., 0.28.
13	43	57½	C'y m'st all day	S. W.				Foggy morning.
S 14	47	50¾	Cloudy	Cloudy	S. W., N.	0.11		Rain 8:30 to 10 A. M., 0.08; 12:30 to 2 P.M., 0.02; part of evening, 0.01.
15	42	53½	Clear	Clear	N. W., S. W.			Cloudy part of afternoon.
16	47	58	Rain	"	S., S. W.	0.04		Rain till 10 A. M., 0.04; cleared 2 P. M.
17	48	58	Cloudy	"	E., N., W.	0.13		Thunder sh'w'r 6 A.M.; cl'rd 9 A.M.; cloudy part P. M.
18	44	56	Clear	"	N. W.			
19	40	53	Cloudy	Cloudy	All points.	0.12		Rain 8:30 to 10 A. M., 0.12; rain 8 P. M.
20	50	56½	"	Clear	N. W., W.	0.36		Rain before day, 0.36; cleared 9 A. M.
S 21	41	48	Clear	"	N. W.			
22	36½	49	C'y m'st all day.	N. W., S. W.				
23	44	52	Rain	Rain	All points.			
24	49	57½	"	Clear	W., N. W.	0.43		Rain till 8:30 A. M., 0.43; cleared 9:30 A. M.
25	42	58	Clear	"	S. W.			
26	43½	56	"	Cloudy	N. E., E.			
27	47	58	Rain	Rain	E.			
S 28	55	59	Cloudy	Cloudy	S. W., N. W.	1.27		Rain before day, 1.17; foggy A.M.; rain 4 to 6 P.M., 0.10. clear part of evening.
29	43	54	"	Clear	S. W.	0.01		Clear part A. M.; cloudy evening with shower, 0.01.
30	42	50	Clear	"	W., N. W.			
31	35	58	"	"	S. W.			Foggy morning.
						5.55		

November, 1888.

Date.	Thermometer. Lowest.	Thermometer. Highest.	Weather. Morning.	Weather. Afternoon.	Prevailing Wind.	Rain and Melted Snow in inches.	Snow in inches.	REMARKS.
1	45	64½	Clear	Clear	S. W.			
2	48½	70	"	"	S. W.			Cloudy evening.
3	58½	63	Cloudy	"	S. W., N. W	0.06		Rain 10:30 A.M. to 1:30 P.M., 0.06; cleared 3 P. M.
S 4	43	57¼	Clear	"	S. W.			
5	45	57½	Cloudy	Cloudy	S., N. E			Partly clear part of morning; clear part of evening.
6	53	70¼	"	Clear	S. W.	0.01		Rain before day, 0.01; clear part of morning.
7	54	59¼	Clear	"	N. W., N. E			Cloudy part of A.M.; cloudy evening.
8	46	52	Cloudy	Rain	N. E., S. E.	0.01		Rain at noon, 0.01; rain 5 P M.
9	50	66	Rain	Cloudy	S. W.	0.24		Rain till 9 A. M., 0.24; rainy evening.
10	65	68	"	Rain	S. W.	1.22		Rain before day, 0.17; 10 A. M. to 4:15 P M., 1.05; clear 9 P. M.
S 11	46½	52	Clear	Clear	S. W., N. W.			
12	38½	52	"	"	S. W., W.			
13	37	51	"	"	N. E., S. E.			
14	37½	54	"	Hazy	S. W.			Foggy morning.
15	47	56	Rain	Misty	N. E.	1.20		Rain till 1:30 P. M., 1.17; misty till 6:30 P. M., 0.03.
16	48	58	Clear	Cloudy	S. W., N.	0.08		Rain 12:30 to 2 P. M., 0.07; 5 to 7 P. M., 0.01; partly clear part of evening.
17	36	44	"	Clear	N. W.			
S 18	30	43	"	Cloudy	N. E., E.			
19	39	54	Rain	"	N. E., N. W.	0.79		Rain till 12:30 P. M., 0.77; misty till 4 P. M , 0 02.
20	40	45	Clear	Clear	N.			
21	23	33	"	"	N. E.			
22	24	36½	"	"	N. E.			
23	17	30	Cloudy	"	N. E.			Cloudy evening.
24	28	39	"	Cloudy	N. E.			Clear part of morning.
S 25	32	35	"	Snow } Sleet }	N. E.	0.01		Light snow 12.30 to 4 P. M., 0.01; sleety evening.
26	32	44	Sleet	Cloudy	N. E.	0.40		Sleet till 7 A. M., 0.40; rainy evening.
27	40	47	Rain	"	N. W., W.	0.20		Rain till 7 A. M., 0.20.
28	37	45	Cloudy	"	S. W., N. W.			Sun rose clear.
29	40	44	"	"	N. W.	0.05		Rain till 7 A. M., 0.05.
30	40	47	"	"	W., N. W.	0.02		Rain before day, 0.02; clear part of afternoon.
						4.29		

December, 1888.

Date.	Thermometer. Lowest.	Highest.	Weather. Morning.	Afternoon.	Prevailing Wind.	Rain and Melted Snow in inches.	Snow in inches.	REMARKS.
1	40	43	Cloudy	Clear	N. W.	----	----	
S 2	33	44	Clear	"	" W.	----	----	
3	33½	39	Cloudy	Cloudy	N. W.	----	----	Clear part of morning.
4	33	41	Snow	Clear	S. W., N. W.	0.02	----	Snow till 9:30 A. M., 0.02; cleared 10:30 A. M.
5	35	47	Cloudy	"	S. W.	----	----	Cloudy evening.
6	36½	38	Rain	"	N. W.	0.11	----	Rain till 8 A.M., 0.11; cleared 9 A. M.
7	30	41½	Clear	"	S. W.	----	----	
8	35½	46	Cloudy	Cloudy	S. W., N. E.	----	----	Clear part of morning.
S 9	38	42½	Rain	"	N. E., N.	0.23	----	Rain till 2 P. M., 0.23; clear evening.
10	34	40	Cloudy	"	N. E.	----	----	
11	36	41½	Rain	"	N. E., N. W.	0.26	----	Rain till 1 P. M., 0.26.
12	32	35½	Clear	Clear	N. W.	----	----	Cloudy evening.
13	28	34	"	"	S. W., N. W.	----	----	Cloudy part of morning, with snow squall.
14	17	26	"	"	N. W.	----	----	
15	21	33½	"	"	W., S. W.	----	----	
S 16	27	44	"	Cloudy	S.W., N.E.	----	----	
17	41	56	Rain	Rain	S. W., N. E.	3.00	----	Bar. 7 A.M., 30.10; rain till 5:30 P. M., 2.90; part of evening till 9 P. M., 0.10; cleared 10 P. M.
18	37	40½	Cloudy	Cloudy	N. W., W.	0.19	----	Rain before day, 0.19; bar. 12:30 A. M., 28.80; clear part of morning.
19	30	32½	"	Clear	N. W.	----	----	Cleared 10 A. M.
20	18	28½	Clear	"	N.W., W.	----	----	
21	22	34	"	Cloudy	S. W., N. W.	----	----	Snow squall 6:30 P.M.; cleared 8 P. M.
22	12	24½	"	Clear	N. W.	----	----	
S 23	19	36	"	"	S. W.	----	----	
24	25	45	"	"	S. W.	----	----	
25	32	49	"	"	S. W.	----	----	
26	35	53	"	"	S. W., S. E.	0.01	----	Clouded over 9 P. M.; rain 10:30 P. M., 0.01.
27	41	53½	Cloudy	Cloudy	S. W., N. W.	0.51	----	Rainbow at sunrise; rain 7:30 to 10 A.M., 0.31; part of afternoon, 0.20; cleared 6:30 P. M.
28	35	40	Clear	Clear	W.	----	----	
29	29	39	"	"	S. W., W.	----	----	
S 30	27	43	"	"	S. W.	----	----	
31	35	43	Cloudy	Cloudy	S. W.	0.08	----	Rain 8:30 to 11:30 A.M., 0.08.
						4.41	----	

Rain and melted snow for 1888, 59.00 inches.

Weather Record for New Brunswick, N. J.

January, 1889.

Date.	Thermometer.		Weather.		Prevailing Wind.	Rain and Melted Snow in inches.	Snow in inches.	REMARKS.
	Lowest.	Highest.	Morning.	Afternoon.				
1	38	44	Cloudy	Clear	W., S. W.			Cleared 8 A. M.
2	35	40	"	Cloudy	S. W., N. W.			
3	34	44	Clear	Clear	S. W.			
4	33	47	"	"	S. W., S.			Cloudy evening.
5	38	40	Rain	Rain	N. E.			Light rain till noon, and heavy after.
S 6	37	42½	"	"	N. E.	1.82		Rain till 8 A. M., 1.72; parts A. M. and P. M., 0.10; rainy evening.
7	40	44	Cloudy	Cloudy	N. W.	0.08		Rain before day, 0.08; cleared 10 P. M.
8	38	47	Clear	Clear	N. W., S. W.			
9	36	58	Rain	Cloudy	S. E., S. W.	0.87		Rain 7 A.M. to 2 P.M., 0.62; violent rain squall 7 P.M., 0.25; cleared 9 P. M.
10	36	43	Clear	Clear	S. W., W.			
11	34	40	"	"	W.			Cloudy part of afternoon.
12	33	40	"	"	N. W.			
S 13	27	41	"	"	All points.			
14	31	39	Cloudy	"	N. E.			Clear part of morning and cloudy part of afternoon.
15	24	36	Clear	"	N., W.			
16	32	46	Cloudy	Cloudy	S. W.			Clear part of morning; rain 6 P. M.
17	41	58	Rain	"	S. W.	1.10		Rain till 12:30 P. M., 1.10; cleared 6 P. M.
18	38½	47	Clear	Clear	N. W.			
19	30	32	"	"	N. W.			
S 20	18	40	Cloudy	Snow	N. E.			Snow 2:30 to 9 P.M. and then sleet; first snow storm of the season.
21	33	37	"	Clear	N. W.	2.00		Rain before day, 2.00.
22	27	34	Clear	"	S. W., N. W.			
23	23	41½	"	"	S. W.			
24	25	40	"	Cloudy	N., S. W.	0.05		Rain part of evening.
25	36	44	"	Clear	N. E., S.			
26	31	43½	"	Cloudy	W., S. W.			Cloudy part of morning.
S 27	36	39	Rain	Rain	N. E.	0.51		Rain till 3 P. M., 0.46; misty afterwards, 0.05.
28	35	38	Cloudy	Clear	W.			Cloudy part of afternoon, with snow flurries.
29	27½	30½	"	"	N. W.			Clear part of morning.
30	21	34	Clear	"	N. W., W.			Cloudy part of evening.
31	27	47	"	"	S.			Cloudy evening, with light rain.
						6.43		

February, 1889.

Date.	Thermometer. Lowest.	Thermometer. Highest.	Weather. Morning.	Weather. Afternoon.	Prevailing Wind.	Rain and Melted Snow in inches.	Snow in inches.	REMARKS.
1.	31	33	Clear	Clear	N. W.			Snow squall at 8:30 A. M.
2	25	39½	"	Cloudy	S. W.			Clear evening.
S 3	32	41½	C'y m'st all day		S. W., N. W.			Snow squalls in afternoon.
4	16	30½	Clear	Cloudy	N. E., S. E.			Clouded over 10 A. M.
5	29	47	Cloudy	"	N. E., S.	0.01		Clear part A. M.; light rain part afternoon, 0.01; rainy evening.
6	19	22	Clear	Clear	N. W., W.	0.19		Snow before day, 0.19; snow squall 10:15 A. M
7	12	24	"	"	W.			Cloudy about noon.
8	16	33½	"	Cloudy	S. W.	0.03		Clouded over 10 A.M.; snow 5:15 to 9 P. M., 0.03.
9	28	41½	Foggy	Clear	S. W., N. W.			Cleared 10 A. M.
S 10	26	37	Clear	"	S. W.			
11	23	36	Cloudy	Snow	N. E.			Snow 12:30 P. M.
12	24	31	Clear	Clear	W.	1.00		Snow before day; first snow this season without rain.
13	14	23	"	"	W.			
14	13	29	"	"	W., N. W.			
15	22	38	"	"	N. W., S. W.			
16	24	39	Cloudy	Rain	N. E.	1.10		Rain 11 A.M. to 10 P.M., 1.10.
S 17	36	45	"	Cloudy	S. W.			Clear part of evening.
18	35	38	Rain	Rain	N. E.	0.55		Heavy rain till 10 A.M., 0.50, and misty till 6 P.M., 0.05; cleared 7 P. M.
19	27	32	Clear	Clear	W., N. W.			Cloudy part of morning.
20	22	31	"	"	N. W.			
21	21	34½	"	Cloudy	S. W.			Clouded over 3 P. M.
22	30	37½	Cloudy	"	S. W.			
23	16	20	Clear	Clear	N. W.			
S 24	5	18	"	"	NW, NE, SE			Cloudy evening.
25	15	29	Snow	"	N. E., N.		0.50	Snow till 7 A.M.; cl'r'd 8 A.M.
26	15	30	Clear	Cloudy	N. E., S. E.			Snow 7 P. M.; ice 6 in. at Weston's, but not cut.
27	28	36	Snow	Snow	E.			Light snow all day.
28	31	36½	Cloudy	Cloudy	N., E., S. E.	0.35		Snow before day, 0.35; clear part of afternoon.
						2.23	1.50	

Weather Record for New Brunswick, N. J.

March, 1889.

Date.	Thermometer. Lowest.	Thermometer. Highest.	Weather. Morning.	Weather. Afternoon.	Prevailing Wind.	Rain and Melted Snow in inches.	Snow in inches.	REMARKS.
1	31½	44½	Clear	Clear	N. W.			
2	34	43	Cloudy	Cloudy	S. W.			
S 3	37	41	Rain	Rain	S. E., E.			
4	36	40	"	"	N. E.			
5	38	48	"	Cloudy	N.	1.33		Rain before day, 1.31; misty till 11 A. M., 0.02; cleared 9 P. M.
6	37½	48	Clear	"	N. W.			Clouded over 3 P. M.
7	37	46½	"	Clear	S. W.			
8	34	42	"	"	S. W., W.			Snow flurries during P. M.
9	31	38	"	Cloudy	W.			
S 10	32	39	Cloudy	"	N. W.			Clear part of afternoon.
11	31	43½	Clear	Clear	N. W.			Cloudy before day.
12	31	53	"	"	S. W.			
13	37½	61	"	"	S. W.			
14	40	47	"	"	N. E., S. E.			
15	34	43	Cloudy	Cloudy	N. E.			Light rain 10:20 P. M.
16	37	53	"	"	N. E.			Rain 6.20 P. M.
S 17	38	44	"	"	N. E.	0.35		Rain before day, 0.35; partly clear evening.
18	37	50	"	"	N., E.			Clear part of afternoon.
19	42	48½	"	"	N. E., S. E.			
20	37	39	"	Rain } Snow	N. E.			Rain noon to 7:30 P. M., and then snow.
21	34	38	Snow	Snow } Rain	N., N. W.	1.34		Snow till 5 P. M., and then rain till 11 P. M.
22	37	50½	Cloudy	Clear	N. E			Cleared 9 A. M; cloudy part of evening.
23	38	59	Clear	"	S. W.			
S 24	41	61½	"	"	S. W.			
25	46	54	C'y m'st all day.		S. W., N. E.			
26	30	46½	Clear	Clear	All points.			
27	33	60	C'y m'st all day.		E., S.			
28	47½	50½	Cloudy	Cloudy	S. W., N. W.	0.05		Rain 11 A.M. to 1 P.M., 0.05; cleared 5 P. M.
29	33	53	Clear	Clear	S. W.	0.03		Cloudy evening with rain and snow squall.
30	28	41	"	"	N. W.			
N 31	33	41	{ Snow Rain	Cloudy	S. E., N. E.	0.13		Snow 7 to 9 A. M., 0.12, and light rain part of morning, 0.01.
						3.23		

Weather Record for New Brunswick, N. J.

April, 1889.

Date	Thermometer Lowest	Thermometer Highest	Weather Morning	Weather Afternoon	Prevailing Wind	Rain and Melted Snow in inches	Snow in inches	REMARKS
1	37	48	Cloudy	Rain	S. E., N. E.	0.56		Rain part of morning; noon to 11 P. M.
2	36½	51	"	Cloudy	N. E., N. W.	0.01		Light rain 3:45 P. M., 0.01.
3	42	62½	"	"	S. W.			Clear part of afternoon.
4	43½	52½	Clear	Clear	N. W.			Cloudy part A. M. and P. M.
5	36	49½	"	"	All points.			Cloudy part of afternoon.
6	35	46	Cloudy	Cloudy	N. E., E.			
S 7	38	48	"	"	N. E.			
8	40	58	"	Clear	N. E.			Clear part of morning.
9	38	63	Clear	Cloudy	N.			Clear evening.
10	46	62½	"	Clear	N. W.			
11	41	68½	"	Cloudy	S. W.			Clouded over 3 P. M.
12	55	69	Cloudy	"	S. W.	0.17		Rain before day, 0.06; part A. M., 0.03; clear part P.M.; rain with lightning part of evening, 0.08.
13	46	58	Rain	Clear	N. W.	0.24		Rain till 7 A.M ,0.24; cleared 10 A. M.
S 14	37	56½	Clear	"	N.			
15	38½	53	"	Hazy	N. E.			
16	37	54	Cloudy	Cloudy	N. E., E.			Partly clear part of afternoon; clear part evening.
17	41	53½	Rain	Misty	N. E.	0.08		Rain before day, 0.06; 7:30 to 10 A. M., 0.02.
18	50	61	Misty	Cloudy	N.E., E., S.W	0.03		Misty till 7 A.M., 0.03; clear evening.
19	50	75½	Clear	Clear	S.			
20	52	72	Cloudy	"	S. W.			Thunder showers after 9 P. M.; cherries flowered.
S 21	61	75	"	"	S. W., N. W.	0.16		Rain before day,0.16; cleared 8 A.M.; cloudy part of ev'g.
22	45	57	Clear	"	N. W.			
23	39	57	"	"	N., S. E.			
24	45	70	"	"	S. W.			
25	54	71½	Cloudy	Cloudy	S. E.			Clear part of A.M. and P.M.; rain 8 P. M.
26	56	60½	Rain	Rain	E., N. E.	2.19		Rain before day, 1.06; 10 A. M. to 5 P. M. heavy, 1.13, and light rest of day.
27	52	56	"	"	E.	1.16		Rain all day till 8 P.M., 1.16.
S 28	52	60	Cloudy	Cloudy	S. W.	0.32		Rain 8 to 11 A.M ,0.30; shower 3:15 P. M., 0.02; clear part of afternoon.
29	52	62½	"	Clear	S. W., N. W.	0.05		Light rain before day, 0.02; cleared 9 A.M.; shower 5 P. M., 0.03; cloudy eve'g.
30	46	60	"	"	N. W., S. W.			Cleared 8 A.M.; cloudy ev'g.

4.97

May, 1889.

Date.	Thermometer.		Weather.		Prevailing Wind.	Rain and Melted Snow in inches.	Snow in inches.	REMARKS.
	Lowest.	Highest.	Morning.	Afternoon.				
1	47	57	Clear	Cloudy	N., S. W.			Clear part of evening.
2	45	56½	"	"	N. W.			Clear part of evening.
3	41	53	"	"	N. W.			Clear evening; frost.
4	42	64	"	Clear	N. W., W.			Cloudy part P. M.; frost.
S 5	48	77	"	"	S. W., N. W.			
6	56	77	"	"	N. W., E., S.E.			
7	52	72	"	"	N. E., S. E.			
8	51	75	"	"	All points			
9	54	81	"	"	N. E., S E.			
10	63	87	"	"	S. W., N. W.	0.61		Rain 5:20 to 8:20 P.M., 0.61; cleared 9 P. M.
11	66	79	"	"	All points.			Cloudy part of evening.
S 12	58	72	"	"	E., N. E.			Cloudy parts A. M. and P. M.
13	57	70	"	Cloudy	N. E., E.	0.03		Rain 2:45 to 3:15 P. M., 0.03.
14	58	75½	Cloudy	Clear	S. W.	0.08		Shower 7:30 A.M., 0.03; cl'dy ev'g with shower 7:40, 0.05.
15	62	76	"	"	N. W., N.			Cleared 8 A. M.
16	59	80	Clear	"	S.			
17	62	83	"	"	S W., S.			
18	59	82	"	"	S., S. E.			
S 19	64	69	Cloudy	Cloudy	S. E., E.			Rain 8 P. M.
20	63	72	"	"	S. E., S. W.	0.86		Rain before day, 0.30; shower 11:30 A. M. to noon, 0.46; rainy evening.
21	63	76½	"	Clear	N. E., W.	0.33		Rain before day, 0.33; cleared 10 A.M.; cl'dy part ev'g.
22	52	66	Clear	Cloudy	N.W., S., S.E.	0.35		Rain 5:20 P.M to 9 P.M.,0.35.
23	51	65	Cloudy	Clear	N., N. W.			Cleared 8 A. M.
24	49	73	Clear	"	S. W.			
25	61	69	"	"	N. W.			Rain 9 P. M.
S 26	50	56½	Cloudy	Cloudy	N. E.	0.74		Rain before day, 0 74.
27	49	53	Rain	Rain M'sty	S. E., N. E.	0.90		Rain 6:40 A. M. to 2 P. M., 0.90; clear part evening, Cleared 7 A. M.
28	51	69	Cloudy	Clear	S. W.			
29	47	65	Clear	"	N., E., S. E.			Clear parts A. M. and P. M.; showers 11:30 A. M. till 3 P. M
30	51	75½	Cloudy	Sh'w'ry	N. E., S.	0.12		
31	62	73	"	Cloudy	S.	0.17		Clear part A. M.; showers 11:40 to noon, 0.02; 4 to 6 P. M., 0.15.
						4.19		

Weather Record for New Brunswick, N. J.

June, 1889.

Date.	Thermometer.		Wind.		Prevailing Wind.	Rain and Melted Snow in inches.	Snow in inches.	REMARKS.
	Lowest.	Highest.	Morning.	Afternoon.				
1	65	69	Rain	Cloudy	S. E.	0.27		Rain till 2 P. M.
S 2	58	73	Clear	Clear	N. W., S. W			
3	55	72	"	"	S.W., N.,S.E.			Cloudy evening.
4	59	75	Cloudy	"	N.E., S., S.W.			Clear part of morning.
5	61	70	Clear	"	N. W., W.	0.08		Shower before day, 0.08; cloudy evening.
6	54	68	Cloudy	"	N. W.			Clear part of morning.
7	52	75	Clear	"	N. W., S. W.			
8	63	78½	Cloudy	Cloudy	S. W.			Clear part of morning and part of afternoon.
S 9	67	85	"	Clear	S.	0.01		Clear part A.M.; cloudy ev'g; with shower 9 P. M.
10	71	87	"	"	S. W.			Cloudy part of afternoon, with sprinkle.
11	70	82½	Clear	"	S. W., N. W.	0.60		Shower 10 A.M., 0.24; shower 5 P.M., 0.36; shower 11 P.M.
12	66	69	Rain	Sh'wery	N. E., S.	0.57		Rain to 8 A.M., 0.51; showers 11 A. M. till 8 P. M., 0.06.
13	60	77	Clear	Clear	S. W.			
14	66	79	Cloudy	Cloudy	S. W.			Cleared 9 A. M.; clear part of afternoon.
15	71	85	"	"	S. W.	0.28		Cleared 7 A. M.; shower 4:10 to 6 P. M., 0.28; shower 10:45 P. M.
S 16	68	83	Clear	Clear	S. W	0.58		Rain before day, 0.58.
17	72	84½	Cloudy	"	SW, NW, NE	0.75		Cleared 7 A. M.; rain 3 to 7 P. M, 0.75.
18	62½	71	Clear	"	N. E., E.			
19	56	72	Cloudy	"	N. E, E			Cleared 9 A.M; cloudy ev'g.
20	65	83	"	"	S W., N. W.			Cleared 8 A. M.
21	63	84	Clear	"	N. E., S.	0.02		Cloudy eve'g; shower 10:30 P. M., 0.02.
22	71	77	Cloudy	"	N. W.			Cleared 7 A. M.
S 23	59	74	Clear	"	N. W.			
24	55	72½	"	Cloudy	N. E., S. E.			
25	57	71	"	"	N. E., E.			
26	65	77½	Cloudy	"	S. E , S. W.	0.22		Rain before day, 0.08; shower 8 A.M., 0.08; 11 A.M. to 1:15 P. M , 0.06; cleared 9 P. M.
27	67	80	"	"	S. W.			Clear part of morning.
28	67	84	Clear	Clear	S. E.			
29	71	83½	Cloudy	"	S. E., S. W.			Clear part of morning.
S 30	69	80	"	"	N. E., E.			Cleared 8 A.M.; cloudy ev'g.
						3.38		

Weather Record for New Brunswick, N. J.

July, 1889.

Date	Thermometer Lowest	Thermometer Highest	Weather Morning	Weather Afternoon	Prevailing Wind	Rain and Melted Snow in inches	Snow in inches	REMARKS
1	70	77½	Cloudy	Cloudy	S. E.	0.07		Light rain till 7 A. M.
2	70	73½	Rain	Rain	S. E.			Light rain, at intervals, all day; very heavy in ev'g.
3	70	78	Cloudy	Show'rs	S.	2.05		Rain before day, 0.97; sh'er 11 A. M. to 6 P. M., 1.08; cleared 9 P. M.
4	71	80	"	Cloudy	S. W., N. W.	0.70		Rain 12:30 to 3 P.M., 0.70; cleared 9 P. M.
5	62	80	Clear	Clear	N. W.			
6	61	77	"	"	N. E., S.			
S 7	64	84	"	"	S. W.			
8	70	87	"	"	S. W., N. W.			
9	72	86	"	"	N W, N.E.,S.E.			Cloudy evening.
10	70	74	Cloudy	Cloudy	S. E.			
11	68	79	Rain	"	S., S. W.	0.10		Rain till 8:30 A. M., 0.08; noon, 0.02; clear parts of afternoon and evening.
12	69	85	Clear	"	All points			
13	71	79	Cloudy	"	S. W.	0.04		Clear part of morning; sh'er 11:50 A. M., 0.03; 4 to 5 P. M., 0.01; clear 6 P. M.
S 14	70	84	Clear	Clear	S. W., N. W.			
15	61½	70	Rain	Cloudy	S. E., N.	1.27		Heavy rain till 6 A. M., and light till 9 A. M., 1.27; cleared 8 P M.
16	57	77	Clear	Clear	N. W.			
17	62	82½	"	"	S. W., N. W.			Cloudy part of evening.
18	65	81	"	"	All points			
19	65	78½	"	Cloudy	S. E., S.			Rain 9 P. M.
20	70	82½	Rain	Clear	S. W., N. W.	1.74		Rain till 6:30 A. M., 1.74; cleared 9 A. M.
S 21	68	80	Clear	"	N. W.			
22	66	82	"	"	All points.			Cloudy part of evening.
23	70	85	Cloudy	"	S. W., N. W.			Cleared 10 A. M.; cloudy part of evening.
24	64	80	Clear	"	N. W.			
25	63	76½	"	"	N. E., S E.			Cloudy part of morning.
26	62	75	Cloudy	Cloudy	S. E.			Foggy A.M.; clear part P.M.; rain 10 P. M.
27	67	72½	Rain	"	N. E., N. W.	0.80		Rain till 11:30 A. M., 0.80; partly clear 5 P. M.
S 28	68	77½	Cloudy	"	E., S.	0.01		Rain 10:30 A. M. to 12:30 P. M., 0.01; cl'r part P. M.
29	72	85½	"	Clear	S. W.	0.01		Clear part A. M., cl'dy ev'g with light showers, 0.01.
30	72	84	"	Cloudy	S. W.	1.96		Clear part A.M.; rain 3:30 to 7 P. M., 1.61; 9:20 to 9:50 P. M., 0.35.
31	69	74½	Rain	"	All points.	1.70		Rain before day, 1 05; showers 8 A.M. to 12:45 P. M., 0.65; freshet.
						10.45		

August 1889.

Date	Thermometer Lowest	Thermometer Highest	Weather Morning	Weather Afternoon	Prevailing Wind	Rain and Melted Snow in inches	Snow in inches	REMARKS.
1	70	78	Rain	Cloudy	S.	0.78		Rain till 6 A. M., 0.44; clear part of morning; showers rest of day, 0.34.
2	70	82	Cloudy	Hazy	S. W.	0.12		Rain before day, 0.12.
3	74	80	"	Cloudy	S. W.	0.41		Clear part A. M ; showers 7 A.M. to 2 P.M., 0.41; cleared 9 P. M.
S 4	67	80	Clear	Hazy	N. W., S. W.			
5	66	75	Rain	Cloudy	All points	0.18		Rain till 10 A. M., 0.18; clear part of afternoon.
6	62	76	Clear	Clear	N. E., S.			Rain 11 P. M.
7	65	77	"	"	N. W., N.	0.14		Rain before day, 0.14.
8	59	75½	"	"	All points			
9	63	78	Cloudy	Cloudy	S. W.	0.07		Rain 6:30 to 7:30 P. M., 0.07.
10	69	80	"	Clear	S. W., N. W.	0.25		Rain 6:15 to 10:15 A.M., 0.25. cleared 2 P. M.
S 11	65	76	Clear	"	N. W.			
12	58	75	"	"	N. W., S. W.			
13	59	78	"	Cloudy	S. W., S. E.	0.53		Sh'rs 3:30 to 4:15 P.M., 0.53.
14	69	80	Rain	"	All points	2.03		Rain till 7:15 A. M., 0.69 ; 2 P M ,0.02; 6 to 9 P.M.,1.32: 1.12 in one hour, 6 to 7.
15	68	76	Cloudy	"	E., S., N. W.			Freshet; partly clear parts morning and afternoon.
16	58	74	Clear	Clear	N. W., W.			
17	60	76	"	"	W., N.W.			
S 18	60	75	Hazy	"	N., W.			
19	61	80	Clear	"	S. W.			Cloudy part of evening.
20	68	81½	Hazy	Hazy	S. W., N. W.			
21	70	85	"	"	S. W.			
22	72½	82½	"	Clear	S. W., N. W.			
23	67	76	Cloudy	Rain	N. E.	0.15		Partly clear part A.M.; rain 3:15 to 8 P. M., 0.15.
24	66	77	Rain	Clear	N. E., S. E.	0.35		Rain till 8 A. M., 0.35.; cloudy evening.
S 25	65	77½	Clear	"	N. E., E.			Cloudy part A.M. and eve'g.
26	64	73½	C'y m'st all day		N. E.			
27	59	72	Cloudy	Clear	N. E., S. E.			
28	55	71	"	"	N. E.			Cleared 9 A. M.
29	58	74	Clear	"	N. E., S. E.			
30	57	79	"	"	N. W.			Foggy morning.
31	64	81½	"	"	W., N. E.			
						5.01		

Weather Record for New Brunswick, N. J.

September, 1889.

Date.	Thermometer. Lowest.	Thermometer. Highest.	Weather. Morning.	Weather. Afternoon.	Prevailing Wind.	Rain and Melted Snow in inches.	Snow in inches.	REMARKS.
S 1	64	77½	Hazy	Hazy	N. E., S. E.			
2	61	77	"	"	N., S. E.			
3	60	78	Clear	Clear	S. W.			
4	60	77	"	"	S. W., S. E.			Foggy morning.
5	64	79	C'y m'st all day		S. E.			Foggy morning.
6	68	84	Cloudy	Clear	S. W., N. W.	0.65		Cleared 7:30 A.M.; showers 5 to 7 P. M., 0.65; 13½ days, long't drought since Aug., 1886.
7	66	77	C'y m'st all day		N. E., S. E.			
S 8	66½	74	Cloudy	Cloudy	N. E.			Clear evening.
9	66	75	"	"	N. E.			Partly clear part of P. M.
10	62	68½	Rain	Rain	N. E.	0.24		Rain till 6:30, A.M., 0.24; rain 9 A.M. rest of day; freshet caused by high tide.
11	62	68	"	"	N. E.	0.39		7 A. M., 0.39.
12	64	67	"	"	N. E.	1.04		7 A. M., 1.04.
13	64	69	"	"	N. E., E.	1.37		7 A. M., 1.37; clear part ev'g.
14	67	75	Cloudy	Cloudy	E.	1.01		7 A. M., 1.01; clear 11 A.M to 4 P. M.
S 15	67½	75	"	"	E., S. E.	0.14		Rain before day, 0.01; clear part A.M.; rain 2 to 5 P.M., 0.13; rain 10 P. M.
16	70	78	Rain	"	S. W.	0.47		Rain till 7 A.M., 0.47; partly clear parts AM. and P.M.
17	70¼	80	Cloudy	Rain	S. W., N. W.	0.02		Rain before day, 0.02; showers after 3 P.M., and steady rain after 7.15 P. M.
18	63	65	Rain	Cloudy	N. W.	1.30		Rain till 10 A.M., 1.30; clear part of evening.
19	53	63	Clear	Clear	N. W.	0.09		Rain before day, 0.03; showers, 2 P. M., 0.03; showers 3, 4 and 5 P. M., 0.03.
20	51	63	"	Rain	S. W.			Cloudy part A. M.; rain 3 P.M.
21	54	63	"	Clear	N. W.	0.16		Rain before day, 0.14; spr'kle at noon and shower 3:45 P.M., 0.02.
S 22	48½	60	"	"	N. W.			Prof. Geo. H. Cook, Rutgers College, died.
23	47	65	"	"	W.			
24	49	60	Cloudy	Rain	N. E.			Rain 3:30 P. M.
25	52	60	Rain	"	N. E.	0.61		7 A. M., 0.61.
26	58½	72	"	Cloudy	N. E., N. W.	0.33		7 A. M., 0.30; rain part of evening, 0.03.
27	50	60	Clear	Clear	N. W.			
28	49	63¼	"	"	S. W.			Cloudy part of morning.
S 29	48	66½	"	"	N. W., S. W.			Cloudy evening.
30	58	69	Cloudy	Cloudy	S. W.	0.01		Rain 4 to 5 P. M., 0.01.
						7.83		

Weather Record for New Brunswick, N. J.

October, 1889.

Date.	Lowest.	Highest.	Weather. Morning.	Weather. Afternoon.	Prevailing Wind.	Rain and Melted Snow in inches	Snow in inches	REMARKS.
1	60	72½	Cloudy	Clear	S. W., N. W.	0.14	---	Showers till 9 A.M., 0.09; clear part of A. M.; 12:15 P. M., 0.01; 5 to 7:30 P. M., 0 04.
2	55½	64	Clear	"	N. W.	----	----	
3	43	62½	"	"	S. W.	----	----	Frost; clear part of ev'g.
4	51	67	"	"	S. W., N	----	----	
5	42	60	"	"	N. W., S.	----	----	
S 6	50	58	Cloudy	Rainy	S., W., N. E.	0.13	----	Rain 6 to 7 A. M., 0.01; 3:30 to 11 P. M., 0.12.
7	47	55	"	Cloudy	N. W.	----	----	Clear 7 to 11 A. M.; clear part of evening.
8	40	52	Clear	Clear	N. W., S. W.	----	----	
9	39	59	"	"	S. W.	----	----	Cloudy evening.
10	48	60½	Cloudy	"	S. W., N. W.	0.03	----	Rain 6 to 7 A M., 0.03; cleared 10 A. M.
11	43	64	"	"	S. W.	0.01	----	Rain 7:30 to 8:30, 0.01; cleared 10 A. M.; hazy even'g
12	47	65	Hazy	Cloudy	S. W., N. E.	0.08	----	Thunder shower 3 P.M., and rain till 6 P. M., 0.08; shower after 8:15 P. M.
S 13	47	52	Cloudy	"	N. E.	0.64	----	Rain before day, 0.64; rain after 8:15 P. M.
14	42	45½	Rain	Rain	N. E.	0.13	----	Rain till 9 A. M., 0.13; rain after 12:30 P. M.
15	43	60	Cloudy	Clear	N. E., N.	0.61	----	Rain before day, 0.61; cleared at noon.
16	44	56½	Clear	"	N. E.	----	----	
17	40	59½	"	"	N. W., S. W	----	----	
18	49½	60	"	Cloudy	N. W., N	----	----	Clouded over 3 P. M.
19	42	62	Hazy	Hazy	N. E., S.	----	----	
S 20	49	67	Clear	Clear	S. W.	----	----	Cloudy evening.
21	45	51½	Rain	"	N. E.	0.26	----	Rain till 7 A.M., 0.26.
22	38	54	Clear	"	All points	----	----	Cloudy ev'g; rain 10:30 P.M.
23	35	42	{ Rain / Snow	Cloudy	N. E.	0.06	----	Rain before day, 0.04; rain and snow 6 to 8 A. M., 0.02; clear part ev'g.
24	33	44	Clear	"	N. E.	----	----	Cloudy part of morning.
25	40	49½	Cloudy	"	N. E.	----	----	
26	46	55	"	Rainy	N. E., E.	0.04	----	Rain before day, 0.04.
S 27	52	62	Rain	Rain	N. E., S. E.	0.75	----	Rain till 7 A.M, 0.29; 10 A. M. to 2 P. M., 0.41; 4:45 to 5:30 P. M., 0.05; clear part of evening.
28	51	56½	Cloudy	Cloudy	S. W., N. W.	0.01	----	Rain before day, 0.01.
29	46	52½	"	"	N. W.	----	----	
30	46	51	"	"	N., N. W.	----	----	
31	47	51½	"	Rain	S. E.	0.24	----	Rain 11:45 A. M. to 5 P. M., 0.20; part of ev'g, 0.04.
						3.13	----	

November, 1889.

Date	Thermometer. Lowest.	Thermometer. Highest.	Weather. Morning.	Weather. Afternoon.	Prevailing Wind.	Rain and Melted Snow in inches.	Snow in inches.	REMARKS.
1	49	60	Cloudy	Clear	All points			Foggy A.M.; cleared 9 A.M.; cloudy evening.
2	52	62	"	Cloudy	S., S. E.	0.20		Clear part of A. M.; rain 11:15 A.M. to 3 P.M., 0.20; rain 10 P. M.
S 3	56	65	Rain	Rain	S W.	0.72		Rain till 4 P. M., 0.72; cleared 6 P. M.
4	43	57	Clear	Clear	N. W., W.			
5	43½	48	"	Cloudy	N. W.			Clouded over 11 A.M.; clear part of evening.
6	39	49	"	Clear	S. W.			
7	36½	54	"	"	S. W.			Cloudy evening.
8	47	49	Cloudy	Rain	S.W,N., N.E.	0.13		Light sprinkles part A. M.; rain at 9 P. M., 0.13.
9	46	54½	Rain	"	All points.	2.14		Rain till 7 P. M., 2.14; rain 10 P. M.
S 10	49	54	Cloudy	Clear	N. E.	0.13		Rain before day, 0.04; rain 10 to 10:30 A. M., 0.09.
11	45	52	"	Cloudy	N. E., S. E.	0.02		Rain 2 to 3 P. M., 0.02.
12	43	58	"	Clear	S. W., S. E.			Foggy A. M.; cl'rd 7 A. M.; cloudy part of evening.
13	47	54	"	Rain	N. E.	0.80		Foggy A. M.; rain 10 A. M. to 7 P. M., 0.80.
14	51	61	Clear	Clear	S. W., N. W.			
15	42	47	"	"	N. W.			
16	31	40	"	"	W., N. W.			
S 17	27	41½	"	"	W.			
18	38	51	Cloudy	Cloudy	N. E.	0.02		Light rain 6 to 7 A.M.; rain part of afternoon, 0.02.
19	44	55	Rain	Rain	N. E., E.	0.94		Rain till 7 P. M., 0.94.
20	44	48½	Cloudy	Cloudy	S. W.	0.01		Clear 7 to 11 A. M.; light rain part of evening, 0.01.
21	41	49	"	Rain	S. W., S. E.			Cl'r part A.M.; rain 2:30 P.M.
22	47	53	"	Cloudy	S. W.	0.43		Rain before day, 0.43; cleared 9 A. M.
23	43	51	"	"	W.			Cleared 7:30 A. M.; clear part of evening.
S 24	40	51	Clear	Clear	W., S. W.			Cloudy part A.M.; cl'dy ev'g.
25	46	48½	Rain	Cloudy	N. W., N.	0.41		Rain till 1 P. M., 0.41; cleared 7:30 P. M.
26	36	43½	Clear	Clear	N. W., S. W.			Cloudy part of evening.
27	37	58	Cloudy	Rain	N. E., S. E.			Rain 11 A. M.
28	54	56	Rain	Cloudy	S. W.	2.54		Rain till 7 A.M., clear parts of morning and afternoon.
29	35	38	Clear	"	S. W.			Snow flurries; clear ev'g.
30	29	37	"	Clear	S. W., N. W.			Cl'dy part of morning with snow squall.
						8.49		

December, 1889.

Date.	Ther-mometer. Lowest.	Ther-mometer. Highest.	Weather. Morning.	Weather. Afternoon.	Prevailing Wind.	Rain and Melted Snow in inches.	Snow in inches.	REMARKS.
S 1	29	42	Clear	Clear	N. W., S. W.			
2	32	50	"	"	S. W.			Cloudy evening.
3	41	51½	Cloudy	Rain / Snow	S.W.,N., N.E.	0.03		Clear part A.M.; rain 2:30 to 6 PM. & snow till 9 PM., 0.03.
4	15	25	Clear	Clear	N. E.			
5	19	37	Cloudy	Cloudy	N. E., S.	0.04		Rain and snow during evening, 0.04.
6	35	44	"	Clear	S. W., N. W.			Clear part of morning.
7	30	45	Clear	"	S. W.			
S 8	33	55	"	Rain	S. W., S. E.	0.14		Clouded over 7:30 A.M.; rain 12:30 to 6 P.M., 0.14.
9	54	60	Cloudy	Clear	S. W.	0.01		Rain before day, 0.01.
10	40	47½	Clear	Cloudy	N. E., S. E.			Clear part of afternoon.
11	44	56	Rain	Clear	N. W.	0.22		Rain till 10 A. M., 0.22.
12	40	52	Clear	"	W., N. W.			Cloudy part of afternoon.
13	40	38	"	"	S. W., N. W.			Cloudy part A.M. & part P.M.
14	30	35	"	Snow / Rain	N. E.	0.62		Clouded over 8 A. M.; snow 10:30 A.M. to 3 P.M., 0.42; then rain till 7 P.M., 0.20.
S 15	26	32	"	Cloudy	N. E., S. E.			Cloudy part of morning; clear part of evening.
16	31	41½	Cloudy	"	S. W.			Clear part A.M. & part ev'g.
17	36	40	Rain	Rain	S. E., N. E.	0.33		Rain till 7 P. M., 0.33.
18	39	45	"	"	N. E.			Fog'y and misty rain all day.
19	43	54	Cloudy	Clear	W.	0.16		Rain before day, 0.16; cleared 7 A. M.
20	40	51	Foggy	Cloudy	S. W.	0.01		Rain before day, 0.01; foggy evening; cleared 9 P. M.
21	42	50	Clear	Clear	N. W.			
S 22	34½	54	Cloudy	Cloudy	All points	0.01		Light rain part A. M., 0.01; cleared 5:30 P. M.
23	42	48	Clear	Clear	N. W.			
24	33	49	"	"	S. W.			Clouded over 4 P. M.; clear part of even'g; bar. 30.45.
25	44	65	Cloudy	"	S. W.	0.01		Rain before day, 0.01; bar. 29.85.
26	46½	65	Rain	"	S. W., N. W.	0.23		Rain till 8:30 A. M., 0.23; cleared 10 A.M.; bar. 29.30.
27	37	43	Clear	"	N. W.			Cloudy part of evening.
28	35	48	"	"	S. W., W.			
S 29	34	52	Cloudy	Cloudy	N. E., S. E.			Clear part of evening.
30	41	47	"	"	N. W., N.			Clear part of morning.
31	25	33	Clear	Clear	N. E., E.			Cloudy evening.
						1.81		

Rain and melted snow for 1889—61.30 inches.

Weather Record for New Brunswick, N. J.

January, 1890.

Date.	Lowest.	Highest.	Weather. Morning.	Weather. Afternoon.	Prevailing Wind.	Rain and Melted Snow in inches.	Snow in inches.	REMARKS.
1	27	53½	Cloudy	Misty	N. E., S. E.	0.01		
2	51	64	Clear	Cloudy	S. W.			
3	43	48½	"	Clear	N. W., N. E.			Cloudy part of A. M., and part of afternoon.
4	29	41	"	"	All points			Clouded over 9 P. M.
S 5	36	52	Rain	Cloudy	S. W.	0.26		Rain till 8 A. M.
6	50	58	Misty	"	S. W.	0.02		Misty till 8 A. M.
7	47	49	Rain	"	N. W., S. W.	0.07		Rain till 12:30 P. M.
8	40	48	Cloudy	Clear	W., N. W.	0.03		Rain before day, 0.03; cl'rd 7:30 A. M.; cl'dy part P.M.
9	28	37	Clear	"	N. W.			Cloudy part of evening.
10	34	38	Rain	Cloudy	E., N. E.	0.03		Light rain till 9 A.M., 0.03.
11	27	39	Cloudy	"	N. E.			
S 12	38	62½	Clear	Clear	All points.			
13	45	66¼	"	Cloudy	S. W., N. W.	0.01		Cloudy 10 A. M. to 6 P. M.; shower 3 P.M, 0.01; clear evening.
14	35	45	"	Clear	N., E.			
15	33	45½	Rain	Cloudy	All points.	0.98		Rain till 1 P M.; Mrs. C. B. Voorhees died.
16	45	55½	"	"	S. W., N. W.	0.30		Rain till 8 A.M.; clear ev'g.
17	26	33¼	Clear	Clear	N. W., S. W.			
18	27	42½	"	"	N. W.			
S 19	28	44	"	Cloudy	N. E., E.			Clouded over 2 P.M.; clear part of evening.
20	37½	56	Rain	"	S. W.	0.31		Rain till 7 A M., 0.24; part of morning, 0.07; clear part of evening.
21	38½	43	Cloudy	Clear	N. W., S. W.			
22	21	30	Clear	"	N. W.			
23	21	31	Cloudy	Cloudy	S. W.			Snow 11 A. M. to 1 P. M.
24	30	36½	"	Clear	N. W.			Snow squall 7:30 A. M.; cl'rd 10 A. M.; cl'dy part P. M
25	24	40¼	Clear	Cloudy	S. W.			
S 26	38½	49	Cloudy	"	All points.			Clear part of morning.
27	41	53	"	Clear	N. W.	0.07		Rain before day, 0.07; cleared 8:30 A. M.
28	30	38	Clear	"	N. W.			
29	29	49	"	"	S. W.			Cl'dy evening; rain 11 P.M.
30	39	48	Rain	"	N. E.	0.50		Rain till 8 A.M., 0.50; cl'rd 9:30 A. M.; cloudy part of afternoon.
31	36	45½	Cloudy	Cloudy	N. E., S.			Misty part of morning; clear part of afternoon.
						2.59		

February, 1890.

Date.	Thermometer. Lowest.	Thermometer. Highest.	Weather. Morning.	Weather. Afternoon.	Prevailing Wind.	Rain and Melted Snow in inches.	Snow in inches.	REMARKS.
1	41	45½	Cloudy	Cloudy	N. W., N.			
S 2	32	39½	Snow	Misty	N. E.			Light snow 7 A. M. till noon and misty rest of day.
3	41½	49	Cloudy	Cloudy	S. W.	0.15		Misty before day, 0.15; clear parts of P. M. and even'g.
4	41	45	Rain	Rain	N. E., E.	0.24		Rain 7 A. M. till 3 P. M.
5	55½	68	Cloudy	Cloudy	S. W., N. W.			Clear 9 A. M. to 2 P. M.
6	33	37	"	Clear	N.			
7	20	36½	Clear	Snow / Rain	N. E., S. E.			Clouded over 11 A. M.; snow 4½ P.M. & soon turns to rain.
8	55½	59½	Rain	Rain	S., N. W.	1.56		Rain before day, 0.54; rain 9:30 A. M. to 6 P. M., 1.02; clear 9:40 P.M.
S 9	30	39	Clear	Clear	W., N.			
10	25	36	Cloudy	"	N. E.			Clear part of morning and cloudy part of afternoon.
11	28	38	"	Cloudy	N. E., S. E.			
12	36	49	"	Clear	S. W., N. W.			Cleared off 10 A. M.
13	33	49	Clear	"	S. W.			
14	35	54	Cloudy	Rain	E., S., S. W.	0.76		Foggy morning; rain 1:30 to 4:30 P.M.; cleared 6:30 P.M.
15	45	50	"	Clear	N. W.			Cleared off 8 A. M.
S 16	27	40	Clear	"	N. W., S. W.			
17	34	49½	Cloudy	Cloudy	S. W., S. E.			Clear part A. M. & part ev'g.
18	39½	64	"	Clear	All points.	0.03		Cleared 8 A. M.; cloudy eve'g; th'nder shower 10:30 P.M.
19	36	40	Clear	Cloudy	N., N. E.			Clouded over 8 A. M.
20	33	43	Snow / Rain	Clear	N. E., N. W.	1.04		Snow, sleet and rain till 7 A.M., 1.04; cl'red 2:45 P. M.
21	22	29½	Clear	Cloudy	N. W.			Clouded over 10 A. M.; clear evening.
22	24	35	"	Clear	N. W., W.			Cloudy part of afternoon.
S 23	27	46	"	Cloudy	S. W., S. E.			
24	36	43	Foggy	Rain / M'sty	S. E., N. E.	0.28		Rain 10 A.M. to 2 P.M., 0.28, and misty and foggy rest of day.
25	40	46	"	Foggy	E.	0.01		
26	44	66	"	Clear	S. W., N. W.	0.02		Cleared 7:30 A. M.
27	38½	48	Clear	Cloudy	N. E., E.			Clouded over 8 A. M.; light sprinkles during evening.
28	42½	46	Rain	M'sty	E.	0.43		Rain till 11:30 A. M., 0.43, and misty rest of day.
						4.52		No ice crop gathered this season.

March, 1890.

Date.	Thermometer. Lowest.	Highest	Weather. Morning.	Afternoon.	Prevailing Wind.	Rain and Melted Snow in inches.	Snow in inches.	REMARKS.
1	43	46	Rain	Cloudy	N. W., N.	0.31		Rain till 11 A. M., 0.31; snow squall 9:30 P. M.
S 2	26½	32	Cloudy	"	N., N. E.			Clear 10 to 11 A. M ; snow 5:30 P. M.
3	18	35	Clear	Clear	N. W., W.		3.50	Snow before day, 3.50; first snow without rain.
4	23	40	"	"	All points			Cloudy part of afternoon.
5	32	40	"	Cloudy	N. W.			Clouded over 3 P M.
6	22	30	Snow Sleet	"	N. E., N.	0.72		Snow and sleet till 9 A. M., and snow till noon, 0.72.
7	12	29½	Clear	Clear	N. W.			
8	18	33	Cloudy	"	N. E.			Clear part of morning.
S 9	21	38	Clear	"	N. W., W.			
10	23	43	"	Cloudy	S. W.			
11	37	47	Rain	"	S. E., S. W.	0.49		Rain till 11 A.M., 0.41; part of afternoon, 0.08.
12	42½	69	Cloudy	Clear	S. W.			Cleared 9 A. M.
13	55	64	Clear	Cloudy	S.W.,N.,N. E.			Rain 6 P. M.
14	41	43½	Rain	Rain	N. E.			
15	36	42	Rain Snow	Cloudy	N. W.	1.15		Rain till 7 A. M., and then snow till noon, 1.15; cleared 4 P. M.
S 16	25	34	Clear	Clear	N. W.			Cloudy part of afternoon.
17	25	40	"	"	S. W.			Cloudy part of afternoon.
18	35	52	Cloudy	"	S. W.			Cleared 8 A. M.
19	30	32	Snow	Snow	N. E., N. W.	0.85		Snow till 4 P. M.; cleared 7 P. M.; greatest snow since March, 1888.
20	21	42	Foggy	Cloudy	S. W.			Cl'rd 8 A.M.; clouded 3 P.M.
21	38	49	"	"	S. W., W.	0.27		Rain before day, 0.24; part A.M., 0.03; clear part ev'g.
22	42	46½	Rain	Rain	N. E., N. W.			
S 23	40	43	Cloudy	Clear	N. W.	1.68		Rain before day, 1.68; cl'rd 8:30 A.M.; cloudy part P.M.
24	32	44	Clear	"	N. W.			Cloudy evening
25	36½	53½	Cloudy	Cloudy	S., S. E.	0.02		Rain 10 A. M. to noon, 0.02.
26	50	56	"	Clear	S. W., N. W.	0.11		Rain before day, 0.11; cleared 8 A. M.
27	37	51	Clear	Cloudy	N. W.			
28	38	44	Show'rs all day.		N. E.	0.98		Thunder showers during day; clear part of ev'g.
29	35½	41	Clear	Clear	N. W.			Cloudy 10 A. M. to 5 P. M., with snow squalls.
S 30	35	45	Snow	"	S. W, N. W.	0.16		Snow till 7 A.M., 0.15; clear part of A.M., snow squalls during day, 0.01.
31	33½	40	Cloudy	Snow	N. W., S W.	0.30		Clear part of A.M.; snow 4 P M. to midnight, 0.30.
						7.04	3.50	

April, 1890.

Date	Thermometer. Lowest.	Thermometer. Highest.	Weather. Morning.	Weather. Afternoon.	Prevailing Wind.	Rain and Melted Snow in inches.	Snow in inches.	REMARKS.
1	32	45	Clear	Clear	N. W.			Cleared 6:45 A. M.
2	32½	52½	"	"	N. W., S. W.			
3	37	64	"	"	S. W.			
4	53	58½	Cloudy	Rain	S. W.	0.53		Rain 7:30 A. M. to 3 P. M., 0.53; clear evening.
5	42	52½	Clear	Clear	N.			
S 6	36	57	"	"	S. W.			Cloudy evening.
7	48	64	Cloudy	"	S. W., N.	0.15		Light sprinkles in morning; shower 1:40 P. M., 0.15.
8	40	51	Clear	Rain	W., S. E.	0.14		Clouded over 9 A. M.; rain 11 A. M. to 3 P. M., 0.14; misty evening.
9	42	47	Rain	Cloudy	E., S. E.	0.64		Thunder showers 2 to 4 A. M., 0.57; part of morning, 0.01; part of even'g, 0.06.
10	44	56½	Cloudy	Clear	S. W., N. W.			Cleared 6:45 A. M.; cloudy part of afternoon.
11	38	52	Clear	"	N. W.			
12	41½	64	"	"	N. W., S. E.			
S 13	45	78	"	"	N. W.	0.06		Cloudy part of evening, with rain, 0.06
14	53	70½	"	"	S. W., S. E.			Cloudy 3 to 8 P. M.; cherries flowered.
15	46½	57	"	Hazy	N.			Clear evening.
16	40	59	"	Clear	N. E., S. W.			
17	41	64	"	"	S. W.			
18	44	59	"	"	N. E., N.			
19	33½	52	"	"	N. E.			
S 20	39	61	"	"	All points.			
21	42½	68	"	"	N. W.			
22	49	70	"	"	N. W., S.			Hazy part of afternoon.
23	45	75½	"	Hazy	S. W.			Foggy morn'g; cloudy eve'g.
24	58	69½	"	Rain	S. W.	0.06		Cloudy part of morning; rain from 12 to 6 P. M., 0.06; cloudy evening.
25	46	50	Rain	Cloudy	N. E.	0.31		Rain till 1 P.M., 0.31; clear evening.
26	42½	48½	Cloudy	Rain	N. E., E.			Clear part of morning; rain 10 A. M.
S 27	44	58	"	Cloudy	N.E., S., N.W.	0.46		Rain before day, 0.40; showery evening, 0.06.
28	47	61	"	Clear	All points.			Cleared 7 A. M.
29	43½	62½	Clear	"	S. E.			
30	47	72½	Cloudy	"	S. W., S.			
						2.35		

STATISTICAL TABLES.

Table of rain-fall at New Brunswick, N. J., for thirty-six years, records of Prof. Geo. H. Cook; and from April, 1862, of P. Vanderbilt Spader, northwest

Month.	1854.	1855.	1856.	1857.	1858.	1859.	1860.
January	2.00	3.05	3.73	3.48	3.30	4.43	2.61
February	4.82	2.51	0.70	1.18	1.91	3.23	1.00
March	1.16	1.80	3.01	0.97	1.90	6.04	0.80
April	9.22	2.21	3.76	6.24	4.01	4.56	1.85
May	4.12	3.54	3.24	5.10	4.80	1.82	5.63
June	3.65	4.80	1.83	3.71	0.24	4.08	2.28
July	3.63	3.17	1.92	4.20	2.85	3.47	2.72
August	1.48	2.48	6.03	6.16	3.00	4.88	11.72
September	2.67	2.66	4.71	3.85	1.54	7.20	4.82
October	1.70	3.84	0.90	3.91	2.01	1.81	3.02
November	3.21	2.48	2.08	0.00	3.56	3.58	6.27
December	2.39	5.81	3.17	5.93	4.23	3.97	3.44
Total for the year	40.05	38.38	36.07	44.23	33.35	49.67	46.06

WEATHER RECORD FOR NEW BRUNSWICK, N. J.   409

from January, 1854, to March, 1862, eight years, taken from the
to April, 1890, twenty-eight years, from the records
corner of George and Church streets.

1861.	1862.	1863.	1864.	1865.	1866.	1867.	1868.	1869.	1870.	1871.	1872.
3.81	5.37	3.84	2.78	3.54	1.74	1.97	3.88	3.49	4.53	4.12	1.70
1.02	2.63	4.25	0.84	4.73	5.04	6.01	2.20	5.84	4.88	3.77	1.06
3.50	3.70	5.35	4.19	4.26	2.24	4.76	2.05	4.87	4.36	5.09	4.19
5.06	3.93	6.60	4.24	3.99	3.20	2.16	4.09	1.62	5.87	3.22	2.15
5.52	2.33	3.77	6.08	6.21	4.50	6.45	7.57	5.18	3.15	3.50	2.45
2.52	7.10	2.46	2.12	2.31	3.10	11.42	6.41	5.57	5.91	5.90	3.85
1.26	5.80	10.59	1.65	7.10	3.22	5.50	6.26	3.01	4.66	8.91	8.97
3.04	1.20	4.08	3.37	3.21	7.80	9.20	8.55	8.70	6.70	9.25	7.12
2.41	3.10	1.13	4.67	2.72	5.47	0.44	7.59	2.34	3.08	2.39	3.01
2.59	5.21	3.20	1.71	4.62	3.88	4.60	1.34	8.53	5.60	5.51	4.00
8.77	5.61	2.42	5.04	2.57	2.82	2.06	4.94	3.76	1.91	4.19	4.04
1.90	1.22	4.75	4.20	5.94	3.58	1.99	3.32	4.86	2.34	2.31	4.70
42.39	47.20	52.50	40.84	51.23	46.59	56.56	54.10	50.37	52.90	58.16	47.93

Table of rain-fall at New Brunswick, N. J., for thirty-six years, records of Prof. Geo. H. Cook; and from April, 1862, to P. Vanderbilt Spader, northwest corner

MONTH.	1873.	1874.	1875.	1876.	1877.	1878.	1879.
January	5.33	4.33	3.64	1.21	3.70	4.01	2.81
February	4.72	2.90	3.81	5.07	1.68	3.56	2.06
March	2.39	2.06	4.30	7.51	6.85	3.39	3.66
April	5.12	8.25	2.84	2.59	3.38	1.38	4.00
May	4.26	1.85	1.77	2.93	0.99	5.71	2.85
June	3.86	3.05	4.56	1.91	4.49	4.34	5.10
July	9.47	4.02	3.94	1.70	4.60	6.23	5.16
August	10.79	2.35	3.08	1.08	4.85	3.02	7.30
September	3.59	8.61	2.19	5.82	1.94	2.22	2.00
October	4.65	2.66	2.62	1.54	6.83	3.42	0.27
November	4.36	2.44	4.37	5.45	7.29	3.65	2.13
December	2.40	2.78	2.77	2.02	1.19	5.43	5.34
Total for the year	60.96	45.30	44.80	39.43	47.20	46.36	43.58

from January, 1854, to March, 1862, eight years, taken from the
April, 1890, twenty-eight years, from the records of
of George and Church streets—Concluded.

1880.	1881.	1882.	1883.	1884.	1885.	1886.	1887.	1888.	1889.	Monthly average.
2.20	6.22	5.49	3.71	5.63	3.72	4.16	4.74	5.22	6.43	3.77
2.63	5.11	4.24	4.67	5.28	4.93	4.94	6.15	3.00	2.38	3.55
4.87	5.57	2.02	1.96	4.23	1.08	3.95	3.59	5.43	3.23	3.62
2.36	0.55	2.85	4.03	2.20	2.14	3.57	3.31	4.68	4.97	3.83
0.67	2.30	5.29	2.82	3.17	2.01	5.30	1.14	5.25	4.19	3.82
1.85	5.86	1.48	5.24	5.34	1.67	4.06	6.28	3.51	3.38	4.05
8.89	0.86	3.04	3.44	4.80	4.29	4.61	6.20	2.66	10.45	4.83
4.08	1.73	3.20	4.40	5.03	5.30	1.90	7.34	5.93	5.01	4.89
1.81	0.94	15.52	3.85	0.37	0.80	1.50	3.07	8.17	7.83	3.74
2.10	2.25	1.42	4.29	3.16	4.00	2.48	2.44	5.55	3.13	3.36
2.45	3.13	1.60	1.49	3.60	4.04	4.81	2.30	4.29	8.49	3.78
3.32	3.92	1.91	3.61	5.63	2.72	3.73	5.28	4.41	1.81	3.58
37.17	38.46	48.06	43.01	48.44	36.70	45.01	51.84	59.00	61.30	46.82

Table of Maximum and Minimum Temperature, by months, at 1857–1890, as observed by P. Vanderbilt Spader,

Year.	January. Maximum	January. Minimum	February. Maximum	February. Minimum	March. Maximum	March. Minimum	April. Maximum	April. Minimum	May. Maximum	May. Minimum
1857	37	−10	65½	8	61½	10½	65½	17	82	39½
1858	61	18	49	−1	55½	7	77	32	76	43½
1859	61½	−5½	57	12	63	19	73½	31½	81½	43
1860	55	2	65	−1	69	24	77	28½	81	41½
1861	47	−1	63	−5	74	14	83	32½	75	85
1862	53	7	45	13	53	19	78	30½	81½	41½
1863	61½	13	52	1½	61½	15½	69½	29½	87	41
1864	58	7	66	3	57½	19½	74	34	84	38½
1865	50	3½	60	2	73	21	76	36	82	41½
1866	47	−11½	62	5	65	15½	77½	32	70	37½
1867	40½	4	53	16	62½	15½	77½	34	82	35½
1868	45	7	43½	−1½	74	2½	70½	22	72	40
1869	35½	13½	50	18	61	7	77	30	82	87½
1870	62½	15½	58	9	57½	19	77½	33	81½	43
1871	54	5	54	2	68	31	82½	34	87½	40½
1872	47½	8	54	12	60½	3½	80½	33	87	42
1873	53½	−12	46	1	55	12½	65	35	85	40
1874	65½	13	70½	7	64	18½	69	22½	85	37½
1875	39	−9	53	3	56½	13	70	24	84	39
1876	66	15	56½	8	65½	15	70	32	84	37½
1877	44	6	55	10	61	15	76	34	87½	35½
1878	50½	12½	54½	10	68½	17	75	42	80½	39
1879	49	−1½	50½	10	63	17	73	27	80½	40
1880	61½	11	65	9	71	18½	78	28½	92	37
1881	39	−6½	53½	0	58	21	76½	24	84½	40
1882	48½	1	54	13	63	20	72½	20	70½	37
1883	47	5½	65	15	60	10½	68	24½	81	39½
1884	45½	5	50	6	62	7	68½	34½	85	44
1885	61½	7	49	1	58½	8	80	29	80	39
1886	56½	0	62½	−1	66½	12	79	29	80	43
1887	60	6	63	16	49½	10	70	29	83	47½
1888	56	4	63	4	64	5	83	32½	82	40
1889	58	18	47	6	61½	28	75½	35	87	41
1890	66½	21	68	20	69	12	78	32	.....	.....

Weather Record for New Brunswick, N. J.

New Brunswick, New Jersey, for thirty-three and one-third years, at the northwest corner of George and Church streets.

JUNE.		JULY.		AUGUST.		SEPTEMBER.		OCTOBER.		NOVEMBER.		DECEMBER.	
Maximum.	Minimum.	Maximum.	Minimum.	Maximum.	Minimum.	Maximum.	Minimum.	Maximum.	Minimum.	Maximum.	Minimum.	Maximum.	Minimum.
85½	52	85	52½	89	54½	80	46	70	85	74	18	58½	14
91	51½	90½	56½	85	49½	84	40	85	33½	62½	23½	65	18½
89	43	90	53½	89	50	77	46½	73	30	66½	30	67	6
91	53	91	50½	88	55½	84	41	74	34½	74½	15	52	10
85	51½	91	55	90	54	82	46½	85	34	64	30	61	17½
84	47	89	55	91½	51	84	45½	82	34	69	27	68	7½
88	50	84	61	90½	52½	80½	41	75½	29½	66	28½	60	10½
95	46½	90½	54½	92½	57½	77½	46	72	34½	68	23	59	8
68½	57½	90	55	86½	49½	86	46	80	33½	68½	26	63	14
89	54	98	56	83	49½	82½	45	72½	34½	67½	21	59½	2
83½	46	88	56	83½	50	81	43½	75	35	69	20	48½	4
87	51	91½	64	85½	56	84½	43	73	30½	66	31	44½	8
86½	48	90½	57	92½	51	85½	41	73½	31	61	23½	57½	10½
91	57	92	59½	89	55½	83	48½	75½	36½	67½	29	54	8½
80½	55	84½	55	85	55½	78	41	73	35	64	17	57	1
88½	51	93½	64	89	57	88	49	76	38	59	18	47	½
90	50	90½	60	88	58	87	45	71½	32	57½	23½	67	20
94	53	89½	59	92	53½	86½	50	72	36	65½	23	49	12½
91½	47½	90	59	83	57	87	41	72	34	60	12	60	5½
92	47	96	59	90	55	87½	48½	72	33½	72	31	47½	5
86½	54	90½	62	88½	61	81	48	76	39	68	26	60	24
86	50	92	63½	90½	56	84	43½	77	36	60	28	60	15
89½	51	94½	59	80½	55½	83	40½	83½	28½	71½	18½	61	11
90½	48½	89	59	88	53	87½	47½	76½	33½	68	14	47	-3½
84½	50	89½	61	95	57	97½	51½	86½	35	68	26	67	22
92½	52	92	56	87½	54½	85	48	73	42	70	21	48½	11
87	51½	91	57	88½	53	81	43	79	34½	66	21½	55	2
89	45	88½	59	89½	51	90	47	79	83	64	23	63	2½
90	50½	94	56½	88½	50½	83	44	75	36	70½	26	60	15
79½	53	90½	56½	86½	54½	85½	47½	77	30½	68	27	53	10
68	51	94½	65½	85½	53	82½	41	75	30½	66	26	57½	18¼
93	52	88½	56	91½	54	78½	42	65½	35	70½	17	56	12
87	52	87	57	85	55	64	47	72½	33	65	27	65	13
....	....	....	....	....	....	....	....	....	....	....	....	....	....

www.ingramcontent.com/pod-product-compliance
Lightning Source LLC
Chambersburg PA
CBHW030550300426
44111CB00009B/929